Canadian Law & Private Investigations

Canadian Law & Private Investigations

Norman J. Groot

IRWIN LAW

A Quicklaw Company

CANADIAN LAW AND PRIVATE INVESTIGATIONS

Published in 2001 by
Irwin Law Inc.
One First Canadian Place
Suite 930, Box 235
Toronto, Ontario, Canada
M5X 1C8

ISBN: 1-55221-059-6

Canadian Cataloguing in Publication Data

Groot, Norman J. (Norman John), 1966-
      Canadian law and private investigations

Includes bibliographical references and index.
ISBN 1-55221-059-6

1. Private investigators — Legal status, laws, etc. — Canada. I. Title.

KE5010.P74G76 2001   344.71'05289   C2001-902577-7

Disclaimer

Although the author has researched all sources to ensure accuracy and completeness of the information con-tained in this book, we assume no responsibility for errors, inaccuracies, omissions, or any inconsistency here-in. Any slights to people or organizations are unintentional. Readers should use their own judgment and/or consult a legal expert for specific applications to their individual situations.

Printed and bound in Canada.

1 2 3 4 5   05 04 03 02 01

For Nan, Marieke, and Juliana,
and all who cherish freedom, responsibility, and the rule of law

SUMMARY
TABLE OF CONTENTS

DETAILED
TABLE OF CONTENTS

PART TWO: AUTHORITIES AND LIABILITIES OF PRIVATE INVESTIGATORS   *13*

CHAPTER 2
Provincial Private Investigators and Security Guards Acts   *15*

CHAPTER 3
The *Canadian Charter of Rights and Freedoms*   99

CHAPTER 4
Criminal Liability   *113*

CHAPTER 7

Confidentiality of Health Information — The Krever Inquiry   *291*

CHAPTER 8
Inquiry on Policing in British Columbia — The Oppal Inquiry   *325*

FOREWORD

You don't write because you want to say something;
you write because you have something to say.

— F. Scott Fitzgerald

The work of private investigators has typically been viewed as a poor cousin to the rest of the Canadian legal system. Misunderstood and seen as practitioners of a black art, private investigators have operated in a world that is perceived as having few rules and therefore no pressing need for scholarly attention.

In his text *Canadian Law and Private Investigations*, not only does Norman Groot have something to say, but his combination of legal analysis and practical insights are a wonderful and much needed addition to Canadian legal writing. Norman has neatly synthesized common law doctrines, *Canadian Charter of Rights and Freedoms* issues, as well as current federal and provincial legislative trends into a highly readable work. The text is very well organized, and it will no doubt both appeal to students pursuing a career in this challenging field and become an indispensable authority to licensed investigators throughout Canada.

Norman Groot is to be commended for this excellent work; in a society where public policing budgets are under severe stress, private sector investigative work is certain to become increasingly important, and this text will set the standard for future legal writing in this field.

Bryan Davies
Ministry of the Attorney General
Whitby, Ontario

PREFACE

This book is a first of its kind in Canada. In all of Canadian literature, there are only three other books devoted to the topic of private investigations. The first book is entitled *If It Wasn't for Sex I'd Have to Get a Real Job — Confessions of a Private Investigator*[1] a war story paperback that is entertaining reading but of little professional value. The second book, *The Canadian Private Investigator's Manual*,[2] a guidebook written by two environmental investigators who discuss various investigative insights and techniques for those seeking to enter the industry. The third book is *The Fraud Examiners Manual, Canadian Edition*,[3] a comprehensive text for those seeking certification as certified fraud examiners. Actually, there was a fourth book: the precursor to this one, a law school thesis I prepared entitled *Legal Liability of the Canadian Private Investigator*.[4]

Obviously, I wrote this book to fill a market and academic void. There is a general consensus, especially in the corporate realm, that the growth of the private sector investigation industry in Canada is strong.[5] Some say it is "booming."[6] There are four primary reasons for this expansion.

---

1   A. Manweiler & J. Burke (Toronto: McClelland & Stewart, 1984).

2   D.J. Hawkins & E. Konstan, (Toronto: Emond Montgomery, 1996).

3   J.T. Wells et al. (Austin, TX: Association of Certified Fraud Examiners, 1998).

4   (Toronto: Andijk Inc., 1998).

5   B. Daisley, "Lawyers Should Check Investigators' Backgrounds" *Lawyers Weekly* (27 June 1977). The estimated national gross annual revenues for the industry in 1996 were over $750 million.

6   N. Pron, "Boom Time for Fraud Artists Sends Victims to Private Firms" *Toronto Star* (7 January 1996) D.1; A. Tanner, "Spies Used to Ensure Employee Honesty" (Edmonton, Canadian Press, 11 June 1995); M. MacLean, "Private Eyes Set Up Canadian Network" *Calgary Herald* (17 December 1994) A19; P. Fraser, "Target: White Collar Crime: Corporate Private Investigators Already Have Cases Lined Up as They Launch Regional Office" *Halifax Daily Times* (22 May 1997) 28; C. Kentridge, "Corporate Fraud Investigative Work Growing" *Law Times* (1 June 1998); D. Hunt, "Private Fraud Investigation Aids Overburdened Public System" *Lawyers Weekly* (29 October 1999) 17.

First, there is the strain on public resources resulting in a shrinking public sector to investigate wrongdoing in the corporate realm.[7] Second, with the erosion of career employers and the advent of contract employment, the loyalty that employees once had towards employers is diminishing to the extent that wrongful acts by employees against corporate employers are more frequently being rationalized as justified.[8] Third, there is an increase in theft of corporate intelligence between corporations owing to increasing market pressures and downsizing.[9] And finally, there is the desire of corporate clients to avoid hanging out their dirty laundry to dry in the public court system.[10] This book is an attempt to provide a body of academic research for this growth industry.

A second reason this book was written is because of an identified lack of industry standards. A major concern in the private sector investigation industry is the lack of expertise of some who practise in this field. Norman Inkster, president of KPMG's Investigations and Security Inc. and a former commissioner of the RCMP, was quoted at a recent World Association of Detectives Annual Conference as urging the adoption of higher standards by private investigation firms and greater cooperation between private investigators and police. This sentiment was echoed by the Quebec Public Security Minister Serge Menard. Other speakers were also quoted as desiring tough hiring standards for the rapidly growing industry, along with courses of study and high ethical standards, as well as the establishment of a professional organization similar to the medical and bar associations.[11]

The concern over lack of standards has also been addressed by other stakeholders. For instance, the Canadian Police Association has stated that the public should be concerned about the areas of policing that are being usurped by the private sector, such as fraud and other financial investigations, because the private sector is under limited accountability.[12]

The concern over lack of standards is under review by some sectors of the industry. For instance, the Canadian Institute of Chartered Accountants (CICA) has established an

---

7   See P. Polango, "Fighting White Collar Crime: The RCMP Can No Longer Get Its Man — Mountie Misery" *Maclean's Magazine* (28 July 1997) 15. Paul Polango reports that the Mounties have largely taken themselves out of the business of investigating white-collar crime. Today, if a corporation is targeted by criminals, it has little choice but to hire forensic accountants and other private investigators. Canada is moving to a two-tier state where the Mounties look after the interests of the state, and business looks after itself.

8   R. Cribb, "Private Sleuths Take on Corporate Crime" *London Free Press* (26 February 1996) 12. See also P. Fraser, "Target: White-Collar Crime — Corporate Private Investigators Already Have Cases Lined Up as They Launch Regional Office" *Halifax Daily News* (22 May 1997) 28.

9   A. Tanner, "Employers Using Private Eyes to Check on Staff" *Montreal Gazette* (17 May 1995) E1.

10 "Cops Can't Beat White-Collar Crime: KPMG" (Toronto: Canadian Press, 22 November 1995); "Police Law Enforcement Monopoly Long Gone: Chiefs" (Fredericton: Canadian Press, 26 August 1997).

11 "Secure Work: PI's Target Fraud, Industrial Spying" (Montreal: Canadian Press, 24 August 1995).

12 D. Kinnear, "Policing Private Security" *Canadian Police Association Magazine* (February 2000) 16.

Investigative and Forensic Accounting Interest Group that has set up a certification program awarding the designation of CA-IFA (Chartered Accountant — Investigative and Forensic Accounting) for successful graduates.[13] Furthermore, the province of British Columbia has instituted an academic process that applicants for private investigator licences are required to pass. Although the Registrar of Private Investigators in Ontario has not yet put into policy any such guidelines, the Urquhart Report to the Registrar's Training and Standards Sub-Committee has pleaded this issue. In addition to industry groups, various community colleges have expressed interest in offering courses on this subject as it seems fundamental that students they educate for the private investigation industry should be well versed on their legal standing and obligations.

The Challenge

One of the difficult aspects of writing this book was presenting it in a style that would be appreciated by each of the three target markets: educational institutions, the private investigation industry itself, and the more common users of investigation services — lawyers, insurance adjusters, and business people.

For academic purposes this book is suitable for a survey-type course on the legal aspects of private sector investigations. The term "survey" is used because my intention is to make the reader aware of issues that have arisen in private sector investigations, or issues that have a real likelihood of occurring. This book is not the final word on any given area of law — volumes have been written on some of the legal issues discussed herein. My hope is that when students find themselves facing a situation that pulls at their conscience, they will recall their studies and take the time to research their legal position.

Notwithstanding that this book is written in a survey format, it is also a useful reference text for those practising in the field of private sector investigations. As mentioned above, this book does not attempt to be the authoritative word on any given area of law. Rather, this text takes legal principles that are well developed and discusses them from the investigation perspective. Most of the cases referenced in this book are not the leading authorities on the given topic. Instead, most of these cases are ones wherein a private sector investigator has been the focus of a court's attention. As such, this text is a useful reference because it includes in one body of literature the law on red-button issues that arise in private sector investigations, as well as extracts from cases and footnotes identifying the case law and legislation relied upon as authority for the commentary made.

For lawyers, insurance adjusters, business people, and others who use investigative services, this book should alleviate that uneasy feeling that results from not knowing how the information sought is obtained. For all users of investigative services, this book provides an easy reference explaining the law as it applies to the private investigation industry. It gives the clients of private investigation services a basis to discuss with their investigators the methods used to obtain the results desired.

---

13   R. Colapinto, "Fraud Squad: Fighting White-Collar Crime" *CA Magazine* (May 1998) 19.

The Term "Private Sector Investigator"

The term private sector investigator was not my creation but was coined by some who are interested in developing a certification process for the industry. In addition to licensed private investigators, there are many persons who investigate in the private sector who are not required to be licensed. Such persons include those employed by insurers, the medical profession, the banks, accounting firms, and so forth. As many of the legal issues discussed in this book apply to licensed and unlicensed investigators alike, and as academic and other stakeholders seek to develop a single certification for all, the term "private sector investigator" has taken on a broader appeal.

Like any other developing field of interest, there may be lack of consensus to this approach. There is an extremely wide degree of sophistication possessed by operators in this industry, probably a range greater than in most industries. The spectrum ranges from chartered accountants specializing in forensic audits employed by large multinational firms to general practice, single person, private investigator agencies. There is no attempt in this book to make an argument for or against certifying persons operating in this industry under one title. However, for the sake of simplicity, the label "private sector investigator" has been adopted as the term of choice.

ACKNOWLEDGMENTS

Anyone who writes a book has a list of people that should be acknowledged for their assistance in making the project happen, and this project is no exception.

Copies of the draft manuscript for Chapter 2 were sent out to each provincial registrar for comment. Special commendations are in order for the input of Brian Millar, registrar of Saskatchewan; Charlene Mulion, registrar of Manitoba; Dean Benson, deputy registrar of British Columbia; and Gerry Gibson, deputy registrar of Ontario.

Copies of this manuscript were also sent out to the private investigator associations of Ontario, Alberta, and British Columbia. Ken Mitchell, Don Wilkinson, and Janet Helm are commended for their input.

Special mention should also be made of Jeff Miller and the team at Irwin Law for their assistance in the production of this book. I would also like to thank Brendan VanNiejenhuis, a law student at the University of Toronto, for his assistance.

Finally, and of course not least, I would like to acknowledge the support I received from my wife, Nan, a Chartered Accountant and senior audit manager with KPMG, LLP.

The Judicial System in Canada

CHAPTER 1

THE MACHINERY OF JUSTICE

This review of the Canadian machinery of justice will briefly touch upon such issues as the types, systems, and sources of law in Canada, and the Canadian court structure.

1.1   WHAT IS LAW?

Before determining who makes laws, it is important to know what is a law. Positive law has been defined as a body of rules for which sanctions are imposed upon their breach. But this definition, although useful, is not complete, for the enforcement of rules must be the responsibility of government and not of private persons. Thus, a restaurant owner who makes a rule that men will not be admitted to dinner unless they wear neckties and jackets has not made a law. Nor are the rules of a private organization, such as a private investigator association, considered law. A private investigator association may impose effective sanctions such as fining or expelling a member who breaks an important club rule, but its rules amount to no more than a private arrangement among club members.

1.1.1   Substantive and Procedural Law

Dividing law into broad categories helps us to understand the legal system. The two most basic categories are *substantive* and *procedural* law.

Substantive law consists of the rights and duties that each person has in society. Some examples are the right to own property, to vote, to travel about the country unmolested, to enter into contracts, to sell or give away property; the duty to avoid injuring others, to perform contract obligations, and to obey traffic laws, customs regulations, and other laws. The substantive laws are further divided into the fields of *public law* and *private law*, referred to below.

Procedural law deals with the protection and enforcement of these rights and duties. Thus, substantive laws decide which of two or more parties is at fault in an automobile accident, but it is through procedural laws that the injured party obtains a remedy against the wrongdoers. Procedural law prescribes the machinery by which the rights and duties recognized by substantive law are actually realized and enforced.

1.1.2   Public and Private Law

Public law is concerned with the conduct of government and the relations between the government on one side and private persons, including organizations such as companies, clubs, or unions, on the other side. Public law is divided into several categories such as constitutional law, criminal law, and administrative law.

Private law comprises the rules governing relations between private persons or groups of persons. A person involved in a dispute may resort to the courts to have his or her rights against the other side decided by the rules of private law. Private law is divided into a number of categories, the largest of which are contract, tort, property, and trusts. Frequently the term "civil law" is used to mean private law. This usage of the term civil law creates an unfortunate ambiguity, especially in Canada, because, as will be explained below, the primary meaning of civil law refers to a different legal system.

1.2   TWO SYSTEMS OF LAW

Two great systems of law have developed in Western Europe since the Middle Ages. They have been inherited by most of the lands that the nations of Western Europe colonized, including Canada.

1.2.1   The Civil Law

The older of the two systems is called the *civil law*. The civil law system covers the whole of continental Europe and to a large extent Scotland, much of Africa, and all of South and Central America. In North America it applies in Mexico and to some degree in several of the southern United States, but particularly in Louisiana, which was French territory until early in the nineteenth century. When the English conquered French Canada, they guaranteed the people of Quebec the continued use of French civil law in most areas of private law. To this day, most of the private law in the province of Quebec is civil law.

Civil law has its roots in Roman law. In the sixth century A.D., Emperor Justinian of the Eastern Roman Empire decided to codify the law of his vast domains. He brought together the leading jurists of the time and had them draft a comprehensive code based on the laws of Rome. This work was a monumental contribution to law and became known as Justinian's Code. It was inherited by the whole of continental Europe and formed the foundation for most of its legal systems. A similar code was ordered by Napoleon in 1804. This version, the French Civil Code, is best known as the Code Napoleon, and was adopted in, or greatly influenced the development of, codes in such countries as the Netherlands, Italy, Spain, Germany, Switzerland, and Belgium.

In these countries the theory is that a court always refers to the Code to settle a dispute. If the Code does not seem to cover a new problem, then the court is free to reason by analogy to settle the problem from general principles laid down in the Code. In theory, a later court need not follow the earlier reasoning in a similar case; the second court may decide that in its view, a just result of the law ought to be the reverse of the earlier decision.

Civil law theory could present practical difficulties. If in any system of law, judges were continually to follow their own biases, values, and personal prejudices, and so contradict earlier decisions, the law would become a jungle. No one could learn what the law on a particular point was. It is a requirement of justice, therefore, that like cases be treated alike. As equal and consistent treatment in like situations is one of the most important aspects of justice and hence of law as well, judges must be interested in, and to some extent influenced by, what other judges have decided in similar cases, whether in civil law or in common law countries.

A second major attribute of law is predictability. If people are to be able to find out where they stand and to act with reasonable certainty, the law itself must be fairly predictable — a strong reason why like cases ought to be decided alike. An important benefit of the concern that like cases be decided alike is the development by judges of principles that link like cases. These principles accumulate into a body of doctrine — a framework of predictable rules that serves as background for the vast majority of legal relations.

As a result, even in civil law countries, judges do decide similar cases in the same way most of the time although they are under no binding rule to do so. Today, in such countries as France and Germany, reports of decisions are regularly published so that lawyers and judges can learn what the courts are deciding and how they are interpreting the Civil Code in modern disputes.

1.2.2   The Common Law

The other great legal system is called the *common law*, and it had its origin in feudal England at the time of the Norman Conquest. It covers the whole of the English-speaking world except Scotland and is a significant part of the law of many non–English-speaking countries that were part of the British Empire, notably India, Pakistan, Bangladesh, and the former colonies in Africa.

The common law judges of England discerned the twin needs of consistency and predictability as early as the thirteenth century. In fact, at certain stages the courts followed previous decisions slavishly, even when the results in new circumstances were nonsensical or manifestly unjust. This custom of following already-decided cases is called the theory of precedent. The Latin phrase for the rule is known as *stare decisis*. The rule dictates that a judge must stand by previous decisions. Followed strictly, such a system, although it has the merits of certainty and uniformity, becomes inflexible, reactionary, and stultifying.

Stare decisis has never been an ironclad rule. In the first place, words are at best relatively inaccurate vehicles for thought. The very vagueness of language permits judges to draw distinctions between similar problems and so refuse to follow obsolete precedents. Second, no two sets of facts are identical in every respect; even when the same parties are involved, the time must be different. Judges, when they feel it to be truly necessary, can distinguish the case before them from earlier precedent by dwelling upon minor differences. In this way they are able to adjust the law rather slowly to changing circumstances and values. Nevertheless, the whole spirit of the common law system is bound to the theory of precedent. We look to past decisions to glean principles and to make new laws. Accordingly, a large part of the study of law is the study of decided cases.

Despite its internal flexibility, the theory of precedent hinders the law in accommodating the rapidly increasing rate of change in society. A decision that seemed quite acceptable in earlier years may be entirely out of step with current social standards. The only way for a court to cope with a marked change may be to ignore *stare decisis* and directly overrule a prior decision.

There is a danger in overruling decided cases too freely. To do so would undermine the needed consistency and predictability in law. The approach to this problem has been different in the United States, Britain and Canada. The Supreme Court of the United States has never considered itself bound to follow its own previous decisions when the result would be manifestly unjust. In a reversal of its traditional position, the English House of Lords recently announced that it will no longer consider itself bound to follow its own decisions. Its announcement is a clear recognition of the need for courts to depart from older decisions when contemporary standards call for change. The Canadian Supreme Court has not committed itself on this subject but it seems highly likely that, following the example of the much respected courts of these senior common law jurisdictions, it too will accept this needed flexibility. Accordingly, we may look forward to an increasing willingness on the part of our courts to disagree openly with past decisions.

An understanding of these significant limitations on *stare decisis* is important for those who will be proposing answers to the legal cases offered for discussion in this book. It is a mistake to assume when one finds an actual reported case with facts seemingly identical to those in the case under discussion that the conclusion in the reported case is the most satisfactory one. It is much more useful to consider the case offered for discussion on its legal and social merits and then look at the reported cases to see what light they may shed on the problem. Some of the reported cases have been severely criticized both by learned writers and by other courts in subsequent cases. They are cited because they offer an opportunity to discuss important problems.

1.3   SOURCES OF LAW

The earliest source of our law is the body of decisions handed down by the judiciary and permanently recorded in England from Norman times to the present day. The second source consists of the statutes passed by Parliament and by provincial legislatures. The Cabinet, in its formal role of adviser to the monarch, can also "legislate" within certain limited areas by issuing orders in council.[1] Every province has also passed statutes providing for the creation of municipal governments and their supervision. These statutes give municipalities the power to make law and to raise revenue for the benefit of their citizens. Municipal bylaws and regulations are thus a form of statute law. In addition to judge made law and statute law, there is a vast area of *subordinate legislation*, usually known as *administrative law*. It derives from authority granted by statute to various administrative agencies of government to make rules and regulations in order to carry out the purposes for which the legislation was passed.

---

1   An order in council is issued by the Privy Council (in effect, the Cabinet) in the name of the monarch, either in exercise of the royal prerogative or under authority of a statute.

1.3.1   Judge-Made Law

1.3.1.1   Common Law

As we have seen, the common law[2] is based on the theory of precedent, which in turn depends on a constant flow of reported cases. An organized national system of courts was therefore necessary to enable the common law to develop. Before a decision would influence judges in subsequent cases, it was necessary to have a judge with a recognized position in society and a court with a wide jurisdiction. Before the Norman Conquest, the courts were mainly local and varied greatly from county to county. William I gave England its first strong centralized government and thus laid the foundation for a national system of courts.

The earliest decisions were, of course, without the benefit of precedent. Courts were often left entirely to their own resources in reaching a decision. It is not always easy to understand their reasoning, but there is no doubt that already established local customs played an important role at the outset. Evidence concerning a local custom would be admitted, influence the judge's decision, and then be incorporated into the common law. As the body of precedents increased, and as the courts developed into a settled order of importance, prior decisions exerted an ever-increasing influence.

Canon law and Roman law also influenced early judicial decisions in England. The Church created canon law when it had a separate legal jurisdiction and held its own courts in matters pertaining to itself and to family law and wills. Roman law left its mark particularly in its distinction between possession and ownership of personal property. The influence of these systems of law was inevitable at a time when practically the only literate people were clerics and scholars trained on the continent. Still another force, feudal law, affected the common law concerning the ownership of land.

1.3.1.2   Equity

The common law by its very nature has always looked to the past for its authority. In its very early stages of development, its judges often sought new remedies when aggrieved parties appeared before them. But as the body of previous decisions grew, the common law became increasingly strict. By the late thirteenth century, it had become very formal and was burdened with cumbersome procedure, much of it rooted in ancient customs and superstitions. An aggrieved person who came before the court had to find one of the ancient forms, called a "writ," to suit the particular grievance. If an appropriate writ could not be found, the court would not grant a remedy. As England developed commercially, these old writs did not provide relief for many wrongs suffered by innocent parties, and great hardship often resulted.

Aggrieved parties without a remedy in the common law courts began to petition the king, who, in the age of the divine right of the monarchy, looked upon himself as the foun-

---

2   Unfortunately, the term "common law" has three possible meanings: (a) common law as opposed to equity, (b) judge-made law including equity as opposed to statute law, and (c) all the law of the common law countries as opposed to civil law countries.

tainhead of all law and justice. The king considered the hearing of petitions an important duty to his subjects and often granted relief. But as the number of petitions increased, the king's chancellor (his chief personal adviser, usually a cleric) took over the task of administering them. The flow continued to increase and the chancellor delegated the work to vice-chancellors. Soon it was apparent that another whole system of courts was growing. These courts were called the courts of the chancellor, which later became known as the courts of chancery, and still later as the courts of equity. The courts of equity developed laws that were labelled principles of equity. The principles of equity rivalled the principles of the common law in their contribution to the legal system developed by our judges.

The approach of the courts of equity was at first different from that of the common law courts because the medieval chancellor was a church official as well as the general secretary of the state. Where the common law courts were nondiscretionary and limited themselves to monetary damages, the courts of equity were discretionary and prepared to decree specific performance. Furthermore, if a defendant refused to comply with an order of the courts of equity, the courts of equity had the power to jail him for contempt of court. Apparently, the threat of medieval jail was highly persuasive.

1.3.1.3   Merger of the Courts

For a long time England continued with these two rival sets of courts. If an aggrieved person did not receive the remedy he sought in one court, he would have to bring a separate cause of action in the other. In 1865, the British Parliament passed an act merging the two systems of courts into the single system we know today. The Canadian provinces passed similar legislation shortly afterwards.

The amalgamation of the common law and equity courts did not mean the abandonment of the philosophy of equity. Every judge now is supposed to have two minds: one for equity and one for legal precedent. Judges may now apply equitable principles when it appears warranted in the circumstances. Equity thus provides a conscience for our modern common law. It prevents the law from straying too far away from reason and fairness.

1.3.2   Legislation

The second main source of our law, statute law or legislation, consists of acts of Parliament and the provincial legislatures and of bylaws passed by municipal governments. A statute overrides all the common law dealing with the same point. Although the volume of statute law is increasing rapidly, the common law still constitutes the bulk of our private law.

Sometimes legislatures enact statutes to codify existing common law rather than to change it. Before the passage of such acts, the related law was to be found in a staggering number of individual cases. The acts did away with the labour and uncertainty of searching through the cases for the relevant law.

Courts are often called on to interpret a statute to decide whether it applies to the facts of a case, and if it does, to decide on its consequences. Their decisions then form part of the judge-made law and are often referred to in subsequent cases. Judge-made law and statutes are thus closely related. The traditional attitude of the courts towards the common law is quite different from their attitude towards statutes. Although the common law is the creation of the courts themselves, statute law, as one writer put it, is "an alien intruder in the house of common law." The courts regularly use principles from earlier decisions, even though the facts may be quite different from the case at issue. On the other hand, the courts are less likely to apply the provisions of a statute unless the facts of the case at issue are covered specifically by the statute. This attitude of the courts is called the strict interpretation of the statutes.

1.3.3 Administrative Law

There are two main classes of legislation. The first and simplest consists of those statutes that change the law: they prohibit an activity formerly permitted or else remove a prohibition thereby enabling people to carry on a formerly illegal activity. This type of legislation is essentially passive in that it provides a framework within which people may legally go about their business. It does not presume to supervise and regulate their activities, but leaves it to an injured party or a law-enforcement official to complain about any activity that has violated a statute of this kind and to initiate court proceedings.

The second class of legislation authorizes the government itself to carry on a program or to supervise and regulate a related trade or activity. Examples of carrying on a program are levying taxes to provide revenue for the purpose of building a hospital, paying pensions to the elderly, and offering subsidies to encourage a particular kind of economic activity. Pertaining to the regulation of trade or activity, the rationale for such legislation is that Parliament itself has never carried on these activities and recognizes it is an inappropriate body to undertake any program requiring continuous supervision. Thus, the government sets up under legislation departments, agencies, and/or tribunals to regulate such activities as a form of consumer protection.

In exercising its regulatory powers and acting in its executive capacity, an administrative agency creates new law, which we defined earlier as "subordinate legislation." Some subordinate legislation sets down broad criteria regulating, for example, the type of guarantee that a licence applicant must supply to carry on a particular activity and the amount and type of investment required as a precondition. Other subordinate legislation may be detailed and technical (fees for applications) and may only require a single ruling on a particular application.

Important regulations — normally those setting out broad standards — require the approval of Cabinet in the form of an order in council. The agency itself drafts these regulations and the minister responsible for the agency brings them before Cabinet. Lesser regulations may be authorized by the minister, the head of the agency, or even a designated officer of the agency.

As noted earlier, the growing complexity of society and government has increased the need for specialized knowledge and control, and the list includes a growing number of business and professional activities that are believed to affect the public interest. As a result, government agencies, each with its own system of regulations and sanctions, continue to proliferate. For a further discussion of administrative law issues as they apply to private investigators, see Section 2.4 — Administrative Law Principles.

1.4   THE COURT SYSTEM IN CANADA

The division of legislative powers between the federal and provincial governments has inevitably led to disputes about which level has jurisdiction over the many problems that defy identification within the categories listed in sections 92 and 93 of the Constitution. Despite the inherent difficulties in federal constitutions, the division of powers in the Canadian constitution has not fared badly. Some aspects of its treatment show great wisdom and have caused little or no trouble. Others appear rather odd at first sight but can be explained by circumstances at the time of Confederation. For example, the Constitution gives the provinces jurisdiction over the administration of justice — the organization and operation of police forces and the system of the courts. At the same time, the Constitution gives the federal government jurisdiction over trade and commerce, banking, bankruptcy, and criminal law — matters frequently litigated before the courts — and also the exclusive right to appoint, and the obligation to pay, all superior court judges.

Why this peculiar division in the administration of the legal system? The explanation lies, at least in part, because at the time of discussions on Confederation in Canada, the United States had just been through a terrible civil war. Many Canadians believed that biased local state legislatures and locally elected judges had fanned internal division in the United States by passing discriminatory laws and by frequently administering laws unfairly against "outsiders" (citizens from other states). The Canadian constitution sought to avoid the problem of local bias by placing jurisdiction over matters peculiarly susceptible to local influence in the hands of the national government. The Constitution also requires that only qualified lawyers be appointed to the superior court benches. Until retirement, they hold office conditional on good behaviour. Superior court judges can be removed only by "joint address," that is, a vote taken before both the House of Commons and the Senate. These provisions are designed to keep judges as unbiased and immune from local pressures as possible.

As in England, there are three tiers of courts: the courts of first instance, the intermediate provincial and federal courts of appeal, and the Supreme Court of Canada. The names and jurisdiction of the courts differ somewhat from province to province, but in general they follow the pattern set out below.

1.4.1   Courts of First Instance

1.4.1.1   Provincial Courts

Provincial judges decide very little, if any, private law. They hear criminal and provincial quasi-criminal cases of almost every type except for the most serious offences. Provincial quasi-criminal cases would include charges laid under provincial legislation such as that pertaining to private investigators. They may hold preliminary hearings in prosecution of serious crimes to decide whether there is enough evidence to proceed to trial. No jury trials are held before provincial judges. If the crime alleged is of a sufficiently serious nature and if an accused elects to have a jury trial, the case must be heard in the Superior Court.

1.4.1.2   Superior Courts

This court is variously known in different provinces as the Court of Queen's Bench, the Superior Court, the Supreme Court, and the Supreme Court Trial Division. It has unlimited jurisdiction in civil and criminal actions. In more remote areas, judges of the Superior Court go on circuit; that is, a judge tours each of a group of county towns periodically and tries the cases that are waiting. The Superior Court in most provinces is divided into various divisions. For example, in Ontario the divisions of the Superior Court of Justice include the Criminal Division, the Civil Division, the Small Claims Court, the Unified Family Court, the Commercial Court, and the Estates Court.

1.4.1.3   Federal Court of Canada

The federal government maintains the Federal Court of Canada in two dimensions: a trial division and an appeal division. Under a 1970 statute, the Federal Court received expanded jurisdiction. Now certain kinds of actions that could formerly be brought in the provincial courts as well are reserved exclusively for the Federal Court, which has exclusive jurisdiction over such matters as patents, copyright and trademarks, disputes concerning ships and navigation, and many sorts of lawsuits against the federal government itself. There remains a large area of concurrent jurisdiction where a plaintiff may still sue in either a provincial court or in Federal Court. For example, a person injured by a careless operation of a federal government motor vehicle may still sue in provincial court.

1.4.2   Appellate Level Courts

1.4.2.1   Superior Courts

Superior Courts, in addition to being courts of absolute jurisdiction in civil and criminal matters, may also act as appellate courts. On the civil side, Superior Court judges may hear appeals from interlocutory orders of a master and appeals from the assessment of costs from a taxation officer. On the criminal side, Superior Court judges may hear appeals on summary conviction matters heard in a provincial court.

1.4.2.2   Divisional Courts

The Divisional Court, created in 1972, is peculiar to Ontario. It consists of the Chief Justice of the Superior Court and such other judges of that court as the Chief Justice designates from time to time. It sits in panels of three judges more or less continuously in Toronto and at various times throughout the year in several other centres. It hears appeals from orders of a judge of the Superior Court in civil matters for single or periodic payments in an amount not greater than $25,000, all interlocutory orders of a judge from the Superior Court with leave, and from all final orders of a master. Divisional Courts also hear applications for judicial review from various provincial administrative tribunals.

1.4.2.3   Provincial Courts of Appeal

Each province has an intermediate appellate court, called variously the Appellate Division, the Supreme Court *en banc* (the whole bench), Queen's Bench Appeals, as well as the Court of Appeal. Provincial Courts of Appeal hear appeals on civil and criminal matters from the Superior Court and appeals from the Divisional Court. Provincial Courts of Appeal usually sit in panels of three appellate court judges. Leave to appeal is required to appeal most matters.

1.4.2.4   Federal Court of Appeal

The Federal Court of Appeal hears appeals from matters tried in the Federal Court — Trial Division.

1.4.2.5   Supreme Court of Canada

The Supreme Court of Canada is the final court of appeal in Canada. It consists of nine judges and hears appeals from both the provincial and federal courts of appeal. In addition, it has special jurisdiction under the *Supreme Court of Canada Act* to rule on the constitutionality of federal and provincial statutes when they are referenced to the court by the federal cabinet. In almost all actions, the appellant must obtain special leave from the Supreme Court of Canada to appeal.

Authorities & Liabilities of Private Investigators

CHAPTER 2

PROVINCIAL PRIVATE INVESTIGATORS AND SECURITY GUARDS ACTS

Legislation pertaining to private investigators falls under provincial jurisdiction. In Alberta, Manitoba, Newfoundland, New Brunswick, Ontario, Prince Edward Island, Saskatchewan, and the Yukon, the legislation is known as the *Private Investigators and Security Guards Act*. In Nova Scotia it is entitled *An Act to Provide for Private Investigators and Private Guards*. Quebec's legislation is entitled *An Act Respecting Detective or Security Agencies*, and British Columbia's is entitled the *Private Investigators and Security Agencies Act*.[1] For the sake of simplicity, this book will refer to each province's or territory's legislation as the "Act" or the "PISGA" for short. Where the Yukon Territory is included, it will be referenced as a province. Finally, where the term "registrar" is used in the commentary, it shall include reference to the respective provincial registrar, administrator, inspector, or commissioner.[2]

The Northwest Territories does not have any legislation pertaining to private investigators. An Act entitled the *Locksmiths, Security Guards and Other Security Occupations Act*,[3] which was to apply to private investigators among others, was enacted by the territorial legislature but it was never brought into force. It was later revoked by the *Reform Measures Act*.[4]

---

1   R.S.A. 1980, c. P-16; R.S.B.C. 1996, c. 374; R.S.M. 1987, c. P132; R.S.N. 1990, c. P-24; R.S.N.B. 1973, c. P-16 consolidated to 31 March 1997; R.S.N.S.1989, c. 356; R.S.O. 1990, c. P.25; R.S.P.E.I. 1988, c. P-20; R.S.Q. 1977, c. A-8; R.S.S.1997, c. P-26.01; S.Y. 1988, c. 23 as amended by S.Y. 1998, c. 22.

2   For a more in-depth explanation of the various titles used, see Section 2.4 — Administrative Law Principles.

3   R.S.N.W.T. 1988, c. 103 (Supp).

4   S.N.W.T. 1998, c. 21, s. 18. No regulations were ever prepared for this Act. Reference <mark_aitken@gov.nt.ca >.

The new territory of Nunavut does not have any such law either, as the legislation in the Northwest Territories was revoked prior to the creation of the new territory.[5]

Because the source of this law is mostly statutory in nature, consideration was given to including the legislative extracts in this book. However, due to space constraints and in recognition that legislation can be difficult to read, overviews of the legislation are included instead. Footnotes will inform the reader if direct reference is necessary. Notwithstanding this omission, although reading legislation may be cumbersome for the uninitiated, it is often the preferable approach, especially when the legislation is complex. As there are often multiple interpretations to the same provisions, any discussion of what the law is cannot be made without direct reference to what the statute says. This is especially true when comparing similar provisions of the various provincial Acts. It is therefore suggested that students of this text acquire their own copy of their respective Act.[6]

Another reason for reviewing the legislation of each province is because increasingly in today's society, investigations cover wider geographical areas. Investigations that commence in one province often continue into other provinces, or even foreign countries. As the jurisdiction of the legislation pertaining to private investigators is provincial, private investigators will find that, when operating in a province not their own, they will be bound by the laws of the province in which they are operating. Accordingly, it is imperative that a private investigator become familiar with the laws of that province. Although most provincial Acts contain similar legislative provisions, there are some significant differences that this chapter will try to impress upon private investigators to assist in avoiding ex-territorial liability.

One more reason to be familiar with the legislation of other provinces is because of the new federal privacy legislation. This legislation, reviewed in Chapter 5 of this book, makes the fee-based transfer of private information across provincial boundaries illegal if the subject of that information does not give express consent. As such, it may become necessary for investigative agencies that acquire private information on subject parties in one province which they intend to sell in another province to set up an agency in the province where the information is to be sold. The reason for this is because current federal privacy legislation does not prohibit the non–fee-based transfer of information across provincial boundaries. Therefore, to sell the impugned information, a private investigative company may be required to transfer the information at no expense from the province where it was acquired to an agency it owns in the province where that information is to be sold. To reiterate, operating in another province will require familiarity with that province's PISGA legislation.

As mentioned, investigations today often not only go beyond the province in which they commence, but also lead into foreign countries. This book does not review the laws of foreign states. If information of this nature is required, advice should be sought from foreign authorities or from appropriate foreign legal counsel.

5   On 1 April 1999, Nunavut assumed the laws of the Northwest Territories as its own, and no legislation existed pertaining to private investigators. Reference <mspakowski@gov.nu.ca>.
6   There is very little case law reported on the various provincial Acts. One registrar reported a reason for this void of case law is because in his five years of conducting licensing hearings, a written decision was never requested, and accordingly he never had a decision reviewed.

Although this chapter is confined to licensed private investigators, many of the comments will relate directly to security personnel as well.[7] Furthermore, notwithstanding that the focus of this book is on the private sector investigation industry, occasionally cases are discussed wherein security personnel were the focus of the court's attention.

Finally, attention should be drawn to the distinction between guidelines, statutes and regulations. Although most of the authority referenced in this chapter is statute, regulatory, and case law, occasionally a registrar's internal guidelines are cited. These guidelines are not law, are subject to frequent change, and are occasionally not followed if the facts of the specific case merit an exception. Accordingly, where a registrar's administrative guidelines are cited, contact should be made with the respective provincial registrar to determine if they apply to the individual case.[8]

2.1   PERSONS AND ACTIVITIES SUBJECT TO THE ACT

This section will discuss

- what activities are included and not included in the definition of a private investigator;
- why it is important to know what activities are included in the definition of a private investigator;
- which types of occupational groups are exempt from requiring a private investigator's licence; and
- which types of occupations are in conflict of interest with that of holding a private investigator's licence.

2.1.1 DEFINITION OF A PRIVATE INVESTIGATOR

The term "private investigator" has been defined in a number of different ways in the various provincial Acts.[9] It is important to be familiar with the term "private investigator" because only those activities that fall within the definition require licensing under the PISGA. Furthermore, as indicated in the introduction to this chapter, the importance of being familiar with the differences in each provincial Act becomes apparent when investigating outside of the province in which one is licensed.

---

7   For discussions of issues relating to security personnel, see C.D. Shearing & P.C. Stenning, *Private Security and Private Justice — The Challenge of the 80s: A Review of Policy Issues* (Montreal: The Institute for Research on Public Policy, 1983); F. Jefferies, ed., *Private Policing and Security in Canada* (Toronto: Centre of Criminology, University of Toronto, 1973); and C.D. Shearing & P.C. Stenning, *Search and Seizure Powers of Private Security Personnel: A Study Paper* (Ottawa: Law Reform Commission of Canada, 1979).

8   Provincial registrars requested that General Guideline section numbers not be cited as they are subject to frequent change.

9   In British Columbia, the Act often uses the term "security employees" and "security businesses" when referring to private investigators and private investigative agencies and other occupational groups covered by the Act such as security guards and locksmiths.

For example, if a person is conducting an investigation inside of Alberta, he or she requires a private investigator's licence to search for and furnish information on a person's personal, business, or occupational character or actions, or to search for missing persons. However, if a person is conducting an investigation in Ontario, not only does he or she require a private investigator's licence to undertake such activities, but also to search for offenders against the law or to search for missing property. In other words, although a private investigator's licence is required to search for missing property or offenders against the law in Ontario, in Alberta, anyone can undertake this activity without a private investigator's licence.

TABLE 2.1

A comparative analysis of the functions included in the definition of a private investigator for each province

Function	Province
Obtaining and furnishing information as to the personal character or actions of a person	All provinces
Obtaining and furnishing information of the character or kind of business or occupation of a person	All provinces except Quebec
Seeking or obtaining information about the activities, character, or repute of a business or organization	Only in British Columbia or Saskatchewan
Searching for offenders against the law	All provinces except Alberta, British Columbia, and Quebec
Seeking or obtaining information about crimes and offences generally	Only in British Columbia and Quebec
Searching for missing persons	All provinces except Quebec
Searching for missing property	All provinces except Alberta and Quebec
Seeking or obtaining information of the causes of fires, accidents, and incidents	Only in British Columbia
Retail store employee integrity checks and retail store loss prevention	Only in New Brunswick, Newfoundland, and the Yukon

Arguably, however, the last function in Table 2.1 is simply part of the first function mentioned, that is, obtaining and furnishing information as to the personal character or actions of a person, which is included in the definition of the term "private investigator" in each province.[10]

---

10 It is the policy of the registrar's office in Ontario that "integrity" shoppers require licensing as a private investigator but that "mystery" shoppers do not.

The phrase "for hire and reward" is included in the definition of private investigator in British Columbia, Newfoundland, Nova Scotia, Ontario, Prince Edward Island, Quebec, Saskatchewan, and the Yukon.[11] Therefore, if the functions listed in Table 2.1 are conducted by someone in Alberta, Manitoba, or New Brunswick, a licence is required even if those functions are performed pro bono.[12]

There have been a couple of cases that have focused on the definition of a private investigator. In both cases, the charge against the individual was operating as a private investigator without a licence. A court from Ontario held that the task of skip-tracing falls under the definition of private investigator.[13] A court from British Columbia held that the task of process serving does not.[14] Notwithstanding this decision from British Columbia, the General Guidelines from Saskatchewan state that the definition of private investigator includes process servers. However, in another section of their General Guidelines it states that a civil process may be served by anyone. In light of this apparent contradiction, the better view is that a private investigator's licence is not required to undertake process serving.[15] It is noteworthy that the function of "executive protection" is not included in the various Acts. Policy statements have determined this function to fall under the title of security guard.[16] The field of electronic countermeasures also remains an unlicensed profession in Canada.[17]

2.1.1.1   Scope of a Private Investigator's Licence

The scope of a private investigator's licence has been the subject of debate. One view determining the scope of this licence is that if the function is not specifically legislated in the Act, licensing is not required to provide that service. An example of this taken from the

---

11   The term "reward" has been held by the Ontario registrar's office to include "gaining experience." Therefore, college students are required to be licensed even if they work for a private investigation agency without compensation.

12   R.S.A. 1980, c. P-16, s. 1; R.S.B.C. 1996, c. 374, s. 1; R.S.M. 1987, c. P132, s. 1 as amended by S.M. 1992, c. 58, s. 25(2)(a); R.S.N. 1990, c. P-24, s. 2; R.S.N.B. 1973, c. P-16, s. 1; R.S.N.S. 1989, c. 356, s. 2; R.S.O. 1990, c. P.25, s. 1; R.S.P.E.I. 1988, c. P-20, s. 1; R.S.Q. 1977, c. A-8, s. 1 and R.R.Q. 1977, c. A-8, r. 1; R.S.S. 1997, c. P-26.01, s. 2; S.Y. 1988, c. 23, s. 1 as amended by S.Y. 1998, c. 22.

13   *R. v. Lillie*, [1988] O.J. No. 1476 (Dist. Ct.).

14   *R. v. Aanar Management Corp.* (1983), 11 W.C.B. 198, B.C.J. No. 1279 (Co. Ct.).

15   R.S.S. 1997, c. P-26.01, General Guidelines; R.S.O. 1990, c. P.25, General Guidelines.

16   R.S.O. 1990, c. P.25, General Guidelines, provides that there is no definition of "executive protection" within the PISGA. A person performing duties of guarding or providing security for a person would fall within the definition of "security guard" as defined in the PISGA. According to the policy, licensed security guards that provide personal security services to a person are not exempt from the PISGA and must display the word "security guard" on their chests as directed while performing their duty. This seems a rather incredulous result. A similar policy statement is included in the General Guidelines of Saskatchewan.

17   D. Ralph, "Minding Your Privacy" *Canadian Security* (June/July 1999) at 20. Doug Ralph is president of COMSEC Services Inc., an electronic countermeasures firm based in Milton, Ontario.

previous section is that a licence is not required to search for missing property in Alberta as Alberta's PISGA does not include this function in its definition of a private investigator.

Another view is that if a person is licensed as a private investigator, that person should not be performing functions that the Act does not provide for. This view was explored by the Federal Court in a tax case.[18] In this case, the issue was whether the function of making "recommendations" came within the definition of "private investigator" under the Act. The taxpayer argued that the functions of investigating and furnishing information, as set out in section 1 of Ontario's PISGA, includes the provision of advice, and in the context of this case, advice as to the compensation to be paid in respect of a claim. The taxpayer further argued that his corporation routinely made recommendations to insurance companies, not as to the precise amount to settle a claim, but with regard to having further investigative work done, if a claim was excessive, or if an individual was malingering.

The court, however, did not agree. It held that the verbs used in section 1 such as "to investigate," "to furnish," and "to search" are clear words, and that a court was not to depart from their ordinary meaning or embark on some search for the supposed intention of Parliament. The court held that the definition of financial services in the Excise Tax Act (ETA) required "the service of investigating and recommending compensation in satisfaction of a claim." The court held that it therefore follows that the reference to "a person . . . who is licenced under the laws of a province to provide such a service" must require that the provincial licence specifically apply to both "investigating" and "recommending." Section 8 of the PISGA authorizes the issuing of a licence to act as a private investigator, a function that by definition does not involve the making of recommendations. Consequently, any recommendation made by a licensed private investigator in Ontario does not form part of the function that the licence authorizes.

In addition to relying on the strict definitions provided by the PISGA and the ETA, the court also referred to the evidence of an insurance adjuster who claimed to have forty years of experience dealing with insurance claims. This witness characterized the distinction between the roles of insurance adjusters and private investigators as follows:

> In my experience private investigators are used by insurance companies to carry out surveillance on individuals, usually in claims relating to bodily injury. They are also used to investigate accident scenes, take statements and do financial or background checks particularly in suspicious circumstances. The investigator then reports to either the staff or independent adjuster, examiner or lawyer who has hired them. In my experience, private investigators are not asked for recommendations as to compensation to be paid in satisfaction of a claim under an insurance policy. It is the job of the adjuster or the claims examiner to decide on the course of action to take, including the compensation to be paid, based on the information provided in the investigator's report.

The court accepted this opinion as accurately depicting the usual functions of insurance adjusters and private investigators in the relevant context. Accordingly, he dismissed the taxpayer's appeal from Revenue Canada's assessment under the ETA.

---

18   *MVSGI v. Canada*, [1998] T.C.J. No. 808 (T.C.C.), aff'd [2001] F.C.J. No. 527 (F.C.A.) [unreported].

With respect to the court, it is believed that the better position is not what a licence authorizes, but those functions for which a licence is required. For this reason, it is submitted that this decision should be confined to tax law, and not to interpretation of the PISGA itself.

2.1.1.2   Powers and Authority of a Private Investigator

In its essence, the powers and authority of a private investigator are those of any private citizen.[19] Notwithstanding that only Alberta, Newfoundland, and Quebec have formally stated this principle in their legislation,[20] the courts in most provinces have recognized this proposition in their decisions.

The issue of a private investigator's authority has been raised in a number of contexts. In criminal cases where the defence of status has been raised, it has been held that no colour of right attaches to unlawful behaviour simply because the accused is a private investigator.[21] The same finding has been made in *Highway Traffic Act* cases.[22] In privacy cases, however, a private investigator's status has been successfully argued as a defence where it has been established the private investigator had a "legitimate interest" in conducting an investigation.[23]

The "legitimate interest" argument has been the subject of some discussion. It has been held that a private investigator may have a legitimate interest if he is acting as an agent of the person with whom he has a contract for services. This legitimacy argument arises from the social utility derived from the immoral and/or illegal acts the private investigator exposes.

Another way of viewing this issue is that the most important source of authority of a private investigator is the instruction he receives from a client. These instructions can vary widely. The investigator may be given free rein by a client to do what he feels is necessary to obtain the information sought, subject only to his own concerns over legality and ethics,

---

19   This point of view has been criticized as too simplistic. See C.D. Shearing & P.C. Stenning, *Private Security and Private Justice — The Challenge of the 80s: A Review of Policy Issues* (Montreal: The Institute for Research on Public Policy, 1983).

20   R.S.A. 1980, c. P-16, r. 15; R.S.N. 1990, c. P-24, s. 34; R.R.Q. 1977, c. A-8, r. 1.

21   *R. v. Andsten and Petrie* (1960), 32 W.W.R. 329 (B.C.C.A.); *R. v. Gibson*, [1976] 6 W.W.R. 484 (Sask. Dist. Ct.); *R. v. Massue*, (1964), 55 D.L.R. (2d) 79 (Que. Q.B.). This is also the position of courts in the United States: *Shultz v. Frankfort Marine Accident and Plate Glass Insurance Company*, 139 N.W. 386 (Wisc. Sup. Ct. 1913); and Australia: *Poznanski v. Stosic*, [1953] S.A.S.R. 132 (Austl.). See Chapter 4 for a further discussion of this issue.

22   *Loncaric v. British Columbia (Superintendent of Motor Vehicles)*, [2000] B.C.J. No. 1032 (S.C.).

23   *Davis v. McArthur*, [1971] 2 W.W.R. 142 (B.C.C.A.); *Druken v. RG Fewer & Associates Inc.*, [1998] N.J. No. 312 (S.C.). This position has also been held in the United States: G. LaMarca, "Overintrusive Surveillance of Plaintiffs in Personal Injury Cases" (1986) 35 Defence L.J. 603; *Forster v. Manchester*, 189 A.2d 147 at 150 (Penn. Sup. Ct. 1963). See *Insurance Corporation of British Columbia v. Somosh and Somosh* (1983), 51 B.C.L.R. 344 (S.C.) for an example of where a private investigator did not have a legitimate interest. See Chapter 5 pertaining to privacy legislation for a further discussion of this issue.

or he may be placed under severe restraints. A client's authority, however, must never result in a breach of the legal constraints a private investigator, as a citizen, is under.[24]

2.1.2 Persons and Activities Exempt from the Act

The main purpose of the various provincial Acts is to protect the public from persons or companies performing the services of private investigation who are of poor character and/or of insufficient financial resources to provide for restitution in case of a judgment against them. In effect, the purpose of the PISGA is a form of consumer protection. For this reason, it is an offence against the Act to perform the activities of a private investigator without a licence.

Notwithstanding that it is an offence to render the services of a private investigator without a licence, some persons or occupational groups are exempt from the legislation. In most cases, each of the exempt persons or groups are governed by their own form of legislation designed to protect the public. Therefore, it would appear that what is prohibited by the Act is not performing the services of private investigation without a licence *per se*, but rather performing the services of private investigation while not being governed by some form of legislation. Generally, each province includes the following professions[25] in this list:

- barristers and solicitors
- police officers
- members of the Canadian Corps of Commissionaires
- insurance company employees
- insurance adjusters
- bailiffs
- collectors of accounts
- employees of financial credit rating companies
- employees of the federal, provincial, and/or municipal governments acting within the scope of their duties

A second form of exemption is private investigators who commence an investigation in their home province and continue that investigation in another province. In most cases, the province in question permits the private investigator to investigate within that province without first obtaining a licence. However, while the private investigator is investigating in that province, she is bound by the laws of that jurisdiction. As stated, most provinces have this form of reciprocal interprovincial agreement. There are, however, some important

---

24 E.F. Geddes, "The Private Investigator and the Right to Privacy" (1989) 17 Alta. L. Rev. 256 at 263.

25 R.S.A. 1980, c. P-16, s. 2; R.S.B.C. 1996, c. 374, s. 2; R.S.M. 1987, c. P132, s. 2; R.S.N. 1990, c. P-24, s. 1; R.S.N.B. 1973, c. P-16, s. 2; R.S.N.S. 1989, c. 356, s. 3; R.S.O. 1990, c. P.25, s. 2; R.S.P.E.I. 1988, c. P-20, s. 2; R.S.Q. 1977, c. A-8, s. 1; R.R.S 2000, c. P-26.01, r. 1, s. 3, General Guidelines; S.Y. 1988, c. 23, s. 2.

exceptions, notably in Quebec, Saskatchewan, and British Columbia. In Quebec, where no such legislation exists, an out-of-province private investigator is required to contact a private investigator licensed in that province to follow up the investigation or become licensed in that province. In British Columbia and Saskatchewan, permission from the provincial registrar is required before the investigation can be continued. For a more in-depth discussion, see Section 2.3.2.4 — Operating Outside of Jurisdiction.[26]

A final form of exemption is investigators who are permanently employed by one employer in a business or undertaking other than the business of providing private investigations and whose work is confined to the affairs of that employer.[27]

There has been some case law on this issue. In an Alberta criminal case, an unlicensed individual took a statement from a young girl who had accused her father of sexual abuse. He did so at the request of the lawyers acting on behalf of the father after the preliminary hearing. The accused then sent a bill to the solicitors for the service. The accused had the solicitor make payment for his services to a numbered company. This was the only evidence before the court of the accused's activities. While the accused was acquitted for other reasons, the court noted that although barristers and solicitors are exempt from the Act, their agents are not.[28]

The question of who is an agent of a lawyer was discussed in an Ontario case where a law firm used its articling students, law clerks, and support staff to make undercover purchases of optical products in contravention of the rules governing the Board of Ophthalmic Dispensers. The law firm was accused of breaching Rule 17 of the Law Society of Upper Canada's Rules of Professional Conduct pertaining to Outside Interests and the Practice of Law, which provides that outside activities of a lawyer should not jeopardize a lawyer's professional integrity. The court, however, held that although such a practice may not be advisable, it is not breach of a lawyer's ethical conduct, particularly when the staff used are instructed to record accurately the facts of the investigation.[29]

In a case from British Columbia, although the court did not find it necessary to decide on the issue, it hinted that process servers would be exempt from licensing as they would fall under the exemption of persons permanently employed by one employer whose business is other than that of providing private investigator services.[30]

The legislation on this issue is quite lengthy and not imperative to the practice of investigating. Reference to the legislation is only required should a private investigator ever take

26 R.S.A. 1980, c. P-16, s. 3(3); R.S.B.C. 1996, c. 374, s. 2; R.S.M. 1987, c. P132, s. 2; R.S.N. 1990, c. P-24, s. 1(h); R.S.N.B. 1973, c. P-16, s. 2(d); R.S.N.S. 1989, c. 356, s. 3(j); R.S.O. 1990, c. P.25, s. 2(1)(i); R.S.P.E.I. 1988, c. P-20, s. 2(j); R.R.S 2000, c. P-26.01, r. 1, s. 3, General Guidelines; S.Y. 1988, c. 23, s. 5(2).

27 R.S.A. 1980, c. P-16, s. 2(e); R.S.B.C. 1996, c. 374, s. 13; R.S.M. 1987, c. P132, s. 2(h); R.S.N.B. 1973, c. P-16, s. 2(h.1); R.S.N.S. 1989, c. 356, s. 3(g); R.S.O. 1990, c. P.25, s. 2(g); R.S.P.E.I. 1988, c. P-20, s. 2(g); R.S.Q. 1977, c. A-8, s. 1(c); R.R.S. 2000, c. P-26.01, r. 1, s. 3; S.Y. 1988, c. 23, s. 2(5).

28 *R. v. Howes* (1991), 14 W.C.B. (2d) 537 (Alta. Prov. Ct.).

29 *Markandey v. Ontario (Board of Ophthalmic Dispensers)*, [1994] O.J. No. 484 (Gen. Div.).

30 *R. v. Aanar Management Corp.* (1983), 11 W.C.B. 198, B.C.J. No. 1279 (Co. Ct.).

issue with an unlicensed practitioner. Although the general exemptions to licensing have been listed, it is noteworthy that some of the various PISGAs contain their own peculiar exemptions and that some of the provincial registrars do not enforce licensing upon certain occupational groups.[31]

2.1.3 Conflicts of Interest

Conflict of interest has been defined as a situation wherein a reasonably informed person would be satisfied that the misuse of confidential information could occur. There are a number of specific professions that legislators have deemed to be in conflict of interest with that of being a private investigator.

The most obvious profession in conflict of interest with private investigators is that of peace officers because of their access to confidential information databanks and their duty to serve public, not private, interests. Each province except British Columbia, Prince Edward Island, and Quebec strictly prohibits the granting of a licence to a peace officer.[32] In British Columbia, the legislation permits the granting of a private investigator's licence to a peace officer upon the discretion of the registrar. The registrar, however, must be satisfied that controls exist that will prevent the peace officer from using confidential information data banks for purposes other than those related to the police.[33] In Prince Edward Island one can hold a private investigator's licence while a peace officer only if the applicant is a peace officer in the capacity of an instructor at the Atlantic Police Academy. Strangely, Quebec's legislation does not speak to this issue. An exception to this general rule is found in the provinces of Alberta, Newfoundland, Ontario, Saskatchewan, and the Yukon where the registrar may grant a private investigator's licence to persons who are peace officers whose sole function is that of parking control bylaw officers.[34] The Saskatchewan registrar reports, however, that this exception is not granted unless an "Approval for Outside Employment" letter is received from the applicant's police service.

---

31 British Columbia includes in this group janitorial staff, agency administrative staff, Crown corporations, engineers, architects, film directors, government liquor and gaming investigators, chartered accountants, and airline reservation personnel. Ontario excludes peace officers and persons appointed as bailiffs under the *Ministry of Correctional Services Act*. Ontario does not enforce licensing upon chartered accountants as they are governed by their own legislation. Certified Fraud Examiners, however, do require licensing as they are only governed by a private association. This review is not exhaustive. See the province's legislation or contact the provincial registrar for further information.

32 R.S.A. 1980, c. P-16, s. 17; R.S.B.C. 1996, c. 374, s. 5(2); R.S.M. 1987, c. P132, s. 35; R.S.N. 1990, c. P-24, s. 34; R.S.N.B. 1973, c. P-16, s. 5.1; R.S.N.S. 1989, c. 356, s. 20; R.S.O. 1990, c. P.25, General Guidelines, Part C, s. 4; R.S.P.E.I. 1988, c. P-20, r. 19; R.S.S. 1997, c. P-26.01, s. 24; S.Y. 1988, c. 23, s. 27.

33 See *Security News*, Issue 7, May 1999. The registrar's office reports the current policy is not to license any police officer as a private investigator for any reason.

34 Note that R.S.O. 1990, c. P.25, General Guidelines, also provides that the prohibition does not apply to special constables or provincial offences officers whose function is escorting prisoners between correctional institutions and courts. See also s. 53(5) of Ontario's *Police Services Act*.

Other than peace officers, the only other profession that is universally held to be in conflict of interest with private investigators is collection agents. One can only surmise the reason for this. Bailiffs are another profession widely deemed to be in conflict of interest with private investigators. Only in Newfoundland, Quebec, and the Yukon is there no prohibition to being licensed as a private investigator while providing the services of a bailiff. Other various conflicts of interest deemed by various provincial legislators include locksmiths in British Columbia and non–peace-officer prison staff in Newfoundland. Because they are licensed under other legislation, there are no prohibitions against consumer reporting investigators being co-licensed as private investigators notwithstanding they have access to confidential credit information about the public.[35]

The provinces that have made the most effort to scrutinize possible conflicts of interest with the granting of private investigator's licences are Ontario and Saskatchewan. In Ontario, the impetus for this effort had its origins in Justice Krever's *Report of the Commission of Inquiry into the Confidentiality of Health Information* of 1980. The Krever Commission Report was a three-volume, 1,600-page report into the misuse of confidential health care information. The Commission made investigation into the practices of at least nine different private investigation agencies operating in Ontario during the 1970s. A review of the findings of the Commission can be found in Chapter 7 of this book.

As a result of the Commission's findings, the registrar of the Ontario PISGA has placed in its discretionary administrative policies the following professions deemed to be in conflict of interest with a private investigator:

- ambulance drivers and attendants
- auxiliary police members
- bailiffs
- bank and other financial institutional employees
- barristers and solicitors and their employees
- bylaw enforcement officers
- civil servants, both federal and provincial
- civilian employees of police services
- collectors of accounts
- correctional services employees
- doctors
- registered nurses and registered nursing assistants
- firefighters

---

35   R.S.A. 1980, c. P-16, s. 16, r. 14; R.S.B.C. 1996, c. 374, ss. 3, 5, & 10; R.S.M. 1987, c. P132, s. 34; R.S.N. 1990, c. P-24, s. 28, r. 12; R.S.N.B. 1973, c. P-16, s. 4.1, & 15; R.S.N.S. 1989, c. 356, s. 19; R.S.O. 1990, c. P.25, s. 29; R.S.P.E.I. 1988, c. P-20, s. 18; R.S.Q. 1977, c. A-8, s. 10; R.S.S. 1997, c. P-26.01, s. 28, General Guidelines; S.Y. 1988, c. 23, s. 27.

- insurance agents and insurance adjusters
- justices of the peace
- military and militia police members
- peace or police officers
- police services board members
- provincial driver examiners
- volunteers with the police services

Although not strictly prohibited, it is the practice of the registrar to deny licensing as a private investigator if the applicant is involved in any of the listed professions unless the applicant can demonstrate that there is no conflict of interest. A similar list is found in the General Guidelines to Saskatchewan's Act.[36]

There have been a number of cases interpreting the issue of peace officers being licensed as private investigators. In one case from British Columbia, a police officer was the owner of an alarm company and was engaged in the alarm business part-time. Although originally licensed, the registrar later retracted his consent to the applicant on the basis that there were not sufficient controls in place within the police department.[37] In another case from British Columbia, a university police officer was terminated for improperly conducting business as a private investigator while on duty and in uniform as a peace officer.[38]

2.2   LICENSING

This section will discuss

- the process of becoming licensed as a private investigator and/or a private investigative agency;
- the term/duration of a private investigator's licence or a private investigative agency licence and when it must be renewed;
- what the registrar permits an executor or administrator to do when a private investigative agency owner dies;
- the purpose and length of time a temporary licence for a private investigator or private investigative agency may be acquired;
- what happens to the licence of a private investigator or private investigative agency when the investigator resigns, the agency closes, or the licensee is suspended or has his or her licence revoked;
- transferring a licence to another person;

---

36   R.S.O. 1990, c. P.25, General Guidelines; R.S.S. 1997, c. P-26.01, General Guidelines.

37   *Active Alarms & Security Systems Inc. v. British Columbia (Registrar of the Private Investigators & Security Agencies Act)*, [1983] B.C.D. Civ. 58.6-03 (S.C.).

38   *Re University of Victoria and CUPE Local 917* (1991), 26 C.L.A.S. 80 (B.C.S.C.).

* having multiple sponsoring private investigative agencies; and
* the issues raised when making application for either a private investigator or a private investigative agency licence.

2.2.1 Licensing Requirements

Licensing requirements vary little across the country and are not onerous. The licensing provisions apply to all new applicants as well as those seeking annual renewals.

All private investigators must be licensed by their respective provincial registrar through a "sponsoring" private investigative agency. Any individual, partnership, or corporation that wishes to operate as a private investigative agency must be licensed by their respective provincial registrar as such. Therefore, if an individual wishes to own a private investigative agency and act as a private investigator, he or she must be licensed both as a private investigator and a private investigative agency. The former is often referred to as the "agent" licence, while the latter is referred to as the "agency" licence.

It is an offence to operate without a licence both as an agent and as an agency. It is also an offence for an agency to employ a person whose functions fit the definition of a private investigator and who is not licensed. Although all private investigative businesses, investigative employees, and investigative trainees must be licensed under their respective provincial PISGA, administrative staff who do not supervise licensed employees are exempt. Further, managers or supervisors of private investigation agencies do not requiring licensing if they are not engaged in investigations. This distinction is drawn as it is possible for a corporation to be licensed as a private investigation agency and then be managed by someone who has not applied for, been refused, or been suspended from, an agency or agent's licence.[39]

If a private investigative business and/or a private investigator is licensed in one province and wishes to conduct an investigation in another province, he or she must comply with the licensing provisions of that province. As pointed out earlier in this chapter, most provinces have reciprocal licensing exemption agreements for these situations. If a private investigative business and/or a private investigator wishes to conduct an investigation in a foreign jurisdiction, he or she must comply with the licensing requirements of that jurisdiction. For an in-depth review of this topic, see Section 2.3.2.4 — Operating Outside of Jurisdiction.

If a foreign corporation, properly incorporated abroad, wishes to operate in any province in Canada, it must be registered or licensed as a business within thirty days after

---

39 R.S.A. 1980, c. P-16, ss. 3, 18, & 21, r. 3; R.S.B.C. 1996, c. 374, ss. 3 & 10; R.S.M. 1987, c. P132, ss. 4 & 5; R.S.N. 1990, c. P-24, ss. 6–9; R.S.N.B. 1973, c. P-16, s. 3; R.S.N.S. 1989, c. 356, ss. 3 & 24; R.S.O. 1990, c. P.25, ss. 4 & 5; R.S.P.E.I. 1988, c. P-20, ss. 3 & 22, r. 2; R.S.Q. 1977, c. A-8, ss. 2, 3, 6, & 12; R.S.S. 1997, c. P-26.01, ss. 5, 6, & 31, General Guidelines; S.Y. 1988, c. 23, ss. 4, 5, & 12. See also the decision of *Rosenberg v. Deputy Registrar of Ontario* (11 January 2001), (Ont. Prov. Ct.) [unreported], as reviewed in Section 2.4.2.4 — Suspending or Revoking a Licence.

commencing the business in the province.[40] This registration and licensing requirement is separate and in addition to the licensing process under the Act. What constitutes "carrying on business" is often defined in the provincial statutes. Various statutory obligations and duties are imposed on foreign corporations. For instance, they must have a solicitor resident in the city or place where the head office or place of business in the province is situated who is authorized to accept the service of process in all suits and proceedings by or against the corporation within that province and to receive all notices. For a further discussion pertaining to foreign corporations operating in Canada, see *Canadian Conflict of Laws*.[41]

A couple of cases were located on the issue of licensing in various legal reporters. An action against a person for holding himself out as a private investigator without a licence was unsuccessful when the Crown failed to prove the means or dates when the accused allegedly committed the offence.[42] In another case, an action was unsuccessful when the accused corporation proved that the investigator was in-house and therefore did not require licensing.[43] However, an action against a skip-tracer has been successful.[44]

Notwithstanding that licensing is one of the most frequently investigated offences by the registrar's office, few charges are actually laid. In some cases the registrar simply deems that although the subject person, such as a forensic chartered accountant, fits the definition of a private investigator, because other provincial legislation governs chartered accountants and because they are self-regulated by the Canadian Institute of Chartered Accountants, the fine letter of the Act will not be applied.[45] In other cases, for various reasons, members of the respective provincial investigative units often "educate" offenders and give them the option of cease and desist, obtain a licence, or face charges. Most of the complaints are received from licensed investigators who learn of unlicensed persons performing the services of a private investigator without a licence, thereby increasing their competition.

---

40 See, for example, Ontario's *Extra-Provincial Corporations Act*, R.S.O. 1990, c. E.27.

41 J.-G.Castel, *Canadian Conflict of Laws* (Toronto: Butterworths, 1977) at 313.

42 *R. v. Howes* (1991), 14 W.C.B. (2d) 537 (Alta. Prov. Ct.). See also *R. v. Brown* (1987), 1 W.C.B. (2d) 257 (Sask. Q.B.).

43 *R. v. Aanar Management Corporation*, [1983] 11 W.C.B. 1983 (B.C. Co. Ct.)

44 *R. v. Lillie*, [1988] O.J. No. 1476 (Dist. Ct.).

45 Recently, the Canadian Institute of Chartered Accountants began awarding the designation CA-IFA (Chartered Accountant — Investigative Forensic Accountant). Because CA-IFAs are often seeking out fraudulent conduct on behalf of clients, a CA-IFA's activities may be described as "investigating and furnishing information for hire or reward including searching for and furnishing information as to the personal character or actions of a person or of a business and searching for offenders against the law." However, as mentioned, because CA-IFAs are governed by their own self-regulating legislation, licensing them would simply be redundant. This is not the case for Certified Fraud Examiners or self-proclaimed forensic accountants. The term "Certified Fraud Examiner" (CFE) is a designation, not a licence. The term CFE is not derived from any provincial or federal legislation. Therefore, if CFEs are performing the function contained in the definition of private investigator, they are required to be

2.2.1.1   Procedure for Licensing

Every province's legislation contains a provision that dictates that an application must be made to the registrar with the prescribed fee and information. Upon becoming licensed, the private investigator or private investigative agency in every province must renew their licence annually, again submitting the prescribed fee and information.[46]

An example of the process and procedure to obtain a licence for an agency is taken from Ontario. It provides the following:

- An agency manager must submit to the registrar a written request for an appointment for an agency interview with personal résumés, a business plan, three letters of reference, and a letter from a bank or financial institution.

- Upon review of the material submitted, the registrar will send the materials back to the applicant for further clarification or as rejected, or, if the materials are acceptable, send out application forms to the applicant and arrange for an interview.

- At the interview, the registrar will orally examine the manager of the proposed business on the manager's working knowledge of the relevant provisions of the *Private Investigators and Security Guards Act* and its regulations, the *Criminal Code*, and other relevant statutes. Managers will also be required to show proof of having three years of investigative experience and sufficient capital to operate the proposed business. If the proposed business is to have employee investigators, the manager will also have to submit an employee policy manual for approval by the registrar.[47]

Appendix 1 — Provincial Contact Information for Licensing lists the various provincial government contacts for obtaining an application package. A detailed review of the licensing requirements is discussed in the following sections. For a listing of current fee schedules, see the footnotes to Section 2.2.1.2.1 — Annual Renewals.

2.2.1.2   Term of a Licence

This section has been broken down into the types of terms by which a private investigator or private investigative agency licence can be limited: the annual renewal, when an agency

---

licensed under the Act. Notwithstanding the nonrequirement of licensing, some chartered accounting firms have approached the provincial registrars and requested that they be licensed. One reason given for the desire to license is because their clients wish to deal only with licensed investigators. Another reason for licensing is because many of these firms employ private investigators as staff investigators. If the latter scenario exists, the chartered accounting firm must be set up as an investigative agency as the staff investigators would not fall under the overseeing body of the chartered accountants.

46 R.S.A. 1980, c. P-16, s. 5; R.S.B.C. 1996, c. 374, s. 3, 10; R.S.M. 1987, c. P132, s. 6; R.S.N. 1990, c. P-24, s. 13, r. 3; R.S.N.B. 1973, c. P-16, s. 4; R.S.N.S. 1989, c. 356, s. 5; R.S.O. 1990, c. P. 25, s. 5; R.S.P.E.I. 1988, c. P-20, s. 4; R.S.Q. 1977, c. A-8, ss. 4 & 5; R.S.S. 1997, c. P-26.01, ss. 8–11; S.Y. 1988, c. 23, ss. 10 & 13.

47 Agency Inquiry Form Letter (Toronto: Ontario Ministry of the Solicitor General and Correctional Services, revised 7 October 1997).

owner dies, when only a temporary licence was issued, and when the licensee quits, is suspended, is terminated, or has his or her licence revoked.

2.2.1.2.1 Annual Renewals

In some provinces, licences must be renewed by a specified date. For instance, in Manitoba, New Brunswick, Quebec, and the Yukon, licences of private investigators and private investigative agencies expire on 31 March of each year and must be renewed before that date. In Alberta, the licences expire on 31 December of each year and must be renewed before that date. Nova Scotia, oddly enough, only requires private investigative agencies to renew on 31 March of each year while private investigator's licence renewals are staggered throughout the year.

As mentioned, in some provinces, renewals are staggered throughout the year. In British Columbia, licences of private investigators and private investigative agencies expire on the date specified, which must be within eighteen months of the original issue date and within twelve months of every successive issue date. In Newfoundland, Ontario, Prince Edward Island, and Saskatchewan, licences of agents and agencies must be renewed twelve months from the issue date.[48] Fees for the initial licensing and renewals vary across the country[49] and are outlined in Table 2.2.

TABLE 2.2
Licensing and Renewal Fees

Province	Agent		Agency	
	Initial Licence	Renewal	Initial Licence	Renewal
Alberta	$50	$50	$500	$500
British Columbia	$100	$40	$500	$275
Manitoba	$25	$25	$400	$400
New Brunswick	$30	$30	$300	$300
Newfoundland	$30	$30	$300	$300
Nova Scotia	$30	$30	$300	$300
Ontario	$30	$30	$500	$500
Prince Edward Island	$100	$100	$200	$200
Quebec*	—	—	$1,136	$1,136
Saskatchewan	$25	$20	$300	$250
Yukon	$10	$10	$50	$25

*Quebec's fees differ for a detective agency, security agency, or detective-security agency. The fee stated in Table 2.2 is for a detective agency.

---

48   R.S.A. 1980, c. P-16, s. 8; R.S.B.C. 1996, c. 374, ss. 3 & 10; R.S.M. 1987, c. P132; R.S.N. 1990, c. P-24, ss. 16 & 18, r. 10; R.S.N.B. 1973, c. P-16, s. 8; R.S.N.S. 1989, c. 356, s. 9; R.S.O. 1990, c. P.25, s. 11, General Guidelines; R.S.P.E.I. 1988, c. P-20, s. 8; R.S.Q. 1977, c. A-8, s. 7, r. 9; R.S.S. 1997, c. P-26.01, s. 39, R.R.S. 2000, c. P-26.01, r. 1, ss. 10, 11, & 14; S.Y. 1988, c. 23, ss. 11 & 15.

49   All figures are on a per annum basis. All fees are not refundable.

2.2.1.2.2   Death of an Agency Owner

In every province except Quebec and Saskatchewan, the registrar has the discretion to grant the administrator or executor of the estate of a deceased agency owner a temporary licence to operate his or her private investigative agency. The intent of this provision is to allow the administrator or executor the opportunity to wind up the affairs of the business.

In Alberta, Nova Scotia, Ontario, Prince Edward Island, and the Yukon, the term of a temporary licence for estate purposes is the same term as for temporary licences generally. In British Columbia, the Act provides that the term of the temporary licence is ninety days and can be renewed for further terms of ninety days. In Manitoba, New Brunswick, and Newfoundland, the term of the licence is determined on a case by case basis.[50]

2.2.1.2.3   Temporary Licences

The most common reason for the issuing of a temporary licence is to allow the applicant private investigator or private investigative agency the authorization to work while the application process is finalized. This situation occurs on a regular basis for new applications and in situations where the private investigator leaves the employ of one agency and starts up with another.

In British Columbia, the registrar may issue a temporary licence for a period of not longer than thirty days. In Alberta, Manitoba, Nova Scotia, Ontario, and the Yukon, the registrar may issue a temporary licence for a period not longer than ninety days. In Newfoundland, the registrar may issue a temporary licence for a period not longer than four months. In New Brunswick, Prince Edward Island, Quebec, and Saskatchewan, there are no provisions for general temporary licences.[51]

Nova Scotia also permits the issuing of temporary licences when a partnership is not properly established and the employees of the private investigative agency are left in limbo temporarily until a partnership is properly constituted.[52]

2.2.1.2.4   Resignation or Suspension of a Licensee

This part of the various provincial PISGAs is somewhat confusing. A strict reading of the legislation suggests that in every province the rules are not the same. The following is an attempt to decipher the relevant provisions of the respective Acts. The distinctions are

---

50   R.S.A. 1980, c. P-16, r. 7; R.S.B.C. 1996, c. 374, s. 7; R.S.M. 1987, c. P132, s. 16; R.S.N. 1990, c. P-24, s. 17; R.S.N.B. 1973, c. P-16, s. 9; R.S.N.S. 1989, c. 356, s. 10(2); R.S.O. 1990, c. P.25, s. 9(2) (*The Government Process Simplification Act,* S.O. 1997, c. 39, repealed s. 9(3), which provided that every temporary licence terminated in accordance with the regulations); R.S.P.E.I. 1988, c. P-20, s. 9; S.Y. 1988, c. 23, r. 5.

51   Notwithstanding the provision for temporary licences in the Act, the policy in Ontario is not to issue temporary licences except in the case of the death of an agency owner. See Section 2.2.1.2.2.

52   R.S.A. 1980, c. P-16, s. 8(2), r. 7(2)(3); R.S.B.C. 1996, c. 374, s. 15(2), r. 1 to 4 of Reg. 294/94; R.S.M. 1987, c. P132, s. 15; R.S.N. 1990, c. P-24, r. 10(2) of Reg. 208/89; R.S.N.S. 1989, c. 356, s. 10; R.S.O. 1990, c. P.25, s. 9(1), (*The Government Process Simplification Act,* S.O. 1997, c. 39, s. 16 repealed s. 9(3), which formerly provided that every temporary licence terminated in accordance with the regulations); R.S.S. 1997, c. P-26-01, General Guidelines; S.Y. 1988, c. 23, r. 10.

important as without legislative authority, the argument can be made that a registrar cannot declare inoperative a private investigator's or private investigative agency's licence. It should be noted that even where there is no legislative provision for ending the licence for change of employment, suspension, or revocation purposes, the licence expires if not renewed.

Cessation of Employment: The licence of a private investigator terminates upon the cessation of employment with his employing private investigative agency in Alberta, Manitoba, Nova Scotia, Ontario, Prince Edward Island, and Saskatchewan. Employment is deemed to cease upon the closing of the agency. In Quebec, the cessation of employment by a private investigator with his employer does not terminate but merely suspends his licence until the private investigator is hired on with another private investigative agency. There is no direct legislation on this issue in British Columbia, New Brunswick, Newfoundland, and the Yukon. This section should therefore be read in conjunction with Section 2.3.3.2.2 — Change of Employee or Company Status, and with Section 2.3.3.2.4 — Surrender of a Licence. These sections indicate that an agency is required to turn in their terminated employee licences to the registrar upon the cessation of employment.

Closing of an Agency: The licence of a private investigative agency terminates upon the closing of the agency in Manitoba, New Brunswick, Nova Scotia, and Prince Edward Island. In Alberta, British Columbia, Newfoundland, Ontario, Quebec, and Saskatchewan, reference must be made to Section 2.3.3.2.2 — Change of Employee or Company Status, and to Section 2.3.3.2.4 — Surrender of a Licence. These latter sections provide indirect authority that the licence of a private investigative agency ceases when its operations end because the agency is required to turn in its licence to the registrar.

Suspension of a Private Investigator: The licence of a private investigator terminates upon the suspension or upon the revocation of her licence by the registrar in Alberta, British Columbia, New Brunswick, Newfoundland, Nova Scotia, Prince Edward Island, and the Yukon. Notwithstanding, however, that in Saskatchewan there is no explicit legislation on this issue, this rule can be inferred from the provisions found in Section 2.3.3.2.4 — Surrender of a Licence, and Section 2.4.2.4 — Suspending and Revoking a Licence. The legislation of Ontario, Manitoba, and Quebec does not speak directly to the issue either. Therefore, a licence suspended in these provinces does not immediately terminate notwithstanding the private investigator is prohibited from carrying out her trade.

Suspension of a Private Investigative Agency: The licence of a private investigator terminates upon the suspension or revocation of the licence of the private investigative agency for which she was employed in Alberta. No other province has legislated this provision. However, because in Manitoba, Nova Scotia, Ontario, Prince Edward Island, and Saskatchewan, the licence of a private investigator terminates upon the cessation of his or her employment at the employing agency, and as an agency cannot provide work when its licence is suspended, these additional provinces in effect suspend the agent's licence when the registrar suspends the agency's licence.

The licence of a private investigative agency terminates upon the suspension or revocation of the licence by the registrar in Alberta, British Columbia, New Brunswick, Newfoundland, Nova Scotia, and Prince Edward Island. Again, as with individual private investigator's licences, the provisions found in Section 2.3.3.2.2 and Section 2.4.2.4 implicitly accomplish the same result in the other provinces.[53]

2.2.1.3   Transferring a Licence

There is legislation that prohibits the transfer of a licence from the private investigator to whom it was issued to a third party in Alberta, Manitoba, Ontario, Quebec, Saskatchewan, and the Yukon. The purpose of this prohibition is to prevent employees of one private investigative agency resigning and commencing employment with another private investigative agency without notifying the registrar. To resign from one employer and commence with another, the Act requires the licensee to submit a formal notice of termination, return his licence to the registrar, and then make application for a new licence. This process is not required when a private investigator transfers from one agency branch to another. However, where a private investigator changes agency branches, he must comply with the change of status notification requirements addressed later in this chapter. This prohibition also includes the obvious situations where a licensee gives his licence to an unlicensed person.

In British Columbia, New Brunswick, Newfoundland, Nova Scotia, and Prince Edward Island, there is no such legislated prohibition. In British Columbia, when a private investigator transfers to a new company, a transfer form must be completed and a fee paid to the Security Programs Division. If the employee licence is still valid, the employee can work for the new private investigation company while the transfer is being processed. There is no need to wait for a new identification card.[54]

2.2.1.4   Multiple Sponsoring Employers

Only Newfoundland and Ontario have a formal policy that dictates that a person will not be issued a licence for two different agencies. Saskatchewan reports that a private investigator can work for more than one company if her application is accompanied by a letter of approval from the owner of each of the sponsoring businesses. The legislation and policy statements from the other provinces did not comment on this practice.[55]

---

53 R.S.A. 1980, c. P-16, s. 8(3); R.S.B.C. 1996, c. 374, ss. 3(8) & 10(8); R.S.M. 1987, c. P132, s. 18; R.S.N. 1990, c. P-24, s. 16; R.S.N.B. 1973, c. P-16, ss. 8(1) & 11(1); R.S.N.S. 1989, c. 356, ss. 9(1) & 14(1)(3); R.S.O. 1990, c. P.25, s. 13, General Guidelines; R.S.P.E.I. 1988, c. P-20, ss. 8(1) & 13(1)(3), r. 12(2); R.S.Q. 1977, c. A-8, s. 6(2); R.S.S. 1997, c. P-26.01, ss. 9(2) & 15(1); S.Y. 1988, c. 23, ss. 11(2) & 15(2).

54 R.S.A. 1980, c. P-16, s. 19(3); R.S.B.C. 1996, c. 374, ss. 3(9) & 10(8); see also *Security News*, December 1995 issue; R.S.M. 1987, c. P132, s. 17; R.S.O. 1990, c. P.25, s. 10, General Guidelines; R.S.Q. 1977, c. A-8, s. 12; R.S.S. 1997, c. P-26.01, s. 30, General Guidelines; S.Y. 1988, c. 23, s. 25(1).

55 R.S.N. 1990, c. P-24, s. 30(4); R.S.O. 1990, c. P.25, General Guidelines; R.R.S 1997, c. P-26.01, policy per the Saskatchewan registrar's office.

2.2.1.5   Replacement of a Licence

Only the province of Saskatchewan has legislation that dictates that an application to the registrar is required for the replacement of a licence. It is assumed this is to deal with situations when a licence is lost or stolen. Ontario has an administrative policy dealing with this issue, stating that declaration must be sent to the registrar along with photographs and a fee. Although the other provinces do not address this issue, it is surmised that such a written request would be accommodated as well.[56]

2.2.2   Requirements for an Agency Licence

This section will review the issues that must be addressed to obtain a private investigative agency licence. The requirements vary from province to province. The issues the various PISGAs address include the character of the applicant, citizenship and residency, insurance and bonding, education and experience, financial position, age, physical and mental well-being, the proposed location of the agency office, the disclosure of the identity of the agency's directors, officers, and shareholders, the obligation to join the provincial private investigators' association, and the requirement of a business permit.

2.2.2.1   Good Character (Criminal Record)

Only the province of Newfoundland does not have legislation pertaining to the character and lack of criminal record of applicants seeking licensing as an agency. However, although explicit legislation is not found in Newfoundland, it is noted that all provinces grant the registrar discretionary power to license, and the test a registrar must apply is what is in the public interest. As virtually all private investigative agency applicants seek licensing as private investigators as well, the requirement of good character by an agency applicant in Newfoundland can be inferred.[57]

Generally, having a criminal record is an obstacle to, but does not necessarily prohibit, the granting of a licence by a registrar. The exception to this rule is New Brunswick, where agency licensing is strictly prohibited to anyone found guilty or convicted of a criminal offence in Canada. In Alberta, a licence will not be granted to an applicant who has been convicted of an indictable offence in the preceding five years while less serious offences are considered on a case-by-case basis. In Manitoba, a licence will not be granted to an applicant who has been convicted of an indictable offence within the preceding five years, or a summary conviction offence within the proceeding two years. In Nova Scotia, Ontario, and Saskatchewan, a licence will not be granted to an applicant who has been convicted

56   R.S.O. 1990. c. P.25, General Guidelines; R.R.S. 2000, c. P-26.01, r. 1, s. 13.
57   R.S.A. 1980, c. P-16, s. 5(2), r. 2; R.S.B.C. 1996, c. 374, s. 8, rr. 2 & 4 of Reg. 3/81; R.S.M. 1987, c. P132, s. 10; R.S.N.B. 1973, c. P-16, ss. 4(6) & 4.1(1); R.S.N.S. 1989, c. 356, s. 6; R.S.O. 1990, c. P.25, s. 7 and General Guidelines; R.S.P.E.I. 1988, c. P-20, r. 2; R.S.Q. 1977, c. A-8, rr. 7 & 8; R.S.S. 1997, c. P-26.01, r. 1, s. 5(2)(d) and General Guidelines; S.Y. 1988, c. 23, s. 9(3)(4).

of an indictable offence within the preceding five years after completing the sentence, or a summary conviction offence within the preceding three years after completing the sentence. Furthermore, in Ontario and Saskatchewan, a licence will not be granted if the applicant received a conditional discharge within the preceding three years, or an absolute discharge within the preceding year. In Quebec, a licence will not be granted to a person who has a record of conviction for an indictable offence, unless pardoned, or who has been convicted of a summary conviction offence within the preceding five years.

In British Columbia and Prince Edward Island there are no strict rules pertaining to licence prohibition in cases where there is a criminal record. In these provinces, the registrar will consider the period of time that has elapsed between the time of conviction and of application and the seriousness of the offence. Offences that were handled under young offenders' legislation or for which a pardon was granted do not have to be reported. For clarification, an absolute or conditional discharge indicates a finding of guilt and must be declared on an application.[58]

In addition to a criminal record, an applicant may be refused a licence because of his poor character if the registrar obtains evidence of excessive use of alcohol or drugs, of a poor business reputation, or other reasons. A registrar may require from an applicant letters of reference to establish good character.[59]

2.2.2.2   Citizenship and Residency

Alberta and Quebec are the only provinces that require the applicant for a private investigative agency to hold Canadian citizenship. In British Columbia and the Yukon, being a resident of Canada is the minimum requirement. In New Brunswick, the applicant must be a resident of the province. In Manitoba, Newfoundland, Nova Scotia, Ontario, Prince Edward Island, and Saskatchewan, there are no citizenship or residency requirements although most provinces ask for proof of citizenship and residency in the application form notwithstanding the lack of legislative authority. Saskatchewan reports that while there are

---

58 In all provinces except New Brunswick, Quebec, and the Yukon, the time periods set out are found in policy statements, and therefore are subject to discretion by the registrar.

59 In Alberta, an information circular accompanying the application package provides that good character interviews are not conducted by the Administrator's office, but rather by either the Calgary or Edmonton Police departments, or by the RCMP. Further, this information circular provides that an applicant for an agency licence must submit three letters of character reference from past employers, business associates, a clergyman, or other third parties. The British Columbia *Security News*, December 1994 issue, a licensing and regulation newsletter, reports that an administrative review must be conducted in all cases where there is a past or present charge or conviction. The reason given for such reviews is because private investigators hold positions of public trust. In Ontario, three letters of reference are required from each applicant who has not been licensed before. In Ontario, if a criminal record exists, the applicant will be subject to a hearing on the issue.

no citizenship and residency stipulations, the Department of Immigration prohibits those on student and visitor visas from working and thus applications from such individuals would be rejected.[60]

2.2.2.3   Bonding and Insurance

Bonding: A bond is a written instrument whereby the person executing it makes a promise or incurs a personal liability to another. In common parlance, a bond indemnifies against loss to third-party beneficiaries when an insured fails to fulfil a specific undertaking for the third party's benefit. For private investigative agency purposes, a bond pledges a specified amount of money as a guarantee of payment for wrongdoing. In other words, bonds for the purpose of the Act are penal in nature.

In every province except Nova Scotia, bonding is required as a prerequisite or condition of licensing. The bond must be in the name of the licence applicant and made payable to the Queen in right of the province and her assigns or the registrar of the respective PISGA. The terms of the bond must mention the faithfulness, honesty, and lawful conduct of the business and its licensed employees. The bond is intended to cover the acts of the agency and any of its employees. An agency licence may be invalidated if the bond is cancelled. Bonds can be purchased from any chartered bank or insurance or guarantee company.

The term of the bond is addressed in the Act of some provinces. For instance, in Alberta, Ontario, and Saskatchewan, the bond must stay in effect for a period of two years after the agency has closed its doors. In Manitoba, the bond must stay in effect for a period of one year. The other provinces do not address this issue.

Another issue is the amount of the bond. In Alberta, New Brunswick, Ontario, Quebec, Saskatchewan, and the Yukon, the minimum amount of bond required is $5,000. In British Columbia, Manitoba,[61] and Newfoundland,[62] the amount of the bond is staggered in relation to the number of private investigators the agency has in its employ. Prince Edward Island has not legislated the amount of the bond, and therefore it is presumed to be at the discretion of the registrar. Whatever the case, the amount of the bond is rarely an adequate source of compensation for a person wronged by a private investigator.

Finally, there is the issue of in what circumstances the bond is forfeited. The Acts of the provinces of Alberta, Manitoba, New Brunswick, Newfoundland, Ontario, and Saskatchewan specifically state the bond is forfeited upon the finding of a court that the private investigative agency is a judgment creditor in a tort action in relation to its business. Although British Columbia, Prince Edward Island, Quebec, and the Yukon do not specif-

---

60   Alberta has no legislation on the issue but sets out its position in a form letter; R.S.B.C. 1996, c. 374, r. 3 of Reg. 4/81; Manitoba has no legislation on the issue but sets out its position in a form letter; R.S.N. 1990, c. P-24, s. 10; however, S.N. 1995, c. A-5.1, s. 13, provides that R.S.N. 1990, c. P-24, s. 10, is no longer in force effective 31 January 1998; R.S.N.B. 1973, c. P-16, s. 4(5)(b); R.S.O. 1990, c. P.25, General Guidelines; R.S.Q. 1977, c. A-8, rr. 7 & 8; R.S.S. 1997, c. P-26-01, General Guidelines; S.Y. 1988, c. 23, s. 9.

61   1–10 employees: $5,000 bond; 11–25 employees: $10,000 bond; 26–100 employees: $15,000 bond; 101–200 employees: $20,000 bond; and over 200 employees: $25,000 bond.

62   1–5 agents: $5,000 bond; 6–10 agents: $10,000 bond; greater than 10 agents: $15,000 bond.

ically address the issue, it is reasonable to expect that a finding of tort liability will also result in the forfeiture of the bond in these provinces. Only in the provinces of Manitoba, Ontario, and Saskatchewan does the legislation specifically state that the bond is forfeitable by a private investigative agency upon conviction of an offence under the PISGA or the *Criminal Code* in relation to its business. Saskatchewan even goes one step further by stating that a bond is forfeitable upon conviction pursuant to *any* Act in relation to its business.

Insurance: Liability insurance is also a prerequisite or condition of licensing in New Brunswick, Newfoundland, Nova Scotia, Ontario, Prince Edward Island, Quebec, and the Yukon. Literature from Alberta states that the holding of liability insurance by a private investigative agency is recommended. British Columbia and Saskatchewan do not address the issue. As to the minimum amounts of insurance that may be carried, New Brunswick, Nova Scotia, and Prince Edward Island require at least $500,000, while Quebec and the Yukon require at least $100,000.

The requirement to have insurance in Ontario exemplifies the discretionary power of the provincial registrar. In Ontario, although there is a statutory requirement to be bonded, there is no specific statutory requirement for private investigators to be insured. However, notwithstanding that the PISGA does not contain an explicit insurance provision, the Act provides:

8(1)   The registrar shall issue a licence or renewal of a licence where in the opinion of the registrar the proposed licensing is not against the public interest, and the licence may be subject to terms and conditions.

In Ontario's General Guidelines, a list of basic requirements for the licensing of private investigator agencies is included. One of the basic requirements is the acquisition of liability insurance. As the granting, renewing, and suspension of licences is discretionary by the registrar, the breach of a guideline, although not stipulated in the Act, is in effect compulsory.[63]

The insurance taken by private investigators is acquired from brokers dealing with specialty risks. The insurance commonly contracted for is comprehensive general liability and failure to perform insurance, as well as the statutorily required bond. The cost of this insur-

---

63   R.S.A. 1980, c. P-16, ss. 6 & 14, r. 8; R.S.B.C. 1996, c. 374, Reg. 4/81, r. 9; R.S.M. 1987, c. P132, s. 7, Reg. 324/87, rr. 10, 11, & 12; R.S.N. 1990, c. P-24, s. 14, Reg. 227/81, r. 5; R.S.N.B. 1973, c. P-16, ss. 6 & 6.1, Reg. 84-103, rr. 3, 6, & 7; R.S.N.S. 1989, c. 356, ss. 4 & 8(2), Reg. 30/85, r. 22; R.S.O. 1990, c. P.25, s. 5, Reg. 938, rr. 5, 6, & 7 (as amended by Reg. 262/99), General Guidelines, Part A, s. 20 (*The Government Process Simplification Act*, S.O. 1997, c. 39, s. 40, repealed the R.S.O. 1990 provisions and substituted the above); R.S.P.E.I. 1988, c. P-20, s. 8, r. 22; R.S.Q. 1977, c. A-8, s. 7, r. 9; R.S.S. 1997, c. P-26.01, s. 5(2), R.R.S. 2000, c. P-26.01, r. 1, ss. 2(d), 5(1)(d), 11(c), & 15; S.Y. 1988, c. 23, s. 10, O.I.C. 1989/073, r. 6.

ance to an individual owner/operator without prior claims is approximately $1,000 per annum. Most provinces only require failure to perform insurance as opposed to the more expensive errors and omissions insurance, although the latter is available.[64]

A form letter sent out by Stewart Insurance Services Limited of British Columbia succinctly reviews the wisdom of errors and omissions insurance. It states:

> As an investigator you are exposed to potential lawsuits arising out of your professional activities. Allegations of wrongful acts causing financial loss to either your client or a third party could arise out of a variety of services such as insurance and fraud investigations, surveillance, background checks, searches of assets, liens, land titles and credit, and loss prevention.
>
> For example, a group of investors contracts your services to provide a background check on an individual prior to investing in his operations. Based on the information you provide, they decide not to proceed with the venture. It is later discovered that your information was incorrect or incomplete. You then face the threat of legal action from either the investors or the individual to recover the potential profit which has been lost as a result of the missed opportunity.
>
> Despite strict adherence to procedures and having tight internal controls, you may be the subject of allegations of wrongdoing causing financial loss. There may be an absence of negligence on your part; however, these accusations would be costly to defend. Errors and omissions liability insurance would respond, and pay defence costs.

Insurers have reported that there does not appear to be much cause for concern over the inherent untrustworthiness of private investigators as few claims are filed against them.[65] The majority of claims that are made are for breach of contract, slander, and harassment (privacy) tort claims. The largest reported claim was a case against a private investigator for failing to deliver a writ, an occurrence when the private investigator was acting as a paralegal. The amount of the claim was $3,000,000.[66]

2.2.2.4   Education and Experience

Surprisingly, only the provinces of New Brunswick and Quebec have addressed the issue of the experience required to own and manage a private investigative agency in their legislation. Quebec requires applicants have five years of investigative experience. In New

---

64   A commonly used insurance broker for private investigators in Ontario is Elliott Special Risks, 130 Adelaide Street West, Suite 1000, Toronto, Ontario M5H 3P5, Tel: (416) 601-1133. In western Canada, a commonly used insurer is Stewart Insurance Services Limited, 1812 - 1177 Hastings Street, Vancouver, British Columbia V6E 2K3, Tel: (604) 669-9600, e-mail: <stewins@direct.ca>.

65   See E.F. Geddes, "The Private Investigator and the Right to Privacy" (1989) 17 Alta. L. Rev. 256. The author reports that between 1976 and 1989 there was only one claim against the security of an Alberta private investigator. Susan Watts of CGU Insurance reports that she is not aware of any successful claims against the private investigative agencies they deal with.

66   Elliott Special Risks. above note 64.

Brunswick, the legislation provides that the standard is what the registrar believes is necessary to operate an agency, which currently is set at five years' investigative experience.

Notwithstanding that the other provinces do not have legislation on this issue, because licensing is at the discretion of the registrar, it is reasonable to expect that where legislation does not exist, the standard is the same as New Brunswick; that is, the registrar decides what is necessary. For instance, Manitoba has stated the same position as New Brunswick in a form letter it sends out to applicants, while in Ontario a form letter to applicants states that three years of experience in an investigation field is required. Further reference can be made to Section 2.4.2.2 — Issuing or Renewing a Licence. The legislation in this section gives the registrars the discretion to issue licences when it is in the public interest, a fairly all-encompassing provision.[67]

The issue of education has not been addressed in the Act of any province pertaining to agency owners. However, it is common that the licensing registrar will conduct an oral examination of applicants pertaining to their knowledge of the Act and other relevant legislation during the interview stage of the agency application process.[68] For the education standards required for a private investigator's licence, see Section 2.2.3.3 — Education and Training.

2.2.2.5   Financial Position

Only Quebec has legislation that explicitly provides that an applicant for a private investigative agency licence shall not be a bankrupt or a debtor and shall be solvent. New Brunswick's and Ontario's legislation makes a vague comment about an applicant's financial position.

Insight for the position of other provinces may be taken from Section 2.2.2.1 — Good Character, and Section 2.4.2.2 —Issuing or Renewing a Licence. In those sections, it is mentioned that a registrar may refuse an applicant a licence if the applicant has a poor business reputation. An example of the evidence a registrar may look for is taken from a form letter to applicants in Ontario. This form letter states that a letter from the applicant's bank or financial institution indicating how the applicant has managed his or her financial affairs in the past is required as a condition of licencing.[69]

2.2.2.6   Minimum Age

Only Quebec has legislated that an applicant for a private investigative agency licence shall be at least twenty-one years of age.[70] Reference here should be made to Section 2.2.3.4 — Minimum Age (for a Private Investigator) and Section 2.2.2.4 — Education and Experience. Obviously, the experience required to attain a private investigative agency

---

67   R.S.N.B. 1973, c. P-16, s. 4.1(1); R.S.Q. 1977, c. A-8, r. 7.

68   R.S.O. 1990, c. P.25, s. 7. Although this provision permits the Ontario registrar to try such examinations to determine competence as the registrar sees fit, in practice only agency owners, not employee investigators, are subject to oral examinations. Ontario encourages agency owners to have policy manuals for their employee investigators.

69   R.S.N.B. 1973, c. P-16, s. 4.1(1); R.S.O. 1990, c. P.25, s. 7; R.S.Q. 1977, c. A-8, r. 7.

70   R.S.Q. 1977, c. A-8, r. 7.

licence can be added to the minimum age to become a private investigator to determine the minimum age required to attain a private investigative agency licence.

2.2.2.7   Physical and Mental Well-being

Only in Quebec is an applicant required to submit a document from a medical practitioner attesting that the applicant is physically and mentally capable of acting as a private investigator. In British Columbia, an applicant must submit adequate and relevant personal information for the registrar to make a determination of mental condition.[71]

Insight for the position of other provinces may be taken from Section 2.4.2.2 — Issuing or Renewing a Licence. The legislation in this section gives the registrars the discretion to issue licences when it is in the "public interest," a fairly all-encompassing provision. Notwithstanding a registrar's discretion, any refusal to grant a licence because of a physical limitation would open the registrar up to a constitutional and/or human rights action. The exercise of discretion by a registrar for mental instability, on the other hand, is obviously legitimate.

2.2.2.8   Location of an Agency Office

An applicant for a private investigative agency licence must have an office located in the province that grants the licence in British Columbia, Manitoba, New Brunswick, Newfoundland, Quebec, Saskatchewan, and the Yukon. The provinces of Alberta, Manitoba, Nova Scotia, Ontario, and Prince Edward Island have not legislated this requirement. However, as a registrar can impose reasonable terms and conditions on a licensee, such a requirement may be made by a registrar in those provinces.[72]

Saskatchewan's General Guidelines impose further conditions. The agency or branch office must be in an office building, or if not in an office building, a home office that is separate and apart from the rest of the residence. Ontario and Saskatchewan's General Guidelines further require evidence that the office complies with all municipal zoning requirements.[73]

2.2.2.9   Disclosure of Identities of Directors, Officers, Shareholders, and Nonlicensed Employees

Only Ontario and British Columbia require a corporation applying for a private investigative agency licence to divulge the identities of its directors, officers, and shareholders.

Saskatchewan requires a person or a corporation applying for a private investigative agency licence to provide a current list of all employees.[74] Saskatchewan's legislation is in

---

71   R.S.B.C. 1996, c. 374, Reg. 3/81, s. 2(b); R.S.Q. 1977, c. A-8, r. 8.
72   Alberta reports their policy is that an agency licensed in their province must have a physical office in the province.
73   R.S.B.C. 1996, c. 374, s. 3(3), Reg. 4/81 with amendments up to Reg. 22/95, r. 3(3); R.S.M. 1987, c. P132, s. 8; R.S.N. 1990, c. P-24, s. 10(2); R.S.N.B. 1973, c. P-16, s. 4(4)(5); R.S.O. 1990, c. P.25, General Guidelines; R.S.Q. 1977, c. A-8, r. 7; R.S.S. 1997, c. P-26.01, General Guidelines; S.Y. 1988, c. 23, s. 9(1).
74   R.S.B.C. 1996, c. 374, s. 6; R.R.O. 262/99 amending R.R.O. 938/90; R.R.S. 2000, c. P-26.01, r. 1, s. 5.

this sense unique as it appears that, in addition to the requirement to identify investigators, the identity of an agency's administrative personnel must be disclosed.

2.2.2.10   Requirement to Join Provincial Private Investigators' Association

There are provincial private investigators' associations in Newfoundland, Quebec, Ontario, Alberta, and British Columbia. However, only Newfoundland requires that agency owners become members of the provincial private investigators' association as a condition of licensing.[75] In all provinces, the operations of the provincial association are separate and distinct from that of the registrar's office. See Section 2.6 for provincial private investigators' association contact information.

2.2.2.11   Business Permit

The administrative guidelines of Saskatchewan expressly provide that a private investigative agency, as a condition of licensing, must have a business permit. In Alberta, this requirement is mentioned in its application package. In all other provinces, reference should be made to provincial and municipal business licensing legislation.[76]

2.2.3   Requirements for an Agent's Licence

This section will review the issues that must be addressed to obtain a private investigator's licence. Although generally consistent, there are some variations between the provinces. These issues include the character of the applicant, citizenship and residency, education and experience, age, physical and mental well-being, language abilities, and the requirement of photographs and fingerprints.

2.2.3.1   Good Character (Criminal Record)

All provinces have legislation pertaining to the character and lack of criminal record of applicants seeking licensing as private investigators.[77]

Having a criminal record in most provinces does not automatically prohibit an applicant from obtaining a private investigator's licence. However, most registrars consider the

---

75   R.S.N. 1990, c. P-24, s. 15, Reg. 227/81, r. 9. The requirements to join the Newfoundland Security Guards and Private Investigators Agencies Association are (1) the applicant company must have at least five years of demonstrated managerial experience in the security industry; (2) a $500 fee; (3) a business plan; and (4) a successful interview with the association. Once accepted, the member must attend a minimum of one meeting per year to maintain membership.

76   R.S.Q. 1977, c. A-8, s. 5 (a form letter to applicants for a detective agency permit provides that in the case of corporate applicants, a copy of its charter with a certificate issued by the Inspector General of Financial Institutions must be sent in with the application form); R.S.S. 1997, c. P-26.01 contains no such provision, but it is included in the General Guidelines, p. 4.

77   R.S.A. 1980, c. P-16, s. 5(3), Reg. 71/91, r. 2(1); R.S.B.C. 1996, c. 374, s. 8(1), Reg. 3/81, rr. 2 & 4; R.S.M. 1987, c. P132, s. 10; R.S.N. 1990, c. P-24, s. 12; R.S.N.B. 1973, c. P-16, s. 4.1(2); R.S.N.S. 1989, c. 356, s. 6; R.S.O. 1990, c. P.25, s. 7 and the General Guidelines; R.S.P.E.I. 1988, c. P-20, E/C 256/88, 475/95, s. 2(1); R.S.Q. 1977, c. A-8, r. 3; R.R.S. 2000, c. P-26.01, r. 1, s. 5(2)(d) and the General Guidelines; S.Y. 1988, c. 23, ss. 13 & 14.

period of time that has elapsed between the time of conviction and the time of application and the seriousness of the offence. Offences that were handled under young offenders' legislation or for which a pardon was granted do not have to be reported. Absolute and conditional discharges indicate a finding of guilt and therefore must be declared on an application. Refer back to Section 2.2.2.1 — Good Character (for Agency Licensing) for further information.

In addition to a criminal record, an applicant may be refused a licence because of his poor character if the registrar obtains evidence of excessive use of alcohol or drugs, of a poor business reputation, or other reasons. A registrar may require from an applicant letters of reference to establish good character.[78]

There is some reported case law on this issue. In a case from Quebec, a registrar refused an applicant because of his past association with known drug traffickers. The registrar claimed he learned of the applicant's character because his actions had been publicized in the local media. Based on this reputation, the registrar held the applicant did not satisfy the requirement of possessing a reputation and moral qualities compatible with that sought in a suitable private investigator. The Court of Appeal upheld the registrar's decision stating that where the issue is reputation and perceived moral qualities, it does not assist the applicant to simply provide explanations for his association. In effect, the court upheld the broad discretion possessed by the registrar for the granting of licences.[79]

In another case from Manitoba, it was held that although a registrar does have broad discretion over licensing applications, his or her discretion is not without limits. In this case, the court held that the only reason for not granting a licence is if it is against the public interest, the onus of which is on the registrar. The court further held that pending charges against the applicant under the federal Bankruptcy Act was not sufficient proof of bad character or dishonesty.[80]

2.2.3.2   Citizenship and Residency

There are no citizenship or residency requirements to obtain a private investigator's licence in the provinces of Alberta, Manitoba, New Brunswick, Nova Scotia, Ontario, Prince Edward Island, and Saskatchewan. An applicant must be a Canadian citizen or landed immigrant to be eligible for a private investigator's licence in British Columbia, Newfoundland, and the Yukon. Strangely enough, the most stringent requirement, that of citizenship, is required only in Quebec. Saskatchewan reports that while there are no citi-

---

78   Ontario requires three letters of reference from each applicant who has not been licensed before.

79   *Maranda v. Quebec* (1997), 71 A.C.W.S. (3d) 207 (Que. C.A.).

80   *Wiens v. Registrar of the Private Investigators and Security Guards Act* (1979), 3 A.C.W.S. (2d) 107 (Man. Co. Ct.).

zenship and residency stipulations, the Department of Immigration prohibits those on student and visitor visas from working and thus applications from such individuals would be rejected.[81]

2.2.3.3   Education and Training

The only two provinces that require a specified formalized education as a condition of licensing as a private investigator are British Columbia and Newfoundland. In Manitoba, New Brunswick, and Ontario, the legislation permits the registrar to require an applicant for a private investigator's licence to take whatever tests or courses he or she deems necessary. This, however, is not carried out in practice. British Columbia has also legislated that applicants for a private investigator's licence report their educational achievements on the application. In practice, the other provinces seek such information as well.[82]

The lack of educational or training requirements by most provinces has been recognized as a point of concern. One commentator reports that the existence of totally untrained investigators can be a serious problem to an investigator's colleagues, to various government departments who administer the legislation, and to the general public. Untrained investigators are far more likely to run afoul of the law, and far more likely to close up their operations after a short time in business. They are also more likely to offer services to clients that they cannot deliver, and in the end, are more likely to give a bad impression to the public about the competence and ethics of the entire profession. Speaking about the situation in Alberta, this commentator also reports that most complaints to the registrar centre around investigators who fail to fulfil their promises to clients, who lose documents, or who simply disappear leaving the registrar to attempt to resolve the problems left behind.[83] For information pertaining to Ontario, see Section 2.7.1 — Report on Training and Standards in Ontario.

It has been reported that the lack of traditional educational requirements by most provinces is because many applicants are in fact retired police officers or graduates of police sciences courses.[84] It has also been recognized that the difficult task of defining qual-

---

81   R.S.B.C. 1996, c. 374, Reg 4/81, r. 3 (note the *Security News*, December 1994 issue, reports that birth certificates, citizenship cards, or immigration papers (landing papers) are acceptable documentation. However, a "working visa" does not meet the requirement); R.S.N. 1990, c. P-24, s. 11; R.S.O. 1990, c. P.25, s. 8(1) and the General Guidelines; R.S.Q. 1977, c. A-8, rr. 3 & 4; R.S.S. 1997, c. P-26-01, General Guidelines; S.Y. 1988, c. 23, s. 9.

82   R.S.B.C. 1996, c. 374, s. 31(2)(n)(i), Reg. 3/81, r. 2; R.S.M. 1987, c. P132, s. 10; R.S.N. 1990, c. P-24, s. 15(1), r. 8, 10(2), Reg.53/89, s. 1, Reg. 123/82, s. 2; R.S.N.B. 1973, c. P-16, s. 4.1(2); R.S.O. 1990, c. P.25, s. 7(1); R.S.S. 1997, c. P-26-01, General Guidelines. One of the reasons for the lack of formal education in many of the provinces may be owing to the lack of text material designed specifically for private investigators. According to the Canadian library records, no such publication exists. This book attempts to fill such a void.

83   E.F. Geddes, "The Private Investigator and the Right to Privacy" (1989) 17 Alta. L. Rev. 256.

84   Mr. Ron Spencer of the Academy of Private Investigation & Security, 1333 Rymal Road East, Hamilton, Ontario, L8W 3N1, Tel: (905) 388-1633 requested that it be noted that he is of the view that most private investigators are not, as Ms. Geddes contends, former police officers or graduates of police sciences courses.

ifications for an occupation such as private investigator lies at the root of the problem. Requirements too narrow in scope to allow licensing for only those who have, for example, taken a particular prescribed course might disqualify applicants with equivalent or even better qualifications. Some persons who could and do make excellent investigators have no specific training for the profession. They come from varied walks of life and bring particular types of expertise to their jobs. For these reasons, it has been recognized that some discretion should remain to allow for the licensing of investigators whose qualifications are other than formal.[85]

Considering the views expressed above, it is appropriate to mention the situation in British Columbia where progress has been made. To qualify for a private investigator's employee licence in British Columbia, the applicant must have at least two years of experience as a private investigator under supervision (PIR1) and letters of reference from former employers. Furthermore, as of September 1999, a mandatory education program is in place. Much of the credit for this initiative should be given to the British Columbia Private Investigators Association, which has taken an active role in the establishment of minimum education standards for that province. The core competencies that were identified were established through consultation with, and participation of, a number of private investigators in this province. Although the course is delivered by Douglas College, it belongs to the association. The association has maintained ownership to ensure that the industry keeps control over the quality and content of the program. The association is pursuing recognition as an "occupation" and in doing so has initiated an apprenticeship-type process for private investigators under supervision.[86]

In addition to entrance educational requirements, the British Columbia Private Investigators Association participated on a joint committee with the Ministry of Education, Skills and Training, the Ministry of the Attorney General Security Programs Division, and the Justice Institute to develop the training standards embodied for a pre-employment course. It is intended that this course will become a prerequisite to licensing. This training will complement the current initiative by the Insurance Corporation of British Columbia to improve the quality of private investigative work in British Columbia's motor vehicle insurance industry.[87]

2.2.3.4   Minimum Age

An applicant for a private investigator's licence must be eighteen years old in Alberta, Manitoba, New Brunswick, Ontario, Prince Edward Island, Quebec, and Saskatchewan. In Newfoundland, Nova Scotia, and the Yukon, an applicant must be nineteen years old.

---

85   E.F. Geddes, "The Private Investigator and the Right to Privacy" (1989) 17 Alta. L. Rev. 256.

86   Information from Janet Helm, Education and Training Committee, the Private Investigators Association of British Columbia, e-mail: <education@piabc. com> or <jhelm@istar.ca>, Tel: (604) 930-0313. Ms. Helm reports the authority for imposing minimum educational requirements is s. 26(p)(i) of the Act.

87   *Security News* (December 1994).

In British Columbia, an applicant must be nineteen years old as well but can apply for a private investigator's training licence known as a "PIR1" at sixteen years of age. Quebec imposes an age limit of seventy years for those holding a private investigator's licence.[88]

2.2.3.5   Physical and Mental Well-being

Only in Quebec is an applicant required to submit a document from a medical practitioner attesting that the applicant is physically and mentally capable of acting as a private investigator. In British Columbia, an applicant must submit adequate and relevant personal information for the registrar to make a determination of mental condition.[89]

As discussed in Section 2.2.2.7 pertaining to agency licensing, registrars have the discretion to issue licences when it is in the "public interest," a fairly all-encompassing provision. Notwithstanding a registrar's discretion, any refusal to grant a licence because of a physical limitation would open the registrar up to a constitutional and/or human rights action. The exercise of discretion by a registrar for mental instability, on the other hand, is obviously legitimate.

2.2.3.6   Language

British Columbia is the only province with minimal English language proficiency standards. Their policy is that an applicant for a private investigator's licence be sufficiently fluent in English to converse during predictable conditions of employment.[90]

2.2.3.7   Fingerprints and Photographs

The taking of photographs and fingerprints has two main purposes: to ensure the identity of the applicant and to provide a basis for a criminal records search.

An applicant for a private investigator's licence is required to submit fingerprints with his or her application in British Columbia, New Brunswick, and the Yukon. The registrar has the discretion to request fingerprints in Alberta, Newfoundland, Nova Scotia, Ontario, Prince Edward Island, and Saskatchewan. The rules pertaining to how fingerprints are to be taken are also dictated in the legislation, usually requiring the applicant to attend a local police service. No legislation exists on the issue in Manitoba and Quebec.

The General Guidelines in Saskatchewan point out that if fingerprints are requested, the application process may be slowed up considerably. Saskatchewan reports that fingerprints sent to Ottawa take four to six months to come back. As a fingerprint search, if requested, must accompany the application for a licence, a person seeking licensing may be prohibited from working as a private investigator for a lengthy period of time.

An applicant for a private investigator's licence is required to submit a photograph with his or her application in British Columbia, New Brunswick, Ontario, and Saskatchewan. The registrar has the discretion to request a photograph in Alberta and Nova Scotia. The

88   R.S.A. 1980, c. P-16, Reg. 71/91 and 270/94, r. 2(1); R.S.B.C. 1996, c. 374, Reg. 4/81, r. 3(1); R.S.M. 1987, c. P132, s. 30; R.S.N. 1990, c. P-24, s. 11; R.S.N.B. 1973, c. P-16, s. 5(1); R.S.N.S. 1989, c. 356, s. 7; R.S.O. 1990, c. P.25, s. 26; R.S.P.E.I. 1988, c. P-20, s. 6; R.S.Q. 1977, c. A-8, r. 3; R.S.S. 1997, c. P-26.01, s. 32; S.Y. 1988, c. 23, r. 1.
89   R.S.B.C. 1996, c. 374, Reg. 3/81, s. 2(b); R.S.Q. 1977, c. A-8, r. 1.
90   B.C. Reg. 4/81, r. 3(6).

rules pertaining to photographs stipulate the necessary dimensions of the photographs. There is no legislation on the issue in Manitoba, Newfoundland, Prince Edward Island, Quebec, and the Yukon.[91]

2.3   REGULATORY LIABILITY OF PRIVATE INVESTIGATION AGENTS AND AGENCIES

This section will discuss

- the maximum penalties in each province that may be imposed upon a private investigator or a private investigation agency for breach of the PISGA or its regulations;

- the operational issues in each province that restrain the conduct of a private investigator and a private investigation agency;

- the administrative issues in each province that a private investigator or a private investigative agency must abide by;

- the judicial process a private investigator or a private investigation agency is subjected to if charged with an offence under the PISGA; and

- the appeal process available to a private investigator or a private investigative agency if he, she, or it is convicted of an offence under the PISGA.

At the beginning of this chapter, it was mentioned that the reason for reviewing the legislation of each province is because it is increasingly common for private investigators today to follow investigations from their home province into another. It was further mentioned that the rules under which private investigators operate are those of the jurisdiction where they find themselves. This reality is especially germane to the subject matter of this section of the chapter.

The types of *operational* regulatory liability issues that will be discussed include identification, confidentiality, weapons and restraints, operating outside of jurisdiction, pretexts, process serving, paid informants, vehicles, in-service training, and the duty to report crime. The types of *administrative* regulatory liability issues that will be discussed include internal record-keeping matters such as employee records and file retention and destruction; external reporting requirements such as annual reports, change of employee or corporate status, incident reporting, and the surrendering of a licence; and other administrative issues such as the displaying of an issued licence, advertising and the name of the agency; civil actions for unlicensed services, part-time employment, and subcontracting.

---

91   R.S.A. 1980, c. P-16, Reg. 71/91, r. 2(2); R.S.B.C. 1996, c. 374, Reg. 3/81, r. 2(3); R.S.N. 1990, c. P-24, Reg. 227/81, r. 16; R.S.N.B. 1973, c. P-16, r. 3(2); R.S.N.S. 1989, c. 356, Reg. 179/83 as amended by Reg. 30/85, r. 5(1); R.S.O. 1990, c. P.25, Reg. 262/99 amending Reg. 938, r. 1(1) and the General Guidelines; R.S.P.E.I. 1988, c. P-20, s. 8; R.S.S. 1997, c. P-26.01, General Guidelines; S.Y. 1988, c. 23, s. 13.

However, before discussing the regulatory sins pertaining to private investigation, it is important to review the authority for laying a charge and the penalties that can be imposed, along with such issues as vicarious liability, limitation periods, how charges are laid, the court of first instance, and how to appeal.

2.3.1   Offences and Penalties

Every province has legislation pertaining to the penalties for committing an offence against the Act. The penalties, both in the form of fines or incarceration, vary widely across the country. Table 2.3 is a schedule of the maximum penalty that can be levied against a first-time offender. It should be noted that incarceration may be imposed in addition to fines.

TABLE 2.3
Penalties for Committing an Offence against the Act

Province	Fine	Incarceration
Alberta	$200	6 months
British Columbia	$5,000	1 year
Manitoba	$1,000	1 year
New Brunswick	$25,000	1 year
Newfoundland	$2,000	1 year
Nova Scotia	$200	no provision
Ontario	$5,000	1 year
Prince Edward Island	$1,000	no provision
Quebec	$700	no provision
Saskatchewan	$5,000	1 year
Yukon	$100	no provision

There are a number of nuances to this schedule. For instance, the maximum fine for a first offender for operating without a licence is $500 in Alberta, Nova Scotia, and Prince Edward Island. For multiple offenders, Alberta raises the maximum period of incarceration to one year. None of the provinces imposes incarceration upon directors or officers of corporate agency offenders. However, the fines in some provinces for corporate agency offenders have much higher maximums. For instance, corporate agency offenders in Manitoba could face a fine of $5,000, in British Columbia and Saskatchewan $10,000, and in Ontario $50,000. New Brunswick has a schedule of fines associated with its provincial offences legislation.

In addition to fines and imprisonment, the registrar or his or her designate in Saskatchewan can seek from the Court of Queen's Bench a restraining order when a person without a licence or whose licence has been suspended or cancelled continues to act as a private investigator or carry on a private investigative business.[92]

This review would not be complete without mentioning the regime in British Columbia in greater detail. In British Columbia, a regulation to the *Offence Act* provides that "inspectors" can levy fines for a host of different offences. Typically during an inspection, an inspector will explain the offences that have been identified and his specific concerns. The inspector will then return to his office to verify the information gathered and mail a notice out to the offending business that explains how compliance can be achieved and a reasonable period of time to correct the offence. If compliance is not achieved within a reasonable period of time, the inspector may recommend to the registrar prosecution, suspension, or cancellation of a licence. Although the registrar will generally determine the action to be taken, inspectors have the authority to hand out tickets to offending private investigative businesses and their owners. Except for serious violations directly affecting public safety, warnings will first be issued for non-compliance.[93] Interestingly, violation tickets issued by the Security Program Division are processed through the Insurance Corporation of British Columbia (ICBC), which oversees the violation ticket process for a number of provincial regulatory agencies. If the ICBC decides to take action to obtain any outstanding fines, they will turn the matter over to their collections department, and if they cannot resolve the matter, the file will be turned over to a private collection agency. Unresolved fines can result in garnishee of wages, court action, or suspension of a driver's licence.[94]

2.3.1.1   Vicarious Liability

Only the province of Quebec has legislated that agencies are vicariously liable for the offences committed by their employee agents. Therefore, if a private investigator contravenes a provision of Quebec's PISGA and is charged with an offence, the agency is automatically charged with the same offence as well.

Only the province of Saskatchewan has legislated that officers, directors, or agents of a corporation are guilty of an offence if they direct, authorize, or participate in an act or omission by a corporation that would constitute an offence by that corporation under the Act. Saskatchewan's legislation further provides that such a person is guilty whether or not the corporation has been prosecuted or convicted.[95]

2.3.1.2   Limitation Periods

Limitation periods are the time periods specified by statute within which an action must be brought or a complaint filed. In British Columbia and Newfoundland, the Act stipulates the limitation period is one year after the commission of the alleged offence. In Manitoba

---

92   R.S.A. 1980, c. P-16, s. 22; R.S.B.C. 1996, c. 374, s. 31(4); R.S.M. 1987, c. P132, s. 37; R.S.N. 1990, c. P-24, s. 39(1); R.S.N.B. 1973, c. P-16, s. 23; R.S.N.S. 1989, c. 356, s. 24; R.S.O. 1990, c. P.25, s. 32; R.S.P.E.I. 1988, c. P-20, s. 23; R.S.Q. 1977, c. A-8, s. 12; R.S.S. 1997, c. P-26.01, ss. 17, 29, 43, & 47 and the General Guidelines; S.Y. 1988, c. 23, s. 29, 30.1.

93   *Security News* (December 1994).

94   *Security News* (March 1998).

95   R.S.Q. 1977, c. A-8, s. 13; R.S.S. 1997, c. P-26.01, s. 43(2)

and Ontario, the Act stipulates the limitation period is one year after the incident first comes to the knowledge of the registrar or minister. In Saskatchewan, the Act stipulates the limitation period is two years after the date of the alleged offence. In Alberta, New Brunswick, Nova Scotia, Prince Edward Island, Quebec, and the Yukon, the Act does not stipulate any limitation period.[96]

Whenever a person is charged with an offence, the limitation period should be one of the first issues researched. If the date of the charge commences after the limitation period has passed, this provision may provide a successful defence.

2.3.1.3   Court of First Instance Procedure

Generally speaking, charges under the Act are laid by summons by the registrar or his or her designate. In most provinces, the summons will require a court attendance. The exception is British Columbia where there is legislative authority that gives inspectors the capacity to issue tickets charging persons with offences under the Act in addition to the powers granted to the registrar. These tickets, which are merely another form of summons, permit an accused to pay an out-of-court fine or seek a court date to dispute the charge. Manitoba and Ontario have set out in legislation that no proceedings may be commenced against a person without the consent of the Minister.[97]

In all provinces, the court of first instance is the provincial court because the Act falls under provincial jurisdiction. In most provinces, the provincial court is simply known as the Provincial Court. In Ontario, the provincial court is known as the Ontario Court of Justice.

Proceedings in provincial courts are summary in nature, which means they are short, concise, peremptory, and without a jury, as opposed to indictable criminal proceedings, which grant the full procedural safeguards to an accused. In Alberta and New Brunswick, the legislation that should be referenced is the *Provincial Offences Procedure Act*; in British Columbia: the *Offences Act*; in Manitoba, Quebec, and the Yukon: the *Summary Convictions Act*; in Newfoundland and Ontario: the *Provincial Offences Act*; in Nova Scotia and Prince Edward Island: the *Summary Proceedings Act*; and in Saskatchewan: the *Summary Offences Procedure Act*.[98]

2.3.1.4   Appeals Procedure

As discussed generally in Chapter 1 — The Machinery of Justice, appeals from the provincial court are made to an "appeal court." In Ontario, the "appeal court" is known as the Superior Court of Justice. In Quebec it is called the Superior Court. In Nova Scotia, the

---

96 R.S.B.C. 1996, c. 374, s. 32(4); R.S.M. 1987, c. P132, s. 38(1); R.S.N. 1990, c. P-24, s. 39(2); R.S.O. 1990, c. P.25, s. 32(4); R.S.S. 1997, c. P-26.01, s. 44.

97 R.S.M. 1987, c. P132, s. 38(2) (The Minister is defined in s. 1 of Manitoba's Act as the member of the Executive Council charged with the administration of this Act by the Lieutenant Governor in Council.); R.S.O. 1990, c. P.25, s. 32(3).

98 R.S.A. 1980, c. P-21.5, see also Alberta Regulation 89/233; R.S.B.C. 1996, c. 338; R.S.M. 1987, c. S230; R.S.N. 1995, c. P-31.1; R.S.N.B. 1973, c. P-22.1; R.S.N.S. 1989, c. 450; R.S.O. 1990, c. P.33; R.S.P.E.I. 1988, c. S-9; R.S.S. 1978, c. S-63.1; R.S.Q. 1977, c. P-15; R.S.Y. 1986, c. 164.

Yukon, and British Columbia, the appeal court is titled the Supreme Court. In the provinces of New Brunswick, Manitoba, Saskatchewan, and Alberta, the appeal court is referred to as the Court of Queen's Bench. Finally, in Prince Edward Island and Newfoundland, it is called the Trial Division of the Supreme Court.[99] Appeals from a decision of an "appeal court" are made to the respective provincial Court of Appeal. Appeals from a provincial Court of Appeal are to the Supreme Court of Canada.

Each province has legislation pertaining to the rules that must be followed to appeal. Table 2.4 lists the legislation to reference in each province.

TABLE 2.4
Provincial Legislation Governing Appeals

Province	Legislation
Alberta	*Judicature Act*, R.S.A. 1980, c. J-1
	Court of Queen's Bench Act, R.S.A. 1980, c. C-29 (see also the Rules of the Court in Reg. 390/68)
	Court of Appeal Act, R.S.A. 1980, c. C-28 (see also the Court of Appeal Rules in Reg. 553/88)
British Columbia	*Justice Administration Act*, R.S.B.C. 1996, c. 243
	Supreme Court Act, R.S.B.C. 1996, c. 443
	Court of Appeal Act, R.S.B.C. 1996, c. 77;
	Court Rules Act, R.S.B.C. 1996, c. 80
Manitoba	*Court of Queen's Bench Act*, R.S.M. 1987, c. C280 (see also the Queen's Bench Rules in Reg. 553/88)
	Court of Appeal Act, R.S.M. 1987, c. C240
New Brunswick	*Judicature Act*, R.S.N.B. 1973, c. J-2
Newfoundland	*Judicature Act*, R.S.N. 1990, c. J-4
Nova Scotia	*Judicature Act*, R.S.N.S. 1989, c. 240
Ontario	*Courts of Justice Act*, R.S.O. 1990, c. C.43
Prince Edward Island	*Supreme Court Act*, R.S.P.E.I. 1988, c. S-10
	Appeals Act, R.S.P.E.I. 1988, c. A-13
Quebec	*Courts of Justice Act*, R.S.Q. 1977, c. T-16
Saskatchewan	*Queen's Bench Act*, 1998, S.S. 1998, c. Q-1.01 (see also the *Queen's Bench Revision Act*, S.S., c. Q-1.1)
	Court of Appeal Act, R.S.S. 1978, c. C-42
Yukon	*Judicature Act*, R.S.Y. 1986, c. 96
	Supreme Court Act, R.S.Y. 1986, c. 165
	Court of Appeal Act, R.S.Y. 1986, c. 37

---

99   *Criminal Code of Canada*, R.S.C. 1985, c. C-46, s. 812.

2.3.2 Operational Issues

The types of operational regulatory liability issues that will be discussed in this section include identification, confidentiality, weapons and restraints, operating outside of jurisdiction, pretexts, process serving, paid informants, vehicles, in-service training, and the duty to report crime.

2.3.2.1 Identification and Uniforms

Private investigators are issued an identification card by their provincial registrar in every province and are prohibited from displaying or using any badge, shield, uniform, or card that is not prescribed by the PISGA. Private investigators are also specifically prohibited from operating as private investigators in a security guard uniform in every province except New Brunswick, Quebec, Saskatchewan, and the Yukon.

An infraction of this nature was reported in British Columbia where the subject party was employed as a university peace officer but also worked part-time as a private investigator. It was alleged that the peace officer attended the office of the secretary of the Department of Psychology in his uniform seeking information concerning one of the staff members. He candidly admitted that he was acting in his capacity as a private investigator engaged by an insurance company. The employer, after investigating the incident, concluded the officer had committed a breach of trust. He was subsequently dismissed.[100]

In every province except New Brunswick and Quebec, private investigators are required to carry their issued identification card on their person at all times while on duty and produce it upon request. The case law pertaining to the requirement to identify oneself as a private investigator varies across the country. In a case from Newfoundland, a court held that if a member of the public merely approaches a private investigator, he is obliged to identify himself at the time, or, if the person inquiring is hostile, as soon as reasonably possible thereafter.[101] However, in a case from Ontario, a court held that a private investigator is not obliged to identify himself unless the member of the public asks specifically to see his prescribed identification.[102]

In British Columbia, the largest employer of private investigation services, the Insurance Corporation of British Columbia (ICBC), has a directive on this issue. It provides:

> ICBC requires, as a condition of retaining any private investigator in British Columbia, that the investigator conduct investigations in a reasonable manner and in accordance with the following standards:
>
> . . .
>
> (3) If asked to identify yourself, give your name and state that you are an owner, partner or employee, as the case may be, of a provincially licenced private investigating firm that has been retained by the ICBC. Name the firm but do not claim to be or give the impression that you are an employee of the ICBC.[103]

---

100 *Re University of Victoria and CUPE Local 917* (1991), 26 C.L.A.S. 80 (B.C.).
101 *Druken v. RG Fewer & Associates Inc.*, [1998] N.J. No. 312, (S.C).
102 *R. v. Shackelton* (1993), (Ont. Prov. Ct.) [unreported].
103 The ICBC Private Investigators Guidelines publication, May 1999 at 8.

In British Columbia, in addition to being required to identify oneself as a private investigator upon demand, private investigators must also disclose the location of their office or place of business. In Saskatchewan, it is the responsibility of the business manager that each employee carry his or her licence card while on duty.

An interesting variance from Ontario and Saskatchewan is that of a hazardous work exception. If a private investigator will be undertaking a project where the revelation of his true purpose and identity may put him in harm's way, he or she can seek prior authorization from the registrar not to carry his private investigator identification. There is no legislation or policy directive on this issue in the other provinces.

Private investigators are specifically prohibited from holding themselves out as police officers in every province except Newfoundland, Prince Edward Island, Quebec, and the Yukon. In the provinces where there is no specific legislation on this issue, reference should be made to section 130 of the *Criminal Code* pertaining to personation of a police officer (see Section 4.3.1 — Personation of a Peace Officer). A similar prohibition exists against the use of the term "detective" or "private detective" in Alberta, British Columbia, Manitoba, Newfoundland, Ontario, and Saskatchewan.

Business cards are also the subject of legislation in some provinces. In Manitoba, Newfoundland, Ontario, and Saskatchewan, business cards possessed by private investigators may not contain any reference to being licensed under the Act. In Saskatchewan, private investigators are further prohibited from stating they are bonded on their business cards.[104]

2.3.2.2   Confidentiality

This section should be read in conjunction with Section 2.3.2.5 on Pretexts and Chapter 7 on the Krever Inquiry.

Confidential information is information that is treated as private and not for publication or release.[105] For information to be recognized as confidential, Canadian courts have held that

- the communications must originate in confidence that they will not be disclosed;
- the confidentiality must be essential to the full and satisfactory maintenance of the relationship between the parties;

---

104 R.S.A. 1980, c. P-16, ss. 11(2), 17, 19, & 20, Reg. 71/91, rr. 9 & 12(2); R.S.B.C. 1996, c. 374, ss. 11 & 27, Reg. 4/81, r. 8(5)(6); R.S.M. 1987, c. P132, ss. 27, 31, 33(2), & 35; R.S.N. 1990, c. P-24, ss. 29 & 30, Reg. 227/81, r. 15(b); R.S.N.B. 1973, c. P-16, ss. 6(2), 13, & 16; R.S.N.S. 1989, c. 356, ss. 17 & 20(1), Reg. 179/83 as amended by Reg. 30/85, r. 7; R.S.O. 1990, c. P.25, ss. 23(1), 25(1), & 30, Reg. 938, r. 12, and the General Guidelines; R.S.P.E.I. 1988, c. P-20, s. 16, E.C. 256/88, 639/93, 475/95, r. 9(5); R.S.Q. 1977, c. A-8, s. 10; R.S.S. 1997, c. P-26.01, ss. 23, 25, & 27, R.R.S. 2000, c. P-26.01, r. 1, s. 17, and the General Guidelines; S.Y. 1988, c. 23, s. 29, O.I.C. 1989/073, r. 7.

105 *LAC Minerals Ltd. v. International Corona Resources Ltd.* (1989), 44 B.L.R. 1 at 77 (S.C.C.).

- the relationship must be one which in the opinion of the community ought to be sedulously fostered; and

- the injury to the relationship due to disclosure of the communication must be greater than the benefit gained for the correct disposal of the litigation.[106]

The duty of confidentiality is an ethical duty owed to all clients. The concept of confidentiality is distinct from that of privilege, which is a rule of evidence. This distinction is significant, for notwithstanding that a private investigator has a duty of confidentiality to his client, he cannot argue that such information is privileged and therefore inadmissible in court unless he is acting under the direction of a solicitor.[107]

Each province's PISGA, except Saskatchewan, contains a confidentiality provision. However, in British Columbia and New Brunswick, the provision does not apply to any information received by a private investigator or private investigation agency during the course of an investigation. In British Columbia and New Brunswick, the provision only imposes a duty of confidentiality upon information obtained for the purposes of the Act.[108] Although there is no legislative direction in British Columbia, the Insurance Corporation of British Columbia (ICBC) Private Investigator Guidelines provide that no files, reports, information, or videotapes may be used for any purpose other than reporting to the ICBC, nor can they be disclosed to any other person except as required to carry out the investigation.[109]

There have been a number of cases that have discussed a private investigator's duty of confidentiality to her client. In a case from Ontario, a husband sought the assistance of an unlicensed person (the investigator) to locate his missing wife. After a number of interviews with the husband, the investigator suspected the husband was responsible for his wife's disappearance, and that she was in fact dead. The investigator took her suspicions to the police who enlisted the investigator as a police informant. The husband later disclosed the location of his wife's body to the investigator and he was subsequently charged with first-degree murder.

At trial, on a *voir dire* to determine the admissibility of the investigator's evidence, the defence argued that the investigator, notwithstanding she was not licensed under the PISGA, had a duty of confidentiality to the accused. The defence further argued that the police had engaged in "dirty tricks" — dirty tricks being acts such as having a police

---

106 *United Services Funds v. Richardson Greenshields of Canada Ltd.* (1988), 24 B.C.L.R. (2d) 41 at 43 (S.C.). Although the concepts of confidentiality and privilege are separate, this definition was also given to information that is privileged in *R. v. Gruenke* (1991), 67 C.C.C. (3d) 289 (S.C.C.).

107 For a further discussion on private investigators and privilege, see Section 10.3.

108 R.S.A. 1980, c. P-16, s. 15; R.S.B.C. 1996, c. 374, s. 29; R.S.M. 1987, c. P132, s. 29; R.S.N. 1990, c. P-24, s. 36; R.S.N.B. 1973, c. P-16, s. 10; R.S.N.S. 1989, c. 356, s. 22; R.S.O. 1990, c. P.25, s. 24; R.S.P.E.I. 1988, c. P-20, s. 20; R.S.Q. 1977, c. A-8, s. 9; S.Y. 1988, c. 23, s. 26.

109 The ICBC Private Investigator Guidelines, effective May 1999 at 5. All files, reports, information and videotapes compiled in the course of an investigation on behalf of the ICBC are the property of the ICBC.

informant pretend that he or she is a religious chaplain or lawyer to obtain the confidence of an accused to get a confession. The court, however, rejected the dirty tricks argument on the basis that the investigator was not in a relationship that society has recognized as being privileged. The court further held that the communications between the accused and the investigator were not confidential on the basis that there was no contractual employment relationship between the accused and the investigator and because the accused had asked the investigator if she was in fact an undercover police agent. The court held that, because the thought that the investigator might not be keeping his confidence had crossed his mind, the accused could no longer complain of a later breach of that confidence.[110]

In another case from Ontario, the German government, through letters of request for judicial assistance, sought an order for the production of documents held by the Canadian Imperial Bank of Commerce (CIBC). The evidence was sought to assist in the criminal investigation of a Canadian landed immigrant who was alleged to have engaged in a fraudulent scheme in Germany. The CIBC had obtained the documents through the use of a licensed private investigator. The Canadian landed immigrant, who was opposing an extradition application, sought and was granted intervenor status on the motion for documents. Among other arguments made, the intervenor contended that the production of documents should not be granted because such an order would breach the confidentiality provisions of the Ontario PISGA, the confidence in this case being that between the CIBC and the private investigator. After analyzing section 16 of the *Canada Evidence Act*, the court stated:

> Clearly, an order this court makes will protect Mr. O'Brien, who is a licenced private investigator, from a violation of this section. In any contest between this section and the interests of lending assistance to the criminal justice system in a foreign state, it is my view that the legitimate protection afforded by this section must give way.

Accordingly, the court ordered the private investigator to provide the impugned documents to the German authorities.[111]

An example of the misuse of privileged confidential information in the hands of a private investigator was demonstrated in an unreported decision from Ontario. In this case, during an adjournment from an unrelated matter but before opening arguments for the case in question, a private investigator who had worked for the plaintiff approached the defendant's lawyers and disclosed his findings. The plaintiff's counsel requested a *voir dire* to argue the applicability of section 24 of the PISGA to this improper action of the private investigator. As a result of this breach of confidentiality, the court ordered the defendant's lawyers be removed from the record on the basis that privileged information must be protected from improper use by an opposing party. The fate of the private investigator for this breach of confidentiality was not reported.[112]

---

110 *R. v. Morgan*, [1997] O.J. No. 5477 (Gen. Div.).

111 *Federal Republic of Germany v. Canadian Imperial Bank of Commerce* (1997), 31 O.R. (3d) 684 (Gen. Div.).

112 *Appleton v. Hawes* (1990), 47 C.P.C. (2d) 151 (Ont. H.C.J.).

Another example of the misuse of confidential information was reported by the Canadian Press pertaining to the widely publicized case of *LAC Minerals Ltd. v. International Corona Resources Ltd.* During the trial, a private investigator's secretary testified that the agency's employees played the stock market with information acquired during investigations. The agency had done investigative work for two Toronto mining corporations, LAC Minerals and Scintilore Explorations Ltd., both of which were engaged in civil actions against Corona. The secretary testified that it was a running joke that the private investigative agency was more of a trading house than an investigative firm. The secretary testified that they knew when an article was coming out in the *Globe and Mail* before it was released and that they knew it would have an effect on the stock. She claimed on two occasions she made quick profits with the information.[113]

Another interesting example of misuse of confidential information is taken from a divorce case in British Columbia in which the defendant solicitor was retained by the plaintiff's wife for the purposes of obtaining a divorce from her husband. The solicitor hired a private investigator whom he had employed with success on prior occasions. The private investigator, in addition to obtaining evidence of adultery on the wife's husband, also struck up a personal relationship with her. The solicitor became greatly alarmed because of the possibility of collusion. In an overreaction, the solicitor notified practically everyone he could reach who had any position of authority including the Attorney General, the RCMP, and the Law Society. Although the action continued to success, the wife brought action against the solicitor, alleging that through the breach of confidential information irrelevant to the retainer and the action, she was injured. The court held that the critical issue of the case was determining what was confidential information. The court found that notwithstanding that the solicitor's actions had always been such that it was obvious that he truly believed he had a continuing duty to expose any real or possible assault upon the purity of justice, the action taken by him exceeded that which the situation warranted. Accordingly, the solicitor breached his contractual relationship with his client. The court, however, held that the damages were nominal.[114]

In summary, case law has held that a private investigator must disclose confidential information if ordered by a court. It has also been held that it is improper for a private investigator to conduct an investigation to a party to litigation and then voluntarily turn over that information to an opposing party. Finally, it has been held that it is improper for a private investigator to acquire information for a party and later use it for his or her own purposes.

Besides being an obligation under the PISGA, the confidentiality obligation makes good business sense. For further information on the requirement of confidentiality, see Chapter 6 on Torts. This issue has not been the subject of many complaints to the registrar.

---

113 Canadian Press (30 September 1988).

114 *Ott v. Fleishman*, [1983] B.C.D. Civ. 2410-09 (S.C.). For another example of a breach of confidence by a private investigator in a family law case, see *Firestone v. Firestone* (1979), 25 O.R. (2d) 314 (H.C.J.).

2.3.2.3   Weapons and Restraint Devices

Although there is legislation or policy in the PISGAs of Alberta, British Columbia, Newfoundland, Ontario, Prince Edward Island, Saskatchewan, and the Yukon pertaining to the carrying of weapons and restraining devices, the legislation is not at all consistent.

In Alberta and Prince Edward Island, the PISGA provides that private investigators are prohibited from carrying restricted firearms unless a permit is received from the local registrar of firearms. In British Columbia, Newfoundland, Ontario, Saskatchewan, and the Yukon, the prohibition is wider, prohibiting the possession of all firearms while conducting any function related to private investigation.

The carrying of pepper spray, truncheons, billy sticks, and other such devices is prohibited by the PISGA in British Columbia and in a policy statement by Alberta. In fact, in Alberta the policy is that flashlights shall be no more than four cells in length. The legislation in the Yukon makes a blanket statement prohibiting the possession of all prohibited weapons by private investigators. In Ontario and Saskatchewan, batons, other special weapons, and self-defence equipment may only be carried by a private investigator if the private investigator has received training in the device and if the registrar has been notified in writing as to when and where the device is to be carried.

The carrying or use of handcuffs is prohibited in British Columbia and Alberta. Ontario and Saskatchewan permit the use of handcuffs if the private investigator is trained in their use and if the registrar is notified as to when and where they are to be carried. When carried, handcuffs must be concealed from public view.[115]

There is no legislation on the issue of weapons or restraints in Manitoba, New Brunswick, Nova Scotia, and Quebec. For these provinces it should be remembered that it is well settled that private investigators have no more power in the carrying out of their functions than that of any ordinary citizen. As the ordinary citizen is prohibited by the *Criminal Code* from carrying a restricted weapon without a permit, and then only under strict conditions for limited purposes, and from carrying prohibited weapons at all, the lawful opportunity for a private investigator to engage in such practices is rare. Prohibited weapons include such devices as spring knives, tear gas, mace, pepper spray, nunchakus, kiyoga batons, and steel cobras. Batons, truncheons, nightsticks, billy clubs, and handcuffs are not prohibited weapons, but carrying such devices for a purpose dangerous to the public peace is a criminal offence.[116]

A Canadian commentator has addressed the issue of private investigators and weapons. She reported that the position of the registrar in Alberta on the issue of permits for the carrying of firearms for private investigative work is such that a permit has never been granted. She further reported that the reasons given by most applicants for such a permit are spurious. The commentator stated that it would be dangerous to approve such permits as the arming of private investigators is not desirable from a public policy point of view. Some

---

115   *Criminal Code of Canada*, R.S.C. 1985, c. C-46, ss. 84, 87, 89, & 90.
116   R.S.A. 1980, c. P-16, Reg. 71/91, r. 16; R.S.B.C. 1996, c. 374, s. 25(1), Reg. 4/81, r. 8(2); R.S.N. 1990, c. P-24, s. 35; R.S.O. 1990, c. P.25, General Guidelines; R.S.P.E.I. 1988, c. P-20, E.C. 256/88, r. 20; R.R.S. 2000, c. P-26.01, r. 1, s. 16(2)(3)(4), and the General Guidelines; S.Y. 1988, c. 23, s. 28(1)(5).

of the desire to carry weapons can be attributed to a number of American investigators who have set up in Canada, or American agencies that have branch offices here. Rules in the United States dealing with the possession of weapons are more lenient and some of these investigators believe it is their right to carry weapons.[117]

A lawyer with the investigative firm of Kroll & Associates in Calgary has suggested that if a person expects to arrest someone, that person should probably carry handcuffs because the arrestor is responsible for the safety of the person in her custody. Pertaining to the use of flashlights, he suggests that it may be wiser to carry a smaller flashlight because complaints about the excessive use of force are commonplace in cases of arrest and there is less likelihood that a small flashlight will be construed as a weapon if the arrest is reviewed.[118]

2.3.2.4   Operating Outside of Jurisdiction

This topic has been raised by many private investigators operating in the field and was touched upon briefly in Section 2.1.2 — Persons and Activities Exempt from the Act. The following is a synopsis of the law on this issue. Reference to the legislation may be made in Section 2.1.2.

The legislation in Ontario is typical of all provinces that have a reciprocal licensing agreement. For ease of understanding, the legislation is broken down into its various parts. In Ontario, the licensing requirement does not apply to a person

- who resides outside Ontario;
- who is an employee of a private investigation agency licensed in a jurisdiction outside Ontario;
- who is working on behalf of an employer or client who resides outside Ontario; or
- who makes an investigation partly outside and partly within Ontario.

In other words, the legislation on this issue is a four-part test. Each part must be fulfilled to avoid breaching a reciprocating province's licensing requirements. Another way of explaining this is that if an investigation is commenced in a location outside Ontario for a client who resides or carries on business outside Ontario, the investigative agency retained does not have to consult the Ontario PISGA registrar or an Ontario private investigation agency to continue their investigation inside Ontario. Of course, the inverse also applies; that is, if the client resides in Ontario, or if the investigation commences in Ontario, the private investigation agency utilized must be licensed in Ontario.

Similar legislation is found in Newfoundland, New Brunswick, Prince Edward Island, Nova Scotia, Manitoba, Alberta, and the Yukon.

Quebec, like every other province, requires licensing. However, unlike other provinces, Quebec does not have an exemption for private investigators following up investigations from other provinces. Therefore, to follow up an investigation, the legal answer is that you must contact a private investigative agency in Quebec to do it for you unless consent is obtained from the Quebec registrar.

---

117 E.F. Geddes, "The Private Investigator and the Right to Privacy" (1989) 17 Alta. L. Rev. 256.
118 D. Ray, "Detaining, Arresting and Using Weapons" *Canadian Security* (June/July 2000) at 34.

The British Columbia and Saskatchewan legislation provides that a person residing out-side British Columbia or Saskachewan, if employed as a private investigator in his home province, *may* conduct an investigation in British Columbia or Saskatchewan *if* he notifies the registrar prior to the investigation and the registrar grants a temporary exception to the licensing requirement. The Saskatchewan registrar reports that the out-of-province private investigative firm must make a written application, disclosing the date, place, and length of time to be devoted to the investigation in Saskatchewan. Upon approval, the out-of-province investigator will receive a letter that must be carried on his person at all times while in Saskatchewan. The letter will only be current for the approved investigation. Any further investigations will require making application for business or employee licences. The Alberta Association of Private Investigators reports that the registrar's office in British Columbia can be quite difficult about this.

For American information, private investigation agencies should contact Max Whittington Investigations, Portland, Oregon, at <mwi@inetarena.com>. Mr. Whittington has published a book entitled *States' Requirements for P.I. Licensing*. Specific to the concerns of Ontario, no private investigator, foreign or out of state, may follow up an investigation within the state of Michigan. To investigate in Michigan, a private investigator must subcontract to a private investigative agency licensed in Michigan.[119] The situation is the same in New York state.[120]

2.3.2.5   Pretexts

A pretext has been defined as an ostensible reason or motive assigned or assumed as a cover for the real reason or motive. A pretext has also been defined as a verbal or physical deception practised on a person to persuade them to provide evidence or information they would not otherwise provide.

Although most PISGAs address the issue of identification, none of the provinces specifically addresses the related issue of pretexts in their legislation. As discussed in Section 2.3.2.1 — Identification and Uniforms, private investigators are specifically prohibited from holding themselves out as police officers in every province except Newfoundland, Prince Edward Island, Quebec, and the Yukon. In the provinces where there is no specific legislation on this issue, reference should be made to section 130 of the *Criminal Code* pertaining to the personation of a police officer, which also prohibits such conduct (see Section 4.3.1 — Personation of a Peace Officer). A similar prohibition exists against the use of the term "detective" or "private detective" in Alberta, British Columbia, Manitoba, Newfoundland, Ontario, and Saskatchewan.

---

119 Michigan Compiled Laws, 1970, *Private Detective Act of 1965*, Act 285, ss. 338.821 to 338.851. For further information, contact Debbie Shaw of the Michigan State Police, P.I. & S.G. Unit, Tel: (517) 336-3424.

120 New York State General Business Law, Article 7, s. 70. For further information pertaining to New York state, contact John Goldman, New York State Department of Licensing, Tel: (518) 474-2651, or see their Internet site at <www.dos.state.ny.us>.

Ontario and Saskatchewan are the only provinces that have an administrative policy pertaining to the use of pretexts. The reason for this may be because only in Ontario has the use of pretexts come under serious judicial scrutiny. It appears Saskatchewan has followed Ontario's lead. The General Guidelines from these two provinces prohibit private investigators from using the following pretexts:

+ lawyers
+ doctors
+ firefighters
+ police officers
+ bylaw enforcement officers
+ armed forced officers
+ government employees
+ telephone company employee
+ other public utility employees

The General Guidelines point out that this list is not considered exhaustive, and that any licensee who uses a ruse that is not justifiable becomes liable to investigation by the registrar. Where the registrar finds that the conduct is not in the public interest, action may be initiated against the licence holder by the registrar.[121]

For a review of the use of pretexts to obtain medical information, which was practised by some private investigative firms and condoned by some in the legal, medical, and insurance fields in the 1970s, see Chapter 7 — Confidentiality of Health Information — The Krever Inquiry.

Although British Columbia does not have legislation on this issue, the major employer of private investigative services in the province does. The ICBC guidelines provide:

> The ICBC requires, as a condition of retaining any private investigator in British Columbia, that the investigator conduct investigations in a reasonable manner and in accordance with the following standards:
>
> . . .
>
> (5)   Do not accept information from or induce employees of public bodies to provide information if, in providing the information, those employees have to violate their employer's policies or laws governing the release of such information.
>
> (6)   Do not induce a person who is being investigated to engage in an activity in which that person would not otherwise be disposed to engage.
>
> (7)   It is important that investigations undertaken on behalf of the ICBC should be conducted in a way that will not alarm claimants or anyone else, nor give them reasonable cause for apprehension for public safety and security. All investigations must be car-

---

121 R.S.O. 1990, c. P.25, General Guidelines; R.S.S. 1997, c. P-26.01, General Guidelines.

ried out in the least obstructive manner possible, and having regard to the circumstances of that investigation:

(a)   do not

◆   enter on the private property of the person being investigated, except where the property is used by that person for commercial purposes and the investigation relates to that commercial purpose, or

◆   use a pretext or misrepresentation to gain access to any premises.[122]

One commentator has made the following observations pertaining to using misrepresentations to obtain evidence:

> The ethical investigator sees himself or herself as a gatherer of information or intelligence. He or she does not make things happen in the sense of creating a situation to which the subject is required or expected to respond. In the investigation of a personal injury case, an investigator might strike up an acquaintance with a subject in a club. She may sit down and introduce herself and talk with him, but she will not ask or encourage him to dance. If he suggests it this would be a different matter as he has initiated the action and the investigator would then be merely responding and observing his physical capabilities. But to place the idea in his head herself would be to make something happen, to create a scenario, rather than insinuate herself into a presently existing one.[123]

It has been said that the art of pretexts is a dying one as more and more information is attainable through electronic sources. Although this may be so, it is naive to think that pretexts are not a necessary tool to extract information in certain cases. When using pretexts, the consequences should be well thought out beforehand. Clearly, the utilization of most pretexts is not illegal in a regulatory sense *per se*. However, their use to obtain entrance into a residence or to obtain privileged information may lead to criminal or civil sanctions. For further information on this subject, see the relevant sections in Chapter 4 — Criminal Liability, and Chapter 6 — The Law of Torts.

2.3.2.6   Service of Documents

As indicated in Section 2.1.1 — Definition of a Private Investigator, the task of process serving does not come under the purview of licensing for private investigators. This policy applies to all civil processes. The service of summons or subpoenas for criminal and provincial offence matters may only be performed by peace officers. For information pertaining to the timing and methods of serving a civil process, see the Rules of Court or the Rules of Civil Procedure for your own province. If the matter litigated falls under federal jurisdiction, see the Federal Court Rules.[124]

---

122 The ICBC Private Investigators Guidelines publication, May 1999 at 8.
123 E.F. Geddes, "The Private Investigator and the Right to Privacy" (1989) 17 Alta. L. Rev. 256 at 268.
124 R.S.O. 1990, c. P.25, General Guidelines; R.S.S. 1997, c. P-26.01, General Guidelines.

2.3.2.7   Paid Informants

None of the provinces has legislation or policies on the use of paid informants. However, as a result of an occurrence in Ontario, it has been suggested that, technically, paid inform-ants should be required to be licensed. In this case, an agency owner was alleged to have hired prostitutes to pose as business clients and lure some businessmen into compromising situations that were surreptitiously videotaped. It was suggested that technically the pros-titutes should have been licensed as private investigators. The registrar's office has not, however, taken action against the agency or the prostitutes in this regard.[125]

An example of a public officer becoming a gratuity-receiving informant of a private investigator was also reported in Ontario. In this case, an experienced OPP officer was found guilty of breach of trust after accepting an all-expenses-paid weekend in Toronto from a private investigator who was probing a fatal traffic accident. The court found as fact that the police officer had been the investigating officer in a fatal crash that killed a couple and injured one of their children in April 1992. The police officer was later contacted by the private investigator. The police officer agreed to come to Toronto to discuss the case if the private investigator would pay for his trip. The private investigator agreed and paid the police officer approximately $650. The police officer in turn provided copies of reports of other accidents from the area of the accident. The court held that the public must main-tain its trust in public officials and that clearly has to be one of the goals of sentencing. The court imposed upon the officer a $3,000 fine. The officer was also required to resign from the force.[126]

2.3.2.8   Vehicles

The use of flashing lights or insignia on vehicles is more of a regulatory concern pertain-ing to security guards than to private investigators. Notwithstanding this reality, the use of flashing lights is expressly prohibited in Alberta, British Columbia, and Saskatchewan. In Quebec, the legislation states that all licensees may not use a vehicle unless its characteris-tics and identification standards are approved of in writing by the registrar. In all other provinces, reference should be made to the respective provincial *Highway Traffic Act*.[127]

---

125 *R. v. Alexander* (1999), (Ont. S.C.J.) [unreported]. For a further review of this case, see Section 4.5.5 — Extortion.

126 *R. v. Martin* (1994), (Ont. Prov. Ct.) [unreported]; see Canadian Press article (12 January 1994). See also *R. v. Rosenberg* (11 January 2001), (Ont. Prov. Ct.) [unreported]; see Bob Mitchell, "Officer Charged with Ticket Fixing" *Toronto Star* (20 October 2000) B7.

127 R.S.B.C. 1996, c. 374, Reg. 4/81, r. 6(1); R.S.N. 1990, c. P-24, Reg. 227/81, r. 14; R.S.Q. 1977, c. A-8; R.R.S. 2000, c. P-26.01, r. 1, s. 18. Alberta's application package further provides that Alberta's *Highway Traffic Act* makes no provision for the use of flashing lights. Should there be a special requirement for this type of equipment, requests can be submitted to the Motor Transport Board for an equipment exemption permit. Once a decision is made, the Administrator of the PISGA must be informed. All prior requests for this exemption by pri-vate investigators have been refused.

2.3.2.9   Training

The educational and training requirements to obtain a private investigator's licence was reviewed in Section 2.2.3.3 — Education and Training. The issue in this section is how the training is conducted.

In British Columbia, private investigators are limited to supervising only two private investigators in training, otherwise known as PIR1s. The General Guidelines of Ontario and Saskatchewan state no on-the-job training may be conducted until the trainee is licensed. The only pre-licence training that may be commenced is in a classroom.[128]

Taking on the task of training junior investigators can result in regulatory liability. In British Columbia, a private investigator took on a trainee who made complaints to the registrar that he was receiving inadequate supervision, instruction, and training. These complaints resulted in the registrar refusing to renew the private investigator's licence. Upon a hearing before the registrar, it was revealed the trainee was untruthful and that the trainee simply did not take advantage of the opportunities provided. The registrar, however, held that the private investigator lacked the necessary training and experience himself to train others. Although the registrar reinstated the private investigator's licence, he refused to permit him to act as a supervisor.[129]

2.3.2.10   Duty to Report Crime

The duty to report crime in this context pertains to criminal activity that a private investigator becomes aware of during the execution of his vocation. It does not include the reporting of criminal activity a private investigator herself has been engaged in, been charged with, or been convicted of. For the self-reporting of criminal activity, see Section 2.3.3.2.3. — Incident Reports (Change in Criminal Status).

The duty of a private investigator to report crime and the liability for omitting to do so has come up in various circles. For example, in a past edition of the Alberta Association of Private Investigators' *Code of Ethics*, one of the provisions read:

> As a private investigator, I will always respect the wishes of my client — except in serious criminal findings, the nature of which I am *legally* bound to disclose to the appropriate law enforcement agency.

Upon further inquiry into the legal basis for this provision in the *Code of Ethics*, a past director of the Alberta Association of Private Investigators stated that the authority for this provision was based on sections 21 to 24, 30, and 494 of the *Criminal Code*. A review of these sections of the *Criminal Code* does not substantiate the proposition that there is a duty upon private persons or private investigators to report crime. Section 21 deals with "Parties to an Offence," commonly known as aiding and abetting a principal accused. In reviewing the definition of "abetting," the editor of *Martin's Criminal Code* asserts that abetting means encouraging. Merely being present is not enough unless the presence is accompanied by

---

128   British Columbia Security Programs Division directive; R.S.O. 1990, c. P.25, General Guidelines; R.S.S. 1997, c. P-26.01, General Guidelines.
129   *Blair v. Bellwood*, [1999] B.C.D. Civ. 530.75.35.00-20 (S.C.).

such additional factors as prior knowledge that the principal was going to commit the offence. Section 22 of the *Criminal Code* deals with persons counselling an offence; section 23 deals with persons who are accessories after the fact; and section 24 deals with attempts to commit criminal offences. These sections are clearly inapplicable to the potential for criminal liability to private investigators for not reporting criminal offences to police. Section 494 of the *Criminal Code*, as dealt with under Section 4.1.1 — Authority to Arrest, deals with a citizen's powers of arrest. Section 494 requires a private person to turn over an arrested person to police as soon as practicable. It does not, however, require the reporting of criminal offences where no arrest has been made. Although not mentioned, a possible applicable provision of the *Criminal Code* would be section 139, Obstructing Justice. See Section 4.5.2 — Obstructing Justice, for a discussion of this issue. No case law with regard to duty to report crime by private persons or private investigators was uncovered.

From the above analysis, it is concluded that there generally is no good Samaritan duty on a private investigator. A private investigator who witnesses a criminal offence, even with prior knowledge that such an offence was going to take place, is in no different position than any civilian person who witnesses a criminal act.[130] The role of private persons is contrasted with police officers, however, who have a duty to report crime. In a case from British Columbia, a court held that a police officer who was the officer in charge of the lock-up could be convicted as a party to an assault committed by another officer on a prisoner if he or she did not investigate and report the incident.[131]

The one exception to the above is a provision found in New Brunswick's *Police Act*. It provides that persons licensed under the PISGA who have knowledge of or are investigating criminal offences shall immediately notify the officer in charge of the area where the offence took place of their knowledge and investigation.[132]

2.3.3   Administrative Issues

The administrative issues to be reviewed fall under the subject headings of internal record keeping, regulatory reporting requirements, displaying of an agency licence, advertising and the name of the agency, civil actions for unlicensed services, part-time employment, and subcontracting.

2.3.3.1   Internal Record Keeping

The issues that arise when dealing with internal record keeping are employee records, investigation file retention and destruction, and business records.

2.3.3.1.1   Employee Records

The rules pertaining to a private investigation agency's duty to maintain its own internal employee records have not been very well addressed in most provinces. In fact, Manitoba, Newfoundland, Nova Scotia, and Prince Edward Island have not addressed the issue at all.

---

130 Section 141 of the *Criminal Code* may apply if a "pay-off" is taken.
131 *R. v. Nixon* (1990), 57 C.C.C. (3d) 97, 78 C.R. (3d) 349 (B.C.C.A.).
132 *Police Act*, R.S.N.B. 1985, c. P-9.2, s. 36.

Of the provinces that have addressed the issue, Alberta, New Brunswick, and Quebec have imposed a statutory duty on private investigative agencies to keep copies of the licences of their private investigators in their agency's offices. Further, there is a statutory duty on private investigative agencies to keep employee records such as name, address, start date, termination date, and licence number in Alberta, British Columbia, New Brunswick, Quebec, and the Yukon. Only Quebec requires that the employee records of a private investigative agency be continually updated and revised every month.

Ontario and Saskatchewan do not have any legislation on the issue but do have policy statements addressing the topic in detail. Among other things, the policies state that records and reports pertaining to employees must be maintained by an agency for a period of two years in addition to the current year. In the event that an agency closes, an agency owner is still obliged to maintain the agency's records and reports for two years plus the current year. Finally, the terms "records" and "reports" pertaining to employees has been defined to include books of account such as payroll records, banking records such as registers of pay cheques, and personnel records such as employment applications, licence and status reports from the registrar, termination notices, and any other correspondence to or from the registrar pertaining to an individual. Photocopies of licences are insufficient; an employer must possess a true copy of the licence.[133]

In addition to the above requirements, every business must comply with the employee record-keeping stipulations of the various federal and provincial tax and business record Acts.

2.3.3.1.2 Business Records

Ontario and Saskatchewan are the only provinces that have a policy stipulating what business records a private investigative agency must maintain. The policy is quite detailed. Ontario's policy provides an agency's records and reports must be kept for two years plus the current year, even after the closing of the agency. Saskatchewan's policy provides that records must be kept for three years plus the current year. The policies define records and reports to include reports to clients for service performed and all business correspondence to and from clients, former clients, or prospective clients. Other reports and records that must be maintained include internal correspondence relating to services, investigator notes, investigation occurrence or incident reports, contractual agreements, employee time sheets, photographs, and video or audio records.

Books of account that must be maintained include account receivable journals, cash receipts journals, cheque disbursement journals, general journals, sales journals, general ledgers, payroll journals, account payable journals, financial statements, expense accounts, payroll records, sales invoices, and customer statements. These records may be removed temporarily from the premises in which they are usually kept for the purpose of auditing or accounting.

---

133 R.S.A. 1980, c. P-16, ss. 11(3) & 12, Reg. 71/91, r. 13; R.S.B.C. 1996, c. 374, Reg. 4/81, r. 5(2); R.S.N.B. 1973, c. P-16, ss. 12(2) & 12.1, Reg. 84-103, r. 9; R.S.O. 1990, c. P.25, s. 8(1) and the General Guidelines; R.S.Q. 1977, c. A-8, s. 7, rr. 15, 16, 17, 18, & 19; R.R.S. 1997, c. P-26.01, General Guidelines; S.Y. 1988, c. 23, ss. 22(2) & 23(1).

Banking records that must be maintained include cheque registers, bank drafts, cancelled cheques, record of pay cheques, bank deposit and withdrawal records, bank statements, and debit and credit memos.[134]

2.3.3.1.3 *Investigation File Retention and Destruction*

The rules pertaining to a private investigation agency's duty to maintain records of their investigations has also not been very well addressed in most provinces. In fact, the provinces of British Columbia, Manitoba, Newfoundland, Nova Scotia, Prince Edward Island, and Quebec have not addressed the issue at all. Of the provinces that have addressed the issue, there is a statutory duty on private investigative agencies to keep records of each investigation or work undertaken in Alberta, New Brunswick, and the Yukon. Ontario and Saskatchewan do not have any legislation on the issue but have developed a policy statement addressing the topic.

Time frames for retaining files is an issue that has been addressed. In New Brunswick, records of investigation files must be maintained for one year. In Ontario, records must be maintained for two years plus the current year, even after the closing of the agency. In Saskatchewan, the rule is three years plus the current year. The legislation in Alberta and the Yukon does not address how long files must be maintained.[135]

Although British Columbia has no formal legislation on the issue, the largest employer of private investigators in that province, the ICBC, has an internal policy by which private investigators that it retains must abide. The policy instructs when the files must be destroyed, how they must be destroyed, and how to handle files when a private investigator leaves an agency or an agency is closed. It provides:

> All notes, files, reports information and videotapes must be retained for a period of seven years from the date of the private investigation firm's closing report.
>
> . . .
>
> (6) Unless otherwise advised, at the conclusion of seven years from submission of the final private investigator's report, all ICBC file material must be entirely destroyed in order that it cannot be used by any other party for any purpose. This information is confidential, so the following safeguards must be followed:
>
> (i) Notes, files, reports and information: All paper documentation must be fully shredded. Paper shredding must be conducted by a bonded, confidential destruction service or arrangements can be made to utilize shredding machines through ICBC.
>
> (ii) Information Stored on a Computer: When computer equipment is disposed of, steps must be taken to ensure that all information contained on the hard drive, all computer disks and any other memory system is rendered irretrievable. Simply deleting or erasing is not sufficient. At the very least, the hard

134 R.S.O. 1990, c. P.25, General Guidelines; R.R.S. 1997, c. P-26.01, General Guidelines.
135 R.S.A. 1980, c. P-16, s. 12; R.S.N.B. 1973, c. P-16, s. 12.1, N.B 84-103, r. 9; R.S.O. 1990, c. P.25, s. 8(1) and the General Guidelines; R.R.S. 1997, c. P-26.01, General Guidelines; S.Y. 1988, c. 23, s. 23(1).

drive should be reformatted. However, even this does not necessarily destroy the data. Please contact the Senior Corporate Information Analyst Data Management Department for proper destruction guidelines.

(iii) Videotapes: It is mandatory that all videotapes be destroyed, or, if reused, fully demagnetized. Erasing videotapes is not sufficient

(7)   If a private investigative firm goes out of business, changes ownership, ceases to do business or is terminated:

(i)   all notes, files, reports, information and videotapes must be returned to ICBC,

(ii)   all computer-stored materials and information must be destroyed in accordance with (6),

(iii)   ICBC reserves the right to demand delivery of all ICBC related file materials.

(8)   In the event that the assigned private investigator transfers out of the private investigative firm, is terminated or resigns, all files assigned to that private investigator must remain with the private investigative firm unless prior approval to transfer those files from the instructing adjuster is obtained.[136]

No case law has been reported on this issue. However, the Canadian Press reported that in the case of *LAC Minerals v. Corona*, a private investigator's secretary testified that her employer instructed her to alter, hide, and discard various records relating to the case and to destroy any information on computer disks if anyone came to their offices with a search warrant. She further testified that the private investigator's motive for these instructions was because his client, LAC Minerals, had previously financed another investigation conducted by him for another company involved in litigation against Corona.[137]

2.3.3.2   Regulatory Reporting Requirements

The issues that arise when dealing with regulatory reporting requirements are annual reports, change of employee or company status, incident reporting (i.e., change in criminal status), and the surrendering of licences.

2.3.3.2.1   Annual Reports

All private investigative agencies in each province are required to renew their licences each year. For the dates of renewal and fees, see Section 2.2.1.2.1 — Annual Renewals.

All private investigative agencies in each province except Manitoba and Newfoundland are required to submit annual reports. In some provinces, however, the date of renewal does not coincide with the date the annual report is due. In Alberta, for instance, an agency licence must be renewed before 31 December of each year while the annual return does not have to be filed until the following month. In Nova Scotia, agency licence renewal applications must be submitted by 1 March and must be renewed by 31 March, while the annual return is not required until 30 April of each year.

---

136 ICBC Private Investigators Guidelines, effective May 1999 at 6.
137 Canadian Press (29 September 1988).

The legislation in Ontario and the Yukon does not detail what must be reported every year, but rather has agency owners and/or managers simply complete a prescribed form. However, other provinces have legislated what the agency annual reports must contain. Examples of what must be reported include the address where the business was carried on during the preceding year, the names of the private investigators whom they employed during the preceding year, including those who were new and those who left or were terminated, the number of investigations and a breakdown by type of investigation, evidence of insurance, and proof of continued bonding. Examples of what must be reported in various provinces by private investigators include changes of address, upgrades in education and training, changes in criminal and mental status, and updated photographs.[138]

A labour case from British Columbia dealt with the issue of an agency that did not report the criminal conduct of one of its employees on its annual return. In this case, a security employee had been convicted of shoplifting in 1983. The security employee was suspended by the registrar, but with the assistance of her employer agency was later reinstated. The security employee received a pardon for the offence in 1986. In 1988 the security employee was again charged with shoplifting. However, because the police were not aware of her prior conviction, the security employee's case was sent to the provincial diversionary program. In 1990, after becoming involved in a dispute with her employer, the agency owner added a note on the security employee's annual return, informing the registrar of the 1988 arrest. On this basis, the registrar again suspended the security employee's licence. In ruling on the propriety of the security employee's dismissal, the arbitrator held that both the security employee and the agency had contravened the PISGA by not reporting the arrest on their annual returns in 1988 and 1989. Notwithstanding this omission, the arbitrator upheld the security employee's dismissal, reasoning that the agency's failure to comply with its annual reporting requirements until two years after becoming aware of the incident was not grounds to reverse the dismissal.[139]

2.3.3.2.2 Change of Employee or Company Status

Every province other than Alberta and Quebec requires private investigative agency owners to report changes in ownership or management personnel of the business within a short period of time after the event. The time frame for reporting such changes is five days in Manitoba, Newfoundland, Ontario, and Saskatchewan; seven days in New Brunswick, Nova Scotia, and Prince Edward Island; fourteen days in British Columbia; and fifteen days in the Yukon.

---

138 R.S.A. 1980, c. P-16, s. 13, Reg. 71/91, r. 13; R.S.B.C. 1996, c. 374, Reg. 3/81, r. 2; R.S.N.B. 1973, c. P-16, s. 8(2), Reg. 84-103, r. 4; R.S.N.S. 1989, c. 356, ss. 9(2), 13(1), & 15, Reg. 179/83 as amended by Reg. 30/85, r. 5(2); R.S.O. 1990, c. P.25, s. 11; R.S.P.E.I. 1988, c. P-20, ss. 12(1) & 14; R.S.Q. 1977, c. A-8, rr. 5 & 14; R.R.S. 2000, c. P-26.01, r. 1, ss. 10 & 11; S.Y. 1988, c. 23, ss. 17 & 24.

139 *Northern Security Guard Services Ltd. v. Construction and General Workers Union Local No. 602* (1993), No. C109/93 (B.C.L.R.B.).

Every province other than Alberta, Quebec, and the Yukon requires private investigative agency owners to report any changes of address of their agency within the time frames given above.

Every province other than Alberta and the Yukon requires a private investigation agency owner to report the termination of any employee within the time frames given above, with the exception of Quebec where the event must be reported "without delay." The Notice of Termination to the registrar must include the employee licence and the reason for termination.

As all applications for licences are made to the registrar, it seems redundant that there would be separate provisions with respect to reporting the start of employment. However, the legislation in Quebec provides that every agency has a duty to report the employment of a new private investigator to the registrar within three days.

There is also a duty in British Columbia, New Brunswick, and Newfoundland on persons holding a private investigator's licence to report a change in their residential address within the time frames given above. In Ontario and Saskatchewan, a private investigator who changes his or her name must notify his or her agency owner, and the agency owner must make application to the registrar for a new licence and identification card.[140]

Where a province does not have legislation pertaining to an issue identified above, reference should be made to Section 2.3.3.2.1 — Annual Reports.

2.3.3.2.3 Incident Reports – Change in Criminal Status

The duty of a private investigative agency owner or a private investigator to report a change in his or her criminal status, be that either a charge or a conviction, to the provincial PISGA registrar only exists upon those licensed in British Columbia, New Brunswick, Newfoundland, and Saskatchewan. In New Brunswick and Newfoundland, the duty is effective immediately upon any change in criminal status, while in British Columbia notification must be made within fourteen days. Saskatchewan does not set out a specified time.

In all other provinces, the duty to report a change in criminal status does not exist. As criminal charges are usually laid by local police departments, such charges can temporarily avoid detection by the registrar as the local police department is not obliged to contact the registrar. However, in most cases it is prudent for private investigative agency owners to report criminal charges laid against an employee to avoid inspections or other inquiries by the registrar. Furthermore, in most provinces, with Manitoba as a notable exception, there is a duty to report any change in criminal status upon the annual renewal. In this regard, reference should be made to Section 2.3.3.2.1 — Annual Reports. In British Columbia, even if a private investigator does not report a criminal charge as required, he

---

140 R.S.B.C. 1996, c. 374, s. 8; R.S.M. 1987, c. P132, s. 9; R.S.N. 1990, c. P-24, s. 21; R.S.N.B. 1973, c. P-16, ss. 7 & 7.1; R.S.N.S. 1989, c. 356, s. 13(2); R.S.O. 1990, c. P.25, s. 6(2), Reg. 262/99 amending Reg. 938, r. 1(3), General Guidelines; R.S.P.E.I. 1988, c. P-20, s. 12(2), E.C. 256/88, r. 22(4); R.S.Q. 1977, c. A-8, rr. 21, 22, & 23; R.S.S. 1997, c. P-26.01, General Guidelines; S.Y. 1988, c. 23, s. 18(1).

or she will not avoid detection for long as the registrar now conducts annual criminal record checks as a matter of course.

Other than criminal matters, Saskatchewan defines "incident" to include situations where there has been an injury to a member of the public, where the police were called, where an employee investigator has been injured while working, or where weapons were involved. For all such incidents, an Incident Report Form must be forwarded to the registrar.[141]

2.3.3.2.4 Surrender of a Licence

Every province except Quebec has legislation requiring private investigative agencies and private investigators to surrender their licences in certain circumstances. If a private investigative agency has its licence suspended or cancelled in Alberta, British Columbia, Newfoundland, Prince Edward Island, Saskatchewan, or the Yukon, it is required to return its agency licence to the registrar forthwith. If a private investigative agency licence expires in British Columbia or Manitoba, the agency must immediately surrender its licence to the registrar. If a private investigative agency ceases to carry on business in British Columbia, Manitoba, New Brunswick, Newfoundland, Nova Scotia, Ontario, Prince Edward Island, or Saskatchewan, the agency must promptly return its licence to the registrar. If a private investigative agency licensee dies in Alberta or Prince Edward Island, the executor or administrator of his or her estate must return the deceased's licence to the registrar forthwith and seek a temporary licence.

The rules for private investigators are similar to those of private investigative agencies. If a private investigator has his licence suspended or cancelled in Alberta, British Columbia, Newfoundland, Prince Edward Island, Saskatchewan, or the Yukon, he is required to return the licence to the registrar forthwith. If a private investigator's licence expires in British Columbia, the licence must be immediately surrendered to his employer, and the employer must surrender the licence to the registrar. If a private investigator in British Columbia does not promptly surrender the licence to his employer, the private investigative agency is required to promptly notify the registrar in writing of the non-compliance. If a private investigator resigns from his employment with a private investigative agency in Alberta, New Brunswick, Newfoundland, or the Yukon, he must return his licence to the registrar forthwith. If a private investigator resigns from his employment with a private investigative agency in British Columbia, Manitoba, Nova Scotia, Ontario, Prince Edward Island, or Saskatchewan, he must return his licence to his employer who will forward it to the registrar. If a private investigator is terminated by his employer, he must immediately return his licence card to his employer, who must in turn forward it to the registrar with a notice of termination. A private investigator's licence surrendered because of resignation from his or her employer in Alberta and the Yukon cannot be reactivated except through a new application and payment of the prescribed fee.

---

141 R.S.B.C. 1996, c. 374, s. 8 (*Security News*, December 1994, reports that the Security Programs Division conducts CPIC screenings of all licensees every five years to ensure compliance. If new criminal information is obtained through the Security Programs Division CPIC screenings, lengthy delays can be expected prior to the renewal of a licence); R.S.N. 1990, c. P-24, s. 21(2); R.S.N.B. 1973, c. P-16, s. 7(2); R.S.S. 1997, c. P-26.01, s. 41(1), r. 1, s. 24, General Guidelines at 57.

If a temporary licence holder in Alberta is issued with a private investigator's or private investigative agency licence, the temporary licence shall be returned to the registrar.[142]

2.3.3.3   Displaying the Licence

Every province except Manitoba expressly legislates that the holder of a private investigative agency licence shall display her licence in a conspicuous position in her principal office or place of business. In British Columbia, duplicate licences are issued by the registrar and shall be displayed in each private investigative branch office.[143]

2.3.3.4   Advertising and the Name of the Agency

There are a number of issues identified by various provincial PISGAs on the topic of private investigative agency names and the advertising of private investigative services.

As a general prohibition, the practice of misleading, deceptive, or false advertising has been expressly forbidden by legislation in Alberta, Manitoba, Ontario, Quebec, and the Yukon. In fact, private investigators are required to forward to the registrar all copies of circulars, pamphlets, and brochures for approval in Alberta and Quebec.

Private investigation agencies may only advertise in the name they are licensed under in Manitoba, Newfoundland, Ontario, and Saskatchewan. No reference or association to law enforcement, peace officers, or police may be made in the name or advertising of a private investigation agency in Alberta, British Columbia, Prince Edward Island, Quebec, and Saskatchewan. No use of the word "detective" may be made in advertising in British Columbia and Saskatchewan. For further information pertaining to the use of the word "detective," see Section 2.3.2.1 — Identification and Uniforms. No reference to being licensed may be made on business cards in Ontario. No reference to being bonded or licensed may be made in the advertising, business cards, or letterhead in Saskatchewan. If the name of an applicant agency is so close to that of an existing agency as to cause confusion, the registrar may reject the applicant agency's application for licence. There is a specific prohibition on advertising depicting or extolling violence against persons or property in British Columbia.[144]

---

142 R.S.A. 1980, c. P-16, Reg. 71/91, rr. 7(3) & 11; R.S.B.C. 1996, c. 374, ss. 9(2) & 12; R.S.M. 1987, c. P132, s. 19; R.S.N. 1990, c. P-24, ss. 20(2), 21(4), & 22; R.S.N.B. 1973, c. P-16, s. 11; R.S.N.S. 1989, c. 356, s. 14; R.S.O. 1990, c. P.25, s. 13 and the General Guidelines; R.S.P.E.I. 1988, c. P-20, s. 13, E.C. 256/88, rr. 12 & 13; R.S.S. 1997, c. P-26.01, s. 15(2)(3), General Guidelines; S.Y. 1988, c. 23, O.I.C. 1989/073, r. 9.

143 R.S.A. 1980, c. P-16, s. 11(1); R.S.B.C. 1996, c. 374, ss. 3(10) & 9(1); R.S.N. 1990, c. P-24, Reg. 227/81, r. 10; R.S.N.B. 1973, c. P-16, s. 12(1); R.S.N.S. 1989, c. 356, s. 16; R.S.O. 1990, c. P.25, s. 12 and the General Guidelines; R.S.P.E.I. 1988, c. P-20, s. 15; R.S.Q. 1977, c. A-8, s. 12(e); R.S.S. 1997, c. P-26.01, s. 38; S.Y. 1988, c. 23, s. 22(1).

144 R.S.A. 1980, c. P-16, s. 21(1), Reg. 71/91, rr. 10 & 17; R.S.B.C. 1996, c. 374, s. 27, Reg. 4/81, r. 7; R.S.M. 1987, c. P132, ss. 28 & 36; R.S.N. 1990, c. P-24, s. 23; R.S.N.B. 1973, c. P-16, s. 4.1(1)(k); R.S.O. 1990, c. P.25, ss. 23(2), 25(1), & 31; R.S.P.E.I. 1988, c. P-20, E.C. 256/88, r. 21; R.S.Q. 1977, c. A-8, rr. 24, 25, & 26; R.S.S. 1997, c. P-26.01, ss. 23, 25, & 46; S.Y. 1988, c. 23, O.I.C. 1989/073.

2.3.3.5   Civil Actions for Unlicensed Services

In New Brunswick and Saskatchewan, there is a statutory prohibition against the commencement, maintaining, or enforcement of any civil action by any person or company for the recovery of fees or other compensation if a private investigator or private investigation agency is unlicensed. In fact, in Saskatchewan, a consumer of investigative services can bring an action to have all payments recovered if the provider of the investigative services is unlicensed.

In all other provinces, reference should be made to the common law. In the common law, it is a well-established principle that a court will not assist a plaintiff whose contract is illegal. As all private investigators and private investigative agencies are required to be licensed by statute, any unlicensed person who enters into a contract for private investigative services commits an illegal act and a court will not enforce the benefits derived from such conduct.[145]

A case on this issue is reported from Saskatchewan. In this case, the solicitor for the plaintiff appealed the decision of a taxation officer who had rejected his claim for the costs of a private investigator who had secured evidence of the defendant's adultery. The private investigator was not licensed under the PISGA. The taxation officer held he would not entertain these fees because Saskatchewan's PISGA provides that no person may bring or maintain an action in any court for the recovery of a fee or other compensation for any act done or expenditure incurred in the course of business as a private investigator unless at the time the action arose the person was licensed. The taxation officer held that to allow the solicitor to claim the costs of this unlicensed private investigator would be to allow the private investigator to do indirectly what he could not do directly. The court agreed, and held the taxation officer was correct to refuse the fees of the investigator in this case.[146]

2.3.3.6   Part-time Employment

There is no prohibition in any provincial PISGA with regard to part-time employment. However, Quebec requires that the agency owner devote a "significant" portion of his time to operating his or her agency.[147]

Private investigators should realize that misconduct while performing their private investigative duties may also bring consequences upon their other source of employment. In a case from Ontario, a registered nurse worked as a part-time private investigator. In the course of her work at her employing private investigation agency, she made pretext calls to various medical institutions seeking confidential medical information for the agency's clients. When this practice was uncovered, the private investigator was charged by the

145 R.S.N.B. 1973, c. P-16, s. 22; R.S.S. 1997, c. P-26.01, s. 48.
146 *Waschuk* v. *Waschuk* (1969), 4 D.L.R. (3d) 78 (Sask. Q.B.). See also *Ripplinger v. Edwards* (1996), 140 Sask. R. 230 (Q.B.).
147 R.S.Q. 1977, c. A-8, s. 5(b).

College of Nurses with professional misconduct under the *Health Disciplines Act*. The private investigator also had her private investigator's licence revoked by the provincial PISGA registrar.[148]

2.3.3.7   Subcontracting

There is no prohibition in the Act or the common law preventing any private investigative business from subcontracting any of its work out to another private investigative agency as long as that agency is licensed.

In British Columbia, the legislation permits a private investigative agency to subcontract employees it has sponsored under its licence to another agency where the employee is not so sponsored.[149] Saskatchewan reports a variation of this theme: a private investigator can work for more than one company if his or her application is accompanied by a letter of approval from the owner of each of the sponsoring businesses. Newfoundland and Ontario have a formal policy that dictates that a person will not be issued a licence for two different agencies. The legislation and policy statements from the other provinces did not comment on this practice.[150]

2.4   ADMINISTRATIVE LAW PRINCIPLES

Before going into the specifics of the authority and obligations of the registrar as provided by the various provincial PISGAs, a general review of the common law as it applies to administrative law is in order. Many of the provinces have not included in their PISGA basic elements of administrative law. Some provinces have enacted fundamental administrative common law legislation in statutes of general application, such as the *Administrative Procedures Act*[151] in Alberta, the *Statutory Powers Procedure Act*[152] and *Judicial Review Procedures Act*[153] in Ontario, the *Judicial Review Act*[154] in Prince Edward Island, and the *Act Respecting Administrative Justice*[155] in Quebec. However, in provinces that have not passed such legislation, reference must be made to the common law.

Governments have created administrative decision makers such as PISGA registrars by statute in response to the growing volume and complexity of legislation in the modern welfare state. With the increasing volume and complexity of legislation, governments have recognized that not all decisions can be made by the courts, and that often the common law is too inflexible for the efficient management of its laws.

---

148 *Re West and College of Nurses of Ontario* (1981), 120 D.L.R. (3d) 566 (Ont. Div. Ct.). For a further discussion of this case and the improper use of medical pretexts, see Chapter 7 —The Krever Inquiry — C IL and PIL.

149 *Security News*, Issue 7, May 1999.

150 R.S.N. 1990, c. P-24, s. 30(4); R.S.O. 1990, c. P.25, General Guidelines, R.S.S. 1997, c. P-26.01, policy statements.

151 R.S.A. 1980, c. A-2.

152 R.S.O. 1990, c. S.22.

153 R.S.O. 1990, c. J.1.

154 R.S.P.E.I. 1988, c. J-3.

155 R.S.Q. 1977, c. J-3.

There are a number of differences between the nature of judicial decision makers, that is, judges, and administrative decision makers such as a PISGA registrar that should be understood. To begin with, administrative decision makers are appointed to limited terms while judges have tenure.[156] Because of this, administrative decision makers are often viewed as not being as objective as judges because to maintain their positions, they are influenced by the policy directions of the government of the day. Second, administrative decision makers are often industry experts rather than lawyers. This fact results in hearings where procedure may be viewed as secondary to the substantive issue to be decided. Third, administrative decision makers are often specialists while judges are generalists. This reality is often helpful, as the learning curve for the decision maker is shorter and he or she is often familiar with what is good for the industry. Finally, administrative decision makers are often active in policy making, while judges, in theory, are tasked to adjudicate the policy or law they are provided with.

There are also differences between the nature of administrative tribunals[157] and the courts. While the courts are strictly adversarial in nature, administrative tribunals often have investigative powers and are inquisitorial to some extent. While the scope of a court action is the dispute between two parties, the scope of an administrative action often includes a public interest agenda. While the courts are generally bound by precedent, administrative tribunals, although mindful of precedent, are not bound by it if the policy of the day dictates differently. Furthermore, while the only review of a judicial decision is to appeal, administrative tribunals may conduct self-reviews. Finally, while the courts have rigid rules of evidence and procedure, administrative tribunals are usually more flexible.

With respect to decision making itself, it is often said that the major purpose behind administrative law is to ensure there is a fair and just system of public administration. As in the court system generally, the two primary areas of concern are procedural safeguards and substantive decision making. However, unlike appeal court reviews of trial court decisions that scrutinize both the substantive and procedural aspects of a trial and the judgment, court reviews of administrative hearings and their decisions focus mainly on procedure while showing significant deference to the substantive decision made.

The procedural aspects a court looks at when reviewing an administrative decision are concepts known in administrative law as fairness and natural justice. Courts do not, however, view procedural matters to a set standard as is often the case in criminal or civil actions. In administrative law, if the decision to be made by the administrative decision-making body is quasi-judicial in nature — such as decisions regarding allegations of wrongdoing which may result in the suspension or revocation of a license — a higher degree of procedural protection will be afforded. When the decision to be made is more

---

156 It has been pointed out that a registrar's "term" of office is indeterminate. In this setting, "term" does not refer to a fixed period of time, but a position from which the person may be transferred at the discretion of another.

157 Administrative tribunals is the term used in administrative law to describe the decision maker or makers. A tribunal can be one administrative decision maker or a panel of administrative decision makers.

administrative in nature — such as the decision whether to issue a license or not — a lesser degree of procedural protection is permitted by the courts.

There are basically two dimensions to the fairness aspect of procedure in an administrative law context. These two dimensions are the right to be informed of an administrator's decision with reasons and the right to reply, that is, a right to a hearing, either orally or in writing. The objective of the doctrine of fairness is to ensure that each individual is given the opportunity to bring to the attention of the decision maker any fact or argument that a fair-minded person would need to be informed of to reach a rational result. As mentioned, the degree of fairness owed by an administrative decision maker varies with the type of decision to be made. Whether a decision is judicial as opposed to administrative in nature is determined by, among other things, the impact of the decision upon an individual, the degree the case is fact-specific as opposed to being of broad public interest, and the legislative context the hearing arises out of, that is, disciplinary versus policy.

There are also two main dimensions to the natural justice aspect of procedure in an administrative law context: the right to be heard and the right to an impartial hearing. Although these two aspects of natural justice seem very similar in title to the second dimension of the fairness doctrine, the courts have held them to be separate, and therefore should be argued as such. Issues addressed when analyzing the right to be heard include a right to notice of when and where a hearing is going to take place, the form of the hearing, and the conduct of the hearing. As mentioned above, there is a spectrum of safeguards depending on whether the decision to be made is quasi-judicial or administrative in nature. If the decision is quasi-judicial, that is, if it may affect the rights of a party, the process should be more adversarial in nature, notice should be more detailed and to a wider body of interested parties, the form of the hearing should be oral and in-person as opposed to written submissions, and the hearing should be open to the public as opposed to private. Finally, if an administrative hearing is quasi-judicial in nature, the subject party should be permitted to retain counsel, call and cross-examine witnesses, bring motions, argue to exclude irrelevant or highly prejudicial evidence, make submissions, and seek written reasons for the decision.

In summary, the procedural rights of an individual facing a decision of a PISGA registrar are far greater if the decision concerns disciplinary matters that may result in suspension or revocation of a licence as opposed to administrative matters such as licensing applicants.

As mentioned above, when courts review the decisions of administrative tribunals, they are far more concerned with procedural safeguards as opposed to the substantive decision. In administrative law terms, it is said that judges will show great deference to the substantive decision made unless that decision is "without jurisdiction." For a substantive decision to be without jurisdiction, the decision maker must have included irrelevant considerations, acted on an improper purpose, acted in bad faith, improperly restricted the decision-making process, failed to recognize the law that applied to the decision to be made, or made a decision that was "patently unreasonable." For a decision to be patently unreasonable, it must on its face not be in accordance with the evidence led at the hearing. For a court to overturn the substantive decision, the accusation must be more than technical or trivial in nature. The degree of error required for a court to overturn a decision will depend, as mentioned above, on the nature of the decision to be made.

As is evident from this discussion, administrative law is complex and not well defined. This reality is paradoxical in the sense that administrative law is intended to be administered by non-lawyers. In practice, administrative decision makers are confined to one specific area of law within which they become familiar with the standards of procedure and substance they must adhere to. As such, most administrative decision makers do not have to concern themselves with lengthy analysis for each case weighing the degree of rights they are required to provide. Of assistance to most areas of administrative law, of course, is the legislation upon which it is founded.

The following sections review the powers and duties of a PISGA registrar. The powers discussed include the power to

- delegate his or her duties;
- issue or renew a licence;
- investigate and inspect;
- suspend or revoke a licence; and
- seize a licence.

The duties a registrar owes to a private investigator or private investigative agency that are discussed in this section include the duty to

- keep a register;
- maintain confidentiality;
- give notice;
- grant disclosure;
- provide a hearing;
- grant attendance by counsel;
- give written reasons; and
- return a licence.

These sections will assist an individual private investigator or private investigative agency to determine what rights they have in their dealings with a registrar.

As mentioned in the introduction to this chapter, where the term "registrar" is used in the commentary, it shall include reference to whatever the respective provincial administrative decision maker's title is, whether that be registrar, administrator, commissioner, or inspector. For the identity of the title of the administrative decision maker in your province, please review the introductory section of this chapter and reference the legislation under the next section: Section 2.4.1 — Delegation to the Registrar.

For further information on administrative law principles, there are a number of excellent texts available.[158]

---

158 D. Mullan, *Administrative Law* (Toronto: Irwin Law, 2001); D.P. Jones & A.S. deVillars, *Principles of Administrative Law*, 3d ed. (Toronto: Carswell, 1999); S. Blake, *Administrative Law in Canada* (Toronto: Butterworths, 1997); J.M. Evans et al., *Administrative Law: Cases, Text and Materials* (Toronto: Emond Montgomery, 1989); and J. Maciura & R. Steinecke, *The Annotated Statutory Powers Procedures Act* (Aurora: Canada Law Book, 1998).

2.4.1   Delegation to the Registrar

Every province except Nova Scotia, Prince Edward Island and Quebec delegates administrative, investigative and adjudicative authority to govern private investigators to the registrar.[159] In Nova Scotia, the Solicitor General directly administers the Act. In Quebec, the Minister of Public Security administers the Act. In Prince Edward Island, the Minister of Justice and the Minister of Community Services and Attorney General administers the Act.[160]

An analysis of the administrative, investigative, and adjudicative authority delegated to a registrar comes from Ontario. In this case, a private investigation agency (the agency) made an application to Divisional Court for judicial review alleging bias on the part of the provincial deputy registrar (the registrar). The agency argued the registrar was biased because he performed the tasks of administrating, investigating, and adjudicating on matters pertaining to private investigators. The court rejected the agency's application. The court held that

> [w]ithout going into detail, it is sufficient to say that the registrar, pursuant to the provisions of the Act, is required to carry out certain administrative functions, certain investigative functions, and certain quasi-judicial functions in connection with hearings pertaining to the suspension or renewal of licences to investigators.
>
> It is argued that the directions of the Act requiring the registrar to both investigate and to conduct hearings raises a reasonable apprehension of bias. Reliance is also placed upon a certain letter sent out by [the registrar]. Even if it is assumed that the document could raise the apprehension of bias as contended by counsel for [the agency], it would not, by itself, constitute a basis for granting the application.
>
> Turning to the Act, it is to be observed that the whole thrust of the legislation is to establish some means of administering and controlling private investigators and security guards. The Act specifically contemplates the registrar acting as administrator, investigator and judicial officer. To hold otherwise would frustrate the whole intent of the legislation. The provisions would give any Court far more concern if the Act did not give very wide powers of appeal. Those powers of appeal set out in s.20 and s.21 of the Act insure that . . . [there is access to a] reasonable review hearing. To contend that by the addition of subsection 3(2) and the appointment of a deputy registrar is sufficient to allow the applicant to bring this motion is to place the matter on too narrow of a ground.[161]

---

159 As pointed out in the introduction to this chapter, the word "registrar" is used to identify the various titles given to the person in the province who governs private investigators. The various titles include "administrator," "commissioner," "inspector," and "registrar."

160 R.S.A. 1980, c. P-16, s. 1; R.S.B.C. 1996, c. 374, s. 1; R.S.M. 1987, c. P132, ss. 1 & 3; R.S.N. 1990, c. P-24, ss. 2 & 3; R.S.N.B. 1973, c. P-16, ss. 1, 2.1, & 2.2; R.S.O. 1990, c. P.25, ss. 1, 3(1), & 33.1; R.S.P.E.I. 1988, c. P-20, s. 1, r. 1; R.S.Q. 1977, c. A-8, s. 16.1; R.S.S. 1997, c. P-26.01, ss. 2 & 4; S.Y. 1988, c. 23, ss. 1 & 3.

161 *Re Centurion Investigations Ltd. and Villemaire, Registrar of Private Investigators and Security Guards* (1979), 23 O.R. (2d) 371 (Div. Ct.). See also *Blair v. Bellwood* [1999], B.C.D. Civ. 530.75.35.00-20 (S.C.).

To summarize, the PISGA (Ont.) delegates powers from the Lieutenant-Governor in Council to the registrar, and in section 3(2) to the deputy registrar. Here the deputy registrar was not acting outside his jurisdiction when he performed the tasks of administrator, investigator, and adjudicator in refusing to renew the licence of the agency. The Act specifically contemplates the registrar acting in an administrative and quasi-judicial capacity as well as in an investigative capacity. Accordingly, the fact that the registrar may both investigate and conduct hearings into the same matter does not raise a legal apprehension of bias calling for judicial review. The agency's application was dismissed with costs.

2.4.1.1   Registrar's Immunity from Prosecution

In ancient times, a royal prerogative was passed that held that no person could bring action against the Crown. In recent times, the legislatures of every province and the federal government have passed legislation overriding this common law rule. This legislation, which is of general application, permits actions against the Crown for the conduct of government employees. In addition to this legislation of general application, some specific statutes set out grounds for actions against the Crown. An example of this is the PISGA in Quebec and Saskatchewan, which provides that actions against the Crown can be brought forth if the plaintiff applicant or private investigator can show bad faith or malicious treatment on behalf of the registrar or his or her representative. Although the other provinces have not specifically addressed this issue in their Act, the same principle pertaining to bringing actions against the registrar would apply through each province's legislation of general application.[162]

2.4.2   Powers of the Registrar

The powers and authority of the registrar vary from province to province. They include the power of the registrar to

* delegate his or her powers generally;
* issue or refuse to issue or renew a licence to a private investigator or a private investigative agency;
* investigate and inspect the records of a private investigative agency and their investigators;
* suspend or revoke the licence of a private investigator or a private investigative agency; and
* seize a private investigator's or private investigative agency licence.

The registrar's burden of proof will also be addressed.

2.4.2.1   Delegating

There is a principle in administrative law that no authority granted to an administrative decision maker may be delegated except as provided by legislation. Pertaining to the

---

162   R.S.Q. 1977, c. A-8, s. 4(3); R.S.S. 1997, c. P-26.01, s. 45.

PISGA, the provinces of New Brunswick, Newfoundland, and Ontario have granted the registrar the authority to appoint subordinates and to delegate powers to them.[163]

2.4.2.2   Issuing or Renewing a Licence

Every province confers upon the registrar the discretionary power to issue or refuse to issue a licence or temporary licence to a private investigator or a private investigative agency. In most provinces, the legislation stipulates that the determining issue is "public interest." In some provinces, what constitutes "public interest" is elaborated upon. "Public interest" has been held to include but not be limited to the following issues:

- a history of drug or alcohol abuse;
- false or misleading statements in the application for a licence;
- false or misleading statements made in an interview with a registrar;
- failure to comply with conditions imposed upon the licence;
- failure to comply with the other operational prohibitions listed in the Act;
- conviction under any federal or other provincial Act;
- outstanding charges related to or probation from a federal offence;
- poor financial history and/or a disreputable business resulting in a reasonable prospect that the business will not be conducted in a fiscally sound manner;
- lack of competence and/or training to manage an agency or to act responsibly in the conduct of the business;
- other evidence that affords reasonable grounds for belief that the business will not be carried on in accordance with law and with honesty and integrity;
- where the person is a corporation or partnership, the officers or directors of the corporation or the members of the partnership are not competent to act responsibly in the conduct of the business, or the past conduct of the officers or directors of the corporation or of a shareholder affords reasonable grounds for belief that the business will not be carried on in accordance with law and with honesty and integrity;
- the person who will manage the agency is not in a position to observe or carry out the provisions of this Act or the regulations;
- the person who will manage and/or others employed with the agency are carrying on other activities that are, or will be if a licence is issued, in contravention of the Act or the regulations or may give rise to a conflict of interest;

---

163 R.S.N. 1990, c. P-24, s. 3(2); R.S.N.B. 1973, c. P-16, ss. 2.2 & 2.3; R.S.O. 1990, c. P.25, s. 3(2); R.S.S. 1997, c. P-26.01, s. 4.

* the proposed name of the agency is so similar to the name of an existing agency as to cause confusion or to mislead persons into believing that the new agency is an existing agency;

* the registration pursuant to the provincial business corporation or business name registration legislation is not current; or

* the person or business is exempted from the Act.

In most provinces, a licence issued can be subject to terms and conditions as the registrar sees fit. The only exception to this general rule is found in the legislation of British Columbia which provides that a private investigator who has surrendered his licence to the registrar because he has ceased employment can demand it back if he finds new employment as a private investigator with another agency and if the licence has not expired.[164]

Any decision of the registrar is subject to review: see Section 2.4.3.5 — Providing a Hearing, and Section 2.4.4 — Appeals and Judicial Review. However, the courts typically grant a decision of a registrar a significant degree of deference, and therefore a decision of a registrar is often difficult to overturn. Further, one should keep in mind the common law principle mentioned in Section 2.4.1 — Delegation to the Registrar: an argument that there is a reasonable apprehension of bias by a registrar will not succeed because the Act grants the registrar the power to both investigate and adjudicate.[165]

2.4.2.2.1   The Charter and the Registrar's Discretion

Section 7 of the *Charter* provides that everyone has the right to life, liberty, and security of the person and the right not to be deprived thereof except in accordance with the principles of fundamental justice.

A case from Ontario has analyzed this *Charter* provision against a private investigator's argument that liberty includes the right to a licence. In this case, the private investigator appealed a decision from an OPP deputy commissioner in which his application for a licence as a private investigator was refused. The private investigator argued that section 8 (the registrar's discretion to license) and section 20 (review of a registrar's decision) of the PISGA were an infringement of his section 7 *Charter* rights to liberty and security of the person because he had been refused a licence to make a living in the field of private investigation. The court held that the right to carry on a business and earn a livelihood is not a right enshrined in the *Charter,* and that section 7 does not extend to economic, commercial,

---

164 R.S.A. 1980, c. P-16, s. 7(1); R.S.B.C. 1996, c. 374, ss. 3(3)(4), 10(5), 12(4), 15(1), & 16, Reg. 294/94; R.S.M. 1987, c. P132, ss. 12, 13, & 15; R.S.N. 1990, c. P-24, s. 15, Reg. 227/81, rr. 6 & 7; R.S.N.B. 1973, c. P-16, ss. 4(1), 4.1, & 5(2); R.S.N.S. 1989, c. 356, ss. 8(1) & 10(1); R.S.O. 1990, c. P.25, s. 8(1); R.S.P.E.I. 1988, c. P-20, s. 7, E.C. 256/88, r. 3; R.S.Q. 1977, c. A-8, s. 4(2); R.S.S. 1997, c. P-26.01, ss. 12 & 13 and the General Guidelines; S.Y. 1988, c. 23, ss. 11(1), 15(1), 20, & 25.

165 *Re Centurion Investigation Ltd. and Villemaire, Registrar of Private Investigators and Security Guards* above note 161; and *Blair v. Bellwood* above note 161.

or property rights, nor does it guarantee a right to work at a specific job.[166] The court held that this point of law had been settled in higher courts.[167]

2.4.2.3   Investigating and Inspecting

Every province except Quebec expressly grants the registrar or a person authorized by the registrar the power to conduct a background investigation on applicants and those seeking renewals for a private investigator's or private investigative agency licence. Such an investigation may include criminal record and fingerprint searches as well as interviews with associates, financial institutions, and others. The registrar may require verification by affidavit for information submitted.

Every province except Alberta and Quebec expressly grants the registrar or a person authorized by the registrar the power to investigate any complaint received from the public. However, unlike legislation pertaining to the police, the Acts of the various provinces do not set out a formal public complaint procedure. This has been cited as one of the reasons why so few formal public complaints are made against private investigators.

The legislation of every province except Alberta and Quebec also expressly grants the registrar or a person authorized by the registrar the power to investigate any suspicion of an offence otherwise obtained and the general business practices of an agency. Such investigations may include an inspection of the books, documents, and records of any licensee. Although the various PISGAs grant the right to inspect, only British Columbia, Manitoba, and Saskatchewan expressly grant the registrar the authority to seek a warrant or an order to inspect. Furthermore, only the legislation of British Columbia, Manitoba and Saskatchewan expressly grant the registrar the power to seize documents and make copies before returning them.

Notwithstanding that only British Columbia, Manitoba, and Saskatchewan expressly authorize this power, such measures could be granted by a court in provinces without such legislation by way of an information to a justice if the matter being investigated was criminal in nature. The provinces of British Columbia, New Brunswick, Nova Scotia, Ontario, Prince Edward Island, and Saskatchewan also make it an offence to in any way obstruct or interfere with an investigation of a registrar. Again, in provinces where there is no such legislation, reference may be made to section 139 of the *Criminal Code* on Obstructing Justice.[168]

---

166 *Maxwell v. Ontario Provincial Police (Deputy Commissioner)* (1988), 30 O.A.C. 56 (Div. Ct.).

167 *R. v. Video Flicks Ltd.* (1984), 48 O.R. (2d) 295 (C.A.); *Edwards Books & Art Ltd. v. R.*, [1987] 2 S.C.R. 713.

168 R.S.A. 1980, c. P-16, ss. 7(1) & 12; R.S.B.C. 1996, c. 374, ss. 17, 22, 23, & 24, Reg. 3/81, r. 10; R.S.M. 1987, c. P132, ss. 10, 11, & 22; R.S.N. 1990, c. P-24, ss. 15(1), 24, 25, & 26; R.S.N.B. 1973, c. P-16, ss. 4(3), 12.1, & 17, Reg. 84-103, r. 9; R.S.N.S. 1989, c. 356, ss. 6 & 12; R.S.O. 1990, c. P. 25, ss. 7 & 17; R.S.P.E.I. 1988, c. P-20, ss. 5, 10, & 11; R.S.Q. 1977, c. A-8, s. 7, rr. 15 & 20; R.S.S. 1997, c. P-26.01, ss. 17, 18, 19, 20, & 21 and the General Guidelines; S.Y. 1988, c. 23, ss. 19 & 23(2).

The only case law on this issue, as mentioned in prior sections, is from Ontario where it was held that there is no legal reasonable apprehension of bias on the part of a registrar on the sole basis that the Act grants the registrar the power to both investigate and adjudicate.[169]

2.4.2.4   Suspending or Revoking a Licence

Licence suspension and revocation is a touchy subject for private investigators, and so it should be. There is the potential for misapplication of the legislation by a registrar, which can have significant consequences for a private investigator, a private investigative agency, and their clients.

Generally speaking, the registrar has wide discretionary powers to suspend or revoke the licence of a private investigator and a private investigative agency. Although the legislation in some provinces sets out in much more specificity the circumstances when a registrar may suspend or revoke a licence, generally the registrar can exercise his or her discretion whenever he or she is of the opinion that the licensee is "unfit" to be licensed. Some of the more common reasons for suspending a licence mentioned in the various Acts include

* complaints being investigated under the Act;
* conditions placed on licences that have not been adhered to;
* failure to make proper information returns;
* failure to comply with the findings of an audit;
* charges pertaining to offences under the Act;
* charges pertaining to criminal offences; and
* failure to pay a judgment.

Some of the more common reasons for revoking a licence mentioned in the various Acts include

* making untrue statements;
* failure to meet the bonding requirements;
* convictions pertaining to offences under the Act;
* convictions pertaining to criminal offences; and
* failure to file a proper renewal application.

Furthermore, as set out in the Saskatchewan legislation, the suspension of an agency licence may also result in the suspension of each of its private investigators.[170]

---

169 *Re Centurion Investigation Ltd. and Villemaire, Registrar of Private Investigation and Security Guards,* above note 161. See also *Blair v. Bellwood,* above note 161.

170 R.S.A. 1980, c. P-16, s. 9; R.S.B.C. 1996, c. 374, ss. 12(5) & 16; R.S.M. 1987, c. P132, s. 20; R.S.N. 1990, c. P-24, s. 20; R.S.N.B. 1973, c. P-16, s. 17(2); R.S.N.S. 1989, c. 356, s. 10; R.S.O. 1990, c. P.25, s. 14; R.S.P.E.I. 1988, c. P-20, s. 10; R.S.Q. 1977, c. A-8, s. 14; R.S.S. 1997, c. P-26.01, ss. 14, 15, & 41 and the General Guidelines; S.Y. 1988, c. 23, ss. 16, 18(2), & 20.

The common law is of assistance in determining the boundaries of a registrar's power. In a case from Alberta, a court held that a registrar cannot suspend the licence of a private investigative agency simply for the reason that he or she had learned that a private investigator from that agency had been charged with a criminal offence. The court held that the registrar must seek out the particulars of the offence to obtain the required grounds to suspend or revoke a licence. Furthermore, a private investigator who is the subject of a registrar's inquiry is not required to provide a registrar with information with which that registrar could rely on to suspend that private investigator's licence.[171]

Expanding the notion of the presumption of innocence even further, a Manitoba case has suggested that a registrar should not exercise his discretion to suspend a licence where a private investigator has been charged with a criminal offence until the matter is disposed of in court.[172] However, in an Ontario case where a private investigator was charged with conspiracy to commit breach of trust relating to allegations of paying off a police officer to conduct CPIC inquiries for him, the registrar's office did suspend the private investigator's licence but not his agency licence while awaiting trial. In this case, the registrar's office relied upon a two-page report and a signed confession it had received from the investigating police agency as grounds for the suspension.[173]

Although there is no clear rule, in cases where the criminal offence is relatively minor in nature and the credibility of the evidence is in question, a registrar should not exercise this most consequential of powers.

For further reference pertaining to the suspension or revocation of licences, see Section 2.4.3.5 — Providing a Hearing, and Section 2.4.4 — Appeals and Judicial Review. Further, the provisions contained in the Yukon's legislation should be kept in mind: upon obtaining new or other evidence, or where material circumstances have changed, a further review of the suspension or revocation should be requested.

2.4.2.5   Seizing a Licence

As noted in Section 2.3.3.2.4 — Surrender of a Licence, every province except Quebec has legislation requiring private investigative agencies and private investigators to surrender their licences under certain circumstances. However, only the provinces of New Brunswick and Saskatchewan have legislated the power to a registrar to seize a licence when a private investigator or a private investigative agency does not voluntarily surrender it.

Notwithstanding the lack of legislation in other provinces, because a licence is the property of the province, a registrar in a province without such legislation could apply to a court for an order requiring the surrender of a licence. Typically, such an order would be issued by a court subsequent to a trial and upon conviction for breaching this section of the Act. Accordingly, there is little purpose in a private investigator or a private investigation agency ignoring a registrar's demand for the surrender of a licence.[174]

---

171 *Forsythe v. Alberta (PISGA Administrator)* (1993), 147 A.R. 300 (Q.B.).
172 *Wiens v. Registrar of the PISGA* (1979), 3 A.C.W.S. (2d) 107 (Man. Co. Ct.).
173 *Rosenberg v. Deputy Registrar of Ontario* (11 January 2001), (Ont. Prov. Ct.) [unreported].
174 R.S.N.B. 1973, c. P-16, s. 11(4); R.S.S. 1997, c. P-26.01, s. 15(7).

2.4.2.6   Registrar's Burden and Standard of Proof

The philosophy behind occupational licensing is that it shall be granted to all suitable applicants. Accordingly, the burden of proof to refuse, suspend or revoke a licence is on the registrar. The standard of proof is the civil standard of the balance of probabilities.

In every province except Quebec and the Yukon there is legislation permitting the registrar to forgo the traditional proof requirements and submit certificates as proof of their contents. Typically, certificates from a registrar may be submitted as proof that a person was or was not licensed. In Alberta, New Brunswick, Nova Scotia, Prince Edward Island and Saskatchewan, the Act permits as *prima facie* evidence for the purpose of proving that a person was engaging in private investigations without a licence such things as a statement in a letter, an advertisement, a card, or other documents. In British Columbia, certificates may be used as proof with regard to copies made as the result of a warrant or inspection.[175]

2.4.3   Duties of a Registrar

The duties of the registrar vary from province to province. The obligations include the duty of

* keeping a register;
* maintaining confidentiality;
* giving notice of an upcoming hearing;
* granting disclosure of the case against a private investigator or private investigative agency;
* providing a hearing prior to suspending or revoking the licence of a private investigator or private investigator agency;
* permitting representation by counsel;
* giving written reasons of the decision made; and
* returning a licence.

2.4.3.1   Keeping a Register

Only in Newfoundland is there an expressly legislated duty upon a registrar to keep a register of all private investigative agencies and private investigators in the province. Notwithstanding that this duty is not legislated in the PISGA of the other provinces, in practice each registrar maintains such a list.[176]

---

175 R.S.A. 1980, c. P-16, s. 23; R.S.B.C. 1996, c. 374, ss. 24(2) & 28; R.S.M. 1987, c. P132, s. 39; R.S.N. 1990, c. P-24, s. 27; R.S.N.B. 1973, c. P-16, ss. 3(3) & 24; R.S.N.S. 1989, c. 356, s. 23; R.S.O. 1990, c. P.25, s. 33; R.S.P.E.I. 1988, c. P-20, s. 21; R.S.S. 1997, c. P-26.01, ss. 5(3), 20, & 40.

176 R.S.N. 1990, c. P-24, s. 4.

2.4.3.2   Maintaining Confidentiality

In every province except Alberta, Newfoundland, and Quebec, the Act contains a provision that the PISGA registrar or his or her designate may not disclose to anyone information acquired during an inquiry or investigation.[177]

This duty of confidentiality has been litigated by persons seeking to obtain information under provincial freedom of information legislation. In two cases from Ontario, the freedom of information and privacy commissioner (the commissioner) denied access to the PISGA registrar's records. In a 1996 decision, the commissioner denied access on the grounds that information received in confidence by a government institution shall not be disclosed by another government institution.[178] Changes in Ontario's freedom of information legislation has now made this decision inappropriate to follow. The reason is because amended freedom of information legislation has included statutory overrides to the confidentiality provisions of other provincial legislation. Although there are exemptions to this override, the PISGA is not included in the list.

Based on a 1997 case, a commissioner in Ontario may now argue that access to records held by a PISGA registrar may be denied on the grounds that the information was obtained during an investigation, and that the release of such information would constitute an invasion of someone else's privacy.[179]

2.4.3.3   Giving Notice

As indicated earlier, PISGA registrars are granted the authority to make decisions on licensing issues pertaining to applicants and licensees.[180] This authority has resulted in various notice obligations being legislated upon registrars in some of the provinces.

One such obligation statutorily imposed upon registrars in Alberta, Manitoba, Ontario, and Saskatchewan is that notice must be given to an applicant or licensee regarding a registrar's initial or proposed decision. Typically, notice is an issue when it pertains to a decision to refuse an applicant for a licence, to refuse to renew a licensee, or the decision to suspend or revoke a licence. In Alberta, Ontario, and Saskatchewan, if the person to whom notice is given is not a licensee, such notice must be in writing and by registered mail.

If the applicant or licensee gives the registrar notice that she would like the registrar's decision reviewed, the registrar is obliged to give notice of where and when the review will take place. In Alberta and Ontario, this notice must be given by the registrar within thirty days from the date the applicant or licensee made application for it.[181]

---

177 R.S.B.C. 1996, c. 374, s. 29; R.S.M. 1987, c. P132, s. 23; R.S.N.B. 1973, c. P-16, s. 10; R.S.N.S. 1989, c. 356, s. 21; R.S.O. 1990, c. P.25, s. 18; R.S.P.E.I. 1988, c. P-20, s. 19; R.S.S. 1997, c. P-26.01, s. 22.

178 *Re Ontario Ministry of the Solicitor General and Correctional Services*, [1996] O.I.P.C. No. 326.

179 *Re Ontario Ministry of the Solicitor General and Correctional Services*, [1997] O.I.P.C. No. 10.

180 See Section 2.4.2.2 — Issuing or Renewing a Licence, and Section 2.4.2.4 — Suspending or Revoking a Licence.

181 R.S.A. 1980, c. P-16, s. 10; R.S.M. 1987, c. P132, s. 24; R.S.O. 1990, c. P.25, ss. 19 & 20(2)(6) and the General Guidelines; R.S.S. 1997, c. P-26.01, ss. 42 & 50.

There is no legislation on this issue in British Columbia, New Brunswick, Newfoundland, Nova Scotia, Prince Edward Island, Quebec, and the Yukon. However, British Columbia reports that it is their policy to inform the applicant or licensee of the registrar's inclination to suspend, cancel, or refuse a licence and then to grant a meeting between the applicant or licensee and the registrar if requested before a final decision is made.[182] In provinces where there is no legislation or policy statements, applicants and licensees must look to administrative common law principles, a statute of general application pertaining to administrative law issues in their province, or consult with their provincial PISGA registrar.

2.4.3.4   Granting Disclosure

Only the unproclaimed Northwest Territories[183] PISGA imposed a duty upon a registrar to disclose the evidence of his or her case to an applicant or licensee relating to the subject matter of a hearing. Although not required by law, British Columbia's practice is also to grant disclosure both prior to a hearing and an appeal.[184]

Although the various PISGAs have not legislated this duty upon the registrars, in some provinces, legislation of general application has addressed this issue. For example, in Ontario the *Statutory Powers Procedure Act* provides that where the character, conduct, or competence of a person is in issue, that person is entitled to disclosure prior to a hearing of any allegation to be made.[185] This requirement obviously would apply to any situation concerning licence applications, renewals, suspensions, and revocations. In provinces where legislation of general application does not exist, each applicant or licensee should request such disclosure prior to any hearing for the purposes of knowing the case they must meet.

2.4.3.5   Providing a Hearing

As indicated earlier, PISGA registrars have the authority to make decisions on licensing issues pertaining to applicants and licensees.[186] Notice of a registrar's decision must be given to the applicant or licensee in most jurisdictions.[187]

After receiving notice, an applicant or licensee unhappy with a registrar's decision may seek a hearing, sometimes referred to as a "review," to alter or overturn it. Typically, reviews of a registrar's decision are granted if the decision pertains to refusing an applicant for a licence, refusing a licensee a renewal, or to suspending or revoking a licence. Alberta, Manitoba, New Brunswick, Nova Scotia, Ontario, and Prince Edward Island have

---

182 Mr. Dean Benson, Deputy Registrar, Private Investigators and Security Agencies Section, Ministry of the Attorney General, British Columbia.

183 The PISGA in the Northwest Territories was never brought into force.

184 Mr. Dean Benson, above note 182.

185 R.S.O. 1990, c. S.22, s. 8.

186 See Section 2.4.2.2 — Issuing or Renewing a Licence, and Section 2.4.2.4 — Suspending or Revoking a Licence.

187 See Section 2.4.3.3 — Giving Notice.

imposed this duty upon registrars in the Act. In British Columbia, the Act provides that the decision to grant a hearing is discretionary upon the registrar.[188] In Saskatchewan, a review of a rejected licence application cannot be made to the registrar but must be made by way of appeal to the Saskatchewan Police Commission. However, on the issue of licence suspensions or cancellations, Saskatchewan permits a licensee a hearing before the registrar imposes this sanction unless, in the opinion of the registrar, it is in the public interest to amend, suspend, or cancel a licence immediately. In Newfoundland, the Act does not provide for a hearing to review a decision of the registrar but rather stipulates any revisiting of a decision of the registrar is directly by appeal to a judge of the trial division.

In some provinces, there are time frames within which requests for reviews must be made after notification of a registrar's decision is received by an applicant or licensee. In Alberta, Nova Scotia, and Ontario, an applicant or licensee must give written notice seeking a review within thirty days of the receipt of a decision of the registrar. If a licence is suspended without a hearing in Saskatchewan, the licensee can demand a hearing within fifteen days of the notice of suspension or cancellation of his or her licence. If an application for a licence is rejected in Saskatchewan, an employer has fourteen days to request an appeal to the Saskatchewan Police Commission.[189]

Hearings in administrative law may be either in person orally or through written submissions without attendance. This decision is usually that of the administrative adjudicator, in this case the PISGA registrar. None of the Acts have addressed this issue. Notwithstanding the lack of specific legislative direction, it is presumed that at least in Manitoba, New Brunswick, and Ontario, hearings are oral and in person because their Acts stipulate that an applicant or licensee may be represented by counsel. British Columbia reports that their practice is that hearings are in person, and that in advance of any licence sanction by the registrar, the licensee is provided a summary of the evidence and is afforded an opportunity to make written submissions.[190] Saskatchewan reports that their discipline hearing may be either in person or in writing, based upon the registrar's discretion.[191] Saskatchewan's General Guidelines provides that appeals of licence applications to the police commission are in person and it is recommended that the employer attend. Consultation must be made with the registrar in the other provinces that allow for hearings to determine the procedure they use.

---

188 Mr. Dean Benson, above note 182, reports there is no written policy on granting a hearing before the decision of the registrar is confirmed. Although the granting of a hearing is discretionary, requests for hearings are usually accommodated.

189 R.S.A. 1980, c. P-16, s. 10(1); R.S.B.C. 1996, c. 374, s. 16; R.S.M. 1987, c. P132, ss. 14, 20, & 26; R.S.N. 1990, c. P-24, s. 38(1); R.S.N.B. 1973, c. P-16, ss. 4.1(3), 5(2), 17(2), & 18.1; R.S.N.S. 1989, c. 356, ss. 8(2) & 11, see also ss. 5(3) & 7 of Nova Scotia's policy and procedures; R.S.O. 1990, c. P.25, ss. 8(2), 14, & 20, General Guidelines, Part B, s. 10; R.S.P.E.I. 1988, c. P-20, s. 10; R.S.S. 1997, c. P-26.01, s. 16(1)(2)(3), General Guidelines at 45–46.

190 Mr. Dean Benson, above note 182.

191 Mr. Brian Miller, Registrar, *Private Investigators and Security Guards Act*, Law Enforcement Services, Ministry of Justice, Saskatchewan.

As mentioned, at common law, administrative adjudicators such as PISGA registrars have the authority to make their own rules to govern the procedure of the hearing, subject to restrictions in the Act or legislation of general application. For example, at hearings in Alberta, the Act stipulates that the applicant or licensee can bring further evidence or make further submissions to the registrar relevant to the issues at hand. In Ontario, the *Statutory Powers Procedure Act* grants a tribunal the authority to issue summons for witnesses and grants a person subject to a hearing the right to adduce evidence, cross-examine witnesses, and make submissions. In a case from British Columbia, a registrar allowed a complainant to testify at an in-person hearing by telephone.[192]

The *Statutory Powers Procedure Act* also grants a person subject to a hearing the right to counsel but only when the subject person is being examined. All other attendance by counsel is discretionary upon the tribunal. Finally, the *Statutory Powers Procedure Act* provides that a tribunal has the discretion to exclude anyone from a hearing except a licensed solicitor. This includes agents of a subject party if they are found to be incompetent.[193] Consultation must be made with the registrars in the other provinces to ascertain the rules governing their hearings. For other statutory authority of general application to administrative hearings, see the legislation listed in Section 2.4 — Administrative Law Principles. For an example of a case that walks through the entire process, see *Maxwell v. Ontario Provincial Police (Deputy Commissioner)* as reviewed in Section 2.4.4 — Appeals and Judicial Review.

If the applicant or licensee is not satisfied with the result of the review, he or she may appeal. In Ontario, however, there is a second form of review to the deputy minister which must be undertaken before an appeal can be made. Case law has held that if an appellant does not seek all lower forms of appeal before proceeding to a court, the court has the jurisdiction to refuse to hear the appeal. For further information on appeals, see Section 2.4.4 — Appeals and Judicial Review.

There is case law on a private investigator's right to a hearing. It has held that in provincial jurisdictions where a registrar has a duty to provide a hearing, the failure to do so may result in the decision being quashed and the applicant or licensee being reinstated to his or her original position. In a case from Alberta, a private investigator was charged with a number of criminal offences. This private investigator had a clear record prior to this incident both in the criminal realm and with the provincial PISGA registrar. When the registrar became aware of the charges against the private investigator, he issued a letter to him indicating that his licence and that of his agency were suspended effective immediately. As the case against the private investigator was not due to reach the criminal courts for approximately a year and a half, the registrar was in effect shutting down his business.

The private investigator brought an application for judicial review of the registrar's decision. The court held that notwithstanding the provision in Alberta's PISGA which grants the registrar the authority to suspend a licence, there still is in this country a presumption of innocence before a trial. The court found that the registrar had made no effort to review

---

192 *Blair v. Bellwood*, above note 161.
193 R.S.O. 1990, c. S.22, s. 9-20.

the evidence that formed the basis of the allegations. The court further held that if the legislature had intended that a registrar could suspend a private investigator's licence on the basis of the mere laying of criminal charges, it surely would have included such a provision in the Act. On this basis, the court held that the actions of the registrar were a clear violation of the private investigator's right to natural justice in administrative law. Accordingly, the court set aside the registrar's suspension of the private investigator's licences. Subsequently, the private investigator's licence was reinstated.[194]

It should be noted that the above case does not stand for the premise that a registrar cannot suspend a licence of a private investigator before the conclusion of a criminal matter. In another case from Alberta, the registrar obtained from the requisite police agency a letter setting out the circumstances giving rise to the criminal charges. In this case, the court held that the letter from a police agency responding to a specific request for particulars surrounding the circumstances of a criminal allegation was sufficient evidence for the registrar to utilize his discretion and suspend the private investigator's licence.[195]

The foregoing exemplifies that judicial reviews of administrative decisions almost always deal with procedure. Most judges will grant deference to administrative decision makers such as a PISGA registrar unless the decision was patently unreasonable. This was the issue in the case from Alberta; the minimum procedural rules of natural justice, that is, notice of a hearing and the right to be heard, were not accorded. The case said nothing of the merits of the allegations against the private investigator. Therefore, the registrar could have suspended the private investigator's licences had the registrar presented sufficient evidence. The registrar in this particular case, however, did not make the effort to obtain it.

2.4.3.6   Permitting Representation by Counsel

The right to be represented by counsel in an administrative law setting is not automatic as it is in a criminal or quasi-criminal action. Only Alberta, Manitoba, New Brunswick, and Ontario provide legislative authority for the right of an applicant or a licensee to appear with counsel, and then only in certain circumstances. In British Columbia and Saskatchewan, there is policy on this issue.

In Alberta, the right to appeal with counsel only applies to an appeal before the Law Enforcement Appeal Board established pursuant to the *Police Act*, not to a hearing before the registrar. In Manitoba, New Brunswick, and Ontario, the right to appear with counsel applies to both review hearings and appeals.[196] In British Columbia the policy of the registrar's office is to permit attendance and representation by counsel on behalf of a licensee

194 *Forsythe v. Alberta (Registrar)*, [1993] A.J. No. 834 (Q.B).
195 [Unreported]. It was referred to in *Forsythe v. Alberta (Registrar)*, ibid.
196 R.S.A. 1980, c. P-16, s. 10(6); R.S.M. 1987, c. P132, s. 26; R.S.N.B. 1973, c. P-16, ss. 4.1(3), 5(2), & 17(2); R.S.O. 1990, c. P.25, s. 22.

on appeal.[197] In Saskatchewan, it is policy to permit counsel at hearings and appeals.[198] In all other jurisdictions, the registrar must be consulted to determine if counsel, or anyone else for that matter, is permitted to attend the hearing with or on behalf of the applicant or licensee.

For further information on the right to be represented by counsel, refer to Section 2.4.3.5 — Providing a Hearing.

2.4.3.7   Giving Written Reasons

The PISGAs of Alberta, British Columbia, Manitoba, Ontario, and Saskatchewan provide that the registrar shall give reasons for his decision to the applicant or licensee in writing upon his or her request. As noted in the introduction, in Ontario such requests are few.[199]

It is also noteworthy that none of the Acts addresses the issue of the time period within which a registrar must return a decision. Therefore, a registrar may reserve his or her decision for an indefinite period of time. Furthermore, if a written decision is requested, there is no legislated time frame upon which such a decision must be submitted. In a case from British Columbia, the registrar said he would attempt to return his decision within thirty days. The registrar did not return his decision for nearly ninety days. The private investigator had no recourse against this delay.[200]

2.4.3.8   Returning a Licence

Only British Columbia's PISGA stipulates that the registrar has a duty to return a licence to a private investigator or a private investigation agency if a suspension is lifted. This duty, however, would seem to be a matter of course in provinces where the PISGA does not contain this provision.

British Columbia's PISGA also stipulates that the registrar has a duty to return a licence to a private investigator who surrendered her licence to the registrar upon leaving her employer when the private investigator has found new employment and if the licence has not expired. There is no such provision in the other PISGAs.[201]

---

197 Procedures on appeals under the *Private Investigators and Security Agencies Act*, Ministry of the Attorney General, British Columbia. Mr. Dean Benson, above note 182, reports that in most cases licensees will attend appeals with witnesses but without counsel. It is the practice in British Columbia that counsel will attend with the registrar at each appeal. See *Blair v. Bellwood* above note 161.

198 Mr. Brian Miller, above note 191.

199 R.S.A. 1980, c. P-16, s. 10, Reg. 71/91, r. 2(3); R.S.B.C. 1996, c. 374, s. 18; R.S.M. 1987, c. P132, s. 21; R.S.O. 1990, c. P.25, ss. 15 & 20(7), General Guidelines, Part A, s. 17(2); R.S.S. 1997, c. P-26.01, s. 16(4).

200 *Blair v. Bellwood*, above note 161.

201 R.S.B.C. 1996, c. 374, s. 12(4)(5).

2.4.4   Appeals and Judicial Review

The appellate body to which an appeal or judicial review is made varies from province to province. In Alberta, the appellate body to which an applicant or licensee can appeal a decision of the registrar is known as the Law Enforcement Appeal Board established under the *Police Act*. In British Columbia, the appellant body is the Director as defined by the *Police Act*. In Manitoba, appeals are to the Court of Queen's Bench. In Newfoundland, appeals are made to the provincial trial division court. In Ontario, appeals are to the Divisional Court. In Saskatchewan, appeals are made to the Saskatchewan Police Commission pursuant to the *Police Act*. The Acts in New Brunswick, Nova Scotia, Prince Edward Island, and Quebec have no formal provisions regarding appeals. In these jurisdictions, applications for judicial review should be made to the appropriate court.[202] For the purposes of this chapter and for the sake of simplicity, the place or person to whom appeals are made from a registrar's decision shall be referred to as the "appellate body."

To appeal a decision of a registrar, the first step is to file a written Notice of Appeal. In Alberta, the Notice of Appeal must be filed not later than fifteen days after the applicant or licensee receives notice of the registrar's decision. However, in special cases, the board in Alberta may extend the time to appeal to up to thirty days. In Newfoundland, Notice of Appeal must be filed within thirty days of the registrar's decision, upon the Deputy Minister of Justice, the PISGA registrar, and the registrar of the court. In Ontario, the Notice of Appeal must also be filed within thirty days of the deputy minister's decision. In Saskatchewan, a Notice of Appeal must be filed within thirty days of the registrar's decision. For all other jurisdictions, time periods to appeal must be ascertained from the provincial registrar.

In some jurisdictions, a prescribed deposit must be paid to file an appeal. In British Columbia, for instance, a deposit must be paid, but if the appeal is successful, the deposit will be returned. However, if the appeal is unsuccessful, the deposit is forfeited and paid into the consolidated revenue fund.[203]

Generally, among other legal requirements, a Notice of Appeal shall include the grounds upon which the appeal is based. This is specifically stipulated in the Acts of Alberta and Newfoundland. There are general requirements when filing appeals in other jurisdictions, requirements that must be ascertained from the registrar.

After filing the Notice of Appeal, some provinces will grant disclosure. For instance, in British Columbia, as soon as the registrar receives a copy of the Notice of Appeal, the registrar will send to the Director of Police Services a certified copy of the prior decision and all other material in their possession relevant to the appeal. A copy of these materials will then be sent to the appellant at least seven days before the appeal hearing. It is also request-

---

202 See "Appeal Courts" as listed in Section 2.3.1.4 — Appeals Procedure.

203 The deposit is payable to the Director of Police Services at the time the appeal is filed. The deposit is $100 for an individual with respect to a security employee licence, $150 for an individual with respect to a security business licence, and $250 for a corporation with respect to a security business licence.

ed that the appellant disclose its documents and submissions in writing through the Director of Police Services to the registrar as well. For the other provinces, see Section 2.4.3.4 — Granting Disclosure.[204]

Unless otherwise ordered, the hearing of an appeal shall be open to the public in British Columbia and Ontario.[205] Saskatchewan has taken the position that all hearings are closed to the public. For all other jurisdictions, this must be ascertained from the provincial registrar.

The procedure during the appeal hearing itself varies from province to province. In Alberta and Newfoundland, the appellate body may decide the appeal from the record from the registrar's decision or upon the presentation of fresh evidence adduced before it. In British Columbia and Manitoba, the appellate body must consider the appeal as if it were a new application. In Saskatchewan, appeals from licence applications are by way of review of the record while appeals from sanctions against existing licences are by way of a new hearing. The difference between new applications and reviews of the record is that with new applications, the attendance of witnesses and the right to cross-examine is granted.[206] In British Columbia, the appellate body must permit representations from the appellant and may hear representations from the registrar or others. In Manitoba and Ontario, the Act stipulates that the registrar may be represented by counsel. This is also the policy of British Columbia.

Generally, an appellate body can confirm, reverse, or vary the decision of a registrar. This is specifically addressed in the PISGA of Alberta, British Columbia, Manitoba, Ontario, and Saskatchewan. In British Columbia, if an appellant fails to appear, the director may dispose of the appeal as he or she sees fit. In British Columbia, decisions are generally reserved and released in writing within two weeks, although verbal decisions at the end of the hearing are permitted.[207]

In most jurisdictions, an appeal to the designated appellate body can be further appealed to the provincial Court of Appeal, and then to the Supreme Court of Canada if necessary. However, the courts have held that all lower forms of appeal must be exhausted before a court is required to hear an appeal from an administrative law context. In British Columbia

---

204 Procedures on appeals under the *Private Investigators and Security Agencies Act*, Ministry of the Attorney General, British Columbia.

205 Procedures on appeals under the *Private Investigators and Security Agencies Act*, Ministry of the Attorney General, British Columbia; *Statutory Powers Procedure Act*, R.S.O. 1990, c. S.22, s. 9.

206 Procedures on appeals under the *Private Investigators and Security Agencies Act*, Ministry of the Attorney General, British Columbia, reports that for licence refusals, the appellant presents his case and makes submissions first, while for licence suspensions and cancellations, the registrar presents his case and makes submissions first.

207 Procedures on appeals under the *Private Investigators and Security Agencies Act*, Ministry of the Attorney General, British Columbia.

and Alberta, because the appeal is to another form of provincial administrative adjudicator, an appeal prior to the provincial Court of Appeal would be to the provincial Superior Court. The Act in Ontario, however, has restricted the option of further appeals and stipulated that an appeal to the Divisional Court is final, but that new applications can be made upon obtaining fresh evidence. In Saskatchewan, appeals to the Court of Queen's Bench are permitted as are questions of law only and may not take the form of a judicial review.

Another issue pertaining to appeals is the effect of filing a Notice of Appeal. In Saskatchewan, the legislation provides that the filing of a Notice of Appeal does not stay the effect of a prior decision. However, the appellant may apply to the commission or Court of Queen's Bench, as the case may be, for a stay pending the disposition of the appeal. Although legislative authority does not exist on this point in other provinces, appellants should make such a request in their Notice of Appeals.

Finally, the issue of costs must be addressed as it may be a determining factor in deciding if an appeal is launched. The awarding of costs is a discretionary remedy in the administrative law context. Only the Saskatchewan Act has specifically addressed the issue. It provides that if the commission finds against the appellant, it may order repayment by the appellant to the registrar costs of the investigation, of the hearing, of its legal representation, and of witnesses. If an appellant fails to comply with the cost order, his or her licence is automatically suspended.[208]

Two short cases are provided here as examples of the administrative law process. In the first case, *Active Alarms v. British Columbia (Registrar)*, the court affirms the principle that all prior avenues of review must be exhausted before making application for a judicial review. In the second case, *Maxwell v. Ontario Provincial Police (Deputy Commissioner)*, the court reviews the entire process from the registrar's initial review to the standard upon which judicial review is conducted.

Active Alarms & Security Systems Inc. et al. v. British Columbia (Registrar of the Private Investigators & Security Agencies Act) [1983] B.C.D. Civ. 58.6-03 (B.C.S.C.)

Taylor J. — The petitioner, Douglas Stephan Martin (Martin), a member of the RCMP, seeks to quash, under the *Judicial Review Procedure Act*, a decision of the registrar under the *Private Investigators and Security Agencies Act*, revoking a licence granted under the Act to enable him to participate in the operation of an alarm system business which he created.

The licence has been revoked by the registrar under s.5(1) of the Act, which provides:

No person licensed under this Act shall, without the consent of the Registrar, act as a . . . peace officer.

---

208 R.S.A. 1980, c. P-16, s. 10; R.S.B.C. 1996, c. 374, ss. 19, 20, & 21; see also the B.C. policy statement on appeals; R.S.M. 1987, c. P132, s. 25; R.S.N. 1990, c. P-24, s. 38; R.S.O. 1990, c. P.25, s. 21 and the General Guidelines; R.S.S. 1997, c. P-26.01, ss. 33, 34, 35, 36, & 37, R.R.S. 2000, c. P-26.01, r. 1, s. 23 and the General Guidelines; S.Y. 1988, c. 23, ss. 21 & 21.1–7.

The registrar says he has not given his consent to Martin acting as a peace officer. Martin says he has.

The reason Martin says he has the registrar's permission to act as a peace officer is that when he first applied for a licence, he disclosed that he was a member of the RCMP. It was, indeed, only after he had provided the registrar with a letter of approval from his superior officer that he was granted the licence. Martin says this means, as a matter of law, that he has received the consent of the registrar under s.5(1) to act as a peace officer, and that his holding a licence under the Act is in violation neither of the statute nor or any condition of the licence. Martin accordingly asserts that the revocation is unlawful and that it ought to be quashed on this application for judicial review.

Counsel for the registrar takes the position that judicial review ought to be refused at this stage because there is a statutory right of appeal from a decision of the registrar canceling a licence to the British Columbia Police Commission under s.17 of the Act. Martin has, indeed, already initiated such an appeal. It is an established principle of administrative law that an application for judicial review may not be entertained if an adequate remedy exists which has not been fully pursued.[209]

Martin says the appeal to the commission is not an adequate remedy, in the sense which should be applied to the expression in this context. He argues that the question he desires to raise is one of law only and therefore one which cannot be finally disposed of by the commission in any event.

I am not persuaded that this objection, if well grounded, would necessarily establish that the statutory appeal procedure is inadequate. But it seems to me that the question raised may well not be a question of law only. It may involve matters of fact. Why did the registrar grant the licence? Why did Martin not specifically ask for the registrar's permission so as to be sure of compliance with the Act? These may be questions the commission will wish to consider. The registrar's consent might be inferred from the fact of the granting of the licence. It would not be inferred if the surrounding circumstances denied or contradicted that inference. I have no reason to doubt that the commission will deal with the matter fairly and expeditiously.

In these circumstances I cannot say that the statutory remedy by way of appeal to the police commission is inadequate. I conclude that judicial review ought not to be undertaken at this stage. Accordingly, the petition should be dismissed.

---

209 *Re Harelkin v. University of Regina* (1979), 96 D.L.R. (3d) 14 (S.C.C.).

Maxwell v. *Ontario Provincial Police* (1988),
9 A.C.W.S. (3d) 393; [1998] O.J. No. 524 (Ont. H.C.J.-D.C.)
per Callaghan, Labrosse and Trainor JJ[210]

Maxwell was issued a private investigator's licence on 10 June 1986 while employed by a Mr. Egan of Detect Investigations. The licence was subject to a condition that he was not to engage in skip-tracing. On 23 October 1986, Maxwell's employment with Detect Investigations was terminated.

A few days later he commenced Colin Maxwell Investigation Agency under the aegis of a numbered Ontario company. In that capacity, he applied for a licence to engage in the business of providing private investigative services as well as a licence to act as a private investigator. On 31 December 1986, the registrar wrote Maxwell advising him that he proposed to refuse the licences applied for on the basis of allegations of skip-tracing and breach of a fee-sharing agreement with his former employer Detect Investigations. The letter advised Maxwell that before a refusal to issue the licence could be made, pursuant to section 19 of the Act, Maxwell had a right to a hearing.

On 19 February 1987, a hearing was held before the registrar. On 4 March 1987, the registrar's decision was released with his reasons for refusal to grant the licences. Maxwell, exercising his rights pursuant to section 20 of the Act, requested a review of the registrar's decision. On 29 and 30 June 1987, this hearing was conducted by way of trial de novo before the commissioner. The commissioner upheld the registrar's decision and refused to issue the licences. Maxwell appealed to the Divisional Court.

Maxwell made a number of arguments at his appeal. He first contended that there was no evidence to support the findings that he was involved in skip-tracing and failing to share a retainer while employed by Detect Investigations. The court, upon reviewing the findings of the commissioner and registrar before him, rejected this argument. The court noted that Maxwell's evidence was in conflict with the other evidence presented, and that the commissioner had rejected Maxwell's version of events. As the evidence on the record was sufficient to support the commissioner's findings, the court felt they were to defer to the findings of fact of the administrative decision makers.

Maxwell's second argument was that sections 8 and 20 of the PISGA violate section 7 of the *Charter* and therefore sections 8 and 20 should be of no force or effect. The court held that the right to carry on a business and earn a livelihood is not a right enshrined in the *Charter;* that section 7 of the *Charter* does not extend to economic, commercial, or property rights, and that it does not guarantee a right to work at a specific job. This point of law had been settled in higher courts.[211]

Maxwell's final argument was that he was not accorded natural justice in the administrative decision-making process. The court, however, found that the duty of fairness was met in both substance and form. The court noted that in each stage of the decision-making process, before both the registrar and commissioner, Maxwell was granted his right to

---

210   The judgment is paraphrased in this section.
211   *R. v. Video Flicks Ltd.* (1984), 48 O.R. (2d) 295 (C.A.); *Edwards Books & Art Ltd. v. R.*, [1987] 2 S.C.R. 713.

a hearing, he was represented by counsel, he was given disclosure of the particular allegations against him, he was given the opportunity to examine and cross-examine witnesses, and he was given the opportunity to make submissions. Furthermore, Maxwell was given written decisions by both decision makers. Accordingly, Maxwell was not in any way denied his right to a fair hearing. The appeal was dismissed with costs against Maxwell.

2.5   STATISTICAL INFORMATION

Requests to provincial PISGA registrars for statistical information have been met with limited success. The reason is not because of lack of cooperation by the registrars, but because many of their offices are not in the practice of keeping detailed statistical information.

Although detailed statistics are not readily available, some general observations are worthy of note. In Ontario, for instance, the registrar's office reports that the number of violations of the PISGA vis-à-vis the number of private investigators licensed in the province is not significant. Of the complaints received by the registrar's office, a significant percentage deal with the failure to perform the terms of the contract between the private investigative agency and their client — an issue not handled by the registrar's office but resolved through the civil court process. The Ontario registrar's office speculates that one of the reasons for the small number of complaints received by their office is because of public unawareness of the PISGA complaint process.

Most of the legislation pertaining to private investigators with the exception of Saskatchewan and British Columbia has remained in its current state for quite some time. Some believe a reason for this lack of government action is because there is no public outcry for such changes — that the legislation is sufficiently workable. The implication is that currently criminal and civil litigation avenues are adequate for dealing with allegations of wrongdoing being made against private investigators.[212]

Table 2.5 lists certain statistical information provided by the registrar's office of the respective provinces, effective July 2000.

2.6   PRIVATE INVESTIGATOR ASSOCIATIONS

Five of the provinces in Canada have provincial private investigator associations: Newfoundland, Quebec, Ontario, Alberta, and British Columbia. Generally, these organizations are loosely knit with little influence over their members. The exception is in Newfoundland where membership is compulsory as a condition of licensing.[213] However, although the current influence of provincial private investigator associations outside of Newfoundland is limited, in Ontario, Alberta, and British Columbia there is a move to evolve from a voluntary membership organization to a self-regulatory body for which all licence holders in the province must seek membership.

---

212 Interview with Mr. Greg Sons, Office of the Solicitor General for Ontario, Police Services Division, 25 Grosvenor Street, 12th Floor, Toronto, Ontario, M7A 2H3, Tel: (416) 326-0050.

213 See Section 2.2.2.10 — Requirement to Join Provincial Private Investigators' Association.

One of the benefits provided by the associations in Ontario, Alberta, and British Columbia is subscription to the association newsletters, which are published quarterly and are quite informative. In Ontario, subscription to the newsletter is provided to all licensed private investigation agencies in the province, regardless of their membership status with the association.

The contact information for the various provincial associations is set out in Appendix 2.

TABLE 2.5

Statistical Information — Agents/Agencies/Registrar Staff/Audits
As of July 2000

Province	Number of Private Investigators	Number of Private Investigation Agencies	Number of People Employed in Registrar's Office	Number of Investigations/ Audits in 1999 by Registrar's Office
Alberta	672	177	3	12
British Columbia	633‡	255	18	n/a*
Manitoba	207	47	2	2
New Brunswick	73	25	1	numerous
Newfoundland	45	12	3	0
Nova Scotia	361	52	3	n/a
Ontario	2,349 (1,200 dual)	502 (150 dual)	8 (OPP)	n/a
Prince Edward Island	42	17	3	0
Quebec	250	78 (71 dual)	3	n/a
Saskatchewan	279	74	3	numerous
Yukon	10	4	1	n/a

‡ With an additional 239 investigators under supervision as of 1997, otherwise known as PIP1s.

* Information not separable from data kept on all security-type agencies, including security guards and locksmiths.

2.6.1 Mission Statements and Codes of Ethics and Privacy

Throughout history and across diverse cultures, ethics vary and continue to change. Societies frequently codify what they regard as ethical into a law. Often, what is considered unethical or illegal in one generation becomes acceptable and legal several generations later. In many situations, people regard law and ethics as means to the same ends.

Codes of ethics, standards of practice, and constitutions often form the cornerstone of admittance and expulsion from an organization such as a provincial private investigative association. As membership often has its privileges, an important issue to private investigators may be the degree to which a decision made by a provincial association can be reviewed by the courts. It is widely held that the decisions of private associations will be granted greater deference by the courts than decisions of government-appointed tribunals adjudicating over specific legislation. Notwithstanding this, the courts will sometimes require private associations to implement the basics of natural justice such as notice, the right to a hearing, and an unbiased tribunal when deciding such issues as membership expulsion. However, the courts will only get involved if the issue to be decided will result in a remedy the courts can enforce.

In Appendix 3 you will find the codes of ethics and mission statements from Alberta, British Columbia, and Ontario. Only the Ontario private investigator association has a Code of Privacy accompanying its Code of Ethics and it is included in Appendix 3.

2.7   GOVERNMENT AND INDUSTRY ADVISORY BOARDS

Only the legislation of British Columbia and Saskatchewan provide that an advisory board may be established.[214] In British Columbia the initial meeting of the board was December 1992. The board meets routinely to discuss industry and government issues of common interest. The board is made up of the registrar, one security member, and a community non-security member.[215] In Saskatchewan the Police Commission advises the industry and produces an annual report.[216]

2.7.1   Report on Training and Standards in Ontario

For an excellent review of the standard and training improvements required in the private investigations industry in Ontario and elsewhere, see the Report from the Ontario Advisory Committee on Training and Standards for Private Investigators, which can be found in Appendix 4 of this text. The report was prepared by William Urquhart of Urquhart Investigations and Research Inc.[217] on behalf of the Best Practices and Training Sub-Committee. The report makes many recommendations to improve the current state of affairs in the industry. Unfortunately, this report has not been given the due care or attention it deserves by those who are in positions to make changes to training standards.

---

214 R.S.B.C. 1996, c. 374, s. 30; R.S.S. 1997, c. P-26.01, s. 49.
215 *Security News* (December 1994).
216 The contact person from the Police Commission is its director, Murray Sawatsky, Tel: (306) 787-6518.
217 110A Hannover Drive, Suite 201, St. Catharines, Ontario L2W 1A4, Tel: (905) 688-9222, e-mail: <urquhart@niagara.com>.

CHAPTER 3

THE *CANADIAN CHARTER OF RIGHTS AND FREEDOMS*

The *Canadian Charter of Rights and Freedoms*,[1] which befell Canadians with the patriation of the Constitution in 1982, has generated more legal analysis than any other legislation in recent memory. This chapter will briefly canvass such topics as

- the liability issues the *Charter* imposes upon private investigators;
- the authority of administrative decision makers to adjudicate *Charter* provisions;
- the *Charter's* applicability to the admissibility of evidence of private sector investigators; and
- an overview of the legal rights the *Charter* bestows upon us all.

3.1 THE *CHARTER* AND LIABILITY ISSUES FOR PRIVATE INVESTIGATORS

Private investigators, generally speaking, will not face direct liability in the form of a *Charter* action. This is because section 32 of the *Charter* has been interpreted to mean that the *Charter* was not intended to pertain to individuals in the private sector. Notwithstanding this limitation, the admissibility of a private investigator's evidence may still be scrutinized under the auspices of *Charter* "values" in a private litigation setting.

Section 32(1) of the *Charter* provides:

32(1) This Charter applies

    (a)   to the Parliament and Government of Canada in respect of all matters within the authority of Parliament including all matters relating to the Yukon Territory and Northwest Territories; and

---

1   *Canadian Charter of Rights and Freedoms*, Part I of the *Constitution Act, 1982*, being Schedule B to the *Canada Act 1982* U.K., 1982, c. 11 [*Charter*].

(b)   to the legislature and government of each province in respect of all matters within the authority of the legislature of each province.

Early in the *Charter*'s evolution, the Supreme Court of Canada held that for the purposes of the rights and freedoms guaranteed by the *Charter*, it is against "agents of the
state" and the executive and administrative branches of government that the *Charter* has
effect.[2] About a year later in another landmark case dealing with similar issues, the
Supreme Court of Canada held that, although the *Charter* applies to the common law, it
does not apply to private litigation in the absence of reliance on governmental action or
authorization. The court held that "government" includes the executive, legislative, and
administrative branches of government. The court further held that to the extent a private
action is justified by, or depends upon, some statutory authority or upon some governmental action, then the government authority or action, and thus indirectly the private
action, is subject to the *Charter*.[3] Providing further clarification to the question of to whom
the *Charter* applies, Professor Hogg, a distinguished constitutional lawyer, stated:

> The *Charter* would apply to a private person exercising the power of arrest that is granted to
> "anyone" by the Criminal Code . . . However, where private party "A" sues private party "B"
> relying on the common law and where no act of government is relied upon to support the
> action, the *Charter* will not apply.[4]

Recently, there has been reported a unique decision in the sense that it was the first
known case wherein a private investigation agency had an action brought against it for
Charter violations while conducting surveillance in an insurance investigation.[5] The facts of
the case are straightforward. The plaintiff had been involved in a motor vehicle accident.
The insurance company of the other party in the accident retained private investigators to
obtain video and photographic evidence to verify the validity of the plaintiff's claims. The
private investigators conducted surveillance of the plaintiff while she was conducting personal business. Unfortunately, the plaintiff's neighbour noticed something was amiss and
informed her she was being followed by a man in a dark grey van with heavily tinted windows and that she was being videotaped. As the plaintiff was alarmed for her safety, she
drove quickly through traffic. The private investigators followed her at the same high rate
of speed. The plaintiff then saw her father in the lot of a local business and stopped and
told him what was taking place. When the plaintiff's father drove over to the van, the private investigators quickly sped away. The plaintiff reported the incident to the police who
determined the owner of the van was a private investigator and informed the plaintiff of his

---

2   *R. v. Therens*, [1985] 1 S.C.R. 613, 45 C.R. (3d) 97 at 124. See also *McKinney v. Board of
     Governors of University of Guelph* (1990), 76 D.L.R. (4th) 545 (S.C.C.).

3   *R.W.D.S.U. Local 580* v. *Dolphin Delivery Ltd.*, [1986] 2 S.C.R. 573. For an in-depth assessment
     of s. 32 of the *Charter*, see E.F. Geddes, "The Private Investigator and the Right to Privacy"
     [1989] Alta. L. Rev. 256 at 291–94.

4   P.W. Hogg, *Constitutional Law of Canada*, 2d ed. (Toronto: Carswell, 1985) at 677. For further
     reading on this topic, see T. Sharback, "Private Law Enforcement: Dodging the Charter"
     (1995) 1 Appeal 42–45.

5   *Druken v. RG Fewer & Associates Inc.*, [1998] N.J. No. 312 (S.C.).

identity. Later, during the plaintiff's action against the insurance company for cutting off her benefits, the videotapes were played. These videotapes showed the plaintiff outdoors on her private property and walking from public place to public place with her child. The plaintiff brought action for breach of privacy under the *Privacy Act* of Newfoundland and under the *Charter*. The plaintiff also asked for the court to comment on possible infringements of the *Criminal Code* and the *Private Investigator and Security Guards Act*.

Pertaining to the *Charter* argument, the major issue was what application the *Charter* has to private litigation. The trial judge quoted the Supreme Court of Canada in *Hill v. Church of Scientology of Toronto* where it was stated:

> It is important not to import into private litigation the analysis which applies in cases involving government action. The most a private litigant can do is argue that the common law is inconsistent with *Charter* values. It is very important to draw the distinction between *Charter* rights and *Charter* values. Care must be taken not to expand the application of the *Charter* beyond that established by s.32(1) . . . [to] creating new causes of action . . Therefore, in the context of civil litigation involving only private parties, the *Charter* will apply to the common law only to the extent that the common law is found to be inconsistent with *Charter* values.

The trial judge then reasoned as follows:

> One such value is the interest affirmed by s.8 of the *Charter* of each person in privacy . . . It remains for me to consider the argument that by commencing proceedings, the plaintiff has forfeited her right to confidentiality. I accept that a litigant must accept such intrusions upon her right to privacy as are necessary to enable a judge and jury to get to the truth and render a just verdict. But I do not accept that by claiming such damages as the law allows, a litigant grants her opponent a license to delve into private aspects of her life which need not be probed for the proper disposition of her litigation.

Based on the foregoing, the trial judge held:

> I must be satisfied that [the private investigator's] actions and production of video surveillance tapes reflect *Charter* values. Were the production of the videotapes at issue before me, then it would be incumbent that I embark on a balancing of the private interest of the plaintiff against the rights of the defendant to fully defend its case in litigation and to have equal benefit of the law bearing in mind the overall goal of the trial process is to discover the truth.
>
> . . .
>
> [Here] the videotapes of the [private investigators] records information which could have been and was being observed by members of the public as it occurred . . . The videotaping of the plaintiff in her yard . . . was readily visible and apparent to the public . . . There was nothing in either the *Charter* cases presented which suggests a *carte blanche* right to privacy . . . An analysis of many *Charter* cases confirms invasions of privacy interests are permitted.
>
> . . .
>
> The [private investigator's] videotaping of the plaintiff was by virtue of a contract with two insurance companies. The plaintiff made a claim for compensation in respect of personal injuries sustained by her. The companies engaged the [private investigators] to conduct video surveillance presumably to test the truth of the plaintiff's position pertaining to the extent of

her injuries. The courts have recognized surveillance as a legitimate tool in defense of personal injury claims . . . to impeach the credibility of the plaintiff.

. . .

On the basis of the foregoing, I am satisfied that the actions of the [private investigators] . . . reflect *Charter* values . . . *Charter* interests . . . must be balanced as between plaintiffs and defendants in civil law suits . . . Surveillance without purpose would engage different considerations.[6]

To conclude, while it appears that *Charter* "values" apply to the actions of private investigators, there does not appear to be any direct pecuniary remedy for a breach of a *Charter* "value." This is because section 24(1) does not provide for such remedies for a breach of a *Charter* "value," only of a *Charter* "right or freedom." However, although section 24(2) also restricts the excluding of evidence by a court to situations where there has been a breach of a *Charter* "right or freedom" by an agent of the state, the courts have expanded this evidence exclusionary power to breaches of *Charter* "values" in private litigation.

For a further discussion on the issue of the staus of an agent of the state as opposed to a private citizen in the eyes of the law, see Section 4.1.1.1 — Agent of the State versus Private Citizen.

3.2   THE *CHARTER* AND ADMINISTRATIVE DECISION MAKERS

An issue that could arise in an administrative hearing under the PISGA is a registrar's authority to grant *Charter* remedies. This issue was addressed by the Supreme Court of Canada in *Weber v. Ontario Hydro*.[7] The plaintiff Weber was employed by the defendant Ontario Hydro. As a result of back problems, Weber took an extended leave of absence, and Ontario Hydro paid Weber sick benefits as stipulated by the collective agreement. As time passed, Ontario Hydro began to suspect that Weber was malingering and hired private investigators to investigate its concerns. The private investigators went onto Weber's property and under a pretext gained entry into his home. As a result of the information obtained, Ontario Hydro suspended payments to Weber on the basis that he was abusing his sick leave benefits.

Weber took the matter to his union. The union filed a grievance against Ontario Hydro, which eventually was settled. Weber then commenced an action based in tort for trespass and under the *Charter* claiming his section 7 right to liberty and his section 8 right to privacy (i.e., the right to be secure against unreasonable search or seizure) were violated.

The court held that since Weber took the matter to his union, and since the union filed grievances that were eventually settled, and since section 45(1) of the *Ontario Labour*

6   [1995] 2 S.C.R. 1130.
7   [1995] 2 S.C.R. 929.

Relations Act states that every collective agreement shall provide for a final and binding settlement by arbitration of all differences between the parties arising from the interpretation, application, administration, or alleged violation of the agreement, it was without jurisdiction to hear the case. On this basis, both the tort and *Charter* claims were dismissed.

Notwithstanding the *Charter* claim was dismissed, the Supreme Court of Canada wrote a split 4 to 3 decision on whether *Charter* issues were arbitrable by administrative decision makers. The four majority judges concluded that the power and duty of arbitrators to apply the law extends to the *Charter* because it is an essential part of the law of Canada. In applying the law to the disputes before them, arbitrators may grant such remedies as the legislature or Parliament has empowered them to grant in the circumstances. Assuming for the purposes of argument that the remedy of damages can be claimed only under section 24(1) of the *Charter*, statutory tribunals created by Parliament or the legislatures may be courts of competent jurisdiction to grant *Charter* remedies, provided they have the jurisdiction over the parties and the subject matter of the dispute and are empowered to make the orders sought. In this case, the arbitrator was empowered to consider the *Charter* questions and grant the appropriate remedies. He had jurisdiction over the parties and the dispute, and was further empowered by the *Labour Relations Act* to award the *Charter* remedies claimed — damages and a declaration.

Although the decision of the three dissenting judges of the Supreme Court is not law, it is useful to understand their reasons. The minority held that although arbitrators must apply provisions of a collective agreement which they determine violate the *Charter*, it does not follow that they have the power under section 24(1) of the *Charter* to grant remedies for *Charter* violations. An arbitrator cannot award a remedy for a *Charter* breach because arbitrators are not courts of competent jurisdiction. The minority held that the use of the word "court" in section 24(1) was deliberate; it was meant to correspond to an adjudicating body with specific characteristics that enable it to grant *Charter* remedies. If a magistrate sitting in a preliminary inquiry does not possess the characteristics of a "court" as found in *R. v. Mills*,[8] it is difficult to accept that a tribunal, which is not even presided by a judge in a traditional courtroom, can be so considered. Like the word "court," the word "tribunal" used in the French version refers to courts of justice. An administrative tribunal does not come within that ordinary meaning.

The minority also held a more purposive approach to interpreting section 24(1) supports the view that labour arbitrators were not intended to be included in section 24(1). Courts must decide cases according to the law and are bound by *stare decisis* while tribunals are not so constrained. As the *Charter* forms part of the supreme law of the country, it is in keeping with its status to have *Charter* claims decided by a system of adjudication that tries to be relatively uniform. Tribunals also differ from courts in their institutional organization and functioning. The flip side of the accessibility of tribunals is that their procedure is often simplified or altered.

---

8 [1986] 1 S.C.R. 863.

The final argument of the minority was that a tribunal such as a labour arbitrator is ill-equipped to deal with the requirements of a section 24(1) application. Structurally, it has not been designed to hold a hearing requiring evidence of a constitutional violation, nor is there a procedure in existence to obtain the participation of the Attorney General before it where legislative provisions are at issue. Its members are not trained in determining appropriate remedies for a constitutional violation and often have no formal legal training. Moreover, a tribunal does not have the same guarantee of independence as a court.

Because of the Supreme Court of Canada's decision that administrative decision makers do have the authority to grant *Charter* remedies, consideration should be given to making *Charter* arguments in hearings before a registrar of private investigators. An example of a *Charter* issue that could arise at a hearing before a registrar is the exclusion of evidence brought by an investigator from the registrar's office which was obtained by a method that breached a *Charter* right or freedom, such as conducting a search without a warrant. *Charter* scrutiny applies to investigators from the registrar's office as they are deemed to be "agents of the state."

A separate issue from appearing as the subject of an inquiry before a PISGA registrar are circumstances where private sector investigators appear as witnesses before other administrative tribunals such as workers' compensation boards and labour relations boards. As seen in the prior section, the courts have held that *Charter* "values" apply to private litigation, and evidence obtained by a method infringing a *Charter* value may be excluded. Because administrative decision makers generally must consider *Charter* values, it follows that administrative decision makers from boards which private sector investigators appear before as witnesses may scrutinize a private sector investigator's evidence in such a light. Accordingly, private sector investigators should respect *Charter* values lest their evidence be excluded on this basis.

3.3 THE *CHARTER* AND THE EXCLUSION OF EVIDENCE

As seen above, it is generally held that the *Charter* does not apply to relations between private individuals. However, on occasion, a private sector investigator will be cast under the auspices of an "agent of the state." Such occasions include whenever a private sector investigator exercises the state function of executing a citizen's arrest[9] or assists police in the execution of a search warrant.[10] It is also argued by some that the *Charter* may apply to the

---

9 The discussion of private investigators as agents of the state for the purposes of arrest is conducted in Chapter 4 — Criminal Liability.

10 The discussion of private investigators as agents of the state for the purpose of search warrants is conducted in Section 10.2 — Search Warrants and Private Investigators.

conduct of a private sector investigator who has embarked upon a criminal investigation.[11] On such occasions, his or her actions may become liable to section 24, the remedy section of the *Charter*.

Section 24(1) of the *Charter* provides:

> 24(1) Anyone whose rights or freedoms, as guaranteed by this Charter, have been infringed or denied may apply to a court of competent jurisdiction to obtain such remedy as the court considers appropriate and just in the circumstances.

Note here that "remedy" can include such things as orders for the payment of damages, orders for specific performance, and declarations.

In addition to the unlimited scope of discretionary sanctions available to a court by virtue of section 24(1), a further nondiscretionary form of sanction is found in section 24(2) of the *Charter*, which provides:

> 24(2) Where, in proceedings under subsection (1), a court concludes that evidence was obtained in a manner that infringed or denied any rights or freedoms guaranteed by this Charter, the evidence shall be excluded if it is established that, having regard for all the circumstances, the admission of it in the proceedings would bring the administration of justice into disrepute

The requirement that evidence be excluded if its admission would bring the administration of justice into disrepute has been the subject of much judicial discussion. The Supreme Court of Canada has held that factors that should be canvassed include

- the nature of the evidence obtained as a result of the violation;
- the nature of the right violated;
- whether the evidence was real evidence that existed notwithstanding the *Charter* violation;
- whether the violation was committed in good faith, inadvertent and technical in nature as opposed to deliberate, wilful, and flagrant;
- whether the violation was motivated by urgency or necessity;
- whether other investigatory techniques were available;
- the seriousness of the offence; and
- whether the admission of the evidence would result in an unfair trial.[12]

---

11 J.T. Wells et al., *The Fraud Examiners Manual,* Canadian ed. (Austin, TX: Association of Certified Fraud Examiners, 1998). The authors of this text opine that whenever a private sector investigator embarks on an investigation where it is foreseeable that criminal charges may result, the investigator is in effect acting as an agent of the state because criminal law is a form of public law. In other words, the term "administration of justice," as discussed in s. 24(2) of the *Charter*, involves not only the court system and public officers involved therein, but also anyone involved in the investigation and detection of crime for the purposes of a publicly administered system. The authors point out that this legal theory is currently not buttressed by any case law.

12 *R. v. Therens*, [1985] 1 S.C.R. 613, and *R. v. Clarkson* (1986), 25 C.C.C. (3d) 207 (S.C.C.).

These seven issues have been summed up by the Supreme Court of Canada in *R. v. Collins*[13] in a three-part test:

+ What was the effect of the admission of the evidence on the fairness of the trial?
+ How serious was the breach of the *Charter* right?
+ What was the effect of the exclusion of the evidence upon the administration of justice and its reputation?

The Supreme Court of Canada has held that the answer to any one of these factors is not determinative of the final conclusion, and that each case must be determined on its own facts.

As stated before, the section 24(2) *Charter* remedy is not a form of liability in the traditional sense. Rather, this section is often viewed as an evidentiary issue. As such, further discussion of section 24(2) will be conducted in Chapter 4 — Criminal Liability, and Chapter 9 — The Law of Evidence.

Although no cases involving private sector investigators have been reported on this issue, there have been a couple of cases wherein a private citizen's actions were brought under *Charter* scrutiny. In a case from Ontario,[14] the accused (Voege) was arrested by a milkman (Letang) for impaired driving. Letang did not explain to Voege his right to counsel. Letang turned Voege over to an Ontario Provincial Police officer approximately twenty minutes later. The OPP officer informed Voege of his right to counsel and then read him the breath demand and took Voege to a police detachment for a breathalyzer test. At trial, Voege argued that the breath test results should be excluded pursuant to section 24(2) of the *Charter* on the basis that Letang was executing a governmental function by arresting him and therefore was required to comply with the *Charter* requirements obligatory on agents of the state.

The court held that on a *prima facie* basis, Letang, acting as an agent of the state, had breached the *Charter* rights of Voege. Pertaining to Voege's section 24(2) argument, the court quoted *R. v. Collins*[15] where Justice Lamer said:

> It is clear to me that the factors relevant to this determination will include the nature of the evidence obtained as a result of the violation and the nature of the right violated and not so much the manner in which the right was violated. Real evidence that was obtained in a manner that violated the Charter will rarely operate unfairly for that reason alone. The real evidence existed irrespective of the violation of the Charter and its use does not render the trial unfair.
>
> However, the situation is very different with respect to cases where, after the violation of the Charter, the accused is conscripted against himself through a confession or other evidence emanating from him. The use of such evidence would render the trial unfair, for it did not exist prior to the violation and it strikes at one of the fundamental tenets of a fair trial, the right against self-incrimination. Such evidence will generally arise in the context of infringement of

---

13   (1987), 33 C.C.C. (3d) 1 (S.C.C.).
14   *R. v. Voege*, [1997] O.J. No. 4804 (Gen. Div.).
15   Above note 13.

the right to counsel. Our decisions in *R. v. Therens*[16] and *R. v. Clarkson*[17] are illustrative of this. The use of self-incriminating evidence obtained following the denial of the right to counsel will, generally, go to the fairness of the trial and should generally be excluded. Several courts have also emphasized the difference between pre-existing real evidence and self-incriminating evidence following a breach of the *Charter*.[18] It may also be relevant, in certain circumstances, that the evidence would have been obtained in any event without the violation of the *Charter*.

The court then discussed the considerations that should make up such an analysis as mentioned above.

In analyzing the law against the facts of the case, the court found that Letang took meritorious action to end the continuation of Voege's driving with an excess of alcohol in his blood. The court found that the breach of Voege's *Charter* rights was committed in good faith and it was not deliberate, wilful, or flagrant. Finally the court found that Letang acted for the good of the community and only in that way, and that there was real evidence available as Letang had observed the manner in which Voege drove. For these reasons, the court held that to exclude the evidence of what occurred prior to the police officer arriving at the scene would bring the administration of justice into disrepute. Accordingly, the court ordered Voege's appeal dismissed.

Another case involving the seizure of evidence by a private citizen wherein the courts reviewed the law as it pertains to section 24(2) of the *Charter* comes from Newfoundland.[19] In this case, the accused (Barnes) was observed by some private citizens (Lloyd and Hann) removing lobsters from traps. Lloyd and Hann suspected that Barnes was fishing undersized lobsters and advised local fisheries officers of their suspicion. Upon being informed that all their enforcement officers were unavailable, Lloyd and Hann embarked on their own surveillance of Barnes. Lloyd and Hann confronted Barnes and demanded that he turn over a knapsack. After Barnes refused, a scuffle ensued and Barnes threw the knapsack over a cliff into the ocean. A boater, at the direction of Lloyd and Hann, recovered the knapsack. The knapsack was eventually turned over to fishery officers. Barnes was later charged with a number of fisheries offences. At trial, Barnes argued that the actions of Lloyd and Hann amounted to illegal detention, search, and seizure. Barnes sought an exclusion of the knapsack as evidence pursuant to section 24(2) of the *Charter* on the basis that Lloyd and Hann had violated his section 8 (right to be secure against unreasonable search or seizure) and section 9 (right not to be arbitrarily detained or imprisoned) *Charter* rights.[20]

---

16   [1985] 1 S.C.R. 613.
17   (1986), 25 C.C.C. (3d) 207 (S.C.C.).
18   See *R. v. Dumas* (1985), 23 C.C.C. (3d) 366 (Alta. C.A.); *R. v. Strachan* (1986), 24 C.C.C. (3d) 205 (B.C.C.A.); and *R. v. Dairy Supplies Ltd.* (1987), 44 Man. R. (2d) 275 (C.A.).
19   *R. v. Barnes,* [1995] N.J. No. 146 (P.C.).
20   This case is also reviewed under Section 4.1.2.2.2 — Search Subsequent to Detention. Further information relating to other aspects of the case included in Section 4.1.2.2.2 may assist the reader in comprehending this analysis.

The court made the following comments:

If the *Charter* is applicable to the actions of [a private citizen] in the recovery of the bags, and if these acts constituted a breach of either or both of s.8 or s.9 [of the *Charter*], I would have to consider the application of s.24(2) of the *Charter*. Would the admission of the knapsack bring the administration of justice into disrepute in these circumstances?

As held in *R. v. Collins*,[21] the onus is on the accused who seeks exclusion of the evidence to establish on a balance of probabilities that admission of the evidence would bring the administration of justice into disrepute. The Supreme Court of Canada has identified three groups of factors the court should consider in assessing such an application. These factors are:

1.   the effect of the admission of the evidence on the fairness of the trial;

2.   the seriousness of the breach of the *Charter* right; and

3.   the effect of the exclusion of the evidence upon the administration of justice and its reputation.

The first factor is not of great significance here as the evidence in question is real evidence which generally would not affect the fairness of the trial. The evidence was not created as a result of the breach.

As to the seriousness of the breach, it is important to note that any breach here resulted from the acts of private citizens unfamiliar with the requirements of procedural law. While this in itself is not determinative, it is an important factor in assessing good faith. I must also consider that there was an attempt to seize evidence by force. However, there was a sense of urgency here.

As to the third factor, if the evidence is excluded, I believe the reputation of the administration of justice could well be negatively impacted. While breaches of any person's *Charter* rights must be seen as serious, when such occurs as a result of actions by private citizens acting to preserve evidence that could reasonably be used in a prosecution, exclusion of the evidence may result in citizens being more reluctant to assist in ensuring compliance of others with the law.

The court concluded that having weighed all the factors, if the *Charter* were applicable and if there was a breach of either section 8 or 9 of the *Charter*, the admission of the evidence would not bring the administration of justice into disrepute. Accordingly, the knapsack and contents were ruled admissible.

A discussion of this topic would not be complete without reference to the Supreme Court of Canada decision in *R. v. Mellenthin*.[22] In this case, the court held that the most

---

21   (1987), 33 C.C.C. (3d) 1 (S.C.C.).

22   [1992] 16 C.R. (4th) 273 (S.C.C.).

important of the three factors listed in *R. v. Collins* is the fairness of the trial. The court went on to say that if the admission of evidence obtained by a breach of the *Charter* would make the trial unfair, the evidence should be excluded even without consideration of the other two factors.

The Supreme Court of Canada made another noteworthy statement in *R. v. Mellenthin*. It held that prior to 1992, courts had often drawn a distinction between the type of evidence at issue in the *Charter* analysis. If, for instance, an accused was forced to give a confession in violation of his or her right against self-incrimination, the evidence was excluded because it was the *Charter* violation that produced the evidence. In other words, if the accused's rights had not been violated, the evidence would not have existed. Therefore, it was considered fundamentally unfair to use the evidence against him at trial. However, if the evidence existed independently and prior to the *Charter* violation, then the risk of unfairness to the accused was not as great. Typically, such evidence was the result of an illegal search. It was argued in these cases that although the search may have been illegal, the evidence existed before the violation and therefore was not created by the *Charter* breach. In *R. v. Mellenthin,* the court held that such reasoning was faulty, and that the fact that the evidence existed before the *Charter* violation is not determinative of whether the evidence should be excluded.

It is in this light that the Ontario and Newfoundland decisions discussed above involving private citizens should be juxtaposed against the Supreme Court of Canada's decision in *R. v. Mellenthin*. Note that the decisions from Ontario and Newfoundland were decided after the Supreme Court's decision in *R. v. Mellenthin*. It can be assumed that the courts in Ontario and Newfoundland were aware of the Supreme Court's findings in *Mellenthin*. On this basis, it is reasonable to believe that the analysis used by the courts in Ontario and Newfoundland referenced above is still good law today.

3.4 THE *CHARTER* AND LEGAL RIGHTS

Following the first three parts of the *Charter* entitled fundamental freedoms, democratic rights, and mobility rights, the *Charter* contains a fourth part made up of sections 7 to 14 known as "legal rights." The legal rights section of the *Charter* deals with provisions most often, although not always, associated with an accused. Section 7 is the right to life, liberty, and security of the person. Section 8 provides for the right to be free against unreasonable search and seizure. Section 9 is the right to not be arbitrarily detained or imprisoned. Section 10 outlines the rights upon arrest or detention, such as the right to be properly informed of the reason for the arrest or detention, the right to retain and instruct counsel without delay, and the right to have the validity of the detention be determined forthwith by a court. Although sections 12 to 14 are also legal rights, the final legal right examined in this book is section 11 — rights pertaining to proceedings in criminal and penal matters.

As mentioned earlier, the intent in this chapter is not to conduct an in-depth analysis of these *Charter* provisions, for *Charter* issues are better analyzed in conjunction with other subject areas, most notably in Chapter 4 — Criminal Liability, and Chapter 9 — The Law of Evidence. Accordingly, in this section, the impugned *Charter* provisions will simply be provided and the relevant subject matter referenced.

3.4.1   Section 7: The Right to Life, Liberty, and Security of the Person

Section 7 of the *Charter* provides:

> 7.   Everyone has the right to life, liberty and security of the person and the right not to be deprived thereof except in accordance with the principles of fundamental justice.

Aspects of this provision involving private investigators are reviewed in the following sections:

- Section 2.4.2.2.1 — The *Charter* and the Registrar's Discretion
- Section 4.1.2.1 — Taking Control and the Use of Force
- Section 4.1.2.5 — Informing the Arrestee of the Right to Silence
- Section 9.3.2 — Statements Taken from Suspects or Arrestees
- Section 9.3.4 — Concealed Tape Recorders
- Section 9.5.1.1 — Conscripted Evidence
- Section 9.5.1.3 — Trading in Confidence and Dirty Tricks

3.4.2   Section 8: Search And Seizure

Section 8 of the *Charter* provides:

> 8.   Everyone has the right to be secure against unreasonable search and seizure.

Aspects of this provision involving private investigators are reviewed in the following sections:

- Section 4.1.1.1 — Agent of the State versus Private Citizen
- Section 4.1.1.2 — Arrest versus Detention
- Section 4.1.2.2 — Search Subsequent to Arrest
- Section 4.1.2.2.2 — Search Subsequent to Detention
- Section 4.2.5.1 — Tracking Devices
- Section 4.2.5.2 — Number Recorders
- Section 9.2.2.5 — The *Charter* and Surveillance Videotapes
- Section 9.2.3.1 — The *Charter* and Insurance Surveillance Evidence
- Section 9.2.4.1 — Off-Site Surveillance — Where Provincial Privacy Legislation Exists
- Section 9.2.6 — Municipal Bylaw Litigation
- Section 9.3.4 — Concealed Tape Recorders
- Section 9.3.5 — Intercepted Cordless Telephone Conversations
- Section 9.3.6 — Intercepted Digital Number Recorder Communications
- Section 9.5.3 — Professional Licensing Administrative Litigation
- Section 9.6.2 — (Property Seizures) The *Charter* — Agents of the State
- Section 9.6.3 — (Property Seizures) The *Charter* — Independent Operatives

3.4.3　Section 9: Detention and Imprisonment

Section 9 of the *Charter* provides:

> 9. Everyone has the right not to be arbitrarily detained or imprisoned.

Aspects of this provision involving private investigators are reviewed in the following sections:

- Section 4.1.1 — Authority to Arrest
- Section 4.1.1.2 — Arrest versus Detention
- Section 4.1.2.2.2 — Search Subsequent to Detention
- Section 4.1.2.6 — Delivering the Arrestee Forthwith to a Police Officer

3.4.4　Section 10: Information, Rights to Counsel, and Release

Section 10 of the *Charter* provides:

> 10.　Everyone has the right on arrest or detention
>
> > (a)　to be informed promptly of the reasons therefor;
> >
> > (b)　to retain and instruct counsel without delay and to be informed of that right;
> >
> > (c)　to have the validity of the detention determined by way of *habeas corpus* and to be released if the detention is not lawful.

Aspects of this provision involving private investigators are reviewed in the following sections:

- Section 4.1.1.2 — Arrest versus Detention
- Section 4.1.2.6 — Delivering the Arrestee Forthwith to a Police Officer
- Section 4.1.2.3 — Informing the Arrestee of the Reason for Arrest
- Section 4.1.2.4 — Informing the Arrestee of the Right to Counsel
- Section 9.3.2.4 — The *Charter:* Section 10

3.4.5　Section 11: Reason for Arrest

Finally, Section 11 of the *Charter* provides:

> 11.　Any person charged with an offence has the right
>
> > (a)　to be informed without unreasonable delay of the specific offence.

Aspects of this provision involving private investigators are reviewed in Section 4.1.2.3 — Informing the Arrestee of the Reason for Arrest.

CHAPTER 4

CRIMINAL LIABILITY

The purpose of criminal law is to protect the health, welfare, morals, and safety of the public by prohibiting conduct that threatens society. This chapter will review Canadian criminal law that is most applicable to the functions of private sector investigators. The sections cover arrest, search, and the use of force; surveillance-related criminal offences; pretext crimes; property offences; and offences pertaining to the administration of justice.

In the book that was the precursor to this one,[1] the topic of search warrants was covered under the chapter on criminal liability. However, because it is generally accepted that the execution of *Criminal Code*[2] search warrants must be supervised by a peace officer, and because the law with respect to peace officer authority and liability is beyond the scope of this book, the topic of search warrants is now covered in Chapter 10 — Litigation Issues.[3]

The initial section of this chapter on arrest, search, and use of force is reviewed in more depth than the sections that follow. The reason for this is because the differences in law between the authorities and obligations of private sector investigators and their public sector counterparts are more pronounced here than in any other area. To more fully understand these differences, a more detailed discussion is included.[4]

4.1 ARREST

Arrests by private persons are generally an uncommon occurrence in Canadian society because of the average citizen's reluctance to get involved and his or her ignorance on such

---

1   Groot, N.J., *Legal Liability of the Canadian Private Investigator* (Toronto: Andijk Inc., 1998).
2   *Criminal Code of Canada*, R.S.C. 1985, c. C-46 [*Criminal Code*].
3   See Section 10.2 — Search Warrants and Private Investigators.
4   For further reference to *Criminal Code* matters, please consult the following annotated Canadian Criminal Codes: J.D. Watt & M.K.Fuerst, *The 2001 Annotated Tremeear's Criminal Code* (Toronto: Carswell, 2000); E.L. Greenspan & M. Rosenberg, *Martin's Annual Criminal Code 2001* (Aurora: Canada Law Book, 2000).

matters. Exceptions are private or store investigators arresting shoplifters for theft and security guards arresting persons who refuse to leave a private premise for trespassing. Outside of the above circumstances, it is only on the rare occasion when a private investigator may find herself in a position where the question of arresting a person may arise.

Regardless of how infrequent the situation occurs, it is essential for a private investigator to have a working knowledge of the citizen's powers of arrest.[5] In this section, a private investigator's authority to arrest and the procedure to be followed will be discussed. Specifically, the issues to be addressed include

- a citizen's (and private investigator's) authority to arrest;
- the distinction between the labels "agent of the state" versus "private citizen" and why this is important;
- the distinction between arrest versus detention and why this is important;
- the importance of being able to identify the grounds for arrest; and
- the procedure required to make a legal arrest.

This section will conclude with a review of the authority to arrest by foreign bail bondsmen.

4.1.1   Authority to Arrest

The authority of a private person, such as a private investigator, to arrest another private person was codified by Parliament in section 494 of the *Criminal Code*. Section 494 provides:

494(1) Any one may arrest without warrant

    (a)   a person whom he finds committing an indictable offence; or

    (b)   a person who, on reasonable grounds, he believes

        (i)   has committed a criminal offence, and

        (ii)   is escaping from and freshly pursued by persons who have lawful authority to arrest that person.

(2)   Any one who is

    (a)   the owner or a person in lawful possession of property, or

    (b)   a person authorized by the owner or by a person in lawful possession of property,

may arrest without warrant a person whom he finds committing a criminal offence on or in relation to that property.

---

5   Further information on a citizen's powers of arrest can be found in "Powers of Arrest and the Duties and Rights of Citizens and Police," [1962] Canadian Bar Papers 131, [1963] Lectures of the Law Society of Upper Canada.

There are a few words from this section that require further explanation. Section 494(1)(a) provides that a private person can only arrest for *indictable* offences. Generally, indictable offences are offences that are more serious in nature.[6] It is imperative that if a private sector investigator is going to attempt to effect an arrest and to avoid criminal and/or civil liability, he should have found the offence being committed *and* be certain that the offence for which the arrest is to be made is an indictable or hybrid criminal offence.

Also note that section 494(1)(b), which refers to the authority of a citizen to arrest a person who is being freshly pursued, is in reference to suspects being pursued by *persons* who have lawful authority to arrest. Therefore, a citizen not only has the authority to arrest a suspect pursued by police, but also the authority to arrest a suspect being pursued by a private citizen who has the authority to arrest found in section 494(1)(a).

Section 494(2) provides that a private person can arrest perpetrators for criminal offences he finds being committed in relation to private property of which he is the owner or the agent. This section is more applicable to security guards in their function of protecting private property. The distinction made between the power to arrest by a private person for any *criminal* offence in section 494(2) and *indictable* offences as dictated in section 494(1) is noteworthy however. The inclusion of summary conviction offences under a citizen's power of arrest in section 494(2) provides a wider power of arrest for an owner of property or his or her agent than for general citizen arrest purposes.

The provisions of the *Canadian Charter of Rights and Freedoms* that are relevant to arrest are as follows:

7.   Everyone has the right to life, liberty and security of the person and the right not to be deprived thereof except in accordance with the principles of fundamental justice.

9.   Everyone has the right not to be arbitrarily detained or imprisoned.

10.   Everyone has the right on arrest or detention

   (a)   to be informed promptly of the reasons therefor;

   (b)   to retain and instruct counsel without delay and to be informed of that right; and

   (c)   to have the validity of the detention determined by way of *habeas corpus* and to be released if the detention is not lawful.

These *Charter* provisions will be discussed in the following sections: 4.1.1.2 — Arrest versus Detention; 4.1.2.3 — Informing the Arrestee of the Reason for Arrest; 4.1.2.4 — Informing the Arrestee of the Right to Counsel; 4.1.2.5 — Informing the Arrestee of the Right to Silence; and 4.1.2.6 — Delivering the Arrestee Forthwith to a Police Officer.

---

6   Section 34(1)(a) of the *Interpretation Act*, R.S.C. 1985, c. I-21, provides that hybrid offences are deemed indictable unless elected otherwise by the Crown. Also see *R. v. Huff* (1979), 50 C.C.C. (2d) 324 (Alta. C.A.).

In addition to the *Criminal Code* provisions pertaining to citizen's arrest, some provinces in their provincial offences legislation also make reference to the citizen's arrest. For instance, in New Brunswick the *Provincial Offences Procedure Act*[7] provides that a "person" may assist a peace officer with an arrest. Other provinces make provision for arrest by a citizen in specific legislation such as that dealing with trespass. Provincial trespass legislation will be reviewed in Chapter 5 of this book.

4.1.1.1   Agent of the State versus Private Citizen

As discussed in Chapter 3 pertaining to a private investigator's liability vis-à-vis the *Charter*, section 32 provides that the *Charter* does not apply to interaction between private parties. As both a private investigator and his or her arrestee are private persons, at first blush it would follow that the *Charter* would not apply to such interaction. This, however, is not the case.

The Alberta Court of Appeal has held that the function of arrest by a private person is a government act. In other words, if a private investigator or any other private person arrests a person, he is acting as an agent of the state. As an agent of the state, a private investigator is obliged to grant an arrestee his or her *Charter* rights, such as the right to be informed of the reason for the arrest, the right to counsel, the right to silence, and the right to have the validity of the detention determined by a court. Any infringement of such rights may result in the evidence obtained from the arrest being declared inadmissible pursuant to section 24(2), the charge being stayed, or some other form of sanction pursuant to section 24(1).

Closely associated with the issue of arrest and conducting a government function is the act of detaining a person on suspicion of a criminal act for police. The courts in Ontario have held that detaining, as opposed to arresting, is not a government act as it applies to private persons if the private person is not acting under the direction of a police officer.

Arrest: Agent of the State or Private Citizen?

The case from Alberta referred to above is worthy of review as it is probably the most comprehensive analysis of the history of the law as it pertains to the authority for a citizen's arrest. In *R. v. Lerke*,[8] the facts of the case were as follows.

The accused (Lerke) went to an Edmonton tavern and was asked to leave because he appeared under age and could not validate his age with identification. A short time later Lerke re-entered the premises and the manager of the tavern asked him to come to the office. When Lerke arrived in the office, the tavern manager asked him if he now had proper identification. Lerke said he did not. The manager told him he was under arrest for "re-entering." Another tavern employee asked Lerke to put the contents of his pockets on the desk. Lerke complied. The tavern employees searched through his papers for proof of age. Lerke then took off his jacket and placed it on the chair behind him. One of the tavern employees reached behind him and, without asking Lerke for authorization, removed a small plastic bag that was subsequently found to contain marijuana. The arrest of Lerke

---

7   R.S.N.B. 1973, c. P-22.1, s. 121.

8   (1984), 13 C.C.C. (3d) 515 (Alta. Q.B.), rev'd (1986), 24 C.C.C. (3d) 129 (Alta. C.A.).

was continued and he was later turned over to police who charged him with possession of narcotics.

At trial, the tavern manager was asked his motive for the search. He first responded: "I haven't got the right to search people." But he said further: "What we were interested in was ID's for the purpose of if he was old enough or if he wasn't old enough. That way we could handle it on the safe side with the liquor board."

At Lerke's initial trial, the court held that the search of Lerke's jacket by the tavern employee was an unreasonable search and seizure contrary to section 8 of the *Charter*. Acting under section 24(2) of the *Charter*, the court held that the admission into evidence of the marijuana seized from Lerke would bring the administration of justice into disrepute and declared it inadmissible. The Crown's case thus collapsed and Lerke was acquitted.

The Crown appealed to the Court of Queen's Bench arguing that the *Charter* does not apply to the actions of one citizen in relation to another. In the alternative, the Crown urged that the search and seizure were reasonable or, in any event, were not of such a nature as to warrant exclusion of the evidence obtained in the search. The Crown's arguments, however, were dismissed. The court held that the right to be secure from unreasonable search and seizure applies to protect citizens against actions by other private citizens as well as by government bodies. The court agreed with the finding that, in the circumstances of the case, the admission of evidence would bring the administration of justice into disrepute. The court therefore held the marijuana was properly excluded.[9]

The Crown appealed again. The Alberta Court of Appeal held the facts of this case did not raise the issue of whether the *Charter* applied to the actions of one private citizen to another. Rather, the Court of Appeal held that the pertinent issue was determining if the arrest of a citizen is a governmental function if the person making the arrest was another private citizen. The court held it reached its conclusion from a consideration of the long legal history of citizen's arrest from its common law origins to the statutory expression of the present powers of arrest contained in the *Criminal Code* and the *Petty Trespass Act*. The court's review of the history of citizen's arrest was as follows.

The system of criminal procedure was, from early times, the function of the sovereign in maintaining "The King's Peace." As one academic reported,

> [t]he foundation of the whole system of criminal procedure was the prerogative of keeping the peace, which is as old as the monarchy itself, and which was, as it still is, embodied in the expression "The King's Peace," the legal name of the normal state of society.[10]

Each citizen had a part to play in this system of criminal procedure with not only the right to make arrests, but the duty to do so in appropriate cases. The right and duty, however, was directly derived from the sovereign himself and the citizen acting in obedience to

---

9   *Ibid.*

10 J.F. Stephen, *A History of the Criminal Law of England*, Vol. 1 (London: Macmillan, 1883) at 184–85.

this royal command functioned as an arm of the state. Reviewing the history of "The King's Peace" from the Assize of Clarendon in 1164 to the time of Edward III, it was reported:

> Shortly the system was described as follows. Upon the commission of a felony any one might arrest the offender, and it was the duty of any constable to do so. If the offender was not arrested on the spot, hue and cry might and ought to be raised. The sheriff and constables from the earliest times, the justices of the peace from the beginning of the reign of Edward III, were the officers by whom the cry was to be raised. In order to render the system effective, every one was bound to keep arms to follow the cry when required. All towns were to be watched and the gates shut at night, and all travelling was put under severe restrictions.
>
> The Assize of Arms and the Statute of Winchester fell into disuse, but the right of summary arrest in cases of felony continues to this day to be the law of the land.[11]

The conclusion of English historians is that the citizen's right to arrest should not be analyzed as being derived from the rights of a peace officer or as consisting of some portion only of the rights and powers of a peace officer. The reverse is true. A peace officer possesses the rights of a citizen with some additions. For the most part, he does as a matter of duty the acts that he might have done voluntarily.

> The police in their different grades are no doubt officers appointed by law for the purpose of arresting criminals; but they possess for this purpose no powers which are not possessed by private persons . . . A policeman has no other rights as to asking questions or compelling attendance of witnesses than a private person has; in a word, with some few exceptions, he may be described as a private person paid to perform as a matter of duty acts which, if so minded, he might have done voluntarily.[12]

Professor Roger Salhany summarizes the application of this history to modern Canada as follows:

> The history of the administration of the criminal law of England has long recognized the duty of all citizens to assist in the capture and arrest of all persons suspected of having committed a crime. The foundation of this duty is based upon the prerogative of the "King's Peace," a concept introduced by the Norman Kings which required the citizens of each community to apprehend all felons, and held them collectively responsible for failing to do so. Accordingly, the common law from its earliest times conferred certain powers on private citizens and on peace officers to arrest without the necessity of a warrant.
>
> In Canada today, the powers of a private person or a peace officer to arrest without a warrant are contained in the *Criminal Code*. The powers listed there are essentially those which existed at common law with some additions. When examining these provisions, it is important to remember that a peace officer possesses all of the powers of arrest of a private citizen plus certain additional powers which will be outlined. There also exists under certain federal

---

11   *Ibid.* at 189.
12   *Ibid.* at 493–94.

and provincial statutes creating offences, specific powers of arrest without warrant with respect to those offences.[13]

The modifications to the common law power of a citizen to make an arrest incorporated in the *Criminal Code* or in the *Petty Trespass Act* do not change the fundamental nature of a citizen's arrest. The power exercised by a citizen who arrests another is in direct descent over nearly a thousand years of the powers and duties of citizens in the age of Henry II in relation to the "King's Peace." Derived from the sovereign, it is the exercise of a state function.

The Court of Appeal also addressed the Crown's argument that governmental function is absent in a citizen's arrest, or at least in this citizen's arrest, because its purpose is to advance a private interest. The court, however, held this argument confuses motive and purpose. A citizen making an arrest, or, indeed, a citizen complaining to a peace officer and setting him in motion may, and usually will, have a personal motive for doing so. He wishes to recover his property, or to see punished one who has injured him, or he wishes to protect his land from crime or trespass. But the purpose of the procedure, the reason for which it exists, is not that of private satisfaction. Rather it is the public purpose embodied in maintaining the King's peace. When a landowner arrests a trespasser and takes him to a provincial court judge as contemplated in the *Petty Trespass Act*, that which results is the trial of an offence prosecuted in the name of the King with any penalty exacted accruing to the public treasury. The landowner is not a party to the proceeding.

On this basis, the Alberta Court of Appeal held that when one citizen arrests another, the arrest is the exercise of a government function to which the *Charter* applies.

Despite the above analysis, in some circles this point of law is still not settled. In *R. v. Asante-Mensah*,[14] a judgment from the Ontario Superior Court, the court refused to answer the question of whether a citizen's arrest attracts *Charter* scrutiny. The court held:

> There is some suggestion that a private citizen, when arresting by virtue of statutory authority, is exercising a power subject to *Charter* scrutiny.[15] Other authorities express reservation as to whether a private arrest engages *Charter* scrutiny.[16] I would think that a federal government employee, with delegated authority from the airport manager, exercising a statutory conferred power of arrest on government controlled property, may well be an instance of governmental conduct.

The court then held that little turned on a determination of this issue in this case.

---

13 R.E. Salhany, *Canadian Criminal Procedure*, 4th ed. (Aurora: Canada Law Book, 1984) at 44.

14 [1996] O.J. No. 1821 (Gen. Div.).

15 *R. v. Lerke* (1986), 24 C.C.C. (3d) 129 at 134–35 (Alta. C.A.); *Sears Canada Inc. v. Smart* (1987), 36 D.L.R. (4th) 756 at 758 (Nfld. C.A.).

16 *Blainey v. Ontario Hockey Association* (1986), 54 O.R. (2d) 513 at 521–52 (C.A.); *McKinney v. Board of Governors of the University of Guelph* (1990), 76 D.L.R. (4th) 545 at 634 (S.C.C.); *R.W.D.S.U. Local 580 v. Dolphin Delivery Ltd.* (1986), 33 D.L.R. (4th) 174 at 195 (S.C.C.); *R. v. Shafie* (1989), 47 C.C.C. (3d) 27 at 31–34 (Ont. C.A.). In *Khan v. El Al Israel Airlines* (1991), 4 O.R. (3d) 502 at 510–13 (Gen. Div.), the court held that airport personnel pursuant to the Foreign Aircraft Security Measures Regulations were considered as exercising governmental powers through their actions.

Detention: Agent of the State or Private Citizen?

In *R. v. Lerke* the issue addressed was if the act of a private citizen arresting another private citizen was a government function making the arrestor an agent of the state. In a case a number of years later from Ontario, a court addressed the issue of whether the act of a private citizen detaining another private citizen is a government function resulting in the detainor being an agent of the state.[17] The facts were as follows.

The accused was observed by a parking enforcement officer (Wylie) driving his motor vehicle at erratic speeds and making abrupt lane changes. Wylie followed the accused and when he and the accused were stopped at a light, he asked the accused to pull over. The accused complied. The reason Wylie asked the accused to pull over was because of his suspicion that he was impaired. Wylie, in a uniform different to that of police, did not identify himself when he asked the accused to get out of his car. Wylie noticed the odour of alcohol on the accused's breath. He contacted his dispatcher and asked for police to attend. Wylie advised the accused accordingly. At no time was the accused advised of his right to counsel. The accused waited about 40 minutes before police arrived whereupon he was arrested.

At trial, Wylie testified that he used his authority as a citizen to stop the accused and that he did not make a citizen's arrest because he could not be certain based on the accused's driving that he was impaired. Wylie further testified that had the accused tried to leave before the police arrived, he would have let him go because he knew he did not have the authority to detain the accused.

The accused testified that he complied with Wylie's directions because he thought Wylie was a police officer and had no choice but to comply. He believed Wylie was a police officer because of his uniform, because he gave directions in an authoritative way, and because he referred to his calling of police as calling for back-up. The accused further testified that had he known Wylie was not a police officer, he would have called a cab and gone home. Further, if he had been advised of his right to counsel, he would have used his cell phone and called a lawyer.

The court held that the relevant case law up to that date did not provide a definitive standard against which the actions of a person might be measured to determine whether he or she was acting as a mere citizen or as a government agent. However, the court did review other cases for assistance. The first case the court cited was a decision of the British Columbia Court of Appeal entitled *R. v. Fitch*.[18] In *Fitch* the accused was a student residing at a university and had been found in possession of stolen property after a university employee had initially checked his room. The room check was conducted to determine if the accused, who was in arrears in his rent, had moved out. Thereafter the police were contacted and a further search of the accused's room was conducted pursuant to a search warrant.

The court concluded on these facts that it had not been shown that the university security personnel were state agents and accordingly there had been no breach of the *Charter*. The court expressly reserved for another case the question of whether, on proper evidence,

---

17   *R. v. Paglialunga*, [1995] O.J. No. 512 (Prov. Div.).
18   (1994), 24 W.C.B. (2d) 576 (B.C.C.A.).

those employed to provide security for large publicly funded institutions took on the mantle of state agents by reason of the character of their employer and the nature of their duties. In this case, the initial security officer had carried out a routine inspection of the accused's room to see if he had moved out. This did not involve the security officer entering upon a criminal investigation. The court refused to conclude that the security personnel should be considered agents of the state because they had gained enough information at the time to support the issuance of a search warrant. The court concluded that the proper procedure for the security officer's superiors was to call in the police, which they did. Based on this evidence, the appeal was dismissed.

The court then reviewed the facts in *R. v. Crimeni*.[19] In *Crimeni* the accused appealed his conviction on a charge of "over 80." He had been stopped by an off-duty police officer who asked for his identification and then took his licence and car keys. The officer asked a passing citizen to contact the nearest police detachment and a short time later police arrived. The off-duty officer did not arrest the accused but conveyed his description of events to the police who then placed the accused under arrest. At no time did the off-duty officer advise the accused of his right to counsel. The British Columbia Supreme Court considered whether the off-duty officer was acting as a mere citizen at the time or whether he was acting as an agent of the state. The court held that because the officer was not on duty at the time did not mean that he ceased to be a police officer. Further, the officer had relied on his capacity as a police officer in his dealings with the accused. Therefore, the off-duty officer was deemed to be an agent of the state in his dealing with the accused.

From reviewing the case law, the court held that a number of criteria could be distilled to assist in the determination of who is a state agent. Although not an exhaustive list, the court held the factors include the following:

1.   The character of employment and the nature of the duties of the person alleged to be a state agent.

2.   The nexus of that person's conduct or status with the state. For example, is the person acting under a specific request or direction of the police or pursuant to any standing arrangements, contractual or otherwise, governing the particular situation in which the person is involved or was the person acting independently and on his or her own initiative?

3.   The time of the person's involvement in the events in question. Was it prior to or during the involvement of the police?

4.   The purpose of the contact with the accused. For example, was the contact as a result of routine duties or inadvertence or specifically for the purpose of conducting a criminal investigation?

The court also held that whether or not a person is an agent of the state for the purposes of the *Charter* should be determined on the basis of an objective analysis of all the circumstances. The court held that an accused's subjective belief that the person is a state agent, even where that belief is objectively reasonable in the circumstances, is not relevant

---

19   (1992), 17 W.C.B. (2d) 489 (B.C.S.C.).

to the threshold issue. The court held that without doubt the subjective belief of the accused is relevant to the issue of any alleged detention. However, the court further held that it could not bear on the assessment of whether a person was acting as a government agent for the purpose of the *Charter*. The court held that it found support for its opinion in the approach adopted by the various courts to the issue of state agent as outlined above. In none of the cases referred to was the subjective belief of the accused a factor considered in determining the application of the *Charter* through the concept of state agency.

Based on this analysis of fact and law, the court held that Wylie was not acting as an agent of the state during his contact with the accused. The court held that Wylie acted on his own initiative in stopping the accused, not as a result of his employment or in further-ance of some state objective that compromised part of his duties. Wylie stopped the accused as a result of his suspicion that the accused had been drinking. Had the accused left the scene, Wylie had no legal authority to stop him. As the act of detention by one pri-vate citizen to another does not attract *Charter* scrutiny, the court held the evidence of Wylie to be admissible.

4.1.1.2   Arrest versus Detention

As seen in Section 4.1.1.1 — Agent of the State versus the Private Citizen, an arrest by a private person is considered in law to be a governmental function. As such, a private citi-zen effecting an arrest must avail the person he or she has arrested of his or her constitu-tional rights. If the private citizen does not do so, the accused person may seek to have evidence resulting from the arrest excluded pursuant to section 24(2) of the *Charter*.

Although such requirements embrace situations where the subject person has been arrested, they do not apply where the person is simply detained. As discussed in the sec-tions pertaining to the *Charter*, statements, and detention in Chapter 9 — The Law of Evidence, the Court of Appeal in Ontario has held that, as a matter of law, the detain-ing of a private person by another private person does not attract the scrutiny of the *Charter*.[20] The rationale for this position is that a private citizen's detaining of another citizen is not authorized by statute, as opposed to the act of arresting another citizen which is. Without the *Charter* as a defensive tactic, evidence that would have been inad-missible if a subject person was arrested by a private person and not informed of his or her *Charter* rights is admissible if the subject person is merely detained. Accordingly, as seen in the case law, knowing the difference between arrest and detention is crucial to successful criminal litigation.

Although the courts have discussed the difference between arrest and detention on numerous occasions, there is little authority on the elements of arrest when the act is per-formed by a private citizen. It is widely acknowledged that the determination of whether an arrest has in fact occurred is dependent upon the circumstances. Pertaining to arrests by peace officers, it is well settled that the elements of arrest include the mentioning of the word "arrest" followed by a touching of the accused. It has also been accepted that if the accused submits or acquiesces because of words other than "arrest" which bring home the

---

20   *R. v. Shafie* (1989), 47 C.C.C. (3d) 27 (Ont. C.A.).

loss of his or her liberty notwithstanding there is no physical contact, an arrest in law is acknowledged to have occurred.

In the case law pertaining to arrests by private citizens, the courts have held that the requirements are virtually the same as those for police. In cases involving citizens' arrests, courts have cited with approval text writers that report that any form of physical restraint is an arrest, and that if merely words are used which cause a subject person to submit to the deprivation of his or her liberty, a valid arrest is recognized in law to have occurred.[21]

Various courts have also addressed the issue of what constitutes detention by a private citizen. It has been held that detention is a submission of liberty without the use or threat of physical force. More expansively, the courts have held that detention is a restraint of liberty other than arrest in which a person may reasonably require the assistance of counsel but may be prevented or impeded from retaining it. Detention may occur by mere psychological compulsion in the form of a reasonable perception of the suspension of freedom of choice. Further, the threat or application of physical restraint is not necessary if the person concerned submits or acquiesces to the deprivation of liberty and reasonably believes that the choice to do so otherwise does not exist.

Some fact scenarios are useful to understand the distinctions here explained. In *R. v. J.A.*,[22] a case from Ontario, two security guards at an apartment building noticed four teenage boys in the lobby. They also noticed that a fire door had been forced open. The security guards confronted the teenage boys about the damage to the fire door. While questioning them about the fire door, they noticed the teenage boys also were in possession of two garbage bags and a gym bag containing some form of property. The security guards ordered the teenage boys to empty the bags. Further investigation revealed that the bags contained stolen property from a local marina. The police were notified and the boys were arrested.

At trial, the defence argued that the evidence of the search by the security guards should be excluded because the security guards did not give the accused his *Charter* rights. The court held that because the search was conducted by security guards who were not agents of the state, the search of the accused would only attract *Charter* scrutiny if in fact the accused was arrested at the time of the search. The court found that because the boys had been informed by the security guards that they were not allowed to leave, because the security guards blocked any reasonable chance of escape, and because the search was conducted under an order from the security guards, the search was not consensual and the boys were in fact arrested. The court further held that there was an arrest notwithstanding that the word "arrest" was not used and the accused was not physically controlled by the security guards. Finally, the court held that *Charter* rights could not be denied on the basis

---

21   *R. v. J.A.*, [1992] O.J. No. 182 (Unif. Fam. Ct.), citing Justice Roger Salhany, *Canadian Criminal Procedure*, 4th ed., above note 13. See also *R. v. Asante-Mensah*, above note 14, and the McRuer Report, Vol. 2, c. 47, "Power of Arrest," at page 726 (Ontario, *Royal Commission Inquiry into Civil Rights: Report*, 5 vols. (Toronto: Queen's Printer, 1968-1971) (Commissioner: J.C.McRuer)).

22   *Ibid.*

that the arrest itself was unlawful. On this basis, the court held that the scenario did attract the scrutiny of the *Charter*, and because the accused was not given his *Charter* rights, the evidence was inadmissible. Without any physical evidence, the Crown's case collapsed and the accused were acquitted.

In *R. v. J.C.*,[23] a case from British Columbia, a music store owner noticed that four tapes were missing from an area of the store the accused had attended but that she had only paid for two. After the accused had left the store, the owner approached her and asked her about the missing tapes. The accused claimed she did not know what he was talking about. The owner then grabbed the accused by the arm, took her back in the store and told her she was not leaving until the missing tapes were found. The accused then surrendered the property. The store owner held the accused for police who, upon their arrival, arrested her and charged her with theft.

At trial, the defence argued that the evidence should not be admitted because of violation of the acccused's *Charter* rights. The court held that the *Charter* would only be relevant to the analysis if the store owner was performing the government function of arrest; that if the accused was merely detained by the store owner, she would not be protected by it. The court held that detention is a submission without the use of a threat or physical force. The court found that, notwithstanding the words "arrest" were not used, by grabbing the accused by the arm and telling her she could not leave until the missing tapes were found, the store owner did more than merely detain her. The court then held that because an arrest had in fact been made, the store owner was obliged to inform the accused of her *Charter* rights to be informed promptly of the reason thereof, of her right to counsel, and of her right to remain silent. Because the accused was not afforded her *Charter* rights, the evidence of the theft was inadmissible. The accused was therefore acquitted.

The case of *R. v. Paglialunga*,[24] another case from Ontario, was discussed in the previous section. By way of review, in this case a parking control officer in uniform, who was not a peace officer, ordered another motorist to pull over to the side of the road because he suspected the motorist was impaired. The motorist complied. The parking control officer radioed his dispatcher to notify police. At no time while waiting for the arrival of police did the parking control officer take physical control of the accused, take his keys, take away his access to his cell phone, or block an avenue of escape. Had the accused chosen to leave, he could have done so.

The court considered a number of senior court cases that analyzed what constitutes detention in the context of actions by police.[25] The court concluded that based on these facts, the accused was not arrested but merely detained. The court concurred with prior decisions that the informing of *Charter* rights is not required by private citizens to individuals who are merely detained. The court held this test was objective, not subjective, i.e., notwithstanding the accused's confusion that the parking control officer was a peace officer. On this basis the court admitted the evidence of impairment and the accused was convicted.

23   [1994] B.C.J. No. 1861 (Youth Ct.).
24   Above note 17.
25   *R. v. Therens* (1985), 18 C.C.C. (3d) 481 at 503 (S.C.C.); *R. v. Moran* (1987), 36 C.C.C. (3d) 225 (Ont. C.A.).

The final case reviewed is *R. v. A.P.*,[26] a decision from Ontario. In this case, the accused was a seventeen-year-old male who was on a recognizance with conditions not to be outside his residence between 10:30 p.m. and 6:00 a.m. The accused was in a friend's apartment building at approximately 11:00 p.m. when he was approached by two security guards. Because the accused did not live in the apartment building, the security guards ordered him against the wall and performed a search of his person. The security guards located the accused's bail papers and realized that he was in breach of his conditions. The security guards then arrested the accused on the basis of criminal breach of recognizance and for trespass to property.

At trial, the defence argued that the actions of the security guards breached the accused's *Charter* rights. The court relied upon the case of *R. v. Whitfield*[27] for the premise that an arrest is an act of compulsory restraint of a person, usually by actual seizure or touching of the body, with a view to detention. The court then stated what must be considered a controversial statement of law:

> I am not aware of any binding authority in Ontario contrary to *R. v. Lerke*.[28] As the issue before the court is related to the question of the application of the *Charter* to the actions of private citizens, I have considered the decision of the Ontario Court of Appeal in *R. v. Shafie*.[29] In that case the court considered the application of s.10(b) of the *Charter* to the actions of a private investigator. The accused (Shafie) had made inculpatory statements to a private investigator hired by his employer to investigate suspected employee thefts. The employee (Shafie) was interviewed in the private investigator's office where he had been taken by his supervisor under circumstances of psychological compulsion. At no time during the interview was Shafie advised of his *Charter* rights. It was not contended that Shafie was arrested, but it was submitted that he was detained within the meaning of s.10(b) of the *Charter*. Mr. Justice Krever held that the *Charter* had no application since the detention was effected by a private citizen and not an agent of the state. It is important for the purpose of the case at bar to consider the reasoning of Mr. Justice Krever:

>> The weight of judicial opinion, although perhaps not authority in the strict sense, is that actions at the hands of the police or other state or governmental agents would not be a detention within the meaning of section 10(b) of the *Charter* when done by private or non-governmental persons. However weakly this conclusion is based on authority, I believe it is supported by principle.

> The principle involved is also set at p.270 of the judgment, as follows:

>> In my view . . . the question as to whether a person's s.10(b) rights were infringed must be tested as at the time alleged detention occurred [in this case the detention being effected by a private investigator]. Any other conclusion would result in the judicialization of private relationships beyond the point that society could toler-

---

26   [1995] O.J. No. 1637 (Prov. Ct.).
27   [1970] 1 C.C.C. 129 (S.C.C.).
28   Above note 15, as discussed in the previous section.
29   Above note 20.

ate. The requirement that advice about the right to counsel must be given by a school teacher to a pupil, by an employer to an employee or by a parent to a child, to mention only a few relationships is difficult to contemplate.

In my view, this principle of avoiding the judicialization of private relationships does not apply to the case of security guards effecting a power of arrest pursuant to a statute. In this context, it is important to recognize that a primary and institutional function of security guards is to effect arrests. Such a role can be contrasted in this regard with the role of parent or school principals where the function of detecting crime and arresting suspected perpetrators are peripheral and extraordinary. Furthermore, that there are good reasons to "judicialize" the relationship between a security guard and a private citizen is illustrated in the case at bar.

In this case the security guard, clothed with the power to arrest without warrant by the *Trespass to Property Act*, took forcible physical hold of [the accused], detained him, and conducted an intrusive search of his person and property. The fruits of the search provided evidence of the commission of the offence. Why should a security guard carrying out the same function as a police officer be less subject to scrutiny for possible abuses of his statutory powers? And what consequences may flow if the state is free to benefit from the fruits of their powers in a manner which respects the democratic rights of others. Furthermore, and of perhaps greater significance, institutional practices could develop in which the police would rely upon or use others operating outside the shadow of the *Charter* to gather evidence for them who employ methods otherwise subject to judicial scrutiny if exercised by the police. In *R. v. Wilson*[30] the point is well put by Mr. Justice Shabbits at p.309:

> There is good reason for the *Canadian Charter of Rights and Freedoms* to apply to the actions of a private individual who is acting under the authority of a statute of the parliament of Canada. If the *Charter* did not apply in that circumstance, the application of the *Charter* could be circumvented by a government that chose to authorize private individuals to do what the *Charter* prohibited it from doing.

Finally, it should be noted that in referring to the decision of the Alberta Court of Appeal in *R. v. Lerke*, Mr. Justice Krever states the following:

> In *R. v. Lerke* the issue was the admissibility of evidence obtained as a consequence of a search by a tavern owner of the person of a customer as incidental to a citizen's arrest. In the result it was not necessary to decide the point now facing us.

Thus Mr. Justice Krever distinguishes the situation in which an arrest is effected by a private citizen from other actions of private citizens in which *Charter* violations may be alleged. In the result, I find that the *Canadian Charter of Rights and Freedoms* has application to the detention and search of the accused by the security guards.

As mentioned in the prelude to this case, it is the opinion of this writer that Mr. Justice Cohen reached the correct result but by erroneous reasoning. There are a number of reasons for this opinion.

---

30   (1994), 29 C.R. (4th) 302 (B.C.S.C.).

First, Justice Cohen finds, quite correctly, that although the word "arrest" was not used by the security guards, the accused was constructively arrested on the basis of the security guards taking physical control of him and his acquiescence. On the basis of that finding, Justice Cohen could have simply followed the decision of *R. v. Lerke* (as well as those of *R. v. J.A.* and *R. v. J.C.* — but those cases apparently were not canvassed). However, Justice Cohen embarked on an analysis of *R. v. Shafie*, rejecting the conclusions of the Ontario Court of Appeal, and concluded that the case at bar illustrated "good reasons to 'judicilize' the relationship between a security guard and a private citizen."

With respect for Justice Cohen, the case of *R. v. Shafie* should never have been included in the analysis. The central difference between the *Lerke* and *Shafie* cases is that in *Lerke* the accused was arrested, while in *Shafie* the accused was detained. In the impugned case, after finding the accused was constructively arrested, Justice Cohen erroneously equates detention prior to arrest with that of detention post arrest. In *R. v. J.C.*, the law was correctly summed up:

> Where a private person merely detains another, the detention is not affected by the *Charter*, and the detainee is not protected by it.[31] It therefore becomes necessary to determine whether Ingram arrested the accused or merely detained her.

Therefore, after finding the accused was arrested, the question should have become: Was the search by the security guards incident to arrest a reasonable search in all of the circumstances? In *Lerke*, the Court of Appeal held:

> Where the search is not for weapons, but only to seize or preserve property connected to the offence, different considerations apply. The urgency present in the search for weapons would not ordinarily be present in those cases. Often the triviality of the offence charged or the improbability, in the circumstances, that any evidence will be uncovered or will be destroyed even if the search is delayed will mean that the search by a citizen would not be a reasonable search. Both the *Petty Trespass Act* and s.449 (now s.494) of the *Criminal Code* contemplates that the offender will be turned over to persons in authority without delay. That being the case, it will be rare that the citizen making an arrest will need to search for evidentiary purposes only. The course of wisdom and the requirement that the search be reasonable will usually dictate that the search for evidence be left until the person arrested is turned over to authority.
>
> There is unfortunately no litmus paper test by which one may know an unreasonable search and seizure when it is encountered. Each case must be resolved on a consideration of the facts and circumstances of it. Though the arrest here was, in my opinion, a valid arrest, the circumstances of the offence for which the arrest was being made were so innocent, the offence itself so minor, and circumstances of urgency so lacking that the tavern employees had no right to make the search. It was an unreasonable search.
>
> The tavern employees did not perceive any danger. Their search was not designed to protect themselves and this conclusion was also reached by the two police officers. They did not search Lerke but merely gave him an appearance notice and released him. The search had

31 *R. v. Shafie*, above note 20.

therefore to be justified, if at all, as need to obtain or preserve evidence in relation to the offence for which Lerke was being arrested. But, of course, proof of age had nothing to do with the offence of "re-entering" for which he was being arrested; he was guilty of that offence regardless of age once he re-entered after being asked to leave. Whatever other motive the tavern employees may have had for the search, they simply misconceived their right to search for proof of age in relation to the charge of reentering. There was no nexus between his age and that charge.

That there must be a nexus between the search for evidence and the offence for which the person is arrested is clear from the authorities previously cited. The search cannot be a fishing expedition.

Based on the reasoning in *Lerke*, the search of the accused would have been found to be unreasonable, and the evidence obtained by the search excluded. If Justice Cohen had used this approach, he could have avoided his statement that

> Mr. Justice Krever distinguishes the situation in which an arrest is effected by a private citizen from other actions [i.e., pre-arrest detention] of private citizens in which *Charter* violations may be alleged. In the result I find that the *Charter* of Rights and Freedoms has application to the detention and search of the accused by the security guards.

Such a statement by Mr. Justice Cohen is an unnecessary muddying of the waters.

A second comment made by Justice Cohen worthy of inquiry is: "Why should a security guard carrying out the same function as a police officer be less subject to scrutiny for possible abuses of his statutory powers?" It is quite clear from a review of the above cases and the legislation that Parliament made a conscious decision to legislate certain powers to police officers and others to private citizens. Parliament, it can be inferred, was aware at the time of the existence of security guards and the functions they served in the community. Had Parliament had concerns that security guards and other trained individuals be treated differently than other private citizens, it is likely that such legislation would have been passed. This applies equally to the inclusion of section 32 of the *Charter*.

As dealt with in other sections of this book, the courts have developed a body of law dealing with when a private citizen is an agent of the state. Such a designation would occur if a private person was under the direction of the police. Therefore, Justice Cohen's concern of what consequences could flow if the state is free to benefit from using private individuals is unfounded. Stated otherwise, as agents of the state fall under *Charter* scrutiny, it is the opinion of this writer that any concerns of the actions of security guards can be argued under this head.

A final comment of Justice Cohen worthy of inquiry is as follows:

> It is unrealistic to expect that the possibility of civil action for false arrest, false imprisonment and assault . . . is not reasonably available to a . . . person like the accused, young, unsophisticated and poor . . . In the circumstances of this case to permit the prosecution to benefit from the actions of the security guards, actions which would not have been acceptable had they been undertaken by the police, would violate the fundamental principles of justice which underlie the community's sense of fairness. Accordingly I am entering a stay of proceedings.

In an age where all poor persons have a right to legal aid, it is likely that the accused would have had access to counsel. Upon reviewing the facts of this case, any counsel should have raised the possibility that such sanctions were available to the accused. To any private individual, especially those whose livelihood is in the quasi-law enforcement field such as a security guard, the prospect of facing civil action is a serious imposition to their career. Furthermore, an allegation of an improper arrest made to the licensing registrar of private investigators and security guards could further jeopardize their careers. Therefore, there exist significant deterrents to security guards to refrain from this sort of behaviour without resorting to the *Charter*.

This is not to say, however, that the *Charter* remedy was inappropriate. It is the opinion of this writer that the evidence would have been excluded, as discussed above, on the basis that the search was unreasonable and therefore in breach of the *Charter*. If the bail papers were excluded from evidence and if the trespass arrest was deemed to be unlawful, the security guards would not have known the identity of the accused and he would not have come into contact with police. On this basis, the accused would have been acquitted. It is submitted that it was unnecessary to resort to "the dramatic and extraordinary remedy" of a stay of proceedings.

Before leaving this section, a few more points are worthy of consideration. Not everyone in the legal community is in agreement on the distinction between arrest and detention. In an article by David Ray,[32] a lawyer with the investigative firm of Kroll & Associates, Calgary office, the author was addressing a question from a reader: "Our administration (a store security department) wants us to detain but not arrest. Can we do this?" The author reviewed some case law and then stated: "The bottom line is that there is no difference between an arrest and a detention."

To conclude, in the cases that were uncovered, the courts have acknowledged that an untrained private citizen cannot be expected to know the formalities of arrest. However, because of the frequency in which security guards undertake arrests, the courts expect a greater degree of adherence to procedure. Because private investigators, like security guards, are also assumed to be more familiar with the procedure to follow when undertaking a citizen's arrest, it is reasonable to assume that the courts will apply a higher standard of adherence to arrest procedure to private investigators as well.

4.1.1.3   Grounds for Arrest: Finds Committing

In Section 4.1.1 — Authority to Arrest, section 494 of the *Criminal Code* was discussed. As was seen there, section 494(1) provides that a ground for a citizen's arrest without warrant is if a citizen finds a person committing an indictable offence or, as per section 494(2), if an owner or a person authorized by an owner finds a person committing a criminal offence in relation to that property. In Section 4.1.1 it was also noted that an indictable offence is deemed to include all offences upon which the Crown may elect to proceed by indictment or summarily. What was not expanded upon was the meaning of "finds committing."

The term "finds committing" has been the subject of judicial discussion. The Supreme Court of Canada has held that "finds committing" is not to be ascertained after a trial to

---

32   "Detaining, Arresting and Using Weapons" *Canadian Security* (June/July 2000) at 34.

determine if an offence was actually committed. Rather, the test for "finds committing" is to be analyzed on the basis of both what the arresting person believed and what is reasonable to believe, and that belief may be based on what was "apparently" being committed.[33] Therefore, the test for "finding committing" has both an objective and subjective component, and does not require absolute certainty or that the charge upon which the person was arrested result in a conviction. Furthermore, "finds committing" does not necessarily require the arresting person to see the actual offence being committed, but rather that the arresting person be satisfied that the offence was apparently being committed at the time immediately prior to arrest.[34]

A review of some cases is helpful to understand these concepts. In *R. v. Devos*,[35] a case from Alberta, the accused was charged with theft under $5,000 and assault. A store investigator, Tony McMillian (McMillian), observed the accused (Devos), while in the store, conceal a pair of jeans from the store inside his jacket. Devos walked by a number of cash registers and approached the front of the store. As he approached the door to leave, McMillian placed his hand on Devos's shoulder and placed him under arrest for theft. McMillian testified he arrested Devos before he actually left the store because it was obvious Devos was not going to pay for the merchandise and if he allowed him to get into the parking lot, there was a greater likelihood the arrest would take on more risk. Upon being informed of the arrest, Devos head-butted McMillian. In the ensuing melee, Devos bit, kicked, and punched McMillian before finally being overcome.

In defence of the assault allegation, Devos argued that McMillian did not have grounds for the arrest because of his position as a store investigator. The court noted that the power of arrest for a store investigator is the same as for any citizen. Section 494(1)(a) of the *Criminal Code* provides that anyone may arrest without warrant a person whom he finds committing an indictable offence. Devos was seen committing the offence of theft. Theft is a hybrid offence and therefore indictable until and unless the Crown elects otherwise. Therefore, at the time of the arrest, the theft allegation was indictable.

The court noted that McMillian could also argue a second justification for the arrest, that of section 494(2)(b) of the *Criminal Code*. As McMillian was under contract with the store, he was an agent of the owner. Section 494(2)(b) provides that anyone who is a person authorized by the owner or a person in lawful possession of property may arrest without warrant a person whom he finds committing a criminal offence on or in relation to the property. Therefore, even if the theft of the merchandise was not an indictable offence, McMillian would still have had the authority to effect the arrest.

As a secondary defence to the assault charge, Devos argued that the force he used was justified because McMillian did not have grounds for the arrest because he was not certain a theft had occurred. The court then discussed the requirements of a private citizen such

---

33   *R. v. Beiron* (1975), 23 C.C.C. (2d) 513 (S.C.C.); *R. v. Roberge* (1983), 4 C.C.C. (3d) 304 (S.C.C.).

34   *R. v. Cunningham and Ritchie* (1979), 49 C.C.C. (2d) 390 (Man. Co. Ct.).

35   (11 October 1999), (Alta. Prov. Ct.) [unreported].

as a private investigator to effect an arrest. The court pointed out that the requirements for arrest have been set out by the Supreme Court of Canada in *R. v. Beiron*[36] and *R. v. Roberge.*[37] *Beiron* stood for the proposition that the arresting person need only believe the accused had apparently committed a criminal offence; that is, a subjective standard. *Roberge* stood for the proposition that the apparent belief of the arresting person also be reasonable on an objective standard; that is, to any reasonable person in the same circumstance as the arresting person at the time. In other words, the arresting person is not required to be certain that an offence has taken place, nor does the offence arrested for have to result in a conviction.

Applying these authorities to Devos, the court held the test to be: Did McMillian believe Devos was apparently committing the offence of theft, and if so, would any reasonable person in his place have reached the same conclusion? The court held that the reasonable grounds requirements of section 495(1) of the *Criminal Code*, dealing with arrest by a peace officer, must be imported into section 494(1)(a), arrest by a private citizen, and therefore, the cases setting out the parameters for arrest by a peace officer where he or she finds the accused committing or has committed an indictable offence are applicable.

Devos raised the case of *R. v. Douglas*[38] as authority that the Crown must prove the offence, in this case theft, beyond a reasonable doubt before the arresting person has the authority to arrest. Devos argued that if the evidence fell short of the necessary degree of proof to convict on the underlying offence, then the arresting person did not have the authority to make the arrest, and he was entitled to resist it on the basis that it was illegal. To this argument the court noted that *Douglas* relied for authority upon *R. v. Pritchard.*[39] In *Pritchard* the court held:

> The general rule seems to be that where a statute confers the power of arrest without a warrant . . . but does not expressly give the right to arrest on reasonable and probable grounds . . . then the arrest cannot be justified if the person in fact was not committing a criminal offence . . . The subsequent trial and acquittal established once and for all that the respondent was not found committing a criminal offence. Under these circumstances the arrest was not a legal arrest and the learned magistrate was right in holding that he could not therefore be guilty of escaping a legal arrest.

The court referenced the *Pritchard* case to that of *Beiron* wherein the Supreme Court of Canada specifically found Pritchard to be wrong on that issue. In *Beiron* at page 524 the Supreme Court of Canada stated:

> [Section 495], paragraph (1)(b) applies in relation to any criminal offence, and it deals with the situation in which the peace officer himself finds an offence being committed. His power of arrest is based upon his own observation. Because it is based on his own discovery of the offence actually being committed, there is no reason to refer to a belief based upon reasonable and probable grounds. If the reasoning in the *Pritchard* case is sound, the validity of an arrest under s.495(1)(b) can only be determined after the trial of the person arrested and after the

36   (1975), 23 C.C.C. (2d) 513 (S.C.C.).
37   (1983), 4 C.C.C. (3d) 304 (S.C.C.).
38   (1972), 8 C.C.C. (2d) 518 (Sask. Q.B.).
39   (1961), 130 C.C.C. 61 (Sask. C.A.).

determination of any subsequent appeals. My view is that the validity of an arrest under this paragraph must be determined in relation to the circumstances which were apparent to the peace officer at the time the arrest was made . . . If the words "committed a criminal offence" are to be construed in the manner indicated in the *Pritchard* case, paragraph (b) becomes impossible to apply. The power of arrest which that paragraph gives has to be exercised promptly, yet strictly speaking it is impossible to say that an offence is committed until that party arrested has been found guilty by the courts. If this is the way in which this provision is to be construed, no peace officer can ever decide when making an arrest without a warrant that the person arrested is committing a criminal offence. In my opinion, the words in paragraph (b), which is oversimplified, means that the power to arrest without a warrant is given where the peace officer himself finds a situation in which a person is apparently committing an offence. It could be read that "apparently" only applies to reasonable grounds and not to finding committing, but I prefer to apply it to all situations.

Based on the passages above, the court held that to answer the test the court must look at the evidence available to McMillian and to what he believed. The basis of McMillian's belief was that Devos selected merchandise and did not attempt to pay for it in the department where it was located, that he concealed the items, that he passed seven cash registers where he could have paid, that he was heading for doors leading to the parking lot, and that he was about to leave the store at the time of arrest. These facts are proof that McMillian believed Devos had apparently committed or was committing a theft. McMillian's belief was reasonable on any reasonable person objective standard. As the test has been met, Devos had no defence to the assault he committed upon McMillian while McMillian was exercising a lawful arrest. Accordingly the accused was found guilty of the assault.

A second case worthy of review is from Manitoba and entitled *R. v. Cunningham and Ritchie*.[40] In this case, the accused were charged with unlawful confinement of a fifteen-year-old boy. The accused were officers in charge of a passenger pleasure cruise ship that travelled the rivers around Winnipeg. During these cruises, there had been several incidents of persons on shore throwing objects at the ship causing damage and, in one case, injuring a passenger. On the evening of the incident, three young boys began throwing stones and apples at the ship, breaking a window. The accused decided to stop the ship and attempt to capture them. The complainant was apprehended near a pile of rocks and apples and taken on board the ship. The court held the accused were legally entitled to arrest the boy for the criminal offence of mischief on the basis of both section 449(1) (now section 494(1)) of the *Criminal Code* pertaining to arrest by a private citizen who finds another committing an indictable offence and section 449(3) (now section 494(2)) pertaining to arrest by an owner or person in lawful possession of property of anyone whom he or she finds committing a criminal offence on or in relation to that property.

---

40 Above note 34.

On the issue of "find committing," the court held:

> Mr. Walsh drew to my attention certain authorities which hold that the phrases used in the section "find committing" does not mean the person effecting the arrest must himself have actually seen the criminal act committed and that it is sufficient if the act has been "apparently committed" irrespective of whether it has been actually committed and regardless of whether a subsequent judicial determination confirms that it has been committed.[41] In the case at bar there was evidence that Captain Cunningham, at least, saw the boys throwing objects at the boat. Further, he received reports that things were being hurled at the ship, that a window had been broken and, after he got off the ship, he actually observed the three boys on the shore in the immediate vicinity with stones and crabapples in their possession. Even if he had not actually seen the boy throwing these at the ship, the reports he had received and his own subsequent observations would have made it readily apparent to him or anyone that the boy had committed the offence of mischief. In my view, the accused found him committing the offence within the meaning of section 449 (now section 494) of the Code.

Notwithstanding the above discussion, some commentators have advised that in the interest of avoiding accusations of false arrest or imprisonment, a private investigator should not make an arrest unless he actually sees the criminal offence taking place. It is further advised that if the identity of the offender is known and if there is no risk of imminent danger to a third party or loss of evidence, that an arrest not be undertaken but rather that the matter simply be referred to police.[42]

4.1.2 Procedure when Making an Arrest

In criminal law, the adherence to procedural rules is imperative to assure the success of an action. In this section, the procedural issues a private sector investigator, as any citizen, must address his or her mind to if making an arrest are discussed. These issues include

- the duty to identify oneself to an arrestee;
- the duty to touch the arrestee;
- the duty to inform the arrestee of the reason for his or her arrest;
- the appropriate use of force that may be used to effect an arrest;
- the right to search subsequent to arrest;
- the duty to inform the arrestee of his or her rights to counsel;
- the duty to inform the arrestee of his or her right to silence; and
- the duty to deliver the arrestee forthwith to a police officer.

---

41 See *Crankshaw's Criminal Code of Canada*, 7th ed. (Toronto: Carswell, 1959) at 595; *Frey v. Fedoruk, Stone and Watt* (1949), 95 C.C.C. 206 at 218–25, rev'd on other grounds, [1950] S.C.R. 517; and *R. v. Beiron*, above note 33.

42 J.T. Wells et al., *The Fraud Examiners Manual*, Canadian ed. (Austin, TX: Association of Certified Fraud Examiners, 1998).

Pertaining to the right to search subsequent to arrest, the collateral issues of consent searches and searches subsequent to detention will also be reviewed.

4.1.2.1   Taking Control and the Use of Force

As discussed in Section 4.1.1.2 — Arrest versus Detention, the requirements to effect a legal arrest are to touch the arrestee, to inform him that he is under "arrest" and to inform him of the reason for the arrest. The preciseness of the reason for arrest is discussed in Section 4.1.2.3. Although not required by law, a private investigator, to avoid resistance by the arrestee, is well advised to identify himself before making this announcement.[43]

There are a number of provisions in the *Criminal Code* that deal with the use of force by a person executing an arrest or a search warrant on behalf of the state. The provision that imperils a person when executing a state function such as an arrest or a search warrant is section 26, which provides:

26.   Every one who is authorized by law to use force is criminally responsible for any excess thereof according to the nature and quality of the act that constitutes the excess.

The protection for a private person making a citizen's arrest against criminal liability for the force used to effect the arrest is covered in section 25 of the *Criminal Code*. Section 25 provides, *inter alia:*

25(1) Every one who is required or authorized by law to do anything in the administration or enforcement of the law

(a)   as a private person . . .

is, if he acts on reasonable grounds, justified in doing what he is required or authorized to do and in using as much force as is necessary for that purpose.

. . .

(3)   A person is not justified for the purposes of subsection (1) in using force that is intended or is likely to cause death or grievous bodily harm unless the person believes on reasonable grounds that it is necessary for the self-preservation of the person or the preservation of any one under that person's protection from death or grievous bodily harm.

As indicated in the preceding sections, because an arrest has been held to be a government function even when performed by private citizens, the *Charter* is a further consideration that must be kept in mind. Section 7 of the *Charter* is relevant to considerations of the amount of force that may be used to execute an arrest. Section 7 of the *Charter* provides:

7.   Everyone has the right to life, liberty and security of the person and the right not to be deprived thereof except in accordance with the principles of fundamental justice.

Case law analyzing sections 25 and 26 has held that even if a court can second-guess a citizen's use of force when executing an arrest, a finding of excessive use of force will not be made if the arresting citizen acted in good faith and with a legitimate purpose. The

---

43   *Ibid.*

courts have held that for a finding of excessive use of force to be made, not only must the accused have committed an illegal act but also done so with guilty intent.[44]

To determine the amount of force permitted in an arrest, the courts have held that the factors to be considered when conducting both a section 25 *Criminal Code* and a section 7 *Charter* analysis include the following:

- the circumstances of the offence;
- the seriousness of the offence;
- the effect of the force that was exerted in executing the arrest;
- the other courses of action open to the arrestor;
- the reputation of the arrestee for violence; and
- the physical prowess of the arrestee.

The courts have held that force used must be reasonable and proportional considering the circumstances.[45]

There are a number of other sections in the *Criminal Code* that are relevant to private persons for which there is not an abundance of case law but of which the private investigator should still be aware. Section 27 deals with the permissible amount of force that may be used in preventing an offence and states:

27.   Every one is justified in using as much force as is reasonably necessary

    (a) to prevent the commission of an offence

        (i) for which, if it were committed, the person who committed it might be arrested without warrant, and

        (ii) that would be likely to cause immediate and serious injury to the person or property of anyone; or

    (b) to prevent anything being done that, on reasonable grounds, he believed would, if it were done, be an offence mentioned in (a).

Section 34 of the *Criminal Code* deals with the authority to use as much force as reasonably necessary to defend oneself against an unprovoked assault and states:

34(1) Every one who is unlawfully assaulted without having provoked the assault is justified in repelling force by force if the force he uses is not intended to cause death or grievous bodily harm and is no more than is necessary to enable him to defend himself.

  (2)   Every one who is unlawfully assaulted and who causes death or grievous bodily harm in repelling the assault is justified if

    (a) he causes it under reasonable apprehension of death or grievous bodily harm from the violence with which the assault was originally made or with which the assailant pursues his purposes; and

---

44   *R. v. Cunningham and Ritchie*, above note 34.
45   *R. v. Wilson* (1994), 29 C.R. (4th) 302 (B.C.S.C.).

(b) he believes, on reasonable grounds, that he cannot otherwise preserve himself from death or grievous bodily harm.

Section 29 is relevant to a private sector investigator because of the following
requirement:

29(3) Failure to comply with . . . (2)[46] does not itself deprive . . . a person who makes an arrest
or those who assist them of protection from criminal responsibility.

In addition to these sections, section 37 pertaining to the use of force to prevent or repel
an assault, sections 38 and 39 pertaining to defence of personal property, sections 40 and
41 pertaining to defence of a dwelling and real property, and section 42 pertaining to assertion of right to a house or real property are worthy of review.

Some case scenarios are helpful to understand these concepts. In *R. v. Cunningham and
Ritchie*,[47] the court analyzed sections 25 and 26 of the *Criminal Code* against an arrest made
by two private citizens, in this case a ship's officers. The facts of this case were reviewed in
Section 4.1.1.3 — Grounds for Arrest: Finds Committing. To summarize the case, the
accused were charged with unlawful confinement of a fifteen-year-old boy. The accused
were officers in charge of a passenger pleasure cruise ship that travelled the rivers around
Winnipeg. During these cruises, there had been several incidents of persons on shore
throwing objects at the ship causing damage and, in one case, injuring a passenger. On the
evening of the incident, three young boys began throwing stones and apples at the ship,
breaking a window. The accused stopped the ship and attempted to capture them. They
apprehended the boy near a pile of rocks and apples and took him on board the ship where
he was put on the floor of the wheel-house with his ankles loosely tied. The police were
immediately contacted by radio, and they instructed the accused to bring the boy to their
regular dock. The boy alleged he had been physically abused at the hands of the accused.

The court held the accused were legally entitled to arrest the boy for the criminal offence
of mischief. Having arrested the boy, the accused were lawfully entitled to hold him prisoner until they could deliver him into police custody. With regard to the unlawful confinement and the excessive use of force, the court held:

Under s.25(1) and s.26 of the Code, the accused were entitled to use as much force as was necessary to effect their purpose of arresting and detaining the boy provided the force was not
excessive. I have already found that the boy was not harmed or abused in any way. Very little
force — if it can be described as such — was employed in his capture and detention. His ankles
were tied, but not tightly, and not in such a way as to hurt him or even cause him undue discomfort. He was not threatened in any way, but, on the contrary, Captain Cunningham was
careful to explain to him that he was going to tie his ankles, that nobody was going to hurt him
and that he was just going to be held until the police picked him up at the Nairn Avenue dock.
Indeed, the boy agreed with this procedure.

---

46   Section 29(2) provides: "It is the duty of every one who arrests a person . . . to give notice to
that person, where it is feasible to do so, of . . . (b) the reason for the arrest."
47   Above note 34.

Crown counsel criticized the accused for having tied the boy's ankles at all. A peace officer effecting an arrest is legally entitled to secure his prisoner, such as handcuffing him or binding him, if he does so reasonably and if he has a good reason for doing so.[48] In the instant case, while it is true that the boy had given no sign that he might attempt to escape, nevertheless, the accused did have a special reason for securing him, for his own protection because they feared that, if they did not do so, he might suddenly run to and jump off the side of the ship, coming to serious harm in the process . . .They should not be criticized for taking simple precautionary measures to minimize the chance that their prisoner would repeat the type of foolhardy act they had witnessed earlier.

In the particular circumstances of this case then, the accused were justified in taking reasonable steps to secure the prisoner. In my view, the measures they did employ were reasonable and did not amount to an excessive use of force. They did not go as far as they might have done by, for example, binding the boy tightly hand and foot.

. . .

It seems to me that the explanation given by Commodore Ritchie with respect to the manner of the boy's detention and for rejecting the options suggested by Crown counsel were reasonable, and I am not prepared to say that the other ship's officers, faced with the same situation and acting reasonably, would necessarily have pursued a different course. Even if I were to "second guess" the accused and find that the choice they made in the circumstances was the wrong one, the fact would still remain that, in acting as they did, they proceeded in good faith with legitimate purpose. The accused, of course, cannot be found criminally liable unless it can be established not only that they committed the act with which they are charged, but that they did so with guilty intent. They must have acted with some "blameworthy condition of mind" or they must have at least an intention to do a wrong or break the law . . . In my opinion, in the case at bar, not only has the prosecution failed to prove that the accused acted with guilty intent, but that the accused have demonstrated to my satisfaction that they acted responsibly throughout with innocent intent.

The issue of what is a reasonable amount of force necessary to effect an arrest by a private person was also dealt with in the case of *R. v. Wilson*.[49] However, the court did not analyze the question solely on the basis of what constitutes excessive force under section 25 of the *Criminal Code*, but rather when the degree of force used constitutes a breach of section 7 of the *Charter*.

The facts were as follows. The accused (Wilson) went into a grocery store in Nanaimo, British Columbia, in the company of a female person. Wilson removed a shopping bag from his person and placed meat, which was the property of the grocer, into the shopping bag. The female person accompanying Wilson then stood in the cashier's lineup in the front part of the store to pay for groceries that she had. Wilson went out an exit of the grocery store without paying for the meat he had placed in the shopping bag and walked to a car with it. Wilson's actions were observed by a store security person, David Hansen (Hansen). Hansen walked to the door through which Wilson had exited and saw Wilson

---

48   See *Hamilton v. Massie* (1889), 18 O.R. 585.
49   Above note 45.

placing the shopping bag containing the stolen meat on the floor of the vehicle by the passenger seat. Wilson then looked up and saw Hansen watching him. Hansen yelled "Stop!" Wilson ran around to the driver's side of the car, got into it, and started it in motion with the driver's door still open. Hansen went to the vehicle and got into the front passenger seat. The vehicle was already moving. Hansen told Wilson to stop the car. Wilson refused. Wilson was an amputee and had no right arm. Hansen tried to put the transmission of the vehicle into park but could not do so as Wilson was pushing him. Hansen was of the belief that other persons in the parking lot were then at risk as the vehicle was moving forward without being controlled. Hansen applied a carotid hold to the throat of Wilson. Wilson fell unconscious. Ten to twelve seconds had elapsed from the time when Wilson got into his vehicle until the time when his vehicle was stopped following his loss of consciousness. After Wilson regained consciousness, Hansen advised him of his arrest and rights under the *Charter*. It is also noteworthy that Wilson had taken $52.00 worth of meat from the grocer, that Hansen was dressed in plain clothes and displayed no identification or badge indicating he was a security guard, and that Hansen did not identify himself before he applied the carotid hold on Wilson. Furthermore, Hansen was aware that people had died as a result of having the carotid hold applied to their necks and that the RCMP used that hold as a last resort in restraining an individual.

The court noted that Hansen's arrest of Wilson was under section 494(1) of the *Criminal Code*. The court further noted some of the trial judge's reasons:

> Not many of us have sympathy for someone stealing meat. How many rights should such a person have? Well, such a person has the same rights as the rest of us. Wilson has the right not to have the security of his person interfered with except in accordance with the principles of fundamental justice. Looking at it only from his point of view, those rights were interfered with. I am not concerned with the point of view of Hansen. I can understand how this happened from his point of view. Things happened quickly. He had to decide under very difficult circumstances what to do, and he did what he did, and I certainly understand how it happened. But the result was, from the point of view of Wilson, that the security of this person was significantly interfered with, and now, with the benefit of hindsight, we can say that that was not reasonable and proportional in the circumstances to the seriousness of the offence.

The appeal court then held:

> As a general proposition, I have concluded that the right to arrest, that is to touch a person and say, "you are under arrest" for a certain offence is not an absolute power to restrain come what may, but if force is to be used, it must be reasonable and proportional to several other factors involved. The factors referred to by the trial judge include the circumstances of the offence, the seriousness of the offence, the effect of the force which is exerted or contemplated in effecting the arrest, and a consideration of what other courses of action were open to the person who was effecting the arrest. He said that the reputation for violence of the person being arrested is of relevance. The trial judge noted that of particular relevance to Wilson was the obvious fact that he had only one arm and had a limited ability to react physically.

> The trial judge did not refer to s.25(1) of the *Criminal Code*. His reasons reflect that he considered the respondent's rights under s.7 of the *Charter* had been breached because of the "quite exceptional force" and "quite drastic action" used in the arrest. The trial judge found

that the security of the person of Wilson was significantly interfered with in a manner that was not reasonable and not proportional to the circumstances prevailing.[50]

. . .

The issue before the trial judge was whether Wilson was deprived of his security of the person other than in accordance with the principles of fundamental justice. Mr. Justice Wood, at p.38 of the *Garcia-Guiterrez*[51] decision, also said this:

> Choking is a life threatening form of force. At the very least it presents the likelihood of serious pain or hurt. At best it endangers life; at worst it causes death. When it is applied to the point of inducing unconsciousness, as it apparently was in this case, it approaches the worst of potential consequences. Thus, in the absence of the circumstances described in s.25(3), it was force not justified under s.25(1).

The *Garcia-Guiterrez* decision dealt with an arrest by a peace officer. Hansen is not a peace officer. His power of arrest was restricted by s.25(3). He was not justified in using force that was intended to, or likely to, cause death or grievous bodily harm.

The trial judge found that Hansen inflicted exceptional and drastic force on Wilson. Wilson, who had limited ability to defend himself and who had neither acted violently nor indicated any violence, was overcome by Hansen while trying to flee. Hansen applied pressure to his carotid artery rendering him unconscious. The trial judge considered that there were other means open to Hansen to apprehend Wilson. Hansen was not required to render Wilson unconscious with the carotid artery hold in order to arrest him. Hansen was not justified by s.25 of the *Criminal Code* in using force which was likely to cause grievous bodily harm. The words "grievous bodily harm" were held by Mr. Justice Anderson of our Court of Appeal in the *Bottrell*[52] decision to mean a "serious hurt or pain". Hansen's actions were actions likely to cause Wilson serious hurt or pain. The evidence does not support the Crown's submission that Hansen's actions were justified by s.25 of the *Criminal Code*.

I am of the view that in the facts of this case, the trial judge proceeded correctly in deciding whether Wilson's *Charter* rights were infringed by analyzing the constitutional protection provided by s.7 of the *Charter*. There was ample evidence supporting the trial judge's findings that Wilson's rights had been infringed.

On the topic of the acceptable degree of force permitted to be used, it is of some comfort that the court in *R. v. Kandola*[53] held that a person cannot be expected to weigh the nicety of the exact measure of the defensive action nor be expected to stop and reflect upon the risk of deadly consequences that might result from taking justifiable defensive action.

---

50 The court also referenced the decisions of *Eccles v. Bourque* (1974), 19 C.C.C. (2d) 129 (S.C.C.).

51 *R. v. Garcia Guiterrez* (1991), 65 C.C.C. (3d) 15 (B.C.C.A.).

52 *R. v. Bottrell* (1981), 60 C.C.C. (2d) 211.

53 (1993), 80 C.C.C. (3d) 481 (B.C.C.A.).

Pertaining to private investigators, *R. v. Constantinescu*[54] is an example of an occurrence where a person who was the subject of the private investigator's surveillance was charged with assault and theft after attempting to steal the film from the private investigator who was photographing him as part of an investigation. The accused was convicted of both the assault and the theft. The case exemplifies the potential for the application of section 34 of the *Criminal Code*.

In another case, *Wilson Roofing Ltd. v. Wayne*,[55] a private investigator was a joint defendant in a tort action along with a police department for defamation, malicious prosecution, trespass, unlawful conversion of documents, illegal seizure, and inducement to breach an employee's contract of employment for his role in investigating, providing information for, and assisting in, a search warrant of the plaintiff's premises. The court, in dismissing the action, held that the protection of section 25(2) of the *Criminal Code* afforded to person(s) required or authorized by law to carry out a sentence or to execute a process applied to the situation of a private investigator as a person assisting a person so authorized.

4.1.2.2   Search Subsequent to Arrest

As we have seen, the authority for a private person to arrest another private person has its roots in the common law and is codified in section 494 of the *Criminal Code*. We have also seen that the courts have deemed a citizen's arrest to be a governmental act, resulting in it attracting the provisions of the *Charter*.[56]

Unlike the authority to arrest, the power to search subsequent to arrest granted to private persons is not found in the *Criminal Code* but rather is a common law measure dating back to the common law authority for the citizen's arrest. Where private citizens have made arrests, the courts have held that at common law, the right to search an arrestee is automatic subsequent to arrest because of the need to protect both the arrestee and arrestor from injury resulting from a weapon, to prevent escape, and to preserve evidence. The courts have further held that the right to search subsequent to arrest is even more important for private citizens than for police because private citizens do not have side-arms, badges, uniforms, or other coercive devices to decrease the likelihood of violence.[57]

Today, however, the imposition of the *Charter* has restricted this right. Because of the *Charter* section 8 right against unreasonable search and seizure, searches subsequent to arrest are now only permitted when it was reasonable in the circumstances. It has been held that every search without a warrant is *prima facie* unreasonable and therefore must be justified by the Crown. Notwithstanding this limit, the courts have generally provided police and private citizens alike with a significant degree of discretion as long as any of the factors listed above are identified as reasons for immediately embarking on a search sub-

54   (1990), 11 W.C.B. (2d) 197 (Ont. Gen. Div.).
55   (1986), 74 N.B.R. (2d) 26 (Q.B.).
56   *R. v. Lerke*, above note 8.
57   *Ibid*. See also C.D. Shearing & P.C. Stenning, *Search and Seizure Powers of Private Security Personnel: A Study Paper* (Ottawa: Law Reform Commission of Canada, 1979).

sequent to arrest. The circumstances in which courts have curbed a private citizen's right to search subsequent to arrest are when the charge is relatively minor, when there is no apparent imminent danger before turning over the arrestee to police, and when the search is not logically linked to the reason for the arrest.[58]

The courts have further held that for a search not to infringe a person's section 8 *Charter* rights, the search must be conducted in a "reasonable manner." The courts have interpreted "reasonable manner" to mean that a search must not be used as a mechanism to intimidate, ridicule, or pressure an accused to obtain a confession, but rather must be conducted in a responsible and appropriately courteous manner. Further, the use of physical or psychological restraints should be limited to what is appropriate in the circumstances.[59]

The parameters of the degree of search permitted by law remains a matter of some contention. Don Stuart, an eminent legal scholar, wrote an annotation to the case of *Cloutier v. Langlois*,[60] a case wherein the Supreme Court of Canada analyzed a police officer's power to search subsequent to arrest. The Supreme Court of Canada followed the decisions of *R. v. Morrison*[61] and *R. v. Miller*,[62] which held that police officers may search for weapons or evidence subsequent to arrest without reasonable grounds to believe that either weapons or evidence would be found on the person. In other words, the Supreme Court of Canada held that the police officer's right to search subsequent to arrest is automatic. Stuart critiqued this reasoning, and noted that in *R v. Lerke*,[63] the Alberta Court of Appeal held that the right of a citizen upon arresting another citizen to search is not automatic, but must be reasonable. Reasonable, according to Stuart, permits searches for weapons where there is an apprehension of danger and for evidence only for what is relevant to the reason for arrest.

4.1.2.2.1 Consent Searches

Consent searches[64] are a valuable investigative tool for police, private security, and private investigators alike. Since a private citizen's arrest is considered a governmental function that triggers the application of the *Charter*, any violation of a person's section 8 *Charter* right to be secure against unreasonable search and seizure may result in evidence being excluded under section 24(2) of the *Charter*. However, when a private citizen engages in a search of his or her own volition, that is, when not exercising the governmental function of arrest or working under the direction of a peace officer, the repercussions of improper searches become less clear.

---

58 *Ibid.* See also *R. v. Deacon*, [1993] B.C.J. No. 973 (P.C.).

59 *R. v. Kozuchar-Thibault*, [1994] M.J. No. 449 (Prov. Ct.).

60 (1990), 74 C.R. (3d) 316 at 318 (S.C.C.).

61 (1987), 58 C.R. (3d) 63 (Ont. C.A.).

62 (1987), 62 O.R. (2d) 97 (C.A.).

63 Above note 8.

64 Assistance on this aspect of law was provided by Robert Gerden, author of *Private Security: A Canadian Perspective* (Toronto: Prentice-Hall Canada, 1998) at 71. Robert Gerden is currently a Senior Adviser, Corporate Security, Nortel Networks, 8200 Dixie Road, Suite 100, Brampton, Ontario L6T 5P6, Tel: (905) 863-5351.

One issue that arises with consent searches is whether the touching of another person for the purpose of searching them constitutes an arrest of that person as opposed to a detention.[65] If the person is deemed, in law, to be arrested, the *Charter* would apply and the search would be held to be unlawful. If the person truly does consent and is only detained, under the common law rule pertaining to the *Charter*'s application to detention by private persons, the *Charter* should not apply and the evidence obtained should be admissible. If the search was not in fact consensual, other criminal and/or civil sanctions may apply.

Consent searches by private persons have not been defined in legislation nor explored in case law. However, in *R. v. Wills*[66] the court dealt with the issue of consent searches as it applies to police. The court held that the Crown must establish, on the balance of probabilities, that the police search was truly consensual. For this to be so, the following must exist:

1.   There was consent, express or implied.

2.   The grantor of the consent had the authority to give the consent in question.

3.   The consent was voluntary in the sense that the consent was not the product of police oppression, coercion, or other external conduct that negated the freedom to choose whether or not to allow the police to pursue the course of conduct requested.

4.   The giver of consent was aware of the nature of the police conduct to which he or she was being asked to consent.

5.   The giver of consent was aware of his or her right to refuse to permit the police to engage in the conduct requested.

6.   The giver of the consent was aware of the potential consequences of giving the consent.

The question of consent searches arises in many aspects of private interaction. Searches are often a condition of entry into premises such as music concerts, bars, and sporting events. A person who refuses consent to be searched should not be searched. However, the refusal to consent to a search often results in the prohibition of entry, even when admission has been paid. Employee contracts also often provide for searches of employee property such as handbags and lockers. This consent, whether express or implied, would be a condition of employment. If an employee refuses to consent to such a search, the option would be open to the employer to dismiss the employee for breach of a term of the employment contract.

As mentioned, no case law has been reviewed on this subject area pertaining to private investigators. It is a matter that will likely be addressed by a court at a future date.

4.1.2.2.2 – Search Subsequent to Detention

As we have seen in Section 4.1.1.2 — Arrest versus Detention, the *Charter* does not apply to the actions of a private person who detains another private person when the reason for the detention is not for a public purpose. In other words, in order for a private person to

---

65   For a further discussion of this issue, see Section 4.1.1.2 — Arrest versus Detention.
66   (1992), 70 C.C.C. (3d) 529 (Ont. C.A.).

detain another private person without attracting the scrutiny of the *Charter*, the purpose of the detention must be for a reason relevant to the private sector. Examples of such conduct are fishermen seizing illegal catches from other fishermen to protect a fishery,[67] or employers hiring private investigators to root out internal thefts by employees.[68]

Case law has further held that since private sector detentions do not come within the realm of the *Charter*, searches and seizures subsequent to a detention by a private person of another private person also fall outside the *Charter's* sphere.[69] This position of the courts again reinforces the importance of distinguishing between arrest and detention.

4.1.2.3   Informing the Arrestee of the Reason for Arrest

The legislation relevant to this issue is section 29 of the *Criminal Code* and section 10 of the *Charter*. Section 29(2)(b) of the *Criminal Code* provides:

> 29(2) It is the duty of every one who arrests a person . . . to give notice to that person, where it is feasible to do so, of . . .
>
> (b) the reason for the arrest.

Section 10(a) of the *Charter* provides:

> 10. Everyone has the right on arrest or detention
>
> (a) to be informed promptly of the reasons therefor.

Pertaining to the mechanics of informing another person of the reason for arrest, in *R. v. Evans*[70] the Supreme Court of Canada held that an arrestee does not have to be informed of the formal section number and words of the offence for which she was arrested. Rather, to fulfil the requirements of the *Criminal Code* and the *Charter*, the arrestee must be informed of the substance of the offence for which she was arrested to the extent, reasonably in all the circumstances, that she would be sufficiently informed to permit her to make a decision to decline to submit to the arrest, or alternatively, to decide whether to exercise her right to consult counsel.

As seen in the prior discussions, most notably in Section 4.1.1.2 — Arrest versus Detention, unlike the act of arrest for which a private person is deemed to be an agent of the state, the act of detaining a person by another private person does not fall under the sphere of the *Charter*. Therefore, although it may be prudent, private persons are not legally required to inform a person they have detained of the reason therefor.

Case law pertaining to this issue vis-à-vis private persons is rare. In *R. v. Asante-Mensah*,[71] the arrestor was an airport ground inspector at Pearson International Airport with the powers and authority only of a private citizen. The airport ground inspector had made an

---

67   *R. v. Barnes*, [1995] N.J. No. 146 (P.C.).
68   *R. v. Shafie*, above note 20.
69   Above note 67.
70   [1991] 1 S.C.R. 869.
71   Above note 14.

arrest of a trespassing "scooper." Pertaining to the impugned issue, the court held that if the *Charter* were applicable to a citizen's arrest,[72] section 10(a) adherence would be necessary with communication of the reason for the arrest. The court also held that section 148(2) of the *Provincial Offences Act* requires notice to the arrestee of the reason for arrest where feasible to do so. The court further noted that in some instances, an arrest is lawful despite the lack of prompt notice of the reason for arrest; that is, where it is obvious[73] or where the accused is clearly aware of the reason.[74]

4.1.2.4 Informing the Arrestee of the Right to Counsel

Section 10(b) of the *Charter* provides:

> 10. Everyone has the right on arrest or detention . . .
>
>   (b) to retain and instruct counsel without delay and to be informed of that right.

Case law has interpreted this provision of the *Charter* with respect to a citizen's arrest. The courts have held that since an arrest by a private person is the performance of a government function, an arrestee must be informed of his *Charter* rights, including his right to counsel. However, although an arrestee may have had his *Charter* rights infringed, the decision of whether the evidence obtained subsequent to the infringement is ruled inadmissible under section 24(2) of the *Charter* is not automatic. Rather, the decision to exclude the evidence must be analyzed against the possibility that the administration of justice would be brought into disrepute by its admission.

The law with respect to the section 10(b) *Charter* right to counsel vis-à-vis detention by a private citizen of another citizen follows previous discussions[75] pertaining to detention by a private citizen and the *Charter*. The courts have held that since the *Charter* does not apply to detentions imposed by a private citizen, there is no obligation on the detainor to inform the detainee of his or her right to counsel under the *Charter*.[76]

The review of some cases is helpful. In *R. v. Easterbrook*[77] the accused was arrested for shoplifting by a store security guard and was not advised of his right to counsel. Subsequent to his arrest, Easterbrook gave a statement to the security guard. At trial, Easterbrook's counsel raised the issue of the admissibility of the statement based on the

---

72 See Section 4.1.1.1 — Agent of the State versus Private Citizen. In this case, the court did not adopt the reasoning of the Alberta Court of Appeal in *Lerke* but rather left the question of the *Charter*'s applicability to citizen's arrest unanswered.

73 *R. v. Beaudette* (1957), 118 C.C.C. 295 at 297 (Ont. C.A.).

74 *Kennedy v. Tomlinson* (1959), 126 C.C.C. 175 (Ont. C.A.), leave to appeal to S.C.C. refused (1959), 20 D.L.R. (2d) 273n.

75 See Sections 9.3.2.3, 9.3.2.4, 9.3.2.5, 9.6.2, and 9.6.3.

76 *R. v. Paglialunga*, above note 17.

77 *R. v. Easterbrook* (18 July 1983), (Ont. Co. Ct.) [unreported].

infringement of Easterbrook's section 10(b) *Charter* right to be informed of his right to counsel. The court made the following statement:

> It is urged by the Crown that the logical extension of this finding would be to require a private citizen, having subdued a thief in his residence, to advise the thief of his rights under the *Charter*. While at first blush this may appear to be an anomaly, the result flows from giving a plain meaning to the wording of the legislation. The *Charter* does not say "Everyone has the right on arrest or detention by a peace officer." Rather, the *Charter* says "Everyone has the right on arrest or detention." It was open to Parliament to restrict the rights to those persons arrested by a peace officer if Parliament had so chosen.
>
> The Crown's concern should not be met by ignoring the plain meaning of the legislation. Rather, the Crown's concern should be met by applying s.24 of the *Charter* which deals with the remedies available to persons whose rights or freedoms as guaranteed by the *Charter* have been infringed or denied.

Not all courts have seen it necessary to impose this procedural requirement upon private citizens.[78]

The wording of the section 10(b) *Charter* rights given by a private person has also been addressed by the courts. It has been held that in addition to the standard warning of "You may retain and instruct counsel without delay," an arrestee must also be advised of how to access legal aid duty counsel and actually given the phone number of legal aid. An arrestee must further be advised that making a call to legal aid duty counsel is free, and that if duty counsel was not immediately available, the arrestee can remain silent and wait until a duty counsel lawyer is available. It has been held that any plain language can be used to fulfil this requirement.[79]

Pertaining to the issue of detention as opposed to arrest, reference again is made to *R. v. Paglialunga*, previously reviewed under Section 4.1.1.1 — Agent of the State versus Private Citizen. In the following extract, the court explained how an accused's right to counsel applies to detention by a private citizen.

> It is not contended the accused was under arrest. There is authority to the effect that although the requirement that the arrested person be advised of the right to counsel does not normally apply to private actions, it does apply in the case of a citizen's arrest because the action of arresting, even by a private citizen, if it is authorized by law, is taken on behalf of the state.[80]
> It was submitted, however, that the accused was detained by an agent of the state and, since there had been a failure to advise him of his right to counsel, all evidence obtained from the point of detention should be excluded under s.24(2) of the *Charter*.

---

78   See *R. v. Asante-Mensah*, [1996] O.J. No. 1821 (Ont. Gen. Div.) where the court held: "No one has suggested the ground transportation inspector (a private person) is required to communicate the s.10(b) *Charter* information to an arrestee."

79   *R. v. Nowoselski*, [2000] S.J. No. 493 (Prov. Ct.).

80   *R v. Shafie*, above note 20; *R. v. Lerke*, above note 8; *R. v. Kozuchar-Thibault*, above note 59.

. . .

In the case of *R. v. Shafie*,[81] the Ontario Court of Appeal considered whether detention within the meaning of s.10(b) of the *Charter* exists where the psychological coercion is brought about by a private person — in that case a private investigator hired by an employer to investigate alleged thefts — and not by a peace officer or other agent of the state. The investigator interviewed an employee who made incriminating statements in the course of an interview. The employee was subsequently arrested by police and charged with theft. As in the instant case, it was not alleged that the employee was under arrest but it was contended that the employee was detained during the interview in the private investigator's office. The employee had been brought to the office for the interview by his superior who believed that it would have been an act of insubordination if the employee had refused to go. The interview was tape-recorded. The office door was closed but not locked. Again, as in this case, there was no physical restraint or touching of the accused and the evidence was that if he had refused to answer the questions or tried to leave, he would have been permitted to do so. On these facts, the Court of Appeal concluded that there existed a sufficient degree of psychological coercion to meet the test of detention.

[In *R. v. Shafie*[82]] Mr. Justice Krever reviewed the cases of *R. v. J.M.G.*,[83] *R. v. Lerke*,[84] and *R. v. MacDonald*[85] and concluded as follows:

> It is apparent from the cases to which I have referred that the weight of judicial opinion is, although perhaps not authority in the strict sense, that actions that at the hands of the police or other state or government agents would be a detention do not amount to detention within the meaning of s.10(b) of the *Charter* when done by private or non-governmental persons. However weakly this conclusion might be based on authority, I believe it is supported by principle.

In *R. v. Shafie*,[86] the defence had submitted that although the private action may not trigger the *Charter*, when the state subsequently seeks to rely on evidence obtained by private action, the earlier breach of s.10(b) would then engage s.24(2) of the *Charter*. Mr. Justice Krever rejected that submission, stating:

> In my view, however, the question of whether a person's s.10(b) rights were infringed must be tested at the time the alleged detention occurred. Any other conclusion would result in the judicialization of private relationships beyond the point that society could tolerate. The requirement that advice about the right to counsel must be given by a schoolteacher to a pupil, by an employer to an

---

81   *Ibid.*
82   *Ibid.*
83   (1986), 29 C.C.C. (3d) 129 (Ont. C.A).
84   Above note 8.
85   (1988), 41 C.C.C. (3d) 75 (N.S.C.A.).
86   Above note 20.

employee or a parent to a child, to mention only a few relationships, is difficult to contemplate.

Therefore the court concluded that the appellant's interview by his employer's private investigator did not amount to a detention within the meaning of s.10(b) of the *Charter*. As no *Charter* right had been breached, the evidence of the statements was properly admissible at trial.

I adopt the reasoning in the *Shafie* case and conclude that there was not a detention within the meaning of s.10(b) of the *Charter* when Wylie stopped the accused on the roadside . . . Therefore, there being no breach of the accused's right to counsel under s.10(b) of the *Charter*, the application to exclude the evidence obtained by the police is dismissed.

4.1.2.5   Informing the Arrestee of the Right to Silence

At common law, a person is not required to answer the questions of another person, whether that be a police officer or a private investigator, unless compelled by some duty in law. This basic tenant of the common law is often discussed in conjunction with a citizen's right not to be arbitrarily detained. If a person does not wish to be questioned, he or she may simply walk away unless reasonable and probable grounds exist upon which only police may arrest. This common law rule is often referred to as the right to silence.

Since the commencement of the *Charter* era, however, the right to silence has taken on a whole new meaning. Under the *Charter*, the informing of an arrestee of his or her right to silence is a duty imposed on police and agents of the state that becomes relevant subsequent to every police officer's detention or arrest or every private citizen's arrest. There is no provision in the *Criminal Code* addressing the issue of right to silence. However, section 7 of the *Charter* has been held by the courts to apply and it provides:

> 7.   Everyone has the right to life, liberty and security of the person and the right not to be deprived thereof except in accordance with the principles of fundamental justice.

As is apparent, the duty to inform an arrestee of his or her right to silence is not expressly stated. The duty was interpreted by the Supreme Court of Canada as one of the principles of fundamental justice in *R. v. Hebert*.[87] In this case, the court considered whether a statement made by a detainee to an undercover police officer violated his right to remain silent. The court concluded that the basis for the right is the freedom to choose whether or not to make a statement to the authorities. The court held that the use of an undercover officer to obtain information violated this right because the accused was tricked into making a statement. The court went on to rule that the duty to inform a person of his or her right to silence, however, is not absolute and does not apply to situations where

* the person is not detained or arrested;
* the person makes voluntary statements to a person who is not a police officer or agent of the state;

---

87   [1990], 2 S.C.R. 151.

- the person is merely observed and no active attempt is made to elicit information; or

- the person has retained counsel notwithstanding that counsel is not present.

Based on the above, it is apparent that this duty does not apply to police or agents of the state who apply tricks to elicit statements prior to detention or arrest. The ruling of the court also means that while a private investigator is required to inform a subject of his right to silence if the person is being detained post arrest for police, there is no such duty on a private investigator if a subject is being detained prior to an arrest or for reasons other than a criminal investigation.

Where private investigators make an arrest, the duty to inform an arrestee of his right to silence must include a warning that the arrestee has nothing to hope from any promise of favour, and nothing to fear from any threats. The arrestee must also be told that anything said by him may be taken down in writing and used as evidence against him.[88]

4.1.2.6 Delivering the Arrestee Forthwith to a Police Officer

The legislation relevant to this issue is section 494 of the *Criminal Code* and sections 9 and 10 of the *Charter*. The *Criminal Code* provides:

> 494(3) Any one other than a peace officer who arrests a person without a warrant shall forthwith deliver the person to a peace officer.

The *Charter* provides:

> 9. Everyone has the right not to be arbitrarily detained or imprisoned.
>
> 10. Everyone has the right on arrest or detention . . .
>
> (c) to have the validity of the detention determined by way of *habeas corpus* and to be released if the detention is not lawful.

The courts have held that the word "deliver" found in section 494(3) of the *Criminal Code* does not mean a private citizen who has made a citizen's arrest must take her prisoner to the police. Rather, the courts have held that it is sufficient that the arrestor simply contact police and upon their attendance turn the accused over to them.[89] The courts have further held that the word "forthwith" does not mean "instantly," but merely as soon as reasonably possible or practicable under all the circumstances.[90]

Pertaining to the issue of "arbitrarily" found in section 9 of the *Charter*, the courts have held that in certain circumstances, such as police R.I.D.E. spot checks, blanket arrest or detention policies are in the public interest and therefore can be saved by section 1 of the *Charter*. However, where store investigators have a policy of holding every arrestee for police regardless of the length of time for police arrival or of the bona fides of the arrest, a court may find such a practice to be arbitrary.[91] To avoid such an accusation, store inves-

---

88 *R. v. Nowoselski*, above note 79.

89 *R. v. Dean* (1991), 5 C.R. (4th) 176 (Ont. Gen. Div.).

90 *R. v. Cunningham and Ritchie*, above note 34.

91 *R. v. Dean*, above note 89.

tigators must be aware that the decision to release an arrestee is discretionary if the arrestee cannot be turned over to police "forthwith."

A final legal issue to address in this section is the difference between arrests by police and arrests by private citizens as it pertains to the release of an arrestee. In a case from Ontario, an accused argued that section 495(2)(e), the section pertaining to arrest without a warrant by a peace officer, should apply to section 494, arrest without a warrant by any person. Specifically, section 495(2)(e) provides: "A peace officer shall not arrest a person without warrant . . . in any case where . . . he has no reasonable grounds to believe that, if he does not so arrest the person, the person will fail to attend court in order to be dealt with according to law." In other words, one reason for arrest is to ensure attendance in court, and if attendance in court is not a concern, then all other things being equal, a subject should be summonsed as opposed to being arrested. Defence counsel was in effect seeking to restrict a citizen's power of arrest to circumstances where a citizen had a concern the subject would not attend court.

In response to this seemingly ridiculous argument, the court stated:

> In my opinion Parliament has chosen to set out different requirements for citizens arresting without a warrant and for police officers doing the same. It is clear from s.495 that police officers are more limited and it is expected they will have definitive knowledge of categories of offences unlike the private citizens acting in a state of urgency or emergency. Paragraph (e) of ss.(2) deals with whether a police officer has reasonable grounds to believe the person is unlikely to attend court if not arrested. Clearly this is not within the purview of the private citizen in circumstances where the private citizen's power would apply. The *Bail Reform Act* gave new powers to police officers in exercising discretion over arrest and release. Such powers are clearly not suitable for private citizens. I find that the restrictions of s.495(2) of the Code do not apply to citizen's arrest under s.494 . . . I conclude that there is nothing unconstitutional in Parliament's having codified two separate rights for warrantless searches, one for private citizens and one for peace officers, with different criteria set for their use.[92]

This statement makes it clear that a private investigator does not have to concern herself with determining if a potential arrestee will or will not attend court. A private investigator may arrest where she has the required grounds and then simply notify the police and turn the person over forthwith.

4.1.3 Forcible Confinement and U.S. Bail Bondsmen

Section 279 of the *Criminal Code* creates the offences of kidnapping and forcible confinement. Pertaining to the offence of kidnapping, section 279(1) provides:

279(1) Every person commits an offence who kidnaps a person with intent

    (a)   to cause the person to be confined or imprisoned against the person's will;

    (b)   to cause the person to be unlawfully sent or transported out of Canada against the person's will; or

---

92 *Ibid.*

    (c) to hold the person for ransom or to service against the person's will.

    (1.1) Every person who commits an offence under ss.(1) is guilty of an indictable offence and liable

        a) where a firearm is used in the commission of the offence, to imprisonment for life and to a minimum punishment of imprisonment for a term of four years; and

        b) in any other case, to imprisonment for life.

Pertaining to the offence of forcible confinement, section 279(2) provides:

> 279(2) Every one who, without lawful authority, confines, imprisons, or forcibly seizes another person is guilty of an indictable offence and liable to imprisonment for a term not exceeding ten years.

Section 279(3) provides that it is not a defence that the person in relation to whom the offence was alleged to be committed did not resist unless the accused proves that the failure to resist was not caused by threats, duress, force, or exhibition of force. In other words, section 279(3) creates a reverse onus on the accused to prove the complainant consented to the confinement.

The offence of kidnapping is of relevance to private investigators involved in assisting foreign bail bondsmen in returning fugitives to their jurisdiction. In *R. v. Kear and Johnsen*,[93] the accused were charged with kidnapping in regard to the element of the offence of transporting a person outside of Canada against his will (section 279(1)(b)). The accused argued that they lacked specific intent as they did not have subjective knowledge that transporting the fugitive they apprehended was unlawful in Canada. The accused further argued that they had lawful authority to apprehend the fugitive on the basis of a contract with the state of Florida and that such common law contracts were recognized across foreign boundaries.

The court, however, held that ignorance of Canadian law is not a defence. The court rejected the accused's second argument as well, and held that even though foreign contracts are recognized in Canada, such recognition does not authorize the violation of Canadian sovereignty. On this basis, the court held that although the accused had the authority to arrest the fugitive in Florida and other parts of the United States, the accused had no such authority in Canada. The accused were therefore without lawful authority when they seized the fugitive and took him out of Canada. The court further noted that even American cases have held that the authority to seize absconding litigants can only be exercised within the boundaries of the United States itself.

4.2 SURVEILLANCE

Investigations involving surveillance are the mainstay of many private investigation agencies. As such, an analysis of criminal law without an examination of charges that may

---

93 (1989), 51 C.C.C. (3d) 574 (Ont. C.A.).

result from improper conduct while on a surveillance would be incomplete. In this section, the provisions of the *Criminal Code* addressed include those related to

+ criminal harassment,
+ trespass by night,
+ intimidation,
+ mischief, and
+ electronic surveillance.

4.2.1   Criminal Harassment

Section 264, introduced by Parliament in 1993, is the anti-stalking provision of the *Criminal Code*. It provides:

> 264(1) No person shall, without lawful authority and knowing that another person is harassed or recklessly as to whether the other person is harassed, engage in conduct referred to in subsection (2) that causes that other person reasonably, in all the circumstances, to fear for their safety or the safety of anyone known to them.
>
> (2)   The conduct mentioned in subsection (1) consists of:
>
> (a)   repeatedly following from place to place the other person or anyone known to them;
>
> (b)   repeatedly communicating with, either directly or indirectly, the other person or anyone known to them;
>
> (c)   besetting or watching the dwelling-house, or place where the other person, or anyone known to them, resides, works, carries on business or happens to be; or
>
> (d)   engaging in threatening conduct directed at the other person or any member of their family.
>
> (3)   Every person who contravenes this section is guilty of:
>
> (a)   an indictable offence and is liable to imprisonment for a term not exceeding five years; or
>
> (b)   an offence punishable on summary conviction.

No reported cases were located pertaining to private investigators being charged under this section.[94] However, the Canadian Press has reported a harassment complaint against a private investigator in which the complainant sought a peace bond. The complainant,

---

94   As mentioned earlier, many cases go unreported. The registrar's office from Ontario has reported that there have been cases where private investigators have been charged under this section. However, Mr. James Cornish, author of *The Criminal Lawyers' Guide to the Law of Criminal Harassment and Stalking* (Aurora: Canada Law Book, 1999), reports that in the research for his book, no cases against private investigators were found.

who was in a custody dispute with her ex-husband, alleged that a private investigator was openly conducting surveillance of her outside of her home. The complainant further alleged that the private investigator even used a pretext on one occasion to gain access to her home. The private investigator admitted she entered the complainant's home under false pretences but claimed the entry was justified as it was what she was hired to do. Manitoba's provincial registrar reported that the private investigator's conduct had not crossed the line to imperil her private investigator's licence. The complainant's motion for a peace bond against the private investigator was denied.[95]

In cases of criminal harassment that have been reported by legal publishers, the courts have held that in order to convict, the Crown must prove the following:

- The accused engaged in the conduct set out in sections 246(2)(a), (b), (c), or (d).

- The complainant was harassed.

- The accused knew that the complainant was harassed or was reckless or wilfully blind as to whether the complainant was harassed;.

- The conduct of the accused caused the complainant to fear for his or her safety or for the safety of anyone known to him or her.

- The complainant's fear was, in all the circumstances, reasonable.

In other words, the Crown is only required to prove a causal connection between the prohibited conduct and the fear that the victim has for her safety or the safety of anyone known to her. It is not necessary for the Crown to prove that the accused knows that the other person feared for her safety, but it is necessary to prove that the accused knows her conduct could cause fear.[96] With regard to the last test for the offence, the court held that pre-charge conduct is admissible as going to the issue of whether the complainant's fear was reasonable in all the circumstances.[97]

By way of defence arguments, the courts have held that for the behaviour listed in section 264(2) to be criminal in nature, there must be an effect on the psychological integrity, health, or well-being of the victim in a *substantial* way. Furthermore, there is a valid defence if the accused can prove that he was acting with lawful authority or with an honestly held belief that his behaviour was not known to the complainant and if his conduct was not wilfully blind or reckless.[98]

---

95 "Anti-Stalking Test" (Winnipeg: Canadian Press, Western Regional News, 22 June 1995).

96 *R. v. Sillipp* (1995), 99 C.C.C. (3d) 394 (Alta. C.A.), leave to appeal to the S.C.C. refused (1998), 123 C.C.C. (3d) vi. This case was cited with approval by Catzman J.A. in *R. v. Krushel* (2000), (Ont. C.A.) [unreported].

97 See Catzman J.A.'s comments in *R. v. Krushel* (2000), (Ont. C.A.), [unreported], where he cited with approval *R. v. Ryback* (1996), 105 C.C.C. (3d) 240 (B.C.C.A.). See also K. Craven, "Anti-Stalking Law Does Not Violate *Charter*" *Lawyers Weekly* (10 March 2000) at 7.

98 *R. v. Sillipp*, above note 96.

This last statement may appear to be a valid line of defence for a private investigator charged under this section as his surveillance function is a lawful and legitimate function of social value.[99] However, the courts have also held that the conduct of a private investigator does not make lawful that which is unlawful for a private citizen.[100] Therefore, caution should be used not to overstep the law in this regard.

A final defensive tactic to address in this section is that of the *Charter*. It has been argued that section 264 of the *Criminal Code* violates section 7 of the *Charter* by being excessively vague, and further that it violates section 2(b) of the *Charter* by infringing freedom of expression. The courts, however, have rejected both arguments. With regard to the section 7 *Charter* argument, the courts have held that the charge was not excessively vague as there is no chance that a morally innocent person could be convicted of the offence. The courts have held that the *actus reus* of the offence as listed in section 246(2) meets discernible standards of nature, cause, and effect. The courts have held that the *mens rea* requires an intention to engage in the prohibited conduct, or at a minimum, to be wilfully blind or reckless of the conduct. The *mens rea* component, therefore, does allow for the defence of honest mistake. Accordingly, the morally innocent accused who honestly believes that his conduct was not known to the complainant and who was not reckless or wilfully blind would escape criminal liability.[101]

With relation to the section 2(b) *Charter* argument, in conducting a section 1 *Charter* proportionality analysis utilizing the *Oakes*[102] test, the courts have held that for the behaviour listed in section 264(2) to be criminal in nature, there must be an effect on the psychological integrity, health, or well-being of the victim in a *substantial* way. In demonstrating the limits Parliament had in place to prevent a miscarriage of justice, the courts have stated that there is a defence if the accused is acting with lawful authority. In one particular case a court reasoned that "[t]his eliminates the risk of lawful labour picketers being caught or anyone else who was acting with lawful authority such as a process server, etc."[103] As stated above, this statement may appear to be a valid line of defence for a private investigator charged under this section as his or her surveillance function is a lawful and legitimate function of social value.

4.2.2 Trespass by Night

Section 177 of the *Criminal Code* is the offence known as Trespass by Night. It provides:

> 177. Every one who, without lawful excuse, the proof of which lies upon him, loiters or prowls at night on the property of another person near a dwelling-house situated on that property is guilty of an offence punishable on summary conviction.

---

99 *Druken v. RG Fewer & Associates Inc.* (1998), 84 A.C.W.S. (3d) 599 (Nfld. S.C.).

100 *R. v. Andsten and Petrie* (1960), 32 W.W.R. 329 (B.C.C.A.).

101 *R. v. Sillipp*, above note 96.

102 *R. v. Oakes*, [1986] 1 S.C.R. 103.

103 *R. v. Sillipp*, above note 96.

With regard to this section, a few issues require further explanation. Section 2, the definitions section of the *Criminal Code*, defines "night" as the "period between nine o'clock in the afternoon and six o'clock in the forenoon of the following day." The term "dwelling-house" is defined in section 2 as the "whole or part of any building or structure that is kept or occupied as a permanent or temporary residence, and includes a building within the cartilage of a dwelling-house that is connected to it by a doorway and a unit that is designed to be mobile and to be used as a permanent or temporary residence."

The section essentially creates two offences, those being prowling and loitering. The essence of loitering is the conduct of someone who is wandering about apparently without precise destination.[104] It is conduct that essentially has nothing reprehensible about it as long as it does not take place on private property where the loiterer has no business. The substance of prowling is to traverse stealthily in the sense of furtively, secretly, clandestinely, or moving by imperceptible degrees. The Crown need not prove that the accused is looking for an opportunity to carry out an unlawful purpose. Where prowling is made out, the accused is required to prove he had a lawful excuse.[105]

There has been a case where two private investigators were charged with this offence. The private investigators were retained by a husband to make inquiries into the infidelity of his wife. The private investigators conducted their surveillance by lingering on the wife's property, hanging around her house, listening at her windows, and finally demanding admission to speak to a man they believed was inside. The Court of Appeal held that the purpose for their investigation did not justify the trespass committed and was not a lawful excuse. The court further held that the accused's belief — which they claimed derived from a custom long followed by private detectives — that they had a right to enter private property and remain thereon to carry out a lawful investigation did not negative intent. The mistake was one of law, not of fact, and the intent lay in the fact that the accused deliberately did those things that were forbidden under the *Criminal Code*. The court also rejected the rather fanciful argument that the accused was not loitering but in fact was working and busy at the time.[106]

4.2.3 Intimidation

It is conceivable that a charge could be laid against a private investigator under section 423 of the *Criminal Code* dealing with intimidation. Section 423 states:

(1)   Every one who, wrongfully and without lawful authority, for the purpose of compelling another person to abstain from doing anything that he has a lawful right to do, or do anything that he has a lawful right to abstain from doing . . .

---

104 *R. v. Cloutier* (1991), 66 C.C.C. (3d) 149 at 154 (Que. C.A.).
105 *R. v. Willis* (1987), 37 C.C.C. (3d) 184 (B.C. Co. Ct.). The prowler acts with a purpose: *R. v. McLean* (1971), 1 C.C.C. (2d) 277 (Alta. Mag. Ct.).
106 *R. v. Andsten and Petrie*, above note 100.

(c) persistently follows that person about . . .

(f) besets or watches the dwelling-house or place where that person resides, works, carries on business, or happens to be . . .

is guilty of an offence punishable on summary conviction.

No cases were found where private investigators were charged or convicted of this offence. However, as private investigators may be seen by the law as agents for their clients, they must ensure that they are not being used for an unlawful purpose. It is noteworthy that section 423(2) provides a defence to a person who approaches a dwelling for the sole purpose of obtaining information. Such a person does not watch or beset within the meaning of this section.

4.2.4 Mischief

The charge of mischief under section 430 is also an offence that could conceivably be laid against a private investigator performing a surveillance function. The offence is found in Part XI of the *Criminal Code* entitled "Wilful and Forbidden Acts in Respect of Certain Property." Section 428 of Part XI defines "property" to mean "real and personal corporeal property."

Section 430 provides:

430(1) Every one commits mischief who willfully

(a) destroys or damages property,

(b) renders property dangerous, useless, inoperative or ineffective,

(c) obstructs, interrupts, or interferes with the lawful use, enjoyment or operation of property, or

(d) obstructs, interrupts, or interferes with any person in the lawful use, enjoyment or operation of property.

The courts have held that "enjoyment of property," as provided for in section (1)(c), refers to "use" or "pleasure," and that "operation" applies to commercial, institutional, or industrial enterprise.[107]

Section 430 must be read in conjunction with section 429. Section 429, which is a defence to the charge, provides:

429(2) No person shall be convicted of an offence under section 430 to 466 where he proves that he acted with legal justification or excuse and with colour of right.

The courts have held that the word "and" should be read as "or." It is sufficient if the accused establishes that he acted with legal justification or excuse, or with colour of right.

---

107 E.L. Greenspan & M. Rosenberg, *Martin's Annual Criminal Code 2000* (Toronto: Canada Law Book, 1999) at 666.

Colour of right means an honest belief in a state of facts which, if they existed, would be a legal justification or excuse.[108]

Similar to the offence of intimidation, there is a further defence to a charge of mischief. Section 430(7) provides:

> 430(7) No person commits mischief within the meaning of this section by reason only that he attends at or near or approaches a dwelling-house or place for the purpose only of obtaining or communicating information.

No reported decisions pertaining to the offence of mischief were found involving private investigators. Elliott Goldstein, a lawyer in Ontario and author of *Visual Evidence: A Practitioner's Manual*,[109] reports that most cases where people have been charged with mischief as it pertains to video surveillance are situations where the video was a stand-alone device and not occurrences where the video was operated by a person. Goldstein further reports that with respect to the defence in section 429, a person undoubtedly would be legally justified in conducting video surveillance to watch his own residence, or to monitor an employer's buildings and contents. Finally, with respect to the defence in section 430(7), Goldstein reports that it could be argued that conducting video surveillance at or near a dwelling house falls within this exception. Goldstein recommends that to protect oneself and an employer from a charge of mischief, an individual is well advised to discuss with his or her lawyer whether legal justification or colour of right exists before commencing any surreptitious video surveillance. All discussions should be documented and records of the events leading up to the surveillance should be kept.[110]

Although no charges have been reported wherein private investigators have been charged with mischief, mischief charges have been laid in relation to the improper use of micro video cameras, a tool commonly used in the private investigative community. In *R. v. Campbell*,[111] the accused, a former high school shop teacher, mounted a micro video camera into a hole in the top of his shoe and attached it to a camera inside a waist pouch. He then proceeded to walk around the Canadian National Exhibition and record the view under the dresses of unsuspecting females. The court referred to such conduct as a serious invasion of privacy, but only imposed a conditional discharge on the accused with probation for eighteen months and 150 hours of community service work. In a similar vein is *R. v. Kewageshig*.[112] In this case the accused, a computer technician at the Canadian Institute of Chartered Accountants, was alleged to have installed a micro video camera under the desk of a thirty-two-year-old female employee. The camera was located when the victim complained about computer problems she was having. When another technician attended

---

108 *Ibid.* at 664. See also *R. v. Creaghan* (1982), 1 C.C.C. (3d) 339 (Ont. C.A.) and *R. v. Ninos and Walker*, [1964] 1 C.C.C. 326 (N.S.S.C.).

109 (Toronto: Carswell) [looseleaf].

110 E. Goldstein, "CCTV and the Law — A Room With A View" *Canadian Security* (November/December 1999) at 22.

111 (1998), (Ontario Court of Justice) [unreported].

112 (1999), (Ontario Court of Justice) [unreported].

her work station, he located the camera and wiring leading to a VCR hidden behind a file cabinet. The accused was charged with mischief for his efforts.

Notwithstanding the lack of charges, various academics have discussed this issue as it pertains to the unethical behaviour of some private investigators who entrap their subjects. Such occurrences are often related to investigations into persons in which there is an issue about the integrity of an injury claim. The commentator alleges that some private investigators have been known to create situations by deflating a subject's tires, leaving objects on a subject's driveway, or other ruses in which a subject party may be tempted to use physical exertion. It was concluded that these types of occurrences could result in a charge of mischief.[113]

Before leaving this section it should be noted that for the current computer age, Parliament has included in this section of the *Criminal Code* a subsection dealing with mischief to data. It provides:

430(1.1) Every one commits mischief who wilfully

(a)   destroys or alters data;

(b)   renders data meaningless, useless or ineffective;

(c)   obstructs, interrupts or interferes with the lawful use of data; or

(d)   obstructs, interrupts or interferes with any person in the lawful use of data or denies access to data to any person who is entitled to access thereto.

4.2.5 Electronic Surveillance

The issues surrounding electronic surveillance are of intrigue to many and are understood by few. It is a very complex area of the law, especially as it pertains to the police and other public sector investigators. The following is not a detailed review of the law with regard to electronic surveillance, but rather an overview of the offences that are applicable to private sector investigators.

According to some Canadian commentators, audio surveillance, or the monitoring or recording of conversations or sounds, is a commonplace activity. The easiest and cheapest method to conduct this surveillance is simply to place a small cassette recorder in the desired location. When it is impossible to gain access to that location, it is not unusual to install remote audio surveillance equipment. These commentators report that the most common remote audio surveillance method is telephone bugging or tapping. Telephone

---

113 See R. Thomas, *Entrapment Issues: Some Surprising Answers and Dangers* (Austin, TX: National Association of Investigative Specialists, 1997) at <www.pimall.com/nais/n.entrap.html>. See also E.F. Geddes, "The Private Investigator and the Right to Privacy" (1989) 17 Alta. L. Rev. 256 at 270.

bugging or tapping is the intercepting of information anywhere between the phone and the exchange, or transmitting directly to a remote receiver.[114]

For the purposes of private investigators in their capacity as private persons, there is a general prohibition against the interception of the private communication of others by the use of electronic surveillance.[115] Section 184, located under Part VI of the *Criminal Code*, which is entitled "Invasion of Privacy," provides:

184(1) Every one who, by means of any electro-magnetic, acoustic, mechanical or other
    device, wilfully intercepts private communication is guilty of an indictable offence and
    liable to imprisonment for a term not exceeding five years.

In addition to private conversations between people together in a place, this section prohibits the interception of private communications on private telephones, e-mail or voicemails to name a few. The issue of e-mails becomes more complex if there is no reasonable expectation of privacy, as may be the case in a workplace.

In addition to the penalty provision of section 184(1), section 194(1) of the *Criminal Code* also grants a punitive tort award as follows:

194(1) Subject to subsection (2),[116] a court that convicts an accused of an offence under s.184,
    s.184.5, s.193 or s.193.1 may, on application of a person aggrieved, at the time sentence was imposed, order the accused to pay to that person an amount not exceeding
    five thousand dollars.

This section is an anomaly in criminal law, as it permits a court that convicts a person of an offence under section 184 (unlawful interception) or section 193 (unlawful possession

---

114 D.J. Hawkins & E. Konstan, *The Canadian Private Investigator's Manual* (Toronto: Emond
    Montgomery, 1996) at 141. At page 144 they report that such devices can be installed by (1)
    hook switch defeat, which picks up all conversations in the area of the telephone and can be
    accessed by tapping the existing telephone line; (2) hot wired microphone, which can take an
    additional feed without interfering with the original wiring allowing monitoring by transmitter; (3) micro phonic bell, in which the mechanism that causes the ring can be rewired as a listening device; (4) spare wires, almost all telephones have them for additional hookups; (5)
    mouthpiece transmitter, which transmits all sounds in the room to a nearby receiver and is
    powered by the telephone's own microphone placed inside the handset; and (6) direct feed
    infinity transmitter, which is powered from a main electrical power supply. Any microphone
    directly attached to such a transmitter will continuously feed a receiver. This tap equipment
    can be purchased inexpensively through retail electrical equipment stores. Further, cordless
    and cell phones can be intercepted by commercially purchased multi-frequency scanners.
115 This is not to be confused with the view of one Canadian commentator who reports that there
    is no offence either under the *Criminal Code* or under the common law of being either an
    eavesdropper or a "peeping tom": see E.F. Geddes, "The Private Investigator and the Right to
    Privacy" (1989) 17 Alta. L. Rev. 256 at 271. She relies upon *The King v. County of London
    Quarter Sessions Appeal Committee*, [1948] 1 K.B. 670 (C.A.), and *Frey v. Fedoruk, Stone and Watt*,
    [1950] S.C.R. 517.
116 Persons who commence actions under Part II of the *Crown Liability Act*.

of interception devices) to order punitive damages be awarded to a person aggrieved of the offence. The order is only to be made on application by the aggrieved person and must be made at the time of sentencing. If the amount of damages is not paid forthwith, section 194(3) permits the order to be treated as if it were a civil judgment for enforcement purposes. Application for this order may not be made where an aggrieved person has already commenced civil proceedings.

Section 183 of the *Criminal Code* provides a number of definitions relevant to section 184. "Electro-magnetic, acoustic, mechanical or other device" is defined as "[a]ny device or apparatus that is used or is capable of being used to intercept private communications but does not include a hearing aid used to correct subnormal hearing of the user to not better than normal hearing." The definition of "intercept" includes "[l]istening to, recording, or acquiring a communication or acquiring the substance, meaning or purport thereof." "Private communications" is defined as follows:

> Any oral communication, or any telecommunication, that is made by an originator who is in Canada or is intended by the originator to be received by a person who is in Canada and that is made under circumstances in which it is reasonable for the originator to expect that it will not be intercepted by any person other than the person intended by the originator to receive it, and includes any radio-based telephone communication that is treated electronically or otherwise for the purpose of preventing intelligible reception by any person other than the person intended by the originator to receive it.

The only exception that applies to private persons is if there is consent by one of the parties to the communication. Section 184(2)(a) of the *Criminal Code* provides:

> 184(2)(a) Subsection (1) does not apply to a person who has the consent to intercept, express or implied, of the originator of the private communication or of the person intended by the originator thereof to receive it.

In 1993 Parliament further clarified the meaning of consent to interception by adding section 183.1 of the *Criminal Code*. It provides:

> 183.1 Where a private communication is originated by more than one person or is intended by the originator thereof to be received by more than one person, a consent to the interception thereof by any one of those persons is sufficient consent for the purposes of any provision of this Part.

Another Canadian commentator reports the most important issue to private sector investigators is that of consent to record a conversation, as frequently conversations may be monitored at the request of a client who would be one of the parties to it. As seen in section 184(2)(a) of the *Criminal Code*, interception of such communications is exempted where the originator or recipient has given implicit or explicit consent. Implicit consent includes situations where the person recording is a party to the conversation notwithstanding the other party or parties are not aware they are being taped.[117]

---

117 E.F. Geddes, "The Private Investigator and the Right to Privacy" (1989) 17 Alta. L. Rev. 256 at 271.

There have been cases wherein the surreptitious recording of a conversation between a private investigator and a subject party has been acknowledged and accepted into evidence by the courts. Typically in these cases the private investigator has acknowledged to the court that he wore a wire unknown to the person he was interviewing and later transcribed the conversation to paper and tendered the written transcription as evidence.[118] In one particular case, a private investigator tape-recorded discussions between two persons where he was a third party to the conversation. The two other parties did not know their conversation was being recorded. The court admitted into evidence the testimony of the private investigator wherein he quoted what he had transcribed from the tapes. The court took no issue with the legality of the private investigator's practice of surreptitiously tape-recording a conversation between two parties where the private investigator was a third party to the conversation.[119] It is noteworthy that section 189, pertaining to notice of intention to produce evidence, does not apply to the taping of a conversation with a recording device where the person recording was a party to the conversation because it is not an interception of private communications under section 184.[120]

It should be noted that in addition to the *Criminal Code* provisions for electronic surveillance, there are provincial statutes, such as the Ontario *Telephone Act*,[121] which prohibit the attachment of any recording or transmitting devices to telecommunications equipment without approval.[122]

It should also be recognized that the prohibition against intercepting private communications does not prohibit the use of video surveillance equipment because it does not necessarily intercept audio communication and because there is no criminal sanction against photographing or filming people or property open to public view.[123] Section 284(1) of the

---

118 *Giffen v. Quesnel* (1995), 16 M.V.R. (3d) 252 (B.C.S.C.); *Nintendo of America Inc. v. 798824 Ont. Ltd.* (1991), 35 C.P.R. (3d) 1 (F.C.T.D.); *GEAC J&E Systems Ltd. v. Craig Erickson Systems Inc.* (1992), 46 C.P.R. (3d) 25 (Ont. Gen. Div.).

119 *Smith v. Smith*, [1983] 23 A.C.W.S. (2d) 187 (B.C.S.C.).

120 In *R. v. Becker* (1978), 43 C.C.C. (2d) 356 (Ont. C.A.), the court held that Part VI has no application where the conversation is merely overheard by a third party without the use of any mechanical or other device. Similarly, in *R. v. Gamble and Nichols* (1978), 40 C.C.C. (2d) 415 (Alta. S.C.A.D.), the court held where the recipient of the conversation testifies as to its contents, the provisions of this Part have no application.

121 R.S.O. 1990, c. T.4, ss. 110–113. For telephone recording legislation by state for the U.S.A., reference: <http://aclu.org/issues/cyber/phonelaw.html> or <http://www.rcfp.org/taping/index.html>.

122 See *Re Copeland and Adamson* (1972), 28 D.L.R. (3d) 26 at 29 (Ont. H.C.J.) for an example of lawyer Clayton Ruby attempting to argue that the court should grant a motion ordering "to apprehend members and civilian employees of the Toronto Metropolitan Police Department who have committed an offence against s. 112 of the *Telephone Act* (listening to another's phone conversation and divulging the information) and to lay informations before the proper tribunal and prosecute and aid in the prosecution of such [police officers]."

123 *Druken v. RG Fewer & Associates Inc.*, above note 99.

Criminal Code would only apply to the use of video surveillance equipment if it was used to intercept private third-party communications. Therefore, when conducting video surveillance, it may be wise to turn the audio-recording equipment off.[124]

Oddly enough, there have been cases where courts have held that pager messages are not private communications since the pager simply broadcast a message to those who may happen to hear or overhear it.[125]

For those conducting investigations in British Columbia, a policy to be aware of is the ICBC Private Investigators Guidelines, which provide as follows:

> ICBC requires, as a condition of retaining any private investigator in British Columbia, that the investigator conduct investigations in a reasonable manner and in accordance with the following standards:
>
> . . .
>
> (8)   Conversations must never be electronically recorded surreptitiously. It is permissible for a conversation (i.e. a witness interview) to be electronically recorded only if it is done openly with all participants agreeing in advance that this is acceptable to them. Investigators should begin a tape-recorded interview by having the interviewee state on tape their agreement to the method of recording.[126]

4.2.5.1   Tracking Devices

Section 492.1 of the *Criminal Code* provides for the granting of a warrant to authorize the use of a tracking device. It provides:

> 492.1(1) A justice who is satisfied by information on oath in writing that there are reasonable grounds to suspect that an offence under this or any other Act of Parliament has been or will be committed and that information is relevant to the commission of the offence, including the whereabouts of any person, can be obtained through the use of a tracking device, may, at any time, issue a warrant authorizing a person named therein or a peace officer
>
> (a)   to install, maintain and remove a tracking device in or on any thing including a thing carried, used or worn by any person; and
>
> (b)   to monitor, or to have monitored, a tracking device installed in or on any thing.

---

124 Hawkins & Konstan, above note 114 at 146. At page 154 Hawkins and Konstan claim that a private investigator may be liable to a charge of Causing a Disturbance under s. 175(1)(a) or Mischief under s. 430 when obtaining videotape evidence in a public area. This notion seems to be a stretch and is not backed up with any examples.

125 *R. v. Labovac* (1989), 52 C.C.C. (3d) 551 (Alta. C.A.); *R. v. Nin* (1985), 34 C.C.C. (3d) 89 (Que. Ct. Sess.).

126 (May 1999) at 8.

(2)   A warrant issued under subsection (1) is valid for a period, not exceeding sixty days, mentioned in it.

(3)   A justice may issue further warrants under this section.

(4)   For the purposes of this section, "tracking device" means any device that, when installed in or on any thing, may be used to help ascertain, by electronic or other means, the location of any thing or person.

This section is unusual in the sense that it allows for the granting of the warrant to "a person" in addition to a peace officer. Accordingly, private investigators may attempt to obtain a warrant to use a tracking device. However, the application for such a warrant is narrow. The section provides that a warrant may be authorized only if reasonable grounds exist to suspect that an offence under the *Criminal Code* or any other Act of Parliament has been or will be committed. Therefore, a warrant may not be obtained to install a tracking device for surveillance purposes in other types of cases such as insurance or domestic investigations. The use of tracking devices without a warrant may attract criminal sanctions.[127]

Because it is perceived that the infringement of privacy is less serious in the case of a tracking device than for a typical warrant to search premises, the grounds for granting this type of warrant are less onerous than the traditional grounds for obtaining a warrant. To obtain a warrant to use a tracking device, a justice needs only to be satisfied that there are reasonable grounds *to suspect* that an offence against the *Criminal Code* or any other Act of Parliament has been or will be committed and that relevant evidence *can be* obtained. The traditional approach to authorizing a warrant is that a justice needs to be satisfied that there are reasonable grounds *to believe* that an offence against the *Criminal Code* or any other Act of Parliament has or will be committed and that relevant evidence *will be* obtained.[128] Enactment of this section follows the decision of the Supreme Court of Canada in *R. v. Wise*,[129] which held that the warrantless installation and monitoring of such a device by police in a suspect's car is a search for the purposes of section 8 of the *Charter*.

Hawkins and Konstan reviewed the legality of electronic surveillance by private investigators in their book. They argued that, although *to record or listen* to a conversation using any equipment is unlawful unless one of the persons to the conversation gives consent, the legality of electronic surveillance depends on what is being recorded or monitored and *when*. They argue that the *Criminal Code* does not prohibit the *monitoring* of a person's activities by use of audio or video equipment.[130]

It is unknown what Hawkins and Konstan base their opinion on. One could argue that the veracity of this argument may be backed up by reference to what the British Columbia

---

127 See s. 430, which provides that "(1) Every one commits mischief who wilfully . . . (c) obstructs, interrupts, or interferes with the lawful use, enjoyment or operation of property."

128 See s. 487.01(1)(a) of the *Criminal Code*.

129 [1992] 1 S.C.R. 527.

130 Above note 114 at 142.

Court of Appeal did not say in their review of an action under the British Columbia *Privacy Act* in the case of *Davis v. McArthur*.[131] In this case, the defendant private investigator had placed an electronic device on the plaintiff's vehicle to monitor a spouse's whereabouts and the court made no mention of the legality of a private investigator using such a device. Further, Elaine Geddes, in her article "The Private Investigator and the Right to Privacy"[132] states that this section applies only to the interception of communication, and probably not to the planting of locator devices.

With respect, it is believed that the better view is that currently the use of tracking devices is a criminal offence if consent is not obtained before its use. Section 492.1 of the *Criminal Code* was made law in 1993 and therefore would override the opinions or lack thereof of Hawkins and Konstan, of Geddes, and of the court in *Davis v. McArthur*, respectively. The use of such devices would be legal if the owner gave consent. It is currently a common practice for owners to put GPS or cellular tracking device technology on their vehicles or equipment. It would also be legal in a case such as *Davis v. McArthur*, a domestic case, if a private investigator installed a tracking device on a vehicle of the registered owner with consent of that person and he or she permitted his or her spouse access to the vehicle. However, other than where consent has been obtained, the use of tracking devices, if detected, may attract criminal sanctions.[133]

4.2.5.2 Number Recorders

Section 492.2 of the *Criminal Code* provides for the granting of a warrant to authorize the use of a number recorder as follows:

> 492.2(1) A justice who is satisfied by information on oath in writing that there are reasonable grounds to suspect that an offence under this or any other Act of Parliament has been or will be committed and that information that would assist in the investigation of that offence could be obtained through the use of a number recorder, may at any time issue a warrant authorizing a person named in it or a peace officer
>
> a) to install, maintain and remove a number recorder in relation to any telephone or telephone line; and
>
> (b) to monitor, or to have monitored, the number recorder.
>
> (2) When the circumstances referred to in subsection (1) exist, a justice may order that any person or body that lawfully possesses records of telephone calls originated from, or received or intended to be received at, any telephone give the records, or a copy of the records, to a person named in the order.

---

131 (1969), 10 D.L.R. (3d) 250 (B.C.S.C.), rev'd (1970), 17 D.L.R. (3d) 760 (B.C.C.A). See Section 5.3 — Provincial Privacy Legislation, for an extract of this decision.

132 (1989) 17 Alta. L. Rev. 256 at 271.

133 For a further discussion of this topic, see E. Goldstein, "Tracking in Transit: A Look at the Legal Implications of Using Tracking Devices in Company Vehicles" *Canadian Security* (April 2000) at 18.

(3)   Subsection 492.1(2) and (3) apply to warrants and orders issued under this section with such modifications as the circumstances require.[134]

(4)   For the purposes of this section, a "number recorder" means any device that can be used to record or identify the telephone number or location of the telephone from which the telephone call originates, or at which it is received or is intended to be received.

This section, like that for the use of a tracking device, is unusual because it allows for the granting of the warrant to "a person" in addition to a peace officer. Accordingly, private investigators may attempt to obtain a warrant to use a number recorder. However, the application for such a warrant is narrow. The section provides that a warrant may be authorized only if reasonable grounds exist to suspect that an offence under the *Criminal Code* or any other Act of Parliament has been or will be committed. Therefore, a warrant may not be obtained to install a number recorder for surveillance purposes in other types of cases such as insurance or domestic investigations. The use of a number recorder without a warrant may attract criminal sanctions unless consent is obtained.[135]

Like a tracking device, because it is perceived that the infringement of privacy is less serious in the case of a number recorder than a typical warrant to search premises, the grounds for granting a warrant are less onerous than the traditional grounds for obtaining a warrant. To obtain a warrant to use a number recorder, a justice needs only to be satisfied that there are reasonable grounds *to suspect* that an offence against the *Criminal Code* or any other Act of Parliament has been or will be committed and that relevant evidence can be obtained. The traditional approach to authorizing a warrant is that a justice needs to be satisfied that there are reasonable grounds *to believe* that an offence against the *Criminal Code* or any other Act of Parliament has or will be committed and that relevant evidence will be obtained.[136]

This section actually envisages two different types of orders. Subsection (1) provides for a warrant to install and monitor the number recorder. Subsection (2) provides that the justice may order that a person in possession of records of telephone calls turn those records over to a person named in the order.

No reported decisions were found involving private investigators in relation to this section. For a case discussing the admissibility of evidence attained by Bell Canada Security who have used this device, see Section 9.3.6 — Intercepted Digital Number Recorder Communications.[137]

---

134 Section 492.1 provides that "(2) A warrant issued under subsection (1) is valid for a period, not exceeding sixty days, mentioned in it; (3) A justice may issue further warrants under this section."

135 See s. 430 of the *Criminal Code*, which provides that "(1) Every one commits mischief who wilfully . . . (c) obstructs, interrupts, or interferes with the lawful use, enjoyment or operation of property." See also the provisions of the *Ontario Telephone Act*, R.S.O. 1990, c. T.4, ss. 110–113.

136 See s. 487.01(1)(a) of the *Criminal Code*.

137 *R. v. Fegan* (1993), 80 C.C.C. (3d) 356 (Ont. C.A.).

4.2.5.3   Cellular and Cordless Phone Communications

The argument that intercepting cellular and cordless telephone communications is not a breach of section 184 of the *Criminal Code* is taken from the definition of private communications. Section 183 of the *Criminal Code* defines "private communication" to include communications that are made in circumstances in which it is *reasonable* for the originator to expect that it will not be intercepted by any person other than the person intended by the originator to receive it. It was argued that in some circumstances it was reasonable for originators to expect that their communications would be intercepted.

Cordless Telephones: This line of defence requires some knowledge about the technology itself. As it pertains to cordless telephones, the "first generation" cordless phones were composed of a base unit that receives the signal and transmits it to the hand-held portion by means of a pair of FM radio channels. Anyone with a scanner can dial the frequency of the FM radio channels, lock the scanner on, and thereby intercept the communication. The newer second- and third-generation cordless telephones utilize various techniques to scramble the signal between the base set and the hand-held portion and thus make the interception difficult. Therefore, communications on second- and third-generation cordless telephones are viewed as private communications because it is not reasonable for such a person to expect that their communication will be intercepted. Communications on first-generation cordless telephones are not viewed as private communications, and therefore it is not an offence to intercept them.[138]

Cellular Telephones: Cellular telephones have historically been held in law as of similar technology to first-generation cordless telephones. In 1993, Parliament passed section 184.5 creating an offence for the interception of cellular telephone communications:

> 184.5(1) Every person who intercepts, by means of any electro-magnetic, acoustic, mechanical or other device, maliciously or for gain, a radio-based telephone communication, if the originator of the communication or the person intended by the originator of the communication to receive it is in Canada, is guilty of an indictable offence and liable to imprisonment for a term not exceeding five years.

This section reversed the line of cases that had held under the predecessor legislation that cellular telephone conversations were not private communications. This section now creates an offence to intercept such communications where the interception was made for gain or maliciously.[139]

---

138 *R. v. Watts* (1997), 47 C.R.R. (2d) 252 (B.C.P.C.).

139 For an example of a case where the court held that, at least in 1990, conversations over cellular telephones were private communications, see *R. v. Cheung* (1995), 100 C.C.C. (3d) 441 (B.C.S.C.). The reasoning the court gave was that while a person sending or receiving a call on a cellular telephone did face some risk of being overheard by someone who just happened to meet the combination of factors which matched a scanner to a call, the chance of someone succeeding in setting out to intercept the calls of a particular individual by scanner was small.

As seen in Section 4.2.5 — Electronic Surveillance, pertaining to section 184, section 194(1) of the *Criminal Code* also grants a punitive tort award in addition to the general criminal liability of section 184.5. Section 194(1) provides:

> 194(1) Subject to subsection (2),[140] a court that convicts an accused of an offence under s.184, s.184.5, s.193 or s.193.1 may, on application of a person aggrieved, at the time sentence was imposed, order the accused to pay to that person an amount not exceeding five thousand dollars.

For an explanation of this award, please review Section 4.2.5 — Electronic Surveillance. No case law was found pertaining to private investigators breaching this section.

4.2.5.4   Possession of Interception Equipment

A further provision in the *Criminal Code* pertaining to electronic surveillance relevant to a private investigator is that of possession of equipment capable of intercepting private communications. Section 191 provides in part:

> 191(1) Every one who possesses, sells or purchases any electromagnetic, acoustic, mechanical or other device or any component thereof knowing that the design thereof renders it primarily useful for the surreptitious interception of private communication is guilty of an indictable offence.

Possession of such equipment for any one other than a police officer requires a licence from the Solicitor General as per section 191(2)(d) of the *Criminal Code*.

In addition to the sanctions that may be imposed for possession of interception equipment, section 192 of the *Criminal Code* also allows the Crown to ask for its forfeiture. Section 192 provides:

> 192(1) Where a person is convicted of an offence under s.184 or s.191, any electro-magnetic, acoustic, mechanical or other device by means of which the offence was committed or the possession which constituted the offence, on the conviction, in addition to any punishment that is imposed, may be ordered forfeited to her Majesty whereupon it may be disposed of as the Attorney General directs.

This is a very infrequently used section of the *Criminal Code*. In *R. v. McLelland*,[141] the accused, a director with the Ontario Charities Lottery Group, was found to have in his office desk a tape recorder rigged up to his telephone, two hidden microphones in his office, and two hidden microphones in a boardroom next door. The device had an activation switch in a locked drawer of his desk. The court convicted the accused on evidence of both the accused and an expert that the design of the device rendered it primarily useful for the surreptitious interception of private communications.

On appeal, Justice Finlayson, in dissent, held that it was improper to convict an accused for possession of such a device where there was no evidence that it was used as such. In

---

140 Persons who commence actions under Part II of the *Crown Liability Act*.
141 (1986), 30 C.C.C. (3d) 134 (Ont. C.A.). Currently, there is a private investigator in Ontario on charge for this offence: *R. v. Alexander* (1999), Ottawa, (Ont. S.C.J.) [unreported].

this case, tapes were seized that contained the recordings of all the interceptions the device had been used for. In all the interceptions, the accused was a party to the conversation. Justice Finlayson further held that Parliament did not intend to make it an offence for people to record telephone calls or conversations in their own offices. He held that even if the equipment was used for an illegal purpose, that does not by itself make the possession of it illegal. He concluded that only if the equipment's exclusive use is for the surreptitious interception of private communications is its possession illegal.

Justice Finlayson's opinion was followed in a recent Ontario case, *R. v. Strano*.[142] In this case, a private investigator gave his client a body-pack micro-cassette recorder equipped with a microphone disguised as a pen. The court held that it was not satisfied that the device was necessarily designed so that its primary purpose was for the surreptitious interception of private communications. The court held that there are numerous situations in which a microphone shaped like a pen would be a useful device. He further held that micro-cassettes are commonplace devices in contemporary society.

On a related note, the courts have held that a radio receiver tuned to a police band is not a device prohibited by this section where the evidence shows that the police are aware that members of the public have receivers capable of intercepting their communications. It has been held that in such circumstances, it could not be said that the device was intercepting "private communications" as those words are defined in section 813 of the *Criminal Code*.[143]

4.2.5.5 Disclosing Private Communications

Even if private communications have been intercepted and the interceptor has not been made the subject of a criminal inquiry, the interceptor or the person who comes into possession of the intercepted communications may become criminally liable for simply disclosing those communications.

Section 193 of the *Criminal Code* provides:

193(1) Where a private communication has been intercepted by means of an electro-magnetic, acoustic, mechanical or other device without the consent, express or implied, of the originator thereof or of the person intended by the originator thereof to receive it, every one who, without the express consent of the originator thereof or of the person intended by the originator thereof to receive it, wilfully

(a) uses or discloses such private communications or any part thereof or the substance, meaning or purport thereof or of any part thereof, or

142 [2001] O.J. No. 404 (Ont. S.C.J.).

143 *R. v. Pitts* (1975), 29 C.C.C. (2d) 150 (Ont. Co. Ct.); *R. v. Comeau* (1984), 11 C.C.C. (3d) 61 (N.B.C.A.). For an overview of state scanner laws in the U.S.A., see <http://www.fordyce.org/scanning/scanning_info/scanlaws.html>; <http://www.afn.org/~jlr/radiolaw.html>; <http://www.fcc.gov>; or <http://strongsignals.net>.

(b) discloses the existence thereof,

is guilty of an indictable offence and liable to imprisonment for a term not exceeding two years.

Section 193(2) provides for a number of exceptions, including for persons who disclose private communications (a) in the course of, or for the purpose of, giving evidence in any civil or criminal proceeding or in any other proceedings in which the person may be required to give evidence on oath; or (b) in the course of, or for the purpose of, any criminal investigation if the private communication was lawfully intercepted.

Section 193.1(1) is similar to section 193 except that it pertains explicitly to radio-based telephone communications. It provides:

> 193.1(1) Every person who wilfully uses or discloses a radio-based telephone communication or who wilfully discloses the existence of such a communication is guilty of an indictable offence and liable to imprisonment for a term not exceeding two years if,
>
> (a) the originator of the communication or the person intended by the originator of the communication to receive it was in Canada when the communication was made;
>
> (b) the communication was intercepted by means of an electromagnetic, acoustic, mechanical or other device without the consent, express or implied, of the originator of the communication or of the person intended by the originator to receive the communication; and
>
> (c) the person does not have the express or implied consent of the originator of the communication or of the person intended by the originator to receive the communication.

Section 183 defines "radio based telephone communication" as "[a]ny radiocommunication within the meaning of the *Radiocommunication Act* that is made over apparatus that is used primarily for connection to a public switched telephone network."

As seen in Section 4.2.5 — Electronic Surveillance, pertaining to section 184, section 194(1) of the *Criminal Code* also grants a punitive tort award in addition to the general criminal liability of section 184.5. Section 194(1) provides:

> 194(1) Subject to subsection (2),[144] a court that convicts an accused of an offence under s.184, s.184.5, s.193 or s.193.1 may, on application of a person aggrieved, at the time sentence was imposed, order the accused to pay to that person an amount not exceeding five thousand dollars.

For an explanation of this award, please review Section 4.2.5 — Electronic Surveillance.

In British Columbia a court found that the disclosure of communications from a first-generation cordless phone that was not a private communication was nevertheless a breach of section 193.1 of the *Criminal Code*.[145] No reported decisions were found involving private investigators charged in relation to this section.

---

144 Persons who commence actions under Part II of the *Crown Liability Act*.
145 *R. v. Penna* (19 June 1997), Prince Rupert No. 18079T, (B.C.) [unreported].

4.3   PRETEXTS

A pretext has been defined as a verbal or physical deception practised on a person to persuade them to provide evidence or information they would not otherwise afford.

There are many examples given in various cases of private investigators using pretexts to gain evidence on subject parties. In *Rusche v. Insurance Corporation of British Columbia*,[146] a private investigator used the pretext of being a potential private buyer of a motor vehicle to trick the plaintiff into coming out of his house to discuss the sale of a car while a second investigator, hidden from view, made a video recording of the plaintiff's activities. In *Law Society of British Columbia v. Gravelle*,[147] a private investigator was retained by the Law Society of British Columbia to determine if Gravelle, a notary public, was engaged in an unauthorized practice of law. The private investigator attended Gravelle's office and posed as someone who needed assistance with her father's estate. During the meeting, Gravelle advised the private investigator on numerous estate law matters. The Law Society of British Columbia successfully used this evidence gained under pretext to obtain a declaration that Gravelle had engaged in a practice of law forbidden by notary publics and a declaration that she cease and desist from such activity in the future. Finally, on an ABC News 20-20 episode entitled "Information Brokers — Secrets for Sale,"[148] a private investigator revealed there are basically four rules to obtaining information by pretext. First, identify the piece of information you are after. Second, identify who the custodian or institution is that maintains it. Third, try to figure out to whom the custodian or institution would release the information and under what circumstances. Then, try to be that person.

In this section, the criminal offences explored that may arise when performing pretexts include

+ personating a peace officer,

+ personation with intent, and

+ entrance under pretext in the form of being unlawfully in a dwelling or break and enter.

After this review, the criminal sanctions pertaining to false messages and indecent and harassing phone calls will be discussed.

For a further discussion on the improper use of pretexts, please see Section 2.3.2.5 — Pretexts, and Chapter 7 — Confidentiality of Health Information — The Krever Inquiry.

---

146 (1992), 4 C.P.C. (3d) 12 (B.C.S.C.).

147 [1998] B.C.J. No. 2883 (S.C.).

148 For a full abstract of the interview on ABC 20-20, see
   <http://www.abcnews.go.com/onair/2020/transcripts/2020_99 0628info_trans.html>.

4.3.1   Personation of a Peace Officer

Section 130 of the *Criminal Code* creates the offence of personating a peace officer. It provides:

130.   Every one who

(a)   falsely represents himself to be a peace officer or a public officer, or

(b)   not being a peace officer or public officer, uses a badge or article of uniform or equipment in a manner that is likely to cause persons to believe that he is a peace officer or a public officer, as the case may be,

is guilty of an offence punishable on summary conviction.

Section 2 of the *Criminal Code* defines "peace officer" and "public officer" as follows:

"Peace Officer" includes, *inter alia,*

(a)   a mayor, warden, reeve, sheriff, deputy sheriff, sheriff's officer and justice of the peace,

(b)   a member of the Correctional Service of Canada who is designated as a peace officer pursuant to Part I of the *Corrections and Conditional Release Act,* and a warden, deputy warden, instructor, keeper, jailer guard and any other officer or permanent employee of a prison other than a penitentiary as defined in Part I of the *Corrections and Conditional Release Act,*

(c)   a police officer, police constable, bailiff, constable, or other person employed for the preservation and maintenance of the public peace or for the service or execution of civil process,

(d)   an officer or person having powers of a customs or excise officer when performing any duty in the administration of the *Customs Act,* or the *Excise Act.*

. . .

"Public Officer" includes:

(a)   an officer of customs or excise,

(b)   an officer of the Canadian Forces,

(c)   an officer of the Royal Canadian Mounted Police, and

(d)   any officer while the officer is engaged in enforcing the laws of Canada relating to revenue, customs, excise, trade, or navigation.

The provisions in this section appear to be clear. It is a summary conviction offence to either misrepresent oneself through oral communication to another person as a peace or public officer or to use a badge of some sort or some other equipment to misrepresent oneself as such.

No case law was located pertaining to Canadian private investigators committing this offence although some registrars have stated it has occurred. However, there have been a number of cases reported where others in the private sector faced this charge. For example, in *R. v. Wallance*,[149] a bailiff attended a residence, identified himself as a peace officer, and attempted to repossess some property. The court held that the term "bailiff" as per section 2 is restricted to certain officials and other persons employed for the preservation and maintenance of the public peace or for the service or execution of a civil process. The court found that Wallance was not executing a civil process because process is defined as the means whereby a court enforces obedience to its order. The court found that here the bailiff was acting as an agent of the landlord and was not acting pursuant to a court order. Accordingly, notwithstanding that Wallance was a bailiff, he was not a peace officer for the purposes of this section. As to the possession of the badges, the court acquitted the accused on the basis of his honest but mistaken belief that he was a peace officer. The court held that because of this mistaken belief, the accused had not formed the requisite intent.

An interesting exception to this section is taken from the case of *R. v. Saleman*.[150] In *Saleman* the court held that this offence could not be proven if the accused had falsely represented himself as a U.S. Sheriff's officer because section 130 requires proof of a misrepresentation as a peace officer or public officer as defined by section 2 of the *Criminal Code*; peace officer being interpreted as a Canadian peace officer. The court further held:

> When the full clothing . . . that the appellant was wearing was observed, it was seen not to be that of a police officer, but seen to what it would appear to any eye to be, I would think, a form of costume.

A final case worthy of note is an allegation of criminal conspiracy made against a firm of private investigators in England when they were found to have obtained confidential personal information from banks and government departments by various misrepresentations, including the impersonation of government officials. The House of Lords, however, held that, although the conduct may have amounted to impersonation of government officials, the facts did not amount to the offence of conspiracy as it was then understood in the criminal law.[151]

4.3.2 Personation with Intent

Section 403 of the *Criminal Code* creates the offence of Personation with Intent. It provides:

   403. Every one who fraudulently personates any person, living or dead,

      (a) with intent to gain advantage for himself or another person,

---

149 (1959), 125 C.C.C. 72 (Ont. Mag. Ct.). Note that a bailiff is included under the current *Criminal Code* definition of peace officer. This case simply demonstrates a possible defence to an action under this section.

150 (1984), 19 C.C.C. (3d) 526 (Ont. Co. Ct.).

151 *D.P.P. v. Withers*, [1974] 3 All E.R. 984 (H.L.). Although the prosecution failed, it was Gerald Dworkin's view that the offence of conspiracy had been made out: "Privacy and the Law" in J.B. Young, ed., *Privacy* (Chichester: John Wiley & Sons, 1978) at 135.

(b) with intent to obtain any property or an interest in any property, or

(c) with intent to cause disadvantage to the person whom he personates or another person,

is guilty of an indictable offence and liable to imprisonment for a term not exceeding ten years or an offence punishable on summary conviction.

The words "to gain advantage . . . [or] to obtain any property or an interest" are not restricted to pecuniary or economic advantage. Advantage is gained, for example, to avoid arrest,[152] or to gain clearance to board an airline.[153] However, the word "person" in this section means a real person, not a fictitious person.[154]

Due to the frequency of the use of pretexts, either by phone or in person, an awareness of the elements of this section is crucial to a private investigator. This section should also be read in conjunction with provincial PISGA legislation. No case law was located on this issue pertaining to private investigators.

4.3.3 Entrance under Pretext (Unlawfully in a Dwelling)

Section 350 of the *Criminal Code* is an interpretation section for section 348 (break and enter) and section 349 (being unlawfully in a dwelling house). It provides:

350. For the purposes of s.348 [Breaking and Entering With Intent to Commit an Indictable Offence, Committing an Indictable Offence or Breaking Out] and s.349 [Being Unlawfully in a Dwelling House],

(a) a person enters as soon as any part of his body or any part of an instrument that he uses is within any thing that is being entered; and

(b) a person shall be deemed to have broken and entered if

(i) he obtained entrance by a threat or *artifice* or by collusion with a person within, or

(ii) he entered without lawful justification or excuse, the proof of which lies upon him, by a permanent or temporary opening. [Emphasis added.]

In the above section, the word "artifice" is emphasized as especially applicable to private investigators who attempt to gain entry by use of a pretext. *Black's Law Dictionary*[155] defines "artifice" as "[a]n ingenious contrivance or device of some kind, and, when used in a bad sense, it corresponds with trick or fraud. It implies craftiness and deceit, and imports some element of moral obliquity." In other words, entrance by artifice equates with entrance under pretext.[156]

---

152 *R. v. Rozon* (1974), 28 C.R.N.S. 232 (Que. C.A.).

153 *R. v. Hetsberger* (1980), 51 C.C.C. (2d) 257 (Ont. C.A.).

154 *R. v. Northrup* (1982), 1 C.C.C. (3d) 210 (N.B.C.A.).

155 *Black's Law Dictionary*, 6th ed. (St. Paul: West Publishing Co., 1990) at 113.

156 In *R. v. Leger* (1976), 31 C.C.C. (2d) 413 (Ont. C.A.), the court held that "artifice" for the purposes of that case meant "a manoeuvre or stratagem such as sneaking into a premises behind someone making a lawful entry."

As mentioned, section 349 of the *Criminal Code* creates the offence of Being Unlawfully in a Dwelling House. It provides:

349(1) Everyone who without lawful excuse, the proof of which lies on him, enters or is in a dwelling-house with intent to commit an indictable offence therein is guilty of an indictable offence and liable to imprisonment for a term not exceeding ten years.

(2)   For the purposes of proceedings under this section, evidence that an accused, without lawful excuse, entered or was in a dwelling-house is, in the absence of any evidence to the contrary, proof that he entered or was in the dwelling-house with intent to commit an indictable offence therein.

Section 2 of the *Criminal Code* defines "dwelling house" as follows:

"Dwelling-house" means the whole or any part of a building or structure that is kept or occupied as a permanent or temporary residence, and includes

(a)   a building within the curtilage of a dwelling-house that is connected to it by a doorway or by a covered and enclosed passageway, and

(b)   a unit that is designated to be mobile and to be used as a permanent or temporary residence and that is being used as such a residence.

The courts have held that a motel unit is a dwelling-house for the purposes of the *Criminal Code*.[157]

There are a few more issues that should be addressed in relation to this offence. In most applications of this section, the "indictable offence therein" is theft. However, as it applies to private investigators who are unlawfully in a dwelling-house to secure information under pretext, the indictable offence arguably would be mischief.[158] It is also important to note that an accused need not have entered with the requisite intent, provided that he formulates the intent while present in the dwelling-house.[159]

No cases were located wherein a private investigator was charged with being unlawfully in a dwelling, the underlying indictable offence being mischief. However, there is a reported case wherein a private investigator was convicted of being unlawfully in a dwelling where the underlying indictable offence was assault when he refused to leave. In this case, the private investigator was retained to gather evidence of adultery. The private investigator rented a room across from the room where the suspected adultery was to take place and kept observation by way of a peep-hole. The private investigator observed the suspected adulterer and a male companion enter the room around 11:00 p.m. At about

---

157 *R. v. Henderson*, [1975] 1 W.W.R. 360 (B.C. Prov. Ct.).

158 In *R. v. E.(S.)* (1993), 80 C.C.C. (3d) 502 (N.W.T.C.A.), the court held that mischief is an included offence to being unlawfully in a dwelling-house.

159 *R. v. Higgins* (1905), 10 C.C.C. 456 (N.S.S.C.). See also E.L. Greenspan & M. Rosenberg, *Martin's Annual Criminal Code 1998* (Aurora: Canada Law Book, 1997) at 569.

4:30 in the morning, the private investigator, with the assistance of three friends, entered the unlocked room without permission. The private investigator and his accomplices immediately started taking pictures. However, the male companion awoke and engaged the private investigator in a brawl. The private investigator, having obtained the desired pictures, left the room.

At trial, the accused private investigator conceded that his entry of the dwelling-house was unlawful. However, the accused refuse to concede to the issue of whether his position as a private investigator and his quest for evidence during an investigation gave him justification to do come what may. The court held that, notwithstanding that his quest for evidence of adultery was not unlawful, there could be no lawful excuse for entering the dwelling without permission. In the alternative, the court held that even if his entry into the room was not proven to be unlawful, the fact that the accused was embroiled in a brawl indicated that he resisted the direction to leave, and was therefore in the room unlawfully after entering and committed the offence of assault therein.[160] This case reaffirms the principle that there is no colour of right attached to unlawful behaviour perpetrated by a private investigator in the realm of criminal law.[161]

4.3.4 Entrance under Pretext (Break and Enter)

As seen under the previous heading, section 350 of the *Criminal Code* explains the application of "entrance" for section 348 (break and enter) and section 349 (being unlawfully in a dwelling-house). It was also explained that the word "artifice" is especially applicable to private investigators who attempt to gain entry by use of a pretext.

The offence of break and enter is of wider application than being unlawfully in a dwelling-house. Section 348 provides:

348(1) Every one who

(a) breaks and enters a place with intent to commit an indictable offence therein,

(b) breaks and enters a place and commits an indictable offence therein, or

(c) breaks out of a place after

(i) committing an indictable offence therein, or

(ii) entering the place with intent to commit an indictable offence therein

is guilty of an indictable offence and liable

(d) to imprisonment for life, if the offence is committed in relation to a dwelling-house, or

---

160 *R. v. Massue* (1964), 55 D.L.R. (2d) 79 (Que. Q.B.).
161 See *R. v. Andsten and Petrie* (1960), 32 W.W.R. 329 (B.C.C.A.), as discussed in Section 4.2.2 — Trespass by Night. See also *R. v. Gibson*, [1976] 6 W.W.R. 484 (Sask. Dist. Ct.).

(e) to imprisonment for a term not exceeding fourteen years, if the offence is committed in relation to a place other than a dwelling house.

(2) For the purposes of proceeding under this section, evidence that an accused

(a) broke and entered a place or attempted to break and enter a place is, in the absence of evidence to the contrary, proof that he broke and entered the place or attempted to do so, as the case may be, with intent to commit an indictable offence therein; or

(b) broke out of a place is, in the absence of evidence to the contrary, proof that he broke out after

(i) committing an indictable offence therein, or

(ii) entering with intent to commit an indictable offence therein.

(3) For the purpose of this section and section 351 (possession of break-in instruments), "place" means

(a) a dwelling-house;

(b) a building or structure or any part thereof, other than a dwelling-house;

(c) a railway vehicle, a vessel, an aircraft or a trailer; or

(d) a pen or an enclosure in which fur-bearing animals are kept in captivity for commercial purposes.

There has been a case where a private investigator was charged with break and enter wherein the Crown argued that he had committed the indictable offence of mischief.[162] In this case the private investigator had passed himself off as a utility worker to gain entry into the complainant's home to obtain evidence of adultery. The court held that the accused gained entry through the use of an artifice, or a pretext, and that his profession as a private investigator was no justification for the unlawful entry. Notwithstanding this finding, the court acquitted the accused because, on the facts of the case, the Crown did not prove beyond a reasonable doubt that the accused's intention was to commit the offence of mischief; that is, to interfere with the use and enjoyment of the property of another. The following is an extract on the issue of intent to commit mischief. It is included to show the precarious grounds on which this private investigator was acquitted.

It was said that Gibson intended to obstruct, interrupt or interfere with Mrs. Boardman in the lawful use, enjoyment or operation of the dwelling house — her home. In *R. v. Wendel*,[163] a judgment of the British Columbia Court of Appeal, the accused was charged that he did unlawfully break and enter an apartment with intent to commit an indictable offence therein. The Crown there, as here, suggested that accused entered with the intention of committing the indictable offence of mischief under s.387(1)(c) or (d).

---

162 *R. v. Gibson, ibid.*
163 [1966] 57 W.W.R. 684 (B.C.C.A.).

For me there is room here for more than one view as to the intent of Gibson. His intention may have been to come and go without obstruction, interruption or interference of any sort. In fact, the interruption or interference, if any, that stemmed from Mrs. Boardman showing Gibson around the house seem not of the sort contemplated by s.387(1) — they seem, with respect, less than the wilful interruption or interference contemplated by the section.

. . .

Here the dwelling house was not vacant. Here there was more than mere entry — there was the misrepresentation. Here, to borrow the words of Tysoe J.A., when Gibson entered (at least on the second occasion) he knew the dwelling house to be occupied and that his conduct would probably cause obstruction to or interference with the lawful use and enjoyment by the owner, albeit in perhaps slight degree, and he was reckless whether this occurred or not. On the other hand, Gibson had some reason to believe and expect that his conduct probably would not cause difficulty — that he would come and go with a minimum of interruption or interference — perhaps even none.

. . .

The Crown characterized this obstruction to or interference with Mrs. Boardman as "taking up her time" — no more. I am not for a moment suggesting that what Gibson was about was an innocent purpose.

. . .

I have read *Massue v. The Queen*[164] . . . The case deals with the activities of private investigators culminating in a charge under then s.293(1) (now s.307(1)) of the Code alleging "entering" as opposed to "being in" with intent. With every respect and likely because of my own limitations, I have difficulty analyzing the decision . . . What happened after entry does not necessarily show intent at the time of entry. It is not open to me to find the offence and work back to the requisite intent at the time of entry.

Tysoe J.A. refers in *R. v. Wendel* to what the Crown must establish in this case as "intent to willfully obstruct, interrupt or interfere with the lawful use, etc." of the dwelling. It seems that this is, for the Crown, a greater chore than to establish simply "intent to obstruct, interrupt or interfere", although the distinction is not altogether clear. The words "intent" and "wilful" are not altogether useful or proper when used in conjunction. In any event, intention is what the Crown must prove. "Wilfulness" is not the key word. The Crown can take no comfort from the use of the word "wilfully" — it may be of comfort to Gibson making proof more difficult for the Crown . . . The difference may well be more apparent than real.

. . .

While Gibson may be said to have had an evil intention with respect to gaining entry by misrepresentation, it is difficult to find that he had an evil intention with respect to obstruction, interruption or interference. In fact, the evidence points the other way — the use of the truck of the Saskatchewan Power Corporation and its guileless employee were designed to gain

---

164 *R. v. Massue*, above note 160.

entrance with the least possible obstruction, interruption or interference. Had the "pretext" worked to the best conceivable hope of Gibson, one of the Boardmans would have met him at the door and given him the run of the basement not bothering to even accompany him.

. . .

All things considered, and on the whole of the evidence, I am not satisfied beyond a reasonable doubt that at the time of entry into the dwelling house, Gibson had the intention to commit an indictable offence therein. I am, of course, referring to the indictable offence of mischief under s.387(1) as that as the only one seriously suggested by the Crown. In result, I find Earnest John Gibson not guilty. Mr. Gibson, you are discharged and free to go.

As alluded to above, this is a case more so than most that is tied to its facts. It is the opinion of this writer that the issue of intent could easily have been decided in favour of the Crown. As permission to enter can only be assessed on informed consent, not consent based on misrepresentation, that is, a pretext, the entry was unlawful. As the intent to obstruct, interfere, or interrupt is an issue open to wide interpretation, a finding of mischief is not beyond conception. Therefore, this case should act as a warning to all those who are considering entering a residence under pretext of the consequences that could follow.

4.3.5   False Messages and Indecent and Harassing Telephone Calls

Section 372(1) criminalizes the tort of intentional infliction of nervous shock. It provides:

> 372(1) Every one who, with intent to injure or alarm any person, conveys or causes or procures to be conveyed by letter, telegram, telephone, cable, radio or otherwise information that he knows is false is guilty of an indictable offence and liable to imprisonment for a term not exceeding two years.

There is no case law reported with respect to this charge pertaining to private investigators. However, during the research of this book, a private investigator discussed a form of pretext of acquiring medical information by telephoning a subject person and advising him or her that a person he or she had been intimate with had tested positive for AIDS. The intent of this ruse was to provide an impetus for the person to discuss their medical and personal background. It is suggested that the conveyance of such false information may alarm the recipient and therefore may fit within the intention of this section.

The remaining two sections deal with what is commonly referred to as indecent and harassing phone calls. They provide:

> 372(2) Every one who, with intent to alarm or annoy any person, makes an indecent telephone call to that person is guilty of an offence punishable on summary conviction.
>
> (3) Every one who, without lawful excuse and with intent to harass any person, makes or causes to be made repeated telephone calls to that person is guilty of an offence punishable on summary conviction.

There is no reported case law in the legal publications on these sections pertaining to private sector investigators either. However, a case was reported in the Canadian Press from British Columbia wherein a private investigator was charged with the offence of harassing phone calls after repeatedly phoning a residence to ascertain if a subject person was home. The outcome of this matter is unknown.[165]

Other decisions interpreting the harassing and indecent phone call legislation have held that the term "harass" is synonymous with the term "annoy" and could include conduct of repeatedly telephoning a person and simply hanging up when the call is answered.[166] It has also been held that the victim of the offence must be the recipient of the harassing telephone calls. Therefore, where the calls were intercepted by someone other than the victim provided in the information, the offence has not been made out.[167] Finally, it has been held that the offence can be made out where the calls were left on an answering machine to be heard by the victim at a later time.[168]

4.4 PROPERTY

Part IX of the *Criminal Code* pertains to offences against rights to property. It contains numerous sections dealing with typical property offences such as theft, fraud, and robbery. As it is obvious that the commission of these crimes should play no part in the role of investigations, such offences are not reviewed here.[169] Rather, in this section of the chapter, "property" issues that private investigators may come up against are identified and explored. These issues include

+ possession of stolen property as it pertains to property obtained during an investigation;

+ theft as it pertains to the obtaining and possession of CPIC information;

+ property rights in garbage; and

+ possession of an illicit sort of property — controlled drugs and substances.

---

165 *Fouracres v. ICBC* (1996), (B.C.S.C.) [unreported].

166 *R. v. Sabine* (1990), 57 C.C.C. (3d) 209 (N.B.Q.B.).

167 *R. v. Wood* (1983), 8 C.C.C. (3d) 217 (Ont. Prov. Ct.).

168 *R. v. Manicke* (1993), 81 C.C.C. (3d) 255 (Sask. C.A.).

169 The Canadian Press reports ("Torture Trial," Edmonton: National General News, 28 February 1989) that private investigators Wayne Clifford Bond and Lynne Lipscobe were charged along with lawyer Alex Hardy with kidnapping, extortion, assault, break, enter, and theft and using a gun while committing a crime. Crown prosecutors alleged that Hardy took the law into his own hands after a local felon named Clifford Fred broke into Hardy's house and stole money and jewellery. Fred claimed he used the $100,000 for drugs, clothes, and a stereo. Hardy used the private investigators to identify, locate, and kidnap Fred. After Fred was kidnapped, he was taken to an office where he was blindfolded, beaten, and burned with an electrical device until he gave up where he was hiding his stolen loot. As mentioned, as this sort of conduct does not fall into the typical activities of private investigators, it has not been further explored.

Mischief, another property offence, is covered in this book under the heading of surveillance crimes as it is under this activity that such an offence more likely would be committed. The obtaining and execution of search warrants is reviewed in Chapter 10.

4.4.1   Possession of Stolen Property

An issue raised by private investigators during the preparation of this book was their liability for possession of stolen property when the property was purchased or obtained as part of an operation they were conducting.

Section 354 of the *Criminal Code* is entitled "Possession of Property Obtained by Crime." It provides:

354(1) Every one commits an offence who has in his possession any property or thing or any proceeds of any property or thing knowing that all or part of the property or thing or the proceeds was obtained by or derived directly or indirectly from

(a) the commission in Canada of an offence punishable by indictment, or

(b) an act or omission anywhere that, if it had occurred in Canada, would have constituted an offence punishable by indictment.

355.   Every one who commits an offence under s.354

(a) is guilty of an indictable offence and liable to imprisonment for a term of not exceeding ten years, where the subject-matter of the offence is a testamentary instrument or the value of the subject-matter of the offence exceeds five thousand dollars; or

(b) is guilty

(i) of an indictable offence and liable to imprisonment for a term not exceeding two years, or

(ii) of an offence punishable on summary conviction,

where the value of the subject-matter of the offence does not exceed five thousand dollars.

The authority for police to possess stolen property is derived from their public duty to investigate crime.[170] Although private investigators have no greater powers than a private person, there is a social utility recognized in law for the function they perform.[171] For this reason, although the section does not contain a clause similar to "in the absence of any reasonable explanation therefrom," it is arguable that the simple possession of stolen property would not necessary lead to an offence provided the property is turned over to its rightful owner or the authorities as soon as it is practicable to do so.

---

170 *Police Services Act of Ontario*, R.S.O. 1990, c. P.15, s. 42.

171 *Druken v. RG Fewer & Associates Inc.*, [1998] N.J. No. 312 (S.C).

Authority for this position is derived from cases in which property was found and converted to personal use. In *R. v. Hayes*,[172] the accused was convicted of possession of stolen property after using identification she had found for the purposes of buying property for her personal use. The court held that, while the documents were originally lawfully in the accused's possession when she found them, she stole them by subsequently fraudulently converting them to her own use. By fraudulently converting the property to her own use, the property was obtained by the commission of an indictable offence within the meaning of the section. *Hayes* indicates implicitly that it is the conversion of the property, that is, for personal use, knowing that it is the property of another, which is unlawful. This is also the reasoning given in a number of other cases where the theft of the property could not be proven, but where ownership of the property and its unlawful use by the possessor was.[173]

No reported decisions were located pertaining to private investigators being charged with this offence. However, a press report alleged such an incident was uncovered. In this case, the private investigator was alleged to have unlawfully negotiated a payment with a company for the return of its stolen video monitor. In addition to the charge of possession of stolen property, he was also charged with unlawfully accepting a reward. The outcome of this case was not reported.[174]

To conclude, in the interest of caution, it may be prudent for private investigators to advise police once they have determined they are undertaking an investigation involving stolen property. For information on coordinating investigations with police, see Section 4.4.5 — Possession of a Controlled Drug or Substance.

4.4.2   Theft

It is obvious that theft has no part in an investigation and therefore is not worthy of discussion in this text. However, there was a case where a private investigator was charged with theft by obtaining information from a restricted computer source — the source being the Canadian Police Information Centre (CPIC). This aspect of the offence of theft is worthy of further examination.

---

172 (1985), 10 O.A.C. 81 (C.A.).
173 See *R. v. Zurowski* (1983), 5 C.C.C. (3d) 285 (Alta. Q.B.); *R. v. Costello* (1982), 1 C.C.C. (3d) 403, [1983] 1 W.W.R. 666.
174 *R. v. Firth* (1984), (Ont. Prov. Ct.) [unreported]; "Demeter" (Toronto: Canadian Press, National General News, 22 January 1984). What also made this case interesting is that the accused private investigator, acting in his own defence, called the infamous Peter Demeter as a character witness. Demeter claimed he retained the accused after somebody used a phony power of attorney and looted his safety deposit box of several hundred thousand dollars. The accused identified and located the thief and only charged Demeter $750 for his efforts. The accused also was retained by Demeter to locate sixteen paintings allegedly of national interest. Demeter testified he was totally satisfied with the results that the accused obtained.

Sections 322 and 334 of the *Criminal Code* formalize the common law offence of theft. They provide:

322(1) Every one commits theft who fraudulently and without colour of right takes or fraudulently and without colour of right converts to his use or to the use of another person, anything whether animate or inanimate, with intent,

> (a) to deprive, temporarily or absolutely, the owner of it, or a person who has a special property or interest in it, of the thing or of his property or interest in it;

> (b) to pledge it or deposit it as security;

> (c) to part with it under a condition with respect to its return that the person who parts with it may be unable to perform; or

> (d) to deal with it in such a manner that it cannot be restored in the condition in which it was at the time it was taken or converted.

334. Except where otherwise provided by law, everyone who commits theft

> (a) is guilty of an indictable offence and liable to imprisonment for a term not exceeding 10 years, where the property stolen is a testamentary instrument or the value of what is stolen exceeds five thousand dollars; or

> (b) is guilty

>> (i) of an indictable offence and is liable to imprisonment for a term not exceeding two years, or

>> (ii) of an offence punishable on summary conviction,

> where the value of what is stolen does not exceed five thousand dollars.

The facts of the case mentioned above were as follows. A retired police staff sergeant had set up a private investigative agency in Alberta. As part of his operations he conducted background checks on potential employees for employers. To fulfil the background checks, the accused sought to determine if the persons he was investigating had criminal records. The accused approached a senior officer within the Edmonton police department to conduct CPIC searches for him. The senior officer advised the accused that such a practice was illegal and denied his request. The accused then approached a constable from the same police department and offered him a fee per name for CPIC information on these persons. This constable advised his managers and the police took steps to set up the accused. The constable had a further discussion with the accused where the accused offered to have the money earned deposited in a separate account in the name of the officer's wife. The accused then gave the officer two names to check. The accused paid the officer upon receipt of the information. The accused was subsequently arrested, charged, and convicted of the offence.[175]

---

175 *R. v. Offley* (1986), 28 C.C.C. (3d) 1 (Alta. C.A.).

On appeal from his conviction, the court held that the crucial phrase in the theft provision of the *Criminal Code* is whether "anything animate or inanimate" includes information from a restricted computer bank. After reviewing conflicting decisions from the Ontario Court of Appeal[176] and the English courts,[177] the Alberta Court of Appeal held that confidential information is incapable of being stolen. In effect, therefore, the Alberta Court of Appeal held that a charge of theft is an inappropriate sanction to deter private investigators from improperly eliciting restricted computer information.

The finding in the Alberta Court of Appeal was affirmed by the Supreme Court of Canada,[178] which held that to be considered "property" for the purposes of the offence of theft, the "thing" stolen had to be capable of being taken away or converted in some manner so as to deprive the victim. As no loss or deprivation of the information had occurred by another's use of it, a theft had not occurred. The Supreme Court of Canada held that to find otherwise would be impractical for the purposes of the *Criminal Code*.[179] Accordingly, there are no property rights in information for criminal law purposes.

Criminal sanctions against private investigators seeking information from CPIC or other restricted computer sources is properly dealt with under section 342.1 of the *Criminal Code*, the "Unauthorized Use of Computers." This offence is reviewed in the next section — Section 4.4.3.

4.4.3 Unauthorized Use of a Computer

Section 342.1 of the *Criminal Code* creates the offence of an unauthorized use of a computer. It provides:

341.1(1) Every one who, fraudulently and without colour of right

(a) obtains, directly or indirectly, any computer service,

(b) by means of an electro-magnetic, acoustic, mechanical or other device, intercepts or causes to be intercepted, directly or indirectly, any function of a computer system, or

(c) uses or causes to be used, directly or indirectly, a computer system with intent to commit an offence under paragraph (a) or (b) or an offence under section 430 (mischief) in relation to data or a computer system

is guilty of an indictable offence and liable to imprisonment for a term not exceeding ten years, or is guilty of an offence punishable on summary conviction.

---

176 *R. v. Stewart* (1983), 5 C.C.C. (3d) 481 (Ont. C.A.).

177 *Oxford v. Moss* (1978), 68 Cr. App. R. 183.

178 *R. v. Stewart*, [1988] S.C.R. 963.

179 It is noteworthy the court left the door open for the conversion of confidential information in a civil form of action.

(2)   In this section,

"computer program" means data representing instructions or statements that, when executed in a computer system, causes the computer system to perform a function;

"computer service" includes data processing and the storage or retrieval of data;

"computer system" means a device that, or a group of interconnected or related devices one or more of which,

    (a)   contains computer programs or other data, and

    (b)   pursuant to computer programs,

        (i)   performs logic and control, and

        (ii) may perform any other function;

"data" means representation of information or of concepts that are being prepared or have been prepared in a form suitable for use in a computer system;

"electro-magnetic, acoustic, mechanical or other device" means any device or apparatus that is used or is capable of being used to intercept any function of a computer system, but does not include a hearing aid used to correct subnormal hearing of the user to not better than normal hearing;

"function" includes logic, arithmetic, deletion, storage and retrieval and communication or telecommunication to, from or within a computer system;

"intercept" includes listen to or record a function of a computer system, or acquire the substance, meaning or purport thereof.

Three people in Alberta have been charged with this offence in relation to a single occurrence, but only two were convicted. One of those convicted was a civilian police security person. She was convicted of the offence on the basis that she personally made unauthorized CPIC searches for a private investigator, thereby directly committing the offence. The private investigator who illicitly requested the CPIC printout was also convicted on the offence on the basis that he indirectly obtained use of restricted computer service. However, the agency owner, although aware that unauthorized CPIC information was in the files of his agency, and although he charged clients for the CPIC information, was acquitted. The basis for the agency owner's acquittal was that he was not actively involved in the fraudulent obtaining of the computer information. In other words, the simple possession of CPIC printouts is not a crime.[180]

In addition to the case discussed above, the Canadian Press reports that an internal inquiry into allegations that some Quebec public servants have sold personal information from confidential government files has resulted in a charge against one such civil servant. The civil servant was alleged to have sold seventy to a hundred welfare files a day for a dol-

---

180 *R. v. Forsythe* (1992), 137 A.R. 321 (Prov. Ct.).

lar a piece. The civil servant was convicted and given a suspended sentence and ordered to donate $500 to charity. The report further comments that such leaks of government information are not limited to welfare files. One private investigator admitted he obtains confidential information from government contacts in exchange for information on those committing welfare and employment insurance fraud, even obtaining information from provincial police files.

For further information pertaining to private investigators utilizing CPIC information, please see the preceding section, Section 4.4.2 — Theft. It is also noteworthy that section 342.2(1) of the *Criminal Code* makes it an offence to possess a device for obtaining the unauthorized use of a computer.

4.4.4   Property Rights in Garbage

A common method of obtaining information by private investigators is the taking of garbage of a subject party. The question that obviously arises is the legality of doing so. As it pertains to the criminal law and in particular the offence of theft, the issue is really one of property rights; that is, has the owner of the property given up possessory rights when the property is placed in the garbage?

The case law on this issue is settled. The Court of Appeal in British Columbia stated:

> Whether or not when the ordinary person puts out his or her garbage there is any thought that others may shift through it will depend on a number of factors . . . Often the expectation is that it will be taken away and disposed of without any intermediate investigation. But by putting it out, the householder puts it beyond his or her control. Any property claim is abandoned . . . Where is the dividing line drawn? In the interest of establishing a uniform rule that can be seen to be easily enforceable by all people, I say the point at which the dividing line should be drawn is where the householder signifies his abandonment of the garbage by putting it off his property in such a way as to indicate an intention to abandon possession of it to others.[181]

In other words, when property is put on the curb for garbage pick-up, an owner's property rights have been abandoned.

An issue that arises from this rule is determining the location of the property boundary, as it may be argued that it is this line that indicates when the property right has been abandoned. For example, in many locations the private property boundary does not extend to the roadway, but is a number of feet back. Therefore, when garbage is put out on the curb, it is off an owner's property. This dividing line is much more difficult to determine in cases such as office towers, apartments, or business parks.

An example of this issue comes from a case from Alberta where the court held that when police entered into the accused's residence, in this case a hotel room, under a ruse and seized items from a garbage container, the accused still had proprietary rights in the garbage, and the seizure, being without warrant, therefore violated his constitutional

---

181   *R. v. Krist* (1995), 100 C.C.C. (3d) 58 (B.C.C.A.).

rights. The court held that notwithstanding that property is put in the garbage, the indication of the intention to abandon the property is not complete until it is off the owner's or occupier's property.[182]

In a case from Manitoba, a plaintiff hired private investigators to search the discarded material in dumpsters on the properties of the defendants, which were situated in a business park. The court held that it could not condone the manner in which the search was conducted or the manner in which the seizures were recorded. The court, however, did not discuss the particular reasons why it could not condone the manner in which the search was conducted. It is surmised that because the dumpsters were still on the property of the defendants, and were not, as stated by the British Columbia Court of Appeal, "put off [the defendant's] property in such a way as to indicate an intention to abandon possession of it to others," it could not condone the practice.[183]

Although there is no criminal sanction for the seizing of property from curb-side garbage, there may be sanctions against such conduct under municipal bylaws. The recycling of paper has developed into an industry unto itself and therefore may be a form of liability imposed on the inquisitive "dumpster diver."

4.4.5   Possession of a Controlled Drug or Substance

The Canadian Press reported a story on 13 August 1989 pertaining to undercover operations within a company that had a drug problem with a number of their employees. The story read as follows:

> The sting operations private investigator Harry Lake stages for companies that want to trap workers selling drugs on the job have an almost surgical precision to them.
>
> Lake, director of Introspec Investigation in Toronto, starts with an operative posing as an employee. "First our agent will set up a buy," explains Lake. "He starts off small, then gets gradually bigger. When we've got a sufficient quantity, we bring the police in."
>
> Orchestrating the arrest is a matter of taste, so Lake gives his client two choices. "Some prefer we do the bust on the premises, to act as a deterrent," he says, "or, we can do it away from the company to avoid publicity."
>
> Introspec, which also investigates corporate fraud, industrial espionage and computer misuse, gets three or four calls a month from clients looking for help with drug problems, Lake says. He says his customers have included a major bank, a brokerage, a large Toronto hospital and an industrial construction company.[184]

The legal question that the above scenario poses is what authority do private investigators have to possess illegal drugs.

---

182 *R. v. Love* (1995), 102 C.C.C. (3d) 393 (Alta. C.A.).
183 *Apotex Fermentation Inc. v. Novopharm Ltd.* (1995), 63 C.P.R. (3d) 77 (Man. Q.B.).
184 R. Carrick, "Budget" (Canadian Press: Weekly Business Focus, 13 August 1989).

Unlike the offence of possession of stolen property — for which there appears to be a defence to a private investigator — is the offence of possession of a controlled drug or substance, for which there appears to be no defence without supervision by police. The *Controlled Drug and Substance Act*[185] provides:

4(1)   Except as authorized under the regulations, no person shall possess a substance included in Schedule I,[186] II,[187] or III.[188]

. . .

(3)   Every person who contravenes subsection (1) where the subject matter of the offence is a substance included in Schedule I

(a)   is guilty of an indictable offence and liable to imprisonment for a term not exceeding seven years; or

(b)   is guilty of an offence punishable on summary conviction and liable

(i)   for a first offence, to a fine not exceeding one thousand dollars or to imprisonment for a term not exceeding six months, or to both, and

(ii)   for a subsequent offence, to a fine not exceeding two thousand dollars or to imprisonment for a term not exceeding one year, or to both.

. . .

(5)   Every person who contravenes subsection (1) where the subject matter of the offence is a substance included in Schedule II in an amount that does not exceed the amount set out for that substance in Schedule VIII is guilty of an offence punishable on summary conviction and liable to a fine not exceeding one thousand dollars or to imprisonment for a term not exceeding six months, or to both.

(6)   Every person who contravenes subsection (1) where the subject matter of the offence is a substance included in Schedule III

(a)   is guilty of an offence and liable to imprisonment for a term not exceeding three years; or

(b)   is guilty of an offence punishable on summary conviction and liable

(i)   for a first offence, to a fine not exceeding one thousand dollars or to imprisonment for a term not exceeding six months, or to both, and

(ii)   for subsequent offences, to a fine not exceeding two thousand dollars or to imprisonment for a term not exceeding one year, or to both.

. . .

---

185   S.C. 1996, c. 19.
186   Opium poppy and its derivatives; Coca leaves and its derivatives (i.e., cocaine); and others.
187   Cannabis and its derivatives.
188   Amphetamines and its derivatives.

7(1) Except as authorized under the regulations, no person shall produce[189] a substance included in Schedule I, II, III, or IV.[190]

. . .

55(2) The Governor in Council, on the recommendation of the Solicitor General of Canada, may make regulations that pertain to investigations and other law enforcement activities conducted under this Act by a member of a police force and other persons acting under the direction and control of a member and, without restricting the generality of the foregoing, may make regulations

(a) authorizing the Solicitor General of Canada, or the provincial minister responsible for policing in a province, to designate a police force within the Solicitor General's jurisdiction or the minister's jurisdiction, as the case may be, for the purposes of this subsection;

(b) exempting, on such terms and conditions as may be specified in the regulations, a member of a police force that has been designated pursuant to paragraph (a) and other persons acting under the direction and control of the member from the application of any provision of Part I (Offences and Penalties) or the regulations.

(56) The Minister may, on such terms and conditions as the Minister deems necessary, exempt any person or class of persons or any controlled substance or precursor or any thereof from the application of all or any of the provisions of this Act or the regulations if, in the opinion of the Minister, the exemption is necessary for a medical or scientific purpose or is otherwise in the public interest.

The *Controlled Drugs and Substances Act (Police Enforcement) Regulations*[191] provides:

3. A member of a police force is exempt from the application of section 5, (trafficking) 6 (importing or exporting) or 7 (producing) of the Act, as applicable, where the member engages or attempts to engage in conduct referred to in any of those sections that involves a substance other than a substance referred to in any of subsections 8(1), 11(1) and 13(1) of these Regulations, of which the member has come into possession during a particular investigation, if the member

(a) is an active member of the police force; and

(b) is acting in the course of the member's responsibilities for the purposes of the particular investigation.

---

189 Section 2 defines "produce," in part, as "a means in respect of a substance included in any of Schedules I to IV, to obtain the substance by any method or process." The definition goes on to give examples of producing.

190 Barbiturates and their derivatives.

191 S.O.R. 97/234, P.C. 1997-632

4. A person is exempt from the application of section 5, 6 or 7 of the Act, as applicable, where the person engages or attempts to engage in conduct referred to in any of those sections that involves a substance, other than a substance referred to in any of subsections 8(1), 11(1) and 13(1) of these Regulations, of which the person has come into possession, if the person

   (a) acts under the direction and control of a member of a police force who the person has reasonable grounds to believe meets the conditions set out in paragraphs 3(a) and (b); and

   (b) acts to assist the member referred to in paragraph (a) in the course of the particular investigation.

. . .

15. A member of a police force who engages in conduct referred to in section 5 or 7 of the Act by offering to engage in that conduct is exempt, in respect of offering to engage in that conduct, from the application of section 5 or 7 of the Act, if the member

   (a) is an active member of the police force; and

   (b) is acting in the course of the member's responsibilities for the purposes of a particular investigation.

16. A person who engages in conduct referred to in section 5 or 7 of the Act by offering to engage in that conduct is exempt, in respect of offering to engage in that conduct, from the application of section 5 or 7 of the Act, if the person

   (a) acts under the direction and control of a member of a police force who the person has reasonable grounds to believe meets the conditions set out in paragraphs 15(a) and (b); and

   (b) acts to assist the member referred to in paragraph (a) in the course of the particular investigation.

. . .

19. A member of a police force is exempt from the application of the provisions that create the offence of conspiracy to commit, being an accessory after the fact in relation to, or any counselling in relation to, an offence under subsection 4(2) or section 5, 6, 7, 8 (possession of property obtained by certain offences) or 9 (laundering proceeds of certain offences) of the Act if the member

   (a) is an active member of the police force;

   (b) is acting in the course of the member's responsibilities for the purposes of a particular investigation; and

   (c) engages in conduct that, but for the application of this section, would constitute a conspiracy to commit, being an accessory after the fact in relation to, or any counselling in relation to, an offence under subsection 4(2) or section 5, 6, 7, 8 or 9 of the Act. SOR/97-281, s. 1.

20.   A person is exempt from the application of the provisions that create the offence of conspiracy to commit, being an accessory after the fact in relation to, or any counselling in relation to, an offence under subsection 4(2) (obtaining a substance) or section 5, 6, 7, 8 or 9 of the Act if the person

   (a)   acts under the direction and control of a member of a police force who the person has reasonable grounds to believe

      (i)   is an active member of the police force, and

      (ii)   is acting in the course of the member's responsibilities for the purposes of a particular investigation;

   (b)   acts to assist the member in the course of the particular investigation; and

   (c)   engages in conduct that, but for the application of this section, would constitute a conspiracy to commit, being an accessory after the fact in relation to, or any counselling in relation to, an offence under subsection 4(2) or section 5, 6, 7, 8 or 9 of the Act. SOR/97-281, s. 1.

From the foregoing legislation, it is apparent that a private investigator, similar to any private person, has no authority to conduct drug investigations and come into the possession of narcotics unless supervised by a police officer involved in this type of investigation. Members of the private investigation community acknowledge that decades ago strict adherence to such regulations was not followed by the industry or the police, and often the police were not notified until long after a significant quantity of drugs had been seized. There are no known occurrences where a private investigator was ever charged with possession of narcotics as the result of an undercover drug investigation carried out solely by private investigators.

Today, in the current age of tighter regulation, the practice of reputable private investigation agencies, upon identifying a drug problem exists at a client company, is to contact the local police drug squad and coordinate their investigations with them. These investigations either take the form of the undercover private investigator introducing an undercover police officer to the individuals in the client company who are involved in the drug trade, or the private investigator making "controlled" buys under the supervision of a police officer and immediately turning over the bought substances to police to hold and analyze for evidence purposes. In other words, the private investigator's actions are now at all times controlled by the police.[192]

---

192 Information pertaining to former and current industry practices was received from Mr. Harry Lake of Introspec Investigations, 1 Yonge Street, Toronto, Ontario, Tel: (416) 362-6666, e-mail at <harryl@introspec.com>, a respected member of the private investigation community.

4.5   ADMINISTRATION OF JUSTICE

Part IV of the *Criminal Code* is entitled "Offences against the Administration of Law and Justice." Pertaining to private investigators, the offences that will be reviewed include

* perjury,
* obstructing justice,
* fabricating evidence,
* public mischief,
* compounding an indictable offence,
* corruptly taking or advertising a reward,
* offences related to affidavits,
* bribery, and
* counselling to commit breach of trust.

Also included in this section is a review of the offence of extortion as it is often cross-referenced with the offence of compounding an indictable offence.

4.5.1   Perjury

By the sheer nature of conducting investigations, there is a greater potential for a private investigator, as opposed to the average citizen, to appear in front of a court as a witness. As such, it is prudent to be aware of *Criminal Code* section 131 pertaining to perjury, which provides:

> 131(1) Subject to subsection (3), everyone commits perjury who, with intent to mislead, makes before a person who is authorized by law to permit it to be made before him, a false statement under oath or solemn affirmation, by affidavit, solemn declaration or deposition or orally, knowing that the statement is false.
>
> (2)   Subsection (1) applies whether or not a statement referred to in that subsection is made in a judicial proceeding.
>
> (3)   Subsection (1) does not apply to a statement referred to in that subsection that is made by a person who is not specially permitted, authorized or required by law to make that statement.

Section 132 is the punishment section associated with section 131. It provides:

> 132. Every one who commits perjury is guilty of an indictable offence and liable to imprisonment for a term not exceeding fourteen years, but if the person commits perjury to procure the conviction of another person for an offence punishable by death, the person who commits perjury is liable to a maximum term of imprisonment for life.

One of the reasons why so few people are convicted of the offence of perjury is because of the requirement of corroborating evidence. Section 133 provides:

> 133.   No person shall be convicted of an offence under section 132 on the evidence of only one witness unless the evidence of that witness is corroborated in a material particular by evidence that implicates the accused.

Perjury is one of the more complex sections in this part of the *Criminal Code*. In order to convict, there must be proof of several discrete elements, including that the statement was false, that the accused knew it to be false, and that there was intent to mislead. The false statement must have been made under oath or solemn affirmation, orally, by affidavit, or solemn declaration. The offence is made out regardless whether the false statement was made during a judicial proceeding or outside the time of the proceeding itself. Another element of the offence is that the person who received the statement must have been authorized to do so, such as a judge at trial, a commissioner for taking oaths, or a notary public.

The evidence amounting to corroboration is also a difficult matter. It is reported that there is a conflict in the authorities as to what element of the offence must be corroborated. In some cases, it has been held that the fact that the testimony was false was sufficient corroboration, while in other cases it has been held that there must be corroboration of the accused's knowledge of the falsity of the evidence. Still further cases report that it does not matter which "material particular" is corroborated, as long as one of them are.[193]

There have been a number of cases where private investigators were convicted of perjury. In a case from British Columbia, the accused were private investigators who conducted their business separately but sometimes assisted each other on various cases. Two married persons, one male and the other female, who were unknown to each other, sought divorces and were directed separately to them. In 1969 no-fault divorces did not exist. As one of the grounds for divorce was infidelity, the private investigators decided that to get evidence the law required, they would set up the spouse of the male client with the spouse of the female client. From this meeting the private investigators claimed they had witnessed events sufficient to prove adultery. After the decree had been granted, the matter was reopened and the alleged adulterous parties denied the evidence given by the private investigators. The private investigators were charged with perjury and conspiracy to commit perjury. The private investigators were convicted of the latter offence.[194]

In a case from Alberta, the accused was a private investigator who gave evidence at a divorce trial. The evidence upon which the accused was convicted was that he attended the back door of a residence of a non-married couple and obtained admission into their kitchen under a pretext. The accused was not granted liberty to look around in the house because he had "muddy boots." At trial, when the issue of adultery arose, the accused claimed he had observed the interior of the home. He testified that the home only contained one bedroom. The house in fact contained two bedrooms, and the couple testified that the accused perjured himself by claiming he had taken a walk through the entire house to ascertain the evidence he provided. The accused was convicted and sentenced to eighteen months imprisonment.[195]

---

193 E.L. Greenspan & M. Rosenberg, *Martin's Annual Criminal Code 1998* (Aurora: Canada Law Book, 1997) at 222.

194 *R. v. Fergusson and Petrie* [1969], 1 C.C.C. 353 (B.C.C.A.).

195 *R. v. Stewart-Smith* (1960), 128 C.C.C. 362 (Alta. S.C.A.D.). The focus of the appeal was whether spouses could provide corroboratory evidence in such a case. The Court of Appeal of Alberta admitted it in this case.

In a case from Quebec, a private investigator was asked during a cross-examination if he had a criminal record; he answered "no." In fact, he had two previous convictions. In his defence to a subsequent perjury charge, the private investigator claimed that he was under stress and may have misunderstood the question. The private investigator further stated he had no interest in lying and that he had just recklessly answered the question. The trial judge found that his testimony had otherwise been precise and showed no sign of recklessness, and that even if his testimony was reckless, he would still be guilty of perjury. On appeal, the court held that the Crown had not discharged its burden of proving that the private investigator intended to mislead the court. The court found that the private investigator had no interest in hiding a theft conviction that occurred when he was seventeen years old for which he was sentenced to a $5 fine, and an assault conviction fourteen years earlier for which he was sentenced a $25 fine. The court held that the absence of interest in misleading the court bears on the question of whether the accused had the required intent. The court held that in the circumstances of this case, it is plausible that the private investigator answered the question automatically without intending to mislead. Since the private investigator's reckless words were insufficient for a finding of intent, the Crown had not proved its case and the accused was acquitted.[196]

In a case from Ontario, a divorce order was set aside when it was determined that the husband had obtained a divorce degree based on perjured evidence of two private investigators. The wife was able to prove that the evidence that she was observed by two private investigators on two separate dates travelling with a male person in an automobile to her apartment and that the male person had come into the apartment was false. The wife was also able to prove that one of the private investigators had arranged for an imposter to stand in the place of her alleged adulterer and receive service of a subpoena to attend court as a witness to that effect.[197]

It should be noted that many of the cases reviewed deal with private investigators who are cross-examined on the veracity of their written notes and statements. With the potential that a prior statement may be the subject of inquiry in a judicial proceeding, a private investigator must be cognizant of the potential for criminal, civil, or regulatory liability in this regard. A private investigator should also be aware that in various provincial application forms for licensing as an agency or an agent, a warning is given that a false affidavit with the application may result in a perjury charge. A registrar may require an affidavit to verify the existence or non-existence of a criminal record.

Closely related to the offence of perjury is the offence of "Witness Giving Contradictory Evidence." Section 136 provides:

136(1) Every one who, being a witness in a judicial proceeding, gives evidence with respect to any matter of fact or knowledge and who subsequently, in a judicial proceeding, gives evidence that is contrary to his previous evidence is guilty of an indictable

---

196 *R. v. Besner*, [1976] 33 C.R.N.S. 122 (Que. C.A.).
197 *Fromovitz v. Fromovitz* (1961), 31 D.L.R. (2d) 221 (Ont. H.C.J.).

offence and liable to imprisonment for a term not exceeding fourteen years, whether or not the prior or later evidence or either is true, but no person shall be convicted under this section unless the court, judge or provincial court judge, as the case may be, is satisfied beyond a reasonable doubt that the accused, in giving evidence in either of the judicial proceeding, intended to mislead.

(2)   Notwithstanding the definition of "evidence" in s.118, "evidence, for the purposes of this section, does not include evidence that is not material.

(3)   No proceedings shall be instituted under this section without the consent of the Attorney General.

Briefly, section 136 states that it is an offence for a witness to give evidence at one judicial proceeding and then give contradictory evidence with regard to a material fact at a subsequent judicial proceeding. To prove this offence, the Crown must show the accused intended to mislead in at least one of the proceedings. Because of the seriousness of this offence, the section requires consent of the Attorney General before a charge is laid. No charges against private investigators for this offence were uncovered during the research of this book.

4.5.2 Obstructing Justice

Private investigators should also be aware of section 139, the offence known as obstructing justice. Section 139 provides:

139(1) Every one who wilfully attempts in any manner to obstruct, pervert or defeat the course of justice in a judicial proceeding,

    (a)   by indemnifying or agreeing to indemnify a surety, in any way, either in whole or in part, or

    (b)   where he is a surety, by accepting or agreeing to accept a fee or any form of indemnity whether in whole or in part from or in respect of a person who is released or is to be released from custody,

is guilty of

    (c)   an indictable offence and is liable to imprisonment for a term not exceeding two years, or

    (d)   an offence punishable on summary conviction.

(2)   Every one who wilfully attempts in any manner other than a manner described in subsection (1) to obstruct, pervert or defeat the course of justice is guilty of an indictable offence and liable to imprisonment for a term not exceeding ten years.

(3)   Without restricting the generality of subsection (2), every one shall be deemed wilfully to attempt to obstruct, pervert or defeat the course of justice who in a judicial proceeding, existing or proposed,

    (a)   dissuades or attempts to dissuade a person by threats, bribes or other corrupt means from giving evidence;

(b)   influences or attempts to influence by threats, bribes or other corrupt means a person in his conduct as a juror; or

(c)   accepts or obtains, agrees to accept or attempts to obtain a bribe or other corrupt consideration to abstain from giving evidence, or to do or to refrain from doing anything as a juror.

The first group of offences mentioned in section 139(1) are not of relevance to private investigators. What is of relevance is subsection (2). The main element of the offence that must be proven is that the accused's actions were wilful. Subsection (3) lists a number of ways this offence may be committed within a judicial proceeding. This list is illustrative, not exclusive.

There are some elements of the offence that are worthy of further explanation. The term "the course of justice" in subsection (2) includes not only judicial proceedings existing or proposed, but also situations wherein the accused contemplates that a prosecution may take place even though no prosecution has been commenced.[198] Therefore "the course of justice" includes the investigatory stage. It is also noteworthy that "the course of justice" includes not only traditional civil and criminal proceedings, but also administrative hearings where the authority for the administrative body is derived from statute and the tribunal is required to act in a judicial manner.[199]

Attempts to obstruct justice can take many forms. Any attempt to pay compensation in any form to a witness that has, as its purpose, a direct tendency to influence a witness not to give evidence in a judicial proceeding is an offence. Any attempt to pay compensation to a complainant to influence a proceeding by persuading a Crown to withdraw a charge is capable of amounting to an offence. The offence, however, is not committed where *bona fide* negotiations take place between a Crown and an accused's lawyer for the purpose of withdrawing or reducing a given charge.[200] For a further explanation of this issue, see Section 4.5.5 — Extortion, and Section 4.5.6 — Compounding an Indictable Offence.

There has been a case where a private investigator was charged with this offence. The court found that the private investigator used threats, bribes, and other corrupt means in an attempt to dissuade a witness from giving evidence at an upcoming trial.[201] In another case, a court found that a private investigator deliberately misled a police officer in providing grounds for a search warrant.[202]

Finally, pertaining to a person's duty to assist in criminal, civil, or administrative investigations, an interesting article has been written by an Ontario lawyer. In this article, it was

---

198   *R. v. Spezzano* (1977), 34 C.C.C. (2d) 87 (Ont. C.A.).

199   *R. v. Wijesinha*, [1995] 3 S.C.R. 422.

200   E.L. Greenspan & M. Rosenberg, *Martin's Annual Criminal Code 1999* (Aurora: Canada Law Book, 2000) at 230.

201   *R. v. Rite* (1980), 6 W.C.B. 19 (B.C.C.A.).

202   *R. v. Butt* (1995), 29 W.C.B. (2d) 328 (Ont. Gen. Div.). In this case, the private investigator was not charged with obstructing justice, although the court implied he could have been. See Section 10.2.2.4 for a further discussion.

suggested that if a crime is recorded on videotape during a surveillance, the investigator who conducted the surveillance is obliged to turn over the impugned videotape to the investigation agency's solicitor, who must in turn decide to

- turn it over to a Crown attorney either directly or anonymously;
- deposit it with the trial judge if it relates to an ongoing civil or criminal matter; or
- disclose the existence of the videotape to the Crown or opposite civil or administrative lawyer and prepare to do battle to retain possession of it.[203]

A classic example of such a predicament often cited in legal circles is that of the criminal defence lawyer who is approached by a person and handed a smoking gun or a bloody knife. To avoid becoming a witness, the advice of the law society to such a lawyer has been to place the property in some form of non-transparent package, call up another lawyer and advise that lawyer to pick up the "package" and take it to a Crown attorney. The lawyer who drops off the package is instructed to advise the Crown attorney that he or she has been asked to drop off the package, and has no knowledge of its contents. By doing so, the initial lawyer who received the potential evidence of a criminal act is protected by solicitor-client privilege by the second lawyer. The initial lawyer also thereby protects the person who turned in the evidence with solicitor-client privilege as well.

As it relates to private investigations, an issue that may arise is whether this obligation to turn in evidence remains notwithstanding that the client of the investigator expressly instructs the investigator that he or she does not wish to be a party or witness to any criminal proceedings. As discussed in Section 2.3.2.10, there is no general duty to report crime. However, when an investigator comes into possession of evidence of a crime, he or she cannot simply withhold or destroy such evidence. Although not obliged to report the time, place, or parties to a crime, it is suggested that the procedure for turning over evidence of a crime discussed above be followed to avoid potential liability for the criminal offence of obstructing justice.

4.5.3 Fabricating Evidence

Section 137 of the *Criminal Code* creates the offence of fabrication of evidence. It provides:

137. Every one who, with intent to mislead, fabricates anything with intent that it shall be used as evidence in a judicial proceeding, existing or proposed, by any means other than perjury or incitement to perjury is guilty of an indictable offence and liable to imprisonment for a term not exceeding fourteen years.

This is a rarely utilized section of the *Criminal Code*, but nevertheless a section that a private investigator should be aware of. No reported decisions were located pertaining to private investigators being charged with this offence.

---

203 E. Goldstein, "Buried Treasure: Determining Whether the Concealment of Videotapes Depicting Crime Is a Crime on Its Own" *Canadian Security* (October 2000) at 24. This article discussed the case of *R. v. Murray* (2000), 48 O.R. (3d) 544 (Ont. S.C.J.).

4.5.4   Public Mischief

Section 140 of the *Criminal Code* creates the offence of public mischief. It provides:

140(1) Every one commits public mischief who, with intent to mislead, causes a peace officer to enter on or continue an investigation by

(a)   making a false statement that accuses some other person of having committed an offence;

(b)   doing anything intended to cause some other person to be suspected of having committed an offence that the other person has not committed, or to divert suspicion from himself;

(c)   reporting that an offence has been committed when it has not been committed; or

(d)   reporting or in any other way making it known or causing it to be made known that he or some other person has died when he or that other person has not died.

(2)   Every one who commits public mischief

(a)   is guilty of an indictable offence and liable to imprisonment for a term not exceeding five years; or

(b)   is guilty of an offence punishable on summary conviction.

This section is relevant to private sector investigators as frequently private sector investigations are turned over to the police for further investigation and processing. In the vast majority of cases, investigators from the private sector are of assistance to their public sector counterparts. However, there have been occasions where private sector investigators have improperly attempted to use the police as a means to secure their own ends. This section creates an offence where a person causes a peace officer to begin or continue an investigation when the true intention was to mislead them. The ways the offence can be committed are by falsely accusing another of committing a criminal offence or falsely reporting that an offence has occurred.

No reported decisions pertaining to private sector investigators committing this offence were located. However, the Canadian Press reports that a private investigator was charged with public mischief for making an allegation that members of the Hamilton Wentworth Regional Police organized and executed a break-in at the home of a Children's Aid Society worker. The social worker was involved in a ten-month-long hearing to decide the custody of two young girls who alleged their mother subjected them to sexual abuse and satanic rituals involving cannibalism and murder. Investigators from the Ontario Provincial Police, after conducting interviews with the Hamilton Wentworth Police, concluded the allegations of the private investigator were fabricated.[204]

---

204 "Child Horrors" (Hamilton, ON: Canadian Press, National General News, 31 July 1986).

4.5.5   Extortion

The charge of extortion is another charge that could befall the unwary private investigator. Section 346(1) of the *Criminal Code* provides:

> 346(1) Everyone commits extortion who, without reasonable justification or excuse, and with intent to obtain anything by threats, accusations, menaces or violence, induces or attempts to induce any person, whether or not he is the person threatened, accused or menaced or to whom violence is shown, to anything or cause anything to be done.

> (2)   A threat to institute civil proceedings is not a threat for the purposes of this section.

This section makes it an offence to induce someone by threat without reasonable justification and with intent to obtain anything. This offence is most applicable to private investigators when conducting interviews and attempting to settle a theft or fraud allegation with a suspect. Subsection (2) permits the use of threat of civil proceedings to induce a person to settle a dispute. By implication, threats of criminal proceedings to settle a dispute are prohibited.

There is a significant gray area associated with determining when a threat of criminal proceedings has occurred. The Supreme Court of Canada has held that when a lawyer approaches another lawyer acting for another party who is on criminal charges and offers without threats to have certain criminal charges dropped in exchange for a sum of money, the offence of extortion is not committed. While permitting this practice, the Law Society of Upper Canada has made it clear that any threats of criminal prosecution prior to the actual laying of charges to induce a settlement of a financial dispute is prohibited.[205] Therefore, negotiations to settle a dispute cannot include the mention of criminal sanctions until after the debtor has been charged with a criminal offence.

There have been a couple of cases in which private investigators were charged under this section. In one case, a private investigator was convicted of extortion after he threatened a party with criminal sanctions unless he wrote a confession statement and agreed to pay a sum of money to his employer.[206] In another case, a private investigator was charged with extortion after he left compromising sexual photographs of a subject party with that party with a note that further pictures would turn up in inopportune places and at inappropriate times unless a civil debt was settled.[207]

The story behind the first case, *McKinnon v. F. W. Woolworth Co.*, is worthy of further review. A manager of a Woolworth store decided to have the store "shopped" by the defendant (Commercial Fidelity). This was an American business that had extended its operations to Canada. "Shopping" consisted of having two or more persons shop in a

205 "Criminal Law May Not Be Used to Collect Civil Debts," *The Law Society Gazette*, Vol. 2, No. 1–3 (Toronto: Law Society of Upper Canada, May–Dec. 1967).

206 *McKinnon v. F.W. Woolworth Co. & Johnson and Matt, Jordison & Commercial Fidelity Audit Agency Ltd.* (1968), 66 W.W.R. 205 (Alta. C.A.).

207 *R. v. Alexander* (1999), Ottawa (Ontario S.C.J.) [unreported].

department of the store at the same time. The cash register tapes were examined afterwards to determine whether the money from the sales had been recorded in the cash register.

One morning, employees of Commercial Fidelity (Matt and Jordison), appeared in the sporting goods department. While the cashier (McKinnon) was waiting upon Jordison, Matt picked up two packages of golf balls and left $6.10 on the counter saying that he did not have time to wait for a bill or to have the purchased articles put in a bag. When McKinnon picked up the money, he realized it was $1.00 more than the correct purchase price. Anticipating that this purchaser might realize his mistake and return to claim the extra money, he placed the whole amount behind the showcase. Later, when going out for coffee, he put the money in his shirt pocket. This was done in the presence and with the knowledge of his assistant. He forgot to ring up in the cash register the $5.10 and to take to the office the $1.00. On his return to the store the following working day, he was called up to his employer's office and accused of having stolen the $6.10.

In addition to "shopping" stores, Commercial Fidelity and its employee Matt were held out as being licensed to "interrogate" any employee suspected of dishonesty. An agreement was made between Woolworths and Commercial Fidelity that any money recovered as a result of the "interrogation" would be divided equally between the latter and the appellant company.

When McKinnon arrived in his employer's office, Matt and Jordison were there. When questioned, McKinnon denied that he had committed a theft and explained what had happened. His explanation, however, was not accepted. At this point, Matt started yelling and screaming. Matt said they had proof of one offence but that there was approximately $1,200 of property missing during the time which he was employed. Matt then stated that they were going to contact the police and have him placed in jail. Matt also threatened McKinnon that they would notify his family, that he would suffer embarrassment, and that he would never get a decent job again. Matt then offered McKinnon a second opportunity to confess on paper to the entire amount of loss claimed and left the room.

During their absence, McKinnon wrote "$25" on the paper. When they returned Matt again went into a rage and repeated the threats he made before. McKinnon testified:

> At this point I was so scared I didn't know what to do and I said, "Well, how much do you want me to give you?" I said, "I will pay you anything." He said, "Let's talk about $1,200." ... He said, "I told him that I wouldn't pay $1,200, $1,200 was supposedly the entire shrinkage of my department." ... He said, "You better put down a figure and it better be close to $1,200" ... And then I wrote down a figure of $200." ... He said "I will give you one more chance" and he said "and this is it, and if you don't up the ante, you are going to gaol." So I wrote down $300 and at that point I don't really know whether that satisfied Mr. Matt or not, but at that point Mr. Johnston stepped in and said, "That's enough, he couldn't have taken more than that," and he stopped the interrogation.

McKinnon was then required to write, at Matt's dictation, a confession of his alleged theft. Except for the reference to the $6.10 purchase of golf balls, the whole statement was false and unsupported by anything that McKinnon had said. It was solely the product of Matt's imagination.

McKinnon was immediately discharged and $75 of the $300 mentioned in the "confession" was paid that day. The balance of the $300 was paid by McKinnon the next day. Some time later the police got in touch with McKinnon and a charge of extortion was laid against Matt. On his conviction, Matt was sentenced to one year in jail.

4.5.6   Compounding an Indictable Offence

Section 141 of the *Criminal Code* creates the offence of compounding an indictable offence. It provides:

> 141(1) Every one who asks for, obtains or agrees to receive or obtain any valuable consideration for himself or any other person by agreeing to compound or conceal an indictable offence is guilty of an indictable offence and liable to imprisonment for a term not exceeding two years.

> (2)   No offence is committed under subsection (1) where valuable consideration is received or obtained or is to be received or obtained under an agreement for compensation or restitution or personal services that is

> (a)   entered into with the consent of the Attorney General; or

> (b)   made as part of a program, approved by the Attorney General, to divert persons charged with indictable offences from criminal proceedings.

To private investigators, this section is applicable to situations where he or she asks for, obtains, or agrees to accept any form of valuable consideration in exchange for agreeing to compound or conceal an indictable offence. Compound an offence has been held to mean entering into an agreement not to prosecute or inform on a person who has committed an offence.[208] The noteworthy exception to this offence is an agreement entered into with consent of the Crown.

No case law involving private investigators was located pertaining to this offence. Indeed, there is little case law on the subject matter at all.[209] However, this offence should cause private investigators some concern. The implication is that if a person is investigated for theft or fraud and the investigators determine that a criminal offence has been committed, and if the suspect then offers payment for his wrongdoing to the investigators in lieu of the investigators proceeding criminally, hypothetically this section has been breached. As seen under the previous heading on extortion, it is the opinion of the Law Society of Upper Canada that this offence had been committed if the criminal justice system is used to collect a civil debt.

---

208 *R. v. Burgess* (1885), 15 Cox C.C. 779 (C.A.).

209 The only case cited by E.L. Greenspan & M. Rosenberg, *Martin's Annual Criminal Law 1998* (Aurora: Canada Law Book, 1997) at 233 was *R. v. H.L.* (1987), 57 C.R. (3d) 136 (Que. Ct. Sess.), where the court held that the Crown does not need to prove that an indictable offence was actually committed. Rather, it is sufficient if the Crown only proves that the accused believed that an indictable offence had been committed.

Doubtlessly, some variance of this behaviour takes place regularly between investigators and suspects in the white-collar corporate fraud world. The "valuable consideration" aspect of this charge includes not only financial compensation, but other offers of value such as a resignation or information that could save a company large sums of litigation and investigation dollars. This offence is the closest requirement known to an investigator's duty to report crime.

Litigation of this offence is required to better determine the extent of the section's authority. It is surmised, however, that to avoid liability, private investigators should insist that all payments of compensation for fraud or theft be made by the culprit to the victim or the victim's counsel, and not to the investigator, and that investigators receive their remuneration via payment from the victim who retained them. In other words, it is advised that private investigators not act as trust accounts for their clients.

4.5.7   Corruptly Taking or Advertising Rewards

There are two separate offences that should be mentioned under this heading. Section 142 creates the offence of corruptly taking a reward for the recovery of goods. It provides:

> 142. Every one who corruptly accepts any valuable consideration, directly or indirectly, under pretence or on account of helping any person to recover anything obtained by the commission of an indictable offence, is guilty of an indictable offence and liable to imprisonment for a term not exceeding five years.

This offence is relevant to private investigators as by definition one of a private investigator's roles is to search for missing property. It would therefore seem incumbent upon a private investigator that she ascertain if the property she is being asked to search for is not property that was obtained by an indictable offence. This offence would seem most relevant to a private investigator who is retained by a rogue client to obtain property illegally obtained by a second rogue.

No case law pertaining to private investigators committing this offence was located. However, there was a case reported in the press of a private investigator charged with corruptly taking a reward for the recovery of goods.[210]

It is noteworthy that the Crown must prove that valuable consideration was accepted "corruptly," and that "corruptly" has been held by the courts to mean "an act done by a man knowing that what he is doing is wrong and doing it anyway with an evil intent or object."[211]

The second offence that should be addressed under this heading is advertising a reward and immunity. Section 143 provides:

---

210 *R. v. Firth*, above note 174.

211 *R. v. Worthington*, [1921] V.L.R. 600 (Austl.), where the court held that on the facts of the case, the accused's acceptance of a reward for obtaining the return of stolen goods was corrupt.

143. Every one who

(a) publicly advertises a reward for the return of anything that has been stolen or lost and in the advertisement uses words to indicate that no questions will be asked if it is returned;

(b) uses words in a public advertisement to indicate that a reward will be given or paid for anything that has been stolen or lost without interference with or inquiry about the person who produces it;

(c) promises or offers in a public advertisement to return to a person who has advanced money by way of a loan on, or has bought, anything that has been stolen or lost, the money so advanced or paid, or any other sum of money for the return of that thing; or

(d) prints or publishes any advertisement referenced to in paragraph (a), (b) or (c)

is guilty of an offence punishable on summary conviction.

As stated above, this offence would seem most relevant to a private investigator who is retained by a rogue client to obtain property illegally obtained by a second rogue. No reported decisions were located pertaining to private sector investigators committing this offence either.

4.5.8   Offences Relating to Affidavits

An affidavit is a written statement supported by the oath of the deponent or by solemn affirmation. It is a common way of bringing evidence before the courts, and by the nature of the profession, private sector investigators are often required to swear to such documents. As such, an awareness of section 138 pertaining to offences relating to affidavits is essential. It provides:

138. Every one who

(a) signs a writing that purports to be an affidavit or statutory declaration and to have been sworn or declared before him when the writing was not so sworn or declared or when he knows that he has no authority to administer the oath or declaration,

(b) uses or offers to use any writing purporting to be an affidavit or statutory declaration that he knows was not sworn or declared, as the case may be, by the affiant or declarant or before a person authorized in that behalf, or

(c) signs as affiant or declarant a writing that purports to be an affidavit or statutory declaration and to have been sworn or declared by him, as the case may be, when the writing was not so sworn or declared,

is guilty of an indictable offence and liable to imprisonment for a term not exceeding two years.

This section prohibits what is often referred to as "phony affidavits." As it pertains to private sector investigators, it prohibits an affiant or a supposed witness from signing a document saying that it is an affidavit when the document was not so sworn or declared.

The section does not require that the contents of the document have to be proven as false, but rather that the document is not what is appears to be, namely a properly sworn or declared document. For criminal liability pertaining to dishonest affidavits, see Section 4.5.1 — Perjury.

No cases were reported where private investigators were the subject of such a charge.

4.5.9 Bribery

In addition to the criminal offence of "Unauthorized Use of a Computer," covered under Section 4.4.3 of this chapter, the offence of bribery has also been used by police to deter private investigators from gaining access to restricted police information such as that contained on CPIC. Section 120 of the *Criminal Code* provides:

> 120. Every one who . . .
>
>> (b) gives or offers, corruptly, to a person mentioned in paragraph (a) [a peace officer] any money, valuable consideration, office, place or employment with intent that the person should do anything mentioned in subparagraph (a) (iv) [to interfere with the administration of justice] or (vi) [to protect from detection or punishment a person who has committed or who intends to commit an offence]
>
> . . .
>
> is guilty of an indictable offence and liable to imprisonment for a term not exceeding fourteen years.

In Ontario, a private investigator has recently been charged with giving a bribe. The Crown alleged the private investigator used his association with a police officer to obtain personal and police information on some of his clients to assist his investigations. In addition to the charge of giving a bribe, the private investigator was also charged with counselling to commit breach of trust and with impersonating a peace officer.[212]

4.5.10 Counselling to Commit Breach of Trust

The offence of counselling to commit breach of trust is really a combination of two criminal offences: counselling an offence and breach of trust. Section 22, pertaining to counselling an offence, provides:

> 22(1) Where a person counsels another person to be a party to an offence and that other person is afterwards a party to that offence, the person who counselled is a party to that offence, notwithstanding that the offence was committed in a way different from that which was counselled.

---

212 *R. v. Rosenberg* (11 January 2001), (Ont. Prov. Ct.) [unreported].

(2)   Everyone who counsels another person to be a party to an offence is a party to every offence that the other commits in consequence of the counselling that the person who counselled knew or ought to have known was likely to be committed in consequence of the counselling.

(3)   For the purpose of this Act, "counsel" includes procure, solicit, or incite.

Section 122, pertaining to breach of trust by a public officer, provides:

122.   Every official who, in connection with the duties of his office, commits fraud or a breach of trust is guilty of an indictable offence and liable to imprisonment for a term not exceeding five years, whether or not the fraud or breach of trust would be an offence if it were committed in relation to a private person.

Commentators report that the offence of breach of public trust by a public officer requires proof that the accused is an official, that the impugned acts were committed in the general context of the execution of his or her duties, and that the acts constituted a fraud or breach of trust. The offence has been interpreted in such a way that proof of corruption is not necessary. Rather, it must be shown that the accused did an act or failed to do an act contrary to the duty imposed upon him or her by statute, regulation, his or her contract of employment, or directive in connection with his or her office, and that the act or omission gave him or her some personal benefit either directly or indirectly. This benefit could be payment of money or merely the hope of a promotion or desire to please a superior. The intention of this section is to prohibit the use of public office for the promotion of private ends by receiving directly or indirectly some personal benefit. However, it is not the intention of this section to punish mere technical breaches of conduct or acts of administrative discipline or administrative fault.[213]

There has been a case in Ontario wherein a private investigator was charged with counselling to commit breach of trust. The Crown alleged the private investigator used his association with a police officer to obtain personal and police information on some of his clients to assist his investigations. The private investigator was also charged with giving a bribe.[214]

4.6   DEFAMATORY LIBEL

The last set of *Criminal Code* offences that are reviewed here are entitled defamatory libel. These offences are rarely prosecuted and for the most part pertain to libel disseminated through the media. Notwithstanding this reality, an awareness of these offences is prudent.

Section 281 defines what defamatory libel is. It provides:

298(1) A defamatory libel is matter published, without lawful justification or excuse, that is likely to injure the reputation of any person by exposing him

---

213 E.L. Greenspan & M. Rosenberg, *Martin's Annual Criminal Code 1997* (Aurora: Canada Law Book, 1996) at 210, which cites *R. v. Perreault* (1992), 75 C.C.C. (3d) 445 (Que. C.A.).
214 *R. v. Rosenberg*, above note 212.

to hatred, contempt or ridicule, or that is designed to insult the person of or concerning whom it is published.

(2) A defamatory libel may be expressed directly or by insinuation or irony

(a) in words legibly marked upon any substance; or

(b) by any object signifying a defamatory libel otherwise than by words.

Of obvious importance to the definition of defamatory libel is the definition of "publishing." Section 299 describes "publishing" as follows:

299. A person publishes a libel when he

(a) exhibits it in public;

(b) causes it to be read or seen; or

(c) shows or delivers it, or causes it to be shown or delivered,

with intent that it should be read or seen by the person whom it defames or by any other person.

As seen by this definition, the scope of publishing is very wide and includes any correspondence sent by one party to another wherein a third person is defamed.

This part of the *Criminal Code* creates two separate offences: section 300, "Libel Known to be False," and section 301, "Defamatory Libel." They provide:

300. Every one who publishes a defamatory libel that he knows is false is guilty of an indictable offence and liable to imprisonment for a term not exceeding five years.

301. Every one who publishes a defamatory libel is guilty of an indictable offence and liable to imprisonment for a term not exceeding two years.

As is evident, the offence of publishing libel known to be false is more serious than simply publishing defamatory libel.

These offences are, however, the subject of a number of defences provided for by the *Criminal Code*. For instance, section 305 provides:

305. No person shall be deemed to publish a defamatory libel by reason only that he publishes defamatory matter

(a) in a proceeding held before or under the authority of a court exercising judicial authority; or

(b) in an inquiry made under the authority of an Act or by order of Her Majesty, or under the authority of a public department or a department of the government of a province.

As well as providing a defence to members of the media, this section also grants an exception to writers of publications such as this text who comment upon cases involving another's conduct. In addition to section 305, similar exceptions are also provided in section 306 pertaining to parliamentary papers, section 307 pertaining to the fair reports of parliamentary or judicial proceedings, section 308 pertaining to the reporting of public meetings, and section 309 pertaining to matters of public benefit.

Of course, the best defence against a defamation action is that what was published was actually true. Section 311 establishes such a defence. It provides:

311.   No person shall be deemed to publish a defamatory libel when he proves that the publication of the defamatory matter in the manner in which it was published was for the public benefit at the time when it was published and that the matter itself was true.

The limitation to this defence, however, is that the accused must prove that the matter published is of public benefit. As a confidential report of a private investigator is not of a nature that is for "public benefit," section 311 is likely to be of little assistance. As such, a private investigator would probably best find solace in section 313, "Answers to Inquiries." It provides:

313.   No person shall be deemed to publish a defamatory libel by reason only that he publishes, in answer to inquiries made to him, defamatory matter relating to a subject-matter in respect of which the person by whom or on whose behalf the inquiries are made has an interest in knowing the truth or who, on reasonable grounds, the person publishes the defamatory matter believes has such an interest, if

(a)   the matter is published, in good faith, for the purpose of giving information in answer to the inquiries;

(b)   the person who publishes the defamatory matter believes that it is true;

(c)   the defamatory matter is relevant to the inquiries; and

(d)   the defamatory matter does not in any respect exceed what is reasonably sufficient in the circumstances.

In summary, section 313 provides that a person will not be found guilty of defamatory libel if he or she publishes a defamatory matter in response to an inquiry made by another person who has an interest in knowing the truth. This defence applies if the person who publishes the defamatory matter believes that it is true, if the matter is relevant to the inquiry, and if the matter is published in good faith for the purpose of responding to the inquiry.

Adjuncts to the defence provided by section 313, "Answers to Inquiries" are section 314, "Giving Information to Person Interested," and section 315, "Publication in Good Faith for the Redress of a Wrong." They provide:

314.   No person shall be deemed to publish a defamatory libel by reason only that he publishes to another person defamatory matter for the purpose of giving information to that person with respect to a subject-matter in which the person to whom the information is given has, or is believed on reasonable grounds by the person who gives it to have, an interest in knowing the truth with respect to that subject-matter if

(a)   the conduct of the person who gives the information is reasonable in the circumstances;

(b)   the defamatory matter is relevant to the subject matter; and

(c)   the defamatory matter is true, or if it is not true, is made without ill-will toward the person who is defamed and is made in the belief, on reasonable grounds, that it is true.

315. No person shall be deemed to publish a defamatory libel by reason only that he publishes defamatory matter in good faith for the purpose of seeking remedy or redress for a private or public wrong or grievance from a person who has, or who on reasonable grounds he believes has, the right or is under an obligation to remedy or redress the wrong or grievance, if

(a) he believes that the defamatory matter is true;

(b) the defamatory matter is relevant to the remedy or redress that is sought; and

(c) the defamatory matter does not in any respect exceed what is reasonably sufficient in the circumstances.

Like section 313, section 314 provides an exemption to a person who publishes defamatory matter to another person who the person believes, on reasonable grounds, has an interest in knowing the truth. This section applies if the conduct of the person who gives out the matter is reasonable, if the defamatory matter is relevant to the subject, and if the person who gives out the defamatory matter does so without ill-will and believes that the published matter is true. Similarly, section 315 provides an exception if the matter published is done so in good faith for the purpose of seeking a redress for a private or public wrong from another person whom he believes on reasonable grounds is obliged to remedy the wrong or grievance. Again, as in section 314, section 315 requires the person who publishes the material to believe that the material is true, that it is relevant to the remedy sought, and that it does not exceed what is reasonable in the circumstances.

No cases were located where private sector investigators were charged with this offence. Although the criminal prosecution for defamation is rare, such actions are commonplace within the civil realm. Therefore, reference for further information on defamation should be made to Chapter 6 — The Law of Torts.

CHAPTER 5

OTHER RELEVANT LEGISLATION

The application packages of some provinces suggest that private investigative agency owners and private investigators should be familiar with other legislation, provincial and federal, in addition to the *Private Investigator and Security Guard Act* (PISGA). For instance, in Ontario, the registrar's suggested list of provincial legislation includes the *Trespass to Property Act*, the *Bailiffs Act*, the *Collection Agency Act*, the *Labour Relations Act*, the *Consumer Protection Act*, the *Consumer Reporting Act*, the *Business Practices Act*, the *Business Corporations Act*, the *Corporation Tax Act*, and the *Partnership Act*. Other provinces include such legislation as the *Freedom of Information and Protection of Privacy Act*, the *Privacy Act*, and the *Human Rights Act*.

Although the *Corporation Tax Act* and a few others may be of questionable relevance to the day-to-day operations of investigating in the private sector, some of the other legislation suggested is clearly germane. The importance of being familiar with other legislation is not because the sanctions that may be imposed are so severe, but because registrars in most provinces have the power to seek suspensions or revocations of licences granted under the PISGA upon conviction of offences under any legislation.[1]

In this chapter, the more pertinent provincial and federal legislation relevant to private investigations is explored. The topics include provincial legislation pertaining to trespass, consumer/credit reporting, privacy, and freedom of information, as well as federal legislation pertaining to privacy.

---

1   See Section 2.4.2.4 — Suspending or Revoking a Licence. In most provinces, the registrar will find authority to suspend or revoke a licence for breach of another Act under the auspices of "public interest."

5.1   PROVINCIAL TRESPASS LEGISLATION

5.1.1   The Scope of Provincial Trespass Legislation

Provincial trespass legislation is a codification of property rights found in the common law.[2] The purpose of trespass legislation is to give greater control over entry to, or use of, an owner's or tenant's premises; to provide penalties and remedies for breaches of the Act; and to facilitate the recreational use of private lands.[3] The legislation, in most cases, does not take away an aggrieved person's right to bring a civil action for trespass, but rather grants the state the authority to seek its own sanctions as a measure to control this sort of behaviour. Every province except Quebec, Saskatchewan, and the Yukon has such legislation. In the provinces without trespass legislation, an aggrieved person may seek redress through a traditional tort action.

The provincial trespass legislation has different titles in the various provinces. (See Table 5.1.) In reading the legislation of the individual provinces, one should be familiar with at least two common definitions. The word "premises" has been variously defined to include lands, structures, water, ships and vessels, trailers and other portable structures, trains, railway cars, vehicles and aircraft except while in operation. The word "occupiers" has been defined to include the owners, their tenants, and anyone put in a position of authority by owners or tenants.[4]

TABLE 5.1
Provincial Legislation Governing Trespass

Province	Legislation
Alberta (two separate trespass statutes)	*Petty Trespass Act*, R.S.A. 1980, c. P-6 *Trespass to Premises Act*, R.S.A. 1980, c. T-8.5(AB)
British Columbia	*Trespass Act*, R.S.B.C. 1996, c. 462
Manitoba	*Petty Trespass Act*, R.S.M. 1987, c. P50
New Brunswick	*Trespass Act*, S.N.B. 1979, c. T-11.2
Newfoundland	*Act to Strengthen Security Measures in Respect of Private Property*, R.S.N. 1990, c. P-11
Nova Scotia	*Act to Protect Property*, R.S.N.S. 1982, c. 13
Ontario	*Trespass to Property Act*, R.S.O. 1990, c. T.21
Prince Edward Island	*Trespass to Property Act*, R.S.P.E.I. 1988, c. T-6.

2   *Russo v. Ontario Jockey Club* (1987), 62 O.R. (2d) 731 at 733 (H.C.J.).

3   Ministry of the Attorney General of Ontario, *Property Protection and Outdoor Opportunities: A Guide to the Occupiers' Liability Act, 1980 and the Trespass to Property Act, 1980* (Toronto: Queen's Printer, 1980).

4   R.S.A. 1980, c. T-8.5, s. 1; S.N.B. 1979, c. T-11.2, s. 1; R.S.N. 1990, s. 1, c. P-11; R.S.N.S. 1982, c. 13, s. 1; R.S.O. 1990, c. T.21, s. 1; R.S.P.E.I. 1988, c. T-6, s. 1.

5.1.2 Prohibitions

The trespass legislation in the various provinces is quite similar in content. Trespassing on privately held land is prohibited in Alberta, British Columbia, Manitoba, New Brunswick, Nova Scotia, Ontario, and Prince Edward Island. Some nuances are included in the various statutes. For example, in Alberta the legislation further stipulates a prohibition of trespassing on Crown land without a permit, while in Newfoundland the prohibition only applies to trespassing on property at shops or stores, factories or warehouses, and schools of various types. Furthermore, while trespassing is typically defined as the unlawful entry onto the private land of another, or performing an unlawful activity on the land of another in Nova Scotia, Ontario, and Prince Edward Island, it also includes the refusal to leave when directed.[5]

5.1.3 Reverse Onus Provisions

Many of the provinces have provided for reverse onus provisions in their trespass legislation. For example, in British Columbia, a person is presumed to be trespassing if he or she is found on land enclosed by a fence, a natural boundary, or if the land is posted as a "no trespassing" zone. In Ontario, a person is presumed to be trespassing if found in a private garden, field or other land under cultivation, inside lands that are fenced for livestock or cultivation, and on lands where notice has been posted. In Alberta, British Columbia, Newfoundland, Nova Scotia, and Prince Edward Island, the legislation provides that notice of trespass is deemed if posters or signboards are visibly displayed at normal access points or at fence corners or the corners of land. Furthermore, the legislation of Alberta, Newfoundland, Ontario, and Prince Edward Island provides that notice is deemed if it is given orally by an owner, occupier, or their agent. Finally, in New Brunswick, notice must be given orally or in writing to be liable for trespassing at a store, shop, shopping mall or plaza, school, or shelter for domestic violence.[6] Trespass is not presumed in privately owned natural areas if it is not posted as prohibited. This point is in accordance with the philosophy of encouraging recreational activity on privately held lands.

5.1.4 Notice

On the issue of notice, Ontario has some unique provisions pertaining to signs. In Ontario, the Act specifically allows for the use of multicoloured signs with symbols to give notice of what activities are prohibited. Therefore, if a sign is posted prohibiting fishing, by default the occupier — assuming the land is not fenced or under cultivation — permits

---

5   R.S.A. 1980, c. P-6, s. 1(1); R.S.A. 1980, c. T-8.5, s. 2(1); R.S.B.C. 1996, c. 462, s. 4; R.S.M. 1987, c. P50, s. 1; S.N.B. 1979, c. T-11.2, s. 2; R.S.N. 1990, c. P-11, s. 2; R.S.N.S. 1982, c. 13, s. 3; R.S.O. 1990, c. T.21, s. 2; R.S.P.E.I. 1988, c. T-6, s. 2.

6   R.S.A. 1980, c. P-6, s. 1; R.S.A. 1980, c. T-8.5, s. 2(2); R.S.B.C. 1996, c. 462, s. 4(2)(3); R.S.M. 1987, c. P50, s. 1(1); S.N.B. 1979, c. T-11.2, s. 3; R.S.N. 1990, c. P-11, s. 2(2); R.S.N.S. 1982, c. 13, s. 3; R.S.O. 1990, c. T.21, s. 2; R.S.P.E.I. 1988, c. T-6, s. 2.

such activities as hiking, skiing, or horseback riding. Furthermore, if a sign has red markings, it means that entry is prohibited; a sign with yellow markings means that entry is prohibited except for certain activities. If a person encounters a yellow sign, he or she must find out what activity is permitted, either from the sign or from the occupier.[7]

5.1.5 Motor Vehicles

The offence of trespassing occurs regardless of how it is committed, whether on foot or by other means. Notwithstanding this reality, some of the provinces have addressed the issue of trespassing by motor vehicle in their legislation. For instance, the driver of a motor vehicle may be liable for trespass in Alberta, Newfoundland, and Ontario. In New Brunswick and Ontario, the legislation provides that unless proven otherwise, the owner of a motor vehicle is presumed to be the driver. In Nova Scotia and Prince Edward Island, the owner of the trespassing vehicle must identify the driver within 48 hours or be charged himself. New Brunswick's legislation is unique in that it only prohibits trespassing with a motor vehicle in environmentally sensitive and agricultural areas or forested lands. In the provinces that have not addressed this issue, it can be assumed that trespassing by vehicle will meet with the same results as trespassing by any other method. In fact, old English law has held that property rights extend from under the earth up into the heavens, thereby theoretically providing protection against those who trespass by air or tunnel. A final issue pertaining to motor vehicles is that of seizure. In New Brunswick, the legislation grants a peace officer the authority to seize a motor vehicle to prevent the continuation or repetition of any offence under this Act and to hold it for up to 48 hours.[8]

5.1.6 Identification

To establish who the trespasser is, some of the provinces have included in their legislation provisions pertaining to the right to demand identification. For instance, in British Columbia and New Brunswick, an owner, occupier, or their agent may demand the name and address of a trespasser.[9] In the provinces without such provisions, the authority to demand identification is implicit in the authority to arrest.

5.1.7 Arrest

The issue of arrest should be of interest to private investigators for proactive and reactive reasons. Proactively, a private investigator should be familiar with the grounds for arrest of a trespasser in case of the odd event where she may be required to execute this measure.

---

7   R.S.O. 1990, c. T.21, ss. 4–7.
8   R.S.A. 1980, c. P-6, s. 3; R.S.A. 1980, c. T-8.5, s. 4; S.N.B. 1979, c. T-11.2, ss. 4, 5, & 8; R.S.N. 1990, c. P-11, s. 3; R.S.N.S. 1982, c. 13, s. 8; R.S.O. 1990, c. T.21, s. 11; R.S.P.E.I. 1988, c. T-6, s. 7.
9   R.S.B.C. 1996, c. 462, s. 7; S.N.B. 1979, c. T-11.2, s. 7.

Reactively, a private investigator should be familiar with what may result if she decides to take such a chance to further an investigation.

In Alberta, Manitoba, and Newfoundland, an owner, occupier, or their agent, or a peace officer may only arrest without warrant a person found *committing* a trespass. If the arrest is made by an owner, occupier, or their agent, the arrestee must forthwith be delivered to a peace officer. The peace officer may hold the arrestee and take her before a provincial court judge or justice of the peace. In Ontario the grounds are wider, permitting an owner, occupier, or their agent to arrest for trespass not only in circumstances of found committing, but also on reasonable and probable grounds. In British Columbia, Nova Scotia, and Prince Edward Island, the power to arrest for trespass is only granted to peace officers on a found-committing basis and on reasonable and probable grounds if the trespasser refuses to identify herself, or to prevent the continuation of the offence. In New Brunswick, an owner, occupier, or their agent may arrest if there is reasonable and probable grounds of trespass on ecologically sensitive or agricultural lands and if the trespasser fails to identify herself. A trespasser arrested in New Brunswick must be delivered to a police officer forthwith, and must be released as soon as her identity is known.[10]

5.1.8 Penalties

The sanctions against trespassing are, for the most part, not of sufficient magnitude to act as much of a deterrent. For first offences, a fine cannot be more than $25 in Manitoba; $100 in Alberta, except in the case of a property with a building on it in which case the fine may be up to $1,000; $200 in New Brunswick[11] and Newfoundland; $500 in Nova Scotia and Prince Edward Island; and $2,000 in Ontario. For subsequent offences a fine may not be more than $1,000 in New Brunswick, and if a vehicle is involved, it may be seized and forfeited to the Crown. The other provinces have not set limits for subsequent convictions.

In addition to fines, orders for restitution are permitted in some provinces. For instance, in Ontario, an aggrieved person may see restitution for an amount up to $1,000; in Nova Scotia and Prince Edward Island an aggrieved person may see restitution for an amount up to $2,000; and in British Columbia there is no limit on what an aggrieved person may seek.[12]

---

10 R.S.A. 1980, c. P-6, s. 4; R.S.A. 1980, c. T-8.5, s. 5; R.S.B.C. 1996, c. 462, s. 10; R.S.M. 1987, c. P50, s. 2; R.S.N. 1990, c. P-11, s. 4; R.S.N.S. 1982, c. 13, s. 6; R.S.O. 1990, c. T.21, s. 9; R.S.P.E.I. 1988, c. T-6, s. 5.

11 Unless the offence takes place at a domestic shelter, in which case the fine shall not be more than $5,000 for a first offence, and shall be imprisonment for not less than 30 and not more than 180 days for a subsequent offence. Subsequent offences at schools also result in a jail term of not less than 30 and not more than 180 days.

12 R.S.A. 1980, c. P-6, s. 2; R.S.A. 1980, c. T-8.5, s. 3; R.S.B.C. 1996, c. 462, ss. 7 & 11; R.S.M. 1987, c. P50, s. 1; S.N.B. 1979, c. T-11.2, ss. 2 & 6; R.S.N. 1990, c. P-11, s. 2; R.S.N.S. 1982, c. 13, ss. 3 & 11; R.S.O. 1990, c. T.21, ss. 2 & 12; R.S.P.E.I. 1988, c. T-6, s. 10.

5.1.9   Defences

There are a number of defences available to a person charged under provincial trespass legislation. The legislation in Alberta, Manitoba, Newfoundland, Nova Scotia, Ontario, and Prince Edward Island provides that, if there is a fair and reasonable supposition that an accused had a right to be on land, an accused may be acquitted. In Ontario, the legislation provides that there is an implied permission to approach a door of a building unless there is a prohibition notice. In British Columbia and Manitoba, the presumption of trespassing may be rebutted if the defendant can prove consent. In New Brunswick, a charge of trespass will not stand if the incident took place at a store, shop, shopping plaza, or school if the accused was engaged in a peaceful public demonstration or a strike. Finally, a charge of trespass will be struck in Nova Scotia and Prince Edward Island if the notice prohibiting entry was illegible.[13]

This brings to an end the review of the provincial trespass legislation. A study of this topic would not be complete without referencing Section 4.2.2 — Trespass by Night, and Section 6.2.2 — Trespass to Land.

5.1.10 Occupiers' Liability

In some of the reading material provided by provincial registrars, it has been suggested that private investigators be familiar with the various provincial occupiers' liability legislation. This suggestion is somewhat curious. Occupiers' liability legislation is designed to impose on owners and tenants of land a duty of care to those who enter their land, to ensure a minimum standard of care to those who may injure themselves on the land of another. The legislation was passed to simplify the complex common law on the subject and to reduce rural land owners' fears of permitting recreational activities on their lands.

Ontario's occupiers' liability legislation is typical of most provinces. It provides that the owner of a premises owes a duty of care that is reasonable in the circumstances to all persons and property brought onto his or her property. This basic duty of land owners and tenants does not apply if

* the risks are willingly assumed by the person(s) entering the premises;
* the person enters for criminal purposes;
* the entrant enters for nonpaying recreational purposes; or
* the entrant is a trespasser under the *Trespass to Property Act*.

As is apparent, occupiers' liability legislation neither creates a liability nor an authority for private investigators. So it is curious that some provincial PISGA registrars make occupiers' liability legislation suggested reading.

---

13   R.S.A. 1980, c. P-6, s. 7; R.S.A. 1980, c. T-8.5, s. 8; R.S.M. 1987, c. P50, s. 1(2); S.N.B. 1979, c. T-11.2, s. 3(6); R.S.N. 1990, c. P-11, s. 6; R.S.N.S. 1982, c. 13, s. 5; R.S.O. 1990, c. T.21, s. 2(2); R.S.P.E.I. 1988, c. T-6, s. 4.

5.1.11 Use of Force to Effect an Arrest

A final word on trespass is a review of a case wherein a court discussed the authority to use force to exact an arrest for trespass under Ontario's legislation. In *R. v. Asante-Mensah*,[14] the accused was a limousine driver without a permit to provide his service at Pearson International Airport. Notwithstanding that the accused had been served personally with papers putting him on notice that he was prohibited from attending the airport grounds, the accused continued to pick up fares from this location. Due to the fact that the summonsing of the accused had no deterrent affect on him, Toronto Airport ground transportation inspectors, who are not peace officers but agents of the owner, laid plans to arrest the accused upon the accused re-offending. During the attempted arrest of the accused when he again attended the airport, the accused shoved a ground transport inspector, slammed his car door, and escaped custody. At trial, one of the issues litigated was an occupier's authority to use force to arrest a trespasser.

The court acknowledged an occupier's authority to use reasonable force to remove an offending party from private property. However, on the issue of arresting a re-offending trespasser when the identity of the trespasser or the vehicle is known, the court held that it is not in the public interest that private persons be authorized to use force for this reason. The court held that where a trespasser does not yield to an arrest effected by word and touching or words alone, the concerned occupier can alert police, follow the trespasser and request police assistance, or report the occurrence to police. In other words, a private citizen in exercising a citizen's arrest is not permitted to use force to effect an arrest for trespassing when the identity of the trespasser is known. The court acknowledged that a trespasser who flees a citizen's arrest may face the prospect of an arrest and criminal charge for escaping lawful custody. However, the court further held that it would be an anomalous result if a private citizen could use force to arrest a person for the criminal offence of escaping lawful custody, deriving from a provincial offence for which force to arrest should not be used.

5.2   PROVINCIAL CONSUMER/CREDIT REPORTING LEGISLATION

5.2.1   The Scope of a Consumer/Credit Report

What is a credit report? A credit report, or consumer report, is a written, oral, or other communication by a consumer or credit reporting agency of "credit information" or "personal information" made for consideration. "Credit information" is defined variously as information about a consumer's credit, which may include the consumer's name, age, place of residence, previous places of residence, marital status, spouse's name and age, number of dependants, particulars of education and professional qualifications, occupation, places of

---

14   [1996] O.J. No. 1821 (Gen Div.).

employment, previous places of employment, estimated income, paying habits, outstanding debt obligations, cost of living obligations, and assets. "Personal Information" is defined variously as information other than credit information about a consumer's character, reputation, medical information, health, physical characteristics, personal characteristics, lifestyle, or any other matter concerning the consumer.[15]

5.2.2   Sources of Credit Information

Credit reports are compiled first from information provided by the credit granters themselves. Added to this is whatever information can be gleaned from searches of court and municipal records, banks, news stories, and credit card companies. This information is then coded and stored so it can be transmitted electronically. Invariably, errors are made in the course of preparing and transmitting such reports.[16]

5.2.3   Purpose of Credit Reporting Legislation

Credit reporting legislation is, in part, a form of privacy legislation as it serves to protect interests in property and reputation. However, its main purpose is a form of consumer protection. The provinces of British Columbia, Newfoundland, Nova Scotia, Ontario, Prince Edward Island, and Saskatchewan have consumer/credit reporting legislation aimed at controlling the collection and use of personal information that is intended to be provided to third parties for profit. The legislation requires licensing of all persons or organizations that wish to practice this trade.[17]

5.2.4   Persons Authorized to Receive Credit Reports

Credit reporters are generally prohibited from releasing information to anyone except persons intending to use the information for purposes of extending credit, collecting a debt, screening for employment, entering into or renewing a tenancy agreement, underwriting an insurance contract, or determining eligibility for benefits conferred by statute. Credit

---

15   R.S.B.C. 1996, c-81, s. 1; R.S.N. 1990, c. C-32, s. 2; R.S.N.S. 1989, c. C-93, s. 2; R.S.O. 1990, c. C.33, s. 1; R.S.P.E.I. 1988, c. C-20, s. 1; R.S.S. 1978, c. C-44, s. 2. Note s. 2(2) of the Saskatchewan legislation provides the statute does not apply to a credit reporting agency where the reports of the agency deal only with industrial or commercial enterprises and the reports are distributed only to such enterprises.

16   The classic work on credit reporters is J.M. Sharp, *Credit Reporting and Privacy: The Law in Canada and the U.S.A.* (Toronto: Butterworths, 1970).

17   R.S.B.C. 1996, c-81, s. 3, but note that the regulations provide that licensing is not required if the person or agency is licensed under the provincial PISGA; R.S.N. 1990, c. C-32, s. 10; R.S.N.S. 1989, c. C-93, s. 4; R.S.O. 1990, c. C.33, s. 3; R.S.P.E.I. 1988, c. C-20, s. 3; R.S.S. 1978, c. C-44, ss. 3 & 4.

reports may also be released if there is a direct business requirement otherwise not listed, or under direct instructions of the consumer.[18]

5.2.5 Prohibitions

It is an offence for a person to knowingly obtain any information from the files of a credit reporting agency for purposes other than those listed above.[19] An exception to this rule is that a credit reporting agency may release identifying information such as name, address, former address, or places of employment to the government of Canada or a province, a government agency, a municipality in Canada, or a municipal agency.[20]

The various laws generally prohibit the seeking of credit reports on a consumer by another person unless that person has first been notified of this in writing or unless the person promptly notifies the consumer in writing that a consumer report will be obtained. Such notice most often occurs at the time of application for credit.[21] In British Columbia, an exception to this rule is if the primary purpose of the report is to supply information respecting the consumer's location or address.[22] On request by the consumer, the reporting agency must disclose to the consumer the names of the recipients of any report respecting that person within the preceding twelve months.[23]

5.2.6 Public Concerns of Credit Reporting

From the foregoing, it is apparent that credit reporters engage in a wide range of exchanges of credit information. This information is often centred in one main data bank. Information is both the foundation of the credit industry and its principal by-product. Notwithstanding this legitimate use for credit information, the potential for misuse exists because of the breadth of information such a report may contain. One researcher found that a large American credit reporting firm, the Retail Credit Corporation of Atlanta with

---

18 R.S.B.C. 1996, c-81, s. 10(1); R.S.N. 1990, c. C-32, s. 19(1); R.S.N.S. 1989, c. C-93, s. 9(1); R.S.O. 1990, c. C.33, s. 8(1); R.S.P.E.I. 1988, c. C-20, s. 8(1); R.S.S. 1978, c. C-44, s. 17.

19 R.S.B.C. 1996, c-81, ss. 10(2), 25, & 26; R.S.N. 1990, c. C-32, ss. 19(2) & 28; R.S.N.S. 1989, c. C-93, ss. 9(2) & 23; R.S.O. 1990, c. C.33, ss. 8(2) & 23; R.S.P.E.I. 1988, c. C-20, ss. 8(2) & 22; R.S.S. 1978, c. C-44, ss. 17 & 30.

20 R.S.B.C. 1996, c-81, s. 10(3); R.S.N. 1990, c. C-32, s. 19(1); R.S.N.S. 1989, c. C-93, s. 9(1); R.S.O. 1990, c. C.33, s. 8(1); R.S.P.E.I. 1988, c. C-20, s. 1; R.S.S. 1978, c. C-44, s. 17.

21 R.S.B.C. 1996, c-81, s. 12; R.S.N. 1990, c. C-32, s. 23; R.S.N.S. 1989, c. C-93, s. 11; R.S.O. 1990, c. C.33, ss. 10(2) & 11; R.S.P.E.I. 1988, c. C-20, s. 10. Note Saskatchewan does not have such a provision in its legislation.

22 R.S.B.C. 1996, c-81, s. 12.

23 R.S.B.C. 1996, c-81, ss. 13 & 14; R.S.N. 1990, c. C-32, s. 24; R.S.N.S. 1989, c. C-93, s. 12; R.S.O. 1990, c. C.33, ss. 10(1) & 12; R.S.P.E.I. 1988, c. C-20, s. 11; R.S.S. 1978, c. C-44, ss. 20, 21, & 22.

whom Equifax is the Canadian affiliate,[24] had openly assembled "character reports" on several million Canadians. The writer stated:

> These character reports are not just a record of whether a person pays his bills. Rather, they are a complete profile of where and how he lives, whether he is in a peace movement or other subversive group, whether his neighbour thinks he drinks too much, whether he is mentally ill, his relationship with his wife and family, his drug habits, his sexual eccentricities. In other words, everything that his friend and enemies care to say about him can be tricked into revealing about him or which can be learned about him from supposedly private files, government records, and the data recorded in the individual's dossier in other interlocking intelligence systems.[25]

The information held by consumer reporting agencies can obviously be very beneficial to a private investigator. For this reason and because of the potential for abuse, it is somewhat surprising that persons who provide credit rating reports are not deemed to be in conflict of interest with the PISGA, and may hold dual licensing as a private investigation and a consumer reporting agency. In fact, in most PISGAs, persons who provide credit reports are exempt from licensing, presumably because they are licensed under their respective credit or consumer reporting legislation.

Notwithstanding that the respective Acts provide no legislated conflict of interest between consumer reporting agencies and private investigators, as mentioned above, the use of credit information on a person is prohibited unless consent is obtained from the person on whom the credit report is subject before its release. Therefore, unless the private investigator is also licensed as a personal information investigator under the respective credit reporting legislation and is employed by a consumer reporting agency, and consent is obtained from the subject person to obtain his or her credit information, this source of information is prohibited to private investigators. An exemption to this rule, however, as alluded to above, is if the private investigator is acting as an agent for a creditor who is his or her client.[26]

Little case law was uncovered with respect to consumer reporting violations by private investigators. In one case, a private investigator in Ontario who also owned a consumer

---

24   Equifax Canada Inc. is the sole distributor of Canadian personal credit information. There are a number of companies such as Dun and Bradstreet and Canadian Credit Reports Inc. that distribute credit information on businesses. For Equifax's operating guidelines on confidentiality, see <www.equifax.ca/Home/Docs/privacy.htm>.

25   Ryan, "Privacy, Orthodoxy, and Democracy" (1973) 51 Can. Bar Rev. 84 at 88. See more recently P. Peladeau, "The Information Privacy Challenge: The Technological Rule of Law" in R.J. Cholewinske, ed., *Human Rights in Canada: Into the 1990s and Beyond* (Ottawa: Human Rights Research and Education Centre, University of Ottawa, 1990).

26   M. Fitz-James, "Investigating People and Their Assets" *Law Times* (1 June 1998). The author reports that historically credit bureaus have been the biggest source of information for private investigators but that the rules have been tightened to prohibit such searches to clients who are creditors wherein the private investigator acts as agent.

reporting agency was fined $400 for using information he obtained under the guise of consumer reporting in one of his private investigation reports.[27]

5.3   PROVINCIAL PRIVACY LEGISLATION

5.3.1   The Creation of the Tort of Invasion of Privacy

The provinces of British Columbia, Manitoba, Newfoundland, Quebec, and Saskatchewan each have legislation creating the tort of invasion of privacy.[28] The legislation is fairly similar in these provinces with the exception of Quebec. The first province to establish privacy legislation was British Columbia.[29] The story goes that the legislation was enacted as a direct result of an incident wherein a meeting of union leaders in a hotel room was monitored electronically by members of a rival union. As a result, there was a Commission of Inquiry into the Invasion of Privacy that recommended the legislative creation of a civil remedy for invasion of privacy. At the time, the *Criminal Code* was silent on the issue.[30]

5.3.2   The Scope of the New Tort

The privacy legislation in the various provinces makes it a tort to invade the privacy of another. Unlike the common law torts, this tort is actionable without proof of damages. In British Columbia, Newfoundland, and Saskatchewan, to commit the tort, the act must be committed wilfully and without claim of right. It would seem therefore that negligent intrusions of privacy do not fall under the scope of the legislation. In Manitoba the standard is lower; while requiring the violation to be substantial, it does not require the violation to be wilful but rather only unreasonable. Thus, negligent acts appear to be included if they are foreseeable.[31]

The legislation provides examples of conduct constituting breach of another's privacy. They include

- surveillance, whether auditory or visual, whether accomplished by trespass or not, of a person, his or her residence, or his or her vehicle;

---

27   *R. v. Gibson and Monarch Protection Services Ltd.* (1984), (Ont. Prov. Ct.) [unreported]. Information taken from Canadian Press reports dated 12 January 1984, 11 April 1984, and 11 July 1984.

28   R.S.B.C. 1996, c. 373; R.S.M. 1987, c. P125; R.S.N. 1990, c. P-22; S.Q. (1993-94), c. P-39.1; R.S.S. 1978, c. P-24.

29   In 1994, the Uniform Law Conference adopted a Uniform Privacy Act that proposed a statutory tort of invasion of privacy. Despite the Uniform Law Conference of Canada's continuing efforts to draft a Uniform Privacy Act, there are dramatic differences in the approach, application, and effect of the existing statutes.

30   I. Lawson, updated and edited by Bill Jeffrey, *Privacy and Free Enterprise: The Legal Protection of Personal Information in the Private Sector*, 2d ed. (Ottawa: Public Interest Advocacy Centre, 1997) at 71–97.

31   R.S.B.C. 1996, c. 373, s. 1(1); R.S.M. 1987, c. P125, s. 2; R.S.N. 1990, c. P-22, s. 3(1); R.S.S. 1978, c. P-24, s. 2.

- eavesdropping or recording a conversation in which that person participates;
- intercepting messages passed through phone lines or other means; and
- the use of letters, diaries, or other personal documents without a person's consent or the consent of the person who is in possession of them.

Violations of privacy may also be committed by other means. In Newfoundland and Saskatchewan, proof of any of the above listed types of conduct is sufficient for a *prima facie* finding of an invasion of privacy thus creating a reverse onus on the accused.[32]

5.3.3 Penalties

The penalties for breach of privacy are those generally available in tort actions. They include awards for damages, injunctions, an accounting of profits, or an order for a defendant to deliver up specific properties that have come into his possession by consequence of the breach. An award for damages shall include a consideration of

- the nature, incidence, and occasion of the act constituting the violation of privacy;
- the effect of the violation of privacy on the health, welfare, social, business, or financial position of the person or his or her family;
- the relationship between the parties to the action, whether domestic or otherwise;
- the distress, annoyance, or embarrassment suffered by the person arising from the violation of his or her privacy; and
- the conduct of the person before and after the incident, including an apology or offer to make amends.[33]

5.3.4 Defences

The legislation makes it clear that privacy is not an absolute right. The legislation provides that the degree and nature of privacy to which a person is entitled is that which is reasonable in the circumstances having regard for the lawful interests of others. Determining the degree of lawful privacy includes an analysis of the nature, incidence, and occasion of the act of invasion of privacy, and to any domestic or other relationship that exists between the parties. Although British Columbia, Newfoundland, and Saskatchewan require these matters to be taken into consideration when determining liability, these issues are only relevant in Manitoba when assessing damages.[34]

---

32 R.S.B.C. 1996, c. 373, s. 1(4); R.S.M. 1987, c. P125, s. 2; R.S.N. 1990, c. P-22, s. 4; R.S.S. 1978, c. P-24, s. 3.
33 R.S.B.C. 1996, c. 373, s. 1(1); R.S.M. 1987, c. P125, s. 4; R.S.N. 1990, c. P-22, s. 6; R.S.S. 1978, c. P-24, s. 6.
34 R.S.B.C. 1996, c. 373, s. 1(2)(3); R.S.M. 1987, c. P125, ss. 2 & 4; R.S.N. 1990, c. P-22, s. 3(2); R.S.S. 1978, c. P-24, s. 6.

The various legislation sets out a number of exceptions or defences to this tort. It excludes an act or conduct that is

* consented to by a person entitled to consent;
* incidental to the exercise of a lawful right of defence of person or property;
* authorized or required by a law, a court, or any process of a court; or
* done by a public or peace officer in the course of his or her duty and not committed by trespass.

The legislation of Manitoba and Saskatchewan further clarifies what constitutes consent by providing that it can be given implicitly or expressly. In Manitoba, a further reverse onus form of defence provides that if the defendant can prove he did not know or should not reasonably have known the act complained of would have violated the privacy of a person, liability cannot be found.[35]

The various legislation also addresses the issue of privacy in printed matter. Generally, the common law has held that the publication of a matter is not a violation of privacy if the matter published is of public interest or if the publication was, in accordance with the rules relating to defamation, a matter that is privileged.[36] Only Manitoba has expressly provided that privilege is a defence to defamation.

5.3.5 Limitation Periods

There are limitations to such tort actions. In British Columbia, Newfoundland, and Saskatchewan, the right of action terminates upon the death of the person who alleged her rights were violated. In Newfoundland, a right to an action also expires two years from the time when the violation of privacy first became known or should have become known, or seven years from the actual violation of privacy. In Saskatchewan, the right to an action expires two years after the discovery of the violation.[37]

5.3.6 Case Reviews

None of the statutory regimes has generated much judicial consideration. An example of an unsuccessful action against a private investigator is taken from the case of *Davis v. McArthur*.[38] In this case, an action was brought against a private investigator on the basis that the plaintiff was aware of the private investigator's surveillance and because the plaintiff had found a tracking device planted on his car. The case stemmed from a domestic investigation wherein a wife had hired the private investigator to keep tabs on her husband.

---

35 R.S.B.C. 1996, c. 373, s. 2(2); R.S.M. 1987, c. P125, s. 2; R.S.N. 1990, c. P-22, s. 5; R.S.S. 1978, c. P-24, s. 4.

36 R.S.B.C. 1996, c. 373, s. 2(2). See *Wooding v. Little* (1982), 24 C.C.L.T. 37 (B.C.S.C.) for a case on this issue. The various legislation also addresses the issue of the unauthorized use of the portrait of another, an issue not of relevance to this book.

37 R.S.B.C. 1996, c. 373, s. 5; R.S.N. 1990, c. P-22, ss. 10 & 11; R.S.S. 1978, c. P-24, s. 2.

38 (1969), 10 D.L.R. (3d) 250 (B.C.S.C.), rev'd (1970), 17 D.L.R. (3d) 760 (B.C.C.A.).

The plaintiff alleged that the private investigator's conduct had caused him to be upset and suffer ill health. In the end, the private investigator was found not to be liable to the plaintiff for breaching his privacy on the basis that the private investigator was acting as an agent of the wife and not out of malice or curiosity and therefore had a legitimate interest in the plaintiff's conduct. The private investigator acted with due circumspection without attracting public attention and otherwise reasonably in all the circumstances.

The issue of legitimate interest was later addressed in *Insurance Corporation of British Columbia v. Somosh and Somosh*.[39] In this case, the private investigator was found to have made telephone calls to the plaintiff's place of work seeking personal information of the plaintiff and to have gained entry into the plaintiff's home under pretext to ask personal questions of the plaintiff's wife. The court held that the conduct of the private investigators was improper because the insurance company had not yet made a claim against the defendants and therefore had no legitimate interest in having private investigators conduct such an investigation.[40]

In another case from British Columbia, a private investigator tricked the plaintiff into coming out of his house to discuss the sale of a car while a second investigator, hidden from view, made a recording of the scene for the information of the I.C.B.C. The court held that such conduct did not breach the *Privacy Act* but was a trespass.[41]

More recently a court had an opportunity to analyze the conduct of a private investigator in Newfoundland.[42] In that case, the plaintiff alleged that a private investigator had filmed her outside her residence and then followed her at a high rate of speed in his vehicle through her town. The court held that consideration must be given to the relationship between the parties and the balancing of interests between those of the complainant and those having a legitimate interest in her. The court concluded that the private investigator had a legitimate interest because the plaintiff was receiving benefits from an insurance company; the private investigator had been retained by an insurance company; and the function the private investigator was performing — that of determining if the plaintiff was a malingerer — had a social utility recognized by the courts.

In cases not involving private sector investigators, the courts have held that unauthorized photographs taken of the front of a plaintiff's residence, which were not obtained by trespass and which were later broadcast on television, were not an invasion of privacy

---

39   (1983), 41 B.C.L.R. 344 (S.C.).

40   Another action where legitimate interest was at issue was *Lee and Weber v. Jacobson* (1992), 87 D.L.R. (4th) 401 (B.C.S.C.), rev'd on other grounds related to the defendant's alibi in (1994), 99 B.C.L.R. (2d) 144 (C.A.). In this case, the plaintiffs alleged their landlord had installed a peephole and a two-way mirror in their bedroom attached to a small shed for the purpose of making observations. The court awarded punitive damages in the amount of $22,500 in addition to compensatory damages of $5,000 on the basis that the defendant's conduct was of such a reprehensible and pernicious nature that it merited condemnation.

41   *Rusche v. Insurance Corporation of British Columbia* (1992), 4 C.P.C. (3d) 12 (B.C.S.C.).

42   *Druken v. RG Fewer & Associates Inc.*, [1998] N.J. 312 (S.C.).

because the front of the home was viewable by the public.[43] The same has been held with respect to surveillance taken of a business from the parking lot of an adjacent business.[44]

With regard to printed matter, it has been held that the disclosure of unpublished financial statements by a firm of chartered accountants to the Crown prior to trial was not a breach of the chartered accountant's client's privacy in circumstances where the documents had been disclosed in a separate judicial inquiry.[45]

The case law was summarized succinctly by a Canadian commentator in a paper prepared by Elaine Geddes for the Alberta Law Review:

> Cases decided under the various Privacy Acts have been rare, notwithstanding that they have been in force for over two decades. Thus, the amount of guidance they offer with respect to what may be considered to be an invasion of privacy is limited. However, the following comments can be made with respect to the private investigator. An investigation which is discreet and unobtrusive will not be an invasion of privacy. Discretion may be shown by minimizing contact with the subject and refraining from any behaviour calculated, or reasonably likely to result in fear or anxiety. Trespassing, while not an invasion of privacy *per se*, substantially increases the likelihood that other behaviour may be considered to be actionable. Surveillance alone is not actionable; there must be other elements present to find an invasion of privacy. Regrettably, no case has dealt with the taking of photographs or films of a subject and so the propriety of this activity cannot be properly judged. In American cases filming alone is not actionable. The cases involving the BCTV appear to stand for the proposition that filming of an individual while on public property or on private property open to the public view is not actionable. The questioning of a subject is not an invasion of privacy, nor is the questioning of third parties, but when these questions deviate from what is pertinent to the investigation, an invasion of privacy may exist.[46]

5.3.7 Quebec

In Quebec there are a number of laws that are privacy driven. They include Bill 68: *An Act Respecting the Protection of Personal Information in the Private Sector*, Article 1457 of the *Civil Code*, and sections 4 and 5 of the Quebec *Charter of Human Rights and Freedoms*.

---

43 *Belzberg v. Broadcasting Systems Ltd.* (1981), 3 W.W.R. 85 (B.C.S.C.). Note in this case the public interest defence was also successfully argued.

44 *Silber v. B.C.T.V. Broadcasting Systems Ltd.* (1986), 69 B.C.L.R. 34 (S.C.). Note here, though, that the television crew was found to be trespassing on the property from which the film was taken. In this case, the public interest defence was also successfully argued.

45 *Bingo Enterprises Ltd. v. Plaxton* (1986), 26 D.L.R. (4th) 604 (Man. C.A.), aff'g (1985), 36 Man. R. (2d) 249, leave to appeal to the S.C.C. refused (1986), 46 Man R. (2d) 160.

46 E.F. Geddes, "The Private Investigator and the Right to Privacy" (1989) 17 Alta. L. Rev. 256 at 299.

5.3.7.1   Bill 68

Bill 68,[47] established in 1994, extended privacy rights to persons who were the subject of information gathering by persons in the private sector. The Commissioner of Access to Information for the public sector had the Commissioner's powers extended to supervise the administration of the new private sector law. Both laws have been accorded quasi-constitutional status in the respect that they are intended to take precedence over other Quebec legislation. Although the new law does not prohibit the exchange of bare nominative lists (lists consisting of only names, addresses, and telephone numbers), it does require that

- the indirect information collected be restricted to what is legitimately required for the intended purpose;
- the person who is the subject of the inquiry be apprised of the secondary purposes of the information gathered with respect to him or her; and
- the person who is the subject of the inquiry be permitted to opt out of any list where his or her data is exchanged.

The exchange of secondary purpose information lists containing information beyond the basic normative data may only be carried out where the subject has opted-in.

5.3.7.2   The *Civil Code* of Quebec

The second source of privacy law is the *Civil Code* of Quebec.[48] Article 1457 sets out definitions for the duty of care and standard of care expected of people in Quebec. It provides:

> Art. 1457: Every person has a duty to abide by the rules of conduct which lie upon him, according to the circumstances, usage or law, so as not to cause injury to another. Where he is endowed with reasons and fails in this duty, he is responsible for any injury he causes to another person and is liable to reparation for the injury, whether it be bodily, moral or material in nature. He is also liable, in certain cases, to reparation for injury caused to another by the act or fault of another person or by the act of things in his custody.

This single provision has been described as embodying the entire law of torts in Quebec.[49]

The *Civil Code* includes a number of provisions dealing specifically with privacy under the heading "Respect for Reputation and Privacy." It provides that everyone has a right to the respect of his or her reputation and privacy. The types of invasions of privacy cited include

- entering the dwelling of another and taking anything therein;
- intentionally intercepting private communications;
- observing a person in his or her private life by any means;

---

47   S.Q. (1993-1994), c. P-39.1.
48   S.Q. 1991, c. 64 (which came into force in 1994).
49   *Regent Taxi and Transport Company Ltd. v. La Congregation des Petits Freres de Mari*, [1929] S.C.R. 650 at 655.

* using a person's name, image or likeness for a purpose other than the legitimate information of the public; and

* using a person's correspondence, manuscripts or other personal documents.

The *Civil Code* further sets out a series of principles on the keeping of files on other persons. It provides no one shall establish a file on another person unless there is a serious and legitimate interest for doing so. Persons who do establish such files must act in good faith and with prudence so as not to damage the reputation or invade the privacy of another. Information in these files must be accessible, and the subject person may examine and cause the rectification of any file kept on him or her. Although access to a file may be denied for serious and legitimate reasons, any dispute or uncertainty as to access may be resolved by an application to a court.[50]

A number of tort actions for breach of privacy have arisen from the *Civil Code*.[51] In one case, the plaintiff wrote an uncomplimentary letter to the defendant about its television show. The show's master of ceremonies decided the plaintiff needed some "cheering up" and broadcast the plaintiff's home address and telephone number. The plaintiff sued for damages for, among other things, the "damaging invasion of privacy" resulting from thousands of viewers causing him harm. The plaintiff led evidence that within minutes of the broadcast, the plaintiff's phone rang continuously for three days, taxis were sent to his address, food parcels were sent to him C.O.D., and he received over 100 abusive letters. The court found the defendant's conduct constituted a "positive wrongful act" and assessed $3,000 in compensatory damages.[52]

In another case, the plaintiff alleged an invasion of privacy after the defendant showed a documentary film of the Woodstock music festival wherein there was footage of the plaintiff running naked in the rain. In this case, the court held there was no such breach as the defendant was able to prove the public interest in showing the tape outweighed any violation of the plaintiff's privacy.[53]

5.3.7.3   Quebec's *Charter of Human Rights and Freedoms*

A final source of privacy law in Quebec is its *Charter of Human Rights and Freedoms*.[54] Although Quebec may have been slower than the other provinces to create basic human rights legislation, its legislation leads Canadian human rights enactments in the realm of privacy protection. Quebec's *Charter* provides that every person has a right to the safeguard of dignity, honour, and reputation, and that every person has the right to respect for his private life. The Quebec *Charter* further provides that a person whose rights have been infringed may apply to a court to prevent the continuation of the violation and seek damages.

---

50   See *An Act to Add the Reformed Law of Persons, Succession and Property to the Civil Code of Quebec*, S.Q. 1987, c. 18, ss. 35 to 41; later replaced by the *Civil Code of Quebec*, S.Q. 1991, c. 64.

51   Actually from its predecessor: *The Civil Code of Lower Canada, 1866*, Article 1053.

52   *Robbins v. Canadian Broadcasting Corporation* (Quebec) (1958), 12 D.L.R. (2d) 35 (Que. S.C.).

53   *Field v. United Amusement Corporation*, [1971] C.S. 283 (Que. S.C.).

54   R.S.Q. 1977, c. C-12, ss. 4, 5, & 49.

The Quebec *Charter* privacy provisions have been judicially considered in at least one case. A plaintiff's estate brought an action against the Montreal *Gazette* for publishing information that identified the plaintiff as being an AIDS victim. The resulting publicity was alleged to have been harmful to the plaintiff's health as he had taken careful steps to ensure that no one knew the nature of the illness, and that the release of the information caused the plaintiff to contemplate suicide. The court held that the Quebec *Charter*'s right to privacy meant that a person has a right to be anonymous — a right to solitude. Although privacy must be balanced against other interests such as a newspaper's publishing public interest matters, such public interest does not include opportunism for the purpose of making a profit of an otherwise private matter. The court further held that the plaintiff did not need to prove fault within the meaning of Article 1053 of the *Civil Code*. Rather, under the Quebec *Charter* the plaintiff merely had to establish an unjustified publication of personal information. The court also held that it was not necessary for the defendant to actually publish the plaintiff's name, but that liability could be found by merely publishing information sufficient for the identification of the plaintiff to be known. The newspaper was ordered to pay $30,000 in compensatory damages and a further $7,500 in punitive damages.[55]

The cases here reviewed pertaining to Quebec's privacy legislation all involve defendants who are members of the media. Quite obviously, private sector investigators are not accustomed to distributing information in a similar fashion. The cases are included, however, because general principles can be taken from them that are useful in understanding the scope of Quebec privacy laws.

5.4   FREEDOM OF INFORMATION AND PRIVACY LEGISLATION[56]

The federal government and every province except Prince Edward Island and Nunavut have a variation of freedom of information and protection of privacy legislation. Table 5.2 lists the titles of the various Acts relevant to this section.

5.4.1   Prohibitions

The various legislation prohibits the collection of personal information by governments unless the collection is expressly authorized by statute; the information is collected for law enforcement purposes; or the information relates directly to, and is necessary for, operating a program or activity of a public body.

Personal information may only be collected directly from the individual concerned unless otherwise authorized by the individual or by statute. The individual from whom personal information is collected must be told the purpose for collecting the information. The legislation imposes a positive duty on public bodies to make sure the information collected is accurate. Public bodies are prohibited from using personal information for purposes other than those for which it was collected.

---

55   *Valiquette v. The Gazette*, [1991] R.J.Q. 1075 (Que. S.C.).

56   Much of the information provided here is from David Johansen, *Federal and Provincial Access to Information Legislation: An Overview* (Ottawa: Law and Government Division of the Parliamentary Research Branch, July 1997).

TABLE 5.2

Legislation Governing Freedom of Information and Protection of Privacy

Province	Legislation
Canada	*Access to Information Act*, R.S.C. 1985, c. A-1
Alberta	*Freedom of Information and Protection of Privacy Act*, S.A. 1994, c. F-18.5
British Columbia	*Freedom of Information and Protection of Privacy Act*, R.S.B.C. 1996, c. 165
Manitoba	*Freedom of Information Act*, R.S.M. 1987, c. F175
New Brunswick	*Right to Information Act*, S.N.B. 1978, c. R-10.3
Newfoundland	*Freedom of Information Act*, R.S.N. 1990, c. F-25
Northwest Territories	*Access to Information and Protection of Privacy Act*, S.N.W.T. 1994, c. 20
Nova Scotia	*Freedom of Information and Protection of Privacy Act*, S.N.S. 1993, c. 5
Ontario	*Freedom of Information and Protection of Privacy Act*, R.S.O. 1990, c. F.31
Quebec	*Access to Documents Held by Public Bodies and the Protection of Personal Information (An Act Respecting)*, S.Q. 1982, c. 30
Saskatchewan	*Freedom of Information and Protection of Privacy Act*, S.S. 1990-91, c. F-22.01
Yukon	*Access to Information and Protection of Privacy Act*, S.Y. 1995, c. 1

5.4.2 Who May Seek Information

Of interest to private investigators, of course, is who may request disclosure of government-held documents. The legislation of Alberta, British Columbia, Manitoba, New Brunswick, Nova Scotia, Ontario, Quebec, and Saskatchewan provides that any "person" (i.e., any individual or corporation) has the authority to seek access to information held by the government. Newfoundland restricts access to its information to Canadian citizens and landed immigrants domiciled in the province. The federal government restricts access to persons who are Canadian citizens and landed immigrants but authorizes the federal

Cabinet to extend these rights to include other persons. The federal Cabinet has extended the right to access information to all individuals and corporations present in Canada.[57]

5.4.3   Who Must Disclose Information

The next logical question is who must disclose government-held information. The statutes generally use one of the following terms to describe who is subject to the legislation: bodies, public bodies, boards, commissions, departments, government departments, foundations, Crown agencies, Crown corporations, school boards, hospital corporations, tribunals, associations, institutions, and government institutions. For the purposes of convenience, hereinafter bodies that are subject to freedom of information legislation will be referred to as "government institutions." Examples of government institutions excluded from the scope of the legislation include legislative counsel, provincial auditors, chief electoral officers, speakers of the legislature, members of the legislature, members of the court, and public archives.[58]

5.4.4   How to Make a Request

Requests for information from most provinces and the federal government must be in writing to the government institution that has control of the record. New Brunswick and Quebec are the notable exceptions to this rule as they allow for oral requests. However, in Quebec if a review is requested, the original request must be in writing. In Manitoba and Saskatchewan, the request must be on an official form. The other provinces do not require the request be made on a special form, although most government institutions have such forms available for the public. The request must provide sufficient detail to enable an experienced employee of the government institution to identify the record with reasonable effort. The required details include information as to time, place, and event.[59]

5.4.5   Exemptions to Disclosure

The legislation of the federal government and each of the provinces except New Brunswick contains mandatory and discretionary exemptions to the general rule of disclosure of information. In New Brunswick, all exemptions are discretionary.

---

57   R.S.C. 1985, c. A-1, s. 4(1)(2); S.A. 1994, c. F-18.5, s. 6(1); R.S.B.C. 1996, c. 165, s. 4; R.S.M. 1987, c. F175, s. 3; S.N.B. 1978, c. R-10-3, s. 2; R.S.N. 1990, c. F-25, s. 4; S.N.S. 1993, c. 5, s. 5; R.S.O. 1990, c. F.31, s. 10(1); S.Q. 1982, c. 30, s. 9; S.S. 1990-91, c. F-22.01, s. 5.

58   R.S.C. 1985, c. A-1, s. 3; S.A. 1994, c. F-18.5, ss. 3 & 4; R.S.B.C. 1996, c. 165, s. 3(1); R.S.M. 1987, c. F175, s. 1; S.N.B. 1978, c. R-10-3, ss. 1 & 2; R.S.N. 1990, c. F-25, ss. 2 & 3; S.N.S. 1993, c. 5, ss. 3(j) & 5; R.S.O. 1990, c. F.31, s. 2; S.Q. 1982, c. 30, s. 3; S.S. 1990-91, c. F-22.01, s. 2.

59   R.S.C. 1985, c. A-1, s. 6; S.A. 1994, c. F-18.5, s. 7; R.S.B.C. 1996, c. 165, s. 5; R.S.M. 1987, c. F175, s. 4; S.N.B. 1978, c. R-10-3, s. 3; R.S.N. 1990, c. F-25, s. 6; S.N.S. 1993, c. 5, s. 6(1); R.S.O. 1990, c. F.31, s. 24(1); S.Q. 1982, c. 30, ss. 42-45; S.S. 1990-91, c. F-22.01, s. 6.

In certain circumstances, a government institution must disclose information notwithstanding there exists an enumerated exemption to disclose. Such circumstances are known as public interest overrides. All the freedom of information legislation contains such provisions with the exception of Newfoundland and New Brunswick. The public interest override means that the public interest in disclosure outweighs the interest any person or government may have in the information being withheld. Examples of public interest overrides include issues such as public health, public safety, and protection of the environment. Again, however, even for the issues listed, the requester must show that the public interest outweighs the government's interest in refusing to disclose the information. Most legislation requires government institutions to notify third parties before the release of such information.[60]

One of the mandatory exemptions to disclosure is where another statute expressly provides that information shall not be disclosed notwithstanding the freedom of information legislation. For the federal legislation, there are approximately fifty different statutes that contain such a provision. In Newfoundland, this rule applies in any statute that requires information gained under it be kept confidential. In New Brunswick, the rule applies to any information that is required to be kept confidential by "law" — law meaning statute or common law. In Alberta, British Columbia, and Quebec, this exemption only applies to statutes enacted after the passing of the freedom of information legislation, and these statutes contain an express provision overriding the *Freedom of Information and Privacy Act*. In Ontario, the disclosure rule supersedes other legislation's confidentiality rules with the exception of eleven statutes listed in a schedule. The rule in Manitoba is the same as Ontario except that it only applies to five statutes. In Saskatchewan, a similar rule applies to twelve statutes. The freedom of information legislation in Nova Scotia is silent on this issue.[61]

Another mandatory exemption to disclosure is for *personal* information not relating to the requester. The exception to this rule is in New Brunswick where such information may be released in certain specified cases. A further exception to this rule in most provinces is if the individual to whom the information relates consents to its disclosure or if the information is publicly available.[62]

Similar in nature to personal information is *third-party* information, which is variously considered to be information that might particularly affect a person other than the gov-

60 R.S.C. 1985, c. A-1, s. 20(6); S.A. 1994, c. F-18.5, s. 31; R.S.B.C. 1996, c. 165, s. 25; R.S.M. 1987, c. F175, s. 42(4); S.N.S. 1993, c. 5, s. 31; R.S.O. 1990, c. F.31, ss. 11 & 23; S.Q. 1982, c. 30, s. 26; S.S. 1990-91, c. F-22.01, s. 19(3).

61 R.S.C. 1985, c. A-1, s. 24 and Schedule II; S.A. 1994, c. F-18.5, s. 5; R.S.B.C. 1996, c. 165, s. 78; R.S.M. 1987, c. F175, ss. 64(4), 65, & 66; S.N.B. 1978, c. R-10-3, s. 6(a); R.S.N. 1990, c. F-25, s. 9(1)(g); R.S.O. 1990, c. F.31, s. 67; S.Q. 1982, c. 30, ss. 168-170; S.S. 1990-91, c. F-22.01, ss. 17(3) & 23.

62 R.S.C. 1985, c. A-1, s. 19; S.A. 1994, c. F-18.5, s. 16; R.S.B.C. 1996, c. 165, s. 22; R.S.M. 1987, c. F175, s. 41; S.N.B. 1978, c. R-10-3, s. 6(b); R.S.N. 1990, c. F-25, s. 10; S.N.S. 1993, c. 5, s. 20; R.S.O. 1990, c. F.31, s. 21; S.Q. 1982, c. 30, s. 59; S.S. 1990-91, c. F-22.01, ss. 29 & 30.

ernment for which it is sought. In other words, the third party is not directly involved in the request for information. All the access statutes provide for an exemption from the disclosure of third-party information. Where it is disclosed, most of the access statutes require that the government institution give the third party notice before its release, and allow third parties to take proceedings to prevent its release. Disputes over the release of third-party information often deal with the trade, scientific, commercial, and financial secrets of third parties that may cause a financial loss.[63]

Information that would endanger an individual's health or safety is another form of exemption. This is a discretionary exemption in the federal legislation and in that of Alberta, British Columbia, Manitoba, Ontario, and Saskatchewan. This is a mandatory exemption in Quebec, except if the information is for public law enforcement purposes. There is no such exemption in Newfoundland and New Brunswick.[64]

Cabinet confidences are another form of exemption. In British Columbia this is a mandatory exemption if the information would disclose the deliberations of the Executive Council or any of its committees including any advice, recommendations, policy considerations, draft legislation, or regulations submitted to Executive Council or its committees. The exemption does not apply to information that has been in existence for fifteen years or more. Alberta's legislation is similar except that it also applies to deliberations of the Treasury Board or any of its committees. The legislation in Ontario, Quebec, and Saskatchewan is the same except that it extends the prohibition to Cabinet information to that in existence for twenty-five years or more. In Manitoba the rule is thirty years. In New Brunswick and Nova Scotia, the exemption is discretionary. The federal legislation is somewhat different in that it does not provide for an exemption, but rather states that its freedom of information legislation does not apply to Cabinet confidences. The significance of this provision is that the usual review procedures are not available to such a request. Federal Cabinet information can be sought if the information is more than twenty years old.[65]

Similar to Cabinet confidences are exemptions against disclosure of certain advice and deliberations about government operations and policy at the ministerial or other subcommittee level, to intergovernmental information exchanges and relations, to state defence

---

63   R.S.C. 1985, c. A-1, s. 20; S.A. 1994, c. F-18.5, s. 15; R.S.B.C. 1996, c. 165, s. 21; R.S.M. 1987, c. F175, s. 42; S.N.B. 1978, c. R-10-3, s. 6; R.S.N. 1990, c. F-25, s. 11(f); S.N.S. 1993, c. 5, s. 21; R.S.O. 1990, c. F.31, ss. 11, 17, & 23; S.Q. 1982, c. 30, ss. 23, 24, & 26; S.S. 1990-91, c. F-22.01, s. 19.

64   R.S.C. 1985, c. A-1, s. 17; S.A. 1994, c. F-18.5, s. 17; R.S.B.C. 1996, c. 165, s. 15(1)(e), 19; R.S.M. 1987, c. F175, s. 49; S.N.S. 1993, c. 5, ss. 15(1)(e) & 18; R.S.O. 1990, c. F.31, ss. 14(1)(e) & 20; S.Q. 1982, c. 30, s. 28(4); S.S. 1990-91, c. F-22.01, s. 21.

65   R.S.C. 1985, c. A-1, s. 69; S.A. 1994, c. F-18.5, s. 21; R.S.B.C. 1996, c. 165, s. 5; R.S.M. 1987, c. F175, s. 38; S.N.B. 1978, c. R-10-3, s. 6(a)(g)(h); R.S.N. 1990, c. F-25, s. 9(1)(b)-(f); S.N.S. 1993, c. 5, s. 13; R.S.O. 1990, c. F.31, s. 12; S.Q. 1982, c. 30, s. 13; S.S. 1990-91, c. F-22.01, s. 16.

and security, to economic interests of the government, and to information relating to law enforcement.[66]

Information protected by solicitor-client privilege is also exempt from disclosure under freedom of information legislation. The purpose of this exemption is to put the government on the same footing as other persons when it seeks legal advice. The exemption is discretionary for the government of Canada and for all other provinces.[67]

5.4.6 Fees

Fees are a part of life when dealing with governments. The various legislation provides for application fees, search fees, and reproduction fees. The fees change from time to time, although they can generally be characterized as nominal. To obtain exact fee information, contact the respective access to information office.

5.4.7 Reviews and Appeals

Finally, a requester who does not succeed in obtaining any or all of the information sought from a government institution is entitled to a "review" of the government institution's disposition. A review is often referred to as an appeal. All reviews must be made within one year from the time when the information request was received by the government institution in the federal realm. In Saskatchewan, the review must be requested within one year from the time the information disclosure report was sent out. In Alberta and Nova Scotia, the review must be made within sixty days of receiving the disclosure requested. In British Columbia, Newfoundland, Ontario, and Quebec, a review must be made within thirty days of the receipt of the information disclosure report. In New Brunswick and Manitoba, there are no time limits.

Another issue pertaining to reviews is to whom an appeal is made. In the federal realm and in Alberta, British Columbia, Ontario, Quebec, and Saskatchewan, a review is to the respective Information Commissioner. In Newfoundland, the review is to a judge of the trial division of the Newfoundland Supreme Court. In Nova Scotia, the review is to a review officer designated by Cabinet. Finally, in Manitoba and New Brunswick, the review is to an ombudsman or a judge of the Court of Queen's Bench.

The review process is adjudicative in nature in Alberta, British Columbia, Newfoundland, Ontario, and Quebec. The review process is investigative in nature in the federal realm and in Manitoba and Saskatchewan. The review process is both investigative

---

66 R.S.C. 1985, c. A-1, ss. 13, 14, 15, 16, 18, & 21; S.A. 1994, c. F-18.5, ss. 19, 20, 23, & 24; R.S.B.C. 1996, c. 165, ss. 13, 15, 16, & 17; R.S.M. 1987, c. F175, ss. 39, 40, 43, 44, & 45; S.N.B. 1978, c. R-10-3, s. 6; R.S.N. 1990, c. F-25, ss. 9 & 11; S.N.S. 1993, c. 5, ss. 12, 15, & 17; R.S.O. 1990, c. F.31, ss. 13, 14, 15, 16, & 18; S.Q. 1982, c. 30, ss. 18, 19, 21, 22, 28, & 35–39; S.S. 1990-91, c. F-22.01, ss. 13, 14, 15, 17, & 18.

67 R.S.C. 1985, c. A-1, s. 23; S.A. 1994, c. F-18.5, s. 26; R.S.B.C. 1996, c. 165, s. 14; R.S.M. 1987, c. F175, s. 40; S.N.B. 1978, c. R-10-3, s. 6; R.S.N. 1990, c. F-25, s. 11(d); S.N.S. 1993, c. 5, s. 16; R.S.O. 1990, c. F.31, s. 19; S.Q. 1982, c. 30, ss. 31 & 32; S.S. 1990-91, c. F-22.01, s. 22.

and adjudicative in nature in New Brunswick and Nova Scotia. An appeal of a review is made to the Federal Court in the federal realm, to the Court of Queen's Bench in Manitoba, Nova Scotia, and New Brunswick if the original appeal was to an ombudsman, to a Superior Court in Quebec on questions of law alone, and to the head of the impugned government institution in Saskatchewan. Secondary appeals are not permitted in Alberta, British Columbia, Newfoundland, and Ontario.[68]

5.4.8   Case Reviews

There are a couple of cases where private investigators have appealed a ruling of the freedom of information and protection of privacy commissioner to further their investigation. In a 1996 decision, an Ontario commissioner denied access on the grounds that information received in confidence by a government institution shall not be disclosed by another government institution.[69] Changes in Ontario's freedom of information legislation have now made this decision inappropriate to follow. The current argument that may be made in Ontario by a freedom of information and privacy commissioner is that access to records held by the PISGA registrar may be denied on the grounds that the information was obtained during an investigation, and that the release of such information would constitute an invasion of someone else's privacy.[70]

5.5   THE FEDERAL PRIVACY LEGISLATION

The *Personal Information Protection and Electronic Documents Act* (the Act or *PIPEDA*)[71] is the new federal legislation designed to further protect personal privacy. It has two distinct sections. Part 1 deals with the protection of personal information in the private sector. It protects personal information that is collected, used, or disclosed by organizations in the

---

68   R.S.C. 1985, c. A-1, ss. 30, 31, 37, 41, & 49-51; S.A. 1994, c. F-18.5, ss. 62, 68, & 69; R.S.B.C. 1996, c. 165, ss. 37, 42, 53, & 58; R.S.M. 1987, c. F175, ss. 14, 25, 27, 30, & 36; S.N.B. 1978, c. R-10-3, ss. 7, 8, 10, & 11; R.S.N. 1990, c. F-25, s. 12; S.N.S. 1993, c. 5, ss. 32, 33, 34, & 41; R.S.O. 1990, c. F.31, ss. 50 & 54; S.Q. 1982, c. 30, ss. 135, 141, 146, 147, & 154; S.S. 1990-91, c. F-22.01, ss. 49, 55, 56, & 57.

69   *Re Ontario Ministry of the Solicitor General and Correctional Services*, [1996] O.I.P.C. No. 326.

70   *Re Ontario Ministry of the Solicitor General and Correctional Services*, [1997] O.I.P.C. No. 10.

71   Section 5.5 was prepared by Ken Mitchell, CSC, CFE, of Mitchell Partners, a leading private investigative firm in Canada. Mr. Mitchell has been a private investigator for twenty-six years and is well respected within the industry. He is the current president of the Council of Private Investigators for Ontario as well as the past chair of the Certified Fraud Examiners Association's Insurance Fraud Committee. Mr. Mitchell has been the leading advocate for revisions of the *Personal Information Protection and Electronic Documents Act* on behalf of private investigators across Canada, appearing before Parliamentary subcommittees and lobbying members of Parliament on behalf of the industry. He can be contacted at (905) 304-5757 or see <http://www.mitchellpartners.com>. For an extensive commentary on the Act, see S. Perrin et al., *The Personal Information Protection and Electronic Documents Act: An Annotated Guide* (Toronto: Irwin Law, 2001).

course of commercial activities. Parts 2, 3, 4, and 5 establish legal protocols for the use of electronic data in business dealings with the federal government.

5.5.1   Background to the Act

The *Personal Information Protection and Electronic Documents Act* was first introduced in Parliament on 1 October 1999. It was sponsored by John Manley, Minister of Industry, and by Anne McClellan, Attorney General of Canada.

The Act is a major component of the Canadian Electronic Commerce Strategy announced by Prime Minister Chretien on 22 September 1998. The Prime Minister was quoted as saying its purpose was to "recreate in cyberspace the same expectations of trust, confidence, and reliability that now exist in everyday commerce."[72]

The impetus for *PIPEDA* can be found in the Data Privacy Directive (DPD) passed by the European Union in 1995 and implemented in October 1998. The DPD stipulates that trade can only take place in personal information among both member and non-member states that have laws protecting personal information in both the private and public sectors. Canada responded to the EU directive with its own legislation to protect international trade with EU member countries.

Canada had been working on privacy legislation for a number of years. The Uniform Law Conference of Canada (ULCC) is an independent group promoting the uniformity of laws across the country. The ULCC began work on a draft Uniform Data Protection Act in 1995. At federal-provincial-territorial meetings in 1998 the ministers agreed to adopt the Canadian Standards Association *Model Code for the Protection of Personal Information* as the minimum standard for privacy legislation in all jurisdictions.[73]

5.5.2   Application of the Act

The *Personal Information Protection and Electronic Documents Act* was passed by the Senate of Canada in December 1999, and was given Royal Assent on 13 April 2000. Part 1 came into force on 1 January 2001 and applies to federally regulated undertakings and business such as broadcasting, telecommunications, banks, airlines, and interprovincial transportation. It also applies to interprovincial and international trade in personal information.

From the perspective of the private sector investigation industry, on 1 January 2001, personal information collected in one province and transmitted to another came under the purview of this Act. On 1 January 2004, this law will apply to all private sector organizations in respect of the personal information that they deal with in the course of commercial activities. This will include business regulated under provincial or territorial jurisdiction. Part 1 of the Act does not apply to provincial government enterprises, municipalities, universities, or hospitals. It does not apply to noncommercial activities. It also does not apply to organizations that collect, use, or disclose personal information for journalistic, artistic, or literary purposes.

---

72   Cited at <http://info.ic.gc.ca/cmb/welcome.nsf>.
73   Industry Canada News Release, 1 October 1998 at 7.

5.5.3   Defining Personal Information

Personal information means information about an identifiable individual, but does not include the name, title, business address, or telephone number of an employee of an organization.

5.5.4   Obligations of Private Investigation Organizations

The *Personal Information Protection and Electronic Documents Act* introduces a new era of privacy regulation in Canada. It has far-ranging effects on the business practice of private sector investigators. The Act imposes strict rules with respect to the collection, use, and dissemination of personal information. Though introduced in Parliament as a result of "high-tech" or e-commerce drivers, the Act, in fact, affects every business entity in the country. This is especially true for firms providing private investigation services, quasi-police, and private police functions in the fight against crime.

The Act regulates all private investigation businesses operating in Canada that collect, use, and/or disclose personal information in the course of commercial activities. The Act sets parameters for the lawful collection of personal information used and distributed by fraud examiners, private investigators, insurance adjusters, or other security professionals. It limits the ability of investigative firms and the investigative units of private business and industry to lawfully collect, use, and disclose personal information of individual Canadians.

The Act further provides a process by which individuals who are the subject of a private investigation can demand access to any "records" held by a firm that pertains to them. It defines "record" broadly to include correspondence, videotapes, photographs, handwritten notes, computer files, sound recordings, drawings, maps, and so forth.

Subject to specific exemptions, the Act requires private investigation businesses to reveal to a requester the nature of any information concerning him or her that has been disclosed to third parties. It requires the identification of any individual who has received such information. Of course, this means the identity of the client of the private investigator.

Private investigation businesses must respond to requests for personal information within specified time frames or risk sanctions. If they do not, a complaint mechanism allows dissatisfied information seekers to appeal to the Privacy Commissioner of Canada who is vested with substantial powers to investigate the complaint.

The Federal Court is empowered to conduct hearings upon application by either a complainant or the Privacy Commissioner concerning alleged violations of the Act. Fines for noncompliance can range up to or beyond $20,000.

Every private investigation business must develop and adopt specific information management practices and policies, train staff to handle information requests and complaints, and facilitate the right of any person seeking access to their personal information.[74]

---

74   Analysis provided by Kris Klein, LLB, McCarthy Tetrault, 26 January 1999.

5.5.5   Incorporation of the Canadian Standards Association Model Code

The Canadian Standards Association Model Code[75] consists of ten interrelated principles:

1. **Accountability:** An organization is responsible for personal information under its control and shall designate an individual or individuals who are accountable for the organization's compliance with the following principles.

2. **Identifying Purposes:** The purposes for which personal information is collected shall be identified by the organization at or before the time the information is collected.

3. **Consent:** The knowledge and consent of the individual are required for the collection, use, or disclosure of personal information, except where inappropriate.

4. **Limiting Collection:** The collection of personal information shall be limited to that which is necessary for the purposes identified by the organization. Information shall be collected by fair and lawful means.

5. **Limiting Use, Disclosure, and Retention:** Personal information shall not be used or disclosed for purposes other than those for which it was collected, except with the consent of the individual or as required by law. Personal information shall be retained only as long as necessary for the fulfillment of those purposes.

6. **Accuracy:** Personal information shall be as accurate, complete, and up-to-date as is necessary for the purposes for which it is to be used.

7. **Safeguards:** Personal information shall be protected by security safeguards appropriate to the sensitivity of the information.

8. **Openness:** An organization shall make readily available to individuals specific information about its policies and practices relating to the management of personal information.

9. **Individual Access:** Upon request, an individual shall be informed of the existence, use, and disclosure of his or her personal information and shall be given access to that information. An individual shall be able to challenge the accuracy and completeness of the information and have it amended as appropriate.

10. **Challenging Compliance:** An individual shall be able to address a challenge concerning compliance with the above principles to the designated individual or individuals accountable for the organization's compliance.

The CSA Model Code is integrated into *PIPEDA* in Schedule 1 of the Act. This Schedule lays out the expectations of the Act and forms the foundation for its interpretation.

Section 4.1 of Schedule 1 deals with Principle 1 — Accountability. This section makes an organization responsible for personal information under its control, or information it

---

75   Canadian Standards Association, *Model Code for the Protection of Personal Information*, CAN/CSA-Q830/96.

has transferred to a third party. It requires an organization to designate specific persons responsible for the organization's compliance with the Act. This section requires organizations to implement policies and procedures, to protect personal information, to receive and respond to complaints, to train staff in the organization's policies and procedures, and to develop information to explain these to the public.

Section 4.2 of Schedule 1 deals with Principle 2 — Identifying Purposes. This section requires that the purpose for which personal information is collected be identified at or before the time the information is collected. This requires documentation of the purpose for the collection, that consent is obtained, and that the persons collecting the information be able to explain the purpose of its collection. If information is to be used subsequently for a different purpose, new authorization must be obtained.

Section 4.3 of Schedule 1 deals with Principle 3 — Consent. This section requires that the knowledge and consent of the individual be obtained for the collection, use, or disclosure of personal information, except where exempted under the Act. This section outlines examples of circumstances that would make the obtaining of consent inappropriate. These include legal, medical, and security reasons, fraud investigation or law enforcement. This principle requires knowledge and consent. For consent to be meaningful, the individual must know the purposes for the collection of his or her personal information. This section allows an individual to withdraw consent at any time.

Section 4.4 of Schedule 1 deals with Principle 4 — Limiting Collection. This section states that personal information collected shall be limited to that which is necessary for the identified purposes. Such information shall be collected by fair and lawful means.

Section 4.5 of Schedule 1 deals with Principle 5 — Limiting Use, Disclosure, and Retention. This section requires that personal information shall not be used or disclosed for purposes other than those for which it was collected. Personal information shall only be kept for as long as needed to accomplish the purpose for which it was collected. Personal information no longer required for its original purpose must be destroyed. If personal information is used to make a decision about an individual, it must be retained long enough to allow the person to access the information after the decision has been made. Organizations must have guidelines for the retention and destruction of personal information in their possession.

Section 4.6 of Schedule 1 deals with Principle 6 — Accuracy. This section requires that personal information collected shall be as accurate, complete, and as up to date as is necessary for the purposes for which it is to be used. The use of the information will determine the extent to which it shall be accurate, complete, and up to date, and must take into account the interests of the individual. Organizations must minimize the possibility that inappropriate information could be used to make a decision about an individual. Regular updating of information should be done only if it is necessary to fulfil the original purpose for which the information was collected.

Section 4.7 of Schedule 1 deals with Principle 7 — Safeguards. This section requires that personal information be protected with safeguards appropriate to the level of sensitivity of the personal information. Personal information must be protected against loss, theft, unauthorized access, disclosure, copying, use, or modification. The more sensitive the information, the higher the level of protection is required. Methods of protection may include physical measures such as locked file cabinets, storerooms, and offices; organizational measures such as security clearances and limited access; and technological measures such as passwords and encryption.

Section 4.8 of Schedule 1 deals with Principle 8 — Openness. This section requires an organization to make its policies and procedures relating to the management of personal information open and available to individuals. This information must include the name, title, and address of the person responsible for the organization's policies and practices, and to whom complaints and requests can be made. It must include the means of gaining access to personal information held by the organization, a description of the type of personal information held, how such information is used, and describe any personal information made available to a third party or subsidiary.

Section 4.9 of Schedule 1 deals with Principle 9 — Individual Access. This section requires an organization, upon request, to inform an individual of the existence, use, and disclosure of his or her personal information and to give access to that information. An individual shall be able to challenge the accuracy and completeness of such information, and be able to have it amended. Exceptions to this rule include information costly to provide, information about other individuals, information sensitive for legal, security, or commercial proprietary reasons, and information protected by solicitor-client or litigation privilege.

Section 4.10 of Schedule 1 deals with Principal 10 — Challenging Compliance. This section requires an individual to challenge an organization's compliance with the above principles. It requires organizations to put policies and procedures in place to receive, review, investigate, and respond to complaints relating to its handling of personal information. These policies and procedures must be simple and accessible. Organizations must investigate all complaints. If the complaint is justified, the organization must take appropriate measures.

5.5.6   Exception to the Principle of Knowledge and Consent

The *Personal Information Protection and Electronic Documents Act* recognizes both the unique role of traditional law enforcement when it comes to collecting personal information and the extent of private sector involvement in the fight against fraud and theft against private business and industry. Section 7(1) deals with the collection of personal information without the knowledge or consent of an individual. It provides:

7(1)   For the purpose of clause 4.3 of Schedule 1, and despite the note that accompanies that clause, an organization may collect personal information without the knowledge or consent of the individual only if

. . .

(b)   it is reasonable to expect that the collection with the knowledge or consent of the individual would compromise the availability or the accuracy of the information and the collection is reasonable for purposes related to investigating a breach of an agreement or a contravention of the laws of Canada or a province;

. . .

    (d) the information is publicly available and is specified by the regulations.

Section 7(1)(b) clearly allows private investigators to collect personal information without the knowledge and consent of the individual in any matter involving contract law, or any other breach of an agreement.

Section 7(1)(d) allows private investigators to collect personal information without the knowledge and consent of the individual if that information comes from a publicly available source as defined by the regulations. (Publicly available sources are discussed later in Section 5.5.9.2.)

Section 7(2) deals with the use of personal information without knowledge or consent of the individual. It provides:

7(2) For the purpose of clause 4.3 of Schedule 1, and despite the note that accompanies that clause, an organization may, without the knowledge or consent of the individual, use personal information only if

    (a) in the course of its activities, the organization becomes aware of information that it has reasonable grounds to believe could be useful in the investigation of a contravention of the laws of Canada, a province or a foreign jurisdiction that has been, is being or is about to be committed, and the information is used for the purpose of investigating that contravention;

    . . .

    (c.1) it is publicly available and is specified by the regulations; or by that section;

    (d) it was collected under paragraph (1)(a) or (b).

Section 7(2)(a) allows private investigators to use any personal information that comes into their possession if that information will further the investigation of the breach of any law of Canada, a province, or a foreign country. Section 7(2)(c.1) allows private investigators to use any personal information that is obtained from a publicly available source as defined by the regulations. Section 7(2)(d) allows private investigators to use personal information if it is collected in the investigation of the breach of an agreement or the contravention of the laws of Canada or a province.

Section 7(3) deals with the disclosure of personal information without the knowledge and consent of the individual. It provides:

7(3) For the purpose of clause 4.3 of Schedule 1, and despite the note that accompanies that clause, an organization may disclose personal information without the knowledge or consent of the individual only if the disclosure is

    . . .

    (c) required to comply with a subpoena or warrant issued or an order made by a court, person or body with jurisdiction to compel the production of information, or to comply with rules of court relating to the production of records;

    (c.1) made to a government institution or part of a government institution that has made a request for the information, identified its lawful authority to obtain the information and indicated that

i)   it suspects that the information relates to national security, the defence of Canada or the conduct of international affairs,

(ii) the disclosure is requested for the purpose of enforcing any law of Canada, a province or a foreign jurisdiction, carrying out an investigation relating to the enforcement of any such law or gathering intelligence for the purpose of enforcing any such law, or

(iii) the disclosure is requested for the purpose of administering any law of Canada or a province;

. . .

(d) made on the initiative of the organization to an investigative body, a government institution or a part of a government institution and the organization

(i)   has reasonable grounds to believe that the information relates to a breach of an agreement or a contravention of the laws of Canada, a province or a foreign jurisdiction that has been, is being or is about to be committed . . .

. . .

(h.1) of information that is publicly available and is specified by the regulations;

(h.2) made by an investigative body and the disclosure is reasonable for purposes related to investigating a breach of an agreement or a contravention of the laws of Canada or a province; or

(i)   required by law.

Sections 7(3)(c), (d), and (i) allow private investigators to disclose personal information to the appropriate government authorities. Section 7(3)(d) allows private investigators to disclose personal information to an "investigative body" as defined in the regulations. The term "investigative body" is crucial to private investigators and will be discussed below. Section 7(3)(h.1) allows private investigators to disclose personal information if it was obtained from a publicly available source. Section 7(3)(h.2) allows investigative bodies to disclose personal information without knowledge or consent if it relates to the breach of an agreement or the contravention of a law of Canada or a province.

5.5.7 Requirement of Private Investigators to Provide Access to Personal Information Collected

All commercial enterprises in Canada must provide individual access to personal information collected in the course of doing business. Section 9 of the Act spells out the organization's responsibilities. It provides:

9(3) Despite the note that accompanies clause 4.9 of Schedule 1, an organization is not required to give access to personal information only if

(a) the information is protected by solicitor-client privilege;

(b) to do so would reveal confidential commercial information;

(c) to do so could reasonably be expected to threaten the life or security of another individual;

(c.1) the information was collected under paragraph 7(1)(b); or

(d)   the information was generated in the course of a formal dispute resolution
       process.

Clearly, most of the work product of a private investigator will fall under one or more of the items listed under section 9(3). When a private investigator has collected personal information and any of the exceptions to disclosure listed in section 9(3) apply, the private investigator need not provide the individual with access to that information.

5.5.8   Contradictions in the Legislation

The legislation has clearly been drafted with an understanding of the needs of private business and industry in the investigation of contract disputes and breaches of the law. Section 7(1)(b) allows for the collection of personal information without knowledge or consent in these instances. Section 7(2)(d) allows for the use of information collected without knowledge or consent. Furthermore the "purpose" clause in section 3 states:

> The purpose of this Part is to establish . . . rules to govern the collection, use and disclosure of personal information . . . and the need of organizations to collect, use or disclose personal information for purposes that a *reasonable* person would consider appropriate in the circumstances. [Emphasis added.]

Reasonableness becomes the standard for all such activity.

Private investigators are able to *collect* and *use* personal information as it may pertain to the breach of an agreement or the contravention of a law. On the flip side, for each transaction under section 7(1)(b) "collection" and section 7(2)(d) "use," there must be an organization that deals with the issue of disclosure. Organizations may only *disclose* personal information to an investigative body. Clearly it was intended that organizations could disclose personal information if it related to an investigation of a breach of an agreement or a contravention of a law; otherwise, section 7(1)(b) would not have been worded as it is.

The inherent contradiction of private investigators being legally able to collect and use personal information, but organizations in possession of this personal information not being able to disclose it to private investigators is reconciled if private investigators are recognized as "investigative bodies" under the regulations. This step would require some consistent and coherent definition of a private investigator that is congruent with the legislated purpose of the Act.

5.5.9   The Regulations

Section 26 of the Act empowers the Governor in Council to make regulations

(a)   specifying, by name or by class, what is a government institution or part of a government institution for the purposes of any provision of this Part;

(a.01) specifying, by name or by class, what is an investigative body for the purposes of paragraph 7(3)(d) or (h.2);

(a.1)   specifying information or classes of information for the purpose of paragraph 7(1)(d), (2)(c.1) or (3)(h.1); and

(b)   for carrying out the purposes and provisions of this Part.

5.5.9.1   Regulations Specifying Investigative Bodies

In October 2000, Industry Canada prepublished the regulations specifying investigative bodies and publicly available information in the *Canada Gazette*.[76] The following is an excerpt.

REGULATORY IMPACT ANALYSIS STATEMENT

Description

Part 1 of the *Personal Information Protection and Electronic Documents Act* (the *Act*) establishes rules to govern the collection, use and disclosure of personal information by organizations in the course of commercial activity. The legislation requires an organization, which is disclosing personal information, to obtain the individual's consent in most circumstances. An exception to this rule is found in paragraphs 7(3)(d) and (h.2) of Part 1 of the *Act* which permit the disclosure of personal information to and by a private investigative body, without the knowledge or consent of the individual, if the investigative body is specified by the Regulations. The purpose of these Regulations is to name the investigative bodies for the purposes of paragraph 7(3)(d) or (h.2) of Part 1 of the *Act*.

Increasingly, many fraud investigations are initially launched by private sector organizations (e.g., a bank or insurance company) by way of an independent, non-governmental investigative body. Should the investigative body's preliminary investigation reveal grounds for suspecting that a fraud has been committed or a law contravened, the organization will then turn the findings over to a police or other enforcement agency for further action. Paragraph 7(3)(d) allows an organization to disclose personal information, without the consent of the individual, to the appropriate private sector investigative body in order to conduct the preliminary investigation. The disclosure is circumscribed, as it must be a reasonable disclosure related to investigations of breaches of agreements or contraventions of the law. Paragraph 7(3)(h.2) allows an investigative body to disclose personal information back to the client organization on whose behalf it is conducting the investigation.

Paragraph 7(3)(h.2) completes the exception provided in paragraph 7(1)(b) for collection without consent for the purposes of the prevention of fraud by extending it to disclosure. Collection alone would be of limited use to those combatting fraud, unless the information could be disclosed to the parties that need the information. However, without paragraph 7(3)(h.2), the flow of information could only go in one direction — from the organization to the investigative body. The investigative body would be unable to disclose the results of its investigation back to the client organization without consent.

The ability to exchange personal information between private organizations without consent for investigative purposes is the only exception granted to these organizations by the regulations. Organizations and investigative bodies which exchange personal information will remain responsible for compliance with all other requirements of the *Act* for this information, and will be subject to oversight by the Privacy Commissioner of Canada and the ability of individuals to seek redress in the Federal Court of Canada.

---

76   Excerpted from the *Canada Gazette*, Vol. 134, No. 41 (7 October 2000).

During the preparation of these regulations, Industry Canada developed a set of criteria that would be used in the assessment of candidates for investigative bodies. These criteria were intended to cover privacy concerns associated with allowing organizations to disclose personal information without consent for investigative purposes. All of the criteria would not necessarily be applicable to each investigative body. The criteria were based on the following considerations:

– The specific contraventions of law or breaches of agreements against which the investigative activities are directed;

– The specific personal data elements which are disclosed by other organizations to the body; the specific personal data elements which flow back to the organizations from the body; the uses and disclosures made of the information by the body; whether audit trails are maintained; the length of time the information is kept; and the security standards and practices in place for retention and disposal of the information;

– Whether the operational structure of the body or process is fully documented and formalized and the authority, responsibility and accountability centres are identified;

– Whether there are specific legal regime, licensing requirement, regulation or oversight mechanisms to which it is subject and whether sanctions or penalties for non-compliance exist;

– The privacy protection policies and procedures, such as a privacy code, followed by the body. The extent to which the policies and procedures comply with Part 1 of the *Act*;

– The extent to which the investigative body is independent from the association of members or client organizations that it serves;

– The extent to which all alternative methods of complying with the *Act*, such as contract or consent, have been exhausted; and

– The amount of information provided to individuals about the existence and operation of the body and about how to make a complaint or seek redress.

. . .

. . . Due to the phased introduction of the legislation and the fact that it is new to the private sector, it is expected that additions to the list of investigative bodies in the Regulations may be necessary. For this reason, the Department [of Industry] will continue to consider applications on a case-by-case basis in the future.

. . .

Alternatives

The legislative framework in Part 1 of the *Act* requires that an investigative body, for the purposes of paragraph 7(3)(d) or (h.2) of the *Act*, be specified by the Regulations. There are no alternatives to deal with the collection, use and disclosure of this information without consent.

. . .

. . .The Governor in Council, Pursuant to Paragraph 26(1)(a.01) [of the Act], Proposes to Make the Annexed Regulations Specifying Investigative Bodies [for the purposes of the Act].

. . . The following investigative bodies are specified . . .

    (a) the Insurance Crime Prevention Bureau, a division of the Insurance Council of Canada; and

    (b) the Bank Crime Prevention and Investigation Office of the Canadian Bankers Association.[77]

5.5.9.2   Regulations Specifying Publicly Available Information

The following is an excerpt from the *Canada Gazette*.[78]

REGULATORY IMPACT ANALYSIS STATEMENT

Description

Part 1 of the *Personal Information Protection and Electronic Documents Act* (the *Act*) establishes rules to govern the collection, use and disclosure of personal information by organizations in the course of commercial activity. The legislation requires an organization which is collecting, using or disclosing personal information, to obtain the individual's consent in most circumstances. Exceptions to this rule are found in paragraphs 7(1)(d), (2)(c.1) or (3)(h.1) of the *Act* which permit the collection, use and disclosure of personal information, without the knowledge or consent of the individual, if the information is publicly available and is specified by the Regulations. The purpose of this regulation is to specify what information and classes of information is publicly available information for the purposes of paragraphs 7(1)(d), (2)(c.1) and (3)(h.1) of the *Act*.

The basic premise underlying this regulation is that the collection, use and disclosure of publicly available personal information for commercial purposes should be subject to the same fair information practices as are required by the *Act* for all other personal information. As a rule, individuals are able to decide for themselves with whom they will share personal information and under what circumstances. However, some personal information enters into the public sphere through a variety of channels, often without the knowledge or consent of the individual. Examples include personal information that appears in telephone or other directories, public registries maintained by governments, public court records or that is published in the media. This personal information is made public for a specific and primary purpose, e.g., individuals allow their name, address and telephone number to appear in the telephone or other directories to enable others to contact them for personal reasons, to enable potential clients to reach them in their professional capacity or to enable others to verify their title, membership or professional qualifications. Some government registries such as land titles, personal property, municipal property tax rolls, are open to the public to promote long-standing public policy purposes. Public access is permitted to some court

---

77   These Regulations came into force on 1 January 2001.

78   See above note 76.

records to facilitate transparency in the justice system, while other personal information is placed in publications to publicize specific information about the individual (e.g., birth and marriage announcements).

Privacy concerns arise because more information is sometimes collected in public registries (many of which were created in an era when privacy concerns were not fully considered) than is required for the fulfilment of the primary purpose. Other concerns relate to the manner in which the information is made publicly available, e.g., whether there are any controls or limitations placed on who may collect and use it and how (increasingly access is possible to an electronic record rather than to the traditional hard copy. Internet access is more common as well). The fact that individuals have continuing expectations of privacy for some publicly available personal information is seldom addressed. Another privacy issue is the growing use that commercial organizations make of this information for purposes that often have nothing to do with the primary purpose for which the information was made public, i.e., to contact individuals and offer them products or services. There is also an increasing tendency to collect and use publicly available information to create comprehensive personal profiles of the individual, including their consumption habits, lifestyles and personal histories for a variety of other purposes, including employment decisions. Many, if not most, of these secondary uses are presently carried out without the knowledge or consent of the individual. A final issue is that, with few rules to govern publicly available personal information, organizations have little incentive to consider obtaining consent from the individual.

The proposed Regulations will permit one exception from fair information practices by allowing commercial organizations to collect, use and disclose certain personal information without consent. The Regulations are based on a recognition that some personal information is publicly available for a legitimate primary purpose, often with the individual's tacit agreement (e.g., the telephone directory and announcements). In these circumstances, it is reasonable to allow organizations to collect, use and disclose this information without adding the requirement to obtain consent. To require an organization to obtain consent to use this information for its primary purpose would not contribute to the protection of the individual's privacy, would add to the organization's costs and could frustrate some public policy purpose. However, it is also reasonable to insist that any purpose other than the primary one should be subject to the consent requirement. This approach is consistent with Principle 2 of Schedule 1 of the *Act* (paragraph 4.2.4) which states that a new purpose requires consent unless required by law. Using the criteria of consistency with the primary purpose or tacit consent as the basis for the regulation of publicly available personal information strikes the appropriate balance between the individual's right of privacy and the business need for information. Organizations will remain responsible for compliance with all other requirements of the *Act* for this information, including the appropriate purpose requirement in Clause 5(3), and will be subject to oversight by the Privacy Commissioner of Canada and the ability of individuals to seek redress in the Federal Court of Canada.

. . .

. . . The Governor in Council, pursuant to paragraph 26(1)(a.01) [of the Act] proposes to make the annexed regulations Specifying Publicly Available Information.

. . .

. . . The following information and classes of information are specified for the purposes of paragraphs 7(1)(d), (2)(c.1) and (3)(h.1) [of the Act]:

(a)   personal information consisting of the name, address and telephone number of a subscriber that appears in a telephone directory that is available to the public, where the subscriber can refuse to have the personal information appear in the directory;

(b)   personal information including the name, title, address and telephone number of an individual that appears in a professional or business directory that is available to the public, where the collection, use and disclosure of the personal information relate directly to the purpose for which the information appears in the directory;

(c)   personal information that appears in a registry collected under a statutory authority and to which a right of public access is required by law, where the collection, use and disclosure of the personal information relate directly to the purpose for which the information appears in the registry;

(d)   personal information that appears in a court record to which public access is permitted, where the collection, use and disclosure of the personal information relate directly to the purpose for which the information appears in the record; and

(e)   personal information that appears in a publication, including a magazine, book or newspaper, that is available to the public, where the individual has provided the information.

5.6   INFORMATION BROKERS

A short overview[79] of the world of the information broker is included to demonstrate that often the investigative world does not have to resort to clandestine methods to provide their work product.

5.6.1   Business Information

The majority of information brokers in Canada are engaged in business research, and, as such, access public information on a fee-paid basis. Dow Jones Interactive, Canada StockWatch, and LEXIS-NEXIS among others provide excellent resources for commercial records. The amount of information available for business varies widely, depending on whether the company is incorporated, publicly or privately held, and if incorporated by province or nationally. For example, SEDAR has Canadian publicly held corporate filings and is searchable online.

---

79   This section was prepared by Mr. Syd Lapan, MSc, a leading information broker in Canada. He can be contacted at True North Research, Comox, British Columbia, Tel: (250) 339-7767, Fax: (250) 339-1867, e-mail: <sydlapan@home.com>.

To find an information broker to handle in-depth business research, check the membership list of the Association for Independent Information Professionals (AIIP) or the Special Librarians Association (SLA). For competitive intelligence, see the Society for Competitive Intelligence Professionals (SCIP). Some major public library systems, such as Vancouver Public Library's Info-Action, have a fee-paid research entity available. Common business records, such as boards of directors and business credit reports, are publicly available and searchable online.

5.6.2 Government Records

A smaller segment of Canadian information brokers are engaged in public records searching. In the United States, many companies claim that they can find out anything about anyone, while failing to mention that their records are out of date, incomplete, and most likely not about *the* John A. MacDonald that the buyer requested. In Canada, with a smaller population, stricter privacy laws, and a certain level of consistency across provinces, the records are more reliably retrieved and creditable.

Table 5.3 lists current access to drivers' abstracts across Canada.

Land titles, property assessments, liens, or personal property records are all publicly available in Canada for a fee. Check with the appropriate provincial offices or contact an information broker who has all the resources.

Other federal information that is available includes a civil aircraft database that offers the names of licensed pilots. Patents and trademarks are also national, public, and searchable.

Corporate records generally list board members' names and provide some financial information of publicly held companies. Strategis Canada is a Web site to promote federally incorporated businesses, import/export, and more. There is very little information available on privately held companies, such as Wal-Mart Canada, whereas Chrysler Canada is publicly owned so much more information can be obtained. Accessibility varies across the country. For example, in Nova Scotia, corporate records are free; in Ontario a fee is charged for access.

In summary, the bulk of public records are fee-based accounts. Availability and access is different for each province. An information broker will know all the rules and will be able to answer your questions.

TABLE 5.3

Access Information to Drivers' Abstracts

Province	Provider	Instructions
Alberta	List of Registry Agents offering different levels of service	Modest fee.
British Columbia	Insurance Corporation of British Columbia (ICBC)	Free fax-back number for owner of the licence
Manitoba	Provincial Government	Signed release. Modest fee.
New Brunswick	Atlantic Canada OnLine (ACOL)	Signed release. Modest fee.
Newfoundland	Provincial Government	Signed release. Modest fee.
Nova Scotia	Atlantic Canada OnLine (ACOL)	Signed release. Modest fee .
Ontario	Ministry of Transport	Available through the Internet. No fax-back. Results are mailed to the requester. Modest fee.
Prince Edward Island	Provincial Government	Signed release. Modest fee.
Quebec	Société de L'Assurance Automobile de Quebec (SAAQ)	Available only to the owner of the licence. Fee required.
Saskatchewan	Provincial Government	Signed release. Modest fee.

CHAPTER 6

THE LAW OF TORTS

A classic example of a tort action against a private investigator was demonstrated in the case of *Weber v. Ontario Hydro.*[1] In this case, Ontario Hydro hired a private investigator to obtain information on an employee suspected of abusing sick leave benefits. The private investigator used a pretext to gain entry onto the employee's property and to subsequently enter into his home. With the information the private investigator obtained under the ruse of an interview, Ontario Hydro suspended the employee's benefits. The employee brought action against Ontario Hydro for the actions of the private investigator for the torts of deceit, trespass, nuisance, and invasion of privacy.[2]

What Is Tort Law?

Notwithstanding that the right to investigate extends to all persons, in addition to regulatory and criminal forms of social control, the conduct of a person conducting an investigation is subject to tort law. Torts are not crimes, breaches of contracts, or infringements of equitable rights. Rather, a tort is a civil wrong for which an individual may seek remedies such as damages, declarations, or injunctions. Although tort law may have indirect consequences of deterrence and social control similar to that in the criminal context, the major function of tort law is to compensate the victim for his or her loss, and in some cases to vindicate oneself publicly while condemning the actions of the offender. It should be noted at the outset that prosecutions of both criminal and civil actions against the same individual arising out of the same conduct are not mutually exclusive. For example, one who commits an unlawful assault on another may be subject to both criminal prosecution by the state and to civil action for damages by the victim.[3]

---

1   [1995] 2 S.C.R. 929.
2   This case never went the distance as a tort action because the plaintiff successfully argued that the allegations had been dealt with internally by arbitration and therefore could not be addressed a second time through the courts.
3   R.M. Solomon & B.P. Feldthusen, *Cases and Materials on the Law of Torts*, 3d ed. (Toronto: Carswell, 1991) at 19.

Torts are basically broken down into two groups: intentional and non-intentional (or negligence) torts. The following is not an exhaustive description of tort law, for volumes have been written on each tort to be reviewed. However, a brief explanation of the torts to be covered is in order.[4]

The behaviour giving rise to intentional tort liability is closer to the elements of criminal liability than that of the other area of tort law. To establish that an intentional tort has occurred, there must have been an act that brought about the intended result by the actor. The intent required, however, is not equivalent to that of criminal intent. Evil motive or the desire to cause injury need not be the end goal; intent to cause the actual result is sufficient.[5]

Traditionally, the intentional torts have included battery, assault, false arrest, false imprisonment, trespass to land, and trespass to chattels. The tort of intentional infliction of nervous shock, also known as the intentional infliction of emotional distress, is a more recent addition to this list.[6] Furthermore, torts such as defamation, invasion of privacy and malicious prosecution have been designated as quasi-intentional torts.[7] Although the above is the conventional way of classifying torts, in this book the torts most relevant to private investigators are considered under headings similar to those used in the chapter on criminal liability, including Arrest and Use of Force, Surveillance, and Pretext. Other aspects of tort law to be reviewed include wrongs associated with a person's reputation, negligence, conspiracy, and the developing tort of invasion of privacy.

Vicarious Liability

The issue of vicarious liability must also be addressed. It is a well-established rule of law that a principal or employer may be held liable for the actions of his or her agent or employee committed within the scope of his or her authority or employment that causes compensable loss to another. Therefore, it is in the interest of employer private investiga-

---

4   For excellent references on tort law, please consult the following texts: P.H. Osborne, *The Law of Torts* (Toronto: Irwin Law, 1999); R.W.M. Dias & B.S. Markesinis, *Tort Law*, 2d ed. (Oxford: Clarendon Press, 1989); J.G. Fleming, *The Law of Torts*, 7th ed. (Sydney: The Law Book Company Limited, 1987); G.H.L. Fridman, *The Law of Torts in Canada*, 2 vols. (Toronto: Carswell, 1989); L.N. Klar, *Tort Law*, 2d ed. (Toronto: Carswell, 1996); W.L. Prosser, *Handbook on the Law of Torts*, 4th ed. (St. Paul: West Publishing Co., 1971); R.M. Solomon & B.P. Feldthusen, *Cases and Materials on the Law of Torts*, 3d ed. (Toronto: Carswell, 1991); and *Winfield and Jolowicz on Tort*, edited by W.V.H. Rogers, 13th ed. (London: Sweet & Maxwell, 1989).

5   A.J. Bilek, J.C. Klotter, & R.K. Federal, *Legal Aspects of Private Security* (USA: Anderson Publishing Company, 1982) at 158.

6   Note the original meaning of trespass is "a wrong." Therefore, to trespass another, or to wrong another, was the basis for all tort law. The term trespass was later restricted to physical contact and to land or chattel interference claims. Because the use of the term "trespass" in this context would only cause confusion, in this book it will only be used as a specific type of tort. See *Winfield and Jolowicz on Tort*, above note 4 at 53.

7   Bilek, Klotter, & Federal, above note 5 at 159.

tive agencies that their employee investigators are well versed in the limitations of their legal rights and obligations.

Notwithstanding that the principle of vicarious liability generally applies to principal-agent relationships, it should also be recognized that it generally does not extend to contractual arrangements. There are, however, exceptions. If the influence of the contracting party is such that the authority and control exerted by it is similar to that of an employer, the doctrine may apply. Evidence of such a relationship will often depend on the terms of the contract. As an independent contractor, the manager of a private investigation business must exercise the due diligence of a reasonable person in his or her field, regardless of the instructions of the person contracted with. Negligent acts committed by a private investigator following the instructions of a party to a contract for investigative services may or may not be imputed to the contracting party.[8]

Invasion of Privacy

Any analysis of tort law pertaining to private investigators would not be complete without a review of the topic of invasion of privacy. Invasion of privacy has many implications. In one sense, it can apply to surveillance-related activities such as videotaping. In another sense, it can apply to pretext-related activities such as obtaining private or confidential information under a ruse. Some studies have reported that many Canadians intuitively feel that the procuring of private information without their consent is improper.[9] However, a review of the law in this area does not bear this out.

In a leading text on privacy law in the private sector, the authors concluded that the subject is dealt with in a smattering of legislation and common law, but that there exists no general right to privacy in the private sector in Canada. The authors state:

> Lawyers advising clients about remedies for the unauthorized use or disclosure of personal information by a person or a company in the private sector may not easily arrive at an opinion. The few federal and provincial statutes applying to private sector activities are unlikely to provide clear solutions . . . If the problem can not be resolved by some legislative provision or informal means, counsel must look to the common law and equity . . . Consultation of leading texts such as Fridman's *The Law of Torts in Canada* (1990), Fleming's *The Law of Torts* (1987) and *Winfield and Jolowicz on Tort* (1989) disclose that privacy invasion is a concept of uncertain legal meaning which has not been recognized as the basis for a legal action. The recent text Rainaldi, ed., *Remedies in Tort* (1990) assigns a brief discussion of privacy to the last chapter entitled "Developing Torts". Even a look at Halsbury's, to which counsel often turn when Canadian law is insufficient, yields disappointment . . .In the volume on torts, infringement of privacy is assigned only one paragraph which states "a person does not commit a tort

---

8   P.C. Stenning & M.F. Cornish, *The Legal Regulation and Control of Private Policing and Security in Canada: A Working Paper* (Toronto: Centre of Criminology, University of Toronto, 1975) at 179.

9   See Ekos Research Associates Inc., *Privacy Revealed: The Canadian Privacy Survey* (Toronto: 1993). Ninety-two percent of the 3,000 Canadians surveyed expressed "moderate" levels of concern about privacy; 52 percent expressed "extreme" concern.

merely because he unreasonably invades the privacy of another," . . . and "there is no general right to privacy in English law." If time is taken to search out legal literature on the topic, it will be found there are no textbooks for the practitioner on the subject of privacy published in Canada . . . Counsel determined to forge a path into this unfriendly territory will be met with frequent signposts bearing the warning "There is no legal right to privacy in common law." Legal scholars along the way will point out that few lawyers attempt to head in this direction, and fewer still manage to achieve the desired result for their clients.[10]

Notwithstanding the reluctance of Canadian and English courts to declare the "invasion of privacy" a tort in and of itself, there are a number of torts in the two countries that more or less cover this notion. Under the torts of nuisance and defamation, the courts have protected individuals against harassing telephone calls,[11] the watching and besetting of a house,[12] the public display of personal papers,[13] the electronic surveillance of a home,[14] and the unauthorized publication of a photograph.[15] These torts will be explored in greater detail later in this chapter.

While Canadian courts have refused to classify these torts under the title of invasion of privacy, American courts have acknowledged this reality. However, notwithstanding that American courts have recognized the tort of invasion of privacy, leading American commentators report that this tort is really a compilation of four separate torts:

1.   the intrusion into another's seclusion or solitude or private affairs concerning actions based on nuisance and trespass to person, land, or chattels or extending beyond physical intrusion to eavesdropping and wiretapping;

2.   public disclosure of embarrassing facts about another, which in reality is an extension of the tort of defamation;

3.   publicity that places another in a false light in the public eye, again which is an extension of the law of defamation with overtones of the intentional infliction of mental distress; and

4.   the appropriation of another's likeness for commercial advantage.[16]

This distinction between common law privacy decisions in the Commonwealth and those in the United States, however, may be more academic than real. In the latter country, a plaintiff can bring an action under the head of "invasion of privacy," while in the former the plaintiff must seek redress under some other more specific cause of action.

---

10   I. Lawson, *Privacy and Free Enterprise: The Legal Protection of Personal Information in the Private Sector*, 2d ed. updated and edited by Bill Jeffery (Ottawa: The Public Interest Advocacy Centre, 1997) at ii. Note this quote was written before the new federal privacy legislation discussed in Section 5.5.
11   *Motherwell v. Motherwell*, [1976] 6 W.W.R. 550 (Alta. C.A.).
12   *Lyons & Sons v. Wilkins*, [1899] 1 Ch. D. 255 (C.A.).
13   *Prince Albert v. Strange* (1949), 64 E.R. 293.
14   *Grieg v. Grieg*, [1966] V.R. 376 (Austl. S.C.).
15   *Williams v. Settle*, [1960] 1 W.L.R. 1072.
16   W.L. Prosser, "Privacy" (1960) 48 Cal. L. Rev. 383 at 406.

Sparse Authority

Finally, it must be acknowledged that although tort law may seem as fertile a legal ground on which to bring action against a private investigator as either the regulatory or criminal areas previously discussed, the case law does not bear this out. One reason for the lack of case law may be due to rather nominal awards levied against such defendants. Other reasons include the reality that the litigation process is slow and expensive, the outcomes of cases are highly unpredictable, and the compensatory value is often vitiated by the financial inability of the defendant to satisfy a judgement.[17]

6.1   TORTS ARISING FROM ARRESTS

As discussed in Chapter 4, arrests by private persons are generally an uncommon occurrence in Canadian society because of the average citizen's reluctance to get involved and his or her ignorance on such matters. Exceptions are private sector store investigators arresting shoplifters for theft and security guards arresting persons who refuse to leave a private premise for trespassing. Outside of the above circumstances, it is only on the rare occasion when a private investigator may find herself in a position where the dilemma of arresting a person may arise.

Regardless of how infrequently the situation occurs, it is useful for a private investigator to be aware of the torts that can arise from the performance of this task. In this section, the torts of assault, battery, false imprisonment, and malicious prosecution are briefly discussed.

6.1.1   Battery

A battery is an unauthorized affirmative act by the defendant that brings about a harmful or offensive contact with the person of another. The person who commits a battery on another is liable for all the resulting consequences whether foreseen or not. If the battery was maliciously intended, punitive damages may also be recovered by the victim. To recover general damages, it is not necessary to prove that any real harm resulted to the victim, but only that the intended contact was unauthorized.[18]

6.1.2   Assault

As opposed to a battery that requires contact, an assault involves an unauthorized act that causes a reasonable apprehension of immediate harmful or offensive contact on the part of the victim. Words alone will not constitute an assault; some threatening gesture is

---

17 Stenning & Cornish, above note 8 at 186. See *Rusche v. Insurance Corporation of British Columbia* (1992), 4 C.P.C. (3d) 12 (B.C.S.C), where the court awarded $1 against a private investigator for trespass. See also M. Zapf, "B.C. Court Lays Down Law on Quantum of Nominal Award" *Lawyers Weekly* (14 February 1992) at 6.

18 W.L. Prosser, *Handbook for the Law of Torts,* 4th ed. (St. Paul: West Publishing Co., 1971) at 34–37)

required. The person who commits an assault must have the intent to cause apprehension by the victim, and the victim must in fact have been apprehensive.[19]

Although battery is simple enough to determine, case law has shown that determining what constitutes assault is not so clear. In one case, it was held that the act of striding towards another with fists clenched was sufficient for the act of assault.[20] In another case, it was held that taking a weapon in hand and stating "if it were another time, I would not take such language from you" does not constitute an assault.[21] Although threats without gestures generally do not constitute an assault, in one American case a court held that a debt collection agent was held liable in trespass to the person for shouting at a pregnant woman that she was a deadbeat and that he was going to send the sheriff after her because of her unpaid account. The court held that the woman's fright from the threat was reasonable in the circumstances, and that although there was no threatening gesture, the principle of granting relief for fright was sufficient for extending the tort in this case.[22]

6.1.3 False Imprisonment

The tort of false imprisonment or false arrest involves the unauthorized restraint of the victim's freedom or movement. The only elements necessary to create liability for false imprisonment are detention and its unlawfulness. Malice and lack of probable cause need not be proven. Any restraint, however brief, if unauthorized, gives rise to a cause of action and the victim may recover for the resulting damages including mental anguish and humiliation. Restraint does not require touching. It is sufficient that the victim is restrained from free movement by threats, demands, or the like, which reasonably cause him to believe that force will be used if he fails to comply.[23]

In one Canadian case, a store owner hired a private investigator to determine if internal thefts were being committed by the cleaning staff. One evening, before leaving at the end of shift and without any prior notice, the private investigator and the store owner took some of the cleaning staff to a locked room where they were subjected to pat-down searches. Nothing was found and the cleaning staff were later released. The court held that it was clearly the intention to hold the cleaners in the premises while an investigation was being made regardless of their consent. The court found this constituted false imprisonment. As the cleaners did not object to being searched, and as the search was conducted with civility, there was nothing objectionable about the search itself. The court assessed damages at $100 and entitled the cleaners to costs.[24]

---

19 *Ibid.* at 37–41.

20 *Tuberville v. Savage* (1669), 86 E.R. 685.

21 *Stephens v. Myers*, 188 S.E. 625 (N.C.S.C. 1840); *Adams v. Rivers*, 11 Barb. 390 (N.Y.S. 1851).

22 *Kirby v. Jules Chain Stores Corp.*, 188 S.E. 625 (N.C.S.C. 1936).

23 Prosser, above note 18 at 42–49.

24 *Cannon & Stephens v. Hudson's Bay Co.*, [1939] 4 D.L.R. 465 (B.C.S.C.).

False imprisonment is also addressed by the Association of Certified Fraud Examiners in their text. They report that in a private investigation, the examiner will seldom be required to restrain a suspect physically. However, a claim of false imprisonment may result from inadvertent or thoughtless acts, such as closing or locking a door to an interview room, standing in front of an exit, conducting a lengthy, overbearing interview under circumstances indicating that the accused is not permitted to leave, or otherwise physically or psychologically detaining a suspect.[25]

6.1.4 Malicious Prosecution

The elements necessary to prove malicious prosecution are as follows:

* A criminal proceeding must be commenced or continued by the defendant against the plaintiff.
* The criminal proceedings must result in the favour of the plaintiff.
* There must be an absence of probable cause for the proceedings.
* There must be evidence of malice.

One who brings a criminal action must have an honest belief in the accused's guilt. The test is whether the ordinary prudent person would have reasonable grounds on which to believe that the accused was actually guilty. With regard to malice, it may be satisfied by ill will or by an improper purpose, one other than bringing the offender to justice.[26] Examples of such a purpose include prosecution as a means to extort money, collect a debt, or compel performance of a contract [27] No reported decisions were found involving private sector investigators.

6.2 SURVEILLANCE TORTS

David Neill, a litigation partner at Toronto's Thomson Rogers, in an interview with the *Law Times* warned that, unless it is very compelling, surveillance evidence is not of much value. He stated:

> The . . . thing about surveillance is that it is very distasteful to most people, especially in jury trials . . . Unless you have the goods, you are better off not using it. It can really damage your case. People find the idea of someone snooping abhorrent. On the other hand, in cases such as soft tissue injuries, insurers do not have many options to test the reliability of the plaintiff.[28]

The primary underlying concern pertaining to surveillance is the breach of another's privacy. Privacy has been defined as the right to be left alone and the right to live one's life

---

25 J.T. Wells et al., *The Fraud Examiners Manual*, Canadian ed. (Austin, TX: Association of Certified Fraud Examiners, 1998).

26 Prosser, above note 18 at 834–35.

27 Bilek, Klotter, & Federal, above note 5 at 164.

28 C. Kentridge, "Surveillance Must Be Used With Caution" *Law Times* (7 June 1998).

in seclusion without being subjected to unwarranted and undesired publicity.[29] When dealing with the issue of surveillance, it is necessary to consider all the circumstances to determine the nature and degree of privacy to which a person is entitled.

In this review of surveillance torts, the torts of the intentional infliction of mental suffering, trespass to land, trespass to chattels, and nuisance are examined. This section concludes with a discussion of motions for injunctions against private investigators conducting surveillance. As the tort of invasion of privacy is an emerging tort, and as it applies to both surveillance and pretext functions, it is discussed at the end of this chapter.

6.2.1   Intentional Infliction of Nervous Shock

The tort of intentional infliction of nervous shock or emotional distress involves an act by a person amounting to extreme or outrageous conduct with an intent to cause emotional distress or shock that actually results in trauma to the victim.[30] The behaviour may be the basis of an independent action or appended to another intentional tort. As stated, the conduct in question must be outrageous; insults, annoyances, and petty oppressions are not sufficient. Canadian law does not protect hurt feelings. The behaviour must be such that an average member of the community would be so aroused that his or her resentment against the actor would lead him to exclaim "Outrageous!"[31]

The tort of intentional infliction of nervous shock resulted from the landmark case of *Wilkinson v. Downton*.[32] In *Wilkinson*, the court permitted recovery where a woman was falsely told that her husband had been severely injured. The court held the defendant was liable on the grounds that, as a reasonable man, he should have known that the effect of his words would be to inflict physical harm through emotional distress. The case established a cause of action for wilful conduct that is calculated to cause and does cause such harm.

Rough Shadowing: This action may be applicable to a form of surveillance known as "rough shadowing." Rough shadowing is surveillance that is so deliberately open and obvious that anyone would be aware of it. In an American case, a firm of private investigators were sued for intimidation after following the plaintiff, threatening him with violence, eavesdropping, lying about him to his neighbours, and keeping him under constant surveillance to prevent him from testifying as a witness at an upcoming trial. The court awarded damages notwithstanding that there was no physical injury to the plaintiff.[33] It is

---

29   *Souder v. Pendleton Detectives Inc.*, 88 So. 2d 716 (1956).

30   There is opinion by some text writers that in Canada there is no longer the requirement of actual physical harm: see Williams, "Tort Liability for Nervous Shock" in A.M. Linden, ed., *Studies in Canadian Tort Law* (Toronto: Butterworths, 1968) at 148. However, there is no case law to back up this proposition: see P.H. Osborne, "The Privacy Acts of British Columbia, Manitoba and Saskatchewan" in D. Gibson, ed., *Aspects of Privacy Law* (Toronto: Butterworths, 1980) at 79.

31   Bilek, Klotter, & Federal, above note 5 at 160.

32   [1897] 2 Q.B. 57.

not unreasonable to speculate that a Canadian court, presented with similar facts, would also find liability under the tort banner of the intentional infliction of nervous shock.[34]

Other Applications: A few other points are worthy of note pertaining to this tort. In addition to the tort of the intentional infliction of mental suffering, nervous shock is itself a separate head of damage in negligence.[35] Furthermore, the tort of intentional infliction of nervous shock may also be a useful supplement to the tort of defamation; that is, where truth is a defence to defamation, the tort of intentional infliction of mental suffering may cover the malicious publication of a true statement.[36]

For a further discussion of this tort in the context of pretexts, see Section 6.3.1.

6.2.2   Trespass to Land

The tort of trespass to land is one of the oldest torts known to the common law as property interests were among the first to be protected by the English courts. The tort of trespass to land has historically been held to occur whenever there has been an actual unauthorized physical intrusion onto the private property of another. The tort has also been recognized when a person remains on an individual's land after permission has been withdrawn.[37] Today, tort writers even argue that the tort of trespass to land may occur whenever there is an unauthorized "interference" to land.[38]

However trespass to land is defined, it is actionable *per se*, that is, without proof of damage.[39] Under normal circumstances, the damages awarded in such a claim will be nominal unless actual damage is sustained.[40] However, if the trespass was conducted for malicious purposes, or if it was arrogant and callous, punitive damages may apply.[41]

For liability to be found in trespass to land, the intrusion must be direct and caused by a positive action. There must be some effect to the land. The effect need not be caused by direct human contact, but may be caused by an object such as a vehicle. Notwithstanding that trespass to land is an intentional tort, liability may still be found if the intrusion was accidental provided there is evidence of negligence. If the intrusion was unauthorized, the

---

33   *Shultz v. Frankfort Marine Accident & Plate Glass Insurance Company*, 139 N.W. 386 (Wis. Sup. Ct. 1913).

34   E.F. Geddes, "The Private Investigator and the Right to Privacy" (1989) Alta. L. Rev. 256.

35   L.N. Klar, *Studies in Canadian Tort Law* (Toronto: Carswell, 1977) at 351.

36   L.N. Klar, *Tort Law* (Toronto: Carswell, 1991) at 53.

37   Prosser, above note 18 at 63–75.

38   P. Burns, "The Law and Privacy: The Canadian Experience" (1976) 54 Can. Bar Rev. 1 at 14.

39   *Entick v. Carrington* (1765), 19 St. Tr. 1029 at 1066.

40   *Rusche v. Insurance Corporation of British Columbia* (1992), 4 C.P.C. (3d) 12 (B.C.S.C.).

41   *Starkman v. Delhi Court Ltd. and Diamond & Mogil Builders Ltd.*, [1961] O.R. 467 (C.A.). See also J.D. Hartman, *Legal Guidelines for Covert Surveillance Operations in the Private Sector* (Toronto: Butterworths, 1993) at 114.

trespasser's motive is irrelevant. Therefore, a person may be liable if he was of an honest but mistaken belief that he was entitled to do the act complained of.[42]

To bring an action in trespass to land, it is not necessary that the plaintiff be the landowner. A tenant acquires the right to bring an action in trespass to land to the exclusion of a landlord. The term "tenant," however, is not extended to guests in a hotel or lodgers in another's house as courts have held that such persons lack sufficient property interest to maintain such an action.[43]

Videotaping: With regard to a private investigator's surveillance functions, it is plausible to envision occurrences where he may directly trespass while filming a subject person. Two British Columbia cases have dealt with the issue of filming and trespass, although not specifically with regard to private investigators. In one case, an owner and his company were engaged in a bitter strike. A local reporter decided to conduct an interview with the owner on his store premises. The owner declined the interview and ordered the reporter and cameraman off his premises. They complied. Later, however, the owner observed the reporter and cameraman on his parking lot again. The owner approached the reporter, reminded him he was not permitted on his lands, and wrestled away his microphone. After a brief scuffle, the police were called and the reporter and cameraman left.

The owner brought action against the media corporation alleging the common law tort of trespass and the statutory tort of invasion of privacy. The court held there was a trespass. The court further held, however, that when the land in question is a retail store parking lot and the trespasser is a media representative in search of a story in which the public has an interest, the measure of damages will be nominal. The court awarded damages of $100 and costs.[44] Oddly enough, in another case where a television reporter stepped on private property momentarily while filming the plaintiff's house, the court held the reporter was not liable in trespass.[45]

Airspace: Another form of direct trespass to land is by invading the airspace above it. The early common law formulated the general principle that whoever owns the surface of land also owns a column of air up to the heavens and the subsurface down to the centre of the earth. However, this principle has been curtailed in recent times. In a case from England, a landowner brought an action in trespass to land against a company that was taking aerial photographs of his property. The court held:

> It may be a sound and practical rule to regard any incursion into the air space at a height which may interfere with the ordinary user of the land as a trespass rather than a nuisance . . . But wholly different considerations arise when considering the passage of aircraft at a height which in no way affects the user of land . . . The plaintiff's complaint is not that the aircraft

---

42   See Klar, above note 36 at 76.

43   G.H.L. Fridman, *Fridman on Torts in Canada*, 2 vols. (Toronto: Carswell, 1990) at para. 5.02.

44   *Silber v. B.C.T.V. Broadcasting Systems Ltd.* (1986), 69 B.C.L.R. 34 (S.C.). The damages awarded were only $100.

45   *Belzberg v. Broadcasting Systems Ltd.* (1981), 3 W.W.R. 85 (B.C.S.C.).

interfered with the use of his land, but that a photograph was taken from it. There is, however, no law against taking a photograph, and the mere taking of a photograph can not turn an act which is not trespass into the plaintiff's airspace into one that is a trespass.

Although the court dismissed the action in trespass to land, the court did state that the plaintiff may have a claim in nuisance if the plaintiff was subjected to the harassment of constant surveillance of his house from the air accompanied by the photographing of his every activity.[46]

Consent: As mentioned in the beginning of this section, remaining on an individual's land after permission has been withdrawn constitutes trespass. In a scenario not uncommon in the days before liberalized divorce laws, private investigators of an estranged wife accompanied the wife at her invitation and entered her husband's home in the middle of the night to obtain evidence of adultery. The husband, who had possession of the home, brought action against the wife's investigators for trespass to land. The court held for the husband, stating that the wife's associates could not be "covered by the cloak of the wife's right to consortium."[47]

Intrusion versus Interference: Also as mentioned above, trespass to land may occur not only by the physical "intrusion" to land, but also by the mere "interference" with land. In a case from England, the defendant continuously ran up and down a roadway adjacent to the land of the Duke of Rutland, waving a handkerchief and opening and closing an umbrella, scaring away grouse the Duke hoped to shoot. The court held:

> So if a man goes on to part of a highway, the soil of which belongs to the owner of the adjoining land, not for the purpose of using such part of the highway as a highway, but only for some other purpose . . . he is in so doing committing a trespass against the owner of the soil . . . [Here] he stood on the highway, and walked up and down on it for the purpose of doing things which interfered with the Duke's enjoyment of the land near the highway. He was, therefore, not there for the purpose of using the highway as such in any of the ordinary and usual modes which people use a highway. Under those circumstances, I think he was a trespasser.[48]

There do not appear to be any cases in Canada that have followed this decision. It does, however, appear to be sufficient authority for a subject of an overt surveillance to base a claim upon.[49]

---

46   *Bernstein of Leigh (Baron) v. Skyviews & General Ltd.* , [1978] 1 Q.B. 479.

47   *Coles-Smith v. Smith*, [1965] Qld. R. 494 (Austl. F.C.).

48   *Harrison v. Duke of Rutland*, [1893] 1 Q.B. 142 (C.A.). This case was followed in *Hickman v. Maisey*, [1900] 1 Q.B. 752 (C.A.). In this case, the defendant walked up and down a road beside a race track to distract the horses.

49   Lawson, above note 10 at 172, where the author states: "The act of standing and watching premises has been found to be actionable trespass [upon] which the courts have not hesitated to award damages for mental distress."

Electronic Monitoring: Another form of trespass to land pertaining to surveillance is through electronic monitoring. An American court awarded damages resulting from a claim in trespass to land based on evidence that the defendant installed a microphone in the plaintiff's home to dissuade the plaintiff from associating with another person.[50] In a case from England, it was held that tapping phones from an outside source was not a trespass to land of the plaintiff homeowner as the telephone lines were owned by a public utility.[51] Similarly, if a listening device is placed in a hotel room, the only person who could bring an action in trespass to land would be the hotel owner as he is the only person in law to have "possession" of the room.[52] Other academic writers have reported that although such activity may not be a trespass to land, it is the type of conduct that a court may find to be an invasion of privacy.[53]

Implied Access: To conclude, other than the grey area of trespassing by way of a pretext as discussed later, the tort of trespass as it relates to the activities of private investigators is not terribly complex. A private investigator, as any private person, can attend onto the property of another during daylight hours where access is implied such as a walk up to the front door of a residence. This implied permission to enter the property of another is subject, of course, to the person in charge of the property revoking the implied permission. As seen in the criminal cases, this implied permission does not extend to trespassing at night,[54] or actually entering a dwelling without permission.[55] Most judicially reported dealings with these sorts of trespass infractions have been dealt with in the criminal, not civil, context.

Insurance Corporation of British Columbia Guidelines: A final note worthy of inclusion for investigators in British Columbia is the ICBC Private Investigators Guidelines of May 1999 pertaining to surveillance. On page 8, the publication provides:

> ICBC requires, as a condition of retaining any private investigator in British Columbia, that the investigator conduct investigations in a reasonable manner and in accordance with the following standards:
>
> . . .

---

50   *Grieg v. Grieg*, [1966] V.R. 376 (Austl. S.C.). The court awarded damages on the basis of the plaintiff's injured feelings. It is noteworthy that "injured feelings" is not yet recognized as a compensable damage in Canada.

51   *Malone v. Commissioner of Police of the Metropolis (No. 2)*, [1979] 2 All E.R. 620 (Ch.D.).

52   Justice (British Section of the International Commission of Jurists), *Privacy and the Law* (London: Stevens & Sons Limited, 1970) at 9.

53   S. Stoljar, "A Re-Examination of Privacy" (1984) 4 Legal Studies 67 at 76. See the latter discussion of the tort of invasion of privacy in Canada.

54   *R. v. Andsten and Petrie* (1960), 32 W.W.R. 329 (B.C.C.A.).

55   *R. v. Massue* (1964), 55 D.L.R. (2d) 79 (Que. Q.B.).

(7)   It is important that investigations undertaken on behalf of the ICBC should be conducted in a way that will not alarm claimants or anyone else, nor give them reasonable
cause for apprehension for public safety and security. All investigations must be carried out in the least obstructive manner possible, and having regard to the circumstances of that investigation:

(a)   do not

- enter on the private property of the person being investigated, except
where the property is used by that person for commercial purposes and
the investigation relates to that commercial purpose, or

- use a pretext or misrepresentation to gain access to any premises.

(b)   surveillance is authorized only:

- when conducted from a public vantage point, and

- in circumstances where the person being investigated is not in a position
where he or she would have a reasonable expectation of privacy.

(c)   surveillance is not authorized:

- where the person being investigated has a reasonable expectation of
privacy,

- while the person being investigated is in the privacy of a home and is in
circumstances where they would have a reasonable expectation of privacy, or

- in, at or near places used predominantly by children, such as school
yards, playgrounds and daycare centers.

(d) do not use audio surveillance under any circumstances.

(9)   It is the ICBC's policy to be sensitive to the beliefs and customs of all sections of our
multicultural community, and this must be reflected in all investigation work done on
the ICBC's behalf. In particular, surveillance and other investigations must not be
conducted during a religious ceremony where there is a reasonable expectation of privacy.

(10)   When a claimant is a minor, particularly careful thought must be given before undertaking surveillance or any other form of investigation to ensure that the proposed
course of action is unlikely to cause apprehension for the claimant's safety. In every
case, the approval of the claim office manager must be obtained before proceeding.

6.2.3   Trespass to Chattels

Trespass to chattels is essentially the same tort as trespass to land with the exception that
it applies to personal as opposed to real property. It requires the direct, intentional, and
unauthorized interference of a chattel in the possession of another. Examples of direct acts
include the destroying or damaging of a chattel, the moving of a chattel from place to
place, or the mere use of it. Similar to trespass to land, it is the lawful possessor of the chat-

tel who is entitled to sue, not the owner who is out of possession.[56] However, the question whether the tort is actionable *per se* is not clear, although most commentators would say that the point is moot as few would sue where there is no reasonable prospect of compensation.[57]

Documents: One grey area pertaining to this tort is the reading of personal papers of another. The courts have recognized the intrinsic value of this asset. In one case it was held:

> Papers are the owner's goods and chattels: they are his dearest property; and are so far from enduring a seizure that they will hardly bear an inspection; and though the eye cannot by the laws of England be guilty of a trespass, yet where private papers are removed and carried away, the secret nature of those goods will be an aggravation of the trespass, and demand more considerable damages in that respect.[58]

An inference that may be taken from this passage, therefore, is that the mere reading of a letter or the listening to a private conversation should not lead to a finding of liability for this tort. Neither should the photographing of a document.[59]

Entrapment: Trespass to chattels would, however, include such entrapment practices attributed to a dubious few private investigators who allegedly have engaged in moving a subject party's possessions around or flattening a tire to set up a situation to videotape. Such allegations have arisen in the context of conducting surveillance for insurance investigations.[60]

Few cases have been reported pertaining to this tort as most claims for property damage are dealt with by way of negligence.

6.2.4   Nuisance

A private nuisance may be defined as a substantial and unreasonable interference with the use and enjoyment of land in the possession of another.[61] The major functional distinction between the action of trespass and nuisance is that trespass protects possession, whereas nuisance protects the quality of that possession. The law of nuisance is concerned with the

---

56   J.G. Fleming, *The Law of Torts*, 7th ed. (Sydney: The Law Book Company, 1987) at 47.
57   Klar, above note 36 at 59.
58   *Entick v. Carrington*, above note 39.
59   H. Rowan, "Privacy and the Law," the Law Society of Upper Canada Special Lectures, *The Law of Torts* (1973) at 267.
60   E.F. Geddes, above note 34 at 274.
61   In an early case, *St. Helen's Smelting Co. v. Tipping* (1865), 11 H.L.C. 642 at 650 (H.L.), the court held that nuisance includes the "interference with one's enjoyment, one's quiet, one's personal freedom; anything that discomposes or injuriously affects the senses or the nerves. In *Poole and Poole v. Regan and the Toronto Harbour Commissioners*, [1958] O.W.N. 77 (H.C.J.), the court held that the test of whether conduct is a nuisance or not is the effect of the conduct on the average reasonable man.

effect of the defendant's conduct on the plaintiff's use and enjoyment of the land and not with the nature of that conduct. Liability may be imposed in nuisance even in cases where the defendant's conduct was neither intentional nor negligent.[62] Like trespass, the plaintiff is only required to have an interest in the land, not ownership.[63] Unlike trespass, nuisance requires damages, therefore demanding an inconvenience at least materially interfering with ordinary comfort. If the conduct complained about is directed solely towards annoyance it may be actionable, but this would only be the case where the conduct is unreasonable.[64]

At first glance, it may seem that the tort of nuisance is more applicable to private investigators than the more outrageous behaviours as required for trespass and intentional infliction of nervous shock. A review of case law reveals that many types of interferences with private property have been identified by the courts. These include overhanging branches, seeping sewage, foul odours, barking dogs, bright lights, vibrations from explosions, machinery or traffic, industrial pollutants, subsidence of supporting soils, obstruction of sunlight or a view, and even unwanted telephone calls. However, notwithstanding the numerous types of nuisances, no case law with respect to actions of nuisance against Canadian private investigators was uncovered.

Notwithstanding the lack of judicial authority, some commentators believe that the law of nuisance is sufficient to provide a remedy. One commentator reported that actionable nuisance has also been found in instances where premises have been watched, where a plaintiff has been followed, and where unpleasant activities have been carried out in one's neighbourhood.[65] Another commentator went even further by stating that the tort or nuisance can cover all forms of unjustified surveillance of another.[66]

Notwithstanding these views, other Canadian academics report that most private investigators do not engage in, or are not detected committing, this form of behaviour. They report that surveillance techniques are usually subtle to prevent the subject from realizing that he or she is under surveillance. It is acknowledged, however, that if a person becomes aware of such surveillance, either while it is in progress or some time afterwards, a reme-

---

62   Solomon & Feldthusen, above note 3 at 118.

63   Note that in *Malone v. Laskey*, [1907] 2 K.B. 141, the wife of an occupier was held unable to sue in nuisance because she lacked a proprietary or possessory interest in the land.

64   Fleming, above note 56 at 388. In *MacNeill v. Devon Lumber Co.* (1987), 42 C.C.L.T. 192 (N.B.C.A.), the court held: "Compensation in nuisance is not dependent upon proof of physical injury. It may consist of the annoyance and discomfort caused to the occupiers of the premises."

65   Lawson & Jeffrey, above note 10 at 188 and 191. No case law was cited other than *Thompson-Schwab v. Costaki*, [1956] 1 W.L.R. 335, wherein an injunction was issued to restrain the use of a house for the purpose of prostitution.

66   R.D. Gibson, "Common Law Protection of Privacy: What to Do until the Legislators Arrive" in L.N. Klar, ed., *Studies in Canadian Tort Law* (Toronto: Carswell, 1977) at 356.

dy may exist in nuisance. Being watched and photographed in the assumed privacy of one's backyard is an example of such a disturbance.[67]

Recognizing the views of the commentators as expressed above, some Canadian law professors report that the law cannot provide a remedy for every minor or transitory interference with a person's use and enjoyment of his or her land.[68] One of the reasons given, besides the obvious lack of sufficient damages to pursue a claim, is drawn from the landmark case of *Victoria Park Racing Co. v. Taylor*.[69] In that case, the plaintiff brought action against the defendant for nuisance because the defendant had erected a platform outside of the plaintiff's property for the purpose of broadcasting racing results. The majority of the court held that there was no general right to privacy and the defendant's actions could not be restrained.

Applying the majority ruling in this case to a private investigator's surveillance activities, it can be inferred that a plaintiff does not have an action against a private investigator making observations of his property from outside his property boundary lines. It is also noteworthy that the case deals with activity from an adjoining landowner, not from a public street where most surveillance by private investigators takes place. Therefore, in most cases, without a privacy right, there can be no cause for an action in nuisance.

It is worth mentioning that the *Victoria Park Racing* case was far from a unanimous decision. One dissenting judge stated:

> There is no absolute standard as to what constitutes a nuisance in law. But all the surrounding circumstances must be taken into consideration in each case . . . An improper or non-natural use or a use in excess of a man's right which curtails or impairs his neighbour's legitimate enjoyment of his property is tortious and harmful and constitutes nuisance.[70]

Another dissenting judge, who found the conduct of the defendant repugnant, stated the following four propositions:

> (A) Although there is no general right to privacy recognized at common law, neither is there an absolute and unrestricted right to spy on or to overlook the property of another person. (B) A person who creates or uses devices for the purpose of enabling the public generally to overlook or spy upon the premises of another will generally become liable for an action in nuisance, providing appreciable damage, discomfort or annoyance is caused. (C) As in all cases of private nuisance, all the surrounding circumstances will require examination. (D) The fact that in such cases the defendant's conduct is openly pursued, or that his motive is merely that of profit making, or that he makes no direct charge for the privilege or overlooking or spying, will provide no answer to the action. [71]

---

67   Geddes, above note 34 at 276.
68   Solomon & Feldthusen, above note 3 at 681.
69   (1937), 58 C.L.R. 479 (Austl. H.C.).
70   *Ibid.* at 524.
71   *Ibid.* at 521.

There is, however, other Canadian authority for the majority finding as laid out in *Victoria Park Racing* in the case of *Re Copeland and Adamson*.[72] In *Copeland* the court held:

> Ancient authority is to be found for the proposition that in English law the natural rights of an occupier do not include freedom from view and inspection by neighbouring occupiers. Of course where there is an actual entry on land, the law of trespass gives a remedy against the invasion of property, but if the defendant commits an annoyance by watching or listening from the other side of the road there is, normally, no protection that the occupier can have under civil law. English law therefore does not accept that freedom from being overlooked exists. It is not a natural right pertaining to land for which a legal remedy is given either by an action for nuisance or otherwise.[73]

Further grounds for inferring that the tort of nuisance does not apply to private investigators performing surveillance can be found in the landmark privacy case referred to earlier as *Motherwell v. Motherwell*.[74] In creating a new category of tort law now recognized as invasion of privacy, the court limited the applicability of it to a form of telephone harassment. The court stated:

> The matters of complaint are unwanted communications made to the respondents. If such acts are properly within the concept of "invasion of privacy" they occupy a niche of their own, *distinct from matters as surveillance, the clandestine gathering and use of personal information by various means*. [Emphasis added.][75]

The court also noted later in the judgment that despite the narrowness of the finding in this case, the category of nuisances will never be closed.[76] Note that this finding was in relation to a private residence. The result may be different if the surveillance is outside of a business and its methods are such that it results in a nuisance.

One case that seems to contradict this apparent right to watch another is the Ontario case of *Poole and Poole v. Regan and the Toronto Harbour Commissioners*.[77] The plaintiffs in that case sought an injunction to prevent the Toronto Harbour Police from continuing to follow them and interfere with their right of navigation in the Toronto harbour. The plaintiffs alleged the harbour police had been following them to and fro across the Toronto Harbour for three months. The defendants claimed they were only doing this to catch the plaintiff violating a city bylaw. No real evidence of the violation existed. The court, without going into the specifics of the surveillance, held that the surveillance was sufficiently outrageous to award punitive damages of $2,000 (in 1957). As an indication that the harbour police went beyond a mere watching or following at a distance, the court stated:

---

72 (1972), 28 D.L.R. (3d) 26 (Ont. H.C.J.).
73 *Ibid.* at 36.
74 [1976] 6 W.W.R. 550 (Alta. C.A.).
75 *Ibid.* at 555.
76 *Ibid.* at 556.
77 [1958] O.W.N. 77 (H.C.J.).

The conduct of the Harbour Police was something more than mere personal inconvenience and interference with enjoyment of one's quiet and one's personal freedom or anything that discomposes or injuriously affects the sense or the nerves . . . I think it would be an affront to the dignity of any man or woman and . . . is actionable in nuisance.

The judge held that the action was a "serious" interference with the plaintiffs' rights and that there was no indication that the defendants planned to stop. On this basis, the court also issued an injunction against the Harbour Police.

As mentioned, this is the only Canadian case found wherein a court made such a judgment. In *Poole* the court referred to an older English decision dealing with illegal picketing of a manufacturing plant.[78] The court in that case held:

The truth is that to watch or beset a man's house with a view to compel him to do or not to do what is lawful for him . . . seriously interferes with the ordinary comfort of human existence and the ordinary enjoyment of the house beset, and such conduct would support an action on the case for a nuisance at common law.

. . .

True it is that every annoyance is not a nuisance; the annoyance must be of a serious character and of such a degree to interfere with the ordinary comforts of life. To watch or beset a man's house for the length of time and in the manner and with the view proved would undoubtedly constitute a nuisance of an aggravated character.

Certainly, if an injunction is available against overzealous police officers, it would also be available against private investigators demonstrating the same degree of zeal. The extent of the nuisance would have to be quite great. For an individual to sue, he must prove special and greater damages above and beyond those of the ordinary public. There seems to be, however, no logical reason why this case would not apply equally to interference with passage along public roadways, a situation far more likely to occur than the impeded passage through a public waterway. An investigator who follows a vehicle too closely or interferes with safe driving on more than one occasion could possibly be restrained by an injunction to prevent the continuance of the nuisance.

A final case worthy of review is *Fouracres v. ICBC*.[79] In this case, the plaintiff Fouracres was awarded $250,000 by a British Columbia jury for losses he had suffered pertaining to a motor vehicle accident he was involved in. Subsequent to the award, the ICBC retained private investigators to obtain further information on the plaintiff. The plaintiff's lawyers successfully argued that the private investigators of the ICBC harassed the plaintiff through his respective customers for years before the lawsuit and continued to do so after the award. Furthermore, the plaintiff alleged that the private investigators telephoned him at all hours of the day. The ICBC disputed Fouracres' claims, taking the position that calls

---

78   *Lyons & Sons v. Wilkins*, [1899] 1 Ch. D. 255 (C.A.). See also *Ward Locke & Co. v. Operative Printers' Assistants' Society* (1906), 22 T.L.R. 327.

79   (1996), (B.C.C.A.) [unreported]. Reported by the Canadian Press on 12 March 1996.

to Fouracres' customers were to investigate tips regarding Fouracres. Notwithstanding ICBC's claims, British Columbia's Court of Appeal ordered ICBC to cease any form of further harassment of Fouracres.

6.2.5 Injunctions against Private Investigators

In the previous section, a case was mentioned where a plaintiff brought a motion for an injunction against a firm of private investigators to obtain an order to have them cease what was characterized as harassing phone calls.[80] Another case from British Columbia that involved a firm of private investigators and which reviewed the law pertaining to the granting of injunctions in more detail is *Unger v. Lutz*.[81] In this case, the complainant brought a motion requesting the court impose an injunction on the respondent private investigators prohibiting them from conducting surveillance on her. The facts of Unger were as follows.

The plaintiff was injured in a motor vehicle accident and made a claim to the ICBC. The ICBC suspected the claim was false and ordered surveillance. Late one evening, while alone in her home, the plaintiff heard someone on her front porch. When she went to investigate, she saw two persons hurriedly leaving the property. The next morning, as she drove away from her home, she observed a van following her. She took the van's plate number and reported it to the RCMP. The RCMP later informed her the van was owned by a private investigator under hire by the ICBC. A day later, she met a friend at a mall and noticed two men watching her. She recognized one of the men as the driver of the van that had followed her. Later that day, she again saw the same man standing on the street outside her friend's home.

The plaintiff claimed the series of incidents made her very tense and anxious. This experience of the plaintiff was in part because she was married to a Canadian Security Intelligence Service agent whose assignments were related to anti-terrorist duties. As such, she was paranoid that her experiences were related to her husband's work. Based on these encounters, the plaintiff brought an application for an injunction to prohibit any further surveillance on her.

Counsel for the applicant stressed that the private investigators committed the criminal offence of Trespass at Night under section 177 of the *Criminal Code* by entering onto her private property. They argued this was sufficient grounds for the awarding of an injunction. The court observed:

> The general rule is that no private individual can bring an action to enforce the criminal law by way of injunction or damages (tort). [However], a private individual whose rights are being interfered with by a criminal act that causes or threatens to cause him damage over and above that suffered by the general public may obtain an injunction.

---

80 *Ibid.*
81 [1996] B.C.J. No. 937 (S.C.).

The court then held as follows:

> The plaintiff has not commenced an action against the ICBC . . . [although] her complaint
> may well be considered a breach of s.1 of the *Privacy Act* . . . Instead the plaintiff seeks an
> injunctive relief . . . In my view this raises a procedural concern . . .The concern has particu-
> lar significance in this case. The plaintiff is asking this court to conclude, on the basis of affi-
> davit evidence alone, that representatives of the ICBC have committed [the criminal and
> tortious acts] of trespass and "harassed" her by putting her under surveillance . . . Those are
> very serious charges. To grant the relief she seeks on this interlocutory application would be
> tantamount to finding the ICBC committed, or may have committed, what Mr. Giroday
> describes as "an outrageous invasion of a citizen's rights". Such issues ought not to be decid-
> ed in this action and on the basis of affidavit evidence alone. If the plaintiff is to obtain the
> relief she seeks, it should be in the context of an action brought against ICBC and its agents
> in which oral testimony is given so that the court will have the opportunity to properly assess
> the reliability of the evidence. In my view it would be unfair and dangerous to proceed in any
> other fashion.

As is apparent, if the grounds upon which an injunction is sought are criminal in
nature, a court may opt to reject such a remedy in the interests of not prejudging the substantive offence without a proper trial.

6.3   PRETEXT TORTS

As mentioned earlier, a pretext has been defined as a verbal or physical deception practised
on a person to persuade her to provide evidence or information she would not otherwise
provide. In this section, the torts of deceit, trespass to property, intimidation, and the intentional infliction of nervous shock are discussed in relation to the investigatory practice of
pretexts.

6.3.1   Deceit

Deceit has been defined as a fraudulent and deceptive misrepresentation, artifice, or device
used by one or more persons to deceive and trick another who is ignorant of the true facts
to the prejudice and damage of the party it is imposed upon.[82] The components of the tort
of deceit include the following:

- The defendant made a false representation of fact by words or conduct.
- The defendant knew the representation to be false.
- The plaintiff relied upon the defendant's false representation.
- The plaintiff sustained damage as a result of the defendant's representation.[83]

---

82   *Black's Law Dictionary*, 6th ed. (St. Paul: West Publishing Co., 1990) at 405.
83   *Bell v. Source Data Control Ltd.* (1988), 66 O.R. (2d) 78 (C.A.).

Pertaining to the first component, the failure to disclose certain facts where there is a duty to do so has been sufficient grounds upon which to found an action.[84] As for the second component, some cases have held that recklessness without regard to the truth is sufficient grounds upon which to found an action.[85] However, conduct that amounts to carelessness or negligent representation is not.[86]

The classic example of the tort of deceit is a situation where a person makes inquiries of another to determine if a party they intend to do business with is of sound financial standing. In such cases, the person to whom the inquiry is made knows the third party lacks business acumen but nevertheless gives a good recommendation because it is in his economic interest to do so. The person making the inquiries subsequently suffers a loss. Cases of this nature are brought in tort because there is no contractual relationship between the plaintiff and the defendant.[87] Another example of an action for deceit is a claim for rescission of contract on the basis of misrepresentation, such as situations where an investor discovers false statements in a prospectus as to how investment funds would be spent and the company became insolvent resulting in a loss for the investor.

As any false statement that causes harm may constitute deceit, some commentators believe the action is also applicable to protecting privacy in the context of credit reporting or other types of investigative reporting.[88] As seen in *Weber v. Ontario Hydro*, the case mentioned in this chapter's introduction, the tort has also been pleaded where a private investigator obtained access to a person's home on the basis of a pretext.[89] The tort of deceit complements the tort of negligent misstatement, which is discussed later in this chapter.

6.3.2   Trespass to Land under Pretext

As discussed earlier in Section 6.2.2 — Trespass to Land, trespass can be committed in a number of ways, one of which is through a pretext. In the case of *Entick v. Carrington*,[90] the court held that agents of the defendant who entered a home under the pretext the owner was suspected of committing seditious libel and searched his papers were liable in trespass to land. The court stated:

> The great end for which men entered into society is to secure their property. The right is preserved sacred and incommunicable in all instances where it has not been taken away or abridged by some public law for the good of the whole . . . By the laws of England, every invasion of private property, be it ever so minute, is a trespass. No man can set his foot upon my ground without my licence, but he is liable to an action, though the damage be nothing.

---

84   *Legh v. Legh* (1930), 143 L.T. 151 (C.A.).
85   *Derry v. Peek* (1889), 14 A. at Case 337 (H.L.).
86   *LeLievre v. Gould*, [1883] 1 Q.B. 491 (C.A.).
87   *Pasley v. Freeman* (1789), 100 E.R. 450.
88   Lawson, above note 10 at 205.
89   [1995] 2 S.C.R. 929.
90   Above note 39.

Canadian case law for trespass to land involving private investigators is rare. One known case is *Rusche v. Insurance Corporation of British Columbia*[91] where a private investigator attended upon the residence of the plaintiff and under pretext asked the plaintiff to discuss a vehicle he was selling while a second private investigator, hidden from view, made a video recording of the scene for the information of the defendant ICBC. The court held that the private investigator was liable in trespass as his pretext vitiated any real consent of the subject allowing the private investigator on his property. The court, however, did not award compensatory or punitive damages but rather awarded only nominal damages of $1 as it found the complainant had not suffered a loss and the private investigators were not activated by malice.

One Canadian commentator, writing on privacy concerns, also addressed the issue of trespass to land committed by private investigators under the guise of a pretext. She wrote:

> One crucial problem in this area is that an investigator who enters a person's house under a misrepresentation, having received permission to enter by the lawful occupant, may be liable for trespass on the grounds that permission to enter was given for a specific purpose, which was not the actual purpose of the investigator. If the investigator identifies himself, then the subject cannot be heard to complain. But if the investigator indicates that he is, for example, taking a survey, and under that guise spends some time speaking with the subject in order to obtain a closer assessment of him, this could be characterized as trespass for which the investigator will be liable in the absence of any damage. This interview technique is one which is not uncommonly used in order to assess persons making bodily injury claims. Investigators are frequently successful in getting such innocent individuals to reveal substantial amounts of material about themselves.[92]

This is also the view of Irene Christie of the firm Osler, Hoskin & Harcourt, when she stated in a speech at a Canadian Institute Conference that employers should not let private investigators trespass on an employee's property or entrap them to gather evidence.[93]

6.3.3   Intimidation

The essential components of the tort of intimidation are (1) the defendant must threaten another person that he will use unlawful means, criminal, tort, or the breach of a contract to compel another to obey his or her wishes; and (2) the person threatened must comply with the demand rather than risk the execution of the threat.[94]

---

91   (1992), 4 C.P.C. (3d) 12 (B.C.S.C.).

92   Geddes, above note 34.

93   D. Pitt, "Scope of Employee's Right to Privacy Unclear — Avoid Future Problems by Hiring Well, Lawyers Told" *Lawyers Weekly* (31 March 1995) at 35. It should be noted that Irene Christie also commented that it is not clear if there really is an actionable common law tort in Canada for invasion of privacy based on a right to privacy.

94   *Roth v. Roth* (1991), 9 C.C.L.T. (2d) 141 at 152 (Ont. Gen. Div.).

The scope of this tort is admittedly narrow. However, some commentators have argued that the action may be useful in cases where information is obtained by unlawful means, particularly in a three-party context, such as when a party employs unlawful means to obtain financial or other personal information. In this regard, the tort of intimidation may also apply to some tactics employed by credit and private investigators or an over-inquisitive press seeking personal and financial information.[95]

An example of such conduct may be taken from the cases discussed in Section 4.5.5 — Extortion. As stated there, the criminal offence of extortion is made out if threats of a criminal action are used to extort money from another. The offence is not made out, however, if threats of a civil action are used as leverage to settle a financial dispute. Accordingly, if threats of a criminal action are used to settle a financial dispute, the tort of intimidation may be applicable, whereas if threats of a civil action are made for the same reason, the tort of intimidation will not apply.[96]

6.3.4 Intentional Infliction of Nervous Shock

As discussed earlier in Section 6.2.1, the tort of intentional infliction of nervous shock resulted from the landmark case of *Wilkinson v. Downton*.[97] In *Wilkinson*, the court permitted recovery where a woman was falsely told that her husband had been severely injured. The court held the defendant liable on the grounds that, as a reasonable man, he should have known that the effect of his words would be to inflict physical harm through emotional distress. The case established a cause of action for wilful conduct that is calculated to cause and does cause such harm.

A dated case from the United Kingdom pertaining to a private investigator using a poor choice of pretext is *Janvier v. Sweeney*.[98] In *Janvier*, the plaintiff was employed by a lady in whose house she resided. The defendant private investigator was under contract by a person who wanted access to some letters in the possession of the plaintiff's employer. The private investigators attended the residence of the plaintiff and, under the pretext that they represented military authorities, told her that her employer was being investigated for corresponding with a German spy. The plaintiff was a French woman who was in fact engaged to a German who was under internment in the Isle of Man. The accusation caused the plaintiff to suffer severe shock and there was medical evidence she became extremely ill. The Court of Appeal found it appalling that the defendant private investigators would resort to such measures to induce the plaintiff to cooperate in obtaining the letters. The court held:

---

95 Lawson, above note 10 at 206.

96 *McKinnon v. F.W. Woolworth Co. & Johnson and Matt, Jordison & Commercial Fidelity Audit Agency Ltd.* (1968), 70 D.L.R. (2d) 200 (Alta. C.A.). See Section 4.5.5 — Extortion.

97 [1897] 2 Q.B. 57.

98 [1919] 2 K.B. 316. It is noteworthy that this case is the only one to follow *Wilkinson v. Downton* in England.

The defendant has . . . wilfully done an act calculated to cause physical harm to the plaintiff — that is to say, to infringe her legal right to personal safety, and has in fact thereby caused physical harm to her.

The court awarded damages against the defendant.

In an American case, the plaintiff brought action against a private investigator for intentional infliction of nervous shock as a result of a phone call she received. At 6:30 a.m. one morning, the defendant phoned the sleeping plaintiff and asked her if the date 22 April 1963 rang a bell. Before the plaintiff could answer, the caller continued: "The daughter you gave up for adoption has been looking for you, and now you have been found." In her pleading, the plaintiff alleged she was immediately overwhelmed with feelings of guilt and the anxiety resulted in her becoming dysfunctional at work. The case is not yet resolved.[99]

Although no reported Canadian cases were uncovered dealing with private investigators in this regard, a local private investigator did reveal one such practice that might elicit such judicial attention.[100] The pretext used was to contact a subject party and reveal to him or her that his or her name had come up as having been in contact with a person who was HIV positive. The subject person, in a fit of despondency, would then provide the information requested, usually information pertaining to his or her address, employment, lifestyle practices, and the like.

One Canadian commentator surmises that the principle enunciated in *Wilkinson* is likely broad enough to cover most cases where there is actual contact between the investigator and the subject under investigation, and where false information is given to the subject in such a manner as to induce some physical harm through emotional distress. In *Wilkinson* the defendant was a mere practical joker who had no clear malicious intent. Therefore, malice is not required to found an action. This commentator contends that, if a court was faced with extreme behaviour by an investigator which results in severe distress to a plaintiff but no clear physical harm, the court could extend the principles in *Wilkinson* to allow for recovery. She reports that the current trend in tort law seems to differentiate very little between severe emotional distress and physical injury.[101]

6.4 TORT LAW AND A SUBJECT'S REPUTATION

A concern of all those who conduct investigations in the private sector should be the reputation of the person they are reporting on. The cause for concern over the subject's reputation is obviously not because of some altruistic philosophy, but rather to protect oneself against litigation. In this regard, the torts of defamation and injurious falsehood are discussed.

---

99 *Austin v. Snyder* (Florida 1998) [unreported]. Karen Testa of the Associated Press reported (1 November 1998) that if Florida's court records had been open to public view, the lawsuit would have no basis. In Alaska and Kansas court adoption records are available for public viewing; however, in Florida such records are not public. The case raises the important competing interests of the right to privacy versus the right to ancestry.

100 This private investigator requested anonymity.

101 Geddes, above note 34.

6.4.1   Defamation

Defamation is the act of making a false statement or other communication about a person that harms the reputation of the person or otherwise deters people from associating with him or her.[102] Stated otherwise, a defamatory statement is one that is false and injures the reputation of another by exposing him or her to hatred, contempt, or ridicule, or which tends to lower him or her in the esteem of right-thinking members of society.[103]

Defamation consists of two different torts: libel and slander. Libel is written defamation and slander is oral defamation. Defamation requires the offending party to communicate the statement to someone other than the victim. The communication need only be made to one other person. The defamation must be understood to refer to the victim person and to no other person. The victim must be able to prove that the statement was a substantial factor in harming his or her reputation.[104] The tort can be committed by innuendo as well as by direct allegation.[105]

Defamation is a tort of strict liability. It does not matter that the defendant did not intend to, or took reasonable steps to avoid causing, harm to the plaintiff's character.[106] As a tort, libel is actionable *per se*. Slander, however, requires proof of damages unless the slander falls into one of the four following categories: a slander in relation to the imputation of a crime, a loathsome disease, unchastity of a woman, or unfitness for a trade or profession.[107] Damages in defamation are intended to compensate the plaintiff for injured feelings akin to emotional distress. This is an anomaly as typically damages are only awarded for actual physical harm. However, some commentators describe damages as the rectification of a person's character; that an attack on character is similar to, or an extension of, an attack on the person or a facet of his property, which is diminished as a consequence of the attack.[108]

Credit Reporting Agencies: There are numerous examples of defamation in the realm of information-gathering professions. Most deal with erroneous credit reports that wrongly assign to the subject the status of a poor credit risk. One such case resulted from a report for an auto insurance company that wrongly described an applicant for insurance as a habitual drunkard. Another such case resulted from a report on an applicant for bonding which wrongly stated that he had been convicted of a crime.[109]

---

102 Hartman, above note 41 at 112.

103 R.W.M. Dias & B.S. Markesinis, *Tort Law*, 2d ed. (Oxford: Clarendon Press, 1989) at 424.

104 Hartman, above note 41 at 112.

105 A.M. Linden, *Canadian Tort Law* (Toronto: Butterworths, 1988) at 634. An innuendo must be specifically pleaded.

106 Fridman, above note 43 at paras. 18.05 & 18.06.

107 Fleming, above note 56 at 388.

108 Fridman, above note 43 at para. 18.02.

109 J.M. Sharp, *Credit Reporting and Privacy: The Law in Canada and the U.S.A.* (Toronto: Butterworths, 1970) at 34. See also H.W. Switkay, "Tort Liability of Credit Investigating Agencies" (1957) 31 Temple L.Q. 50.

In an early case from the Supreme Court of Canada, a credit reporting company was held liable in defamation for making a credit report on the plaintiff that caused him to suffer heavy losses, almost to the point of bankruptcy. The court made the following observations:

> Whenever, by culpable negligence or the want of proper precaution, not truthful but false information is supplied, whereby a third party is damnified in his business, property or credit, why should the party so injured by the wrongful act of the agency not be indemnified for the loss he has sustained by the injury done to him by the agency who by their act caused the damage? . . . In this case no proper precautions appear to have been exercised. Surely no man has a right to propagate a false statement, injurious to the credit of another, without having satisfied himself of its truth or falsity before adopting and promulgating it as truthful and useful information. Would it not be a most dangerous and unreasonable doctrine to hold that a man's reputation and credit could be destroyed by secret false information, furnished, as it were, behind his back, and the knowledge of which is withheld from him, and the truth of which the agency is under no obligation to guarantee? [The complainant] does not appear to have had any connection with the agency. They had no interest in his business, but appear to have intermeddled with it for certain reward, paid them without his authority, and made statements, unfounded in fact, in reference thereto, with a view to such statements being acted upon and which were acted upon to his injury. There was no duty, as I have said, cast upon the agency to furnish this information except their contract to do so, to which [the complainant] was no party. They furnished it voluntarily for pure gain. I cannot conceive that if a man who for gain and reward voluntarily intermeddles with another man's business, and issues false reports in reference thereto to be acted upon by the party receiving it, is in any way privileged to do so; if he does it I think he does it at his peril . . . This company may be useful in the mercantile world, but it is clear its usefulness must depend upon the care they take to promulgate only truthful information. I think, therefore, the damage in this case was solely by the fault of the agency; that there was on their part and on the part of those whom they employed the greatest and most culpable negligence, carelessness and impropriety without taking any reasonable or proper precautions to ascertain the truth of the statements.[110]

Private Sector Investigators: There is little reporting in case law of private investigators being held liable for defamation.[111] That is not to say, however, that such actions have not been commenced. In addition to the types of slander that are actionable *per se*, the applicability of the tort of defamation to private sector investigators is foreseeable in cases where he or she reveals a report; that is, fails to retain confidentiality or makes statements

---

110 *Cossette v. Dun* (1891), 18 S.C.R. 222.

111 Allegations of defamation have been made both against and by private investigators. In one particular story from the United Kingdom (J. Burns, "Private Eye Sues Reynolds for Libel" *Sunday Times* (23 October 1994) Home News section), a private investigator brought an action for defamation against a client because, after informing the client about his investigation of a failed investment bank, the client used the information to demean the private investigator's investigation and reputation.

to others with regards to information obtained from an investigation. One commentator explained defamation in relation to private investigators this way:[112]

> An investigator may be liable for defamation if he or she publishes untrue statements at any time during the course of, or subsequent to, an investigation . . . A private investigator could easily find himself in a possible defamatory situation, either as the originator of the statement or as the individual passing it on. The very nature of the investigator's business leads to the obtaining of possibly damaging information, and the undertaking of an inquiry can raise imputations of wrongful conduct. An investigator is very likely to come into contact with people who are more than willing to make untruthful statements about others, or statements tainted with a disregard for accuracy . . . What an investigator needs to avoid is a situation where he states or implies wrongdoing with no sure knowledge that his statements are true. If a statement is published by a third party, it will be actionable if the facts turn out to be false . . . Imputation of the commission of a crime is actionable per se and so the investigation of a suspected fraud or theft would have to be dealt with carefully as to avoid alleging guilt against a subject in the absence of any actual proof. Slandering an individual in relation to his fitness for his profession is also actionable per se. Any employment related investigation would require equal caution so as to avoid the possibility of injuring an individual's professional reputation. Defamation can be committed by innuendo as well as by direct allegation. In the ordinary sense, innuendo includes all reasonable inferences which can be drawn from words, but in the technical sense, innuendo means words which bear a special meaning not on their face defamatory, but understood as such because of circumstances. Thus an investigator needs to be cautious with respect to hints or leading statements which will convey a definite impression on either all or part of a select audience. In the words of Lord Devlin: "Loose talk about suspicion can very easily convey the impression that it is a suspicion that is well founded.[113]

Defence of Actual Truth: According to some commentators, the battleground in a defamation action occurs with reference to the defences instead of the threshold level of whether a statement is defamatory.[114] There are a number of defences to the tort of defamation. The most obvious and commonly employed is that the statements are actually true. Actual truth is a complete defence, but it must not be confused with holding an honest belief that the statements are true. An honest but ill-founded belief in the truth of a defamatory statement is no defence at all.[115] However, it is sufficient for the defendant to prove that the statements were substantially true without being exactly true.[116]

---

112 Geddes, above note 34 at 278.

113 *Lewis v. Daily Telegraph*, [1964] A.C. 234, cited in Geddes, *ibid.*

114 Klar, above note 36 at 484.

115 J.E. Smyth, D.A. Soberman, & A.J. Easson, *The Law and Business Administration in Canada*, 6th ed. (Scarborough: Prentice Hall Canada, 1991) at 103.

116 Fridman, above note 43 at para. 18.58 referring to *Alexander v. North Eastern Railway Co.*, 6 B. & S. 340 (1865).

Defence of Absolute Privilege: A second exception to this general applicability of the tort of defamation is absolute privilege. Absolute privilege applies to statements made in relation to judicial proceedings; that is, solicitor-client and litigation privilege. Litigation privilege is wider in scope than solicitor-client privilege. It pertains to all communications made between a lawyer and those assisting a lawyer in preparation of litigation. Solicitor-client and litigation privilege even protects untrue and malicious statements. The reason for this is because the passions of litigation would otherwise fuel endless lawsuits and witnesses would be reluctant to appear. Therefore, it has been said that absolute privilege applies to the occasion, not the content, of a statement.[117]

Litigation Privilege: An example of litigation privilege comes from a case where a private investigator had been retained by the defendant to uncover evidence for an upcoming civil suit. In interviewing the defendant's witnesses, one of them made some defamatory statements. The defendant's words were republished in a subsequent transcript. The defendant private investigator argued that the defence of absolute privilege applied to all communications made in the course of judicial or quasi-judicial proceedings. The defendant further argued that the defence of absolute privilege extends to all steps taken in contemplation of litigation, including statements made by potential witnesses even if never called upon to testify. The court agreed, finding that the investigation of the private investigator was reasonably close or intimately connected to a judicial proceeding.[118] This ruling and the cases reviewed under the section on confidentiality in Chapter 2 of this book provide authority for the position that a private investigator who is acting for a solicitor with respect to actual or pending litigation is protected by absolute privilege with respect to his or her communications for the purpose of the litigation.

Qualified Privilege: Another form of privilege is qualified privilege. Qualified privilege affords protection to the statement itself, as opposed to the occasion on which it is made, and is defeated by any malice on the part of the defendant.[119] It exists when one party is under a duty — legal, social, or moral — to make disclosure to another person and the other person has a corresponding duty or interest to receive the information.[120] It is often cited in cases of performance reviews by an employer of an employee.

An example of pleading qualified privilege comes from another credit reporting case. In this case a former employer deliberately gave a false reference to a credit reporting agency alleging dismissal for dishonesty and mishandling of company money because he was angry that his employee had left his company. Upon the employee's action for defamation, the court held that the employer's defence of qualified privilege did not apply to a credit reporter's communication with clients for the purpose of profit. The court held:

---

117 Lawson, above note 10 at 347.
118 *Larche v. Middleton* (1989), 37 C.P.C. (2d) 174 (Ont. Gen. Div.).
119 Lawson, above note 10 at 348.
120 *Adam v. Ward*, [1917] A.C. 309 at 334.

In my view the welfare of society does not require that such reporting agencies enjoy a qualified privilege. The commercial and business world has adopted sophisticated methods of gathering information concerning all phases of its operations. The extent to which this information is accurate and truthful may determine the financial health of each corporate unit. But the individual in society, who often must limit his self-interest for the common good, should not be required to accept diminished safeguards for the protection of his reputation in order to accommodate agencies that perform a useful business service.

On this basis, the court found the credit reporting company, its employee who recorded the defamatory report, and the employer equally liable in defamation. Damages were assessed at $3,000, one-third of which was an award of exemplary damages against the employer.[121]

Some commentators argue there should be a defence of qualified privilege for private investigators. They contend that private investigators' relationships with their clients should be protected because of (1) the confidential nature of their employment; (2) the restrictions placed on them by legislation to prevent the disclosure of information obtained during the course of that employment; and (3) the duty private investigators are under to disclose information to their clients.[122] The merit of this argument is exemplified in cases where a spouse contracts with a private investigator to make inquiries regarding the activities of his or her significant other. If qualified privilege was permitted, the publication of a defamatory statement should only be protected to the extent that it is legitimately made and not actuated by malice. Absence of belief as to the truth of the statement could make it malicious and thus the privilege would be forfeited. As inferred above, a reckless statement is as culpable as a deliberate lie.

Vicarious Liability: If a defence of qualified privilege is not accepted in an action against a private sector investigator, liability may also fall on the person who retained the investigator. One Canadian commentator reported as follows:

> If an investigator were to make a malicious statement on an occasion of privilege to his client, not only will he be liable for the defamation but so too will the client. By the principle of *respondent superior*, the principal can be made liable for the defamatory statements of his agent.[123]

In conclusion, the limitations of the tort of defamation should be recognized. It has been stated that defamation can at best deal only with the question of accuracy of the information. Where inaccuracy amounts to untruth and where one is certain that the information was in fact transferred, defamation exists. However, both are far from easy matters

---

121 *Gillett v. Nissen Volkswagen Ltd.* (1975), 58 D.L.R. (3d) 104 (Alta. S.C.T.D.). The court here followed *MacIntosh v. Dun*, [1908] A.C. 390 (J.C.P.C.), which has been quoted with approval in *Halls v. Mitchell*, [1928] S.C.R. 125 at 132. Note that non-profit co-operatives have been permitted qualified privilege: *London Association for the Protection of Trade v. Greenlands*, [1916] 2 A.C. 15.

122 Geddes, above note 34 at 280.

123 Geddes, *ibid.*, referring to *Egger v. Chelmsford*, [1965] 1 Q.B. 248.

to prove. If nothing false is included in the statement, the tort of defamation provides no remedy however much a person is aggrieved or harmed.[124] The publication of true but embarrassing facts is not actionable in defamation.

Case Review: Before leaving this section, it is worthwhile to review a corporate case dealing with the issue of privilege and defamation pertaining to private investigators from the United Kingdom.[125] In this case, a group of business persons from India brought action against a British bank, in part for comments made to another financial institution by a private investigator the defendant bank had retained. The original slander, as alleged in the statement of claim, by the private investigator was to officials of the Bank of England. They reported the words of the private investigator as follows:

> In the early months of 1992, Suresh Shah knowingly helped Bhupen Dalal, one of those charged in India in connection with the securities market scandal, to launder the substantial proceeds of this fraud via Dubai through Mount and then back to India. The Shahs may not be Mount's beneficial owners but acting as a front for Dalal. $150 million of funds from Bhupen Dalal has been laundered by Mount Banking Corporation. Suresh has arranged for the purchase of $70M of India Development Bonds and $80M of Non-Resident deposits on Dahal's behalf. The funds for the purchase were routed through ANZ Dubai.

This slander was followed by a libel attributed to the private investigator for the following report given by him to officials of the Bank of England:

> I am a private investigator with considerable experience in finance-related investigations. My client this time is Standard Chartered Bank and I am currently undertaking an investigation into Mount Banking Corporation related to the recent Indian Government security scandal in which Standard Chartered have been effected and have incurred losses of £200M . . . Mount Banking Corporation is linked to the scandal . . . The funds realized from that scandal are likely to have been remitted from Dubai, a known stop-off point for funds washed from India. Bank of America, one of Mount Banking Corporation's agent banks in India, was also used in the transaction chain . . . The corporate route of the funds to Mount Banking Corporation could have been direct from Snow India, or via a UK company called CIFCO UK Ltd. to whom Mount Banking Corporation are bankers . . . There is a correlation between Mount Banking Corporation's increases in capital and previous financial scandals in India . . . Have Mount Banking Corporation's activities come to the Bank of England's attention's before now?

The court reviewed the alleged slander and libel and made the following comments pertaining to the private investigator's conduct:

---

124 *Winfield and Jolowicz on Tort*, edited by W.V.H. Rogers, 13th ed. (London: Sweet & Maxwell, 1989) at 131. Note that another form of defence is fair comment on matters of public interest.
125 *Shah v. Standard Chartered Bank*, [1998] T.N.L.R. No. 351, [1998] E.W.J. No. 394 (England & Wales C.A.).

In my view, a proper balance between freedom of speech and protection of reputation is achieved by rejecting the plaintiff's submission. Those who publish without malice defamatory statements to the effect that there are reasonable grounds to suspect a plaintiff of discreditable conduct are protected if the occasion is privileged. If the occasion is not privileged, they may justify the publication by proving objectively that there are such reasonable grounds. Allegedly credible hearsay may not contribute to such proof. Defendants will have to call their informants or provide other direct evidence. If this is in individual cases difficult, that only emphasizes that reputation should not be put at risk by publication on occasions which are not privileged of unsubstantiated hearsay.

This quote highlights some of the dangers of relying on third-party information and the limits of qualified privilege. The subpoenaing of informants highlights the awkwardness of defending a defamation claim.

6.4.2 Injurious Falsehood

The tort of injurious falsehood has been described as a false statement about a person which is not defamatory but published maliciously with the intent of producing an economic loss. The tests that must be met to find liability in this tort include the following:

- There must be a statement made that was false.
- The statement was made maliciously or recklessly as to its truth.
- The statement must have caused injury or damages.

The tort originated to protect from slander a person's goods or services. It is this point that distinguishes it from defamation, which is designed to rehabilitate a person's reputation or character. Today, the tort of injurious falsehood is broader in scope, compensating people who have suffered an economic loss as a result of a false statement intended to have others not deal with the person, as well as injury from nervous shock.[126]

Commentators have reported that there is potential that the tort of injurious falsehood may be a significant weapon for dealing with credit reporters and other investigative reports that are inaccurate or deliberately false and cause an economic loss. The application is obvious. However, no case law was reported in which the action was utilized.[127]

Besides being a complement to the tort of defamation, the tort of injurious falsehood is very similar to the tort of intentional infliction of nervous shock. It is relevant in the context of making pretext calls. In one case, a defendant told the plaintiff's family members that the plaintiff's son had hung himself. The plaintiff suffered a violent shock and became ill. The statement of the defendant, however, was false. The court held:

When the defendant circulated the false report he must surely have known that it would be repeated to the mother, and, in my opinion, he is liable for the damages suffered by the mother on account of the false report he started, just as much as if he personally made the false statement to her the plaintiff.

---

126 Fridman, above note 43 at para. 21.56.
127 Lawson, above note 10 at 283.

In other words, the court rejected the defence that the defendant's words were slanderous and therefore not covered by this tort but a component of the tort of defamation. The result is that today the tort of injurious falsehood is not limited to false statements respecting another's business or property interests.[128]

6.5   NEGLIGENCE

Simply stated, negligence is the absence of due diligence. The law requires that all persons conduct themselves with due regard to the safety and rights of others. The failure to do so constitutes negligence. Unlike intentional torts, negligence encompasses a multitude of situations in which the law imposes a legal duty on an individual to conform to an objective standard of reasonable care.

In order for a victim to recover for negligence, the victim must prove that the tortfeasor acted in a manner contrary to his duty to act prudently, and that his or her lack of due care was the cause of certain compensable losses. There must also be proof of damages. The standard by which the particular conduct is tested to determine whether such conduct constitutes negligence is that of the fictitious "reasonable person." The test is often stated as "would a reasonable person of ordinary prudence have acted similarly under the same or similar circumstances."[129]

This standard of a "reasonable person" is an issue often litigated. The courts have held that the standard of care imposed by law is higher when the impugned conduct of the defendant took place while the defendant was in his or her professional capacity. Therefore, if one holds oneself out to the public as being an expert in a particular field, one thereby assumes the duty of conducting one's activities in accordance with the generally accepted standards of others in the same profession. As such, the conduct of someone who holds himself out to the public as an investigator will be measured against a higher standard than the common man who professes no such expertise. Accordingly, those who advertise themselves as specialists such as private investigators have a legal obligation to inform themselves of the standards of the industry and meet those standards in the conduct of their operations.[130]

6.5.1   Surveillance

An example of a negligent investigation by a private investigator comes from Alberta. In this case, the plaintiff brought action because her disability payments were withheld by the defendant insurance company. The insurance company stopped payment based on reports from private investigators it had retained. The private investigators reported that the insured was working forty hours a week in a bookstore when her insurance policy only allowed benefits for up to sixteen hours a week. The court, however, took a different view

---

128 *Bielitzki v. Obadisk*, [1921] 3 W.W.R. 229 (Sask. Q.B.), aff'd [1922] 2 W.W.R. 238 (Sask. C.A.).
129 Smyth, Soberman, & Easson, above note 115 at 86–88.
130 Bilek, Klotter, & Federal, above note 5 at 158.

of the private investigator's findings. The court characterized the private investigator's report as "replete with assumptions" and "mute but graphic evidence of the ineptness and inadequacy of the surveillance conducted." The court further held:

> The most obvious error of the private investigators' reports is that they equate attendance at the bookstore with hours of work. None of the investigators were in the store to determine if the plaintiff was in fact working except for three or four very short interludes. Most of the surveillance was conducted from vehicles parked outside the store with totally inadequate visibility of the activities going on in the store.

With regard to the insurance company, the court held that although the duties owed by an insurer to its insured have rarely been discussed in case law, there is a duty to act in good faith. This good faith was breached by ignoring the medical opinions and relying on incompetent surveillance. The court awarded punitive damages of $7,500 plus costs.[131]

6.5.2   Credit Reporting

One commentator has suggested that, pertaining to the standard of care, no credit bureau will be regarded by a court as an absolute guarantor of the truth of the contents of its reports. Credit bureaus are not expected to double-check in minute detail every fact included in a credit report. They are, however, expected to take reasonable measures, where possible, to check their sources of information, particularly where the source is new or suspect. It may also be considered reasonable to expect that credit bureaus check any information that may be verified easily and cheaply by reference to public records such as bankruptcy, garnishee of wages, and others rather than report on a second-hand source.[132] This level of standard of care is also applicable to other forms of private sector investigators.

6.5.3   Loss of Confidential Information

One commentator reports that the greatest risk of a negligence pertaining to invasion of privacy claims arises from the lack of control of data on computer-based information systems. The main dangers include impersonations where a remote user of the system masquerades as someone entitled to use it, accidental leakages where information is erroneously sent to the wrong terminal, and wiretapping. All of these forms of leakage are preventable with known technology. Therefore, failure to provide protection from any of these dangers would likely amount to negligence.[133]

---

131 *Adams v. Confederation Life Insurance Co.* (1994), 152 A.R. 121 (Alta. Q.B.).
132 Sharp, above note 109 at 77–78.
133 Barron, "People, Not Computers" in J.B. Young, ed., *Privacy* (Chichester: John Wiley & Sons, 1978) at 321.

6.5.4 Nefarious Locates

Investigators should be wary of the purpose of their client. In an Ontario case, an accused was charged with first-degree murder. The accused was a former stock promoter who hired a private investigator to find his "buddy," using the words "I want you to find my old friend. I want to talk business with him." The private investigator informed the accused that the person he was seeking was staying at the Royal York hotel for a convention. The accused attended the hotel and shot his "buddy" twice at close range. Allegedly, the accused and his victim had known each other for a long time. The victim had become wealthy and the accused had fallen on hard times. The accused believed the victim owed him money. The hit was his way of settling the debt.[134]

In Alberta, a private investigator also fell victim to a nefarious locate request. A man retained a private investigator to find the address of his estranged wife who had moved to Edmonton four months earlier. The client told the investigator that his wife had left him, and he was concerned about her welfare, where she was working, and how she was living. The client stated he had his wife's unlisted phone number and simply needed her address. The private investigator thought his client came across like a guy who wanted to straighten things out and write her a letter. Upon being forwarded his wife's address, the client flew to Edmonton and shot his wife dead as she pleaded with him in a parking lot near her apartment. He then shot himself with a semi-automatic handgun. On the seat of his rented mini-van was the one-page report of the private investigator, complete with photos of the outside of his wife's apartment, an arrow penned in to indicate her apartment.[135]

In a British Columbia case, a Vancouver lawyer contacted an Alberta private investigator and asked him to locate a woman living in Calgary. The private investigator, acting on the request without question as it came from a lawyer, completed the file. The investigator later explained that in many cases, requests from lawyers are for the purposes of serving divorce papers or other documents. In this case, however, the information found its way into the hands of the woman's brother who travelled to Calgary and gunned down his sister, her husband, and a family friend in a shopping mall parking lot.

Based on experiences such as these, many private investigators agree to locate persons on condition that they notify the person located and the located person is given the choice of contacting the private investigator's client. Some clients get agitated and angry at this arrangement, but for most investigators, this has simply become a responsible way to conduct business.

6.5.5 Negligent Misrepresentation

In 1963, the House of Lords in England expanded the common law by creating a tort for negligent misrepresentation causing an economic loss. The torts of fraud and deceit historically dealt with intentional false statements that caused damages. However, there was

---

134 *R. v. Bissonnette* (1998), (Ont. S.C.J.) [unreported]. See "Miner Murder" (Toronto: Canadian Press, 1 February 1988).
135 "Investigators — Violence" (Edmonton: Canadian Press, 21 August 1992).

no cause of action against persons who made innocent but negligent misrepresentations unless there was a contract between the parties or there was a fiduciary duty owed by one of the parties. Thus, for example, when providers of financial information such as bankers, accountants, and stock brokers provided information that they knew would be disseminated to a wider audience than its direct recipient, there was no recourse if that information was in fact false and negligently reported. This new tort expanded liability to those who made negligent false statements that caused damages to third parties who relied upon those statements.

The elements of the tort of negligent misrepresentation are as follows:

• There must have been a representation that was false.

• The representation must have been carelessly given.

• There must have been a duty owed by the representor to the representee to take reasonable care to ensure the representation was accurate.

• The loss must have been a reasonably foreseeable consequence of the misrepresentation at the time it was made.[136]

The case that was the basis of this new legal principle originated in a situation where a company asked an advertising agency to handle its account in placing ads. Since the advertising agency had to extend credit to the company, it asked its own bank to obtain credit information on the company. The advertising agency's banker made inquiries from the company's bankers about the company's creditworthiness without revealing that the purpose of the credit check was for one of its own clients. The company's bank reported to the advertising agency's bank that the company was considered good for its ordinary business obligations but that the size of the transaction was larger than experienced by the company's bank. At no time did the advertising agency communicate directly with the company's bank. The advertising agency accepted the company's account based on their banker's information. Shortly afterwards, the company became insolvent. The advertising agency sued the company's bankers for their loss, claiming it was caused by their negligent misrepresentation of the company's creditworthiness.

The court held that a person providing information or advice in response to a request is under a duty to take reasonable care to reply accurately, provided that person knew or ought to have known that his or her statement would be relied upon by the person to whom it was made, and to third parties who were in a foreseeable special relationship with that person, and that such reliance might cause damage to that person. This case was also significant for establishing the principle that pure economic loss as a result of a negligent act was a basis for compensation. It is noteworthy that in the end, the advertising agency's bank was relieved of liability because it had marked its report with the terms "confidential" and "without responsibility."[137]

---

136 *Rainbow Industrial Caterers Ltd. v. Canadian Railway* (1991), 84 D.L.R. (4th) 291 (S.C.C.).
137 *Hedley Byrne v. Heller & Partners*, [1964] A.C. 465 (H.L.).

There are no reported cases where private sector investigators have been sued under this branch of tort law. However, there are cases where analogies can be made. For example, pertaining to reporting between private persons, a doctor has been held liable in negligent misrepresentation for a plaintiff's distress when he negligently told her that her husband had committed suicide when there was no basis for concluding his death was in fact a suicide.[138]

In scenarios where the tort is used to recover losses incurred by third parties, commentators have speculated on its applicability to those who provide investigative reports:

> A credit report does not have to be defamatory or invade the subject's privacy in order to make its author liable; if the report, as issued, is negligently complied so as to contain inaccurate information, which, in due course, causes loss or injury to a third party who acts upon the report, then that third party may sue the author of the report for damages for his loss, provided always that it was reasonably foreseeable that the plaintiff third party would act in reliance upon the report.
>
> . . .
>
> A negligent misstatement may damage the person about whom it was made without necessarily being defamatory. If, for example, a credit report negligently misstates the financial standing of the subject without actually defaming him, but nonetheless causing him to be denied credit, then he may well be able to sue for the negligent misstatement as a result of which he suffered loss, even though there was no privity [of contract] and even though he might not have sued for the tort of defamation. The action for negligent misstatement thus fills the gap left by the other tort remedies where a credit report causes loss.[139]

6.6 CONSPIRACY

Conspiracy is both a tort and a crime. It is established where an agreement is made between two or more persons to cause harm to the plaintiff by unlawful means. The determination of "unlawful means" has been an issue of some debate. While the breach of a contract amounts to unlawful means for the purpose of the tort of intimidation, it may not be sufficient wrongdoing for the tort of conspiracy. However, the tort may be established even if otherwise lawful means are employed but with the purpose of injuring the plaintiff.[140]

A leading Canadian authority on the tort of civil conspiracy is *Canada Cement LaFarge Ltd. v. B.C. Lightweight Aggregate Ltd.*[141] In this case, the Supreme Court of Canada dealt with the requisite elements in a conspiracy action:

---

138 *Jinks v. Cardwell* (1987), C.C.L.T. 168 (H.C.).
139 Sharp, above note 109 at 75.
140 See Dias & Markesinis, above note 103 at 263; *Winfield & Jolowicz on Tort*, above note 124 at 514.
141 [1983] 1 S.C.R. 452.

Although the law concerning the scope of the tort of conspiracy is far from clear, I am of the opinion that whereas the law of tort does not permit an action against an individual defendant who has caused injury to the plaintiff, the law of torts does recognize a claim against them in combination as the tort of conspiracy if:

(1)   whether the means used by the defendants are lawful or unlawful, the predominant purpose of the defendants' conduct is to cause injury to the plaintiff; or

(2)   where the conduct of the defendants is unlawful, the conduct is directed towards the plaintiff (alone or together with others), and the defendants should know in the circumstances that injury to the plaintiff is likely to and does result.

In situation (2) it is not necessary that the predominant purpose of the defendants' conduct be to cause injury to the plaintiff but, in the prevailing circumstances, it must be a constructive intent derived from the fact that the defendants should have known the injury to the plaintiff would ensue. In both situations, however, there must be actual damage suffered by the plaintiff.

There are a couple of cases where this tort is known to have arisen against private investigators. In England, the public prosecutors tried a firm of private investigators for criminal conspiracy alleging the private investigators had obtained confidential personal information by making representations to government officials and banks. The private investigators were convicted at trial by a jury on the basis that they agreed to do deceitful acts that could cause extreme injury to the community. The House of Lords, however, later overturned the conviction as the facts did not amount to a conspiracy that should have resulted in a criminal conviction. Some commentators have suggested the complainants would have had better success if they had proceeded in tort, rather than criminal law.[142]

In Canada, a successful tort action for conspiracy against a firm of private investigators has been reported. In this case, the defendant department store retained the defendant private investigative firm to investigate some suspected internal thefts. One agreement between the department store and the private investigators was that any money recovered as a result of interrogations would be divided equally between the two. The private investigators had reasonable grounds to suspect the theft of a $6.00 box of golf balls. However, the private investigators sought a confession to a larger dollar amount. Based on the conduct of this interview and the agreement between private investigators and the department store, the court convicted the private investigators of criminal extortion and held the department store and the private investigators liable for the tort of conspiracy.[143]

---

142 D.P.P. *v.* Withers, [1974] 3 All E.R. 984 (H.L.).

143 *McKinnon v. F.W. Woolworth Co. & Johnson and Matt, Jordison & Commercial Fidelity Audit Agency Ltd.* (1968), 66 W.W.R. 205 (Alta. C.A.). For a more detailed review of the facts of this case, see Section 4.5.5 — Extortion.

6.7   INVASION OF PRIVACY

The tort of invasion of privacy has been left to the end of this chapter because it is one of the most controversial areas of tort law. At best, the tort of invasion of privacy can be described as a developing tort; at worst, it is argued by some to be no tort at all in Canada. Whatever the position taken, no discussion of tort law as it applies to private investigators would be complete without a review of this topic.

As discussed in the introduction of this chapter, privacy is for most people a cherished concept. The right to retreat into the sanctity of one's own home and private life undisturbed by others is one most people would be outraged to discover had been violated. Many Canadians believe that they may not be followed, photographed, spied on, or reported on, nor may their personal lives, finances, history, or occupations be investigated without their consent, or at the least their knowledge. Many would likely react with indignant protest if they were made the subject of such inquiries and demand the inquiries cease. Most would be even more outraged to discover that in Canadian law the explicit recognition of a right of privacy *per se* is very limited.

In Chapter 5 it was revealed that the majority of provinces do not have legislation creating the tort of invasion of privacy. With regard to the Canadian jurisdictions that have passed a privacy Act and do recognize the tort, it may be said that it provides for an illusionary level of protection. In the "have-not" provinces, privacy issues with regard to specific concerns are legislated in various other Acts. However, their application is very limited. The federal *Privacy Act* is not applicable in such cases as it mainly pertains to breaches of confidential information held by state agencies. The *Charter* is not applicable because section 32 provides that it applies to only the affairs of state agencies. The *Criminal Code* is applicable, but only in certain instances such as electronic surveillance.[144] Personal investigation legislation provides for limitations on the types of inquiries that can be made in certain circumstances and the information that can be recorded. Still, there remains a large area where the concern of the individual to prevent intrusions into his or her personal life is unmet by any statutory protection.[145]

Recourse must then be had to the common law where protection of privacy interests is scattered among a variety of torts, and where the general right to privacy receives little judicial sanction. Although in England no court has ruled in favour of the tort of invasion of privacy, it is now well established in American law. In Canada and other common law jurisdictions, commentators continue to publish articles asserting that such a tort exists or that it should exist. This section will review the case law from Canadian courts that have recognized the legitimacy of the tort of invasion of privacy.

The first decision in Canada to suggest the possibility of an independent tort of invasion of privacy was a case where a professional football player learned his photograph

---

144 In certain cases, individuals convicted of violating federal wiretap legislation may be ordered to pay the aggrieved party up to $5,000 in punitive damages. See the *Criminal Code*, R.S.C. 1985, c. C-46, ss.183 to 196.

145 Geddes, above note 34.

appeared without his consent in an advertisement for an automobile dealer. The football player sued on the basis of invasion of privacy and passing-off. The automobile dealer brought a motion to have the action for invasion of privacy struck from the lawsuit on the grounds that it disclosed no reasonable cause of action. However, the court dismissed the motion, allowing the action to go to trial, stating that although the cause of action was novel, no case law was presented that indicated that a Canadian court would not recognize a right to privacy. The case was later settled on the basis of passing-off.[146]

The breakthrough case for the common law tort of invasion of privacy originated out of an action in Alberta known as *Motherwell v. Motherwell*.[147] In that case, the defendant made recurrent contacts to the plaintiffs by telephone and mail, fabricating numerous unfounded statements and accusations concerning the affairs of the plaintiffs and refusing to cease from this behaviour. The plaintiffs argued this behaviour was both a breach of their right to privacy and a nuisance. The plaintiffs pleaded for nominal damages and an injunction. The court held that the behaviour the plaintiffs complained about did not fit the existing categories permitted in tort law; that an invasion of privacy does not come within the principles of private nuisance. The court concluded:

> The interests of developing jurisprudence would be better served by approaching the invasion of privacy by abuse of the telephone system as a new category of tort rather than seeking to enlarge the third category [of nuisance]. We are dealing here with a new factor. Heretofore the matters of complaint have reached the plaintiff's premises by natural means: sounds through the air waves, pollution in many forms carried by air currents, vibrations through the earth, and the like. Here the matters complained of arise within the premises through the use by the defendant of communication agencies in the nature of public utilities available to everyone, which the plaintiffs have caused to serve their premises. They are non-selective in the sense that so long as they are employed by the plaintiffs, they have no control over the incoming communications.[148]

A motion to strike an action for invasion of privacy was also set aside in a case between a wife and her estranged husband. In this case, the wife alleged that her estranged husband made repeated unauthorized entries into her home, made persistent telephone calls to her home and work, and on several incidents had physically and sexually assaulted her. The court held that although the allegations fit well within the accepted torts of nuisance, trespass, and assault, the allegations could fit into the proposed head of action of invasion of privacy. The case was therefore permitted to go to trial.[149]

The next case that looked at this tort commenced in a municipal council meeting in Niagara Falls, Ontario. Here the defendant played a tape recording at a council meeting

---

146 *Krouse v. Chrysler Can. Ltd.* (1974), 1 O.R. (2d) 225 (C.A.). *Krouse* was later followed in a similar motion in *Heath v. Weist-Barron School of Television (Canada) Ltd.* (1981), 18 C.C.L.T. 129 (Ont. H.C.J.).

147 [1976] 6 W.W.R. 550 (Alta. C.A.).

148 It is noteworthy that the court did not extend this form of invasion of privacy to incoming mail.

149 *Cappan v. Cappan* (1980), 14 C.C.L.T. 191 (Ont. H.C.J.).

which he had made of the plaintiff over the phone without the plaintiff's consent. The defendant's purpose was to vindicate himself from allegations of deceit and breach of confidence. The playing of the tape and its contents was duly reported in a local newspaper and became the subject of an editorial. The result of the disclosure embarrassed the plaintiff sufficiently that he became reclusive. The plaintiff brought an action that by the time of trial was narrowed down to one issue: Could a plaintiff be awarded damages for invasion of privacy with malice? The court reviewed the few cases in which invasion of privacy had been argued and found as fact in this case that the plaintiff had not suffered any economic loss but was embarrassed and felt his confidence had been betrayed. On this basis the court held:

> Be that as it may, it's my opinion that certainly a person must have the right to make such a claim as a result of a taping of a private conversation without his knowledge and also against the publication of the conversation against his will or without his consent. Certainly, for want of a better description as to what happened, this is an invasion of privacy and despite the very able argument of the defendant's counsel that no such action exists, I have come to the conclusion that the plaintiff must be given some right to recovery for what the defendant has in this case done.

The court found there was no malice in the defendant's actions and awarded damages of $500 along with costs in the same amount.[150]

In another case from Ontario, a court awarded $7,000 in damages for invasion of privacy as well as for defamation. In this case, the defendant sought to embarrass the plaintiff into acceding to a proposed modification to a mortgage of farmland. The defendant's chief tactic was to endorse the back of mortgage payment cheques with comments respecting the plaintiff's integrity and creditworthiness. The defendant knew these cheques would cause the plaintiff stress and damage the plaintiff's reputation as they passed through the plaintiff's bank and the tobacco marketing board. The defendant also approached a number of businesses in the plaintiff's community alleging various improprieties respecting the plaintiff's activities and honesty. On these facts, the court adopted the reasoning of the Alberta Court of Appeal in *Motherwell* and concluded the defendant's actions constituted an invasion of privacy.[151]

A case dealing with the conduct of debt collection has also been addressed in Ontario in the context of invasion of privacy. In this case, a female defendant had borrowed a sum of money from a male plaintiff and failed to repay it. The female plaintiff, who was married to the male plaintiff, proceeded to harass the defendant by making numerous telephone calls to her residence, attending the defendant's residence and forcing her way into her bedroom when she was ill, demanding payment, and attending the defendant's place of employment on two occasions demanding payment, using a loud voice and profanity in front of her co-workers and physically assaulting her in the parking lot. The court award-

---

150 *Saccone v. Orr* (1981), 34 O.R. (2d) 317 (Co. Ct.).
151 *S.&A. Nagy Farms Ltd. v. Repsys* (13 March 1987), St. Thomas No. F54/85, (Ont. Dist. Ct.) [unreported].

ed the plaintiff the amount of money the defendant owed, but then went on to review the defendant's counterclaim for invasion of privacy. The plaintiff argued that the defendant's claim should be dismissed as the ridicule she subjected the defendant to was true. The court held:

> Should a creditor attempt to force payment of the debt by subjecting the debtor to public contempt, insult and ridicule because of the importance in a free society of the circulation of true information? To ask the question, in my view, is to answer it.

On this basis the court held that the question of whether there was an invasion of privacy depends on the circumstances of the particular case and the conflicting rights involved. The court further held that it would be a monstrous injustice to deny a remedy to a victim of privacy invasion in circumstances where the rights of the individual outweigh society's interest in the circulation of true information. Referring to the *Motherwell* case, the court held that the law is not confined to the existing categories of tort law and that the common law can expand to deal with situations not dealt with before. The court awarded the defendant $2,500 for the invasion of privacy.[152]

Finally, a trespass case also argued in the context of invasion of privacy was based on an acrimonious dispute concerning the use of an access road to a cottage. In this case, one of the defendants assaulted one of the plaintiffs, removed articles from the plaintiff's cottage, and repeatedly locked a gate at the entrance of the disputed access road. The plaintiffs made their claims in trespass, assault, intimidation, harassment, and invasion of privacy. The court held that taken altogether, the facts were of a kind that a person of normal sensitivity would regard as offensive and intolerable and an invasion of the plaintiff's right to privacy. The court awarded damages of $20,000 for mental distress and exemplary damages of $5,000 as a result of the invasion of privacy.

From the foregoing, one commentator has concluded that currently, actions for invasions of privacy have been accepted for the unauthorized recording and disclosure of a telephone conversation, for unreasonable behaviour in the collection of a debt, and for conduct involving harassment, trespass, and interference with the enjoyment of real property. The actions all appear to be rooted in the judicial reluctance to allow reprehensible conduct to go unremedied. Each of the decisions addresses privacy as a "right": the right to be left alone, the violation of which could be remedied by way of damages in tort. The courts seem to be in agreement that for an intrusion to be actionable, the conduct must be substantial and of a kind that a reasonable person of normal sensitivity would regard as offensive and intolerable.[153]

The number of situations to which an action for invasion of privacy could be extended are numerous. For example, although a plaintiff could succeed in a trespass to land action against someone who has planted a listening device on his property, he or she would be entering into new tort territory by proceeding with an action for invasion of privacy against an individual who intercepts his conversations without entering his land.

---

152 *Palad v. Pantaleon* (14 June 1989), No. 266930/86 (Ont. Dist. Ct.) [unreported].
153 Lawson, above note 10 at 220.

It is noteworthy that in the United States there are two forms of the tort of invasion of privacy that are very relevant to private investigators. The first is known as invasion of privacy — making private facts public. The second is known as invasion of privacy — unwarranted intrusion.

In the first case, a person may be held liable for invasion of privacy, making private facts public, if he publishes broadly private facts about another, which could be highly offensive to a reasonable person, about a matter in which the speaker does not have a legitimate interest. The focus of this tort is the unwarranted publicity of private facts, not their discovery. In the United States, courts have held that the publicity must be broad and pervasive for liability to be found. Thus, when a bank gave information on a customer to a respective employer, a court found no liability. Likewise, where an investigator reported credit information of a subject to an insurance company, a court found no liability.

In the second case, however, the scope is wider. The elements of invasion of privacy, unwarranted intrusion, include the unreasonable, deliberate prying into private matters of the "seclusion" of another without a legitimate interest or authority. This tort has been held to apply to situations such as an unwarranted search of a person's personal property, intensive physical surveillance, and the obtaining of private bank account information absent a court order or subpoena. As discussed in Section 5.3 — Provincial Privacy Legislation, "legitimate interest" would appear to be the key defence to an action for this tort.

The Association of Certified Fraud Examiners has also addressed the parameters of the tort of invasion of privacy — unwarranted intrusion. In their text, it is stated that the mere gathering of information is not a tort. However, where the conduct is the gathering of confidential information, and where the intrusion is unreasonable and/or without predication or grounds, the tort may be made out. They also note that no tort is committed if the information is public or disclosed to others.[154]

To conclude this topic, it is important to note how accessible information is on any person from both unrestricted[155] and quasi-restricted sources.[156]

---

154   J.T. Wells et al., above note 25.

155   There are sources of information that are generally viewed as unrestricted. These sources include a subject party's family and friends, neighbours, employers, financial transactors (e.g., real estate agents), memberships to organizations or periodicals, utility companies, government land titles and mortgages, liens, bankruptcy registries, voters lists, divorce records, P.P.S.A., corporate search, county, civil, criminal, or sheriff court filings, library telephone books (criss-cross directories for home ownership, renters and occupants, and home businesses), business indexes, trade magazines, student yearbooks, and newspapers, to name a few.

156   Restricted sources of information include motor vehicle registration, drivers' licence search, credit information (credit information is not permitted for location of witnesses, missing persons, or matrimonial matters), birth/death/marriage records, occupational associations, bureaus of registered trade, municipal assessment offices, better business bureaus, municipal licensing, etc.

6.7.1   Inducement to Breach Confidentiality

Confidentiality is also an issue that should be addressed here as it is often raised in discussions pertaining to invasions of privacy.

Confidentiality rights are often found in contracts. A definition of the tort of inducement to breach a contract has been described as the intentional and unjustified act of inducing or procuring anyone to break a contract made by him or her with another. The tort requires damages to have resulted from the breach.[157] The concept that interference with certain relationships could be tortious has ancient roots in the common law dating from the early protection of the relationship between master and servant.[158]

Although the majority of such actions deal with cases where contracts have been broken in the more traditional sense, some cases have furthered this type of action by including situations where a person induced another to breach his promise of confidentiality included in the contract. A typical example of this form of breach is in the context of employment where a competitor or a competitor's agent induces the disclosure of trade secrets. Another example of this tort has occurred with regard to credit information.

In the Montreal *La Presse*, it was reported that Equifax made a proposal to Quebec's major credit union, Desjardins, to provide credit references at no charge if the credit union gave Equifax details of credit card transactions by customers using a Desjardins VISA card. Equifax's proposal was to allow it to have access to Desjardin's entire customer data bank, and this proposal was made in the course of efforts commenced by Equifax in early 1992 to solicit similar arrangements with businesses honouring Desjardin's VISA cards. Desjardins strongly resisted Equifax's efforts.[159]

Another form of action for breach of confidence was alluded to in Section 4.4.2 — Theft (of CPIC Information). In *R. v. Stewart*,[160] the Supreme Court of Canada suggested that an action for breach of confidence may take over where the Criminal Code leaves off in protecting against the unauthorized disclosure of confidential information. The court held: "It is possible that, with time, confidential information will come to be considered as property in the civil law or even be granted special legal protection by statutory enactment." The court further stated that even if confidential information was property for the purposes of the civil law, it does not follow that such information would be property for criminal law purposes.

General statutory enactment to protect confidential information remains lacking. However, the common law has continued to develop. Where no contract has been formed pertaining to confidential information, courts have held that a confidence is formed when-

---

157 R.F.V. Heuston & R.A. Buckley, *Salmond and Heuston on the Law of Torts*, 19th ed. (London: Sweet & Maxwell, 1987) at 404.

158 Fridman, above note 43 at para. 21:30.

159 "Equifax à l'oeil sur la banque de données Desjardins" *La Presse* (29 February 1992) F2.

160 (1988), 50 D.L.R.(4th) 1 (S.C.C.).

ever one party imparts to another private or secret matters on the express or implied under-standing the communication is for restricted purposes.[161] The principal elements of an action for an action for breach of confidentiality include the following:

- The information itself must have the necessary quality of confidence about it.
- The information must have been imparted in circumstances imposing an obligation of confidence.
- There must have been an unauthorized use of the information by the party under an obligation of confidence.[162]

Information for which breach of confidence actions arise pertain to commercial, finan-cial, personal and governmental information, and addresses information in any form, from documents and drawings to recorded conversations.[163] One Canadian commentator reports that an action for breach of confidence respecting personal information given to a compa-ny or an individual for a limited purpose is just as effective a remedy for invasion of pri-vacy as an action for trespass to land by a private investigator, albeit for commercial purposes.

Defences to an action for breach of confidence include the obvious — consent, often referred to as the voluntary assumption of risk in negligence cases, or by the Latin phrase *volenti non fit injuria*: One who has invited or assented to an act being done towards him cannot, when he suffers from it, complain of it as a wrong. Consent can be implied or given expressly.

Because breach of confidence is an equitable doctrine, a plaintiff must come with clean hands. Plaintiffs who themselves have breached a confidence in relation to the defendant will often be refused a remedy. Furthermore, the equitable duty of confidence does not apply to prevent the disclosure of inequity, today deemed to be criminal offences or civil wrongs. Other defences to breach of confidence include delay and public interest.[164]

---

161 F. Gurry, *Breach of Confidence* (Oxford: Clarendon Press, 1984) at 111.

162 *Coco v. A.N. Clark (Engineers) Ltd.* , [1969] R.P.C. 41 at 47–48.

163 P.M. North, "Breach of Confidence, Proposals for Reform" in C.M. Campbell, ed., *Data Processing and the Law* (London: Sweet & Maxwell, 1984) at 175.

164 Lawson, above note 10 at 350.

CHAPTER 7

CONFIDENTIALITY OF
HEALTH INFORMATION —
THE KREVER INQUIRY

In 1980, Mr. Justice Horace Krever released the *Report of the Commission of Inquiry into the Confidentiality of Health Information* (the Inquiry).[1] The Inquiry was undertaken in response to allegations that there was an ongoing and lucrative trade in confidential and private health care information among police, private investigators, insurance companies, lawyers, and the medical profession itself. Among the various other functions of the Inquiry of relevance to private investigators is the examination made of the practices of various private investigation agencies in eliciting information through the use of pretexts. Krever reviewed the practices of at least eight separate private investigative agencies and his findings were very critical. Krever's report set back any public perception gains the private investigative field may have had for a number of years.

By way of background, the Inquiry found that various pieces of legislation impose confidentiality obligations on five categories of health care professionals: dentists, physicians, nurses, optometrists, and denture therapists. Each of these professions was and still is prohibited by legislation from disclosing health information without patient consent unless required to do so by law. Breach of these obligations constitutes professional misconduct as well as possibly a statutory offence. The governing bodies of the respective disciplines may investigate any suspected misconduct. Penalties imposed may range from reprimands to suspension or revocation of a licence to practice.

In this chapter, the findings of Krever with respect to each of the private investigative agencies that faced the Inquiry will be reviewed. This approach is not intended to reflect negatively upon the private investigation agencies mentioned as it will be seen that the practices found to be unethical were seemingly condoned by many people in the legal,

---

1   Krever, H.J., *Report on the Commission of Inquiry into the Confidentiality of Health Information* (Toronto: Queen's Printer, 1980).

insurance, medical, and private investigation fields at the time. The intent of this section is to explain the pretext practices that were used formerly by private investigators and the reasons why these pretext practices are improper. As will be seen, many variations of pretexts were exposed by the Inquiry. As such, this chapter offers a good insight into how pretexts are used to acquire information, and it will conclude with a review of Krever's findings pertaining to the lawyers who instructed the private investigators who were named.

The language found in this review for the most part paraphrases that used by Justice Krever himself and retains many of his expressions. Some stylistic revisions were required as Justice Krever wrote much of the report in the first person, whereas this review is mostly written in the third. For those readers who would like to review the Inquiry report itself, the review of the conduct of the private investigators is contained in Volume 1 of the three-volume report. This chapter's excerpts are taken from the 583 pages of Volume 1. Because this chapter is included strictly for educational purposes, the names of all persons and agencies have been replaced by initials to protect the identity of any persons who may still be active in their professions.

7.1   CIL AND PIL

On 14 April 1977, ML, a medical record technician employed by the St. Catharines General Hospital, received a telephone call. The caller identified herself as being from Toronto General Hospital and said to ML that a patient, one JM, was unconscious from a drug overdose in the Toronto General emergency department. The caller requested that ML obtain JM's hospital records and provide her with JM's medical history, particulars of JM's hospital attendance, and any other information on the file. ML noted the caller's telephone number as 225-1486 and was advised by the caller that this was a direct dial number. ML told the caller that she would check JM's chart and return the call. JM had been a psychiatric patient at the hospital and ML reviewed the chart. She was suspicious and therefore checked the telephone directory listing and telephoned Toronto General Hospital to verify that 225-1486 was one of its phone numbers. ML was informed that it was not a Toronto General Hospital telephone number and that JM was not being treated in that hospital's emergency department.

ML then telephoned the caller back. Her call was answered by "Mrs. Robinson, medical records department." ML told "Mrs. Robinson" that she had telephoned Toronto General Hospital and had been informed that JM was not in the emergency department. ML was then told that she had misunderstood and that she was speaking to someone at the Toronto East General Hospital, and not the Toronto General Hospital. ML, displaying unusual perception, again said that she would return the call. ML obtained the telephone number of the Toronto East General Hospital, called the number, and was advised that 225-1486 was not a number associated with the Toronto East General Hospital either.

While ML was making this telephone call to the Toronto East General Hospital, another telephone call was received in the hospital's medical records library. The caller identified himself as "Dr. Henderson" calling from the emergency department of the Toronto East General Hospital. The recipient of this call told "Dr. Henderson" that there was difficulty in verifying the legitimacy of the request for information and requested that he wait a moment. "Dr. Henderson" became irate and warned that JM's life was in jeopardy. ML, who was informed of the "Dr. Henderson" call, transferred "Dr. Henderson's" call from the hospital's medical record library to the emergency department. ML then reported the incident to her department head and faithfully recorded the sequence of events and the telephone number 225-1486. Mr. Barr, Q.C., the solicitor for the St. Catharines General Hospital, was notified and reported the particulars of the incident to the Ontario Provincial Police Registrar of the Private Investigators and Security Guards section.[2]

The OPP investigation determined that PIL, an investigation company, had been retained by WMCI, an insurance company, to carry out an investigation of JM's medical condition. JM had been injured in a motor vehicle accident and was seeking benefits from WMCI. The OPP, although they believed the calls had originated from CIL, another investigation company, were unable to prove to its satisfaction who had made the call to the hospital. The OPP had PIL surrender its agency licence. No member of the OPP, however, reviewed CIL's files to determine whether calls of a similar type had been made by them despite the fact that the *Private Investigators and Security Guards Act* (the Act) conferred the power to undertake such a review. For all practical purposes, the surrender of the licence by PIL terminated the OPP investigation.

The Inquiry's investigation went further. It established that one or more of the MG brothers, the principals of CIL, was or were the beneficial owner or owners of the issued shares of PIL. It was apparent that PIL surrendered its licence in the hope that the surrender would terminate the OPP investigation and thereby protect from disclosure the practice by CIL of obtaining access to health records of claimants without their authorization.[3]

The Inquiry further learned that PIL had been retained by WMCI to carry out an investigation of JM. PIL, in turn, had retained CIL to obtain medical information on JM. Bell Canada records revealed that on 14 April 1977, the telephone number 225-1486 was registered to CIL, and on that date CIL had the number changed to 226-1704. The OPP investigated CIL in relation to this incident. Their investigation disclosed another occurrence wherein CIL had attempted to obtain medical information without authorization.

Based on this and other information, on 19 April 1978 the Inquiry obtained a search warrant for the premises of CIL. The Inquiry's investigators seized 720 files of which 326 contained evidence of confidential health care information being requested or obtained.[4]

CIL was licensed in 1972 pursuant to the requirements of the Act. At all material times the shareholders were four brothers: JMG held approximately 50 percent of the shares; DMG, approximately 30 percent; BMG, approximately 15 percent; and TMG, approximately 5 percent.

Around September 1973, KPM, an investigator with CIL Investigations, was promoted to the position of director of field operations. At that time, the jurisdiction of insurance investigations was handled by DMG. During that time, KPM and DMG had several dis-

2   *Ibid.* at 166.
3   *Ibid.* at 167.
4   *Ibid.* at 168.

cussions pertaining to the success of some staff investigators in obtaining confidential medical information through the use of pretexts. KPM and DMG concluded that substantial quantities of health information were passed within the medical community as a matter of expediency by telephone without any security precautions being taken to ensure that the person requesting and receiving the health information was acting legitimately. They concluded that since this dialogue within the medical community was carried out mainly by women (nurses, receptionists, technicians, and medical record librarians), female investigators would make less suspicious pretext investigators.[5]

In the beginning, two female employees were given the sole responsibility of making pretext phone calls to hospitals and physicians' offices for the purpose of obtaining medical information. In August 1976, a registered nurse, JDW, was hired by DMG expressly and solely to make pretext phone calls.[6] She was familiar with medical terminology and DMG believed this knowledge would make the pretext seem all the more reasonable and successful. JDW was never licensed under the Act. Later, in January 1977, another registered nurse, RM, was employed by DMG. RM believed she was being hired as a private investigator and was licensed as such. She did the usual investigator's work including surveillance for the first few weeks of her employment. She was then introduced to JDW who taught her how to make pretext calls to physicians' offices and hospitals. These pretext calls were referred to as "medicals." On more than one occasion RM asked DMG if making medicals was proper. DMG's response was that CIL's lawyers had sanctioned this practice. RM accepted DMG's answer. In fact, no evidence was presented that DMG had ever made such inquiries. During this time period, RM and JDW made their pretext calls from CIL's offices while two other non-licensed investigators made their pretext calls from their own homes.[7]

The "CIL System" was described by Krever as follows. Instructions to CIL from its clients to carry out investigations were usually received by telephone, although both WMCI and the Co-operators Insurance Company (Co-operators) used a preprinted form addressed to CIL that set out the nature of the investigation required. When CIL received instructions from a client, it sent out a written confirmation to the client so that there would be no dispute as to the nature of the investigation services requested. Invariably, the written confirmation would contain the word "medical" as part of the assignment to be carried out. Thus, it was apparent that the insurance companies were aware that this form of information gathering was taking place.[8]

On receipt of a client's instructions, an "assignment sheet" was completed. This sheet was circulated among several investigators depending upon what the client had requested. For example, if a surveillance was to be carried out in addition to an attempt to obtain medical information without authorization, the surveillance would be carried out by the

---

5   *Ibid.* at 169.
6   For a further discussion, see the case of *Re West and College of Nurses* as found in Section 2.3.3.6 — Part-time Employment.
7   Above note 1 at 171.
8   *Ibid.*

field investigator and the pretext calls by the employee whose function was limited solely to the making of such calls. Before a pretext call could be made to a hospital or physician, it was necessary to know the name of the treating physician and the hospital that the patient had attended. The client (insurer) sometimes provided this information. The client could properly obtain this information from police reports or from the voluntary disclosure from the patient. When CIL did not provide the necessary information, it used various pretexts to discover the names of the treating physicians and hospitals.[9]

CIL used a number of "market survey" pretexts to extract information from unwary subjects of their investigations. One of the methods was under the guise of a bogus survey form entitled "Traffic Inquiry Researchers of Canada," which was a fictional entity. As DMG later admitted, this fictional name was probably chosen because it closely resembled in name the Council of Independent Traffic Researchers of Canada which was a bona fide research organization. A CIL investigator would call at the subject's residence and represent that he or she was conducting a survey on behalf of Traffic Injury Researchers of Canada. The answers to the questions would disclose any hospital attendance, names of treating physicians, whether therapy had taken place, and other relevant information.[10]

Another form of pretext used was a market poll called a "Neighbourhood Survey." This survey was purported to be prepared by Metro Marketing Services, another fictional entity. Survey forms were prepared in large quantities for CIL investigators. They would then attend the subject's residence and represent they were employed by the fictitious Metro Marketing. The ruse would gain the investigator entry into the subject's home. As investigators were required to be glib, the conversation would soon turn to the subject's injuries and the circumstances of the accident. During the conversation, the investigator would elicit the name of the treating physician and the hospital the subject attended.[11]

Yet another form of subterfuge was known as the OHIP pretext. For this pretext, JDW, RM, or another CIL employee would telephone the subject and represent that she was employed by OHIP and that OHIP was undertaking an investigation or audit and ask the subject to name all the physicians whom the subject had visited as well as the hospitals attended within a specific time period. Almost without fail, the use of this pretext gave the investigators the names of treating physicians and the particulars of any hospital attendances.[12]

JDW, RM, and other CIL investigators who engaged in pretext inquiries were equipped with tape recorders, and almost all the pretext calls were recorded. Every CIL file contained a work sheet that had an area headed "Pretext" where the pretext used was to be inserted. Every pretext call was transcribed. The files contained the transcribed notes, the work sheets, and other information such as surveillance reports. All were delivered to DMG. DMG then dictated the report for CIL's client. Once the report had been dictated, the transcript of the pretext calls and the worksheet were destroyed as a matter of course.[13]

---

9   Above note 1 at 172.
10   *Ibid.* at 173.
11   *Ibid.* at 174.
12   *Ibid.* at 175.
13   *Ibid.* at 176.

Of all CIL's clients, the Co-operators provided the most cases. Of the 326 files seized during the Inquiry's search warrant which contained evidence of health information requests, 194 files were from the Co-operators. The Co-operators had been doing business with CIL since 1974. At the beginning of their relationship, CIL only emphasized surveillance services. Gradually, however, CIL began to provide medical information. The Co-operators accepted this medical information and began to expect it. It was apparent from the files that the Co-operators had retained CIL specifically for the purpose of obtaining medical information on their claimants, and that they knew CIL was obtaining this information using methods that were without patient authorization. In fact, the practice was so widespread that letters were found from Co-operator adjusters indicating that if the information sought was not obtained, the Co-operators would not pay, notwithstanding the fact that CIL had to put the same time investment into a file whether they were successful or not.[14]

By 1977, around the time that the Inquiry was starting, a manager of the Co-operators, DG, consulted a solicitor and was informed of the danger and impropriety of the types of medical investigations being utilized by CIL. As a result of this, DG prepared guidelines for the investigators it contracted with. DG sent CIL a letter containing the following provisions:

The following guidelines will be observed when conducting an investigation for any office of the Co-operators in Ontario:

1.   When interviewing a claimant who is not represented by a solicitor, a representative of an investigative service or other person acting on our behalf will correctly identify himself and the fact that he is representing the Co-operators;

2.   There will be no pretext interview or direct contact with any claimant represented by a solicitor unless the claimant has properly and of his own accord withdrawn his retainer or unless the claimant's solicitor has given his permission for such interview or contact;

3.   Medical information will not be sought or obtained from any medical practitioner or hospital without the written consent of a party who is the subject of the enquiry;

4.   A surveillance may be carried out but during the course of such surveillance no affirmative action to entrap a claimant will be taken;

5.   There will be no use of paid informers to obtain information on claimants other than the payment of rewards through proper law enforcement authorities.

Extraordinary circumstances such as suspected fraud may necessitate some deviation from these guidelines. However, any deviation must be authorized by the division claims manager.

---

14   *Ibid.* at 177 and 212.

Effective immediately, we may utilize the services of any investigation service to interview neighbours, employers, acquaintances, etc. of claimants or to carry out surveillances of claimants.[15]

When questioned as to his justification for conducting the impugned pretexts, KPM testified that DMG considered the release of medical information to be an ethical matter for the physician as opposed to a legal matter. KPM testified that they had concluded that the truth was being hidden behind the ethics of the medical profession, that their client's right to know was in conflict with the patient's right to privacy, and that on balance their client's right to know was more important. KPM went on to say that he had been unaware that there was a legal obligation upon physicians and hospital employees to keep patient medical information confidential. However, KPM did acknowledge that an investigator had an obligation pursuant to its enabling statute to keep information confidential.

Krever found that KPM appeared to be an intelligent and well-informed person, and that it was incredible that he did not realize that a medical professional would have at the very least a similar legal obligation to his own. Furthermore, CIL carried on a large business and had access to corporate solicitors who were in a position to define their precise legal obligations. No legal opinion was sought. Krever concluded that KPM and DMG knew generally that physicians had an obligation of confidentiality and that health information could not be obtained from a hospital without written authorization by the patient. Therefore, KPM and DMG consciously decided to implement a carefully organized system, the aim of which was to obtain health information without authorization of the patient. Krever rejected that this was done after a philosophical analysis of competing interests. Krever found that the system was instituted because KPM and DMG knew that health information was a commodity that had a pecuniary value and could be sold to their clients for a large profit.

As for the conduct of JDW and RM, Krever found they must have known from their professional training that the making of these pretext calls was improper. Krever accepted RM's statement that she found the making of these pretext calls to be distasteful, and that the only reason she continued to make them was because she could not find any other form of suitable employment. Notwithstanding her employment situation, Krever found that the choice should not have been difficult for her considering her professional training. She should have chosen not to work at all rather than become involved in this form of pretext calling.[16]

At the inquiry, DMG claimed that the destruction of worksheets and transcripts of pretext calls was carried out as a matter of good housekeeping and to conserve filing space. Krever did not accept this explanation. Krever found that there was other irrelevant material in the files which could have been destroyed to conserve space but was not. Krever found that CIL's principals knew that the OPP, under the authority of the *Private Investigators and Security Guards Act*, had the right to attend to review the files if they had received a complaint. If the work sheets and transcripts of the pretext calls remained in the

15 *Ibid.* at 212–14.
16 *Ibid.* at 171.

files, there would be the risk that the practice would be exposed. Therefore, the destruction of the worksheets and transcripts was carried out as part of a concerted effort to conceal the improper manner in which health information was being obtained. By oversight, some of the worksheets and transcripts were not destroyed. They ended up being the basis for discovering the practice.[17]

From reviewing the files and based on the evidence of RM and JDW, Krever found that health information was obtained from every imaginable source, and that no source was immune. Some of the sources were physicians, physicians' employees, chiropractors, dentists, physiotherapists, teachers, principals, school nurses, occupational health professionals, social workers, private laboratories, police departments, finance companies, insurance companies, pharmacists, clergy, universities, lawyers, psychologists, and all types of hospital departments including admitting, accounting, physiotherapy, records, emergency, and X-ray. Krever further found that CIL had numerous insurance companies and adjusters as clients, and that these insurance companies and adjusters were aware of, and in fact condoned, the improper investigative methods of CIL. A typical example of Krever's findings with regard to the insurance companies and adjusters is taken from the extract dealing with the WMCI. Krever reported as follows.

WMCI is a casualty insurance company that carries on business in Ontario. The Inquiry revealed ten files in which WMCI's employees requested CIL to obtain, or in which they received, health information without patient consent or authorization. For these assignments, CIL received a preprinted assignment form from WMCI requesting it to determine the claimant's "type of injury and medical information." The medical information contained in these reports was often obtained by RM by the use of pretext calls. For a typical file, she would lie to the claimant's general practitioner that she was calling from, for example, the offices of "Dr. Martin, Neurologist."

WMCI's instructions to CIL were given with the intention that it should obtain medical information without the claimant's authorization. The words "discreet inquiries," which were often found in CIL's reports, meant that a pretext or some other impropriety had been used. In one report to WMCI, it was even expressly stated that information could not be obtained from the Etobicoke General Hospital Medical Records Department without authorization from the patient. The fact that the instructions to CIL were made on a preprinted form strongly suggests that WMCI did a volume of business with CIL. WMCI's employees had obtained this sort of information from CIL on other occasions. WMCI knew it was being obtained on a regular basis.

Another common colloquialism found in the reports to WMCI from CIL was that "the investigator was advised by a confidential source." DMG testified that the words "confidential source" were not used to mislead the client into believing that CIL had a source, that is, a person with a special relationship who provided the information. Rather, to DMG the expression "confidential source" simply meant that a pretext call had been made. DMG further testified that he believed the clients did not know that pretexts calls were made to obtain health information. No one, to his knowledge, had ever explained to the clients how the subjects' medical histories were acquired.

---

17   *Ibid.* at 176.

Krever found that CIL did not have a "confidential source" in any hospital. Krever found that the term "confidential source" meant information obtained from an unknown person or from a known person by the use of a pretext. Krever found that the words were used to mislead clients into believing CIL employees were able to obtain information the clients themselves could not obtain because of a position of access to the confidential health care information. Krever found that even DMG conceded that anyone reading a CIL report would conclude that the health information provided had been obtained by CIL investigators by some improper manner. Krever held that what was significant is that no customer of CIL ever complained about, or took issue with, the manner in which that information had been obtained.

Krever noted that DMG attempted to justify the practice of obtaining health information by pretext as serving a legitimate purpose such as to enable an insurance company to settle a claim, and therefore the method of obtaining the information was irrelevant. In other words, the use of pretexts was not improper because the ends justified the means. Krever rejected this rationalization stating that it is an entirely unacceptable solution to a problem of conflicting interests.[18]

Krever did not simply set his sights on WMCI as being an accomplice to CIL's improper pretext information-gathering practice. He also set out examples from files seized of thirteen other insurance and adjuster companies that utilized CIL and were aware that the acquisition of medical information for them was through improper means.[19] Krever's explanations of CIL's involvement with these companies was similar in nature to that of WMCI and does not require additional explanation. Krever further noted that five other insurance companies acknowledged their use of CIL as well for the acquisition of medical information.[20] Krever further reported that other private investigation companies and lawyers also used this service of CIL.[21] A discussion of the role of various lawyers is included further on in this chapter under Section 7.10.

7.2   AA

RM was a private investigator who operated an agency entitled AA. Under his employ or in association were private investigators including DE, TJ, JL, and CM. The following is a review of Krever's findings pertaining to the private investigators of this agency.

RA[22]

RA was retained by insurance companies, adjusters, and lawyers. He was occasionally requested to obtain from hospital employees confidential medical information without the patient's consent. RA admitted that he knew that hospital employees had an obligation to keep health information confidential. Despite this knowledge, he had personally gone to

---

18   *Ibid.* at 240–47.
19   *Ibid.* at 216–72 and 286–90.
20   *Ibid.* at 272–73.
21   *Ibid.* at 260.
22   *Ibid.* at 277–80.

hospitals and identified himself as a private investigator and sought health information. On a few occasions, he obtained information although he did not indicate on whose behalf he was acting. RA claimed he did not engage in pretext calls because he was not good at it due to his thick English accent. RA did admit, however, that he had retained others to make them for him.

The veracity of RA's claims were not verified by review of his files. When RA heard about the Inquiry, he suddenly began a reorganization of his files and destroyed more than sixty files. RA claimed that he conducted the purge because he was concerned about the confidentiality of his clients. He claimed that on two prior occasions, the OPP, under the auspices of the Registrar of their Private Investigator and Security Guard section, had inspected his files. On these occasions, RA felt that the confidentiality of his clients was compromised. To ensure his client's confidentiality was not compromised on this occasion, RA took the further precaution of destroying his invoices. This further measure prevented the Inquiry from obtaining copies of the investigation reports from the clients themselves.

In a classic understatement, RA admitted that the destruction of his files would certainly look suspicious in the mind of a reasonable person. Krever found that the destruction of the files was neither in accordance with any usual or accepted business practice nor in accordance with common decency or business morality. Rather, the destruction of these files was done to eliminate the possibility of review by the Inquiry to determine the extent to which he was engaged in the practice of improperly obtaining medical information. Krever found that RA's professed concern for the confidentiality of his documents and information was insincere. RA knew confidential information was being obtained by the use of pretexts. He did not care. He believed the industry viewpoint to be that nobody cared what means were used to obtain confidential information. Although he never disclosed to his clients how he obtained the information requested, RA did concede that anyone who read his reports would have had to have known that some trick or other means were used.

DE[23]

DE was described as a Runyonesque character who provided one of the most enlightening and entertaining moments of the Inquiry. Known as "Ike" and "the Old Man," he was an expert in the locating or skip-tracing business. Almost all his work was done by telephone pretexts. Approximately 5 percent of his work was done by trick mail. For example, Ike would forward an unsolicited cheque stamped "for deposit only" payable to a debtor and then wait for the return of the cancelled cheque and thus discover the bank in which the debtor had an account. Ike was retained by creditors, law firms, adjusters, and insurance companies.

According to Krever, Ike gave a remarkably introspective and perceptive account of the investigation industry. Ike believed that the "real villains" were the people who paid "weak men" like private investigators such as himself for their efforts. Ike cast himself and his cohorts in the role of "victim" or "exploited," and asserted that most of the blame

---

23   *Ibid.* at 281–83.

belonged to the "masters rather than the servants." Ike thought that the "perceived dignity" of the insurance industry must be diminished by its readiness to resort to the subculture of which he was a part. Ike explained that private investigators wanted to make their clients believe that they had paid informers as contacts because this enabled the investigator to pad his account to the customer — since all payments to informers are made in cash. Ike's experience was that clients accepted the fact that cash payments would have to be made to informants from time to time. It was Ike's practice to call his client to obtain express authorization before making a payment of that sort. Ike claimed he would never tell a client that he had, for example, an OHIP contact, but if the subject arose, he would protest somewhat meekly against the idea, hoping to leave the impression with his client that he indeed did have such a contact. Ike expressed the opinion that the client preferred to believe that he had contacts in the medical industry and was usually willing to pay for something unlawful.

Ike testified that he frequently telephoned OHIP and identified himself as the person whom he wished to locate. In a typical inquiry, he would mention the OHIP number (which he obtained from the person instructing him) and expressed the concern that his employer was not making the required contributions and that therefore he was without OHIP coverage. The person handling the inquiry at OHIP would then begin to discuss the nature of the coverage. By feigning confusion, Ike could usually extract the name and address of the debtor's employer and the address of the debtor. Ike testified that this technique was common in the investigation field, and was used by finance companies, banks and private investigators regularly when they were attempting to locate debtors. The OHIP information bank was a favourite source because is was the most up-to-date list of addresses in the province on account of the fact that even persons who were bad credit risks wanted to keep their OHIP coverage in order.

Ike testified that he never contacted OHIP for the purpose of obtaining medical information without authorization. Ike claimed that he received medical information from another private investigator named JL. Ike claimed JL was his protegé but had gone into business for himself and now was his competitor. Ike claimed that JL frequented taverns in close proximity to OHIP's offices in order to make contact with female employees of OHIP who were less than attractive and who were therefore thought to be more likely to breach their obligation and impart confidential information in exchange for companionship.

Notwithstanding Ike's explanations, Krever found that Ike did contact OHIP for the purpose of obtaining medical information. Krever based this finding on the contradictory testimony from a representative of the Hartford Insurance Company who testified that he received medical information from Ike. Krever found that Ike was quite glib and accurate when he portrayed himself as a "master" in the use of the telephone pretext. Krever found that he had no doubt that Ike was able to extract medical information from an unsuspecting employee of OHIP by using a telephone pretext. Krever found that Ike had no contacts at OHIP, and that Ike would not pay money to a source for information that he could obtain by his wit. Furthermore, with regard to JL, Krever found that there was hostility between JL and Ike, that the assertion that JL had sources at OHIP was simply an act of a member of the subculture "conning" the investigators (to use the jargon of the trade), and that whatever drinking habits JL may have had, there was no creditable evidence that any such liaisons existed.

JL[24]

JL was another "telephone man" specializing in locating or skip tracing. He learned his trade from Ike. However, as alluded to above, JL's relationship with Ike soured when he went to work for AA.

Krever found that while working for AA, JL obtained confidential medical information by the use of telephone pretexts from time to time. If his instructing investigator did not provide JL with an OHIP number, JL would obtain it by telephoning the subject's employer using the pretext that he was a physician who had just treated the employee and had failed to obtain his OHIP number from him. If that did not work, JL would phone the wife of the subject and represent that he was calling from OHIP and that the OHIP number was required to properly process the subject's claim. JL testified that he was successful in almost all his attempts made to hospitals. Krever found that JL did not have a source at OHIP although he would lead fellow investigators to believe that he did.

TJ[25]

TJ was a private investigator who had been employed by Ike and later by AA. It was TJ who introduced RA to Ike. TJ testified that from time to time RA retained Ike to obtain medical information through the use of pretexts. TJ claimed that Ike was the master at pretext phone calling and that he had been made aware that Ike obtained information from OHIP among other sources. TJ did not believe that JL, Ike, or CM had confidential sources at OHIP. Krever found that TJ knew of, and took part in, the trade of confidential medical information obtained surreptitiously from OHIP and other sources.

CM[26]

CM was also a "telephone man" in the employ of AA as a private investigator. CM's expertise originally was in the locating of absconding debtors. However, during his employ at RAs, CM began to make pretext calls to hospitals and physician's offices for the purpose of obtaining confidential medical information without patient consent. RA promised CM that he would destroy CM's reports after their use.

One of the techniques utilized by CM was that of contacting an accounting department at a hospital, representing that he was calling from "the audit department" and requesting confirmation of an OHIP number. The impression left was that he was, in fact, calling from OHIP and acting in some type of auditing capacity. CM also developed the technique of telephoning the medical records department representing that he was calling from the accounting department of the hospital itself. He would change a digit or transpose two digits of the OHIP number and would request such information as the date of the patient's admission to the hospital and the extent of his or her injuries in order, ostensibly, to ensure

---

24   *Ibid.* at 285.
25   *Ibid.* at 280.
26   *Ibid.* at 284.

that he was dealing with the correct individual. CM indicated that all hospital personnel would cooperate because they thought it was an internal call and believed they were simply ensuring that the hospital would be properly credited by OHIP for the care given to the patient. He used a similar approach to obtain information from physicians' offices, for example, by representing that he was calling from a department of OHIP, distorting the OHIP number, and telling a nurse or receptionist that the physician would not be paid unless he was given the required information.

Krever found that at no time in fact did CM have a source at OHIP whom he paid to provide information. CM claimed that it was his customers who believed that he did have such a contact and he deliberately did nothing to dissuade them from this belief.

7.3 QIL

In March 1976, KPM left CIL Investigations Ltd. and obtained a licence to operate his own agency. KPM named his agency QIL.[27] Because of his experience at CIL, KPM was fully aware of the use to which improperly obtained medical information could be put and the price he could demand for it in the marketplace. During Krever's Inquiry, KPM cooperated fully with the Inquiry's investigators and gave them full access to his files.

KPM informed the Inquiry that to successfully obtain medical information by pretext, he adhered to a number of guidelines. These guidelines included avoiding physicians in favour of nurses, avoiding nurses in favour of clerks, and utilizing an officious, demanding, and authoritative manner when dealing with any health care personnel.

One of the techniques utilized by KPM was that of using unpronounceable names when telephoning the health care personnel. He identified himself as "Sterandolvsky" or "Jarislav Dubrovnic"; "Sterandolvsky" being the name of an Eastern European forwarding company and "Jarislav Dubrovnic" being the name of a ship. KPM claimed that often the nurse or clerk would be too embarrassed to ask for the proper spelling, and that although he did not specifically identify himself as a physician, the health care personnel would assume that he was. KPM testified that after revealing his name, he would tell the nurse or clerk that he required information because he was being "consulted about" or "taking a look at" a patient.

Krever found that while KPM never identified himself as a physician, his intention was that the person with whom he spoke believe he was. Krever found that the deliberate omission of the title "Doctor" did not mitigate his unjustifiable misrepresentation. Krever found that KPM's intention was to deceive, and that in most cases his deception was successful. Therefore, whether or not KPM used the title of "Doctor" was of no consequence because the result was the same. Krever found that this pretext technique utilized by KPM was unethical and designed to prey upon the medical profession's sloppy security.

Another technique utilized by KPM was that of contacting the subject's employer. As learned through the Inquiry, large stores of medical information are held by employers in Ontario for the purposes of workers' compensation and group sickness and accident insur-

---

27   *Ibid.* at 291–310.

ance. When an employee has been injured, either at work or elsewhere, he or she may be entitled to certain benefits. To receive those benefits, the employee is obliged to file proof of his or her injuries. At most companies, the benefits are administered through the personnel department. Often, employees of the impugned personnel department were lax in their guard of employee personal information. As KPM testified, "[i]n many circumstances the personnel department of a company is sympathetic to the investigator who is investigating an employee who is goofing off."

When approaching an employer, KPM adopted one of two approaches. The first approach was to identify himself as a private investigator who had been retained by an insurer to investigate the employee. The second approach was that of utilizing a pretext. The pretext approach involved contacting the personnel department and advising the company representative that he was considering entering into a business arrangement of some sort with the employee who was the subject of the investigation. Before entering into this arrangement, he wanted some information relating to the employee's financial background and job security. After asking some questions relating to the continuity of the employee's income, the questions would turn to whether the employee would continue to be paid should he become injured. According to KPM's explanation, the personnel department employee would reply affirmatively, saying that the company sponsored a sickness and accident insurance plan for its employees. The conversation would then unfold thus:

Q: Has Mr./Ms. [employee] ever collected accident insurance before?

A: Yes, on one occasion.

Q: What was that related to?

A: He/She had a back problem arising out of an automobile accident.

Q: Well, I am a little concerned about getting into an arrangement with a person who is possibly not fit.

A: Well, he/she's been treated and he/she seems to be alright. He was treated by Dr. X.

With such a phone call, KPM would then have the information of where to obtain a more detailed medical background.

In addition to attempting to determine how private investigators were obtaining confidential medical information, the Inquiry sought to determine an explanation for what it considered to be the brazen conduct of private investigators such as KPM. KPM gave the Inquiry two justifications. The first justification was discussed under the section dealing with CIL Investigations; that is, the private investigator took it upon himself to balance the patient's right to privacy against his client's right to know, concluding the latter was more important than the former. On this issue, an extract of question and answer exchanges was instructive:

Q: In any event, you say that you perceived this as an ethical problem. Did you perceive it as your ethical problem or did you perceive it as an ethical problem of the physician?

A: It wasn't the physician's problem. Our problem was that the medical profession has a code of ethics that prevents them from releasing information and we had to find a method of by-passing it.

Q: You didn't consider that it was an ethical problem for you?

A: From a point of view of our ethics, our client's right to know superseded the patient's right to privacy.

Q: Why did you think that you had an ethical problem?

A: It was a judgment decision as to what was right and what was wrong.

Q: Whether it was right or wrong to make pretext calls to the hospitals or doctors' offices?

A: No, whether it was right as to whether our clients' right or need to know superseded a patient's right to privacy.

Q: Was this in substance the discussion you had with the DMGs?

A: The substance of it, yes.

Q: So you were under the impression that the difficulty standing in the way of getting information for your client was a code of ethics on the part of the medical profession?

A: Correct.

Q: So you had a belief that there was no legal impediment in the way of your doing so? You had to devise a technique which would deceive them into betraying the confidence which ethically they were obliged to keep?

A: The technique was already in existence.

Q: Well, to use that technique?

A: To continue to use it, yes.

Q: Continue to use that technique. The decision that, as between the two competing interests of the right of your client to know and the . . .

A: . . . Need to know. The right to privacy.

Q: The need to know and the privacy of the patient — and I suppose we can also say the ethical requirement of the physician. You thought the paramount interest, as far as you were concerned, was the client's need to know and that justified deceiving the physician in order to get around his obligation to maintain confidentiality?

A: *Based on my perception of the type of patient we were dealing with and some of the types of physicians we were dealing with, the answer is yes.* [Emphasis added.]

Krever found that KPM's position was untenable and that KPM's economic interests deprived him of the objectivity that is essential for the process of weighing the competing interests, regardless of what KPM's knowledge of the law was. Krever held the balancing of those interests was accomplished in legislation, and in our society, it is simply not acceptable for a contrary solution to be preferred by private interests. Krever held that except where modified by the legislature, the insurer's right to know must yield to the patient's right to privacy.

KPM's second ground of justification for using medical pretexts was that the provincial overseeing body for private investigators, the registrar assigned from the Ontario Provincial Police, condoned the technique by approving course material that included an explanation of its utilization. KPM testified that in 1974, while still employed at CIL, he was involved in the tendering for a contract to supply security guards to the federal government. As part of the contract, the security guards were required to pass an examination set by the federal Department of Supply and Services. After examining the course material, KPM came to the conclusion that the subject matter of the course was neither relevant nor necessary. KPM, therefore, set about to develop his own course of instruction for security guards and private investigators. These materials formed the basis of a manual that KPM and CIL Investigations proposed to use in their own private school for private investigators and security guards. However, before opening their doors to students, CIL was advised that it required approval from the Private and Vocational Schools branch of the Ministry of Colleges and Universities. The Ministry of Colleges and Universities advised CIL that in order to approve their application, CIL would be required to have their course material approved by the registrar of Private Investigators and Security Guards. The registrar at that time was Chief Inspector Lyle of the Ontario Provincial Police. After a number of meetings between Lyle and KPM, and after various modifications to the manual, the manual received the necessary approval.

KPM testified that when the manual received approval, it contained a section dealing with obtaining medical information by pretext. The manual was divided into a number of chapters, each dealing with separate subjects of interest to private investigators. One of the chapters was entitled "Contact Investigation Procedure." This chapter discussed the uses to which pretexts could be put during the course of an investigation. An excerpt from the chapter reads as follows:

> The correct use of a pretext is a valuable asset to the good investigator. It can be used when its use does not violate any law. The investigator should in no way attempt to impersonate a police officer or the representative of any legal organized union or institution or government department, or represent himself as the agent of any company that exists. Furthermore, the investigator should not take unto himself a badge or insignia or pass himself off as a fireman or the fire marshall or a utility inspector or a public officer, etc. Thus, for all practical purposes, when the investigator presents himself as representing an organization or a company, the said organization or company should be fictitious, that is nonexistent.

In a chapter entitled "Standard Fraudulent Insurance Claims Investigation," there was a discussion about the various sources of information that a private investigator should approach. Under the subheading "Medical," the following passage was found:

> Here the investigator should endeavour to obtain all information possible from hospitals, doctors, nurses, chiropractors, physiotherapists, and particularly from the claimant himself in respect of past and present illness and injuries.

KPM testified that these chapters were in the manual when it was delivered to Lyle and that it was approved by the registration branch without comment. Accordingly, KPM considered himself entitled to rely upon that approval and to employ pretexts to obtain medical information.

In response to KPM's assertions, the Ontario Provincial Police led evidence to the effect that the manual to which KPM had referred was not the same manual as that submitted to the registration branch.

Krever found that even if the manual submitted by KPM was the same manual as approved by the registration branch, the approval could not have the consequences that KPM suggested it should. Krever held that no approval given by the registration branch to unjustifiable conduct could ever justify KPM's conduct, and that in fairness, the matter must be put into perspective. CIL wanted to obtain the approval of a branch of the Ministry of Colleges and Universities for its proposed school. The Ministry of Colleges and Universities was not prepared to approve the course of study without some indication that it was appropriate. To satisfy the Ministry of Colleges and Universities on that score, the registration branch, which at the time was an understaffed, overworked, and overextended unit of the Ontario Provincial Police, was asked to examine the manual and simply advise its opinion of the material. The excerpts from the manual referred to are very small portions of a volume 1.5 inches thick. Furthermore, the chapters from which they are extracted do not immediately follow each other. Therefore, in effect, what KPM has done is to attempt to isolate two brief passages from the manual, taking them separately and out of context. The action of the registration branch of the OPP in approving the teaching of the technique of pretexts was unexceptional. There are as many situations in which a pretext can lawfully, and perhaps justifiably, be used as there are situations in which it is unlawful and unjustifiable.

Krever further found that not every approach by an investigator to a health care provider to obtain medical information is improper. Indeed, as long as the investigator makes full and complete disclosure of the reason for his request, an authorization executed by the patient may not even be necessary for the request for information to be proper. But to place together two statements, one dealing with pretexts and the other with medical information, and to rely on the failure of the registrar to object to those unconnected statements as an acknowledgment that the practice of obtaining medical information by the use of pretexts is proper is to place an interpretation upon approval which was never intended and is unreasonable. The registration branch was not asked to approve a code of conduct for private investigators. It was asked to examine study materials for a proposed school of investigators to determine if the subject matter was appropriate. It was not requested to approve of the practice sought to be covered in the lecture material. It was asked generally to review the material so that the Ministry of Colleges and Universities could be satisfied that what was proposed to be a course of study for private investigators would be satisfactory and potentially of some practical use. Nothing more was sought and nothing more was provided. No effect can be given to KPM's claim that he used pretexts to obtain confidential medical information in the belief that this technique of extracting information had been approved by the government agency responsible for regulating his conduct.

In short, Krever found KPM's second ground of justification as equally untenable as the first.

7.4 ESL

ESL was a wholly owned subsidiary of EI. At the time of the Inquiry, EI was the largest company in the American investigation industry. The estimated earnings of ESL's Ontario operations alone in 1979 were three to four million dollars.

ESL was put under the scrutiny of the Inquiry for their use of pretexts. However, officials from ESL added another dimension to the discussion. Officials from ESL placed their Field Investigation Manual into evidence to demonstrate their view of the ethical dilemma. The manual stated: "It is sometimes justifiable to attempt an interview of a physician even though an authorization was not available . . . In these cases we may obtain only non-privileged information which is limited to the names of doctors and the dates of treatment."

Krever did not buy into the distinction between privileged and non-privileged medical information. ESL management testified that investigators were trained and ordered to seek only non-privileged medical information. However, if the investigator innocently came into possession of privileged medical information during the course of his conversation with his "source," he and his supervisor had to make a decision whether that privileged information was to be included in the report to the customer, or simply disregarded and discarded. ESL management later retracted this statement and admitted ESL's investigators actively sought privileged medical information when one of ESL's files was placed into evidence which contained the following quote: "Obtain as much confidential medical information as possible through Dr. A, B & C."

In addition to the file evidence, Krever found that the distinction drawn by ESL between privileged and non-privileged medical information had no basis in law. Krever noted that in Ontario the *Public Hospitals Act*, R.S.O. 1970, c. 378, and the *Health Disciplines Act*, 1974, S.O. 1974, c. 47, make no such distinctions. Krever found that at no time did ESL seek to determine the legality of its practice in Ontario . Krever held that while it is not expected that a non-lawyer be able to cite the title and section of a particular statute that prohibits the impugned disclosure, it is reasonable to expect that ESL would know that there was some statutory provision that prohibited the practice. Krever concluded that the absence of such knowledge on ESL's management represented a wanton and reckless disregard for the laws of Ontario, or, at the very least, a willful blindness.[28]

A variation to the discussion ESL attempted to prove was the distinction between the concepts of an "indirect approach" as opposed to a pretext. The apparent reason ESL chose to make this distinction was because their investigation manual clearly stated that ESL investigators were not to engage in pretexts or affirmative misrepresentations when seeking information. According to ESL's manual, pretexts were forbidden because the source would be tricked or deceived into disclosing the requested information. The only practice ESL officially permitted was the use of indirect approaches. These indirect approaches were only permitted when conducting third-party investigations. Examples of indirect approaches included the following:

---

28   *Ibid.* at 311–16.

+ Hi, I am [John Doe] from ESL. I'm completing a claim for [Jane Doe]; or
+ I'm processing a claim for [Jane Doe]; or
+ I'm doing a business reference on [Jane Doe].

If the claimant or source asked the reason for the inquiry, the ESL investigator was to advise the source that the investigator was not permitted to divulge it.[29]

ESL's rationalization for the use of indirect approaches was that it was necessary to obtain truthful and unbiased information. ESL claimed that insurance companies have learned through experience that in a third-party claim situation where the company is dealing with an adversary claimant (as opposed to its own insured), it is not possible to develop the information needed if the interviewer discloses that insurance is involved. If the person "speculating" on the claim has something to cover up, such as a fraud, he will not provide the honest responses necessary to evaluate a claim fairly. Thus, insurance companies that order claim reports based on the indirect approach have a legitimate interest in having the report completed through this method.[30]

The extent to which the use of the indirect approach could and did give rise to confusion and misapprehension of the facts is best exemplified by a situation involving ESL investigator HB. This occurrence was referred to the Ontario Provincial Police PISGA registrar for investigation. On this occasion, HB telephoned the offices of Dr. Ralph Wright to obtain medical information relating to two of Dr. Wright's patients. HB spoke to Dr. Wright's wife who worked in his office. Mrs. Wright testified that she thought that HB said he was "Dr. HB from ESL Claims." Mrs. Wright stated she assumed HB was an employee of OHIP who was attempting to verify the claims submitted for payment. Thinking that OHIP had a right to the information requested, Mrs. Wright continued to answer HB's questions.[31]

Another example was taken from a receptionist, NI, who worked at the medical records department at North York Branson Hospital. NI testified that when contacted by the ESL investigator, she thought she was helping the patient by releasing the information requested. NI was convinced the information was needed to speed up the payments to the patient. In fact, NI operated under the misapprehension that ESL itself was an insurance company.[32]

Krever found that on any objective analysis, the distinction that ESL tried to make between pretexts and indirect approaches was semantic quibbling. Krever found that the examples of indirect approaches given above are misleading explanations of the function of the investigator and, as such, are pretexts just as much as a misdescription of the investigator's identity would be from the point of view of the effect on the person addressed. While ESL investigators did not generally hold themselves out to be physicians, law

---

29   *Ibid.* at 334.
30   *Ibid.* at 339.
31   *Ibid.* at 336.
32   *Ibid.* at 340.

enforcement officers, or health care workers, the indirect approach used by ESL investigators represents the most sophisticated and subtle misrepresentation examined during the Inquiry.[33]

Krever further found that, aside from the medical information obtained from physicians, hospitals, and insurers, ESL investigators, usually successfully, sought medical information from school board employees and school nurses, the Workers' Compensation Board, the Unemployment Insurance Commission, OHIP, police forces, employers, and various government and public agencies including probation officers, immigration department investigators, municipal social assistance departments, the Ministry of Community and Social Services, and the Ministry of Transportation. In short, there was no storehouse of information safe from ESL investigators. ESL investigators freely admitted that if an individual refused to disclose the information sought because of some obligation of confidentiality, whether imposed by statute or by contract of employment, the matter did not rest. The investigators simply closed off the conversation and contacted another individual employed by the same "source."[34]

When asked about the propriety of obtaining information that was required to be kept confidential, the ESL investigators maintained that they carried on business in accordance with the law and ethical business standards. ESL took the position that if a person was under a duty to keep information confidential, it was that person's decision whether or not to disclose it in breach of his obligation. ESL further took the position that there was no impropriety in attempting to induce that individual to breach his obligation of confidentiality.

Krever found this position to be unacceptable. Krever held that even if it were acceptable to attempt to gain confidential information from a "source," it must certainly be incumbent upon the investigator to fully and frankly advise his source of his identity and the purpose for which the information is requested. Only if the holder of the information was fully apprised of all the circumstances could he be fairly charged with culpability in the decision to breach his obligation of confidentiality. The approaches used by ESL investigators was anything but full and frank. Although perhaps not amounting to a positive misrepresentation, the introductions used by ESL investigators were calculated to mislead the holder of the information with respect to the real purpose for which that information was sought. Krever held that ESL is a company that sells only one commodity, and that commodity is information. Accordingly, it is expected that ESL would have made the effort to inform all its investigators the law with respect to the relevant legislation that might affect the business of obtaining and selling that commodity. ESL, as the largest private investigation firm in Ontario and considered by most to be the industry leader, has plainly shown itself to be incapable of responsible self-regulation.[35]

---

33 *Ibid.* at 335.
34 *Ibid.* at 326.
35 *Ibid.* at 329–31.

7.5 FIS

Since 1969, CF had carried on the business of FIS in Ontario. During 1978, he employed an average of approximately ten persons, mostly on a part-time basis. CF admitted that at all material times, he knew that physicians and hospital employees had an obligation to keep health care information confidential. Despite this knowledge, like many others in the investigation and insurance industry, CF accepted the practice of attempting to obtain confidential health information. According to CF, in each case in which his employees attempted to obtain confidential health information without the patient's consent, his clients expressly directed him to seek that kind of information. Because of his accent, CF claimed he never made pretext calls himself. Rather, CF's employees made the pretext calls with his consent. CF accepted responsibility for their actions.

In 1974, CP began to work for CF. CP made CF's pretext phone calls. CP testified that she called both hospitals and physicians' offices. When she called hospitals, she normally spoke to someone in the business office and asked whether the patient was still hospitalized and what the status of the OHIP claim was. She intended to leave the impression that she was entitled to receive the information she sought and that she was from another part of the same hospital or from OHIP, although she was careful never to make that representation expressly. On occasion, she attempted to obtain medical information from the medical records department of various hospitals but she was usually unsuccessful. Sometimes she claimed to be a close family member of the patient's family and to be calling from out-of-town to inquire about the patient's condition. When CP called physicians' offices, she usually stated she was calling for a patient to confirm the patient's next appointment. She occasionally alleged to be calling with regard to an OHIP claim. Once the physician's employee began talking, CP was usually able to extract confidential health information. CP admitted that when she alleged to be calling about an OHIP claim, it was implicit in what she said that she was calling from OHIP itself.

CP admitted that, at the time she made pretext calls, she knew that physicians, physicians' employees, hospitals and hospital employees were obliged to keep health information about their patients confidential. She admitted that she never asked CF, any insurance company, or any lawyer whether the practice was improper. CP testified that she believed that the ethics of her profession permitted her to make pretext calls of the kind described.

Krever found CP to be rather naive. Krever accepted her statement that she assumed that, since CF's clients were reputable insurance companies, adjusters, and law firms, they would not do anything illegal and that, therefore, if they requested her to make pretext calls, those calls must have been legal. This was the circumstance until June 1977. However, in June 1977 a directive regarding pretext calls from the registrar of the Private Investigators and Security Guards came to her attention. This directive had been sent to all licensed private investigators in the province. The letter is reproduced in its entirety:

Ontario Provincial Police

June 13, 1977

To All Private Investigation Agency Heads and Branch Offices

Re: Misrepresentation of Investigation

Dear Sir:

The Registration Branch has received a number of complaints concerning private investigators who are deliberately misrepresenting their identity in attempts to obtain information. For example, a private investigator has recently misrepresented himself as a doctor to obtain information from hospital records. Such conduct is a matter of concern to medical groups and the public in general, and I share this concern. It is sometimes difficult to discern the permissible limits, but I urge you to consider carefully whether the ruse is justified in the circumstances of the case.[36] I am forced to take action under the *Private Investigation and Security Guards Act* where I find that such conduct is not in the public interest.

Among those misrepresentations which I do not consider to be in the public interest and which I will not countenance are the following:

(a)   impersonation of a doctor or a person working under his authority;

(b)   impersonation of a lawyer or one working under his authority;

(c)   representing oneself as being in any way connected with government (federal, provincial, municipal, Crown Corporation, etc.);

(d)   representing oneself as being in any way connected with the administration of justice (Crown Attorney, Judge, Sheriff or their staff);

(e)   representing oneself as being in any way connected with the police. This is, of course, an offence under the *Private Investigator and Security Guards Act*, and may be an offence under the *Criminal Code of Canada*.

There may be other ruses and pretexts which are equally objectionable. However, at this time I am most concerned with those mentioned above. Accordingly, you are requested if you or anyone under your direction are engaging in these misrepresentations, to refrain from doing so immediately. You are further requested to bring the contents of this letter to the attention of the private investigators licensed with your firm.

As I have mentioned, these investigative techniques are not in the public interest, and should it come to my attention that firms or private investigators persist in using these subterfuges, then I will proceed against their licences in accordance with the *Private Investigators and Security Guards Act*.

Yours truly,

J.C. Villemaire

Acting Chief Inspector

Registrar/Director

Private Investigation and Security Guards Section

Registration Branch

---

36   This sentence indicates there is no legislation explicitly prohibiting the use of pretexts generally.

Krever found that when CP became aware of this directive, she ought to have realized that she should stop making calls of that sort. At the very least, she should have sought an explanation from the registrar or an opinion from CF or his solicitors. In June 1977 she must have known that this memorandum was directed to the kind of pretext she had been using because, by her own admission, she knew that OHIP was part of the Ministry of Health and therefore part of the provincial government.

As stated earlier, CF testified that he accepted responsibility for all the actions of CP. CP was, after all, at all times working under his direction. Despite the knowledge of the duty of confidentiality on the part of physicians and hospitals, CF accepted assignments from insurers and adjusters that required him to attempt to cause persons to breach this obligation. He did so because he wanted to remain competitive in the investigation industry. It is clear that from about 1974, about the time when CIL had begun to refine the technique of obtaining confidential medical information without authorization, there was enormous pressure on all its competitors to provide a similar service to their clients who had come to expect and demand such information.

Krever listed six insurance and adjuster companies who were CF's clients and who received investigation reports containing confidential health information obtained without the claimant's consent. Each of these companies expressly instructed CF to obtain information that they ought to have known they were not entitled to.[37]

7.6 GIA

AO became a licensed private investigator in 1967 and in 1974 opened GIA. In 1976, AO began to obtain confidential health information using pretexts. These pretexts were made by him and his employees.[38]

Frequently, GIA's staff used a shopping-survey pretext similar to the CIL pretext discussed earlier. GIA's employees also used a "Night Out Magazine" pretext. This was an attempt to sell to the subject a magazine that highlighted the nightlife in Toronto. The theory was that a totally disabled person would be uninterested in such a magazine. If there was a refusal by the subject to purchase the magazine, an opportunity for a discussion would ensue about the reason for the refusal. This discussion would often lead to a description by the subject of his physical disability.

The mainstay of the GIA repertoire of pretexts was to attend upon a hospital employee and identify himself or herself as an independent insurance adjuster. AO testified that he and his employees used the independent insurance adjuster pretext because, in his opinion, the description of "private investigator" had an unsavoury connotation. AO attributed this perception to television shows such as *Rockford Files*. Krever rejected this explanation. Krever found that AO used the term "independent insurance adjuster" to project the image of being neutral or even of common interest with that of the subject. Krever

---

37   Above note 1 at 345–53.
38   *Ibid.* at 354.

held that by using that term, physicians and their employees would be lulled into thinking they were aiding their patient in the resolution of a claim.[39]

AO testified that he did not know that hospital employees and physicians had an obligation in law to keep health information about their patients confidential. AO testified that he believed that physicians could freely tell anyone anything about their patients. Krever found this incredible. Krever noted that during his testimony, AO admitted that he knew that physicians ran the risk of having their licences to practice suspended if they divulged confidential health information about their patients. Krever found that this admission was evidence that he realized there existed a legal sanction that could be used against a physician if he or she violated his or her obligation of confidentiality.[40]

Recommendation of the Inquiry

Based on his review of GIA's files, Krever recommended that private investigators be prohibited from representing that they were insurance adjusters.[41]

7.7 WAK AND CCR

WAK was a corporation licensed as independent insurance adjusters. CCR was a corporation licensed as private investigators. Both corporations were held by the same three shareholders. Throughout the period the Inquiry was conducted, WAK and CCR were located in the same building. The insurance adjuster business was separated from the private investigation business by an unlocked door. Both operations shared a common bookkeeper. The adjusters had access to all the investigator's files and there was no restriction preventing the investigators from gaining access to the adjuster's files. Krever's examination of CCR's files indicated that approximately 16 to 20 percent of their work was assigned by WAK.

Krever found that CCR's investigators regularly obtained confidential health information without the patient's consent from physicians, physicians' employees, and hospital employees. In that respect, CCR was similar to other investigative agencies put under the scope of the Inquiry. What Krever found that set CCR apart was the quality and quantity of information CCR obtained from OHIP.[42]

Krever reviewed the work of a number of private investigators, the most stimulating of which was AW. AW was an extremely experienced private investigator with over sixteen years of experience before joining CCR in 1973. AW knew that physicians, physicians' employees, hospital employees, and other health care providers have a duty to keep their patient information confidential and not to release any information without authorization. AW knew that every physician had a licence and that physicians could loose their licences for breaches of professional misconduct. AW also knew that he, as an investigator, had an

---

39 *Ibid.* at 355.
40 *Ibid.* at 354.
41 *Ibid.* at 361.
42 *Ibid.* at 363.

obligation to keep information that came into his possession confidential. Krever found that despite this knowledge, AW contacted health care providers and persuaded them to provide confidential patient information. AW did this, as he stated, because "[t]hat was the whole basis of the insurance investigation business . . . to gather information which is not readily available."[43]

In thirty-nine of the fifty-seven reports filed by AW that were exhibits at the Inquiry, AW referred to the person from whom he obtained OHIP medical information as a "confidential source." As Krever pointed out earlier, many investigators equated an anonymous source with a confidential source, when in fact these investigators did not have any inside informer at all. That was what made AW distinguishable. He truly had a confidential source at OHIP. That confidential source was CG.[44]

AW testified that he believed that every OHIP employee had an obligation to keep information that came to him in the course of his employment confidential except such persons as CG who were involved in the operation of OHIP's subrogation department. AW stated the subrogation department, like any other insurance company, was involved and interested in claims settlement. As such, employees involved with subrogation would provide information verifying the medical aspect of claims to others interested in insurance claims. The subrogation department, by providing information, was cooperating with the insurance industry and was acting within the rules of the *Health Insurance Act, 1972* that governed OHIP's activities. Therefore, AW reasoned, CG, in providing this information, was simply doing his job and there was nothing improper in AW seeking out this information. AW testified that any other investigator would be as able as he to obtain this type of information from CG and others in the subrogation department. However, stated AW, although any other investigator could obtain this information from CG, he was, according to an internal arrangement at CCR, the sole person permitted to contact CG and all inquiries at OHIP were to be channelled through him.

Krever set out a number of AW's reports in detail to show that the tone and content of the reports were inconsistent with AW's professed beliefs. AW repeatedly used the phrase "confidential source" and "[W]e must caution you about the use of this information so that the source is not identified."[45] Krever further relied upon the evidence of the supervisor from OHIP's subrogation department, Mr. G., who testified that his practice was to deal only with adjusters and lawyers and not to provide any information to private investigators as private investigators do not have the authority to settle claims. Mr. G. testified that if OHIP had retained a solicitor to deal with its subrogated interests, the investigator should have sought information from the solicitor. If OHIP dealt directly with a liability insurer, the liability insurer or the adjuster retained by the liability insurer would receive all the necessary information and the intervention of an investigator was unnecessary. Mr. G. testified that, although he had never been contacted by a private investigator, he would have refused him information for the reasons given above.

---

43   *Ibid.* at 372.
44   *Ibid.* at 373.
45   *Ibid.* at 388.

With regards to CG, CG was an experienced casualty claims adjuster in the private insurance industry prior to his employment in the subrogation department at OHIP. CG became acquainted with AW in 1973 and came to know that AW was a private investigator. CG acknowledged he gave information to AW. CG's explanation was that his actions were perfectly proper because he was excluded from the general obligation of confidentiality imposed by the *Health Insurance Act, 1972*. CG further claimed that his treatment of AW was no different that what he would have accorded to any other private investigator had he been contacted by one. Krever found the problem with this aspect of CG's testimony was that in a file seized from CIL, there was a note from a private investigator indicating that he had contacted CG at OHIP and that CG had refused to disclose medical information on the basis that such information was protected by patient confidentiality rules. The note of the CIL investigator stated:

> He was not able to release any information if they have it because of the Health Insurance Act. There was nothing he can do because he and all civil servants are bound by the Act dealing with disclosure of information and suggested that the information required should be obtained from the plaintiff's lawyers. He stated that he regretted he could be of no assistance but had no choice in the matter.

Based on this note from the CIL file, Krever found that if CG had honestly held the view expressed above, there would have been no reason for him to refuse to provide information to the CIL investigator. Krever concluded that he was providing information to AW and he knew that he had no authority to do so.[46]

Although he had no trouble finding that CG improperly gave confidential information to AW, Krever did acknowledge the reason for CG's actions was much more difficult to ascertain. Krever indicated that the most obvious reason — compensation — was not a factor. Krever found that CG believed AW to be his friend, and that CG was quite surprised at the amount of detail AW attributed to CG in his reports. Krever found that CG was more than disappointed with the way AW had used the information he provided him. Krever found that AW was an articulate, personable man who persuaded CG that he was of use to CG because from time to time he brought to OHIP's attention the existence of accidents and injuries to subscribers of which OHIP was unaware. CG unwittingly become involved in a situation in which he was trading information with AW. It is probable that he never really appreciated that this had happened. In short, CG was another example of an individual permitting his friendship or relationship to blind him in the execution of his duty.[47]

Recommendations of the Inquiry

Based on the above findings, Krever recommended:

1. With regard to CG, the subrogation department of OHIP should refuse to provide any information to private investigators. The department should only deal with

---

46   *Ibid.* at 400.
47   *Ibid.* at 422.

licensed insurance adjusters, insurance companies, or solicitors in attempts to settle its subrogated claims.[48]

2.   With regard to CCR, no individual, partnership or corporation carrying on business as an insurance adjuster be permitted to carry on business as a private investigator or own an interest of any kind in a corporation licensed as a private investigator under the *Private Investigators and Security Guards Act*.[49]

7.8   CSL

CSL was an Ontario corporation in the business of private investigations. Throughout the relevant time period, it was licensed as a private investigation agency. The shareholders of CSL were MC and KL. The name of the company was derived from a syllable taken from the names of each of the principals. Both MC and KL had prior experience at ESL before commencing their own business.

MC and KL both testified that they did not believe that physicians, hospitals, or hospital employees had any obligation to keep the health care records of their patients confidential. Any restriction of the release of health information, they thought, was a matter of individual ethics and hospital policy rather than a matter of law. They testified that as private investigators, they were entitled to obtain from hospitals and physicians without a patient's consent a patient's OHIP number, the dates of admission and discharge from hospital, the names of the patient's family physician and specialist, and the amount billed and paid to and by OHIP. However, Krever found that both MC and KL could not reasonably have held such beliefs.

One of the bases for Krever's findings was the approach used by MC when he contacted physicians or hospitals. Evidence indicated MC would use the following introductions:

- We have been asked to assist in the processing of a disability claim.
- We are working in connection with a disability claim.
- We are working on a disability claim.
- We are processing a disability claim of your patient.
- We have been asked to assist in the processing of an injury claim.
- We have been asked to verify the dates X was in hospital.

Krever found that if MC genuinely believed that there was no impediment to having the information, he would not have resorted to the introduction that he invariably employed. Krever found that the approaches were misleading and were intended to be misleading. Not only were the approaches not fully informative, they were quite inaccurate. MC used the verification approach even when he had nothing to verify. Krever concluded that had MC truly believed he was entitled to the information he sought, MC would have said something to the effect of "I am Michael MC of CSL Services Limited. I am a private

---

48   *Ibid.* at 424.
49   *Ibid.* at 427.

investigator. I have been hired by the X Insurance Company to obtain information about your patient who is probably going to sue X's insured. Your patient does not know I am seeking this information and has not authorized its release. Can you please tell me . . . ." Had MC used such an introduction, there is no doubt he would not have received any information at all. Thus MC engaged in the use of pretexts.[50]

7.9   JTI

JTI was a partnership established in 1973 by JT and GJ. JT and GJ carried on business in the Windsor area and from time to time in Detroit, Michigan, although not licensed to do so. Both JT and GJ were experienced private investigators at the time of the Inquiry. Both received their original training at ESL.

JT admitted that he knew that at all material times physicians had an obligation to keep health care information about their patients confidential and that this obligation arose as a matter of law, or as he put it "as a matter of oath." GJ denied knowing that a physicians' obligation to keep health care information confidential arose as a matter of law. GJ testified that he believed it was a matter of ethics, and that hospitals were not to release medical information as a matter of policy. Krever found that GJ and JT did not actually contemplate the distinction between policy, ethics, or law as it pertained to patient medical information confidentiality. Krever found that their use of pretexts was consistent with their knowledge that a full and frank disclosure of the interests would have resulted in a refusal of the information they sought.[51]

Krever's account of the practices of JT and GJ was similar to much that has already been reviewed. The interesting aspect of the practices of this particular private investigation agency dealt with their use of a confidential source. Krever reiterated that throughout the Inquiry, many investigators equated an anonymous source, that is, a person who provided information in response to a pretext, with a confidential source, a confidential source being a person who because of his or her relationship with the investigator provided information. JT was a special case because he truly did have a special confidential source. JT's confidential source was his wife (MT).

MT appeared before the Inquiry and gave evidence. She was a registered nurse employed by the Metropolitan Hospital in Windsor. MT was aware that as an employee of the hospital, she had an obligation to abide by the written hospital policy that, among other matters, stated that no information about a patient was permitted to be released to an adjuster, an insurer, or a private investigator without the patient's written authorization. MT also knew that as a registered nurse, it was her professional duty to keep confidential all information about every patient. In fact, MT even advised her husband of these obligations. Despite this knowledge, JT began asking his wife to acquire information for him. At first she refused to give him any information but he kept at her. He was upset when she refused to acquiesce and he subjected her to pressure. She finally relented. JT told his wife

---

50   *Ibid.* at 432.
51   *Ibid.* at 438.

he was only seeking the truth and therefore it would not hurt the patient. She believed him, even though her training ought to have told her this reasoning was faulty. She provided information to him but did not know this information was finding its way into reports prepared by the private investigation agency of which he was a part.

Krever found that it was improper for MT to have given any information to her husband and she knew it. However, Krever found that JT's conduct of inducing his wife to breach her obligations was much more culpable, characterizing them as "unforgivable." Krever held that JT ought to have respected his wife's obligations as an employee and as a professional person and ought not to have exercised his influence over her to induce her to breach her obligations.[52]

JT and GJ were also forced to expose a second confidential source they had for information. This source was EF. EF was an employee of Ford assigned to its workers' compensation section. As a workers' compensation administrator, EF had the task of processing employee applications for workers' compensation benefits. EF followed up the applications with requests for information from physicians, the employee, and the Workers' Compensation Board. In addition, EF had access to the health information in hospitals. Before his employment at Ford, EF had been a private investigator in Detroit as well as a clerk at a law firm. While working for Ford, EF occasionally retained the services of GJ & JT Investigations to do work for Ford. Notwithstanding that he was aware it was against Ford policy to release confidential medical information about employees at Ford, EF did so on at least ten occasions. Krever found there was no reasonable lawful explanation that EF or JT & GJ could give for their actions.[53]

Krever summed up the issue of breaches of confidentiality by stating that privacy has been defined as the right to choose to whom information about oneself should be released. When a special relationship is established and a person chooses to release confidential information about herself to, for example, a physician, a physician's employee, or a hospital employee, she does this in the expectation that the recipient of this information will respect the confidence and refrain from releasing the information to another. Krever stated that the Inquiry has shown that recipients of confidential health care information must be more careful in their handling of this information. However, where it has been proven that a pretext was used to trick the health care provider, it is difficult to speak of findings of misconduct by the health care professionals. The conduct of the pretext callers is undoubtedly of greater culpability. Furthermore, the act of capitalizing on friendships and relationships to obtain information to trade for profit is even more disturbing.[54]

7.10 THE INSURERS AND LAWYERS

A review of what Krever determined to be the improper use of pretexts by private investigators would not be complete without a review of the conduct of those who gave the private investigators the instructions to pursue the information — the insurers and lawyers.

---

52   *Ibid.* at 467–68.
53   *Ibid.* at 477.
54   *Ibid.* at 475 and 493.

Krever wrote that insurance companies have an obligation to provide a defence for those whom they insure. This often means that they have an obligation to retain a lawyer to act on behalf of the insured. Of course, not all claims lead to litigation. The evidence from the Inquiry indicated that investigation reports were obtained in approximately 5 percent of all bodily injury claims. There is no doubt that a high percentage of the cases in which investigation reports were obtained were cases that eventually would be put into the hands of lawyers retained by insurance companies to represent the individuals insured. Insurers are sophisticated in the personal injury field and normally retain experienced, competent counsel who traditionally have been among the leaders of the bar in Ontario. Krever found that it was therefore exceedingly disturbing and distressing that the evidence revealed that only one lawyer retained by an insurance company had advised his client about the danger and impropriety inherent in the receipt of investigation reports containing medical information obtained without patient authorization.

The Inquiry's investigation revealed twenty-five lawyers who through private investigators had sought or received confidential medical information without patient authorization. Krever divided these lawyers into two groups. The first was lawyers who ordered investigations using shorthand terms such as "background investigations" and "activities checks" and who repeatedly received investigation reports containing confidential health information obtained without authorization. Krever held that at some point these lawyers ought to have realized that to order an investigation report using such a shorthand designation was equivalent to expressly asking the investigator to obtain or to attempt to obtain confidential health information. The second group was lawyers who expressly directed investigators to obtain confidential health information from persons and institutions having an obligation to keep that information confidential.

Throughout the Inquiry, many private investigators testified that they were unaware of the precise statutory provisions requiring physicians, for example, to keep health information about their patients confidential. Whatever the law may say, as a matter of fact, ignorance of the law on the part of non-lawyers may be understandable and even excusable. However, as has been mentioned above, insurance companies usually retain experienced and competent lawyers. It cannot be said that the lawyers who appeared before the Inquiry were ignorant of the statutory obligations of confidentiality imposed upon physicians, hospital employees, OHIP employees, and others in the health field. That these solicitors had actual knowledge of these obligations was beyond question. Nevertheless, they failed to use their abundant analytical skills and continued to follow inherited practices. In their behaviour they were slaves to precedent. In short, these lawyers failed to ask themselves the fundamental question of whether it was proper to retain investigators to carry on in this fashion.

The Inquiry was prepared to call all the lawyers it identified to testify and explore their conduct. However, the impugned lawyers sought and were granted the opportunity to provide an agreed statement of facts and thus eliminate the need for an exhaustive examination of every lawyer's conduct on a case-by-case basis. Krever claimed this was not a concession to these individuals because they were lawyers. Krever claimed receiving agreed statements of fact was consistent with the practice followed by the Inquiry in its dealings with everyone who appeared before it. Krever claimed the aim of the Inquiry was to determine if confidential health information had been sought or received, and if so, by whom, and whether instructions were given in circumstances in which the person giving them knew or ought to have known that such activities were wrong, the manner in which the information was obtained, and precisely what information had been obtained. If a witness was prepared to admit that he had engaged in this kind of conduct, knew or ought to have known at the relevant times that it was improper, undertook to discontinue it, and to cooperate with the Inquiry in the future, Krever claimed it was unnecessary to engage in an examination. On this basis Krever permitted twenty-one lawyers to put in an acknowledgment of facts.

These lawyers acknowledged the following as facts:

1. Hospitals and their employees and doctors and their employees have an obligation to keep the contents of health records of patients confidential and this was and is a subsisting and recognized principle.

2. The solicitors knew or ought to have known that the principle of confidentiality subsisted and ought to have recognized and accepted same.

3. For many years it has been a practice among the members of the legal profession and their staff engaged in personal injury litigation to instruct private investigators to obtain, and in consequence to receive, investigation reports that would contain, on occasion, among others, information from hospitals, hospital employees, doctors, doctors' employees, without the consent of the patient. Therefore, these solicitors ought to have known that such instructions were likely to result in the receipt of investigation reports that contain, on occasion, information from hospitals and hospital employees, doctors and doctors' employees, obtained without the consent of the patient.

4. Some solicitors, on occasion, specifically instructed private investigators to attempt to obtain medical information from hospitals, hospital employees, doctors, and doctors' employees without authorization.

5. These instructions, under the current state of the law, cannot be justified.

6. The practice described had its roots in what was a very restricted system of production and discovery.

7. Recent changes in the *Evidence Act* and the Rules of Practice consequent thereon widely expanded the scope of discovery available, and it is conceded by the solicitors that there was no fresh look taken at the long-standing practice in the light of their significance or these significant changes and that the practice cannot be justified.

8. As a matter of principle, on the current state of the law, solicitors recognize that hospitals, hospital employees, doctors, and doctors' employees have an obligation to keep the contents of health records of their patients confidential. These solicitors agreed that they would not seek to obtain such information without authorization, subject to the existing right granted by legislation and the Rules of Practice, and that if such information is tendered, they will actively discourage the obtaining of such information on the part of private investigators and others.[55]

---

55   *Ibid.* at 532–35.

Krever reviewed the conduct of a number of lawyers notwithstanding his acceptance of their agreed statement of facts. One such lawyer was WR. Krever noted that six investigation reports were found prepared by ESL for which WR had either instructed ESL to seek health information without the patient's consent or in respect of which that company had provided information of that kind to WR. WR usually gave instructions in writing. His letters of instructions requested ESL to determine "what disabilities, if any, she may have had together with any previous records on accidents or illnesses claimed"; or "I would appreciate if you would check out the background of these people for previous accidents, claims and for illnesses or sicknesses, as well as employment earning times lost from work, if any"; or "I would appreciate if you would check on this man's claims background for sickness, accident or ill health as well as his earnings, lost time from work and what, if any, benefits were available to him." These instructions were interpreted as instructions to seek confidential health information without authorization and were so intended.

In one of WR's files, it was learned he was retained to defend an action with respect to a motor vehicle accident where a fourteen-year-old girl and her mother were injured. WR, by letter, requested ESL to conduct an investigation to "determine from the school whether the girl has had any previous physical problems of this nature prior to the accident." As ESL proceeded with its investigation, its investigator, HB, kept in contact with WR's law clerk. The clerk supplied the investigator with the names of physicians and specialists who saw the claimants. Through his law clerk, WR obtained updates on HB's investigations and was aware that HB was seeking confidential health information from physicians and hospitals without the claimant's authorization.[56] Krever found that while WR may not have known precisely how HB was misrepresenting himself, there is no doubt that after having expressly instructed ESL to obtain confidential health information without authorization, WR must have expected that some trick or ruse would be resorted to. Accordingly, WR must be taken to know that the giving of the type of instructions he gave was improper.[57]

Krever further pointed out that the names of the twenty-five lawyers discovered in the files seized by the Inquiry were not the only lawyers in Ontario engaged in the practice of retaining private investigators to obtain confidential health information without patient authorization. The Insurance Bureau of Canada polled its members and learned that the practices referred to in the earlier acknowledgement of facts were generally followed throughout the province by lawyers involved in insurance litigation.

Krever went on to say that it was his recommendation that none of the persons identified by his Inquiry should be subject to criminal prosecution as a result of the exposure of their improper or illegal acts. With respect to the lawyers identified, Krever stated it would be unfair to single out this specific group, especially since it would not be possible to identify all the lawyers who were engaged in similar practices. Krever further stated that the insurance industry in effect is the client of the lawyers practising at the defence bar, and that it could act as a check upon the lawyers. Krever found that because of the undertak-

---

56   *Ibid.* at 568.
57   *Ibid.* at 580.

ings given, the publicity that the hearings generated, and the identification of those named, there was a sufficient impetus that the deplored practices would not occur in the future.

Krever did acknowledge that during the Inquiry, one witness (Ike) made and then withdrew an allegation that the Inquiry would not fully explore the involvement of the legal profession in the obtaining of confidential health information. The essence of Ike's allegation was that although the Inquiry was prepared to expose others such as private investigators, the Inquiry would protect its own who were culpable of the same conduct. Krever stated that the fact that such a comment was even made demonstrates a general attitude that exists and necessitates extreme diligence on the part of the legal profession to ensure its actions are scrupulously proper. Krever concluded that because the lawyers submitted an agreed acknowledgment of facts, and knowing how difficult it is to have two lawyers agree to any statement that is controversial, the matter was sufficiently addressed.

Notwithstanding the respect due to Justice Krever, one must query if this is a reasonable analysis of these lawyers' motives. Any litigation lawyer knows the horror of cross-examination. The findings of the Krever Inquiry arguably leave an impression that these solicitors were able to circle their wagons and retreat with the most minimal of losses that could have been incurred, given their situation.

The final matter addressed by Krever was why would such competent and reputable professionals engage in such an indefensible practice. He found that these lawyers probably did not direct their minds to what they were doing, and found it significant that civil procedure discovery provisions were much more primitive in the time before the Inquiry, and that lawyers learn their practice, as opposed to their theory, from practising lawyers. Krever opined that one generation teaches the next. The practices discussed at the Inquiry are old and originated with a generation of lawyers at a time when consciousness of the importance of privacy and confidentiality was not high and when discovery mechanisms were rudimentary and inadequate for modern needs. The learning generation of lawyers inherited the practice and never stopped to ask themselves why they were continuing it and why it was still necessary. The power of analysis that every good lawyer has was not used. Precedent, good or bad, is still too often the guide. [58]

Again, with all due respect for Justice Krever, this excuse, too, is suspect. Decide for yourself if Krever's procedure with respect to the conduct of the lawyers involved was appropriate. Decide for yourself if the practice of allowing these learned professionals to escape the rigours of cross-examination while forcing it upon a far less organized and ill-equipped group of private investigators was fair in the circumstances. Krever's analysis with respect to the lawyers is arguably grounds for cynicism — something not uncommon outside of the legal profession.

---

58   *Ibid.* at 582-83.

CHAPTER 8

INQUIRY ON POLICING IN BRITISH COLUMBIA — THE OPPAL INQUIRY

Justice Oppal's Commission of Inquiry on Policing in British Columbia (the Inquiry)[1] was a major initiative of the British Columbia government to address issues of importance to the general public about policing and other related activities in the province. Although the majority of the report focused on the recognized police agencies and their practices, the Inquiry also made an effort to address concerns relating to the private sector players who performed police-like services.

Although the Inquiry addressed many issues discussed in prior chapters of this book, the recommendations were not incorporated because many of them were addressed by other sources and because the recommendations of an inquiry are not law. Notwithstanding that the recommendations are not law, the findings are very insightful to understanding liability issues pertaining to private investigators. It is reasonable to assume that the Inquiry will form the basis of review of the private sector investigation industry in other provinces in the future.

The following are paraphrased sections from the Inquiry report, retaining many of Justice Oppal's expressions, and setting out some of the Inquiry's recommendations.

8.1 REGULATION UNDER THE *PRIVATE INVESTIGATORS AND SECURITY AGENCIES ACT*

Private security agencies are regulated by the Security Programs Division of the Ministry of Attorney General (the Division) in accordance with the *Private Investigators and Security*

---

1   Oppal, W.T., Policing in British Columbia Commission of Inquiry, *Closing the Gap: Policing and the Community* (Victoria: Queen's Printer, 1994).

Agencies Act (the Act). The director of the Division (the registrar) determines whether to license a firm or individual. Both security employees and security businesses must be licensed, including businesses in private investigation.[2]

There are few licensing criteria and they are relatively easy to satisfy. However, the registrar has considerable discretion to refuse, suspend, or cancel a licence on the grounds that

◆ the applicant or licensee is undesirable in terms of education, training, experience, skill, mental condition, character, or repute;

◆ it is not in the public interest to license the person;

◆ the applicant or licensee has done something contrary to the Act or licensing conditions;

◆ the applicant or licensee is convicted of a specified crime; or

◆ the person is a peace officer.

Licensees or applicants may appeal decisions of the registrar to the police commission. There have been forty-nine appeals in British Columbia since 1988 and six between 1991 and 1993. Most of these appeals have been regarding employee licences. Since 1988 there have been five appeals regarding agency licences.

Licensees are required to report such things as changes of address and criminal charges or convictions, to display licences, and to surrender them upon cancellation, and to refrain from using terminology, uniforms, or vehicles that might suggest they are police. The Act prohibits a security business or employee from engaging in work without a valid licence, and it is also an offence under the regulations to fail to disclose required information. However, there is no specified power for the registrar to investigate offences. On the other hand, the regulations do permit the registrar to inspect businesses to ensure licensees comply with the Act.

8.2   REGULATION BY THE *CANADIAN CHARTER OF RIGHTS AND FREEDOMS*

Recent cases suggest that the *Charter* applies to private security personnel only when they are making an arrest. When they are acting for a private employer, they may not be subject to *Charter* provisions that would apply to the same actions by a police officer. Thus, for example, the Ontario Court of Appeal determined that a private security agent might be able to detain a person without having to comply with the *Charter*, although the agent would have to comply if the detention amounted to an arrest. In Alberta, the Court of

---

2   The terms "Private Security Agents" and "Private Security Agencies" are used in the *Private Investigators and Security Agencies Act* to include, in addition to private investigators, security guards, alarm service providers, armoured-car service providers, locksmiths, and security consultants.

Appeal determined that evidence collected by private security agents is not subject to the unreasonable-search-and-seizure provisions of the *Charter*. The case considered whether the search-and-seizure provisions applied to evidence of illegal activities videotaped by security personnel prior to arrest by police. The court found that the security personnel were acting as private persons rather than exercising a government function so that the *Charter* did not apply.

The Inquiry found that allowing security guards to be excluded from these provisions is an anomaly and is not acceptable. The *Charter* provides fundamental protection to citizens during the law enforcement process that private security agents should not be permitted to circumvent. They should have the same rights to detain people and gather evidence that other private citizens have. However, it should not be possible for police to use private security agents to, for instance, obtain evidence that would be inadmissible in court if police had obtained it themselves by the same means.

Recommendation of the Inquiry

128: The province amend the *Private Investigators and Security Agencies Act* to ensure that

    (a) private security agents cannot unfairly take advantage of their status as private persons to deprive citizens of *Charter* protections; and

    (b) police cannot use private security agents to avoid *Charter* protections for citizens during the law-enforcement process.

8.3   REGULATION UNDER THE *CRIMINAL CODE* AND COMMON LAW

Private security agents have the same authority to arrest and detain people that all private persons have under the *Criminal Code*. However, their authority to search people is limited under the common law to

- searches incidental to valid arrest;
- the need to prevent injury; and
- the preservation of evidence related to the alleged offence.

On the other hand, where an employee or an accused person gives consent, private security agents may have additional powers. The *Criminal Code* also gives private security agents certain powers to use force. However, an agent who uses excessive force may be subject to both criminal penalties and civil liability. Additionally, the *Criminal Code* requires private security agents to assist police on request, unless they have a reasonable excuse.

Invasion of privacy is a common concern with private investigations. Both federal and provincial statutes and the common law restrict the activities of private investigations in relation to people's privacy. In addition, private security agents may also be liable for torts such as assault, false imprisonment, and malicious prosecution.

Some people in the private security industry have argued that the current legal framework governing the private security industry is sufficient. They say that criminal penalties and the fact that a citizen can sue an agent civilly for such things as assault or false imprisonment are sufficient to ensure agents will enforce the law with fairness and integrity.

The Inquiry does not agree with this view, nor did members of the public in their submissions to us. Many people, for economic reasons or other reasons, do not have the resources to launch civil suits seeking recompense for wrongs against them, and this creates an opportunity for abuse by security agents. The province must ensure that all those who enforce public laws within its borders act with integrity and fairness.

8.4   UNREGULATED GROUPS

The Inquiry believes that currently unregulated groups such as in-house security employees, the Corps of Commissionaires and armoured-car service employees should be required to meet provincial standards for training and accountability.

8.4.1   In-House Security Personnel

Many companies that are not security businesses assign particular employees, or proprietary security personnel, the same duties as they would to licensed security agents hired on a contractual basis. Yet these employees are not subject to the *Private Investigators and Security Agencies Act*. People have made the following arguments in favour of this exception:

- Proprietary security personnel have better background qualifications than contract security personnel because of their prior experience in law enforcement or private security.
- Better working conditions and benefits for in-house personnel attract better candidates.
- In-house security departments provide more and better training for personnel.
- In-house security departments exercise more care in selecting personnel than contract security.
- In-house security departments provide better supervision of personnel.

Moreover, some have argued that government resources are insufficient to regulate this sector and that the industry would simply reclassify employees to avoid regulation. However, survey research for the Inquiry found the following:

- A significant proportion of in-house security personnel have had no prior security-related experience.
- Security personnel may not be sufficiently checked through criminal records to ensure their integrity.
- Training may not be consistently adequate.
- There are no external controls to ensure security personnel are accountable and adhere to performance standards and safeguards.

Thus, the traditional rationales for exemption are not borne out by empirical research. The province must ensure that citizens are treated fairly, safely, and competently by law enforcement personnel, whether private individuals or police. Therefore, basic standards regarding competence, accountability, and training for in-house employees are appropriate. Regulation should include all proprietary security employees whose tasks are wholly or principally devoted to security duties. In the case of employees who have a variety of security and non-security related duties, regulation should include those employees who spend the majority of their time interacting with the public.

In principle, concerns about lack of enforcement resources or reclassification by employers should not prevent the province from establishing such standards. On the other hand, regulation must be sensitive to the unique structure of this sector of the security industry and should provide flexibility to industry to ensure competence through employer-delivered training programs and hiring practices.

Recommendation of the Inquiry

129: The province amend the *Private Investigators and Securities Agencies Act* to regulate competence and accountability of both employers and employees with the in-house or proprietary-security sector.

8.4.2 The Corps of Commissionaires, Armoured-Car Employees, and Other Unregulated Security Services

The B.C. Corps of Commissionaires (the Corps) is a non-profit organization that was founded to provide employment to former members of the armed services and the RCMP. The Corps has the right of first refusal on contracts to provide certain security services for the federal government. These services make up 62 percent of its work. The Corps also competes directly with other members of the contract security industry to provide security services for businesses and institutions.

The Inquiry found that the Corps imposes some competence and accountability standards during hiring and training. However, the Corps appears to receive a competitive advantage from its exemption, which may not be justified, and it is impossible to deny the inherent contradiction in requiring different levels of training for persons performing the same tasks. Moreover, the province cannot ensure public safety through an *ad hoc* approach to training and performance standards.

Armoured-car employees are also currently exempt from the Act, and it is therefore difficult to ensure that they and their employers are accountable to the public. Regulation of this group should provide flexibility for the industry, requiring the employer to undertake comprehensive screening of applicants, including criminal background checks. All the submissions to the Inquiry from armoured-car personnel, including those from their union, complained of lack of standards. The need for training armoured-car personnel in the use of force is discussed in the "High-Risk Policing" section of this report.

Such services as those provided by bouncers, bodyguards, and guard dogs also have a significant effect on public good and the expenditure of resources on public law enforcement. For example, bouncers are often accused of using excessive force. Yet the current Act does not regulate such activities. A more flexible approach to definitions within the Act should allow for inclusion of new and existing security sectors. Regulation of guard dog operations would be relatively easy since amendments to the regulations are all that is required.

Recommendation of the Inquiry

130: The province amend the *Private Investigators and Security Agencies Act* to

(a) include the Corps of Commissionaires;

(b) include all people employed for the purpose of maintaining order and control at an establishment or event and who may be required to use force in carrying out their duties;

(c) include any person employed for the purpose of protecting the safety of another person or group of persons, whose duties may require the use of force;

(d) require licensing of armoured-car employees; and

(e) ensure that the Act is flexible enough that other security services can be included as needed.

8.5 LICENSING: ENSURING COMPETENCE AND INTEGRITY

8.5.1 The Need for Measurable Standards

Currently, the *Private Investigators and Security Agencies Act* provides very few requirements that will ensure that security businesses and employees are competent and honest enough to enforce the law without threatening the public interest. Although the registrar may refuse a licence application or cancel a licence on the grounds of the applicant's or licensee's education, training, experience, skill, mental condition, character, or repute, these criteria are not further defined. As a result, the Security Programs Division of the ministry has developed policies such as requiring a credit check to ensure an applicant is financially stable, or a criminal record check to evaluate the applicant's integrity.

The Division also has policies on mental condition, repute, and undesirable candidates, as well as policies requiring interviews with candidates for investigator licences that require police references. However, these policies seem for the most part designed merely to acquire and evaluate limited information as to the integrity of candidates. They do not provide specific prerequisites that will ensure licence applicants are competent.

An applicant for a private investigator's business licence must have two years' previous experience as a licensed investigator. Otherwise, the Act and regulations are virtually silent about specific licence qualification criteria. Nor has the registrar developed a comprehensive set of policies or requirements to establish the competence and integrity of new and renewal applicants. Although the registrar should retain discretion to refuse licences to applicants who are generally undesirable, the Inquiry believes that the registrar must be required to apply specific qualification standards to ensure competence and honesty in law enforcement. Many other jurisdictions provide more specific criteria than those current in British Columbia, including, for example, the successful completion of examinations.

To ensure competence and safeguard the public interest, the province must require the industry to meet reasonable standards concerning background, repute, and experience. These standards should clearly indicate to prospective applicants their chances of success. An appeal of the registrar's decision should be made under the *Judicial Review Procedures Act*.

8.5.2   Assessing Integrity through Record Checks

The present system requires the registrar to assess integrity through criminal record checks, and the registrar may dismiss an application where the applicant has been charged with certain crimes, such as theft, fraud, or assault. Contrary to the principles of natural justice, the applicant has no opportunity to challenge this decision.

However, although applicants and licensees are required to report certain crimes, they are not required to report many provincial offences. This means the registrar has a limited amount of information on which to judge their integrity. This is unacceptable. The registrar should be aware of an applicant or licensee who has committed a provincial offence, since a tendency to disregard the law suggests that the individual would not be above reproach in enforcing the law.

Recommendation of the Inquiry

131: The province, in consultation with affected stakeholders, amend the *Private Investigators and Security Agencies Act* and regulations to

(a) prescribe, for both business and employee licence applicants, specific, measurable qualification criteria regarding experience, education, skill, mental condition, character, and repute of the applicant; and

(b) oblige licensees and applicants to report convictions for any offence, including offences under provincial statutes.

8.6   ONUS ON APPLICANTS TO DEMONSTRATE THEY ARE QUALIFIED

As noted previously, the registrar currently presumes that an applicant is entitled to a licence. The Inquiry believes such a presumption makes it too easy for people to obtain licences and does not assist the registrar in safeguarding the public interest.

Recommendation of the Inquiry

132: The province, in consultation with affected stakeholders, amend the *Private Investigators and Security Agencies Act* and regulations to

(a) place on the applicant the burden of demonstrating that the applicant meets specified qualifying criteria; and

(b) remove any presumption that an applicant is entitled to a licence unless, as a minimum requirement, the applicant satisfies the qualifying standards, subject always to the registrar's discretion to reject any applicant as undesirable.

8.7   FOCUSING REFORM ON BUSINESS APPLICATIONS

Currently, the number of employee applicants causes considerable pressure on administrative resources. However, if we focus on reform on specific criteria for business licence applicants rather than employee applicants, and on licensing only competent and honest businesses, these operators in turn will most likely employ competent and honest security personnel. Training, as opposed to qualifying criteria such as experience, is a more appropriate method for ensuring the competence of security employees.

Some states in the United States require administrators to fully investigate business licence applicants. The opportune time to assess business licensees is when the licence comes up for renewal. The licensee's business operations provide a good source of data for the registrar to assess the licensee's performance and suitability.

Recommendation of the Inquiry

133: The province, in consultation with affected stakeholders, amend the *Private Investigators and Security Agencies Act* and regulations to

(a) develop for security business applicants more thorough and rigorous qualifying standards and assessment procedures that would, in addition to criminal record checks, include specific screening procedures; and

(b) ensure that, at licence renewal, the registrar reviews the actual performance of the licensee in business.

8.8   INCREASING ADMINISTRATIVE RESOURCES

The large number of applicants is making it increasingly difficult for administrators to adequately administer the Act. To enable the province to administer tighter regulations, it should consider means of increasing its resources, including such options as the following:

- Develop responsibility of assessing employee licence candidates to security businesses.
- Increase licence fees in accordance with the user-pay principle.
- Use temporary licences with conditions to ensure public safety.
- Increase the duration of the licences.

Temporary licences should include safeguards such as penalties for employers who fail to follow guidelines for screening temporary employees and who hire an employee who causes harm to persons or property.

Recommendation of the Inquiry

134: The province ensure that any interested member of the public, including licence applicants, has easy and direct access to all current policies of the registrar and the Security Programs Division for the administration of the *Private Investigators and Security Agencies Act* and regulations.

8.9   TRAINING PRIVATE INVESTIGATORS

Currently, applicants for business licences in the private investigator category must have two full years' experience as an unrestricted investigator. To obtain this experience, applicants can work as employee investigators under supervision. All applicants, whether for business licences or employee licences, must be interviewed by the Security Programs Division. At the time of writing, the Division was preparing guidelines for the under-supervision category to specify the requirements for satisfactory apprenticeship and to give the public notice that the employee is not fully qualified. The Act does not contain any qualifying standards for the training of investigators.

Private investigators potentially have a significant impact on the privacy of individuals and research shows that the training currently provided by most employers is incomplete and fails to address privacy issues. Although few other jurisdictions have established formal guidelines for training, the Inquiry believes that the present review of policing in British Columbia provides an important opportunity to make British Columbia's standards among the best. Training should include course work, examinations, and apprenticeship periods. To ensure that apprenticeship programs are effective, guidelines should delineate the task to be performed, the degree of supervision required, and reporting requirements. The fact that private investigators can access technology and techniques that enable them to greatly intrude on privacy makes the need for training very important.

Recommendation of the Inquiry

137: The province, in consultation with affected stakeholders, amend the *Private Investigators and Security Agencies Act* and regulations to require specific qualifying standards with respect to training for all private investigative applicants.

8.10 ACCOUNTABILITY

With the growing use of private security, there is need that security personnel be accountable for their actions. Yet current legislation provides relatively few options for ensuring that accountability.

Under the present system, the registrar may hold people accountable by (1) suspending, cancelling, or refusing to renew a licence; or (2) prosecuting offences under the Act. Statistics identifying the degree of enforcement through licence sanctions are not available. Of the forty-nine appeals to the police commission from the registrar's decisions since 1988, less than five have included the suspension, cancellation, or revocation of an existing licence. However, many of the industry representatives consulted indicated that there is significant non-compliance with the Act. A frequent offence involves unlicensed personnel; this has led to licence sanctions being brought against the employer or refusal of the employee's application.

Research also shows that there have been only three prosecutions in the twelve years since the Act came into effect. However, the relatively low number of prosecutions may have resulted from some confusion as to which agency — the police or the Security Division — is responsible for investigating allegations and initiating prosecutions.

To ensure that provincial regulation of the security industry is effective, we must give the registrar clear authority to investigate and prosecute alleged offences. We must also give the public an opportunity to bring complaints to the attention of the registrar and the industry through fair and equitable complaint procedures.

Recommendations of the Inquiry

138: The province amend the *Private Investigator and Security Agencies Act* and regulations to provide the registrar with clear authority to initiate prosecution of offences under the Act.

139: The province either amend the *Private Investigators and Security Agencies Act* and regulations or establish guidelines to set out comprehensive public complaint procedures for administrators, the public, and the industry.

8.11   THE REGISTRAR'S POWERS TO INVESTIGATE COMPLAINTS

Under the present system the registrar can inspect a business but has no clear power to investigate alleged offences. We can significantly enhance the registrar's ability to promote accountability by giving the registrar specific and significant powers to investigate applicants and alleged offences.

Recommendation of the Inquiry

140: The province amend the *Private Investigators and Security Agencies Act* and regulations to enable the registrar to conduct a full investigation into any allegation of misconduct under the Act.

8.12   THE CREATION OF SUMMARY SANCTIONS

The lack of prosecutions may also be due to the lack of alternatives to either expensive and lengthy prosecutions or overly harsh licence suspensions to penalize less serious violations. Providing a wider range of sanctions would enhance the registrar's ability to ensure that the industry is accountable. For example, in California, administrators of similar legislation may fine offenders up to $1,000 for less serious infractions, or increasing amounts for repeat offences. Florida and Illinios statutes contain similar provisions, as well as penalties such as censure, probation orders, and orders for professional instruction. A system of such sanctions, with the opportunity for an offender to dispute them, would be flexible and efficient without compromising fairness or natural justice.

Recommendation of the Inquiry

141: The province amend the *Private Investigators and Security Agencies Act* and regulations to

(a) include a system of regulatory fines, official reprimands and probation with conditions; and

(b) provide for informal settlements in the case of disputed violation notices.

8.13 REPORTING REQUIREMENTS FOR LICENSEES

Under the current system, the registrar may discover infractions or offences through the following methods:

- inspecting businesses;
- requesting the police to investigate;
- receiving reports from licensees under current reporting obligations;
- requiring licensees to produce a licence upon request; and
- receiving informal complaints from industry and the public.

These sources of information are insufficient to provide timely and full information that would ensure the industry is accountable. For instance, the registrar must refer investigations to police who have little expertise concerning the Act. The investigation is limited to the background of the licensee and may not concern the licensee's full conduct. Moreover, there are few requirements for record keeping and no formal requirement that industry report public complaints.

To be effective, the registrar must have full information systematically provided from a number of sources. By requiring the industry to report public complaints, civil actions, and other industry conduct, we can ensure that the registrar has sufficient information to enforce accountability.

Recommendation of the Inquiry

142: The province amend the *Private Investigators and Security Agencies Act* and regulations to require licensees to disclose or report to the registrar and keep records of the following matters:

   (a) all complaints made regarding conduct relating to the business or employees;

   (b) all civil suits instituted against businesses or employees;

   (c) all instances where a firearm or other weapon has been used by a licensee;

   (d) all particulars relating to the dismissal of employees for cause;

   (e) all petitions for bankruptcy commenced by or against a licensee; and

   (f) declarations that all provincial and federal taxes have been paid as due.

8.14 BONDING AND INSURANCE COVERAGE

Other mechanisms that hold the private security industry accountable include bonds and criminal and civil liability. However, the bonds required by law are very small and the registrar has no notice of the status of the bonds. These mechanisms are inadequate and should be supplemented by mandatory insurance for civil liability.

Inasmuch as the activities of the private security industry will necessarily involve frequent interaction with members of the public, it is appropriate that agencies and individuals employed by agencies carry insurance in order to protect the public and ensure that loss occasioned through civil wrongdoing can be compensated.

Recommendation of the Inquiry

143: The province amend the *Private Investigators and Security Agencies Act* and regulations to require all licensees to carry a specified minimum amount of liability insurance as a condition of obtaining or retaining a licence.

8.15 ACCOUNTABILITY OF THE REGISTRAR

Administrators should also be accountable. Currently, the registrar is held accountable in part by the right of applicants and licensees to appeal the registrar's decisions. However, this accountability is limited to licensing decisions. To ensure the registrar is accountable for other aspects of administration, the province should require the registrar to report to the legislature in a form that would be distributed directly to the public and the industry.

Recommendation of the Inquiry

144: The province amend the *Private Investigators and Security Agencies Act* and regulations to require the registrar to submit an annual report to be tabled in the legislature which should

(a) include statistics relating to the issuance and renewal of licensees, disciplinary action taken, expenditures and revenues, and other information relevant to the administration of the Act; and

(b) be made available to the public after review by the legislature.

8.16 HEARINGS ON LICENCE SANCTIONS

Presently, licences may be revoked, cancelled, or suspended without a hearing where the registrar deems this to be in the public interest. Although this power does not appear to have been abused, a fair system should ensure that a licensee has an opportunity to challenge the information on which the registrar's decision is based.

Recommendation of the Inquiry

145: The province amend the *Private Investigators and Security Agencies Act* and regulations to

(a) require a hearing before the registrar where there is a substantial likelihood that a licence will be cancelled or suspended; and

(b) give a licensee the right to waive this requirement.

8.17 INCREASING THE RESOURCES OF THE SECURITY PROGRAMS DIVISION FOR INVESTIGATIONS

A growing workload, a greater range of duties, lack of staff, and the office location in Victoria make it increasingly difficult for the Division to enforce the Act and regulations. Thus, in its current form, the Division cannot ensure accountability of the industry. Not surprisingly, submissions to the Inquiry repeatedly called for additional administrative resources, a clear and realistic compliance policy, and a greater range of penalties for offenders. To effectively administer the regulations proposed in this report, the Division needs much greater investigative resources.

Recommendations of the Inquiry

146: The province amend the *Private Investigators and Security Agencies Act* and regulations to allow the registrar to engage inspectors and investigators to carry out proposed additional investigations.

147: The province ensure there is a realistic budget for the registrar's mandate under the Act.

8.18 CONSULTATION, SELF-REGULATION, AND THE ROLE OF THE ADVISORY BOARD

Most regulatory schemes are more effective when stakeholders consult periodically with administrators. We must ensure that the security industry has adequate opportunity for such involvement. One such opportunity is the Private Investigators and Security Agencies Advisory Board (the Board), appointed by Cabinet to advise the attorney general and registrar on the Act and regulations of the industry. Other options include informal consultation and formal mechanisms for self-regulation. This section of the report discusses means of achieving effective stakeholder participation through such things as the Board, informal consultation, and self-regulation.

8.18.1 Mandate of the Advisory Board

The Advisory Board is responsible for the following:

- advising the attorney general through the registrar on the Act or matters referred to the Board by the minister;
- advising the registrar on policies, procedures and practices relating to the Act;
- consulting, informing, and advising the industry regarding standards and code of ethics that should be adopted in the public interest; and
- making recommendations to the registrar concerning training of licensees.

The first Board was appointed in 1992, and it has established several procedural rules, including the use of discussion papers. As well, Board members may invite other stake-holders, including industry associations, to make submissions to the Board.

By comparison, Newfoundland requires all business licensees to become members of an association that the government hoped would consult with administrators and take responsibility for self-regulation. Unfortunately, this approach to consultation and accountability has not developed effectively.

The belief that the process of self-regulation has not worked was expressed by both the Newfoundland Deputy Administrator of the *Private Investigation and Security Services Act* and the current chair of the Newfoundland Security Guards and Private Investigation Agencies Association (the Association). From the Newfoundland government's point of view, the Association has produced no recommendations relating to ethics or standards, and the heavy competition between individual firms for business undermines the Association. However, according to the Association chair, their members believe that their business interests are private and are no concern of the government. They also believe that wage differences between union and non-union firms creates unfair competition. Both parties suggested to the Inquiry that it will likely require government regulation to rectify the inequality.

This stalemate does not necessarily condemn the Newfoundland project to failure, nor is Newfoundland the only jurisdiction where advisory boards operate. For example, boards in California and Illinois have much broader responsibilities than are found in British Columbia, including mediating complaints and hearing appeals of licensing decisions.

This suggests that, although the province must proceed carefully, the Board's role could be usefully expanded to include discipline proceedings or hearings involving allegations of unethical or unprofessional conduct. If the province adopts proposals for summary sanctions, the Board could carry out initial fact-finding and make non-binding recommendations to the registrar concerning penalties. Such a system would encourage informal resolution and reduce the registrar's workload. On the other hand, it would likely require Board members to be paid.

Recommendation of the Inquiry

148:   The province amend the *Private Investigators and Security Agencies Act* and regulations to give the Advisory Board a role in disciplinary proceedings.

8.18.2 Advisory Board Membership

In British Columbia, there are no qualifications specified in the Act for Board membership and there are no provisions relating to tenure or replacement of members. By comparison, Illinois requires members on a similar board to have three years' experience in their field and limits members to a four-year non-renewable term. The director has power to remove members for cause.

It is important to appoint members who have sufficient knowledge, experience, and respect throughout the industry in order for them to be valuable contributors. Research into consultation schemes of other jurisdictions suggests that industry members must be mature, organized, and willing to participate effectively in regulating the industry. In addition, the province must ensure that the sole criterion for membership is merit. We can achieve this through statutory qualification requirements, public guidelines on membership, consultations with industry, and nomination of candidates for the stakeholders.

Recommendation of the Inquiry

149: The province amend the *Private Investigators and Security Agencies Act* and regulations to

   (a) include minimum qualifications for Advisory Board membership including specified experience and evidence that candidates are respected within the industry for their integrity, impartiality, and competence; and

   (b) ensure there is thorough consultation with industry and other stakeholders prior to appointing members.

8.18.3 Size and Constitution of the Advisory Board

Several industry representatives told the Inquiry they were concerned that the present Advisory Board does not adequately represent all stakeholders. Specifically, there are no members solely designated to represent the interests of investigators, armoured-car services, security consultants, security employees, or consumers of security services. Research into consultation procedures in other jurisdictions shows that, to make consultation work, stakeholders must have a meaningful role in regulation. We must therefore ensure that all interests are represented.

Recommendation of the Inquiry

150: The province, in consultation with affected stakeholders, amend the *Private Investigators and Security Agencies Act* and regulations to expand the Advisory Board to include additional members from industry and other stakeholder sectors not currently represented.

8.18.4 Accountability of the Advisory Board and the Registrar

As with any administrative body, the Advisory Board should be accountable. Accountability can be achieved by ensuring that through formal and informal mechanisms, members must consult a wide range of opinions in their sectors. However, we can create additional public scrutiny of the actions of the Board and the registrar by asking the Board to report to the legislature and ensuring that the registrar must respond to the Board's recommendations. To ensure that the Board is regularly refreshed with new insights and is not dominated by inflexible interests, we should limit the terms of members and provide that they can be removed for cause.

Recommendations of the Inquiry

151: The province amend the *Private Investigators and Security Agencies Act* and regulations to

   ◆ require the Advisory Board to submit an annual report to the registrar;

- require this report to be tabled in the legislature or at least distributed to all stake-holders;
- require the registrar to formally respond to recommendations and initiatives from the Advisory Board;
- specify non-renewable terms for members; and
- specify that members be removable for cause.

152: The province ensure that the Advisory Board and the Division establish formal and informal mechanisms for regular consultation with industry.

8.18.5 The Registrar's Involvement with the Board

The registrar's position as chair of the Board may undermine the independence of both the registrar and the Board. We can prevent this result from happening by placing the registrar or a designate on the Board as an *ex officio* member to ensure an arm's length relationship between the Board and the registrar. This would be consistent with principles of account-ability, independence, and control, and with the Inquiry's recommendation respecting community police boards and committees.

Recommendation of the Inquiry

153: The province amend the *Private Investigators and Security Agencies Act* and regulations to place the registrar or designate on the Advisory Board as an *ex officio* member with no voting rights.

8.18.6 Mandatory Membership in an Industry Association

Requiring all security business licensees to be involved in an industry association could enhance opportunities for consultation and self-regulation. An association's constitution and operations would be developed by industry members themselves. Such an association would unite the various small industry groups that now exist.

Recommendation of the Inquiry

154: The province, in consultation with affected stakeholders, amend the *Private Investigators and Security Agencies Act* and regulations to require that all security busi-ness licensees be members of an industry association.

PART THREE

Evidence & Litigation Issues for Private Investigators

CHAPTER 9

THE LAW OF EVIDENCE

This chapter does not claim to be a comprehensive treatise on the law of evidence. The *Canada Evidence Act* and the various provincial evidence Acts are not specifically reviewed. Neither does this chapter claim to be a comprehensive summary of all evidentiary issues applicable to private sector investigations.[1] Rather, this chapter reviews case law where the courts have specifically addressed the conduct of private investigators or the circumstances upon which private investigations were conducted. As such, this chapter gives an overview of evidence issues that are relevant to private investigators.

General Principles for Admissibility

Generally, the goals of the laws of evidence are (1) to search for the truth, (2) to increase the efficiency of a trial, and (3) to bring fairness to the trial process.[2] The criteria for the admissibility of evidence are (1) relevance, (2) reliability, (3) authentication, and (4) juristic discretion, also known as the probative value versus prejudicial effect test.[3] If the evidence is obtained legally, and if it passes the qualifiers listed above, it is admissible. However, if evidence is obtained by a method that contravenes some law, different considerations arise.

Admissibility of Illegally Obtained Evidence

Historically, the admissibility of illegally obtained evidence has, at common law, been very liberal, both in the criminal and civil realms. As stated by Justice Crompton in the nineteenth century, "[i]t matters not how you get it, even if you steal it, it would be admissible as evidence."[4] Only a few exceptions have arisen over the years at common law to this strict

---

1   For a comprehensive treatise on the law of evidence, one should visit leading texts such as J. Sopinka, S.N. Lederman, & A.W. Bryant, *The Law of Evidence in Canada*, 2d ed. (Toronto: Butterworths, 1999); D. Paciocco & L. Stuesser, *The Law of Evidence*, 2d ed. (Toronto: Irwin Law, 1999).
2   Sopinka, Lederman, & Bryant, *ibid.*
3   E. Goldstein, *Visual Evidence: A Practitioner's Manual* (Toronto: Carswell, 1999) at 2-14 to 2-20.
4   *R. v. Leatham*, [1861-73] All E.R. Rep. Ext. 1646.

inclusionary rule; for example, confessions obtained through improper conduct or illegal interception of private communications. However, even in these cases, derivative evidence has been admissible unless a judge found that its inclusion would bring the administration of justice into disrepute.

The rationale for the general inclusionary rule is that the trier of fact should have the benefit of all relevant evidence irrespective of how it was obtained. If illegal or improper acts committed in the acquisition of evidence do not affect its probative value, these acts should not distract the court from its primary task of finding facts and determining the truth. The laws of evidence are not to be used as a means of disciplining its collectors. Rather, if someone is prejudiced by evidence obtained illegally, such an aggrieved person can resort to other proceedings, criminal or civil, to obtain recourse against the wrongdoing investigator.[5]

The *Charter*

The liberal stance of the common law has, however, been reined in since the passing of the *Canadian Charter of Rights and Freedoms.* Section 24(2) provides that where a court concludes that the evidence is obtained in a manner that infringes or denies any rights or freedoms guaranteed by the *Charter,* the evidence shall be excluded if it is established that, having regard to all the circumstances, the admission of it would bring the administration of justice into disrepute.

It is now trite law that the *Charter* does not apply to private litigation but only to actions involving either the executive, legislative or administrative branches of government.[6] Therefore, for typical private actions, the historic common law rules of the admissibility of evidence still apply. However, due to recent decisions in various contexts, the courts have imported into private litigation a concept called *Charter* values.[7] This concept, while not allowing for a remedy as per section 24(1) of the *Charter,* may result in the exclusion of evidence if it was obtained by conduct deemed unsavoury by the courts. The concept of *Charter* values is discussed in various sections of this chapter.

Ignoring for now the concept of *Charter* values, it can be said that it is only if the evidence is in support of governmental criminal, quasi-criminal, or administrative action that its admissibility falls under the direct *Charter* spotlight. If the evidence is obtained in breach of a *Charter* right, then section 24(2) provides it is inadmissible unless it does not bring the administration of justice into disrepute. Such an analysis requires a consideration of factors such as:

- What kind of evidence was obtained?

- What *Charter* right was violated?

- Was the *Charter* violation serious or was it of a merely technical nature?

- Was the violation deliberate and flagrant or inadvertent and committed in good faith?

---

5   Sopinka, Lederman, & Bryant, above note 1 at 379–80.

6   *R.W.D.S.U. Local 580 v. Dolphin Delivery Ltd.*, [1986] 2 S.C.R. 573.

7   *Hill v. Church of Scientology of Toronto*, [1995] 2 S.C.R. 1130.

- Did it occur in circumstances of urgency or necessity?
- Were there other investigatory techniques available?
- Would the evidence have been obtained in any event?
- Is the offence serious?
- Is the evidence essential to substantiate the charge?

This list is not exhaustive, and no one factor is determinative.[8]

As most private investigations take place in the civil context, these complex *Charter* analyses are often not required. However, as *Charter* jurisprudence continues to develop, its impact cannot be ignored. Accordingly, reviews of the *Charter*'s implications are included in the sections that follow.

9.1   THE PREJUDICE AGAINST A PRIVATE INVESTIGATOR'S EVIDENCE

The courts have historically held a prejudice against the evidence of private investigators for a number of reasons. Such reasons include being paid witnesses, acting without a licence, being retained on a results only basis, obtaining evidence through entrapment, the inclusion of irrelevant derogatory information in reports, and appearing biased while testifying. The courts have also discussed the admissibility of reports where the investigator or the witness the investigator spoke to becomes deceased prior to trial. These various issues are reviewed individually.

9.1.1   Paid Witnesses

A common criticism of the evidence of private investigators is that they are paid witnesses and therefore have a vested interest in the outcome of a matter and may slant their evidence accordingly. For example, in a divorce case from Manitoba, the court found that two private investigators colluded with a married couple to produce evidence of adultery so that the couple could obtain a divorce. The court stated: "Without casting any slurs, I think I must be on guard against and scrutinize testimony of witnesses whose gainful profession it is to obtain evidence."[9] Another example is taken from a case in Nova Scotia where a court stated:

> My general reaction is that evidence of this kind must be received with definite reservations. It must be remembered that the tape was taken by persons who were paid to gather evidence tending to discredit the plaintiff and who have more than an immediate interest in obtaining that kind of result.[10]

---

8   *R. v. Collins* (1987), 38 D.L.R. (4th) 508 (S.C.C.).
9   *Boivin v. Boivin*, [1944] 3 W.W.R. 70 (Man. K.B.).
10 *Smith v. Avis Transport of Canada Limited and Harvie* (1979), 35 N.S.R. (2d) 652 at 673 (S.C.).

Again, in another case from Nova Scotia a court held that "[t]he private investigator's evidence had to be accepted with caution. This type of witness, since he was paid to produce his evidence, was likely to slant his evidence in favour of his sponsor."[11]

A Workers' Compensation Board has also voiced this concern. In one particular case, the panel held:

> A private investigator is by definition hired to represent an interested party. Therefore, the report from a private investigator that is submitted as evidence is necessarily one-sided . . . The investigator is most likely contracted to support an allegation that a particular claim is not valid. And one can presume that the "diligent" investigator would therefore attempt to maximize or exaggerate every adverse observation and to minimize or ignore every observation which would support a worker's claim.[12]

Most recently an Ontario court stated: "There is something I find disquieting about a private investigator going out and gathering evidence after getting paid. That could taint the objectivity of the evidence."[13]

Although such concerns are legitimate, it must also be acknowledged that many witnesses have an interest in the outcome of a case, and very often their interest is monetary in nature. In fact, all expert witnesses would fit into this category, let alone a party to an action. Accordingly, a private investigator's evidence cannot simply be disregarded as unreliable for this reason alone.

9.1.2 Unlicensed Private Investigators

Another reason the courts have given for viewing a private investigator's evidence with suspicion is if he or she is not licensed. In an Ontario case, a court held that evidence given by a private investigator who has not secured the licence required by the Act should not be readily accepted unless it is fully and strongly corroborated and the opposite party fails to adduce evidence in refutation.[14] It is noteworthy, however, that other courts have not expressed this concern.[15]

9.1.3 Success-Based Retainer Contracts

A third reason the courts have given for negative findings against a private investigator is because of the arrangement the private investigator was under to be remunerated. In a Manitoba case, a private investigator revealed the arrangement with his client was he would charge $250 if he produced evidence, but if he did not, he would charge nothing. The court held that such a financial arrangement could, in some cases, be an inducement to an investigator to colour his testimony, or worse. The court stated that it hoped that such

---

11 *Mitchell v. Trainor* (1993), 123 N.S.R. (2d) 361 (S.C.).
12 *Decision No. 918/941*, [1995] O.W.C.A.T.D. No. 170.
13 *R. v. Hadjor* (2000), O.J. No. 2978 (S.C.J.). See also N. Pron, "Verdict in Fraud Trial May Not Stand" *Toronto Star* (15 March 2000).
14 *LaMarche v. LaMarche*, [1961] O.W.N. 15 (H.C.J.) (decided under R.S.O. 1960, c. 306).
15 *R. v. Morgan*, [1997] O.J. No. 5477 (Gen. Div.).

a practice is generally not prevalent in the industry, and that to the extent that it does exist, the profession should recognize its dangers and put an end to it.[16]

9.1.4   Entrapment

Some forms of entrapment have resulted in judicial rebuke, while others have been held to be acceptable tactics for investigating. For example, in an intellectual property case in Ontario, a private investigator knowingly purchased a cartridge from an employee of a corporation that had been served a notice of injunction with regard to the sale of certain products. The methods used by the private investigator in making the purchase were found to be lawful as he made no threats or inducements when purchasing the product. Further, the private investigator was deemed to have taken the appropriate actions as the property, which was restricted from sale, was immediately turned over as evidence.[17]

Another example of an acceptable form of entrapment is taken from an internal theft investigation in Alberta. In this case, two private investigators posed as bus passengers and paid cash to a bus driver of Greyhound Bus Lines. The company believed the driver was pocketing cash sales. As suspected, the accused did not record the sales to these two passengers and failed to pay the funds received to his employer. In his theft trial, the defence raised the issue of entrapment. The court, however, admitted the evidence of the two private investigators and the accused was convicted.[18]

One of the most scorned forms of entrapment is the infamous "coin drop." In these cases, one private investigator will walk in front of an unsuspecting disability claimant and "accidentally" drop some coins onto the sidewalk in front of him or her. Typically, the plaintiff will bend down to help the private investigator retrieve the coins while another private investigator records the behaviour with a hidden video camera. Such recorded behaviour is then used to refute a claim of injury. Although raising suspicions of the legitimacy of a disability claim, such tactics are generally frowned upon as they induce a person into an activity they would not have undertaken but for the private investigator's actions. They are also discouraged because they could actually induce a claimant to injure themselves to a greater extent. In other words, there are public policy reasons a court will hold such evidence as inadmissible.[19]

For a further discussion of entrapment cases, see Section 9.2.4.6 — Entrapment in a Labour Litigation Setting, and Section 9.5 — Undercover Operations later on in this chapter.

9.1.5   Inclusion of Irrelevant Derogatory Information in Notes and Reports

The courts look for objectivity in reporting. In an Ontario employment case, an employer suspected that an employee had been drinking on the job. The employer retained a firm of

---

16   *Klassen v. Klassen* (1968), 62 W.W.R. 192 (Man. C.A.).
17   *Nintendo of America v. 798824 Ont. Ltd.* (1991), 41 F.T.R. 161 (F.C.T.D.).
18   *R. v. Gallagher*, [1993] A.J. No. 681 (P.C.).
19   C. Kentridge, "Surveillance Must Be Used with Caution" *Law Times* (1–7 June 1998).

private investigators who made observations and inquiries about the employee. A written report submitted to the employer did not contain any evidence of lack of sobriety at the workplace. However, it did disclose that the employee had been convicted of impaired driving and that his licence had been suspended for three months. In addition, the investigator reported a "property search" that disclosed that a bank had registered a mortgage against the employee's home to collaterally secure a loan.

In relation to this fact, the investigators volunteered the gratuitous observation "We can only speculate as to the purpose of the loan, but one might consider the possibility of capitalizing a new business." The report concluded with commentary in which the employee's general demeanour was adversely analyzed. The court held the report appeared to attach somewhat of a sinister innuendo to a list of observations or facts of an apparently innocuous character. The court concluded that such commentary only diminished the weight to be given to it.[20]

How notes and reports should be prepared was set out in an Ontario case wherein a law firm used its own students to conduct an undercover investigation. The students were given the following instructions:

* Prepare a detailed memorandum setting out your observations immediately after the event.

* The memorandums must be complete and accurate as they may be used for refreshing memory at a later time.

* All handwritten notes must be kept and they should not be rewritten for any reason.

* Memorandums should not comment on the legal implications of the facts observed.

* Memorandums should not comment on the best way to obtain evidence for a conviction.

* Memorandums should not make reference to a person being engaged in an illegal practice.

* Memorandums should only include the facts observed and the investigator's conduct.

The instructions from the partner to the students concluded with a comment that making judgments on the facts observed is for a court to decide.[21]

9.1.6 Conduct while Testifying

The courts on occasion have made negative comments about the quality of a private investigator's testimony. One critique has been the lack of objectivity. For example, in one case a court held:

> There are problems with the credibility of at least one of the private investigators hired by the defendant. I find that in his zeal to prove that the plaintiff was implicated in starting the fire, he sought to have at least one of the witnesses he interviewed change his evidence in accord with what his view was of the matter.[22]

---

20   *Housepian v. Work Wear Corp. of Canada Ltd.* (1981), 125 D.L.R. (3d) 447 (Ont. Co. Ct.).

21   *Markandey v. Ontario (Board of Ophthalmic Dispensers)*, [1994] O.J. No. 484 (Gen. Div.).

22   *A.K. v. Dominion of Canada General Insurance Co.*, [1997] B.C.J. No. 576 (S.C.).

In another case, a court held:

> The plaintiff's action fails to be determined upon the evidence of two private investigators
> . . . I gave most careful attention to their demeanor in the witness-box, and to the manner in
> which they gave their evidence. I have also given careful consideration to what they swear to
> have seen and heard and done in connection with this case. I have come to the conclusion that
> the evidence of these two witnesses is entirely unreliable, and that they were willing to give
> any evidence which might advance the interests of the plaintiff. I can not and will not accept
> their evidence.[23]

Another critique has been the error of using derogatory adjectives to describe observations. An example of this is taken from a Nova Scotia case:

> Their observations were totally unconvincing and in some cases were clearly beyond the scope
> of their competency. They gave the appearance of being unreliable witnesses. For example, the
> private investigator described the plaintiff's walking as "waddling" and he attempted to ascribe
> the subject's overweight as the reason for her gait. His observations of her shopping at a
> supermarket failed to remark upon the significance of the fact that she had the assistance of
> her young son in performing that task and ultimately she was met by another person who
> assisted her in unloading the vehicle.[24]

The courts have also pointed out what they view as favourable characteristics in the manner in which private investigators have given their evidence. For example, a court noted private investigator Andrea Scott's apparent disinterest in the outcome of the trial and her detailed notes.[25] In another case, a court found that private investigator David Andrews of the Atlantic Bureau of Investigation Inc. gave his testimony without embellishment or exaggeration.[26] In yet another case, the court stated that private investigator Frank Drundia gave evidence that was credible and not unduly partisan.[27] A key feature to appearing disinterested is to give short answers that respond to the specific question, and to avoid any superfluous anecdotes that may reflect a bias in favour of either party.

9.1.7   Evidence of a Deceased Witness

There has been a case where a court declared inadmissible the notes of a private investigator who died before the case to which he was a witness went to trial. On appeal, the court held that under the ordinary rules of evidence, such notes are admissible as an exception to the hearsay rule on the basis that they were made in the ordinary course of business by a person who later became deceased. The court found that the investigator's supervisor gave sufficient evidence on the issue of whether the investigator's notes were made in the course of his duties.[28]

---

23   *DeFalco v. DeFalco and Barbier*, [1950] 3 D.L.R. 770, rev'd [1951] 4 D.L.R. 128 (Ont. H.C.J.).

24   *Clark v. O'Brien*, [1995] N.S.J. No. 8 (S.C.). See also *Knipple v. Bulizuik*, [1995] S.J. No. 130 (Q.B.).

25   *L'Herbier de Provence Ltd. v. Amarsy* (1995), 59 C.P.R. (3d) 367 (F.C.T.D.).

26   *Mitchell v. Trainor,* above note 11.

27   *Boodhai v. Allstate Insurance Co. of Canada*, [1994] O.I.C.D. No. 135.

28   *Conley v. Conley*, [1968] 2 O.R. 677 (C.A.). The court relied upon *Wigmore on Evidence* (original by J.H. Wigmore as *Evidence in Trials at Common Law*), vol. 5, 3d ed., rev. by J.T. McNaughton (Boston: Little, Brown, 1961) at 372-3, s. 1524, and again at 370-1, s. 1522.

There has also been a case where a court declared inadmissible a statement received by a private investigator from a witness who died before trial. In this case, a private investigator had made notes of a telephone conversation he had with the witness. The private investigator had informed the witness that he was a private investigator conducting an investigation on behalf of an insurance company. However, the witness was not made aware that his statement could later be used in court. The court held that without a written statement, an opportunity to correct, and a warning of the importance of the statement, the required guarantees of trustworthiness and reliability had not been met.[29]

9.2 SURVEILLANCE REPORTS, VIDEOS, AND PHOTOGRAPHS

This section commences with a general review of various judicial impressions of surveillance evidence tendered by private investigators. It then discusses how surveillance evidence has been received in insurance, labour, family, and municipal by-law litigation settings.[30]

9.2.1 Judicial Opinions on the Value of Surveillance Evidence

9.2.1.1 The Court's Historic View of Videotape Surveillance Evidence

When motion picture technology was first introduced into courtrooms, the results could have been foretold. Just as there are those in the general populace who embrace change and those who fear it, so judges took various positions as to the changes in evidentiary techniques.

For example, in 1968 a court from Ontario held that it was unable to find any precedent for the use of motion pictures at a jury trial. Believing he was a court of first instance and being cautious as to change, the judge held:

> In my view the introduction of visual evidence in the form of motion pictures to a jury is a dangerous and unacceptable form of demonstrable evidence. One must consider that members of the jury are being put in the position of witnesses of certain alleged motions or actions. Experience has shown beyond doubt that eyewitnesses of matters under consideration by the court themselves vary to an extraordinary degree in their recollection and appreciation of what they have actually seen. It is a familiar game or test, even employed at the university level, for a scene to be enacted rapidly in the space of a few minutes before an audience which has been warned to use their best powers of observation and then to ask members of the audience to describe what they have seen. From the results of these tests it is well known that the most extraordinary diverse recollection is then described by those participating . . . I also note that the use to which viewing a videotape by a trial judge sitting alone may be put is carefully restricted to the assisting of his understanding of the evidence and not to converting the trial judge into a witness.[31]

---

29 *Guthmiller v. Krahn* (2000), 268 A.R. 369 (Q.B.).

30 For a comprehensive review on the law and visual evidence, see E. Goldstein, *Visual Evidence: A Practitioner's Manual*, above note 3.

31 *Nag v. McKellar*, [1968] 1 O.R. 797 (H.C.J.).

In fact, the issue of the admissibility of motion pictures as evidence had been discussed in Canadian courts prior to this. As early as 1950, a court had this to say about motion picture evidence:

> The plaintiff employed a commercial moving picture company to take various moving pictures at different dates showing the nature of the streets, the weather, the congestion caused by the picketing and the presence of the defendants named.
>
> . . .
>
> It demonstrated to me also the possibility that with modern inventions, old rules should not necessarily remain static. It did appear to me that it might well develop in a case in the future that moving pictures themselves might be tendered and admitted as evidence. I could well imagine a case where pictures were being taken and at that very moment, in focus, an automobile accident occurred.
>
> . . .
>
> I mention this to illustrate that my finding in respect of the moving pictures only applied to the present case and I did not intend, by such finding, to lay down a universal rule in regard to the use of moving pictures. With the scientific development of moving pictures, there might arise, in the future, an action when the pictures themselves, properly proved, would be the very best evidence of what occurred.[32]

9.2.1.2   Early Decisions Accepting Videotape Surveillance Evidence

The evolution of photographic and video technology eventually resulted in a more general acceptance of such evidence by the courts. An example of this change in judicial opinion is found in a 1978 case from Nova Scotia where a court stated:

> A video tape taken by the investigators was shown to both the trial judge and to this court. The evidence of the investigators, *corroborated in part by the video tape*, would indicate that the respondent has a higher, or more normal, physical activity level than perhaps his evidence would lead one to believe. The fact is, however, that all this evidence was before the trial judge and indeed he said: "I found the evidence of these investigators and the video tape useful as indicating the way in which the plaintiff went about his daily affairs, and I find it of assistance in assessing the evidence given by the plaintiff and his description of his disabilities.[33] [Emphasis added.]

9.2.1.3   The Persuasiveness of Videotape Surveillance Evidence

There have been cases wherein the courts have commented upon the persuasiveness of surveillance evidence provided by a private investigator to assist the finding of facts. For example, in a Nova Scotia case a plaintiff alleged that she was unable to hang clothes since the date of the accident because of the injuries she had incurred. However, the court, upon reflecting upon the video and still photos admitted into evidence, held that the evidence

---

32   *Army & Navy Department Store (Western Ltd.) v. Retail Wholesale & Department Store Union, Local No. 535* (1950), 97 C.C.C. 258 (B.C.S.C.).

33   *Guy v. Trizec Equities Limited* (1978), 26 N.S.R. (2d) 1 (S.C.A.D.).

clashed with that of the person shown in the video and indicated that the plaintiff was inclined to exaggerate.[34]

In an Alberta case, a plaintiff complained of stiffness in her neck and lack of mobility. However, surveillance evidence showed her to walk energetically, turn her head with no apparent restriction and load bags of groceries into the trunk of her car. Based on this surveillance evidence, the court rejected the testimony of the plaintiff, two of her friends, and the plaintiff's medical expert.[35]

In an Ontario case, a court summed up the beneficial nature of surveillance evidence:

> It must be remembered that the purpose of such surveillance is either verification or contradiction. A trial is a search for truth and surveillance is a tool used in pursuit thereof. A truthful witness will not suffer by having been under surveillance; prevarication and exaggeration may be exposed.[36]

Videotape surveillance evidence is made more persuasive when it is used in conjunction with other integrity tools such as lifestyle questionnaires, interviews with neighbours, and acquaintances and medical examinations.[37]

9.2.1.4   Video Surveillance Evidence versus Medical Opinion

One of the main reasons to use videotape surveillance evidence is to discredit a medical opinion a plaintiff seeks to have a court accept. In a case from Alberta, a court held:

> The videotape evidence and surrounding evidence is very demonstrative of the plaintiff's condition . . . The observations I have made of the plaintiff on the videotape are inescapable . . . The relationship between the medical evidence and what a trier of fact sees on a videotape is an important one. Clearly, where medical evidence is specifically directed at certain points of the videotape, the trier of fact must accept the medical evidence or the preponderance of that medical evidence. General powers, however, of observation are as much within the purview of the trier of fact as anyone else, medically trained or otherwise.
>
> . . .
>
> Had it not been, perhaps, for the compelling videotape evidence, the plaintiff's evidence delivered in a relatively creditable manner, supported, in part, by medical evidence . . . may well have left the court with the option of accepting the claim being put forward in large measure. The unrehearsed, spontaneous nature of the videotape evidence after the plaintiff's evidence of her predicament, however, changed that assessment and put the plaintiff directly in a position of a credibility problem of serious magnitude.

---

34   *Mitchell v. Trainor*, above note 11.

35   *Stevens v. Okrainec*, [1997] A.J. No. 1158 (Q.B.). See also *Laube v. Juchli*, [1997] A.J. No. 1029 (Q.B.); *Alnashmi v. Arabi*, [2000] 8 W.W.R. 710 (Alta. Q.B.).

36   *Murray v. Woodstock General Hospital Trust* (1988), 64 O.R. (2d) 458 at 463 (H.C.J.).

37   *Ritch v. Sun Life Assurance Company of Canada* (1998), 8 C.C.L.I. (3d) 228 (Ont. Gen. Div.).

The medical evidence in support of the plaintiff simply does not, in my view, overcome these difficulties . . . Clearly the evidence as depicted by that videotape and surrounding evidence indicates that there is little residual or continuing problem, if any, with the plaintiff as a result of the injuries sustained in the motor vehicle accident.[38]

In short, frequently a court will prefer objective videotape surveillance evidence provided by a private investigator over medical evidence based predominantly on subjective complainants of a plaintiff given to his or her doctor.[39]

That is not to say that surveillance evidence necessarily undermines medical evidence in every case. In an action from Ontario, the defence did not cross-examine the plaintiff's medical witness with their surveillance videotape, choosing rather to submit it as part of the case for the defence. The court held that since the plantiff's medical witness was not given a chance to see the videotape and thereby change his opinion, the medical evidence was not directly challenged and therefore not discredited.[40]

9.2.1.5   Limits of Videotape Surveillance Evidence – Recording Pain

Although it is commonly accepted that videotape surveillance evidence is admissible for the purpose of impeaching the plaintiff's credibility with regard to the extent of his or her injuries, the courts have also been careful to point out that videotapes cannot record pain.[41] One commentator observed that although a videotape may show a man digging in his garden, it cannot show the pain and discomfort he may have felt while doing it, nor will it show how he may have felt the next day after his over-optimistic efforts.[42] Another commentator noted that counsel should not have an investigator giving a medical opinion such as "He looked perfectly normal to me" or "He did not look to be in pain." Such evidence is valueless. The investigator is not in that person's shoes.[43]

9.2.1.6   Other Reasons for Using Videotape Surveillance Evidence

In many cases, video surveillance conducted by private investigators will simply confirm what the plaintiff alleges. In other cases, the video surveillance will indicate that the claims made are in part exaggerated. Notwithstanding that it is only on the odd occasion that a private investigator's video surveillance will provide proof of a black-and-white fraud, many litigators believe that surveillance is money well spent to verify a claim one way or another, especially in motor vehicle and personal injury cases.[44]

---

38 *Laube v. Juchli*, above note 35.

39 *Mitchell v. Trainor,* above note 11; *Ritch v. Sun Life Assurance Company of Canada*, above note 37.

40 *Valletta v. MacKinnon*, [1992] O.J. No. 1889 (Gen. Div.).

41 *Stevens v. Okrainec*, above note 35.

42 G. LaMarca, "Overintrusive Surveillance of Plaintiffs in Personal Injury Cases" (1986) 35 Defense L.J. 603 at 619.

43 C. Kentridge, "Surveillance Must Be Used with Caution" *Law Times* (1–7 June 1998).

44 *Ibid.*, quoting Bill Scott, a litigation partner at McCarthy Tetrault's Toronto office.

9.2.1.7 Reasons for Not Using Videotape Surveillance Evidence

Although the verification aspect of video surveillance evidence is generally agreed upon, not all litigators believe that such evidence will have its desired impact at trial. One senior litigator warned that, unless it is very compelling, surveillance evidence is not of much value. He commented that video surveillance is very distasteful to most people, especially in jury trials; that most people find the idea of someone snooping abhorrent, and that unless the evidence is unequivocal, it may be wiser not to use it. He also acknowledged, however, that in cases such as soft tissue injuries, insurers do not have many options to test the reliability of the plaintiff.[45]

Another reason for not seeking video surveillance evidence is if the plaintiff is aware that he or she is likely to be taped. This is more likely to occur after a defendant discloses to the plaintiff that surveillance reports exist as required by the discovery process.[46]

9.2.2 General Admissibility Considerations

As mentioned in the introduction to this chapter, the criteria applicable to the issue of admissibility are relevance; reliability, that is, the accuracy in representing the facts and the absence of any intention to mislead; verification under oath; and judicial discretion.[47] These criteria apply equally to videotape and photographic evidence.

9.2.2.1 Relevance

A private investigator's videotape surveillance and photographs are relevant in an insurance case refuting a plaintiff's medical evidence, whether it be his or her subjective account or that of a medical practitioner called by the plaintiff or the defence. It is also relevant to the issue of damages.[48] Private investigator videotape surveillance evidence has also been held relevant to the same issues in labour arbitration[49] and Workers' Compensation cases.[50] Surveillance evidence is also relevant for the purpose of clarifying oral testimony. It has been held that relevancy is to be determined by an inquiry as to whether or not a witness would be permitted to describe the scenes filmed.[51]

---

45 *Ibid.*, in an interview with David Neill, a litigation partner at Thompson Rogers in Toronto.

46 *Ritch v. Sun Life Assurance Company of Canada*, above note 37.

47 *R. v. Creemer and Cormier*, [1968] 1 C.C.C. 14 (N.S.S.C.A.D.); *Ball v. Vincent,* [1993] O.J. No. 3289 (Gen. Div.).

48 *Ball v. Vincent, ibid.*

49 See *Re Toronto Star Newspaper Ltd. and Southern Ontario Newspaper Guild Local 87* (1992), 30 L.A.C. (4th) 306 (Ont.) (Springate). In this case, the arbitrator relied upon *Army & Navy Department Store (Western Ltd.) v. Retail Wholesale & Department Store Union Loc. No. 535*, [1950] 2 D.L.R. 850 (B.C.S.C.), and upon *Greenough v. Woodstream Corp.*, [1991] 24 A.C.W.S. (3d) 1253 (Ont. Gen. Div.).

50 *Decision No. 918/941*, [1995] O.W.C.A.T.D. No. 170.

51 *Simpson Timber Co. (Sask.) Ltd. v. Bonville*, [1986] 5 W.W.R. 180 (Sask. Q.B.).

9.2.2.2   Reliability

For surveillance videotape to be admissible as evidence at trial, a court must find that the evidence tendered is reliable. There are a number of aspects of reliability discussed here, including the identity of the subject party, the quality of notes made at the time of the observations to support the videotape surveillance evidence, editing concerns, the hearsay rule, the duration of the surveillance, and issues pertaining to digital enhancement.

9.2.2.2.1 Identifying the Subject Party

One of the requirements for admissibility is correctly identifying the person who is the subject of the surveillance. In a Nova Scotia case, the plaintiff alleged that while most of the still photos tendered as evidence were in fact her, some of the photos were that of her sister. The court, however, chose not to accept the testimony of the plaintiff. The court held that from his own observations, the party in the pictures appeared to be the plaintiff. Furthermore, the private investigator's observations were aided by the use of binoculars. Accordingly, the allegation of improper identification of the plaintiff was rejected.[52]

In an Ontario case, a court allowed the identification of the subject party even when the party was not identifiable in the film with the naked eye. The court held the videotapes accurately depicted the activities of the plaintiff, albeit at a distance. The court further found that the private investigators who had the plaintiff under surveillance and who operated the camera could testify as to what they saw in many cases through binoculars as the camera ran. The court concluded that in this way the film was corroborated by oral evidence.[53]

There have been cases, however, where the identification of the subject party has been rejected. In a British Columbia case, evidence was presented by a private investigator hired by the employer. The employee later brought evidence corroborated by others working at the logging operation that the private investigator had identified the logging contractor who was using the employee's truck and not the employee himself. Upon hearing this evidence, the arbitrator dismissed the employer's claim that the employee was engaged in fraudulent conduct against his employer.[54]

9.2.2.2.2 Notes and Reports Verifying Videotape Surveillance

The Insurance Corporation of British Columbia (ICBC) Private Investigators Guidelines provide a good overview of what is required of a private investigator's notes and reports pertaining to an insurance investigation. They state:

> All reports submitted to the ICBC should be an objective accounting of relevant facts. It is not necessary to repeat information given by the adjuster except to confirm instructions, nor should you include material which does not add value or clarity to the report. An account of

---

52 *Mitchell v. Trainor*, above note 11. See also *R. v. Nikolovski*, [1996] 3 S.C.R. 1197, and *R. v. Leaney and Rawlinson*, [1989] 2 S.C.R. 393.

53 *Ball v. Vincent*, above note 47.

54 *Finlay Forest Industries Ltd. v. I.W.A. Canada Local 1-424*, [1989] B.C.D.L.A. 190-18 (B.C.). See also *Guy v. Grosfield*, [1994] O.J. No. 1965 (Gen. Div.), and *Parkes v. Kaneff Properties Limited*, [1997] O.J. No. 2037 (Gen. Div.).

the investigation written in plain language is all that is required. Reports must not contain an investigator's opinions, nor unsubstantiated and gratuitous comments.[55]

In addition to these guidelines, private investigation agency reports should not include statements that cannot be substantiated from a field investigator's notes. In a case from Ontario, field surveillance investigators made notes that they provided to a supervisor. The supervisor used the notes to prepare reports summarizing a claimant's activities and abilities. In several instances, the supervisor elaborated on what the court labelled as "his investigator's rather sketchy notes."

For example, the notes of one investigator stated: "Wednesday, September 30, 1992 13:20 — subject departs in passenger seat of taxi." The supervisor translated this passage in his report as follows: "She walks a short distance from the doorway to an awaiting taxi cab parked on her driveway. She boards the rear seating area of the cab in a normal manner, lowering herself from a standing position to a seated position in one continuous maneuver." The supervisor explained this elaboration on the basis that his investigators are trained to record "abnormal" movements and since no abnormality was noted, the subject must be assumed to have boarded the taxi in a "normal" manner.

The court held these extrapolations seriously undermined the value of the investigation agency's report. He held the supervisor not only summarized the observations of his investigator, but he also elaborated on them. Accordingly, the court concluded that little, if any, weight could be placed upon the supervisor's written reports of his field investigator's observations. The court accepted the limited evidence contained in the field investigator's notes where the investigator recorded that the plaintiff remained inactive or indicated that she visited a bank. The court concluded, however, the investigative evidence tended to confirm, rather than undermine the plaintiff's claims of disability.[56]

Other factors relevant to notes and reports are authorship and how the notes or reports came about. In an Ontario Workers' Compensation case, a panel noted that a private investigator's report submitted as evidence did not mention who the author was. Further, the report only referred to the impugned worker as "the subject." The panel was also concerned about a twenty-two-minute conversation between a worker and the investigator wherein it was not apparent whether the account was reconstructed from the investigator's memory or transcribed from an electronic recording. Additionally, it could not be ascertained whether the report was transcribed from notes dictated simultaneously as the events occurred, if it was prepared entirely from memory, or if it was an expanded text from shorthand notes recorded intermittently during the day.

Pertaining to the investigation itself, the panel noted that nothing was known about the conditions under which this investigator was retained, what kind of reports he or she was assigned to prepare and what background information he or she was provided with before commencing this assignment. It was also not known whether the dates provided in the report were the only days during which the investigator conducted this surveillance and

---

55   Effective May 1999 at 5.
56   *Turner v. Economical Mutual Insurance Company* (14 May 1999), F.S.C.O. Judgment No. A-012411 (Ont. F.S.C.).

what criteria, if any, factored in the selection of the particular dates for this surveillance activity. Because the report lacked this information, the panel adjourned the case and subpoenaed the private investigator to testify.[57]

9.2.2.2.3 The Editing of Surveillance Videotapes

One of the primary concerns of the courts in accepting videotape evidence is its susceptibility to manipulation, thus reducing or eliminating its usefulness to a court. In a Nova Scotia case, a court held that surveillance videotapes must be received with reservations because of the possibility that they may be edited by the person who operated the camera.[58]

In an Ontario case, a plaintiff argued that because there were occasions during the surveillance of him where he was not videotaped, the admissibility of the videotapes would be unfair or alternatively would give an inaccurate impression of the true state of his affairs. The defence argued that the reason the plaintiff was not videotaped at all times during the surveillance was because at certain points, the private investigator was driving his vehicle following the plaintiff, and on other occasions the plaintiff would come into view unexpectedly and leave before the camera could be operated again. The court noted that during each of these occasions the private investigator could describe what the plaintiff was doing and there was no evidence that the private investigators edited out parts of the tape that showed the plaintiff in a more favourable light. The court further noted that any manipulation or editing of the film was denied by the private investigators under cross-examination. On this basis, the court held that the omissions in the videotape did not taint the films with inaccuracy or unfairness. The videotapes were admitted into evidence.[59]

An example of the courts taking a very dim view of a private investigator's videotape surveillance evidence comes from British Columbia. In this case the court increased costs by 60 percent against the defendant insurers because the private investigator had repeatedly turned off the camera when the plaintiff's activities were not beneficial to the defendant. The court held that the result was that the surveillance evidence was neither a fair nor an accurate representation of the plaintiff's condition. The court noted that the private investigator claimed this conduct was not intentional. However, he went further to state:

> If I had had evidence of a deliberate attempt . . . to deliver misleading surveillance evidence by either party, I would not have hesitated in ordering special costs against the party tendering such evidence. Such conduct would clearly be reprehensible . . . and deserving of rebuke . . .
> In my judgment it is important to consider conduct which may preclude early resolution or unduly protract litigation.[60]

A court has also made similar findings in a Nova Scotia case where a private investigator turned off the video camera immediately after some activity by the plaintiff which prevented the court from seeing how the plaintiff reacted to it.[61] Likewise, in a criminal case in Ontario, a court overturned a conviction based on what it viewed as improper editing of

---

57 *Decision No. 918/941,* [1995] O.W.C.A.T.D. No. 170.
58 *Smith v. Avis Transport of Canada Limited and Harvie* (1979), 35 N.S.R. (2d) 652 at 673 (S.C.).
59 *Ball v. Vincent,* above note 47.
60 *Houseman v. Sewell,* [1997] B.C.J. No. 1478 (S.C.).
61 *Clark v. O'Brien,* [1995] N.S.J. No. 8 (S.C.).

surveillance videotape by a private investigator when the camera was turned off immedi-ately after the taking of some inculpating activity.[62] For a court to rely upon videotape evi-dence, it is clear that it must contain footage both before and after the parts that are being relied upon to address an issue in an action.

9.2.2.2.4 The Speed at Which the Videotape Evidence Is Depicted

Videotape evidence may not be admissible if it is not depicted at the actual speed of the event it is portraying. In *R. v. Maloney (No. 2)*,[63] the accused, Detroit Red Wing Don Maloney, was charged with assault causing bodily harm resulting from an incident with Toronto Maple Leaf Brian Glennie. The Crown sought to introduce a videotape film of the game. Part of the film was shown in slow motion. Counsel for the defence argued the film should not be admitted into evidence.

The court held that videotape reproductions of film are admissible on the same basis as are still photographs; that is, if they represent a true and accurate reproduction of the events depicted. The court held that "true" means consistent with fact and agreeing with reality. Accordingly, film depicted at actual speed in the proper sequence that the events occur is admissible. However, where time is a crucial factor, as in this case, slow-motion film and film containing excerpts that are out of sequence are inadmissible as not meeting this test. The court also noted that if counsel from both sides agreed that the film as edit-ed would assist the jury in determining the proper sequence of events and that the distor-tion could be explained, the film could be admitted on consent.[64]

In cases of videotape surveillance taken at strike scenes, the courts have made similar findings. In a British Columbia case, a court noted that if the speed of the film was accel-erated, it would indicate a mob scene, while if it was run at a normal rate of speed, it might appear the picketing was conducted in a lawful manner.[65]

---

62 *R. v. Tran*, [1995] O.J. No. 1513 (Gen. Div.).

63 (1976), 29 C.C.C. (2d) 431 (Ont. Co. Ct.). See also *R. v. (Tiger) Williams* (1977), 35 C.C.C. (2d) 103 (Ont. Co. Ct.).

64 Justice LeSage conducted a thorough review of the jurisprudence in deciding this case. At the end of the judgment, as an appendix, he cited the Canadian and American authorities he ref-erenced. The Canadian cases include *Nag v. McKeller* (1969), 4 D.L.R. (3d) 53 (Ont. C.A.); *R. v. Creemer and Cormier*, [1968] 1 C.C.C. 14 (N.S.S.C.A.D.); *Niznick v. Johnson* (1961), 28 D.L.R. (2d) 541 (Man. Q.B.); *Montreal Tramways Co. v. Beauregard* (1939), 67 Que. K.B. 578 (C.A.); *Army & Navy Department Store (Western Ltd.) v. Retail Wholesale & Department Store Union Local No. 535* (1950), 97 C.C.C. 258 (B.C.S.C.); *R. v. Sim* (1954), 108 C.C.C. 380 (Alta. S.C.); *Chayne v. Schwartz*, [1954] Que. S.C. 123 (S.C.); *R. v. Gallant* (1965), 47 C.R. 309 (P.E.I.S.C.); *R. v. O'Donnell* (1936), 65 C.C.C. 299 (Ont. C.A.); *R. v. Green* (1972), 9 C.C.C. (2d) 289 (N.S.A.D.); D. Cragg Ross, "Motion Pictures as Evidence" 12 Chitty L. Rev. 249; P. Meyor, "Evidence in the Future" 51 Can. Bar Rev. 107; B.A. MacFarlane, "Photographic Evidence: Its Probative Value at Trial and the Judicial Discretion to Exclude it from Evidence" 16 Crim. L.Q. 149.

65 *Army & Navy Department Store (Western Ltd.) v. Retail Wholesale & Department Store Union, Local No. 535* (1950), 97 C.C.C. 258 (B.C.S.C.).

9.2.2.2.5   The Hearsay Rule

Challenges to the admissibility of videotape surveillance evidence have been made under the rule against hearsay evidence. For example, in an employment case from Saskatchewan, a preliminary objection was made to the admission of three affidavits offered by the applicant employer. The affidavits related to evidence depicted on videotape of a certain newscast on a television station. To the respondent's arguments against the videotapes' admissibility, the court held:

> At the heart of the admissibility of these videotape films is whether I am satisfied that there is some evidence upon which I might reasonably be certain that they are an accurate reproduction of what they purport to reproduce and that they are of a content and quality and that they will not mislead or prejudice but rather assist in providing relevant evidence. Any controversy as to accuracy goes to weight and not admissibility. This evidence, with respect, has nothing to do with the hearsay rule as suggested by counsel for the respondents. Is the tape authentic? If so, it is admissible. It is admissible. So is the affidavit.
>
> I have considered the "illustrative testimony" or "pictorial testimony theory of videotape films" only. I was not asked to and did not consider the videotape film as a silent witness which "speaks for itself" . . . That is for another day.[66]

Reports of private investigators have also been challenged on the basis of breaching the hearsay rule.[67]

9.2.2.2.6   Duration of the Surveillance

A Canadian commentator reported that one problem with the use of surveillance videotape is that it may not be as accurate as it purports to be if it is conducted for too short a period of time. For example, if the surveillance is only conducted for one day, a claimant may argue that the videotape was taken on a non-representative day or that he or she spent the next two days in the hospital recuperating. To present more credible evidence, surveillance must take place over a longer period of time. Single-day surveillances are generally only useful in those cases where the plaintiff claims that his or her injuries are so severe that he or she cannot work at all.[68]

Another commentator points out that there are many reasons for plaintiffs to attempt to perform certain activities. He reports that surveillance often penalizes the non-malingering plaintiff who attempts to return to a normal life as quickly as possible but has misjudged his or her physical ability at the particular time. It also penalizes the non-malingering plaintiff who, despite the actual disability, simply performs an activity out of frustration, ego dynamics, or social pressure. As such, an investigator must have enough material in an

---

66   *Simpson Timber Co. (Sask.) Ltd. v. Bonville*, [1986] 5 W.W.R. 180 (Sask. Q.B.). See also *Re Toronto Star Newspaper Ltd. and Southern Ontario Newspaper Guild Local 87* (1992), 30 L.A.C. (4th) 306 (Ont.) (Springate).

67   *First Choice Haircutters Canada Inc. v. Miller*, [1997] O.J. No. 1940 (Gen. Div.).

68   E.F. Geddes, "The Private Investigator and the Right to Privacy" (1989) 17 Alta. L. Rev. 256 at 267.

activity report to show the context in which a certain activity was performed in order for the activity to be of probative value.[69]

In cases where surveillance indicates that the degree of disability or impairment is different from what the plaintiff has claimed, it is the opinion of some practitioners that a minimum of two or three consecutive days of surveillance is required.[70] In a Workers' Compensation case, a panel has held that four days of surveillance are required.[71]

9.2.2.2.7 Digital Enhancement

Digital filming is the latest technology and has been the subject of little judicial discussion. In a criminal case from British Columbia, a court held that for identification purposes, the isolation, extraction, enhancement, and presentation of surveillance images is admissible as long as the original is presented with the augmented pictures.[72] In another criminal case involving digital surveillance evidence, a court held that both still images from videotapes and enhanced video stills are admissible. It further held that digitization and video analysis assist the court, and that a trier of fact may draw his or her own conclusions from the manipulation of an original recording.[73]

9.2.2.3   Verification/Authentication by a Witness

Generally, videotapes and pictures are only admissible if a proper foundation has been laid as to their accuracy.[74] In a labour case, a court held that a videotape, like a tape recording, should only be admitted into evidence if its authenticity is established and if it is shown to be a true and unaltered record that has properly been identified.[75] Such a finding has also been made in Workers' Compensation cases[76] and in the criminal realm.[77] Arguably, this is part of the reliability test, but for instructive purposes, it is covered separately.[78]

One issue that has been raised is whether the private investigator who actually took the videotape or picture is required to verify its authenticity, or if a third party can provide this evidence to a court. It has been held that videotapes can only be received as non-verbal expressions of testimony of a witness. Accordingly, it is immaterial who prepared the videotape, provided it is represented to the court by a competent and qualified witness, and as a representation of his or her knowledge. In other words, the person who took the film

69 G. LaMarca, "Overintrusive Surveillance of Plaintiffs in Personal Injury Cases" (1986) 35 Defense L.J. 603 at 619.

70 C. Kentridge, "Surveillance Must Be Used with Caution" *Law Times* (1–7 June 1998), quoting Bill Scott, a litigation partner at McCarthy Tetrault's Toronto office.

71 *Decision No. 918/941*, [1995] O.W.C.A.T.D. No. 170.

72 *R. v. Coelen*, [1999] B.C.J. No. 2867 (S.C.).

73 *R. v. Cooper* (February 2000), (B.C.S.C.) [unreported]. For a comprehensive review of the law of visual evidence, see Elliott Goldstein at <http://www.videoevidence.ca>.

74 See *Niznick v. Johnson*, [1961] 34 W.W.R. 101 at 107 (Man. Q.B.); *Teno v. Arnold* (1975), 7 O.R. (2d) 276 (H.C.); *Hauer v. Hauer* (1959), 18 D.L.R. (2d) 742 (Sask. C.A.).

75 *Simpson Timber Co. (Sask.) Ltd. v. Bonville*, above note 66.

76 *Decision No. 918/941*, [1995] O.W.C.A.T.D. No. 170.

77 *R. v. Sommerville*, [1963] 3 C.C.C. 240 (Sask. C.A.).

78 See above Section 9.2.2.2.2 — Notes and Reports Verifying Videotape Surveillance.

is not required to testify to its authenticity. However, someone is required to testify where and under what circumstances the videotape or picture was taken, and that it accurately portrays what it shows.[79] Obviously, the best person to do this would be the person who made the tape.[80]

9.2.2.4   Judicial Discretion: Prejudicial Effect Exceeds Probative Value

The final common law argument commonly made against the admissibility of videotape surveillance evidence is that its prejudicial effect is greater than its probative value, a factor sometimes referred to as judicial discretion.

In a Workers' Compensation case from Ontario, a panel adopted the view of Sopinka and Lederman pertaining to the relationship between prejudicial effect and the admissibility of evidence. They held that evidence may be excluded, even though it is relevant, if it is of slight probative value to a fact in issue in relation to its prejudicial effect.[81] The panel acknowledged that evidence brought by an employer to defeat a claim is by nature prejudicial against the employee. However, the question is not whether the report is prejudicial on its face, but is it so prejudicial as to warrant its exclusion from evidence.[82]

In personal injury insurance cases, courts have found that a private investigator's videotape evidence is of sufficient probative value to support its admission if the evidence depicted on the videotape addresses the core issue of the injuries to the plaintiff, and in particular the degree and nature of the incapacity as a result of those injuries.[83]

9.2.2.4.1   Subjective Comments Contained in Surveillance Reports

The issue of prejudicial effect has been raised with regard to subjective comments made by private investigators in their reports. In a Workers' Compensation case in Ontario, a private investigator included such descriptive phrases as "a normal unencumbered gait," a "hurried pace," and "neither undue exertion nor visible discomfort" in his report. The report also made reference to a wide variety of movements made by the subject as "without any visible medical aids." However, the report also mentioned the subject was wearing an arm support under his left shirt sleeve and that in conversation with the investigator, the subject mentioned that he was wearing a brace on his left knee without which he would be unable to walk. The panel held that subjective comments made by the private investigator in his report were of little probative value, and that to the extent that such interpretive comments were embedded into a text that was otherwise detached and clinical, they were potentially misleading.[84]

---

79 *Niznick v. Johnson*, above note 74.

80 *Ball v. Vincent*, above note 47.

81 Sopinka, Lederman, & Bryant, *The Law of Evidence in Canada*, above note 1, chapter 6; J.D. Ewart, *Documentary Evidence in Canada* (Toronto: Carswell, 1984), chapter 2; and the *Ontario Evidence Act*, R.S.O, 1990, s. 35.

82 *Decision No. 918/941*, [1995] O.W.C.A.T.D. No. 170.

83 *Ball v. Vincent*, above note 47.

84 *Decision No. 918/941*, [1995] O.W.C.A.T.D. No. 170.

9.2.2.4.2 Audio Narratives Contained on Surveillance Videotapes

In a Workers' Compensation case, a surveillance videotape was submitted as evidence which contained a running narrative of mostly subjective editorializations and interpretations of the private investigator. The panel held that the tape was admissible without the audio narration, as the investigator's speculative comments were of insufficient probative value to warrant inclusion.[85] In an insurance case, a plaintiff agreed to the admission of surveillance videotapes but submitted that no weight should be given to interpretative commentary provided by the private investigators.[86]

9.2.2.4.3 Selective Recordings

It has been successfully argued in cases where the videotapes only represented short and selective recordings of the activities included in the surveillance report that the prejudicial effect outweighs the probative value. This issue is related to reliability and is discussed more fully above in Section 9.2.2.2.3 — The Editing of Surveillance Videotapes.

9.2.2.5   The *Charter* and Surveillance Videotapes

The issue of collecting video surveillance evidence being akin to the government action of arrest and therefore attracting *Charter* considerations has also been addressed by the courts.[87] In a criminal case from Manitoba, the issue was whether the *Charter* rights of employees had been violated when the store management conducted a surreptitious video surveillance of them in a public washroom. The court concluded that the *Charter* did not apply to searches carried out by strictly private actors. The court noted that had the surveillance been carried out by an agency of the state, it would have constituted an unreasonable search under section 8 of the *Charter*. However, surveillance, unlike arrest, by itself is not deemed to be an action of the state.[88]

Although breaches of *Charter* rights may not apply to surveillance conducted by investigators in the private sector, as seen in the discussions below, a breach of *Charter* "values" may.

9.2.3   Insurance Litigation

In the following sections, specific concerns to the admissibility of private investigative surveillance evidence is discussed with reference to various types of litigation. Pertaining to insurance litigation, the topics reviewed are *Charter* arguments, insurer no-contact clauses, videotape from inside a residence, public view video in bad taste, unsatisfactory surveillance, and an insurer's duty of good faith.

9.2.3.1   The *Charter* and Insurance Surveillance Evidence

The first and only known case where a private investigation agency has had an action brought against it for *Charter* violations while conducting surveillance on an insurance investigation is *Druken v. RG Fewer & Associates Inc.*[89]

---

85   *Decision No. 688/87*, [1987] 6 W.C.A.T.R. 198 (O.W.C.A.T.).
86   *Venier v. Osei and Guardian Insurance Company of Canada*, [1999] O.J. No. 4946 (S.C.J.).
87   Recall the *Lerke* case from Section 4.1.1.1 — Agent of the State versus Private Citizen.
88   *R. v. Swanarchuk*, [1990] M.J. No. 686 (Q.B.).
89   [1998] N.J. No. 312 (S.C.).

In this case, the plaintiff (Druken) had been involved in a motor vehicle accident. The insurance company of the other party in the accident retained a private investigation agency (Fewer) to obtain video and photographic evidence to verify the validity of Druken's claims. Fewer conducted surveillance of Druken while she was conducting personal business. Unfortunately, Druken's neighbour noticed something was amiss and informed her that she was being followed. As Druken was alarmed for her safety, she drove quickly through traffic. Fewer followed her at the same high speed. Druken then saw her father in the lot of a local business. She stopped and told him what was taking place. When Druken's father drove over to Fewer's van, he quickly sped away. Druken reported the incident to the police. The police identified the owner of the van as Fewer and informed Druken that he was a private investigator.

Among other claims, Druken brought action for breach of privacy under the *Charter*. The court held the main issue to be decided was what application the *Charter* has to private litigation. The court quoted the Supreme Court of Canada in *Hill v. Church of Scientology of Toronto*[90] where it was stated:

> It is important not to import into private litigation the analysis which applies in cases involving government action. The most a private litigant can do is argue that the common law is inconsistent with *Charter* values. It is very important to draw the distinction between *Charter* rights and *Charter* values. Care must be taken not to expand the application of the *Charter* beyond that established by s.32(1) . . . [to] creating new causes of action . . . Therefore, in the context of civil litigation involving only private parties, the *Charter* will apply to the common law only to the extent that the common law is found to be inconsistent with *Charter* values.

Based on this passage, the court in *Druken* recognized that one such value is the interest affirmed by section 8 of the *Charter* of each person in privacy. The court held that in the Canadian system of justice, a litigant must accept such intrusions upon her right to privacy as are necessary to enable a judge or jury to get to the truth and render a just verdict. However, the mere commencement of an action does not grant a defendant a licence to delve into private aspects of a plaintiff's life which need not be probed for the proper disposition of the litigation. Accordingly, to reflect *Charter* values, the admissibility of videotape evidence depends on a balancing of the private interest of the plaintiff against the rights of a defendant to fully defend its case in litigation, bearing in mind the overall goal of the trial process is to discover the truth.

Applying this statement of law to the facts, the court found that the videotapes of the defendants recorded information that could have been observed and was observed by members of the public. The court noted that there was nothing in the *Charter* cases to suggest a *carte blanche* right to privacy. The court also found that the defendant's videotaping of the plaintiff was by virtue of a contract with an insurance company. The court noted that it has been recognized in law that surveillance is a legitimate tool in defence of personal injury claims to impeach the credibility of a plaintiff. Based on these findings, the

---

90   [1995] 2 S.C.R. 1130.

court held that the actions of the defendants reflected *Charter* values. The court concluded by stating that surveillance without purpose would engage different considerations.

Based on this case, a succinct statement of the law is that a private investigator's video surveillance evidence will not attract *Charter* scrutiny if (1) the surveillance is observable by any member of the public; (2) if the investigator is under retainer at the time of conducting the surveillance; and (3) if the reason for acquiring the surveillance evidence is for a proper purpose. If these conditions are not met, however, it is within judicial discretion to not admit a private investigator's videotape surveillance into evidence for infringing upon a *Charter* value.

9.2.3.2 Insurer No-Contact Clauses

Some insurance contracts contain clauses that state that after an insured has retained counsel, all further contact between the insurer and/or its agents must be made directly and only to the insured's counsel. The following scenario demonstrates the difficulty such clauses may cause.

An investigator is assigned by an insurer to conduct surveillance on a suspected malingering claimant. The claimant alleges to be paraplegic and totally wheelchair bound. The claimant lives in a very rural area. His driveway is quite long and it is not possible to see the home or yard area due to woods and a hill. However, neither the driveway nor any area of the home or acreage have any "keep out" or "no trespassing" signs. Just down from the claimant's home and acreage is a real estate sign stating the property is for sale. No one is home or present in the area of the listed property.

The investigator drives into the claimant's driveway to ask about the property for sale; that is, is it theirs, what do they know about it, how large a parcel is it, can it be walked on to look at, area schools, and type of neighbours. The investigator is alone and his investigative equipment is hidden from view. The investigator observes the claimant walking in the garage area of his home. The investigator exits his vehicle and has a ten-minute conversation with him. The claimant is observed standing, walking, and lifting items. No wheelchair, walker, or other persons are observed in the area. The insurance contract contains a no-contact clause. An issue that arises is: Is this evidence legally obtained?

American practitioners state such evidence has been ruled inadmissible. If the claimant is represented by an attorney, any direct contact such as talking to the claimant by a private investigator is interference with that attorney's representation. There is also the issue of trespass to the claimant's property. Although trespass will not nullify admissibility, if the private investigator shows up to testify at trail and the claimant remembers him, the claimant's action may very well expand to an invasion of privacy, interference of representation, and a trespass claim.[91]

9.2.3.3 Videotape Obtained from Inside a Residence

The admissibility of videotape evidence from the cases reported where private investigators have entered people's homes under pretexts and obtained videotape surveillance evi-

---

91   John Grogan: <http://www.JohnGrogan.com> and e-mail: <jgroganpi@aol.com>. Richard W.J. Baxter, CFE: <http://www.baxtereyes.com> and e-mail: <ricbaxter@baxtereyes.com>.

dence is not consistent. For example, in a case from Alberta it was reported that a private investigator gained entrance into the insured's residence on the pretext of having her complete his income tax return. While inside the residence, the private investigator videotaped the insured with a hidden camera. Videotape footage revealed the insured in her residence sitting casually in a chair and speaking to someone she believed to be a client. The insured was also videotaped showing prospective tenants a duplex that she was renting. With regard to evidentiary concerns, the court reported that no issue was taken during the trial concerning the admissibility of the videotapes. Accordingly, the videotapes were properly admissible including those taken inside her residence.[92]

In a case from British Columbia, the plaintiff, a nineteen-year-old hairdressing student, reported suffering soft-tissue injuries, urinary incontinence, and pain to her neck and back as the result of a traffic accident. Later she reported she could not perform full-time work as a hairdresser because she could not hold her hands up as required, do fine work with her fingers, or remain on her feet for extended periods of time. The defendant's insurer hired a private investigator to establish the extent of the plaintiff's injuries. The private investigator arranged to have a haircut at the plaintiff's house. When this evidence was presented at trial, the plaintiff blamed the private investigator for being pushy and insisting on an appointment. Nevertheless, the court admitted the evidence and held that the plaintiff was not candid in disclosing the extent to which she ran a hairdressing business out of her home.[93]

In a case from Ontario, an insurer sought to introduce a private investigator's reports, photographs, and video surveillance obtained during a lengthy investigation of an insured on an income replacement disability claim. During this investigation, private investigators were welcomed into the insured's home under the pretext of seeking her professional printing services on one occasion and seeking piano lessons on another. The insured sought to exclude portions of the investigation evidence on the basis that the investigative techniques were unduly invasive of her privacy. The insurer argued that these were routine investigative techniques and were justified because the insured was conducting her business out of her home. The arbitrator held the entry into the insured's home under the pretext was unduly intrusive. The arbitrator further held that it was inappropriate for the private investigators to do more than simply observe or record her activities; that it is inappropriate to lure a claimant into activities they do not initiate. As the investigation was an unnecessarily intrusive breach of the insured's reasonable expectation of privacy, the arbitrator held the evidence was inadmissible.[94]

In another Ontario case, an adjudicator excluded video surveillance of the interior of the applicant's home after 10:00 p.m. on the basis that the breach of privacy outweighed whatever probative value the tape contained.[95]

---

92   *Stevens v. Okrainec*, [1997] A.J. No. 1158 (Q.B.).

93   *Armstrong v. Oliveria*, [1992] B.C.J. No. 2003 (S.C.).

94   *Turner v. Economical Mutual Insurance Company* (14 May 1999), F.S.C.O. Judgment No. A-012411 (Ont. F.S.C.).

95   *Levy v. Traders General Insurance* (30 June 1998), O.I.C. A96-001590.

In a case from Scotland, a private investigator gained entry into a home under the pretext of being a researcher investigating the possibility that the subject person might be the beneficiary of an inheritance. Once in the house, he engaged the subject in conversation wherein the subject told him of his activities. In response to this evidence, the court held that he totally deplored the method whereby the private investigator gained entry to the house, being a total deception. He further held that while such methods do not make the evidence inadmissible, the fact that it was wholly uncorroborated and positively contradicted by three witnesses rendered the whole of the evidence worse than useless.[96]

It is worthy of note that in the cases where this sort of evidence was accepted it does not appear that it was actively opposed. And harkening back to the comment of Judge Crompton,[97] it is fair to say that at common law, such evidence would be admissible, although the private investigator's conduct could result in an action against the insurer and private investigator for invasion of privacy, interference of representation and trespass. However, given the recent development of applying *Charter* values to private litigation, it is more likely that if an argument is made for exclusion, a court will disallow such evidence for the reason that it upsets the balance between privacy and the need for truth.[98]

9.2.3.4   Public View Videotape in Bad Taste

The courts have commented on a private investigator's video surveillance that is not illegal or inadmissible but is in poor taste. For example, in an Ontario case, a private investigator observed an insured leave a physiotherapy clinic and then drive a short distance to a cemetery where she parked and walked about 30 yards to her mother's grave. The investigator videotaped the insured at the gravesite. The arbitrator commented that he was troubled by the nature of this evidence. He stated that surveillance is always intrusive by nature, but that videotaping an insured while they are involved in activities as personal as visiting the grave of a loved one is in bad taste. He concluded by stating that if the purpose is to show that the person is more active than he or she claims, surely there will be another opportunity to do the videotaping.[99]

Using a telephoto lens for videotaping into a residence through an open window from a public street, while not illegal or necessarily rendering the evidence inadmissible, is also a practice frowned upon.[100]

9.2.3.5   Unsatisfactory Surveillance

Adams v. Confederation Life Insurance Co.[101] was an action for a declaration that the plaintiff was entitled to benefits under a long-term disability policy issued by the defendant. The plaintiff also sought punitive damages claiming the defendant had acted in bad faith on the

---

96 *Lindsay v. T.N.T. Express (UK) Ltd.*, [1996] Scott J. No. 236 (Scot. Ct. Sess. O.H.).

97 *R. v. Leatham*, [1861-73] All E.R. Rep. Ext. 1646: "It matters not how you get it, even if you steal it, it would be admissible as evidence."

98 *Hill v. Church of Scientology of Toronto*, above note 90.

99 *Puopolo v. Wellington Insurance Co.*, [1996] O.I.C.D. No. 124 (Ontario Insurance Commission).

100 *Levy v. Traders General Insurance*, above note 95.

101 [1994] I.L.R. 1-3096 (Alta. Q.B.).

basis that the insurer staked its case solely on very questionable surveillance evidence. The rehabilitation agreement permitted the plaintiff to work four hours per day up to sixteen hours per week. The insurer tendered surveillance evidence to prove the plaintiff was working in excess of that amount. With regard to the surveillance evidence, the court stated:

> To prove the alleged breaches, the defendant chose to rely on surveillance evidence alone. Realistic assessment of that evidence demonstrates that it fell far short of proving on a balance of probabilities that the plaintiff breached the rehabilitation agreement. The most obvious error of both reports is that they equate attendance at the bookstore with hours of work. None of the investigators were in the store to determine if the plaintiff was in fact working except for three or four very short interludes. Most of the surveillance was conducted from vehicles parked outside the store with totally inadequate visibility of the activities going on in the store. There are no exact details on the attendances of the staff or even their arrival or departure from the store.
>
> The [private investigator's] investigation is highly questionable as to accuracy and detail because of its limited surveillance and because it alleges the plaintiff was at work for two days when she was not there at all . . . The insufficiency of the second surveillance is proven beyond any doubt by the videotapes taken by [the private investigator]. The videotapes, taken mostly from a motor vehicle parked near the front of the bookstore, are mute but graphic evidence of the ineptness and inadequacy of the surveillance conducted of the plaintiff by this investigator. They prove the limited observations of the plaintiff during the term of surveillance. They reveal nothing of the activities within the store or who is on duty. The video of the school book fair shows the plaintiff seated at a table and speaking to the odd person. [The investigator's] observations and inquiries of the school authorities add some detail but are inconclusive as to hours worked or duties performed.
>
> Neither of these reports nor the videos were shown to the medical experts for assessment, and it is obvious why this was not done. They reveal nothing that would provide a basis for evaluation. Nor were the two surveillances of the plaintiff long enough on which to base an accurate assessment of her ability to work in excess of four hours per day or sixteen hours per week on a consistent or any basis.

The court awarded punitive damages of $7,500 against the insurer.

9.2.3.6   An Insurer's Duty of Good Faith

The case often touted as the leading authority on an insurer's duty of good faith is *Whiten v. Pilot Insurance Co.*[102] In this case, the insurer's counsel rejected all reports from independent investigators that a fire was accidental and chose to breach the insurer's duty to pay out on an accidental fire claim. A jury awarded a million dollars in punitive damages on top of the compensatory damages against the insurance company. In this case, the investigator's conduct was not a contributing factor to the claim.

---

102 (1999), 170 D.L.R. (4th) 280 (Ont. C.A.), leave to appeal to the S.C.C. allowed (14 October 1999), Doc. 27229.

The leading case wherein private investigators were a contributing factor in a bad faith finding against an insurer is *Adams v. Confederation Life Insurance Co.*[103] The facts of this case were discussed in the section above. Pertaining to the issue of an insurer's duty of good faith, the court stated:

> It is clear from the authorities that an insurer owes a yet undefined duty of good faith to its insured. It is a duty which in certain circumstances resembles a fiduciary duty but is always governed by fair play in every dealing.
>
> Did the actions of the insurer in this case amount to a breach of its duty of good faith under the principle of *uberrima fides*? My answer is yes. The decision to embark on covert surveillance without reason or cause is obvious from the facts. By this I do not mean to be taken as saying that surveillance is an improper investigative technique for insurers to prove an unmeritorious claim. But in this case . . . the defendant [insurer] had requested and received additional medical information from the attending physician . . . No inquiry or request was made [by the defendant insurer] of the plaintiff to provide any certification of the hours worked. It simply launched an unwarranted and unmerited investigation without reason . . . It acted solely on the basis of two totally inadequate investigative reports.
>
> . . .
>
> During proceedings, the defendant [insurer] applied to this court for an order permitting further medical examinations of the plaintiff for the purpose of evaluating the claim. On receipt of a report favourable to the plaintiff, the defendant again chose to ignore it. It pursued further covert surveillance of the plaintiff without first addressing its concerns to the plaintiff or providing her the opportunity to respond to its concerns. It clearly breached its duty of good faith.
>
> . . .
>
> An appropriate award of punitive damages in this case . . . is $7,500 . . . [In addition] the plaintiff is entitled to her costs and all related disbursements.

For a general review of the legal principles pertaining to an insurer's duty of good faith, see Professor Craig Brown's text, *Insurance Law in Canada*.[104]

9.2.4 Labour Litigation

Although the traditional considerations pertaining to the admissibility of evidence applies to the field of labour law, there are also further factors that must be considered if the surveillance is being conducted on unionized workers. The case law reveals that arbitrators in provinces where there is privacy legislation have utilized an evidentiary analysis pertaining to privacy rights that is similar to that used when considering the section 8 search and seizure provisions of the *Charter*.

---

103 Above note 101.
104 (Toronto: Carswell, 1999).

In provinces where privacy legislation does not exist, the views of arbitrators pertaining to privacy rights are not so clear. Although many legal practitioners believe that the same admissibility rules apply regardless of the province, the case law indicates some arbitrators believe there is a separate standard for admissibility in provinces where a legislated tort of invasion of privacy has not been passed. As a result, in provinces without privacy legislation, two lines of admissibility rules have developed — one imputing a section 8 *Charter*-like analysis, and another that does not. For instructive purposes — in provinces where the tort of invasion of privacy has not been legislated — the analysis that does not embrace the *Charter* will be reviewed.[105]

9.2.4.1   Off-Site Surveillance – Where Provincial Privacy Legislation Exists

Re Doman Forest Products Ltd. and I.W.A. Loc. 1-357[106] was an arbitration involving the discharge of an employee. The employee had been employed for seventeen years and had a normal record of attendance. In October 1989 he phoned in sick for seven days followed by five days of booked vacation. On the last day of his vacation, a Friday, the employee telephoned his supervisor informing him that he would be sick on the following Monday. The supervisor told him not to be silly and asked how he knew he would be sick on Monday when it was only Friday. The employee responded by saying that he would call on Monday. The employee was not asked if he was attending a physician nor did he volunteer this information. Later that day, a decision was made by the company to conduct surveillance commencing Monday if the employee failed to show up for work. On Monday morning the employee telephoned to say that he was sick and could hardly get out of bed. With that phone call, surveillance was commenced.

The evidence that the company sought to produce entailed videotape and visual observations of a private investigator. The union objected to its admissibility on the basis that it was a breach of the employee's implied right to privacy under the collective agreement. The union further argued that the company had no right to invade the employee's privacy unless there was a reasonable basis for so doing and all alternative means had been exhausted. It submitted that the employer had not made such efforts and accordingly the evidence should not be admitted. The union also argued that the section 8 *Charter* right to be secure against unreasonable search or seizure is a "value" that should be imported into labour litigation of this type.

The company responded by saying that it recognized the jurisprudence pertaining to personal private rights. However, the right to privacy is not absolute. The company further argued that the *Charter* provisions did not apply, particularly where there is a provincial statute applicable to the right to privacy.

The arbitrator reviewed the Supreme Court of Canada decision in *R. v. Duarte*[107] where the court considered whether participant surveillance sanctioned by section 178.11(2)(a)

---

105 For non-unionized workers, the traditional considerations discussed in the above section apply. See also S.L. Parkin, *Surveillance in the Workplace* (Toronto: Council of Private Investigators — Ontario Professional Development Conference, 12 May 2000).
106 (1990), 13 L.A.C. (4th) 275 (B.C.) (D.H. Vickers).
107 [1990] 1 S.C.R. 30.

(now section 184) of the *Criminal Code* offended the constitutional guarantees contained in the *Charter*. In *Duarte* the court concluded that the electronic recording of conversations of individuals with the police and informers was improper in the absence of judicial authorization (i.e., a search warrant).

On the issue of a labour dispute being an action between private parties, the arbitrator relied upon the Supreme Court of Canada decision in *R.W.D.S.U. Local 580 v. Dolphin Delivery Ltd.*[108] In *Dolphin Delivery* the court opined that the judiciary ought to apply and develop the principles of the common law in a manner consistent with the fundamental values enshrined in the *Charter*. The arbitrator further acknowledged that electronic surveillance by the state is a breach of an individual's right to privacy and is only countenanced by application of the standard of reasonableness enunciated in *Hunter v. Southam*.[109]

The arbitrator then reviewed section 1 of the *Privacy Act* of British Columbia.[110] The arbitrator agreed with the employer that the right to privacy is not absolute. Privacy must be judged against what is reasonable in the circumstances and, amongst other things, is dependent upon competing interests such as the relationship between the parties. It may be violated by surveillance, both visual and electronic. The arbitrator concluded that the *Privacy Act* gives an employee a legal right to privacy in certain circumstances, quite apart from any contractual right which he or she may have with his or her employer.

The arbitrator then held that while no specific provisions existed in the collective agreement insuring the right to privacy, it was impossible to read the collective agreement outside of the value system imposed by the *Charter* and the statement of law contained in the *Privacy Act*. Accordingly a balance must be struck between the right of the company to investigate what it considers to be an abuse of sick leave and the right of an employee to be left alone. The arbitrator held it would be improper to countenance disciplinary action against an employee in circumstances where the company may have offended its employee's privacy rights.[111]

Based on this analysis, the arbitrator held the following test should be applied to determine the admissibility of videotape surveillance evidence tendered by an employer:

1.   Was it reasonable, in all the circumstances, to request a surveillance?

2.   Was the surveillance conducted in a reasonable manner?

3.   Were other alternatives open to the company to obtain the evidence it sought?[112]

---

108   [1986] 2 S.C.R. 573.

109   [1984] 2 S.C.R. 145. For a further discussion of this topic, see Section 3.1 — The *Charter* and Liability Issues for Private Investigators.

110   *Privacy Act*, R.S.B.C. 1979, c. 336. For a review of provincial privacy legislation, see Section 5.3 of this book.

111   The arbitrator further cited *Re Canada Post Corporation and C.U.P.W.* (1988), 34 L.A.C. (3d) 392 (Bird), a case dealing with an employee's right to refuse to give his fingerprints to his employer.

112   In *Doman Forest Products Ltd. v. I.W.A. Canada Loc. 1-357*, [1991] B.C.I.R.C. 30-13, the panel held that on the balancing of interests, the videotape evidence should be excluded because the privacy rights of the employee had been violated by the company.

Subsequent to the *Doman Forest Products* decision, the results of an arbitration titled *Re Steels Industrial Products and Teamsters Union Local 213 (Sidhu)*[113] was released. In addition to relying on the decision of *Doman Products Ltd.*, the arbitrator also relied upon the Supreme Court of Canada decision in *R. v. Wong.*[114] The *Wong* case dealt with a police video surveillance of a hotel room suspected of being a location of illegal gambling. The video surveillance was conducted without a search warrant. The court reviewed in detail its earlier decision in *R. v. Duarte,*[115] where it held that an unauthorized police electronic audio surveillance was in violation of section 8 of the *Charter* dealing with unreasonable search and seizures. In *Wong* the Supreme Court of Canada held that it would be erroneous to limit Duarte to that particular technology, and found on similar principles that the unauthorized surreptitious videotaping in a private place by police and agents of the state also violated section 8 of the *Charter*.

The arbitrator went on to state that as a general principle, a private citizen — specifically an employer — should have greater freedom or authority to monitor another private citizen than does the state, even if the private citizen is one's employee. The arbitrator also acknowledged that the law has not developed in the area of private surveillance to the same extent that surveillance by the police is monitored by the courts. However, the arbitrator held that even within the employer-employee context, great circumspection is called for when an employer seeks to electronically monitor the activities of an employee off the job — albeit during working hours. The employer-employee relationship is based on an employment contract and the videotaping of an employee clearly is at the extreme of the employer's authority under such a contract.

The arbitrator then further refined the earlier analysis presented in the *Doman Forest Products* case. He reduced the three questions to two:

1.   Was it reasonable, in all the circumstances, to request a surveillance?

2.   Was the surveillance conducted in a reasonable manner?

This arbitrator held that the third question posed in *Doman Forest Products* can be considered as part of the first. If the answer is "no" to either question, then the evidence is not admissible.

In the introductory paragraph, it was mentioned that all provinces with privacy legislation would likely follow the decision of *Doman Forest Products*. In *Re Albright & Wilson Americas and S.T.E.C. Local 165,*[116] a Quebec arbitrator rejected the notion that an employee's right to privacy was protected under the *Charter* notwithstanding that Quebec has privacy legislation. The arbitrator held that the relationship between an employer and an employee is not a relationship of individual and state as protected in the *Charter*. This arbitrator ruled that on the balance of interests, the employer was entitled to conduct surveillance and that the evidence was admissible. It is noteworthy that Quebec's privacy legislation is different in form and content than that found in British Columbia, Newfoundland, Manitoba, Saskatchewan, and soon New Brunswick.

---

113 (1991), 24 L.A.C. (4th) 259 (B.C.) (Blasina)
114 [1990] 3 S.C.R. 36.
115 Above note 107.
116 (1992), 28 C.L.A.S. 198 (Quebec).

9.2.4.1.1 Reasonable Grounds for Conducting Surveillance

A number of cases including and since *Doman Forest Products* and *Steels Industrial Products* have refined what is and what is not considered to be relevant to determining at what point surveillance may be conducted and when surveillance evidence would be admissible in a union setting. Factors considered relevant include the following:

* disclosure to the subject employee that he or she is suspected of malingering if the problem is not habitual;
* length of service record;
* the number of prior occasions when the employee was suspected of fraudulently not attending his work;
* independent evidence from co-workers or others that the subject employee is engaged in other forms of work;
* change of address while the employee is on disability leave;
* inability of the employer to contact the employee at his home phone number;
* evidence provided by a medical practitioner that the subject employee may be exaggerating or faking the injuries claimed;
* refusal to attend the offices of a medical officer appointed by the employer for the purposes of evaluating the injury;
* an unexplained change in medical opinion;
* observations by supervisors or co-workers that the subject employee is conducting his activities at variance with the injuries claimed;
* an unusual pattern of on-the-job injuries which exceeds that of employees generally;
* discipline record of dishonest conduct;
* prior denial of wrongdoing when confronted with an accusation;
* attribution of blame to fellow employees or the employer for the subject's conduct;
* prior record of damaging company equipment or products; and
* a general attitude that would lead the employer to believe the subject employee would not provide honest answers.

Generally, the longer the service record, the greater the moral and ethical duty an employer owes to an employee to confront him or her personally for an explanation to the problem. Similarly, where the problem is a first occurrence, it is not reasonable to immediately conduct surveillance. Finally, the mere existence of a disciplinary record is not a factor that may be relied upon if the record is not relevant to the problem at hand.[117] Conducting

---

117 *Re Canadian Pacific Ltd. and Brotherhood of Maintenance of Way Employees (Chahal)* (1996), 59 L.A.C. (4th) 111 (Canada) (M. Picher); *Re Air Canada and Canadian Union of Public Employees*, [1995] C.L.A.D. No. 114 (C.L.A.); *Re Alberta Wheat Pool and Grain Workers' Union, Local 333* (1995), 48 L.A.C. (4th) 332 (B.C.) (Williams); *Re Canada Safeway Ltd. and United Food and Commercial Workers International Union, Local 2000 (Falbo)* (1998), 71 L.A.C. (4th) 97 (B.C.); *Re Greater Vancouver Regional District and G.V.R.D.E.U.* (1996), 57 L.A.C. (4th) 113 (B.C.).

surveillance after an employee has been dismissed to secure evidence in an arbitration has also been frowned upon.[118]

In suspicious circumstances surrounding the medical condition of an employee, the employer has the right to conduct a full investigation. However, only as a last step should an employer choose the intrusive alternative of invading the employee's privacy by conducting surveillance. Where there are other methods that can be taken such as discussions with the employee, interviews of his or her doctors, and other matters referred to above, those methods must be followed before employing a private investigator to conduct surveillance. If these preliminary steps are not taken, the videotape evidence will likely be deemed inadmissible.

9.2.4.1.2   *Conducting Surveillance in a Reasonable Manner*

The second part of the admissibility test for videotape surveillance evidence in a unionized environment is whether the surveillance itself was conducted in a reasonable manner. Factors that arbitrators have identified include who conducted the surveillance, and if the employee was aware that he or she was under surveillance. If the surveillance results in harassment or a nuisance, and/or if the surveillance was conducted by the employer itself instead of a third-party specialist such as a private investigator, the evidence may be held to be unreasonable.[119]

9.2.4.2   Off-Site Surveillance – Where No Provincial Privacy Legislation Exists

As mentioned in the introduction to this part, many labour law practitioners believe that the same rules apply in provinces with and without the legislated tort of invasion of privacy. However, for teaching purposes, the views of arbitrators who do not hold this view is explored. In *Re Kimberly-Clark Inc. and I.W.A. Canada Local 1-92-4 (Meo)*,[120] an employee was discharged for dishonesty in connection with his absence from work. The employer based its decision to fire for the most part on its investigator's reports and videotapes. The employee had a long history of health-related absences from work. He had sustained injuries several years before that led to the amputation of the fingers of his left hand. He had also injured his left knee in an industrial accident and his lower back in a motor vehicle accident.

The employer first began to suspect the employee of malingering on disability when it was reported by other employees that he had been observed doing various things, including dancing at a night club, that appeared to be inconsistent with his claim of disability. After consultations with counsel, the employer decided to retain the services of a private investigator.

The results of the private investigator's surveillance was videotape footage of the employee working at a construction site at a commercial property he owned on an after-

---

118 *West v. Eaton Yale Ltd.* (1999), 107 O.T.C. 48 (S.C.J.).

119 *Re Steels Industrial Products and Teamsters Union Local 213 (Sidhu)* (1991), 24 L.A.C. (4th) 259 (B.C.). For a critique of the reasoning of B.C. arbitrators on this issue of off-site surveillance in the labour context, see D. Majzub, "Employee Privacy: A Critical Examination of the Doman Decision" (Appeal: Review of Current Law and Law Reform) (1998) 4 Appeal 72.

120 (1996), 66 L.A.C. (4th) 266 (Ont.).

noon when he was not scheduled to be at work. The videotapes also show the employee walking, getting in and out of cars, driving, shopping, talking to various people, taking out the garbage, changing outdoor light-bulbs and entering and exiting cafes. At no time were the investigators on the employee's property or on any other private property. Everything they videotaped was in public view.

Submissions on the Admissibility Issue: The union argued that arbitrators are required to strike a balance between the right of the employer to control abuse of disability leave and the right of the employee to privacy. The union argued there were alternative strategies the employer could have followed to determine the legitimacy of the absence from work such as confronting the employee with its suspicions, talking to the employee's doctors, and having the employee examined by an independent doctor. The employer had done none of this but had jumped straight into the intrusive investigation of the employee's activities and movements while away from work. The union argued the videotapes and the private investigators' reports should therefore be inadmissible, as well as their testimony.[121]

The employer submitted the approach taken in cases chiefly from British Columbia should be rejected. The courts, the employer noted, have had no hesitation in admitting videotapes into evidence, subject only to concerns about accuracy, reliability and relevance.[122] The Workers' Compensation Appeals Tribunal had also admitted such evidence in comparable circumstances.[123] The employer argued that it was apparent from numerous arbitral awards that surveillance videotapes have routinely been admitted in arbitrations without any objection from the other party.[124] Still photographs of employees has also been consistently admitted into evidence. The employer noted that the British Columbia cases were distinguishable since they relied on British Columbia's privacy legislation, which had no counterpart in Ontario.

The employer further argued that although the British Columbia cases had also invoked the *Charter*, other cases had questioned the relevance of the *Charter* to an employment relationship.[125] The employer opined that employee locker searches or drug-testing cases had

121 This was exemplified in decisions such as *Re Alberta Wheat Pool and Grain Workers' Union, Loc. 333* (1995), 48 L.A.C. (4th) 332 (Williams); and *Re Air Canada and C.U.P.E.*, [1995] C.L.A.D. No. 114 (Simmons), unreported but summarized in 37 C.L.A.S. 453 (Ont.).

122 See *R. v. Creemer and Cormier*, [1968] 1 C.C.C. 14 (N.S.S.C.A.D.); *Guy v. Trizec Equities Ltd.* (1978), 26 N.S.R. (2d) 1 (N.S.S.C.A.D.); and *Ball v. Vincent* (1993), 24 C.P.C. (3d) 221 (Ont. Gen. Div.).

123 See *Decision No. 688/87*, [1987] 6 W.C.A.T.R. 198 (O.W.C.A.T.).

124 See *Re Midas Canada Inc. and U.S.W.A. (Honigan)* (1993), 37 L.A.C. (4th) 1 (Briggs); *Re Canadian National Railway and I.B.E.W. (Sesak)* (1991), 25 C.L.A.S. 485 (M. Picher); *Re Kimberly-Clark of Canada Ltd. and Canadian Paperworkers Union, Loc. 307* (1987), 4 C.L.A.S. 66 (Weatherrill); *Re Thunder Bay (City) and C.U.P.E. Loc. 87* (1986), 3 C.L.A.S. 36 (Haefling); *Re London (City) and London and District Service Workers' Union Loc. 220 (Flanagan)* (1993), 29 C.L.A.S. 499 (Hunter).

125 See *Re Canadian Pacific Ltd. and Brotherhood of Maintenance of Way Employees (Chahal)* (1996), 59 L.A.C. (4th) 111 (Picher); *Re Labatt Ontario Breweries (Toronto Brewery) and Brewery, General and Professional Workers Union Loc. 304* (1994), 42 L.A.C. (4th) 151 (Brandt).

no application to the far less intrusive activity of videotape surveillance.[126] The employer submitted videotape surveillance is essentially no different from taking a series of still photographs. The employer further submitted that the tests developed in the British Columbia cases for determining whether the results of such surveillance should be admitted had been criticized as unpractical.[127] The only pertinent test, according to the employer, was whether the surveillance had been conducted in a reasonable manner.

Decision on the Admissibility Issue: At the outset, the arbitrator pointed out that there is little that medical practitioners can do to confirm that a person is indeed suffering pain in the knee and back of the kind the employee reported. A conclusion by a physician that a patient has such symptoms depends largely on what the patient tells the physician. The arbitrator found as fact that at no time did the employer speak to any of the employee's doctors about his condition, or ask him to attend for examination by a doctor of its choice. Nor did it confront the employee with its suspicions before ordering the covert surveillance.

The arbitrator then discussed the applicability of the *Labour Relations Act, 1995*,[128] which empowers an arbitrator, among other things, to accept oral or written evidence as the arbitrator in his or her discretion considers proper, whether admissible in a court of law or not. The arbitrator held that the *Labour Relations Act, 1995*, is not limited to admitting evidence that would be inadmissible, but extends to excluding evidence that would be admissible in a court of law.[129]

Pertaining to an arbitrator's power to exclude evidence, the arbitrator stated that three principles relevant to the *Labour Relations Act, 1995*, emerge from the case law. First, arbitrators must not fetter their discretion by a mechanical application of the rules of evidence applied by courts. It follows that arbitrators may, when appropriate, exclude evidence that a court would admit. Second, relevance is the most important criterion in determining admissibility in arbitration proceedings. And third, if the evidence is admissible in a court of law, it would not appear prudent or proper for an arbitration board to exclude it.[130]

In keeping with the final point, the arbitrator held that other arbitrators have generally been reluctant to exclude court-admissible evidence. They have traditionally been unwilling to deny a party the opportunity to prove its case by relevant evidence.[131] The arbitrator noted that situations where relevant evidence has been excluded is where its use is prohibited by the collective agreement, or if it was obtained (1) in violation of the collective

---

126 *Re Labatt Ontario Breweries (Toronto Brewery) and Brewery, General and Professional Workers Union Loc. 304, ibid.*

127 *Re Ottawa-Carleton Regional Transit Commission and A.T.U. Loc. 279 (Desjardins)* (1995), 40 C.L.A.S. 252 (Eberlee). See also D. Majzub, above note 119.

128 S.O. 1995, c. 1, Sch. A. s. 48(12)(f).

129 *Re Greater Niagara Transit Commission and A.T.U. Loc. 1582* (1987), 43 D.L.R. (4th) 71 (Ont. Div. Ct.).

130 *Ibid.* at 88–90.

131 M.R. Gorsky, S.J. Usprich, & G.J. Brandt., *Evidence and Procedure in Canadian Labour Arbitration* (Toronto: Carswell, 1991–) [looseleaf] at 11-4.

agreement, (2) during grievance procedure discussions, (3) during a polygraph test, (4) from privileged discussions between a union representative and an employee, or (5) from confidential management documents.[132]

Because the disputed evidence was relevant to these proceedings and would be admissible in a court of law, the arbitrator then inquired as to why videotape evidence should be scrutinized with a view to possible exclusion. He noted four distinct reasons given by arbitrators in other cases.

First is the *Charter*. The view has been expressed by some arbitrators that it is legitimate for reference to be made to the principles or policies contained in the *Charter* in a determination of the admissibility of evidence. For example, in *Re Doman Forest Products Ltd. and I.W.A. Loc. 1-357*,[133] the arbitrator said: "It seems to me that while s.8 of the *Charter* does not apply to this dispute, as an adjudicator, I am called upon to bear in mind those fundamental *Charter* values." The arbitrator held that the correctness of this approach was rejected by the Divisional Court in Ontario; that the admission of evidence by a board of arbitration constituted under the *Labour Relations Act* should not depend on the admission or rejection of that evidence in a court of law pursuant to section 24(2) of the *Charter*.[134]

Second is provincial privacy legislation. The arbitrator noted that the cases from British Columbia[135] had been followed by some cases in Ontario.[136] The arbitrator held that the British Columbia cases are not persuasive in Ontario arbitration given the admonition by the Divisional Court regarding the proper use of the *Charter* and given the reliance on the British Columbia privacy legislation in these awards.[137] The arbitrator concluded that the right to privacy has no legal underpinning in Ontario of the kind found in the British Columbia legislation and relied on in the two principal British Columbia cases, and this calls into question the persuasiveness of this line of cases in Ontario arbitrations.

Third is the rationale that surreptitious videotaping is, in principle, as offensive an invasion of privacy as other forms of search and seizure to which employers have resorted such as drug testing and searches of personal effects.[138] The cases relied on to support this ratio-

---

132 See *Re Miracle Food Mart and U.F.C.W. Loc. 175 and 633* (1983), 11 L.A.C. (3d) 320 (Swan); *Re Greater Niagara Hospital and O.P.S.E.U. Loc. 215* (1989), 5 L.A.C. (4th) 292 (Ont.) (Joyce); *Re Canadian Broadcasting Corporation and C.U.P.E. (Broadcast Council)* (1991), 23 L.A.C. (4th) 63 (Thorne); and *Re Canada Post Corporation and C.U.P.W.* (1992), 27 L.A.C. (4th) 178 (Swan).

133 (1990), 13 L.A.C. (4th) 275 (B.C.) (Vickers).

134 *Re Greater Niagara Transit Commission and A.T.U. Loc. 1582* (1987), 43 D.L.R. (4th) 71 (Ont. Div. Ct.).

135 *Re Alberta Wheat Pool and Grain Workers' Union Loc. 333* (1995), 48 L.A.C. (4th) 332 (B.C.) (Williams), which followed *Re Steels Industrial Products* and *Re Doman Forest Products*.

136 *Re Toronto Star Newspaper Ltd. and Southern Ontario Newspaper Guild Local 87* (1992), 30 L.A.C. (4th) 306 (Ont.) (Springate); and *Re Walbar Canada Inc. and U.S.W.A. Loc. 9236* (1993), 31 C.L.A.S. 124 (Marszewski).

137 *Re Greater Niagara Transit Commission and A.T.U. Loc. 1582*, above note 134.

138 *Re Labatt Ontario Breweries (Toronto Brewery) and Brewery, General and Professional Workers Union Loc. 304* (1994), 42 L.A.C. (4th) 151 (Brandt).

nale, however, arose, for the most part, after employees refused to submit to the search in question and were disciplined for their refusal. The issue there was whether it was reasonable for the employer to have attempted to conduct such forms of search and seizure, and not whether evidence obtained thereby was admissible.

The arbitrator stated that this distinction is an important one. The common law has traditionally concluded that even the illegal acquisition of evidence is admissible.[139] A Canadian court will only exclude illegally obtained evidence if the *Charter* has been violated and if the court concludes that the admission of the tainted evidence would bring the administration of justice into disrepute.[140] In other circumstances, the common law has generally held that disputed evidence is admitted for the simple reason that parties should not lightly be denied the opportunity to prove their case through relevant evidence.

The fourth basis for excluding the product of surreptitious videotaping is the "obligation which boards of arbitration have to safeguard the integrity of their own procedures, and the credibility of the arbitration process generally."[141] Stated otherwise, the fundamental question that has to be asked is whether an arbitrator, in the exercise of the discretion conferred by the *Labour Relations Act, 1995*, is entitled to rely on such considerations.

The courts have been called upon on several occasions to explain what they see as the purpose of the impugned provisions of the *Labour Relations Act, 1995*.[142] Essentially, the courts view the purpose of vesting a discretion in arbitrators with regard to the admission of evidence as two-fold: (1) to keep the proceedings informal and expeditious; and (2) to insulate awards from judicial review on the basis of arbitrators' rulings on the admission of evidence. Accordingly, it is questionable that this discretion is available to arbitrators to allow them to sanction employer conduct of which they disapprove.

The arbitrator found that for these four reasons the cases do not reveal a convincing basis for excluding videotape evidence of the kind tendered in this case. Additionally, he added, there is a further problematic aspect of excluding other forms of covert surveillance evidence. What if a private investigator took still photos instead of videotapes? What if a private investigator simply made a written report to the employer of what he had seen and testified at the hearing on that basis? What if a manager or member of the public without having been specifically assigned to keep the employee under surveillance, just happened to see the employee engaged in questionable activities, and captured his or her activities electronically or gave a non-electronic report of them?

The arbitrator held the awards endorsing possible exclusion of surveillance evidence do not explain whether the offensiveness of such evidence lies in the electronic means used for gathering it, in the use of outside specialists, or in the planned nature of the informa-

---

139 *R. v. Wray*, [1971] S.C.R. 272.

140 See s. 24(2) of the *Charter*.

141 *Re Canadian Pacific Ltd. and Brotherhood of Maintenance of Way Employees (Chahal)*, above note 125.

142 *Re Toronto (City) and C.U.P.E. Loc. 79* (1982), 133 D.L.R. (3d) 94 at 106–9 (Ont. C.A.). More recently, the Supreme Court of Canada addressed the issue in *Re United Brotherhood of Carpenters and Joiners of America Local 579 and Bradco Construction Ltd.*, [1993] 2 S.C.R. 316.

tion gathering. In the absence of a carefully defined rationale for scrutinizing such evidence, the arbitrator held it is not immediately apparent why the product of some of these types of covert surveillance should be potentially inadmissible but not others.[143]

In the result, the arbitrator held that the union's objections were not well-grounded and were therefore dismissed. The videotape evidence was ruled to be admissible.[144]

9.2.4.3   On-Site Surveillance — The Four Levels of Privacy

In *Re Saint Mary's Hospital and Hospital Employee Union*,[145] an arbitration from British Columbia, an electrician was doing a routine wire inspection at a hospital when he came across a cable that was unfamiliar to him. He followed the wire to the office of the manager of housekeeping where he discovered a video camera above the ceiling tile approximately in the middle of the room. The union was outraged at what it considered was a substantial encroachment on the rights of privacy of the employees who had been subjected to surreptitious surveillance. The employer stated it was necessary to determine who was responsible for a number of thefts. A grievance was filed.

General Arbitral Jurisprudence Relating to the Right to Privacy: The arbitrator held that there is a kind of hierarchy of protection afforded by the right to privacy. From the arbitral jurisprudence, he found the following principles to emerge.[146]

---

143 See *Re Toronto (City) Board of Education and U.A. Local 46 (Hughes)*, (1993), 38 L.A.C. (4th) 288 (M. Levinson).

144 Much of the reasoning of this case was followed in *Re Toronto Transit Commission and Amalgamated Transit Union Local 113 (Fallon)*, (10 November 1998), (Ontario) [unreported] (Solomatenko, Reistetter, & Crockett). Cases that rejected the analysis of *Kimberly-Clark* and which were in turn rejected in *Toronto Transit Commission (Fallon)* include *Re Toronto Transit Commission and Amalgamated Transit Union Loc. 113* (1997), 61 L.A.C. (4th) 218 (Saltman). Arbitrator Saltman relied upon *Re Labatt Ontario Breweries (Toronto Brewery) and Brewery, General & Professional Workers Union Loc. 304* (1994), 42 L.A.C. (4th) 151 (Brandt); *Re Toronto Star Newspaper Ltd. and Southern Ontario Newspaper Guild Loc. 87* (1992), 30 L.A.C. (4th) 306 (Ont.) (Springate); and *Re Toronto Transit Commission and Amalgamated Transit Union Loc. 113 (Collins)*, (31 January 1999) [unreported] (J. Johnston).

145 (1997), 64 L.A.C. (4th) 382 (D.L. Larson). Note this case also included an analysis of British Columbia's privacy legislation.

146 The arbitrator discussed at length the cases of *Re Thibodeau-Finch Express Inc. and Teamsters Union Loc. 880* (1988), 32 L.A.C. (3d) 271 (Burkett); *Re Algoma Steel Corporation Ltd. and United Steelworkers, Local 2251* (1984), 17 L.A.C. (3d) 172 (Davis); *Re Johnson Matthey & Mallory Ltd. and Precious Metals Workers' Union Federal Loc. 24739 CLC* (1975), 10 L.A.C. (2d) 354 (H.D. Brown); *Re University Hospital and London and District Service Workers' Union Local 220* (1981) 28 L.A.C. (2d) 294 (P.C. Picher); *Re Alberta Wheat Pool and Grain Workers' Union Loc. 333* (1995), 48 L.A.C. (4th) 332 (Williams); *Re Doman Forest Products Ltd. and I.W.A. Loc. 1-357* (1990), 13 L.A.C. (4th) 275 (Vickers); *Re Steels Industrial Products and Teamsters Union Loc. 213 (Sidhu)* (1991), 24 L.A.C. (4th) 259 (B.C.) (Blasina); and *Re Puretex Knitting Co. and Canadian Textile and Chemical Union* (1979), 23 L.A.C. (2d) 14 (Ellis).

First, actions by employers which involve actual body intrusions are protected by the law of trespass and assault, and accordingly, an employer is not entitled to do anything that would involve touching the employee except with the employee's consent, express or implied.[147] In such cases, there can be no question of the balancing of interests because the employer does not obtain a right to commit a trespass or an assault on an employee by virtue of the employment relationship. There are no cases that have held that consent can be implied from the mere existence of the employment relationship. In fact, where there is a collective agreement, it has been specifically held that consent cannot be implied from the management rights clause or the health and safety provisions.[148] Examples of intrusions that are accorded the highest level of protection include such things as mandatory medical examinations[149] and body searches.[150]

Second, actions by employers that involve searches of personal effects and spaces are an unsettled area of law. Some arbitrators have expressed the view that a distinction between bodily searches and searches of personal effects is not warranted since some incursions, although not involving a body search, may be so intimate as to make the distinction invidious.[151] Although this conclusion may be justified based on a subjective analysis of human values, it ignores that the body search cases are founded upon torts of trespass and assault which are absolute rights. The only permitted exception is where the employee consents to an intrusion. But when it comes to searches of personal effects, those rules have no application. Accordingly, such actions are properly governed by the right to privacy. Indeed, it is precisely by making the distinction that the interests of the employer may be properly balanced against those of the employee.

Third, there is a range of privacy protection which applies to surveillance cases. At one end of the scale is what may be called benign surveillance, where it is used for the benefit of the employees. For example, the videotaping of work activities for purposes of training and to assist key supervisors who are temporarily disabled. In those kinds of cases, there would be little evidence required to justify the surveillance.[152] Next are cases involving surveillance conducted to provide security to both the employees and the employer. Security surveillance would typically involve open electronic monitoring. The cameras are not hidden and will often be installed with the implicit consent of the union. If they are installed with the full knowledge of the union, the union would likely be taken to have acquiesced in any infringement of privacy inherent in the installation.

---

147 *Re University of British Columbia and A.U.C.E. Loc. 1* (1984), 15 L.A.C. (3d) 151 (McColl). In some cases, an order may be obtained from an arbitration board.

148 *Re Air Canada and Canadian Airline Employees Assn.* (1982), 8 L.A.C. (3d) 82 (Simmons).

149 *Re Thompson and Town of Oakville* (1963), 41 D.L.R. (2d) 294 (Ont. H.C.J.).

150 *Re Riverdale Hospital (Board of Governors) and C.U.P.E. Loc. 43* (1977), 14 L.A.C. (2d) 344 (Brent).

151 *Re Algoma Steel Corporation Ltd. and United Steelworkers, Local 2251* (1984), 17 L.A.C. (3d) 172 (Davis); *Re Lornex Mining Corp. and U.S.W. Loc. 7619* (1983), 14 L.A.C. (3d) 169 (Chetkow).

152 *Re Puretex Knitting Co. and Canadian Textile and Chemical Union* (1979), 23 L.A.C. (2d) 14 at 30 (Ellis).

Finally, there is surreptitious surveillance. It has the greatest potential to affront the privacy rights of employees. It is this kind of surveillance that arbitrators require strict justification by the employer. If the surveillance is directed at a particular individual rather than a whole group of employees, or where it is not constant, it may require less justification. Examples of the most serious kinds of infringement against the right to privacy include surveillance of production work or monitoring employees for disciplinary purposes or to conduct surveillance of the social or sensitive areas of the workplace such as locker rooms, washrooms, and lunchrooms.

After having determined the type, purpose, and frequency of the hidden surveillance, the balance of interests involves the application of specific tests. The onus is on the employer to justify the encroachment upon the employees' rights to privacy by demonstrating that there is a substantial problem and that there is a strong probability that surveillance will assist in solving this problem. The employer must demonstrate that not only is there cause to initiate surveillance, but that it is not a contravention of any of the terms of the collective agreement.[153] It must show that it has exhausted all available alternatives and that there is nothing else that can be reasonably done in a less intrusive way.[154] Finally, it must ensure that the surveillance is conducted in a systematic and non-discriminatory manner.[155]

Conclusion: The arbitrator found as fact that there was a serious problem of vandalism and theft at the hospital. Further, because the hospital was a large institution to which the public had ready access and where employees were not closely supervised, it would be difficult to apprehend the offender. The arbitrator held, however, that other things could have been done within the office to secure the documents. The documents that were stolen had not been kept in a locked drawer. Therefore, without in any way purporting to exonerate the person who may have taken the documents, some responsibility for the loss must be attributed to the failure to take that very basic precaution. Because there was an alternative to using a hidden camera, the use of it was improper in the circumstances. Therefore, the arbitrator ordered that the tape was to be surrendered and erased to protect the innocent who may have been filmed.

9.2.4.4 Workers' Compensation Evidence Thresholds

Decision No. 918/941[156] is a case that, for the first time in Workers' Compensation hearings, provided a comprehensive review of the law as it is applied to the admissibility of evidence of private investigators. The case was an appeal from a decision of a hearing officer in

---

153 *Re Thibodeau-Finch Express Inc. and Teamsters Union Loc. 880* (1988), 32 L.A.C. (3d) 271 (Burkett).

154 *Re Algoma Steel Corporation Ltd. and United Steelworkers, Local 2251* (1984), 17 L.A.C. (3d) 172 (Davis).

155 *Re Steels Industrial Products and Teamsters Union Loc. 213 (Sidhu)* (1991), 24 L.A.C. (4th) 259 (B.C.) (Blasina).

156 [1995] O.W.C.A.T.D. No. 170.

which a worker's claim for entitlement was denied, based on an eighteen-page report that documented the surveillance observations of a private investigator. No surveillance video-tape was presented. The worker sought to have the report held inadmissible.

9.2.4.4.1   General Considerations

At the outset of this inquiry, the panel members agreed the issue of admissibility of a private investigator's surveillance report is an important one that brings into apparent conflict some of the fundamental principles upon which notions of administrative justice are founded. They also found that surveillance reports are of essentially the same nature as videotape evidence because they are prepared under circumstances where the worker is unaware that he or she is being observed; because they purport to approximate the visual images of a video recording; and because they can be highly influential in shaping a decision maker's factual findings. For these reasons, the panel held that a high degree of caution is warranted, not only in the analysis of the admissibility of this evidence, but also in determining the appropriate weight to be given to it if it is admitted as evidence.

The panel further noted that its own policies indicated that audio or visual recordings should not be accepted as evidence except under stringent circumstances that include consideration of (1) relevance, (2) authenticity, and (3) probative value versus prejudicial content.[157] The panel pointed out that the utilization of this sort of evidence can lead to an unhealthy adversarial relationship between workers and employers. The panel also stated that in addition to entrenching the parties in a far more adversarial process, the use of private investigators also tends, in the long run, to denigrate the role of the Workers' Compensation Board in adjudicating claims.[158]

9.2.4.4.2   Authenticity

In *Decision No. 918/941*,[159] the panel concluded that the surveillance report was relevant to determining the legitimacy of the claim, that it was of significant probative value, and that the potential evidentiary value of the surveillance report outweighed its prejudicial effect. However, the panel concluded the authenticity of the surveillance report was not established.

The panel acknowledged that nowhere in its jurisprudence had it dealt explicitly with the question of whether deficiencies in the authenticity of a report would constitute an appropriate basis for the exclusion of such evidence. The panel noted that as a rule, a very broad approach to the question of the admissibility of evidence is generally taken.[160] For example, it has been stated:

---

157 WCB Operational Policy Document #09-01-06.

158 See "Additional Reasons" to Decision No. 467/87.

159 Above note 156.

160 See s. 74(b) of the former *Workers' Compensation Act*, which applied to Tribunals by virtue of s. 92 of the Act and authorized the Tribunal to accept such oral or written evidence as in its discretion it considered proper whether admissible in a court of law or not. [This Act has been repealed and replaced with the *Workplace Safety Insurance Act*, S.O. 1997, c. 16, Schedule A.]

One of the hallmarks of administrative law adjudication as contrasted with the court system is that administrative tribunals are generally willing to accept any evidence which is relevant to the inquiry subject to submissions about what weight or importance ought to be attached to the evidence. This avoids the lengthy dispute about admissibility of documentary or other evidence and, in the workers' compensation context, makes the hearing less formal and more accessible.

The Workers' Compensation Appeals Tribunal has an obligation to decide cases upon their merits and justice. Unless evidence is entirely irrelevant, it should be admitted and considered by the hearing panel.[161] A review of Tribunal jurisprudence confirms that only in rare and unusual circumstances have panels decided to exercise their discretion to exclude evidence.[162] Far more commonly, panels will admit relevant but controversial hearsay evidence but accord it less weight than other evidence which has been subjected to cross-examination.[163]

The panel further noted that the position of common law and statutory authority is that relevant evidence, whether documentary or demonstrative, can be considered admissible even in the absence of sworn testimony from a witness with personal knowledge to establish its authenticity.[164] Because the authenticity of the private investigator's report was in question, the Panel decided to invoke its investigative authority and directed that the private investigator attend and give oral evidence under oath regarding the authenticity of it.[165]

9.2.4.4.3   Prejudicial Effect: Privacy Intrusions

Workers' Compensation Tribunals have held that as a matter of policy in a labour setting the right to privacy is important because of the ideal of creating a non-adversarial process of investigating and adjudicating workers' compensation claims. Generally, the right to privacy depends on the degree of intrusion and the nature of the activity observed. Tribunals have held that where a worker is observed performing commonplace physical activity in a public area, there is nothing inherently private about it.[166]

9.2.4.4.4   Prejudicial Effect: Evidence of Illegal Activity

Ontario Workers' Compensation Tribunal policy states that videotape surveillance cannot contain prejudicial information such as the worker admitting to or being shown performing an illegal activity. Such a recording could unfairly influence the decision maker's opinion of the worker and adversely affect the worker's credibility.[167]

---

161   See *Decision No. 905/89* and *Decision No. 968/90R*.

162   See, for example, *Decision No. 77/91* and *Decision No.968/90R*.

163   See, for example, *Decision No. 776/93I* and *Decision No. 774/91*.

164   *Ontario Evidence Act*, R.S.O. 1990, s. 35. See also the general discussion of this question in Sopinka, Lederman, & Bryant, *The Law of Evidence in Canada*, above note 1 at 950ff.

165   Pursuant to s. 74(a) and s. 92 of the Act., see above note 160.

166   *Decision No. 688/87*, [1987] 6 W.C.A.T.R. 198 (O.W.C.A.T.).

167   WCB Operational Policy Doc. #09-01-06. See *Decision No. 918/941*, [1995] O.W.C.A.T.D. No. 170 and *Decision No. 688/87*, [1987] 6 W.C.A.T.R. 198 (O.W.C.A.T.).

9.2.4.5   Nanny Cams

In the March 2000 issue of *Canadian Security*, the issue of nanny cams was discussed. A Toronto lawyer reported that there are no Canadian legal decisions reported on nanny cams but that traditional labour law principles would probably apply. He further reported that workplace surveillance is an invasion of an employee's right to privacy akin to searching of an employee's personal property, and that an employer would have to justify its use by providing other evidence giving rise to suspicion of wrongdoing. Without proper foundation, the evidence obtained would probably not be admissible in a case for wrongful dismissal.[168]

9.2.4.6   Entrapment

Entrapment cases in a non-unionized setting were briefly outlined in the beginning of this discussion on evidence and surveillance in Section 9.1.4. The following discussion pertains to the issues of surveillance and entrapment by private investigators in a unionized work place.

In a British Columbia case,[169] a union and employer jointly brought forward an issue on admissibility of surveillance video obtained through entrapment. An employee's residence was kept under surveillance for two days and nothing untoward was observed. On the third day, one of the investigators telephoned the employee's residence and arranged a hang-gliding lesson. During the ensuing lesson, still photographs and a video-tape were taken. The employee was asked if he had any objection to the video. He said he did not. He did not know, however, for what purpose it was taken.

The arbitrator held there are two tests an employer must satisfy to justify video surveillance. *Re Doman Forest Products Ltd.*[170] set out as a first principle that an employer must act reasonably when determining to undertake a surreptitious surveillance. The arbitrator recognized that the *Charter* does not bear on the relationship between private parties. Instead, he relied on section 1 of the *Privacy Act* (B.C.). It follows, he said, that in determining whether or not to admit surveillance evidence, an employer is required to balance the need for surveillance against other ways of obtaining the evidence it seeks.

To support its grounds for surveillance, the employer submitted that the employee was absent from work allegedly as a consequence of a car accident. The employer had suspicions that he was working elsewhere. The employer was also concerned about the employee's absenteeism record. The triggering event that led to the surveillance was the employer's inability to contact the employee at home. In the course of conducting routine claims management inquiries, the employer made a telephone call to the employee's house. The

---

168 S. Hunt, ed., *Canadian Security* (March 2000), quoting lawyer Philip Spencer of Cassels Brock & Blackwell. Mr. Spencer also noted that, notwithstanding such evidence may be inadmissible in a court action, it is understandable parents may undertake such surveillance to achieve their peace of mind.

169 *Re Pacific Press Ltd. and Vancouver Printing Pressmen, Assistant and Offset Workers' Union, Local 25* (Dales) (1997), 64 L.A.C. (4th) 1 (B.C.).

170 *Re Doman Forest Products Ltd. and I.W.A. Local 1-357* (1990), 13 L.A.C. (4th) 275 (B.C.) (Vickers).

announcement at his answering machine invited callers to leave a message for him, his spouse, or for his school of hang-gliding. Against this background, the employer decided it was reasonable to invoke surreptitious surveillance.

The union argued that other methods could have been employed such as confronting the employee with its suspicions. It might have asked around to inform itself of his interest in hang-gliding and the operation of the hang-gliding school. The arbitrator held that neither of these options was likely to disclose the employee's activities while away from work. The arbitrator concluded that there were no other reasonable or practical alternatives except to engage in surreptitious surveillance.

As for the reasonableness of the investigation, the union argued it was unreasonable to expect the employee to turn down the opportunity, given his love for the sport and the infrequency with which he was asked to teach. The employer, on the other hand, submitted that it was open for him to simply say that he was injured and unable to comply with the request for a lesson.

The arbitrator held that this case was unlike any described in the authorities. In all of the surveillance jurisprudence reviewed, the employer performed a passive role in observing the activities of its employee. The union argued consideration should be given to criminal cases of entrapment. In *R. v. Mack*[171] the Supreme Court of Canada ruled that the police may only provide an opportunity for an accused to commit an offence where there is reasonable suspicion that the individual is engaging in criminal activity of the same type. The mere fact that an individual had engaged in the same form of criminal activity in the past is not sufficient.

The arbitrator held that although criminal law is not directly applicable, it is consistent with the principle that an employer's suspicions concerning the activities of its employees must be well founded in order to lay a trap in this manner. It is analogous to cases of theft in which there is some concrete evidence that an employee engaged in similar activities in the past. In such cases, an employer is permitted to arrange for an opportunity in which the employee might be observed stealing company property.

The arbitrator held that apart from the name of the hang-gliding school on the answering machine and the knowledge that the business was running, there was no other concrete evidence to suggest that the employee was engaging in teaching on a routine or regular basis while away from work. The arbitrator concluded that in such circumstances, it was unreasonable for the private investigators to set up the employee in order to secure surveillance videotape evidence of him breaching the conditions of his employment. The videotape was therefore inadmissible.

9.2.4.7   E-mail and Internet Surveillance

The law pertaining to the admissibility of evidence obtained by monitoring the email of employees in Canada is in its infancy. American courts have held that an employer has the right to monitor e-mail on the basis that the computer is property of the employer and

---

171 [1989] 1 W.W.R. 577 (S.C.C.).

there is no reasonable expectation of privacy.[172] In private employment scenarios, it is likely that Canadian courts will follow similar common law principles.

In unionized workplaces, the principles of privacy discussed above pertaining to videotape surveillance will likely apply. Therefore, in order for an employer to monitor a unionized employee, the employer will likely require a policy advising the employee that his or her e-mail is being monitored. The employer will also require a reason to conduct the monitoring, and ensure that the monitoring is conducted reasonably.

In one case, an arbitrator admitted evidence taken from a workplace computer's hard drive where the employee was warned not to use the computer assigned to her for personal use and the employer regularly backed up the contents of the PC assigned to employees onto its server. The fact that the computer was owned by the employer, that the hard drive is a fixture within the computer, and that the employee was cautioned before being caught was critical to this decision.[173]

Other examples where computer surveillance evidence has been admitted in unionized labour arbitrations include allegations of downloading pornography from the Internet,[174] receiving and distributing e-mail with pornographic materials,[175] reviewing child pornography for 25 percent of a shift,[176] accessing a manager's e-mails without authorization,[177] and for spending excessive time on personal e-mails.[178] In all these cases, the employees used employers' computers on company time.

Pertaining to non-work environments, there has been a case in the criminal context where an Internet provider intercepted an e-mail of a subscriber containing child pornography and forwarded it to police. The court held that e-mail with a Web provider does carry a reasonable expectation of privacy and that for a seizure of such information by police to be admissible, a search warrant is required.[179] As the *Charter* does not apply to the investigations of private investigators prior to arrest, such admissibility concerns would not apply, although other forms of liability may result.[180]

---

172 *Smyth v. Pillsbury Co.,* 914 F. Supp. 97 (E.D. Pa. 1966); *Bohach v. City of Reno,* 932 F. Supp. 1232 (W.D. Nev. 1996).

173 *Re International Association of Bridge, Structural and Ornamental Ironworkers Local 97 and Office and Technical Employees Union, Local 15,* [1997] B.C.D.L.A. 500.24.00-12.

174 *Dorrian v. Canadian Airlines International Limited,* [1997] C.L.A.D. No. 607

175 *Consumers Gas v. Communication Energy and Paperworkers Union,* [1999] O.L.A.A. No. 649.

176 *Chronicle Journal v. Thunder Bay Typographical Union, Local 44 (Barichello)* (2000), O.L.A.A. No. 575 (Ont.).

177 *Fraser Valley Regional Library v. Canadian Union of Public Employees, Local 1698 (Matthews)* (2000), 91 L.A.C. (4th) 201 (B.C.).

178 *Mount Royal College v. Mount Royal Staff Association* (1998) (Alberta) [unreported].

179 *R. v. Weir,* [1998] 8 W.W.R. 228 (Alta. Q.B.).

180 See Section 4.2.5 — Electronic Surveillance.

9.2.4.8   Collateral Use

It has been held that in balancing the interests of employers and employees, videotape evidence can be received to show it is reasonable to further investigate an employee's conduct. For example, videotape evidence can be received for the limited purpose of requesting a medical review.[181]

9.2.4.9   Case Law Reviews of Evidence Required for Discharge

The following cases are reported to give an indication of the amount of surveillance evidence required for an employer to successfully dismiss an employee.

Where an employee was discharged for dishonesty after being videotaped shovelling dirt with no apparent mobility impairment while off work with a non-occupational back condition, an arbitrator held that the discharge was based on suspicion rather than proof of abuse and therefore reinstated the employee. Medical reports diagnosed spondylitis. The arbitrator held that occasional shovelling is not inconsistent with the disease in question.[182]

Where an employee was terminated for fraudulently misrepresenting a medical condition of being totally disabled, an arbitrator found that the employer did not meet the required standard of proof and reinstated the employee. The employee was observed by a private investigator at the job site of another employer while collecting workers' compensation benefits. The union argued that the private investigator's evidence never indicated the employee was working — only that he attended another employer's job site.[183]

Where an employer dismissed three bartenders and suspended another for a month after receiving a private investigator's report alleging theft, an arbitrator held that while the standard of proof remains on the balance of probabilities, evidence must be scrutinized with greater care where the allegations are so serious. In the circumstances of this case, the investigation did not establish sufficient cause. The bar conditions were chaotic on the nights in question and the errors and omissions in the private investigator's reports and the inconsistency of his testimony brought the findings into question.[184] However, in another bartender theft dismissal case, an arbitrator upheld the discharge, finding that the private investigator's reports contained sufficient detailed evidence that till tapes and cash in the till at the end of shift were not consistent with the amount of liquor disbursed during the impugned shifts. The arbitrator rejected the grievor's explanation of spillage and mistaken record keeping.[185]

It has been held that the standard of proof required of an employer in cases involving allegations of serious misconduct of a criminal nature is higher than the civil standard of balance of probabilities but not as high as the criminal standard of beyond a reasonable

---

181 *Re Canada Post Corp. and A.P.O.C. (Knox)* (1996), 56 L.A.C. (4th) 353.

182 *Re Pacific Brewers Distributors and Brewery, Winery and Distillery Workers' Union Local 300,* (1988), 9 C.L.A.S. 124 (B.C.).

183 *Re Camco Inc. and C.A.W. Local 504,* (1994), 37 C.L.A.S. 216 (Ont.).

184 *Re Capri Hotel and Hotel Restaurant and Culinary Employees and Bartenders Union Local 40,* (1988), 10 C.L.A.S. 5 (B.C.).

185 *6K Investments Ltd. v. Hotel, Restaurant and Culinary Employees and Bartenders Union, Local 40,* [1996] B.C.D.L.A. 500.15.40.25-08 A-05/96.

doubt. The evidence to meet the test must be clear, strong, and cogent. Where an employee was terminated for selling drugs on the employer's premises while on shift based on the evidence obtained in a private investigator's report, the arbitrator held the required standard of evidence did not exist. The grievance was allowed.[186]

Where an employer discharged an employee for dishonesty and theft, an arbitrator reinstated the employee, holding that employees are only obligated to provide explanations to theft accusations where the employer finds the employee in possession of company property. A private investigator was contracted by the employer to conduct video surveillance of the store in response to concerns that employees were "grazing." The private investigator made a videotape that verified the employer's concerns. The arbitrator held that the videotape evidence was not clear as to the exact food the employee was eating. On this basis, the arbitrator held that the allegation of theft was based on "less than convincing" evidence.[187]

9.2.5 Family Law Litigation

No case law was found on this issue. However, an interesting scenario was submitted by a private investigator. A woman who was concerned about the fidelity of her husband retained a private investigator to conduct surveillance of her property and to videotape any and all activity at her residence. The woman's name was on title of the property. The woman instructed the private investigator that he could attend anywhere on the grounds of the residence, but not inside. The private investigator videotaped the woman's husband with another woman inside the residence through an open window. The client sought to introduce the videotape into evidence at a divorce proceeding. The husband argued that the tape should be inadmissible as it was a breach of his privacy.

In today's world, litigating such a scenario would be uncommon due to liberalized no-fault divorce laws and stipulated distribution of wealth provisions in provincial family law legislation. However, it does still pose an interesting question. A lawyer from California had some views on it. He submitted that one spouse does not have the general authority to waive the rights of another, except in cases such as where there is a power of attorney. Pertaining to property that is co-owned or co-leased, a reasonable expectation of privacy would apply to rooms such as bathrooms and marital or significant other bedrooms. The question essentially is: Does the person at the time and place in question have a reasonable expectation of privacy? The trend in civil law is towards granting greater privacy expectations in all domains of life.[188]

---

186 *Re Weston Bakeries Ltd. and B.C.T. Local 246* (1993), 29 C.L.A.S. (3d) 567 (Ont.).

187 *Re Overwaitea Food Group and U.F.C.W. Local 1518*, [1995] B.C.D.L.A. 190-20 (B.C.).

188 Greg H. Walker, Attorney at Law, President, RisKontroL — Risk Management, Security Consulting & Investigations, Houston, Texas, Tel: (713) 850-0061.

9.2.6   Municipal Bylaw Litigation

It has been held that video surveillance of businesses in a strip plaza conducted by private investigators retained by a municipal government for the purpose of procuring evidence of a breach of a city bylaw does not offend the section 8 search and seizure provisions of the *Charter* and is admissible. The court characterized an application by the city for a declaration that a city bylaw was being breached as a civil dispute that does not fall under the nomenclature of government action. The court distinguished this scenario from that in *R. v. Wong*[189] where video surveillance was taken by police of an accused in a criminal matter in his hotel room. The court held that whereas people generally have a reasonable expectation of privacy in a hotel room, there is no reasonable expectation of privacy where a business is open to the public view.[190]

9.3   INTERVIEWS AND WITNESS STATEMENTS

Private investigators are regularly retained by lawyers, employers, and others to take statements from various persons. Often, the person who requests the statement will wish to use the statement as evidence in a criminal or civil proceeding. Accordingly, it is imperative that private investigators know how the courts view their role in the taking of statements.

9.3.1   Property in Witnesses

It is commonly held that there is no property in a witness. Therefore, a private investigator can approach any person who may have information relevant to the case at hand.[191] There are, however, some exceptions to this general rule that every private investigator should be aware of.

9.3.1.1   Party to an Action

The Law Society of Upper Canada's Rules for Professional Conduct prohibit a lawyer from dealing directly with the client of another solicitor.[192] If a private investigator is retained by a solicitor, by extension, the private investigator is also prohibited from taking statements from any person who is then a party to an action opposite that solicitor. The answer, however, is not so clear if the private investigator is not retained by the solicitor of the litigant but by the litigant herself. In such situations, a private investigator is well advised to ask the litigant if she has retained counsel, and if she has, to operate under counsel's direction.

---

189 [1990] 3 S.C.R. 36. See Section 9.2.4.1.

190 *Toronto (City) v. 1291547 Ontario Inc.* (2000), 16 M.P.L.R. (3d) 104 (Ont. S.C.J.).

191 *Ward v. Magna International Inc.* (1994), 28 C.P.C. (3d) 327 (Ont. Gen. Div.); *R. v. Keukens* (1996), 23 O.R. (3d) 582 (Ont. Gen. Div.).

192 See Law Society of Upper Canada, 41st Bar Admission Course: Phase Three Materials, at 2-6.

Notwithstanding this prohibition, it is lawful and indeed often tactfully wise to interview a party who may potentially be adverse in interest before an action is commenced. As long as at the time of the interview a decision has not conclusively been made that the person will be a party to the action, an interview of such a party is not prohibited. If such conduct is questioned, a reasonable explanation is that it was not until after the interview of the party that it was concluded the person would or would not become a party to the action.

9.3.1.2   Third Party Witnesses

Although there may be limitations on contacting a party to an action, there are no property rights in third-party witnesses. In a British case where a man was charged with murder, the accused instructed his solicitors that he had an alibi and wished to provide details to the police. At the police interview, the accused stated that around the time of the victim's death, he was in a hostel. The solicitor retained a private investigator to make inquiries at the hostel and gave him a picture of the accused. At the same time, the police proposed to hold an identification parade. The solicitor informed the police that she had instructed a private investigator to make inquiries. The police advised her that showing the accused's photograph to potential identification witnesses would hinder their investigation and threatened to charge her with obstructing justice.

The accused's solicitor applied for a contempt of court order against the police. The court held that there is no property in a witness, and that England is a country where everything is permitted except that expressly forbidden by law. Therefore, the court held, the solicitor's and private investigator's actions in attempting to identify the accused's potential alibi witnesses, even though it may hinder a police investigation, was not an offence of obstructing justice. Furthermore, the threat to prosecute for an offence not grounded in law is a form of contempt of court.[193]

There are no general rules against contacting third-party witnesses, but some witnesses may be reluctant to cooperate due to other professional obligations. In an Ontario case involving an allegation of sexual assault against a school teacher, defence counsel retained a private investigator to interview and take statements from fellow teachers and students. The school principal intervened, arguing that confidentiality rules under the *Education Act* prohibited certain information from being released. The accused brought a motion claiming the actions of the principal prevented him from being able to make full answer and defence, and that the confidentiality rules under the *Education Act* only applied to documents, not conversations. The court held that the purpose of the confidentiality rules under the *Education Act* is to prevent the release of personal information and accordingly, it must apply not only to documents held by the school but also to knowledge of the contents of the documents which a school employee may have. The court held that while such confidentiality rules may deter a teacher from cooperating with an investigator, such a balance is required to give the legislation its intended effect.[194]

---

193 *Connolly v. Dale*, [1995] N.L.O.R. No. 122 (England H.C.J.-Q.B.D.C.).
194 *R. v. Keukens*, above note 191.

9.3.2   Statements Taken from Suspects or Arrestees

The considerations that must be addressed by a private investigator when taking a statement from a suspect or an arrestee include the following questions:

1.   Does the suspect or arrestee believe the investigator to be a person in authority?

2.   Does the suspect or arrestee believe the investigator to be a threat or holding out an inducement?

3.   What effect does the *Charter* have on the process?

9.3.2.1   Is the Interviewer a Person in Authority?

The first test to determine the admissibility of an inculpatory statement, otherwise known as a statement against self-interest, is if it was given to a person in authority. The courts have held that if a statement is made to a person in authority, the person offering the statement must first prove that it was given free of threats or inducements. If a statement is not given voluntarily, its reliability is at issue. This determination is usually made during a *voir dire*. A question that flows from these requirements, therefore, is: Who is a person in authority?

It is well settled in law that a person in authority includes anyone whose promise or threat would likely influence an accused and induce him or her to make a statement against interest from fear or hope. Whether a person is or is not in authority for the purpose of the rule is a question of fact that can be determined only by evidence. The test is subjective rather than objective. The burden of proof is the evidentiary burden.[195] Generally it has been held that a person in authority includes anyone connected with the arrest, detention, examination, or prosecution.[196]

In a case involving a medical doctor and a person under his care charged with murder, the court made the following statement, which can be applied to all such analysis:

> It appears . . . logical to use the subjective test. The main reason for questioning the admissibility of a confession appears to be that it may not be true. It is more likely to be true if it is freely and voluntarily given, rather than procured by fear or prejudice or hope of advantage. In other words, one must see if there is any reason for lying. What the accused thinks and feels will be what motivates the giving or not giving the confession. It is not what someone else or a reasonable man thinks or feels that is important. If the accused genuinely perceives the person who is questioning or examining him is a person in authority who has offered him an inducement, he may falsely confess.

The court then held that it would be impossible, without having examined the circumstances, to categorize all doctors and psychiatrists as being or not being persons in author-

---

195   *R. v. Hodgson* (1998), 127 C.C.C. (3d) 449 (S.C.C.).
196   *R. v. Postman* (1977), 3 Alta. L.R. (2d) 139, 3 A.R. 524, aff'd [1978] 2 S.C.R. 392.

ity. Accordingly, the test should be: Is the person in a position, to the knowledge of the confessor, to influence the course of the prosecution? His profession *per se* is irrelevant.[197]

Where a private investigator has taken a statement at the behest of police, he has been found to be a person in authority.[198] However, private investigators often take statements where they are not acting under the direction of the police. In such situations, determining if a statement taker is a person in authority is not so clear and must include the subjective analysis described above. For example, where a loss prevention supervisor was known to an employee to have investigated other employees for theft, and where the loss prevention supervisor told the employee that his role included the investigation of staff shortages, it was held the loss prevention supervisor was a person in authority.[199]

9.3.2.2   Was the Statement Given Voluntarily?

After determining that a person who is offering a statement is a person in authority, the next question is if such a person made a threat or a promise of a temporal advantage that should render the statement unreliable and therefore inadmissible. In such cases, the party seeking to have the statement admitted must prove it was given voluntarily beyond a reasonable doubt in criminal cases, and on the balance of probabilities in civil cases.

Referring back to the case of the medical doctor discussed above in *R. v. Stewart*, the court found as fact that while no threat was made, there was the promise that any information the accused gave would remain confidential. However, there was no element of trick or stratagem. The doctor testified at trial only because of a subpoena. As a result, there was nothing about the doctor's handling of the matter which would cast doubt upon his evidence that the statement was voluntary, and there was no pressure through fear or hope that would cause the statement to be untrue. Rather, the doctor offered the accused protection, which allowed the accused to deliver the truth without fear of consequences. The court accordingly admitted the statement.[200]

Referring back to the case with the loss prevention supervisor, the court held that the statement was not voluntary because there was evidence that the employee did not under-

---

197 See *R. v. Stewart* (1980), 12 Alta. L.R. (2d) 303 (C.A). In this case, the court found as fact that the accused believed the doctor to be in a position of authority. The doctor regarded himself as an agent for the Attorney General conducting examinations and that he had been instructed to conduct the examination by the office of the Clerk of the Provincial Court. The doctor had made it clear to the accused that he was aware of the charge and that he had seen the body in his capacity as coroner. The doctor advised the accused of his conclusion that he was fit to stand trial and asked the accused to speak to the prosecutor about bail and a change of venue. Based on these facts, the court concluded the doctor was a person in authority.

198 See *R. v. Wray* (1970), 11 D.L.R. (3d) 673 (S.C.C.), where it was held that a private investigator who administered a polygraph examination at the request of police was acting under the direction of police and was, from the perspective of the accused, a person in authority. For an opposite result where the police solicited two private individuals to obtain a statement, see *R. v. Todd* (1901), 4 C.C.C. 514 (Man. K.B.A.D.).

199 *R. v. Nowoselski*, [2000] S.J. No. 493 (Prov. Ct.). See also *R. v. Shafie* (1989), 47 C.C.C. (3d) 27 (Ont. C.A.), discussed in Section 9.3.2.4.

200 *R. v. Stewart*, above note 197.

stand what was going on at the beginning of the interview, the employee was not a sophisticated person, the employee was misled into thinking a human resources manager was looking out for her best interests, and the loss prevention officer could not verify if he was or was not wearing handcuffs at the time. The court also found the loss prevention officer wrote up his notes and reports approximately fifty minutes after the confession and was imprecise in some significant respects. The court further held that while the loss prevention supervisor was not required to give the employee her *Charter* rights or right to silence, he was required to give her a warning as to the possible consequences of making any statement to him.[201]

9.3.2.3 The *Charter*: Section 7

The *Charter* has added further scrutiny to the admissibility of confessions. *R. v. J.C.*[202] was a case where a private citizen, a shop owner, arrested a person he suspected of theft from his premises. The court held that a right of an accused under section 7 of the *Charter* is not to be deprived of liberty except in accordance with the principles of fundamental justice. The principles of fundamental justice require that an accused shall not be convicted except on legally admissible evidence. The court declared a *voir dire* to determine if the shop owner was a person in authority, and if so, whether the accused's conversation with him was free and voluntary.

The court referred to the decision of *R. v. A.B.*[203] as an exhaustive and authoritative analysis of the concept of a person in authority. In that case, the court summarized seven categories of such persons. One such category is a person engaged in the arrest, detention, examination or prosecution of an accused. The court found that the storeowner fell into this category. Another such category is a person who, from the subjective point of view of the accused, has some degree of power over him or her. The court found the storeowner, by taking physical control over the accused, fell into this category as well.

With regard to whether the statement was freely and voluntarily given, the court held that the accused was under compulsion because of the physical restraints put upon her by the storeowner when she spoke to him. Accordingly, the court found the accused's statement was not voluntary and therefore inadmissible.

9.3.2.4 The *Charter*: Section 10

As seen in Section 4.1 — Arrest, pertaining to the discussion of *R. v. Lerke*, if a private investigator arrests a person, she is performing a state function and therefore is bound by the duties imposed on her by the *Charter*. Therefore, any statement taken by a private investigator after she arrests someone must be preceded by informing the person of his or her section 10(b) *Charter* right to counsel. However, in most cases, private investigators are not taking statements subsequent to an arrest but in the course of an investigation. The issue therefore is: What are the *Charter* requirements upon a private investigator if he or she is merely detaining someone?

---

201 *R. v. Nowoselski*, above note 199.
202 [1994] B.C.J. No. 1861 (Youth Ct.).
203 (1986), 26 C.C.C. (3d) 17 (Ont. C.A.).

Summing up this difficult issue to its simplest form, the law is that a private investigator is not required to give a person subject to an interview, from which a statement is sought, his or her section 10(b) *Charter* right to counsel if at the time the statement is taken, the private investigator is not an agent of the state. A private investigator is only an agent of the state if he or she has been "recruited" by an agent of the state to take the statement. If a private investigator is retained by a private person, the interview is seen in law as an interaction between two private parties and the *Charter* does not apply. This is the law regardless of whether the intent of the private parties before the statement is taken is to forward the statement to police at a later time. As long as no state intervention was involved before the statement is taken, the *Charter* does not apply.

The leading case on this point is *R v. Shafie*.[204] Shafie was employed by the owner of a parking facility. His employer became concerned about dwindling receipts and caused an audit to be done. The audit revealed a discrepancy between the receipts and the number of parking tickets issued by the facility. The employer sought, unsuccessfully, to have the Metropolitan Toronto Police investigate the matter. When the police declined to become involved, it entered upon its own investigation and engaged a licensed private investigator to assist it by interviewing some of its employees of whom Shafie was one.

Shafie was taken by his employer to an office where a private investigator awaited. The employer indicated to Shafie that he would consider it an act of insubordination if he refused to accompany him. The door was closed but not locked. The meeting was tape-recorded. In the course of the interrogation, Shafie made some incriminating statements. Based on the statements taken, the employer had Shafie charged with theft.

Both the Crown and defence agreed that although the private investigator was a person in authority, the statements were voluntary and thus admissible under the common law rule relating to the admissibility of confessions. It was also determined that Shafie was not under arrest but rather was detained.[205] The only issue that remained in dispute was whether the private investigator was required to inform Shafie of his *Charter* section 10(b) right to counsel. If the private investigator was required to advise Shafie of his right to counsel, the Crown conceded Shafie's statement would be excluded under section 24(2) of the *Charter*.

The court formulated the issue this way:

> The question that must now be addressed is whether a detention within the meaning of s.10(b) of the *Charter* can be said to exist when psychological coercion is brought about by a private person — in this case an employer in the private sector of the economy, or by its agent — and not by a peace officer or other agent of the state.

Section 10(b) of the *Charter* provides as follows:

> Everyone has the right on arrest or detention . . .
> to retain and instruct counsel without delay and to be informed of that right.

204 (1989), 47 C.C.C. (3d) 27 (Ont. C.A.).
205 For the analysis to determine if Shafie was detained, please see Section 4.1.1.2 — Arrest versus Detention.

The court noted that in *R. v. Therens*,[206] the issue was considered in relation to the conduct of police. However, no express consideration was given to detention by non-state agents. Recognizing the lack of direct authority on this issue, the court held:

> It is apparent from the cases to which I have referred that the weight of judicial opinion, although not perhaps authority in the strict sense, is that actions that at the hands of the police or other state or government agents would be a detention do not amount to a detention within the meaning of s.10(b) of the *Charter* when done by private or non-government persons. However weakly this conclusion may be based on authority, I believe it is supported by principle.[207]
>
> In a very able argument, Mr. Taylor (on behalf of Shafie) submitted that the *Charter* must be given a liberal interpretation to ensure that the rights guaranteed by the *Charter* are best protected. In determining whether Shafie was denied his right to be advised of the right to counsel before his incriminating statement was taken, we should, he submitted, consider the purpose for which the interrogation was taken. It is not clear to me that the statement was taken for the purpose of a prosecution, but for the present purposes I am prepared to assume that it was.
>
> Another way, perhaps, of putting the argument is that, although private action may not trigger the application of s.10(b) of the *Charter*, when the state later proposes to use a statement as part of a prosecution, state action then occurring, the earlier breach of s.10(b) would then engage s.24(2) of the *Charter*. In my view, however, the question of whether a person's s.10(b) rights were infringed must be tested at the time the alleged detention occurred. Any other consideration would result in the judicialization of private relationships beyond the point society could tolerate. The requirement that advice about the right to counsel must be given by a schoolteacher to a pupil, by an employer to an employee, or by a parent to a child, to mention only a few relationships, is difficult to contemplate.

The court concluded that, although Shafie was detained in the ordinary sense of the word, the interview by his employer's private investigator did not amount to a "detention" within the meaning of section 10(b) of the *Charter*. As no *Charter* right of Shafie was infringed, the evidence was admissible. Accordingly, the appeal from conviction was dismissed.

The case of *R. v. Shafie* has been the subject of some discussion. One commentator has opined that the lines here are somewhat blurry, and that the reasoning in *Lerke* is not entirely reconcilable with the outcome in *Shafie*. He argues, however, that it cannot have been intended by the framers of the *Charter* to superimpose the *Charter* on every form of interaction between private citizens where criminal law is implicated. This commentator concluded that the main and decisive issue was whether the private investigator was engaged for the purposes of not only the internal aspects of the investigation, but also for the public aspects. He stated:

---

206 [1985] 1 S.C.R. 613.
207 Referring to *R v. MacDonald* (1988), 5 M.V.R. (2d) 283 (C.A.); *R. v. Easterbrook* (18 July 1983), (Ont. Co. Ct.) [unreported]; and *R. v. Lerke* (1986), 24 C.C.C. (3d) 129 (Alta. C.A.).

The intent of the person to implicate state power later is not determinative. The person must be a state agent at the time of the alleged infringement . . . In the view of the writer, *Shafie* is a wise decision, balancing social interests in a proper way . . . It is not . . . reasonable to attribute to the state a responsibility for an alleged constitutional wrongdoing simply because the acts of a private citizen are in contravention of the law . . . [especially if it produces] evidence which is probative in a criminal proceeding. If, for instance, prison inmates decide to inform on other [inmates] . . . without having been earlier invited to do so by a state authority, it is difficult to imagine why such a source of valuable information should be effectively suppressed by the Constitution. *Shafie* is rightly decided.[208]

In a later case, a court commented that Shafie's detention was a private matter between him and his employer. If Mr. Shafie's detention was tortious, his remedy is in a private suit. The court rejected the idea that the *Shafie* decision is in conflict with that of *Lerke*.[209]

In a case involving a loss prevention supervisor who detained and interviewed an employee with the intention of obtaining a confession that could be used later in a criminal action, the court held:

The concern is that a person in authority may abuse his or her position by postponing arrest and obtaining a statement to facilitate intended prosecution. In some circumstances it may be that a court will find the conduct so questionable and the atmosphere so oppressive that the accused may be found to have been detained for the purpose of s.10(b) of the *Charter*. It is not necessary for me to decide this issue as I have found that the statement was not voluntarily made.[210]

This statement indicates the concern held by some in the legal community of the private sector making an end-run around the *Charter*.[211]

9.3.2.5 Derivative Evidence

For years before the imposition of the *Charter*, it was settled law that where the discovery of some fact confirms the truth of an involuntary confession, the part of the confession that is confirmed by the discovery of the fact is admissible. This was known as the Rule of St. Lawrence.[212] For example, where a private investigator was recruited by police and obtained a confession that a murder weapon was in a swamp, the Supreme Court of Canada held that although the confession involved trickery, because it was confirmed by the finding of the weapon, the part of the statement that led police to the weapon was admissible.[213]

---

208 See *R. v. Shafie*, annotation by Jack Watson, Appellant Counsel, Attorney General of Alberta, Edmonton, Alberta, (1989) 68 C.R. (3d) 260. The author also points out that the jurisprudential support for the position reached is not as scarce as the court may have felt, pointing out the cases of *R. v. Fisher (sub nom. R. v. Alexander)* (1987), 49 Alta. L.R. (2d) 293 (C.A.); *R. v. MacDonald*, above note 207; and *R. v. Dyment*, [1988] 2 S.C.R. 417.

209 *R. v. Wilson* (1994), 29 C.R. (4th) 302 (B.C.S.C.).

210 *R. v. Nowoselski*, above note 199.

211 See the discussions in Sections 4.1.1.2, 9.3.5, and 9.6.3.

212 *R. v. St. Lawrence* (1949), 93 C.C.C. 376 (Ont. H.C.J.).

213 *R. v. Wray*, [1970] 4 C.C.C. 1 (S.C.C.).

Since the passing of the *Charter*, the rules have changed. In a recent case from Toronto, an accused robbed a taxi operator at gunpoint. The police identified and interviewed the accused. The accused confessed his knowledge pertaining to the location of the gun. Before getting a search warrant, the police told the accused that they would "trash" his mother's home if he did not tell them the precise location of the gun. The gun was located. At trial the accused did not raise the *Charter* but did argue his confession was not voluntary and therefore the gun was inadmissible. The Crown argued that the gun was admissible based on the Rule of St. Lawrence. The accused argued the Rule of St. Lawrence offended section 7 of the *Charter*.

The court held that the *Charter* introduced a marked change in philosophy with respect to the reception of improperly or illegally obtained evidence. No longer was reliability the only key issue for evidence to be admissible pursuant to the confession rule. Rather, in addition to reliability, the discretion to exclude relevant prosecution evidence depends also upon the probative effect of the evidence balanced against the prejudice caused to the accused. The court held that such measures are required to ensure that the coercive powers of the state are held in check and to preserve the principle against self-incrimination. The court held that the Rule of St. Lawrence no longer applies with respect to police conduct. The gun was ruled inadmissible for breaching the *Charter*.

The question that remains is whether the Rule of St. Lawrence is still good law for investigators in the private sector. In the above case, the court stated:

> The confession rule is only concerned with voluntariness where statements are made to a person in authority . . . In my view, these rationales explicitly endorse a focus on the relationship between individuals and the state or its representatives, and should define our notion of "person in authority".
>
> . . .
>
> Therefore any instances of private coercion fall beyond the scope of the confession rule. The general unfairness of utilizing involuntary statements resulting from private coercion has never been the focus of the confession rule, even when the rule was justified by policy concerns for reliability.
>
> . . .
>
> Its modern rationales explicitly affirm that the rule is concerned only with voluntariness within the relationship between the state and the individual . . . A state which arbitrarily intrudes upon its citizens'personal sphere will inevitably cause more injustice that it cures . . . The policy basis for the rule . . . [includes] deterrence of improper police conduct and fundamental principles of fairness such as the rule against self-incrimination.[214]

No cases were reviewed which specifically addressed this issue. However, applying the principles of *Lerke* and *Shafie*, it would appear that the Rule of St. Lawrence would no longer apply to private investigators who take involuntary statements from an arrested person. However, where a suspect is merely detained, while not condoning the use of threats

---

214 *R. v. Sweeney* (2000), 50 O.R. (3d) 321 (C.A.).

or promises by private investigators, it does appear that derivative evidence obtained from involuntary statements by private investigators would likely be admissible.

9.3.2.6   Demands for Resignation by Private Investigators

Private investigators are often retained by companies to ferret out employee breaches of criminal law or company policy. Upon receiving sufficient evidence, corporate management occasionally will request a private investigator to conduct an interview with the subject employee, obtain a confession, and seek a resignation.

Case law has set out parameters with regard to the conduct of employers and the private investigators they retain when they engage in the seeking of confessions and demands for resignation. In a union context, a union representative must be present with the subject employee at the time of the interview and request for resignation, or minimally, the subject employee must be given an opportunity to consult with a union representative before making a final decision. Furthermore, there must be no threat of police intervention or criminal charges made to obtain some other objective.[215] Finally, there must be no threats of violence or other forms of intimidation.

Private investigators, as agents for the company, may confront a subject employee with wrongdoing and inform the employee of the company's intention. As the options of discharge or resignation by reason of personal circumstances are open to employers, these are alternatives a private investigator may put to an employee. So is the threat of civil action for restitution for losses an employee has caused his or her employer. The threat of civil action is an exception to criminal extortion. However, a threat of civil action may nullify the prospect that the statement is voluntary and therefore admissible later in court. The following cases discuss situations where companies have retained private investigators to obtain resignations from wayward employees.

In *Re Dubord & Rainville Inc. and M.U.A. Local 7625*,[216] a company was experiencing difficulties in its warehouse during the shift the subject employee was assigned to. These difficulties manifested themselves in numerous accidents, damage to equipment, errors in preparing orders for shipment, and high levels of absenteeism. As well, company officials received complaints from a number of other employees of the behaviour of the subject employees, including allegations that some were under the influence of drugs while at work or were using drugs while on duty.

The company resolved to address what it perceived as a serious problem. It engaged private investigators to maintain surveillance in its warehouse over a two-week period. Following the presentation by the private investigators of a report, the company concluded that some fourteen of its employees were implicated to some degree in the use of drugs while at work. It decided that it would proceed to discharge eight of these employees.

At the commencement of an evening shift, the company, with private investigators in attendance, summoned the union president and advised him of its intentions. It then summoned the eight employees targeted for discharge. During the course of an interview con-

---

215 See Section 4.5.5 — Extortion. A threat of criminal charges could result in the offence of extortion.

216 (1996), 53 L.A.C. (4th) 378 (Que.).

ducted in private by the private investigators, each employee was informed that the company had conducted surveillance and had gathered evidence of drug use on its premises. Each was informed that it was the intention of the employer to discharge the employee concerned for that reason. Each employee was advised of his right to have a union representative in attendance during the interview. Each employee was presented with the choice of either being made the object of a discharge or resigning. Those employees who chose to resign would be provided with a letter of reference. The subject employee, with some misgivings, chose to resign.

After a period of sober second thought, the subject employee argued that his resignation was not freely and voluntarily given. He submitted he was convoked without prior notice to an interview conducted by private investigators engaged by the company at which he was confronted with accusations of serious wrongdoing. He pointed out that he was alone in a room with the private investigators during the course of what amounted to an interrogation. He was then issued an ultimatum to the effect that he would be discharged for reasons that could reflect upon his reputation unless he preferred to resign his position.

The board held that the principles surrounding voluntary resignations are well known and have been made the object of numerous decisions. In law, a resignation is a unilateral act of an employee that must be freely and voluntarily given. The board pointed out that in order to claim a resignation was not freely and voluntarily given, an employee must show more than that the employer would have simply discharged the employee in the absence of a resignation. This is particularly so where the employee was given the opportunity to consult with his union representative upon the decision to be made. The board found as fact that the conduct of the employer in this case did not go beyond the simple request for a resignation in lieu of a discharge.

The board also held that the case law presented by the union was distinguishable. In a Quebec case, an employee was accused of a criminal offence involving drugs and made the object of intimidation and threats during the course of an interrogation conducted by company private investigators. A union representative was not in attendance at the time despite a provision in the collective agreement providing for such a requirement. The employee had no intention of resigning and only did so following considerable pressure. The board in this case held that the absence of the union delegate in the face of an express requirement that such a delegate be present at the interview was the determining factor to overturn the dismissal.[217]

In another case from Quebec, an employee was accused of drug use. Police intervention was threatened. The employee was convinced to resign and at no time was extended an opportunity to consult with a union representative. The board, in overturning the dismissal, held the employee had been subjected to undue pressure and the employer had acted improperly.[218]

---

217 *Re Provigo Distribution Inc. et Travailleurs et Travailleuses Unis de l'Alimentation et du Commerce, Section Local 501* (14 October 1991), (Quebec) Grievance No. 15806 [unreported] (J.-P. Lussier).
218 *Messageries de Presse Benjamin Inc. et Teamsters-Quebec, Local 1999 (Godin)*, (25 August 1994), (Quebec) [unreported] (P. Imbeau).

9.3.3 Interview Individually

In a case from Ontario, it was reported that a private investigator took statements from fifteen victims of a fraud as a group. The defence argued that such a procedure contaminated the reliability of the witnesses' accounts. The court agreed. The court, however, concluded that there was sufficient documentary evidence upon which to convict the accused.[219]

9.3.4 Concealed Tape Recorders

The tape or video recording of a confession can be critical to assisting a court determine if a statement was given voluntarily later at trial. For example, in a situation where a loss prevention supervisor did not make any notes until fifty minutes after an interview, a court held:

> [Although] the failure to have a record of the interview is not necessarily fatal . . . all of the surrounding circumstances are pertinent to the issue of voluntarines . . . In the circumstances I find that the failure to record the interview as it was occurring . . . to be significant . . . Given the inaccurate provisions of the rights and warning, I have no confidence in his testimony about what he did or what he recorded . . . Had he properly recorded what took place, perhaps we would know whether the handcuffs were in view and whether they were used to or had the effect of intimidating.[220]

As pointed out in Section 4.2.5 — Electronic Surveillance, it is not uncommon for private investigators to keep a concealed recording device on their person when conducting an interview. The courts have accepted into evidence the notes transcribed from such recordings in numerous civil cases.[221] The acceptance of such evidence has been more controversial in criminal cases.

In a recent Ontario case, *R. v Strano*,[222] a private investigator supplied a body-pack micro-cassette recorder with a microphone disguised as a pen to a client. The client then had a conversation with a government official who attempted to have the client make payoffs to him for government contracts. The government official's conversation was recorded on tape and later supplied to a government internal auditor who, in turn, turned over the tapes to the Ontario Provincial Police. The government official was charged with breach of trust and accepting secret commissions.

At his trial, the accused argued that the evidence on the tapes should be excluded as being the fruits of an illegal search pursuant to section 8 of the *Charter*. The court, however, held that pursuant to the ruling in *R. v. Shafie*,[223] the question of whether a person's

---

219 *R. v. Hadjor* (2000), O.J. No. 2978 (S.C.J.).

220 *R. v. Nowoselski*, above note 199

221 *Giffen v. Quesnel* (1995), 16 M.V.R. (3d) 252 (B.C.S.C.); *Nintendo of America Inc. v. 798824 Ont. Ltd.* (1991), 35 C.P.R. (3d) 1 (F.C.T.D.); *Smith v. Smith*, [1983] 23 A.C.W.S. (2d) 187 (B.C.S.C.); *GEAC J&E Systems Ltd. v. Craig Erickson Systems Inc.* (1992), 46 C.P.R. (3d) 25 (Ont. Gen. Div.).

222 [2001] O.J. No. 404 (C.J.).

Charter rights have been infringed must be tested at the time the alleged infringement occurred. Because the police were not involved in this case when the alleged infringement occurred, the *Charter* did not apply. Accordingly, the evidence was admissible unless there was some other reason for its exclusion.

In *R. v. Strano* the accused further argued that the evidence should be excluded because it was obtained illegally and therefore violated the accused's section 7 *Charter* right to life, liberty, and security of the person. The court, however, held that it was not illegal to possess or use the device used to obtain the evidence. Additionally, as mentioned above, at the time the device was used, the police were not involved in the investigation. Accordingly, the accused's section 7 *Charter* rights were not infringed and the evidence was held admissible.

9.3.5   Intercepted Cordless Telephone Conversations

In *R. v. Watts*,[224] an accused was charged with breach of trust and obstructing justice. The evidence to support the charges were recordings from a scanner of conversations on a cordless telephone made by a neighbour. When the neighbour realized the contents of the conversation contained elements of a criminal offence, he turned over the recordings to police. The accused argued that this evidence was inadmissible for breaching section 8 of the *Charter*. The court agreed and held that notwithstanding that the police were not involved in the securing of the evidence, it is the utilization of the evidence that triggers the *Charter* right. The court held that to allow such a practice would be to let police get in through the backdoor evidence that requires proper judicial authorization.

The *Watts* decision, a decision from British Columbia, has not been followed in Ontario. In *R. v. Strano,* discussed above, it was held that the court in *Watts* did not take into consideration well-established *Charter* jurisprudence as to when *Charter* rights crystallize. The court in *Strano* followed *R. v. Shafie*,[225] where the Ontario Court of Appeal held that the question of whether a person's *Charter* rights were breached must be tested at the time when the alleged *Charter* infringement occurred. In *Watts* the police were not involved in the case at the time the neighbour recorded the cordless telephone conversation. Accordingly, the *Charter* should not apply. *Watts* is another example of the contentious aspect of the *Charter*'s application to private investigations.[226]

9.3.6   Intercepted Digital Number Recorder Communications

In *R. v. Fegan*,[227] the accused was charged with making obscene telephone calls. Bell Canada and a radio station had been receiving complaints of annoying and offensive telephone calls from women stating that the caller would falsely identify himself as a radio

---

223   Above note 204.
224   (1997), 47 C.R.R. (2d) 252 (B.C.P.C.).
225   Above note 204.
226   See the discussions in Sections 4.1.1.2, 9.3.2.4, and 9.3.6.
227   (1993), 80 C.C.C. (3d) 356 (Ont. C.A.).

announcer. Although police were contacted, they deferred the investigation to Bell Security. Bell Security chartered a detailed record of the calls, which resulted in a lead. With the consent of a residential phone client, Bell Security installed a digital number recorder (DNR). The DNR produced evidence of the accused's phone number and the timing of the calls. As a result of this evidence, Bell Security contacted police who attended the accused's residence and arrested him.

At trial, the accused argued the DNR evidence should be excluded pursuant to section 8 of the *Charter* because it was seized without warrant. The court, however, held that Bell Security was not an agent of the state when it made the seizures and therefore, pursuant to the Ontario Court of Appeal in *R. v. Shafie*,[228] the *Charter* did not apply. Furthermore, even if the *Charter* did apply, the court held that DNR communications are not private communications for the purpose of *Criminal Code*. Finally, the court held that even if the communications were found to be private in nature, Bell Security was a party to the communications by waiver of the residential client and therefore had consent to record them.

9.4   AFFIDAVITS

Issues that have been addressed by the courts pertaining to private investigators who submit affidavit evidence include

* when hearsay is permitted;
* when hearsay is prohibited;
* summary judgments and the divulging of sources;
* the prohibition against double hearsay; and
* improper inducements to obtain an affidavit.

The following review is confined to principles taken from case law where the affidavits of private investigators were at issue. This review does not purport to make specific reference to each province's rules of civil procedure. Such a review is beyond the scope of this book.

9.4.1   Hearsay Permitted – Evidence Given on Information and Belief

The general rule is that affidavits shall be confined to facts within the personal knowledge of the deponent. There are a number of exceptions. Affidavits in support of applications may contain hearsay evidence, otherwise known as evidence given on information and belief, if the evidence is not contentious.[229] Affidavits in support of motions may contain evidence based on information and belief provided the source of the information and the reason for the belief are specified.[230] Affidavits in support of motions for summary judg-

---

228 Above note 204.
229 Rule 39.01(5), Ontario Rules of Civil Procedure.
230 Rule 39.01(4), Ontario Rules of Civil Procedure.

ment may also contain evidence based on information and belief. However, a negative inference may be drawn from such evidence if it is otherwise possible to obtain an affidavit from a person having personal knowledge.[231]

Where a private investigator gave evidence in an affidavit on information and belief that certain persons who attended a picket line were in violation of an injunction, a court found that the evidence did not result in such a conclusion. The injunction prohibited activity interfering or obstructing the business of a company. The court found the persons were only "peacefully communicating." The court held that while evidence in labour injunction cases invariably involves affidavits containing information provided on information and belief, this case fell short of the certainty required.[232]

9.4.2   Hearsay Prohibited — Applications Where Evidence Is Contentious

In Section 9.4.1, it was stated that affidavits in support of applications may contain hearsay evidence if the evidence is not contentious. In *Green v. Minister of National Defence*,[233] an application was made to strike out two affidavits submitted by private investigators in support of an application for judicial review on the basis that the affidavits contained hearsay evidence. The applicants argued that the private investigators' affidavits contained the subjective reports of telephone interviews with reluctant witnesses. The court held that the reluctance of otherwise available witnesses did not constitute necessity, an exception to the hearsay rule, particularly where the evidence was a subjective, speculative, and prejudicial collection of statements. Accordingly, the court struck out the private investigators' affidavits as not meeting the necessary criteria.

9.4.3   Summary Judgments and Divulging Confidential Sources

The courts generally reject affidavits of private investigators where they have not disclosed the source of their information.[234] However, on occasion, it is accepted. An example of a case where a court admitted into evidence an affidavit where a private investigator did not disclose his sources is *Mele v. Royal Bank of Canada*.[235] In this case, the defendant bank brought a motion for summary judgment against the plaintiff. As evidence against the granting of a summary judgment, the plaintiff submitted an affidavit of a private investigator.

In his affidavit, the private investigator stated he was retained by the plaintiff to conduct inquiries into claims of the plaintiff being a victim of a fraud perpetrated or facilitated through the bank. The private investigator disclosed some aspects of his investigation and

---

231 Rule 39.01(4), Ontario Rules of Civil Procedure.
232 *683481 Ontario Ltd. v. Beattie* (1990), 73 D.L.R. (4th) 346 (Ont. C.A.).
233 [1997] F.C.J. No. 1489 (F.C.T.D.).
234 *Sherman v. National Life Assurance Company of Canada* (1995), 130 D.L.R. (4th) 752 (Ont. Gen. Div.).
235 [1996] O.J. No. 230 (Gen. Div.).

certain information he received. Among other things, the private investigator stated his sources included a resident of the Bahamas who had acted on his behalf in the past and provided reliable and accurate information. The private investigator further stated that this individual imposed a condition that his identity not be disclosed as it would imperil his present position and prevent him from maintaining present employment. This individual's information was that a certain bank employee had been the subject of a police force investigation in the Bahamas and an internal inquiry by various officials of the bank.

The private investigator further quoted other individuals who had known this bank employee but would only provide information on condition that their identities remained anonymous to protect their current positions of employment and ability to obtain similar or more responsible positions in the future. The private investigator asserted that these individuals stated the bank employee had a bad reputation and that he had been involved in criminal activity while employed by the bank, and that the bank was aware of it.

Counsel for the bank objected to the admissibility of the private investigator's affidavit on the grounds that it was hearsay or double hearsay, that the time of retainer or when the information was obtained was not apparent on the face of the affidavit, and that there was no indication the information would be admissible if the anonymous sources testified.

The court recognized that Ontario's Rules of Civil Procedure provide that an affidavit for use on a motion may contain statements of the deponent's information and belief if the source of the information and the fact of the belief are specified in the affidavit.[236] However, specific to the facts of this case, the court held that it had to look at the ultimate evidence that was sought to be admitted on information and belief. In this case, it was evidence that verified the bank had conducted an internal investigation with regard to a specific employee and that a report had been made. The court held that the information the private investigator reported was not some vague allegation of obscure events but rather a pinpointing of documentary evidence in the hands of the bank. The judge concluded that in the circumstances of this case, and bearing in mind that it is a motion for summary judgment and not a trial, the affidavit was admissible.

A more typical reaction of a court to such evidence is taken from the case of *Mooney v. Orr*.[237] In this case the defendant sought a Mareva injunction[238] as to the *ex juris* assets of the plaintiff. As evidence to obtain the injunction, the defendant submitted an affidavit of a private investigator it had retained to inquire into the plaintiff's foreign assets. The plaintiff opposed the admissibility of the private investigator's affidavit, arguing the private investigator did not state the source of his information.

---

236 See Rule 39.01(4), Ontario Rules of Civil Procedure.

237 (1994), 98 B.C.L.R. (2d) 318 (B.C.S.C.).

238 A Mareva injunction is an "injunction preventing a defendant in a civil action from removing his or her assets from the jurisdiction prior to the court delivering its judgment. Such an injunction will only be granted if the applicant can persuade the court that there is a real risk that the assets will otherwise disappear": *Canadian Law Dictionary* (New York: Barron's, 1998) at 162. See also R.N. Ough & W. Frenley, *The Mareva Injunction and Anton Piller Order, Practice and Precedents*, 2d ed. (Toronto: Butterworths, 1993).

The court found that there were some serious evidentiary difficulties. In particular, the investigations manager of the private investigation firm had deposed to the results of the firm's investigation as reported to him by the individual investigator assigned to the file. However, that investigator's name was contained only in a second affidavit that was provided under seal. Second, the sources of the investigator's information were not disclosed since, according to the manager, his firm's methods are closely guarded trade secrets and cannot be revealed without jeopardizing all its future inquiries and operations.

Counsel for the defendant acknowledged the general rule that where affidavit evidence is based on information and belief, the deponent must state the source of the information applied with particular stringency to *ex parte* applications. The defendant's counsel argued, however, that the rule that permits a chambers judge to admit "other forms of evidence," taken together with another rule that creates a discretion to admit affidavit evidence that might otherwise be inadmissible, should be exercised here in the same way that information received from police informants is admitted without the disclosure of the identity of the informant.[239]

The court, however, held that the same reasoning does not apply to private investigators involved in carrying out the wishes of private litigants in civil cases. It stated that one would require very strong authority before extending it to private investigators, notwithstanding that the disclosure of their sources might be embarrassing to their sources or jeopardize future investigations. The court held the affidavits to be inadmissible.

9.4.4 The Prohibition Against Double Hearsay

In *R. v. E.J.B.*[240] the accused appealed his conviction of sexual assault. Concurrent with his appeal, he filed an application to admit fresh evidence. The accused argued that his trial counsel was incompetent because he advised against retaining a private investigator who would have discovered the information that he now sought to adduce as fresh evidence.

In response to this argument, the court held that any analysis of fresh evidence must start with an examination of the nature of the evidence. In this case, the appellant swore an affidavit that after conviction he retained a private investigator and that the investigator had informed him that he had interviewed a number of persons who had told him things that contradicted evidence given by the complainant at trial.

The court then quoted the rules of fresh evidence on appeal, which include (1) the evidence should generally not be admitted if, by due diligence, it could have been adduced at trial; (2) the evidence must be relevant in the sense that it bears upon a decisive or potentially decisive issue in the trial; (3) the evidence must be credible in the sense that it is reasonably capable of belief; and (4) the evidence must be such that if believed it could reasonably, when taken with the other evidence adduced at trial, be expected to have affected the result.[241]

---

239 Rule 52(8)(b) and Rule 57(10)(b) respectively of British Columbia's Rules of Civil Procedure. See *R. v. Hunter* (1987), 34 C.C.C. (3d) 14 (Ont. C.A.) *per* Cory J.A., quoted in Sopinka, Lederman, & Bryant, above note 1 at 804.

240 [1992] S.J. No. 546 (C.A.).

241 *R. v. Palmer*, [1980] 1 S.C.R. 759 at 775.

The court found that the affidavit the accused sought to enter as fresh evidence did not meet the first or third requirements. With regard to the first point, the court held that a deliberate decision was taken by counsel after discussion with the appellant to not undertake the investigations that would have uncovered the evidence. With regard to the third requirement, the court held that the fresh evidence was double hearsay: the affidavit of the appellant was to what a private investigator told him as to what yet other persons told the investigator. The court found that there was no indication whether the investigator took oral or written statements from the person he interviewed. There was nothing to indicate that, if the statements were written that they were either signed or sworn. Accordingly, the material was insufficient because there was nothing from which the court could determine whether the proposed fresh evidence was credible in the sense that it was reasonably capable of belief.

9.4.5 Improper Inducements to Obtain an Affidavit

Some private investigators are also qualified as commissioners for oaths and therefore can take affidavits from persons, have them sworn to, and then submit them to a lawyer or client as part of an investigation. Although having the qualification of a commissioner for oaths is laudable, it does bring with it the responsibility that the affidavits are taken in an appropriate manner. One concern of the courts in such cases is that which arises with the taking of statements generally, that of inducements or fear of reprisal.

In *Re Bernstein and College of Physicians and Surgeons of Ontario*,[242] a hearing before the discipline committee of the College of Physicians and Surgeons, the committee had to decide on the admissibility of two affidavits from private investigators. It came out in evidence that the private investigators had been hired by a disgruntled business partner of a doctor to obtain any sort of slanderous evidence possible on him to have him comply with a business arrangement. The private investigators maintained surveillance on the doctor for twenty-five days without making any observations of abnormal behaviour. However, one particular evening they observed a female being turned away by the doctor from his office door. After being rebuffed by the doctor, the private investigators picked her up. After a considerable period of time and questioning, the female made a short affidavit in which she stated that she had been having sexual intercourse with the doctor and had had an affair with him.

During the hearing, it was revealed that the female investigator told the complainant that she was an ex-patient of the doctor and had also been having an affair with him but now was getting the runaround. In fact, this female investigator had never been a patient of the doctor nor had she ever had anything to do with him. Counsel for the discipline committee did not have the opportunity of hearing from this female investigator at their hearing. However, the complainant later submitted a second affidavit to a lawyer in which she indicated she was not truthful on her original affidavit. She further alleged that she had signed the affidavit because of the pressure she was under from the private investigators. It was further learned that the complainant had psychiatric problems.

---

242 (1977), 15 O.R. (2d) 447 (Ont. Div. Ct.).

The court found that it did not know exactly how the private investigators obtained the statement but that it was obvious there had been a good deal of discussion before it was signed. The court held that what was really significant about the evidence of the private investigators was that even though they had followed the doctor on numerous occasions, they had not witnessed anything improper. The court also took note of the fact that shortly after taking the affidavit, it was forwarded along with other material that was before the court to a columnist for the *Toronto Sun* newspaper. It was this columnist who apparently lodged the complaint with the College of Physicians and Surgeons. Based on these reasons, the court held that the affidavit was unreliable and accordingly inadmissible as evidence.

9.5   UNDERCOVER OPERATIONS

A number of cases where the courts admitted evidence from undercover operations of private investigators in the civil litigation context were located during the research for this book. However, only one case where contentious issues were addressed in this regard was found pertaining to the criminal realm.

9.5.1   Criminal Litigation — Agents of the State

Covert, otherwise called undercover, assignments where the police have recruited a private investigator as an agent of the state have raised *Charter* concerns. In *R. v. Morgan*[243] the accused was charged with first-degree murder. Critical for the Crown was the admissibility of statements and observations obtained by an unlicensed private investigator who had befriended the accused.

The unlicensed private investigator came into contact with the accused through her own efforts after reading about the disappearance of his wife in the local media. For some time, she attempted to assist the accused to locate her. However, after a period of time, the private investigator became uncomfortable with assisting the accused because of certain discrepancies in his story. At approximately the same time, the private investigator was contacted by police. The police were familiar with her activities because they had wiretaps on the accused. At the behest of police, she agreed to befriend the accused with a goal to obtaining a confession and locating his wife's body.

The accused argued the police conduct amounted to an abuse of process and therefore the charges should be stayed. He argued that although he was not manipulated into committing an offense, he was connived into a course of conduct that provided compelling and damning evidence against himself. He argued the police authorities used fraud and trickery and that there was persistent importuning on the part of the police agent private investigator. The court held the authorities to answer this allegation fall into three categories: the entrapment cases; the dirty tricks cases; and the conscripted evidence cases.

---

243 [1997] O.J. No. 5477 (Gen. Div.).

9.5.1.1   Conscripted Evidence

The court held that in conscripted evidence cases, what must be considered is whether or not the accused is compelled to participate in the creation of evidence. If the accused is compelled to create evidence, a section 7 *Charter* breach occurs and it is then the obligation of the Crown to demonstrate on a balance of probabilities that the evidence would have been discovered by alternative non-conscriptive means.

The court held that while the police agent private investigator encouraged the accused to search for his wife, it cannot be said that there was "persistent importuning" on her part. Moreover, the evidence was not being created; it already existed and was being located. Further, the encouragement to find the body did not overwhelm the accused's freedom of choice. The accused could have easily declined her invitation. Accordingly, the accused's freedom of choice was not so fettered by virtue of the police conduct that a remedial order should have been considered by the court.

9.5.1.2   Entrapment Evidence

The court held that in entrapment cases, what must be considered is whether or not the accused was compelled to commit a crime. The limits of this rule are (1) a trap for a person cannot be laid unless that person is already under a reasonable suspicion of being involved in the specific type of criminal activity; and (2) if there is reasonable suspicion, a trap cannot go beyond the providing of an opportunity to commit an offence. Random virtue testing is not an acceptable practice by police.

The court held that in the present case, it could not be said the police were acting in a random fashion through the private investigator. They clearly believed that the accused was a suspect and provided him with an opportunity to incriminate himself. Accordingly, the accused was not entrapped in a fashion that a court would provide a remedy for.

9.5.1.3   Trading on Confidence and Dirty Tricks

The accused argued that the police employed a "dirty trick" by enlisting the private investigator to become a police informer. He argued that she was working for him and had an obligation to maintain confidence by virtue of being a private investigator notwithstanding that she had not yet obtained her private investigator's licence or was formerly retained or being paid by the accused. The accused pointed out that similar "dirty tricks" had been criticized by the courts such as a police informant pretending to be a religious chaplain hearing a confession and a police informant pretending to be a legal aid lawyer obtaining a statement.

The court held that "dirty tricks" contemplate a relationship of confidence and privilege that society has traditionally recognized. The court further held that if the relationship between a suspect and an informer meets the "Wigmore criteria" of privilege or confidentiality, then the evidence obtained would fall into the "dirty trick" category and be excluded.[244] The four Wigmore criteria are:

1.   The communications must originate in a confidence that they will not be disclosed;

---

244 *R. v. Gruenke* (1991), 67 C.C.C. (3d) 289 (S.C.C.).

2.   The element of confidentiality must be essential to the full and satisfactory mainte-
     nance of the relation between the parties;

3.   The relation must be one which, in the opinion of the community, ought to be sedu-
     lously fostered; and

4.   The injury that would inure to the relation by the disclosure of the communications
     must be greater than the benefit thereby gained for the correct disposal of litigation.[245]

The court determined that a case-by-case analysis should be employed.

On the facts of this case, the court held that the first criteria had not been established, namely, that the communications originated in confidence that they would not be disclosed. At the very first meeting between the private investigator and the accused, the private investigator asked if she could tape-record the interview. No objection was taken. Further, the private investigator was not employed by the accused. At least three times thereafter during the relationship between them, the accused made suggestions that she might be an undercover agent. Clearly, the thought crossed his mind that he might be dealing with an individual outside his confidence. In fact, he was; he could not now complain.

With respect to the issue whether the lies told by the private investigator to the accused constituted "dirty tricks," the court held that a review of the case law confirms that the false information given to the accused as a result of which he took certain steps would not shock the conscience of the community. The cases show that far more serious conduct than that engaged in by the private investigator has passed the muster of the courts. For example, in *R. v. Skinner*,[246] an undercover officer became acquainted with the accused and posed as an escorted prisoner. He befriended the accused and lied to him and received incriminating statements. The evidence was found to be admissible. In *R. v. Unger*,[247] police officers falsely held themselves out to be members of a gang and enticed the accused to join. To become a member, the accused was encouraged to demonstrate that he had killed somebody. The accused confessed to a killing, was charged and convicted. The police conduct was found to be within acceptable boundaries by the Manitoba Court of Appeal. In *R. v. McIntyre*,[248] two undercover police officers were investigating the killing of a nun. They believed the accused was the guilty party. They pretended to be involved in prostitution and created a friendship with the accused. They offered the accused a job on condition that he be able to kill if necessary and asked for proof that he was capable. He refused to answer. The police officers continued to push him for answers, specifically on the subject of the nun who had been killed. Finally, after much encouragement, the accused realized that the only way to get a job was to confess, which he did in detail.

In the circumstances, the court held that it could not be said that the police conduct or that of the private investigator amounted to a "dirty trick." The conduct was well within the parameters of acceptable police activity in the pre-detention phase. The court held that tricks employed in this phase are not only acceptable but necessary. It is only when the

---

245   Above note 28.
246   (1992), 17 C.R. (4th) 265 (Man. Q.B.).
247   (1993), 83 C.C.C. (3d) 228 (Man. C.A.).
248   (1993), 135 N.B.R. (2d) 266 (C.A.).

tricks become repulsive to fundamental societal values, viewed objectively, that they become subject to an overarching rule of exclusion. The court concluded that the accused had not demonstrated on a balance of probabilities that his section 7 *Charter* rights had been violated. Accordingly, the application to exclude the evidence of the private investigator was denied.

9.5.2 Labour Litigation

Evidence obtained by undercover operations is admissible in a labour litigation context, subject to concerns about privacy and entrapment discussed earlier.[249] Examples include private investigators posing as kitchen employees to obtain evidence of tobacco smuggling,[250] and private investigators posing as patrons in a bar to obtain evidence of employee theft.[251]

9.5.3 Professional Licensing Litigation

In a case involving a doctor charged with illegally dispensing optical products in contravention of his professional body's rules of conduct, it was argued that evidence obtained by a law student posing as a customer in the doctor's store breached the doctor's section 8 *Charter* right against unreasonable search and seizure. The court, however, held that the undercover operation in a public place is not an unreasonable breach of a person's right to privacy. The court admitted the evidence obtained.[252]

Law societies have accepted evidence of private investigators posing as clients to unlicensed persons providing legal services.[253]

9.5.4. Insurance Litigation

Evidence obtained by undercover operations is admissible in an insurance litigation context, subject to concerns about privacy.[254] For example, while the courts have accepted the evidence of private investigators who have entered an insured's home where the insured was running a business out of the home,[255] they have also been very critical of this practice.[256]

---

249 See Section 9.2.4.

250 *Re Beaver Foods Ltd. and Hotel Restaurant and Culinary Employees and Bartenders Union Local 40,* [1996] B.C.D.L.A. 500 (B.C.).

251 *6K Investments Ltd. v. Hotel, Restaurant and Culinary Employees and Bartenders Union, Local 40* (1996), B.C.D.L.A. 500.15.40.25-08 A-05/96.

252 *Markandey v. Ontario (Board of Ophthalmic Dispensers),* [1994] O.J. No. 484 (Gen. Div.). See also *Manitoba Association of Optometrists v. 3437613 Manitoba Ltd. (c.o.b. Eye-Deal Eyewear)* (1997), 124 Man. R. (2d) 61 (Q.B.).

253 *Law Society of British Columbia v. McLaughlin,* [1992] 6 W.W.R. 569 (B.C.S.C.); *Law Society of British Columbia v. Gravelle,* [1998] B.C.J. No. 2883 (S.C.).

254 See Section 9.2.3.3.

255 *Stevens v. Okrainec,* [1997] A.J. No. 1158 (Q.B.); *Armstrong v. Oliveria,* [1992] B.C.J. No. 2003 (S.C.).

256 *Turner v. Economical Mutual Insurance Company* (14 May 1999), F.S.C.O. Judgment No. A-012411 (Ont. F.S.C.); *Levy v. Traders General Insurance* (30 June 1998), O.I.C. A96-001590; and *Lindsay v. T.N.T. Express (UK) Ltd.,* [1996] Scott J. No. 236 (Scot. Ct. Sess. O.H.).

9.6   PROPERTY SEIZURES

The issues covered in this section are the requirement to maintain continuity of evidence, evidence obtained from garbage, and *Charter* considerations.

9.6.1   Continuity of Physical Evidence

As a general rule, there must be a trail of continuity for evidence to be found reliable for a court. The typical practice of most investigators is to place an identifying mark, such as an initial, on the evidence in an innocuous part of it. If the evidence itself cannot be marked, the evidence may be placed in a bag or container suitably marked and initialled. Either way, the evidence should then be placed in a secure place for which access is regulated. Any change of possession of evidence must be carefully logged to maintain the trail of continuity.

An interesting example of a court rejecting evidence in a civil matter due to failing to maintain proper continuity is taken from the case of *Havana House Cigar & Tobacco Merchants Ltd. v. Naeini*.[257] In this case, the allegation was that the defendants were selling counterfeit Cuban cigars. The case is summarized as follows.

A private investigator was hired by Havana House. He was not knowledgeable about cigars. He purchased part boxes of cigars, six in one box and ten in another, that were on display at Pacific Tobacco and Cigars. He had a clerk write on the back of the receipt what was purchased. He put his signature on a sticker that he affixed to the boxes to identify them. The cigars in the boxes were not marked to allow for later analysis. The boxes were open at the time of purchase. They were not sealed subsequently except in the sense that they were packaged for delivery to the director of Havana House, a Mr. Ortego (the plaintiff), by courier. The boxes containing the cigars were then sent by Federal Express from Vancouver to Toronto to the custody of Mr. Ortego.

The court held that there were a number of steps that could have been taken by the plaintiffs to increase the court's confidence in the integrity of the evidence. The cigars that were purchased could have been deposited by the private investigator with the court immediately after purchase for safekeeping. The cigars could have been deposited with some independent third party who was knowledgeable about cigars for both evaluation and safekeeping. The private investigator could have retained custody subject to making them available for inspection. Instead, the cigars were delivered into the custody of Mr. Ortego (the plaintiff) and they remained there throughout. The private investigator did not even have them in front of him when he signed his affidavit. There was no assurance that the cigars evaluated by Mr. Ortego and that were in the boxes before the court were the same as those that were purchased at Pacific Tobacco and Cigars. The court held that due to this loss of confidence, the balance of convenience favoured the defendants, not the plaintiffs. The evidence was deemed inadmissible and the injunction application was dismissed.

---

257 [1997] F.C.J. No. 1059 (F.C.T.D.).

9.6.2   The *Charter* — Agents of the State

The issue of property rights in garbage was reviewed in Section 4.4.4 — Property Rights in Garbage. The issue discussed here is whether such evidence is admissible.

It is well settled in law that in a civil context, such evidence would be admissible subject to the usual qualifiers of relevance, reliability, and judicial discretion. As noted in the introduction of this chapter, at common law it matters not how you get it, even if you steal it, it is admissible as evidence.[258] However, if a private investigator is operating as an agent of the state, other concerns arise.

In *R. v. Krist*[259] the accused was facing a charge under the *Narcotic Control Act*. The issue was whether a warrantless search of garbage left on the street for collection adjacent to the accused's home violated his section 8 rights under the *Charter*. On this issue the court stated:

> The issue boils down to the right of the police to seize garbage put out for collection and to search it for evidence without a warrant. I am told that there is no decided case in Canada.
>
> . . .
>
> In my view, it is preferable that the law be drawn with a clear line of demarcation as to when garbage may be seized and searched without a warrant and when it may not. The right to be secure against unreasonable search and seizure is the product of a right to be private. Whether or not when the ordinary person puts out his or her garbage there is any thought that others may sift through it will depend on a number of factors . . . Often the expectation is that it will be taken away and disposed of without any intermediate investigation. But by putting it out the householder puts it beyond his or her control. Any property claim is abandoned.

With this statement the court held that evidence derived from garbage placed on a curb off an owner's property is not an illegal seizure rendering it inadmissible regardless of whether the context is criminal or civil or whether it was seized by police or private investigators.

There have been other cases that have further clarified the law pertaining to garbage. In a case from British Columbia, police found garbage bags outside the fenced portion of a property and removed them. To obtain the garbage, the police had to step over the property line and temporarily onto the property of the accused. The accused argued that because the police actually trespassed onto his land, they breached his reasonable expectation of privacy. The court, however, held that the police did no more than what a garbage collector, for whose attention the bags were obviously left, would have done. Accordingly, the accused had no reasonable expectation of privacy. The evidence was deemed admissible.[260]

Stepping on someone's property, however, is distinguished from entering their home. In a case from Alberta, police entered into a residence, in this case a hotel room, under a ruse and seized items from a garbage container. The court held that the accused had not yet

---

258 *R. v. Leatham*, [1861-73] All E.R. Rep. Ext. 1646, subject to concerns of other types of liability.
259 (1995), 100 C.C.C. (3d) 58 (B.C.C.A.).
260 *R. v. Tam* (23 March 1993), File No. CC920382 (B.C.S.C.) [unreported].

abandoned his proprietary rights in the garbage. Therefore, the seizure, being without warrant, violated his section 8 *Charter* right. This case reinforces the notion that property rights are not abandoned until after garbage is put off the property of the owner.[261]

9.6.3 The *Charter* — Independent Operatives

The cases discussed in the section above each pertained to the conduct of police in seizing evidence. These cases are instructive for determining admissibility if a private investigator is acting as an agent of the state. In most cases, however, private investigators are not acting in this capacity. The question that then arises is what effect is there on admissibility if a private investigator obtains physical evidence illegally.

During this chapter the famous quote from Justice Crompton has been mentioned a number of times: It matters not how you get it, even if you steal it, it would be admissible as evidence.[262] This principle has been verified recently in a case from Saskatchewan.[263] In this case private investigators entered into a private vehicle without authorization and obtained a sample of DNA that they later turned over to a private laboratory for analysis. When the results of the DNA investigation came back, the evidence was forwarded to police who used it to obtain a search warrant. The accused argued that the search warrant should be quashed on the basis that the private investigators were essentially agents of the police and therefore fell under the scope of the *Charter*, and as such had breached the accused's section 8 *Charter* rights. The Saskatchewan Court of Appeal, however, did not agree. They stated:

> We are of the view the private investigators can not be said to have been agents of the state so as to render their actions in gathering samples of material . . . a violation of the appellant's constitutional rights. We are also of the view that, even if the private investigator . . . gathered the sample . . . illegally, this did not preclude the judge who issued the warrant from acting on the strength of the results of the DNA analysis. The evidence of the results . . . came to the knowledge of the police after the fact, and they placed it before the judge disclosing what had occurred. We see no reason for concluding that this evidence was inadmissible or could not have been relied upon by the judge in issuing the warrant.

This statement affirms the principle from *R v. Shafie* discussed in Section 9.3.2.4 pertaining to the taking of statements. There it was said that the section 10(b) *Charter* requirements do not apply to private investigators if the police have not been contacted before the investigation, regardless of whether the intention of the private investigators is to turn the evidence over to police at a later time. This statement also affirms the principle from *R. v Barnes*, discussed in Section 4.1.2.2.2 — Search Subsequent to Detention. There it was said that the section 8 *Charter* requirements apply to private investigators only after arrest, a state function, not detention, which in the private sector is not a state function.

---

261 *R. v. Love* (1995), 102 C.C.C. (3d) 393 (Alta. C.A.).
262 *R. v. Leatham*, above note 256.
263 *R. v. Schneeberger*, [2000] S.J. No. 640 (C.A.).

The position of the courts on this issue will be contentious to some. In Section 4.1.1.2 — Arrest versus Detention, the cases of *R. v. J.A.* and *R. v. Wilson* were reviewed. In those cases, the courts raised concerns about agents of the state using private investigators to do what the *Charter* prohibited them from doing. Although those cases do not have direct bearing on the discussion here, it is apparent that while agents of the state cannot circumvent the *Charter* by using private investigators, other private actors such as defence lawyers and private citizens can. However, if such private actors do entertain these thoughts, they must bear in mind that they leave themselves open to liability in different forms.

9.7 ASSET TRACING

In a family law division of assets case, a spouse retained a private investigator to investigate her husband's business affairs and locate any assets outside of their province of residence. The private investigator retained other investigators who specialized in this type of investigation. The private investigator produced a list of bank accounts held in the names of various companies to which he claimed the husband was a signatory. Prior to trial, the private investigator confirmed these accounts were still operational by making small deposits into each of them, which were not returned. The court held that while the deposits may prove the accounts are still operational, it does not prove who the signatories to the accounts are. Furthermore, because the contracted investigators were not identified, did not disclose the basis upon which they obtained their information, or the basis upon which they were retained, let alone testify, the evidence was not sufficiently reliable to be admissible.[264]

---

264 *Matthews v. Matthews*, [1999] B.C.D. Civ. 360.60.72.00-01 (S.C.).

CHAPTER 10

LITIGATION ISSUES

This chapter discusses a number of topics of possible interest to private investigators in their role in the litigation process. These topics are separate and distinct in nature. They include a review of the law pertaining to private prosecutions, the law pertaining to executing search warrants, the law of privilege, and the law of costs.

10.1 PRIVATE PROSECUTIONS

There has been a rather sensational case where a private investigator commenced a private prosecution on behalf of fifteen fraud victims who were bilked out of approximately $650,000. The group originally took their complaint to Metro Toronto Police Service and were advised that because their complaint was for less than a million dollars, it would take more than a year for them to get around to investigating it. The group then sought out a certified fraud examiner who commenced an investigation immediately. Upon completion of his investigation, this investigator took the evidence to a justice of the peace where he swore out an information against the accused. The private investigator also convinced the justice of the peace to issue an arrest warrant.

At trial, the court acknowledged that corporations and citizens are increasingly taking their fraud allegations to private investigators because of the lack of response from police. The court, however, had a number of criticisms in this particular case. The court opined that when private investigators investigate fraud cases, they should take their findings to police instead of proceeding by way of private informations themselves. The court also noted that the private investigator did not take sufficient notes during his investigation, that he arranged for a camera crew to be present at the time of the arrest, and that he did not make adequate disclosure to the defence. Despite these procedural shortcomings, the court convicted the accused. The court held that because the jury was apprised of the flaws in the private investigator's conduct and procedure and because of the serious nature of the offence, the finding of guilt by the jury would stand.[1]

---

1   *R. v. Hadjor*, [2000] O.J. No. 2978 (S.C.J.).

Although private prosecutions are not common in Canada, their existence is relevant to a review of Canadian law and private investigations because of the increasing unwillingness or inability of police to conduct timely investigations and prosecutions of financially related offences. The most comprehensive review of private prosecutions in Canada is found in a 1986 Working Paper of the Law Reform Commission of Canada entitled *Private Prosecutions*.[2] In their study, the Law Reform Commission found that "[t]he power of private prosecution is undoubtedly right and necessary . . . The frequency of the use of the power is not in our view an accurate measure of its value.[3] The following is a summary of that report.

10.1.1 Definitions

The *Criminal Code*[4] defines the term "informant" to mean any person who lays an information. The term "justice" means a provincial court judge or a justice of the peace. In most cases, an informant will deal with a justice of the peace. The *Criminal Code* defines the term "prosecutor" to mean the Attorney General, or if the Attorney General does not intervene, the informant, or counsel acting on behalf of either of them.[5] The term "information" is commonly understood to be the evidence given to a justice which forms the basis of a criminal charge. Finally, the term "indictable" includes offences that may proceed by either indictment or summary conviction.

10.1.2 Laying an Information

All criminal proceedings are initiated by the "laying of an information." The *Criminal Code* provides that anyone who, on reasonable and probable grounds, believes that a person has committed an indictable offence may lay an information in writing and under oath before a justice.[6] It provides that a justice who receives an information shall hear and consider the allegations of the informant *ex parte*. A justice has discretion on whether to hear evidence of witnesses.[7] It further provides that summary conviction offences shall be commenced by laying an information in Form 2. Form 2 does not restrict who may lay an information.[8]

If all the formal requirements of the alleged offence are met, a justice is obliged to receive the information. If a justice of the peace refuses to receive the information, his or her decision is reviewable by a superior court as a matter of law. An informant's other option is simply to seek out a different justice for a second opinion.

---

2 *Working Paper 52: Private Prosecutions* (Ottawa: Law Reform Commission of Canada, Catalogue No. J32-1/52-1986).

3 *Ibid.* at 21 & 29.

4 *Criminal Code*, R.S.C. 1985, c. C-46.

5 *Ibid.*, s. 2.

6 *Ibid.*, s. 504.

7 *Ibid.*, s. 507.

8 *Ibid.*, s. 788.

The informant does not have to be a witness or a victim to the alleged offence. Rather, an informant must simply have reasonable and probable grounds, that is, objectively reliable information, for his or her belief that the accused committed the offence alleged. Accordingly, an aggrieved person can have his or her counsel or agent lay an information. Indeed, as seen in the case above, a private investigator was permitted to act as agent on behalf of fraud victims for the purpose of laying an information.

10.1.3 Compelling Appearance by the Accused

Once an information has been laid and been accepted by a justice, the next issue is notifying the accused of the charge, a concept also known as issuing and confirming process. The *Criminal Code* provides that, upon accepting an information, a justice shall issue either a summons or a warrant for arrest of the accused to compel the accused to attend court to answer to a charge. The section further provides that no justice shall refuse to issue a summons or warrant only because the alleged offence is one for which a person may be arrested without warrant. A justice shall issue a summons unless there are reasonable grounds to believe that it is necessary in the public interest to issue a warrant for arrest.[9]

10.1.3.1   Summons

If a justice chooses to issue a summons, it shall state the name of the accused; the offence for which the accused is charged; and the time, date, and location of the court at which the accused must attend. The summons may only be served by a peace officer. It must be served personally or to someone who is over sixteen years old at his or her usual place of residence. If the offence with which the accused is charged is indictable, the accused must also be fingerprinted and photographed pursuant to the *Identification of Criminals Act*.[10]

10.1.3.2   Warrant to Arrest

A justice may issue an arrest warrant if the justice has reasonable and probable grounds to believe that it is necessary in the public interest to do so.[11] Arrest warrants must state the name of the accused, the offence he or she is charged with, and the court the accused must be returned to. Arrest warrants remain in force indefinitely.[12] Arrest warrants shall be directed to peace officers in the jurisdiction of the court where the accused is to be returned. Arrest warrants may only be executed by peace officers.[13]

10.1.4 Title of the Prosecution

The name under which to prosecute a criminal private prosecution is an issue that has been addressed by the courts. It is settled law, at least in Ontario, that all proceedings are carried on in the name of the Crown, even though a representative from the Attorney General's

---

9   *Ibid.*, s. 507.
10   *Ibid.*, s. 509.
11   *Ibid.*, s. 512.
12   *Ibid.*, s. 511.
13   *Ibid.*, ss. 513 & 514.

office may not have intervened. The rationale for this approach is taken from a Court of Appeal case where it was stated:

> The distinction between the information and the summons is an essential one and one which should be readily apparent. The information is the subject's remedy to bring to the attention of the Sovereign the alleged offence against the Sovereign. The summons is the Sovereign's act in calling the accused before her "justice."
>
> The prosecution commences when the "justice" issues the summons addressed to the accused. Viewed from this angle it is clear that the laying of an information does not entail any act on part of the Sovereign and therefore it is not required to be laid in the name of the Sovereign; it is equally clear that by the summons issued under the Criminal Code or the Summary Convictions Act the Sovereign intervenes and the proceedings are commenced in the name of the Sovereign.[14]

From this passage it is clear that once a justice issues a summons, the prosecution is in the name of the Crown, notwithstanding the Attorney General decision to not intervene.

10.1.5 Summary Conviction Offences

The procedure for all summary conviction offences is dealt with in Part XXVII of the *Criminal Code*. If process has been confirmed and if the prosecutor and accused attend, a summary conviction court shall proceed to arraign an accused.[15] If the prosecutor does not attend and the accused appears, a summary conviction court may dismiss the information or may adjourn the trial to some other time.[16] If an accused pleads not guilty to a charge, a summary conviction court shall proceed to trial and take evidence from witnesses.[17]

At a summary convictions trial, a prosecutor is entitled to examine and cross-examine witnesses personally or by counsel or an agent.[18] Although the *Criminal Code* provides that a prosecutor is entitled to conduct his case personally, it has been held that a provincial Crown attorney continues to have the right to intervene and take over the prosecution of the offence.[19]

10.1.6 Indictable Offences

In summary conviction cases, the Attorney General has the option of whether to intervene and take over a case from a private prosecutor. At issue here is whether the same can be said when the offence is an indictable one. The answer is not so clear because for most indictable offences, there are three modes of trial an accused can select: (1) trial before a judge and jury with or without a preliminary hearing; (2) trial before a judge alone with or

---

14 *R. v. Devereaux* (1966), 48 C.R. 194 (Ont. C.A.).
15 *Criminal Code*, above note 4, s. 800.
16 *Ibid.*, s. 799.
17 *Ibid.*, s. 801.
18 *Ibid.*, s. 802.
19 *Re Bradley and the Queen* (1975), 24 C.C.C. (2d) 482 (Ont. H.C.J.).

without a preliminary hearing; and (3) a summary trial before a provincial court judge. For some very serious offences, the accused cannot select a summary trial before a provincial court judge. Likewise, there are a number of offences for which the Crown can elect whether to proceed summarily or by indictment.[20]

In a case from British Columbia, a court set out what it believed to be the rules under which a private prosecutor could prosecute an indictable offence. It held that on summary trials before a provincial court judge, as dealt with in the section above, a private prosecutor may handle the case unless the Attorney General intervenes. If the accused seeks trial by either superior court judge or judge and jury and a preliminary hearing, the preliminary hearing may be conducted by a private prosecutor. If the accused seeks trial by a superior court judge and waives his or her preliminary hearing, or, upon having a preliminary hearing, is committed to trial, a private prosecutor cannot proceed with a case unless the Attorney General "prefers" a charge; that is, files the charge with a Superior Court of Justice or gives permission to a private prosecutor to prefer a charge. Trials by judge and jury may only be conducted by a private prosecutor with leave of the court or the Attorney General.[21]

These requirements are actually stricter today. A review of the *Criminal Code* reveals that any prosecution conducted by a private prosecutor in which the Attorney General does not intervene requires a written order of a judge in a court where the information was laid before an indictment may be filed.[22] Cases considering this issue have held that a court must consider the nature of the alleged offence; that is, whether it is of a public nature, such as murder, or a private nature, such as criminal libel. A court should also consider the position of the Crown on the matter. Where a preliminary hearing has been held, a judge's consent should only be given to prevent a miscarriage of justice. Therefore, consent will not automatically be given simply because a *prima facie* case was made out at the preliminary hearing. Where no preliminary hearing has been held, the test is stricter: consent should not be granted unless some urgency or other strongly persuasive reason exists.[23]

10.1.7 Right of Attorney General to Intervene

Despite all the good intentions of a private prosecutor, the *Criminal Code* provides that at any time after an information is laid, whether the alleged offence is indictable or summary conviction, an agent of the Attorney General can intervene and stay proceedings.[24] If the proceedings are not recommenced within one year, the proceeding is deemed to have never commenced.[25] The stay of proceeding provisions do not prevent a Crown attorney

---

20 *Criminal Code*, above note 4, ss. 469, 536, 553, 558, 561, & 568.
21 *R. v. Schwerdt* (1957), 27 C.R. 35 (B.C.S.C.).
22 *Criminal Code,* above note 4, s. 574(3).
23 *Re Johnston and Inglis* (1980), 52 C.C.C. (2d) 385 (Ont. H.C.J.); *Re Garton and Whelam* (1984), 14 C.C.C. (2d) 449 (Ont. H.C.J.).
24 *Criminal Code,* above note 4, s. 579(1).
25 *Ibid.*, s. 579(2).

from seeking to withdraw charges with leave of a court prior to a plea having been taken. After a plea has been taken, a Crown attorney can only have charges withdrawn with leave of a court.[26]

Although a proceeding is stayed by an agent of the Attorney General, all is not lost. Subsequent to a proceeding being stayed, an informant can lay a new information with identical allegations.[27] Alternatively, a Crown attorney's decision to stay proceedings can be reviewed by way of motion to a court. It is noteworthy, however, that a recognized ground for staying proceedings is where the criminal proceedings have been instituted to collect a debt or realize on some civil claim. This ground, however, must be more than a mere admission under cross-examination that if the victim had been repaid, a criminal information would not have been laid.[28] It must amount to evidence that the victim had threatened the accused to go to police if payment was not made, and then followed through with that threat.[29] As discussed above, this is a form of extortion.[30]

Note also that the authority of the Attorney General is not limited to the right to stay or withdraw charges. In cases where an accused voluntarily decides to make restitution to a victim, a victim cannot on his or her own accord decide to have charges withdrawn. Once an information has been laid, a Crown attorney can intervene and pursue prosecution against the wishes of a private prosecutor.

10.1.8 Application to Private Sector Investigations

The complexity of the process should not act as a deterrent to investigators in the private sector whose clients are turned away by police. It has been recognized in policy that private prosecutions are a legitimate form for individuals to seek vindication for personal grievances. Arguably more important, private prosecutions have been recognized as a necessary part of the justice system to prevent victims of crime from resorting to unregulated forms of self-help. Other arguments for private prosecutions include reducing the burden on overworked Crown attorneys and promoting citizen participation and democratization in our justice system. Critics of private prosecutions argue the propensity for abuse of this power. However, if a victim's allegations or motives are truly nefarious, an accused may seek redress through counter-allegations of extortion or civil actions for malicious prosecution.[31]

As discussed in the beginning of this section, the consideration of commencing a private prosecution really only arises in fraud investigations wherein the police indicate their lack of interest or inability to conduct a timely investigation. In *R. v. Hadjor*, the case discussed in the beginning of this section, the court held that a private investigator should take the findings of his or her investigation to police before laying a private information. The

---

26 *R. v. Grocutt* (1977), 35 C.C.C. (2d) 76 (Alta. S.C.T.D.).
27 *R. v. Judge of the Provincial Court, Ex parte McLeod*, [1970] 5 C.C.C. 128 (B.C.S.C.).
28 *R. v. Laird* (1983), 4 C.C.C. (3d) 92 (Ont. H.C.J.).
29 *R. v. Janvier*, [1985] 5 W.W.R. 59 (Sask. Q.B.).
30 See the discussion in Section 4.5.5 of this book.
31 See *Working Paper 52: Private Prosecutions*, above note 2, Chapter 3.

court held the reason for this procedural step was to ensure an aspect of the investigation was not overlooked or improperly conducted. In other words, filing a completed investigation report with police prior to the laying of a private information is a form of checks and balances. Following such a procedure is also wise for the purposes of appearing objective, to establish a defence to an allegation of malicious prosecution, and to increase one's credibility with the courts. If the police remain uninterested, it is recommended that consideration be given to retaining a private solicitor to pursue the process until it is taken over by a Crown attorney. Arguably, there are few private investigators who can claim such a familiarity with criminal law that they would feel comfortable seeing the process through to its conclusion.

10.2   SEARCH WARRANTS AND PRIVATE INVESTIGATORS

During preliminary discussions before this book was written, some private investigators queried whether a search warrant could be issued to, and executed by, a private investigator to further an investigation as opposed to going through the conduit of the police or an attorney. This issue must be separated into search warrants issued under the *Criminal Code* and search orders arising from what are colloquially called, in civil litigation, "Anton Piller orders."

The short answer to this question is that it is highly unlikely a private investigator will ever be issued a criminal search warrant or its civil equivalent, an Anton Piller order. And even if one were issued to a private investigator, the opportunity for him or her to be in charge of its execution is even more remote because of the court's reluctance to permit this sort of authority to anyone who is not a peace officer or an officer of the court.

As seen in the cases reviewed below, the role of a private investigator is that of collecting evidence in order for a peace officer or an attorney to submit an information for a search warrant. Under the supervision of a police officer or lawyer, a private investigator may assist in its execution. As discussed, these are important roles that should not be taken lightly.

10.2.1 Civil Search Warrants: The Anton Piller Order

An Anton Piller order is very intrusive — it has been called the nuclear weapon among civil remedies.[32] The Anton Piller order was invented as the ultimate weapon against fraudulent copyright pirates. The original purpose of the Anton Piller order was to preserve the subject matter of a cause of action by directing defendants to permit representatives of the plaintiff to enter their premises for the purpose of inspecting and removing certain specified classes of documents and things. Although its use has been expanded, this still is the main reason for obtaining the order today.

---

32   See C. Pibus, "Seeking Anton Piller? Meet John Doe" *Lawyers Weekly* (22 January 1999) at 13. See also R.N. Ough & W. Frenley, *The Mareva Injunction and Anton Piller Order, Practice and Precedents*, 2d ed. (Toronto: Butterworths, 1993).

Anton Piller orders are received upon a motion to the court. Most motions proceed *ex parte*[33] and in camera[34] to ensure an element of surprise so as to prevent the defendant from destroying evidence. Most motions are sought either before or at the onset of a court proceeding.[35] On these "searches," plaintiffs are permitted to copy those things capable of being copied and are permitted to seize those not capable of being copied on condition of ensuring their safe custody pending resolution of an action.[36]

10.2.1.1 The Development of the Anton Piller Order

Early Conditions and Rationale: Since 1765 it had been clear that under the common law, no court would authorize searches in civil cases.[37] In 1974, all this changed. The order received its name from the case in which it originated: *Anton Piller K.G. v. Manufacturing Processes Ltd.*[38] In this case, Ormund L.J. summarized the essential preconditions for the granting of this order:

1. There must be an extremely strong *prima facie* case;

2. The damage, potential or actual, must be very serious for the plaintiff; and

3. There must be clear evidence that the defendants have in their possession incriminating documents or things, and there must be a real possibility that they may destroy such material before any application can be made.

The first element is usually proven with proof of trademark, copyright, or industrial design registration. The second element is usually proven with estimates of financial loss. The third element, the likelihood that infringers will dispose of important evidence, is the crucial element of proof required to obtain an Anton Piller order. This is very often difficult to prove with tangible evidence. A plaintiff must somehow obtain evidence of dishonest character, such as a history of destroying evidence or obstructing the judicial process.[39]

Much judicial comment has been made as a result of the court's awarding of this extraordinary power. In *Anton Piller* itself, Shaw L.J. added:

> The overriding consideration in the exercise of this salutory jurisdiction is that it is to be resorted to only in circumstances where normal processes of the law would be rendered nugatory if some immediate and effective measure was not available.

---

33 An order made at the request of one party without the other party having had notice of the application.

34 Without publicity, privately, and, if possible, in the private office of the judge or a private room.

35 *Castlemore Marketing Inc. v. Intercontinental Trade and Finance Corp.* (1995), 64 C.P.R. (3d) 462 (F.C.T.D.).

36 *Grenzservice Speditions Ges.m.b.H. v. Jans* (1995), 64 C.P.R. (3d) 129 (B.C.S.C.).

37 *Entick v. Carrington* (1765), 19 St. Tri. 1029, 2 Wils. K.B. 275, 95 E.R. 807.

38 [1976] 1 All E.R. 779 (C.A.).

39 See C. Pibus, above note 32 at 13.

In his reasons in *Anton Piller*, Lord Denning M.R. made these observations about the newly developed order:

> During the last 18 months, the judges of the Chancery Division have been making orders of a kind not known before. They have some resemblance to search warrants. Under those orders the plaintiff and his solicitors are authorized to enter the defendants' premises so as to inspect papers, provided the defendants give permission.
>
> Let me say at once that no court in this land has power to issue a search warrant to enter a man's house so as to see if there are papers or documents there which are of an incriminating nature, whether libels or infringements copyright or anything else of the kind. No constable or bailiff can knock at the door and demand entry so as to inspect papers or documents. The householder can shut the door in his face and say: "Get out." That was established in the leading case of *Entick v. Carrington*.[40] None of us would wish to whittle down that principle in the slightest.
>
> But the order sought in this case is not a search warrant. It does not authorize the plaintiffs' solicitor or anyone else to enter the defendants' premises against their will. It does not authorize the breaking down of any doors, nor the slipping in by a back door, nor getting in by an open door or window. It only authorizes entry and inspection by the permission of the defendants. The plaintiffs must get the defendants' permission. But it does do this: it brings pressure on the defendants to give permission. It does more. It actually orders them to give permission — with, I suppose, the result that if they do not give permission, they are guilty of contempt of court.
>
> We are prepared, therefore, to sanction its continuance, but only in an extreme case where there is grave danger of property being smuggled away or of vital evidence being destroyed.

Although Anton Piller orders are usually sought in cases dealing with alleged infringement of proprietary rights relating to intellectual property, the Court of Appeal in Anton Piller recognized that the order extended well beyond the simple inspection of documents and included an element of discovery and inspection of property. This was because the Anton Piller order was derived from the inherent jurisdiction of the court to do what was necessary in the interest of justice.

Expanding the Scope of the Order: As time passed, the courts widened the scope of the order. In 1977, an order for discovery of the names and addresses and of the defendant's suppliers and customers was added.[41] By 1978, Lord Denning commented that Anton Piller orders were "in daily use" when he extended the order to encompass "bootleggers" who made unauthorized audio recordings of live performances that were then made up and sold as records and cassettes.[42] At some point, a further refinement was introduced with the addition of a direction to the defendants to answer specified questions about their property.

---

40   Above note 37.
41   *E.M.I. v. Sarwar and Haidar,* [1977] F.S.R. 146 (C.A.).
42   *Ex parte Island Records Ltd.,* [1978] 3 All E.R. 824 (C.A.).

In 1980, the scope of the order was again expanded when an Anton Piller order was granted with respect to nonindustrial property that was not itself a subject matter of the action. In that case, the Court of Appeal authorized the search for two files containing accounts and a diary listing details of transactions between the plaintiff and the defendant. These were alleged by the plaintiff to be the best possible evidence of the debt founding the action and were thought to be in danger of destruction.[43] It should be noted that to date no Canadian authority exists which considers an Anton Piller order of this type.

In 1981, the rule of privilege against self-incrimination interrupted the enthusiasm for the order.[44] However, Parliament shortly thereafter withdrew the privilege against self-incrimination from defendants in civil proceedings accused of infringing rights pertaining to intellectual property or passing-off. The privilege remains important in Canada because of the penal provisions in sections 25 and 26 of the *Copyright Act*, R.S.C. 1985, c. C-42.[45]

Adoption of the Order by Canadian Courts: In 1982 a Canadian court adopted the Anton Piller order to obtain and preserve evidence of infringement of the plaintiff's copyrights in the coin-operated audio-video games known as Donkey Kong and Donkey Kong Junior.[46] For the purposes of private investigators, the case is instructive insofar as it demonstrates the extent to which the court relied upon the affidavits of the plaintiffs' private investigator Harry Lake. The court stated:

> According to the Lake affidavit, an infringer can create an entirely new audio-video game merely by replacing the game board and then installing a different front name plate with the entire process taking only approximately 20 minutes . . . By way of example, I quote from only a few of the conversations which the deponent, Lake, a licensed private investigator, swore he had with some of the defendants.

Applying the Order to Ongoing Litigation: More recently the courts have further expanded the use of Anton Piller orders. In a 1997 case, a plaintiff alleged that, prior to receiving an amended affidavit of documents, the plaintiff's private investigator rented an infringing videocassette tape from the defendant's store. The affidavit listed only two infringing videos as being in the defendant's possession. Not included in this list was the program rented by the private investigator. The plaintiff, to test the accuracy of the defendant's affidavit of documents, again sent a private investigator to the defendant's retail store. The private investigator rented three further copies of other programs. None of these programs were disclosed in the defendant's affidavits of documents either.

The plaintiff brought a motion for an Anton Piller order on the basis that the defendant failed to provide an accurate and complete affidavit of documents. The court, after reviewing the burdensome three-factor test set out in the original *Anton Piller* case, held that a

43 *Yousif v. Salama,* [1980] 3 All E.R. 405 (C.A.).
44 *Rank Film Distributors Ltd. v. Video Information Centre,* [1981] 2 All E.R. 76 (H.L.).
45 The review above was largely taken from *Grenzservice Speditions Ges.m.b.H. v. Jans* (1995), 64 C.P.R. (3d) 129 (B.C.S.C.), *per* Huddart J.
46 *Nintendo of America Inc. v. Coinex Video Games* (1982), 69 C.P.R. (2d) 122 (F.C.A.).

fourth test should be added for situations where a defendant submitted a misleading affidavit of documents. If application for an Anton Piller order is sought after an action has been commenced and the opposing parties both have counsel, a court must be satisfied that there is compelling evidence that the other party is bent on flouting the process of the court by refusing to abide by the ordinary discovery process, and there remains no other effective option but to proceed in the absence of the other party.[47]

The court found that the evidence demonstrated that there was a probability the defendant would dispose of the videotapes if given notice of the motion, and that the plaintiff's litigation would therefore be unfairly and improperly frustrated as a result. The court stated:

> In my view, the affidavit evidence of the plaintiff's private investigator provides compelling evidence . . . The private investigator's evidence is that he rented several programs which properly should have been disclosed, but have not been . . . In my view this is one of those rare cases where the evidence demonstrates that the ordinary discovery process will not have its intended effect and an Anton Piller order is appropriate.
>
> It should be noted that the courts are careful to ensure that Anton Piller orders are not used as tools for fishing expeditions. I am satisfied, in light of the private investigator's evidence with respect to his having rented several allegedly infringing videos, that the plaintiff is not seeking this motion as part of a fishing expedition. On the evidence, I draw the inference that there are additional allegedly infringing video-cassette tapes at the defendant's retail premises.[48]

Rolling John Doe Orders: A further development in Anton Piller orders is what is known as the "Rolling John Doe order." This type of order has radically changed the scope of the order by permitting the naming of a fictitious defendant John Doe to allow the order to extend to defendants who have not been identified prior to the moment of enforcement. The "John Doe" order came about as a result of the courts recognizing that it is virtually impossible to identify purveyors of counterfeit goods in typical situations like flea markets, street stalls, or concerts, given the temporary nature of their business. The effect of the order is that once served, defendants must identify themselves and are thereafter named as defendants to the litigation. The other part of the order, the "rolling" component, refers to the time limit imposed upon the order. Such "rolling" orders are often sought for a year and can be renewed upon further motion.[49]

One commentator said that these John Doe orders represent a departure from the normal tests required for an Anton Piller order. By definition, since one is dealing with a fictitious party, the evidence must deal with unknown premises and unknown goods. A strict

---

47 Rule 453 of the Federal Court Rules, C.R.C. 1978, c. 663, does not require that a party who has received an inaccurate affidavit of documents find a remedy under that rule. The party can proceed under Rule 470, which contemplates the making of an Anton Piller order.
48 *Profekta International Inc. v. Mai* (T.D.), [1997] 1 F.C. 223, [1996] F.C.J. No. 1133 (F.C.T.D.).
49 *Fila Canada Inc. v. Doe (T.D.)* (1996), 68 C.P.R. (3d) 1 (F.C.T.D.).

application of the three-fold test becomes problematic. How can one argue that the unknown defendant has a dishonest character? Is it possible to claim a strong *prima facie* case of infringement if the products in question are unknown? In answer to these questions, the courts have adjusted the test to apply to marketplace realities such as vendors fleeing at the first hint of enforcement. Drawing on evidence of the conduct of the class — that is, vendors who have sold counterfeit products in the past — the court has concluded that future members of that group are likely to have the same characteristics and exhibit the same conduct.[50]

10.2.1.2 *Charter* Concerns and the Anton Piller Order

In the original "Rolling John Doe order" case, the court placed a number of limitations on its use. It held that because the orders are for terms of up to a year, a motion for an order is not urgent, and normal motion rules such as filing at least two days prior must be adhered to. Second, because the identity of the defendants is not known at the time of the hearing, there is no need for the proceeding to be held in camera in most cases. Finally, because there is an obligation to make complete disclosure to a court, a court must be informed if evidence can be obtained by investigators without an order and if the action could proceed against the vendor in the normal way. If it can, a case has not been made out for an Anton Piller order.[51]

The context for these restrictions was the court's perspective of the *Charter's* applicability to Anton Piller orders. The court held:

> Anton Piller orders are, in effect, search and seizure orders. The fiction is that the defendant gives permission to the plaintiff to search and seize. The defendant does so under threat of being found in contempt of court if permission is not granted. The penalty for contempt of court, at least theoretically, can be a term of imprisonment. Also, while the theory is that the goods seized are to be retained as evidence for use at trial, the seizures in fact often operate as executions before or sometimes even without judgment. Plaintiffs are using these orders as self-help measures in circumstances in which, in other days, the police may have played a more active role.
>
> Section 8 of the *Charter* provides that individuals are entitled to be free from unreasonable search and seizures. That section is not confined to search and seizures by police officers or investigators pursuant to statutory powers. It is at least arguable that it applies to the civil search and seizures authorized by order of the Court under an Anton Piller order. An unreasonable search and seizure, as I understand the jurisprudence, encompasses one which has been conducted pursuant to an invalid order, or pursuant to an order which was too broadly

---

50   See C. Pibus, above note 32 at 12. For further reading see M. Dockray, "Liberty to Rummage — A Search Warrant in Civil Proceedings?" (1977) Public Law; R.J. Sharpe, *Injunctions and Specific Performance* (Aurora: Canada Law Book, 1995); A.M. Rock, "The Anton Piller Order: An Examination of Its Nature, Development and Present Position in Canada" (1984-85) 5 Advocates Q. 191; and G. Takach, "Exploring the Outer Limits: The Anton Piller Order in Canada" (1985) 23 Alta. L. Rev. 310.

51   *Fila Canada Inc. v. Doe (T.D.)*, above note 49.

drafted, or to an order which has been unreasonably executed: see *Hunter v. Southam*, [1984] 2 S.C.R. 145. When an Anton Piller order is sought from this court, it is important to place them within this context.

Recently, this point of view was rejected. In an Ontario case, a court held that an Anton Piller order is not a civil search warrant. Its origins are found in the inherent jurisdiction of the court, and it enables the court to control and render efficacious its own process and to maintain the integrity of the process. The form of the order shows that it is not ordering or granting anything equivalent to a search warrant. The order is an order on the defendant to permit inspection at the risk of being guilty of contempt. There is no authority in an Anton Piller order to demand entry into any location, be it a home or place of business, with the right and authority to force entry if that demand is not acceded to. Rather, an Anton Piller order allows a request for entry and that request may be denied, but the denier faces contempt proceedings for failure to give the permission that the court has ordered.

As the Anton Piller order is grounded in the inherent jurisdiction of the court, it is unnecessary and misleading to deal with the *Courts of Justice Act* or the Rules of Civil Procedure. As an order of the court exercising its inherent jurisdiction, an Anton Piller Order is not a government action subject to the *Charter*. However, assuming that section 8 of the *Charter* did apply, Anton Piller orders meet the high standard required for a criminal search. Anton Piller orders generally have safeguards that exceed the requirements for a search as established by the Supreme Court of Canada. Further, if section 8 of the *Charter* were infringed, then the infringement is justified under section 1 of the *Charter*. The pressing and substantial objective of Anton Piller orders is to protect the judicial process from being undermined by those who are *prima facie* untrustworthy enough to suppress or destroy evidence.[52]

A Toronto legal practitioner has also reported that notwithstanding the *Charter* concerns, the track record of cases supports its use. Since John Doe orders have been in existence, at least 2,000 John Doe defendants have been identified in counterfeit litigation. Many examples of John Doe defendants have been doing precisely the conduct predicted, such as burning documents and running down fire escapes with bags of evidence. As such, it would appear this "made in Canada" development will be part of the Anton Piller order evolution.[53]

10.2.1.3 Execution of Anton Piller Orders

From the very beginning, Lord Denning M.R made these observations about the newly developed order:

> In the enforcement of this order, the plaintiffs must act with due circumspection. On the service of it, the plaintiffs should be attended by their solicitor, who was officer of the court. They should give the defendants an opportunity of considering it and of consulting their own solicitor. If the defendants wish to apply to discharge the order as having been improperly obtained,

---

52 *Ontario Realty Corporation v. P. Gabriele & Sons Limited* (2000), 50 O.R. (3d) 539 (S.C.J.).
53 See C. Pibus, above note 32 at 12.

they must be allowed to do so. If the defendants refuse permission to enter or to inspect, the plaintiffs must not force their way in. They must accept that refusal, and bring into the notice of the courts afterwards, if need be on an application to commit.[54]

Since that time, much has been said about the requirement for safeguards pertaining to the execution of Anton Piller orders. For example, in the first Canadian case that adopted the order, the court summarized the language of Lord Denning as follows:

1) the subject order together with copies of all supporting material must be served forthwith and with all due dispatch;

2) the plaintiff must undertake to be bound by any order of the court as to damages and further agree to provide a surety bond in the amount of $75,000 as security for the undertaking as to damages;

3) the documents or things seized shall be transmitted by the plaintiff's solicitor to the sheriffs in the appropriate jurisdiction of the respective defendants and may be utilized solely for the purpose of civil proceedings against the defendants or other persons in relation to the plaintiff's copyrights;

4) entry to the defendant's premises on behalf of the plaintiff is restricted to not more than four persons in number;

5) the right of entry and removal is restricted to documents and [things] specifically and particularly described in the order; and

6) the defendants may move the court to (a) vary or discharge the order, or (b) to increase the amount of security ordered on 24 hours notice to the plaintiff's solicitor.[55]

In Britain, Anton Piller orders were routinely granted in the 1980s and early 1990s. However, during the 1990s, a series of reported cases began to focus on wrongful executions and abuses committed by overzealous plaintiffs. Predictably, this led to a new set of safeguards under a 1994 practice direction including the requirement that executions must be supervised by an *independent* solicitor.[56]

In Canada, allegations of wrongful executions have rarely been made.[57] The most striking example is taken from a 1995 British Columbia case.[58] In this case the plaintiff made claim for restitution for unjust enrichment based on a customs fraud perpetrated on the state of Germany by the defendants. The defendants had by fraud and false pretences imported meat into Germany through an Austrian customs broker who, when the scam

---

54   *Anton Piller K.G. v. Manufacturing Processes Ltd.,* [1976] 1 All E.R. 779 (C.A.).

55   *Nintendo of America Inc. v. Coinex Video Games,* above note 46.

56   See C. Pibus, above note 32 at 13.

57   See *Procter & Gamble Inc. v. John Doe (c.o.b. Clarion Trading International),* [2000] F.C.J. No. 61 (F.C.T.D.). Here the defendant alleged the private investigator was abusive. The court, however, found no wrongdoing.

58   *Grenzservice Speditions Ges. M.B.H. v. Jans,* above note 36.

was exposed, became liable to the German government for approximately $4,000,000 in duties. To recover their losses, the plaintiffs, in addition to obtaining a Mareva injuction[59] to restrain the defendants from dealing with their property in any way, also obtained an Anton Piller order to seize Deutschmarks that may have been stored at the defendant's residence. The court made the following comments regarding the execution of the order:

> After the order was obtained, Mr. S., an experienced counsel who has conduct of this proceeding for the plaintiffs, instructed Mr. F., at the bar for only 13 months, to accompany Mr. H. of Coopers & Lybrand Limited to the defendants' property at 127 Mile House. He told him to take with him Mr. L., a lawyer from New York State acting for the insurance adjusters, and Mr. T., an investigator for the plaintiffs from Austria. He arranged for local members of the RCMP at 100 Mile House, one of whom was known to Mr. Jans (a defendant), and a member of the RCMP's commercial crime unit at Kamloops to accompany them.
>
> . . .
>
> So seven men arrived at the ranch in three or four vehicles . . . Two of them were unauthorized. Mr. T. carrying a video camera with which he was going to create a permanent photographic record of the search. This was also unauthorized.
>
> . . .
>
> Mr. F. spoke first to Mrs. Jans . . . Mr. F. says that he gave Mrs. Jans a copy of the order, the writ and the statement of claim and then explained the terms of the order to her . . . He introduced himself to Mrs. Jans as counsel for the plaintiff and an officer of the court. Mrs. Jans denies having received any paper or an explanation of the order from Mr. F.
>
> Mr. H., Mr. L., Mr. T. and the three RCMP officers searched the house and the outbuildings looking for Deutschmarks and any documents that might lead them to the currency, whether on the premises or on deposit in financial institutions or elsewhere. Mr. F. did not accompany them . . . Mr. F. interviewed Mr. Jans about his assets . . . Mr. L. also asked questions . . . relevant to issues about liability, but irrelevant to the present financial circumstances of the defendants. Some of the questions were about documents that Mr. L., Mr. T. or Mr. H. had located in the house. It is not disputed that at least two and possibly three of the documents were privileged communications to or from Mr. Jans' lawyer.
>
> . . .
>
> These facts reveal [the following] unauthorized conduct by the representatives of the plaintiffs:
>
> 1)   Two unauthorized persons [Mr. T. and Mr. L.] accompanied the representatives of Coopers & Lybrand Limited to the ranch. Neither is a resident of British Columbia or Canada;

---

59   A prejudgment remedy intended to freeze assets until judgment is obtained and a writ of execution issued. It was named after the case *Mareva Compania Naviera S.A. v. Int. Bulkcarriers S.A.*, [1980] 1 All E.R. 213 (C.A.).

2)   Those two non-residents assisted Mr. H. with his search for Deutschmarks and in the process looked at whatever documents they were able to locate in the Jans' home;

3)   The search by Mr. H., Mr. T. and Mr. L. was assisted by the police officers extended beyond searching for and taking possession of Deutschmarks;

4)   Mr. F. did more than request that Mr. and Mrs. Jans provide a sworn declaration of their property. He examined Mr. Jans about his property and that of his wife;

5)   Mr. L. participated in the unauthorized questioning of Mr. Jans;

6)   Mr. T. filmed parts of the search, the interview, and documents located during the unauthorized aspects of the search; and

7)   Premises rented to third parties were searched.

The defendants also established that the usual practice with regards to Anton Piller orders was not followed in these respects:

1)   The materials supporting the granting of the *ex parte* order (capable of being copied) were not served upon the defendants or any of them;

2)   A detailed list of the items copied or seized was not made. No written receipts were offered;

3)   The supervising solicitor did not file a written report to the court forthwith after the search. Nor did he deliver a copy of such report to the defendants, nor did he produce any notes he may have kept to the defendants or to the court. He did file an affidavit two weeks later. By then it had become apparent that the Jans had complaints about the search;

4)   The supervising solicitor did not explain the order in everyday language to Mr. Jans. Nor did he advise him or his wife that they had the right to obtain legal advice before permitting entry; and

5)   The police attendance was not limited to prevention of breach of the peace.

It is clear that Mr. and Mrs. Jans were extremely cooperative . . . What is not anticipated, by good citizens or by the court, is that a solicitor attending premises under the authority of a court's search order will go outside the terms of the order. This is especially true when that solicitor relies on the defendant's co-operation which has been induced by the court order and member of the RCMP, and when the search is made outside the ordinary business hours of [the defendant's] law firm.

The court induces co-operation by an Anton Piller order where there is reasonable grounds for believing that a defendant is unwilling or refuses to respect the rules of the adversary system. It ill behooves a plaintiff who seeks a remedy at the limits of the court's jurisdiction to take advantage of whatever relief he obtains.

I have reviewed the execution of this order at some length because of its importance to the administration of justice. There is little to distinguish what I have called the search order from an Anton Piller order. Both are in effect civil search warrants. Every counsel who seeks a mandatory order designed for immediate execution in a civil action to accompany a Mareva injunction should read the decision of Scott J. in *Columbia Picture Industries v. Robertson*.[60]

In applying the foregoing to the impugned case, the court held:

While the evidence before me does not permit a finding as to whether the defendants have suffered any significant material harm from the execution of the order, the circumstances of this case show that the procedure is fallible and capable of abuse. If the remedy is to be granted and is to survive constitutional scrutiny, responsibility for supervision of civil search and seizure orders should include at a minimum the obligation to ensure that fundamental individual rights guaranteed by the *Canadian Charter of Rights and Freedoms* are respected. This case suggests that safeguards cannot remain implicit in the supervision of the order. They must be specified. In determining the safeguards, regard can be had to the statutory search and seizure provisions that have been adjudged and justified under s.1 of the *Charter*.

The court then listed the following as safeguards that must be included in every Anton Piller order:

1)   an undertaking to advise the defendants of their right to consult counsel before being required to permit entry to their premises;

2)   an undertaking to advise the defendants of their right to assert privileges, particularly the solicitor-client privilege and the privilege against self-incrimination;

3)   an undertaking to search only during ordinary business hours;

4)   a list of the specific items sought;

5)   an undertaking to serve upon the defendant at the execution of the order the materials filed in support of the order;

6)   the identity of the persons who may conduct the search and seize items;

7)   an undertaking as to the use that can be made of the items seized;

8)   an undertaking to make a detailed list of all items seized and an undertaking to provide a receipt to the defendant of this list; and

9)   an undertaking that the supervising solicitor will prepare a written report for the delivery to the defendant and for filing with the court within a specified time after the execution of the order.

The court also recommended that whenever an Anton Piller order is sought, it be supervised by an experienced solicitor who is not a member of the firm acting for the plaintiffs.

On the basis of the foregoing factual scenario — especially the inadequate supervision by the leading counsel — the court concluded the proper remedy was to remove counsel for the plaintiff from the case. The court stated:

---

60   [1986] 3 All E.R. 338 (Ch. D.).

The Mareva and Anton Piller orders were conceived not so much to protect the plaintiffs as to protect the court's jurisdiction against defendants bent on dissipating or secreting their assets or evidence in order to render inconsequential the judicial process against them. They represent an extraordinary assumption of power by the judiciary. Judges must be prudent and cautious in their issue. It follows that counsel must be discerning in their execution and particularly sensitive to the rights of unrepresented defendants who have not been heard.

In this case the duty was more onerous because the solicitor acted as an officer of this court in attending the home of the unrepresented defendant; he was told to supervise a search for specified items without specific guidelines, and he was provided with the assistance of the police force.

Certainly, Mr. F. can not act as counsel in this proceeding. He has given evidence and may be required to do so again. The real issue is whether Mr. S. and other members of his firm may do so. Mr. S. says that hindsight is perfect, that he has learned from this experience, that he now recognizes that the order was flawed, that the instructions given to Mr. F. were flawed, that Mr. L. and Mr. T. should not have attended without authority, and that he should have asked a more experienced solicitor to supervise the search.

. . .

There is no evidence to establish that anything Mr. L., Mr. T., or Mr. F. did was dishonest. Dishonour usually requires some element of shame or disgrace. Since Mr. and Mrs. Jans co-operated so fully with Mr. T. and Mr. L., their behaviour might not be considered sufficiently appalling to be dishonourable. Mr. T. may not have understood the sensitivity to the defendants' rights required by the search and the listing orders . . . Failure to perform duties of which one is not aware is regrettable and may have serious consequences, but it is not dishonourable.

. . .

It is obvious from what I have said that the integrity of the judicial system is challenged whenever a solicitor, authorized to supervise the execution of a court order that infringes an individual's privacy, permits those who seek to benefit from it to go beyond a strict interpretation of the order . . . The only way a court can express its disapproval of such egregious behaviour is by removing counsel from the record . . . Ancillary to that order, there will be orders requiring the plaintiffs and their agents . . . to return everything they garnered from the search . . . Lastly, Mr. H., Mr. F., Mr. L., and Mr. T. must disclose the names and addresses of all those whom they may have provided information acquired during their attendance at the premises of the defendants . . . with a brief summary of the information provided.

In response to this case, Canadian courts have instituted several new procedural requirements. A model order was released by the same judge who prohibited private investigators from executing unsupervised *Criminal Code* search warrants. The court made further observations on the conduct of solicitors in executing such orders:

A solicitor attends on the execution of these orders in two capacities: as counsel for the plaintiff and as an officer of the Court. It is the plaintiff's solicitor who attends. I accept that this may not be ideal. In the United Kingdom a practice has developed of having licensed Anton Piller officers, independent of the plaintiff, attend and supervise the execution of these orders. This practice may be worth adopting. We do not have it at present, however, I prefer to have a solicitor present at the execution of these orders, albeit the plaintiff's solicitor, rather than no solicitor at all.

A solicitor, as an officer of the Court, owes duties to the Court as well as to his or her client. Solicitors attend and supervise the execution of these orders to ensure that their boundaries are not exceeded and to be in a position to give the Court an accurate and complete description of what occurred. They have the legal expertise and are expected to be able to explain to those enforcing the order and to those against whom it is being executed what is and what is not allowed thereunder. This gives some assurance that the boundaries of the order will not be exceeded. Counsel understand that a misstep or mischaracterization of a situation can lead not only to the particular execution of the order being invalid, but also to the vacating of the Anton Piller order itself.[61]

In summary, solicitors are required to be present at the execution of the order to ensure its boundaries are not exceeded and to be in a position to give a court an accurate and complete description of what occurred.

10.2.2 *Criminal Code* Search Warrants

This section will review the authority for issuing *Criminal Code* search warrants to private investigators, the authority prohibiting private investigators from executing them on their own, guidelines for private investigators assisting in their execution, and considerations when providing information to police for the purpose of search warrants.

10.2.2.1 Issuing Search Warrants to Private Investigators

The issuance of search warrants is covered by section 487 of the *Criminal Code*, which provides:

(1)   A justice who is satisfied by information on oath in Form 1 that there are reasonable grounds to believe that there is in a building, receptacle or place:

   (a)   anything on or in respect of which any offence against this Act or any other Act of Parliament has been or is suspected to have been committed;

   (b)   anything that there are reasonable grounds to believe will afford evidence with respect to the commission of an offence, or will reveal the whereabouts of a person who is believed to have committed an offence, against this Act or any other Act of Parliament, or

   (c)   anything that there are reasonable grounds to believe is intended to be used for the purpose of committing any offence against the person for which a person may be arrested without warrant,

may at any time issue a warrant under his hand *authorizing a person named therein* or a peace officer

---

61   *Fila Canada Inc. v. Doe (T.D.)*, above note 49, *per* Reed J.

(d) *to search* the building, receptacle, or place for any such thing and to seize it, and

(e) subject to any other Act of Parliament, to, as soon as practicable, bring the thing seized before, or make a report in respect thereof to, the justice or some other justice for the same territorial division in accordance with s.489.1. [Emphasis added.]

The wording of this section is somewhat ambiguous. It appears that a warrant may be *issued to a person named therein*, implying a private person may apply for and be issued a search warrant. The question that remains outstanding therefore is if a private person can actually execute the warrant he or she is issued.

10.2.2.2   Execution of Search Warrants by Private Investigators

The wording of section 487(1) states that a warrant issued authorizes the person to whom it is issued *to search*. At first blush, it may appear that the section implies that a private person who is issued a search warrant can execute the warrant as well. However, related provisions in the *Criminal Code* as well as a reflection on relevant case law does not bear this out.

To begin with, section 487.07, entitled "Execution of Warrant," provides:

(1) Before executing a warrant, a *peace officer* shall inform the person against whom it is executed of [and a list is provided]. [Emphasis added.]

There is no mention in this section of a *person* with respect to executing a warrant. The section implies the execution of a general warrant is strictly the function of a peace officer. Furthermore, Form 5 entitled "Warrant to Search" with respect to section 487 commences with the phrase: "To the *peace officers* in the said (territorial division)."

Perhaps the most persuasive of arguments against a private investigator ever receiving the exclusive authority to execute a search warrant comes from a civil action known as *Fila Canada Inc. v. Doe (T.D.)*,[62] a case discussed above pertaining to the execution of an Anton Piller Order. In this case, the court held:

I turn then to the need for a supervising solicitor in attendance on all executions of the order. It is on this point that counsel on behalf of his client felt most strongly. He argued that such a requirement would make the use of these orders too expensive for his clients, that it is dangerous in some situations because executions of the order can result in physically abusive confrontations, that it is impractical when a number of executions are to take place in different locations simultaneously and, that it is unnecessary because the investigation agency which is employed is knowledgeable in these matters.

I recognize the force of these arguments, but I am also mindful of the fact that there is enormous potential for abuse in issuing these orders. The Court is putting in the hands of the plaintiff the power to search the premises and to seize the goods, equipment and records of others.

---

62   Above note 49.

These powers are exercised in each particular situation when the plaintiff determines that particular goods are or relate to an infringement of its intellectual property rights. *There is no public official involved in the execution of the order.* If the Court is going to assist a plaintiff in the assertion of its rights by giving orders as invasive as Anton Pillers, then, I do not think the cost to the plaintiff should weigh too heavily in the balance when the protection for the defendants is the competing consideration

. . .

It may be that there are situations for which the individual Anton Piller orders can be obtained . . . where a solicitorless seizure is justified. *Counsel painted a picture of a circumstance in which police officers and the plaintiff's private investigators work together* through a crowd. I leave open the question of whether there are situations in which solicitorless search and seizures can be justified. All that is necessary to say for the present purposes is that I am not prepared to provide for such in the present case.

I am asked to put the search and seizure powers in the hands of an investigation agency. *The Court has no way of knowing why a particular agency should be granted such authority as opposed to any other. The plaintiff has chosen and pays that agency. The agency's loyalty in any actions taken by its staff will naturally be to the plaintiff.* [Emphasis added.]

From the foregoing, it is quite evident that search warrants will not be executed by those who are not sworn, either as police officers, or as officers of the court; that is, solicitors.

Finally, although these cases are not exactly on point, the general view of the courts with respect to an invasion of one's privacy was laid out in the seminal *Charter* case of *Hunter v. Southam.*[63] In this case the court held:

The function of the *Charter* is to provide for unremitting protection of individual rights and liberties . . . Like other *Charter* rights, [s. 8] must be interpreted in a broad and liberal manner so to secure the citizen's right to reasonable expectation of privacy against governmental encroachments. Its spirit must not be constrained by narrow legalistic classifications based on notions of property and the like which served to protect this fundamental human value in earlier times.[64]

From reviewing the cases on arrest where a private person is deemed to be acting under the auspices of the state for the purpose of making an arrest, it can be extrapolated that a private person would be deemed to be acting under the authority of the state for the purposes of executing a *Criminal Code* search warrant as well. Because a private person, when acting as an agent of the state, is subject to the *Charter*, the chances of making a case for the reasonableness of the execution of a search warrant by a private person would appear to be remote.

There is a wide spectrum of other issues with respect to search warrants that may be of interest to private investigators. However, as a private investigator will not execute a search warrant without the assistance of public sector police or an attorney, and as public sector

---

63   (1984), 14 C.C.C. (3d) 97 (S.C.C.).
64   *Ibid.* at 105 & 109.

police or an attorney should be aware of the issues relating to search warrants, these issues are not dealt with extensively in this book.

10.2.2.3 Private Investigators Assisting in the Execution of Search Warrants

The case of *R. v. B.(J.E.)*[65] gives a comprehensive review of the law on the topic of persons other than those listed on warrant assisting in its execution. In this case, the accused was convicted at trial of sexual assault and gross indecency. On appeal, the accused argued that evidence obtained during a search warrant should be excluded pursuant to section 24 of the *Charter* because a child protection worker, who was not a peace officer, assisted police in the execution of the search warrant and therefore breached his section 8 *Charter* right to be secure from unreasonable search and seizure.

The court reviewed a number of cases. In *Re Purdy and the Queen*,[66] the court struck down search warrants and the seizures made under them. The warrants were issued to a police officer, but the actual search was carried out by a solicitor. In that case, the court stated:

> Section 443(1) provides the Justice "may . . . issue a warrant under his hand authorizing a person named therein or a peace officer to search . . ."
>
> The right to search is restricted to the person named or a peace officer. This provision must be given its ordinary meaning. No other person has the right to compulsory access to the private premises to be searched and unrestricted access to private records and documents in the absence of a warrant directed to him. More particularly, a solicitor, who may acquire information concerning other matters not connected with the proposed prosecution which may be of use to that solicitor in other matters, [may not search] unless he is specifically authorized in the warrant.
>
> Section 443 provides for the invasion of privacy of the home and the prerequisites therein must strictly be complied with. The order quashing the warrant to search is upheld.

In *R. v. Heikel and MacKay*,[67] a warrant to search was issued under section 37 of the *Food and Drugs Act*, R.S.C. 1970, c. F-27. Section 37 provides that only police officers named in the warrant are authorized to conduct the search. The officer named in the warrant enlisted the aid of three fellow police officers. The trial judge excluded the evidence because the police had not kept to the terms of the warrant. On appeal, the court held "others" can assist, and their mere assistance does not render a search and seizure unlawful.

In *R. v. Fekete*,[68] another narcotics case where the search warrant was "issued to a peace officer named therein", the court held that the named peace officer could enlist the aid of other officers in conducting the search. The court held:

> Left to my own devices I would have no difficulty whatsoever in concluding that it follows as a matter of common sense that if a power of search and seizure is conferred upon a named officer, he is entitled to enlist aid in the execution of this power. That is not to say that he may

---

65   (1989), 52 C.C.C. (3d) 224 (N.S.S.C.).

66   (1972), 28 D.L.R. (3d) 720 (N.B.S.C.).

67   (1984), 57 A.R. 221 (C.A.).

assign or delegate this power, only that he may execute his power assisted by others. The fact of assistance does not change the essential fact that it remains the search and seizure of the named police officer.

Because there have been decisions in the provincial and county courts of this province which are inconsistent with the above view, it is perhaps fitting that the matter be examined more carefully.

At common law, search warrants were authorized only in cases of larceny or suspected larceny, but it appears that in those cases the officer to whom the warrant was issued could enlist the aid of others in executing the warrant. [Hale's Pleas of the Crown, Vol. 2, p. 135.][69]

Equally, in the case of a warrant issued for the arrest of a person, the common law recognized that the person to whom the warrant was issued might be assisted by others in its execution [Hawkins, Pleas of the Crown, Vol. 2, p.135]. The appellant sought to distinguish this latter principle on the ground that it concerned only the arrest of the person. However, I can not accept this proposition that the common law was less concerned with the liberty of the subject than with the security of his dwelling. It would seem only reasonable to conclude that s.10(2) of the *Narcotic Control Act* should be interpreted in a manner that is consistent with these long standing common law principles.

In *R. v. Strachan*,[70] Dickson C.J.C., after referring to the requirement in section 10(2) of the *Narcotic Control Act* that the officer to search for narcotics must be named in the warrant, went on to say:

> This requirement is met when the officer or officers named in the warrant execute it personally and are responsible for the control and conduct of the search. The use of unnamed assistants in the search does not violate the requirement of s.10(2) so long as they are closely supervised by the named officer or officers. It is the named officers who must set out the general course of the search and direct the conduct of any assistants. If the named officers are truly in control, participate in the search, and are present throughout, then the use of assistants does not invalidate the search or the warrant.

Based on this review, the court in *R. v. B.(J.E.)*[71] held that unlike the solicitor in the Purdy case, who had apparently had control of the search, the child protection worker was, at most, an assistant to the police officers carrying out the search. Therefore, the participation of the child protection worker in the search of JEB's house did not invalidate the search, the seizure, or the warrant.

---

68   (1985), 17 C.C.C. (3d) 188 (Ont. C.A.). See also *R. v. Baylis* (1986), 28 C.C.C. (3d) 40 (Sask. Q.B.), and *R. v. Lebrocq and Plaska* (1984), 35 Alta. L.R. (2d) 184 (Q.B.).

69   This principle was recognized in this country in *Re Old Rex Café (sub nom. R. v. Laramee)* (1972), 7 C.C.C. (2d) 279 (N.W.T. Terr. Ct.).

70   (1988), 46 C.C.C. (3d) 479 at 492 (S.C.C.).

71   Above note 65.

An example of private investigators assisting in a search warrant is taken from *R. v. Aquintey*.[72] In this case an American company, which was the holder of copyright in various videocassettes, retained a private investigation firm to determine whether videotapes of movies in which it held copyright were being unlawfully copied and rented to the public in the Toronto area. The investigation revealed that some videocassettes that the accused was renting out from his variety store were not authorized copies. The investigators reported the results of their investigation to Metropolitan Toronto Police. Based on the information received, officers obtained a *Criminal Code* search warrant for the accused's store. Four police officers and two private investigators executed the warrant, seizing numerous knock-off tapes and records of movie rentals. The court in this case did not mention any concern over the procedural correctness of the private investigators assisting in the execution of the search warrant.

10.2.2.4 Providing Information to Police for Search Warrants

Although private investigators cannot execute search warrants on their own, their involvement in providing the grounds for police or an attorney to obtain one is critical. Accordingly, it would be remiss not to note cases where, to further their investigations, overzealous private investigators have deliberately provided misleading information in order that a warrant may be secured.

In *R. v. Butt*[73] the accused was charged with possession of devices to fraudulently obtain telecommunication services. At trial, the accused brought a section 8 *Charter* motion to suppress the evidence obtained by a search warrant of his home, business, and storage facility. The accused alleged that the search warrant the police obtained was based on unreliable information provided to police by a private investigator.

The court found as fact that the private investigation agency spent a significant portion of their resources investigating the unauthorized use of television decoders and descramblers on behalf of a cable company. As part of that investigation, the agency owner had two of his investigators keep surveillance on the accused and one of their storage garages. During the surveillances, the investigators made observations wherein they could not draw conclusions from what they saw. The agency principal, however, took the statements of his investigators and prepared "grounds for belief" statements indicating that his investigators had made positive observations of the accused in possession of the illegal devices. The agency principal then took these statements to police.

The court further found as fact that the agency principal had been a police officer in Toronto for twenty-five years prior to opening a private investigation agency. The police officer in question had been referred to the agency principal through other officers who had known the agency principal as a police officer years before. The police officer did not make any attempts to corroborate the information of the agency principal, nor could he say that he had had prior dealings where his information was accurate. The police officer simply

---

72   [1998] O.J. No. 3469 (Prov. Div.).
73   (1995), 29 W.C.B. (2d) 328 (Ont. Gen. Div.).

took the prepared statements of the agency principal and submitted them to a justice of the peace to obtain a search warrant.

The court held that the agency principal deliberately manipulated and distorted the observations of his staff investigators for the purpose of his "grounds of belief" statements. The court further held that the private investigator then deliberately, through the agency of a police officer, misled a justice of the peace to obtain a search warrant. The court concluded that when police choose to rely on untested material given to them by persons who seek to deliberately mislead a justice of the peace into issuing a search warrant, a serious breach of the accused's section 8 *Charter* rights has taken place. The court held that as such conduct should not be condoned and as the charge was not serious, it must be excluded pursuant to section 24(2) of the *Charter*.

Although it cannot be understated that the conduct of this private investigator fell below that which is acceptable by a court, it is noteworthy that the search warrant did result in the seizure of the illegal property sought. What is clear from this case, therefore, is that the courts are more concerned with attempts to mislead the court than the end result. To validate this point, see *R. v. Schneeberger*[74] discussed in Section 9.6.3 — The Charter — Independent Operatives. In that case, the court held that evidence obtained by private investigators where they illegally obtained access to a person's vehicle to seize DNA evidence was admissible because it was not done at the behest of police and because the private investigators were honest in explaining how they obtained the evidence. In other words, being honest about illegal activity during an investigation will result in legally obtained search warrants while attempting to mislead a court about what is otherwise legal activity (surveillance) results in a search warrant that is quashed for being illegal. As pointed out in Section 9.6.3, this is stated not to advocate illegal activity, for other forms of liability may result, but to emphasize the attempts to mislead the court is the more egregious of sins.

10.3   PRIVILEGE AND PRIVATE INVESTIGATORS

As mentioned in Section 2.3.2.2, while the duty of confidentiality is an ethical duty owed to all clients, privilege is a rule of evidence. The distinction is significant. Communications, whether oral or in writing, which are intended to be confidential between a solicitor and his or her client or prospective client for the purpose of giving or receiving legal advice are privileged. Privilege is that of the client, not the lawyer. The effect of privilege is that neither the client nor the solicitor, without the client's consent, can be compelled to disclose the communications. However, where a client voluntarily waives the privileged character of a communication, both the client and his or her solicitor may be fully examined if called as a witness to a proceeding.[75]

The following review of the law of privilege and disclosure requirements in civil and criminal matters is confined to principles taken from case law where the evidence of pri-

---

74   [2000] S.J. No. 640 (C.A.).
75   *R. v. Solosky* (1979), 105 D.L.R. (3d) 756 (S.C.C.).

vate investigators was at issue. This review does not purport to make specific references to the Rules of Civil Procedure of the various provinces pertaining to discovery. Such a review is beyond the scope of this book. This review does provide, however, an insight into the considerations made by Canadian courts on this issue and accordingly is useful to private investigators in the operation of their practice.

10.3.1 Litigation Privilege

Most applicable to investigators in the private sector is a concept known as litigation privilege, sometimes referred to as legal professional privilege. Whereas solicitor-client privilege attaches to all confidential communications made between a lawyer and his or her client where the client is seeking the lawyer's advice, litigation privilege is broader in scope in that it attaches to communications with or for documents prepared by third parties.[76] This includes such situations as where a lawyer retains an independent insurance adjuster, who in turn retains a private investigator. Although the lawyer has not directly retained the private investigator, the private investigator's communications with the insurance adjuster are privileged by virtue of the insurance adjuster being retained by the lawyer.[77] Litigation privilege may even attach to such material if a client decides to represent himself or herself and no lawyer is to be briefed.[78]

The courts are faced with two competing principles pertaining to privilege. On the one hand, all relevant evidence should be made available for a court to determine the facts, and on the other hand, communications between a lawyer and his client should remain confidential and privileged to encourage open and full discourse between them to preserve the client's rights.[79] It has also been recognized that in the adversary system, which purports the legal myth that truth will best be determined if each side vigorously pursues and presents its own case, parties may rely too heavily on the work of others if disclosure of privileged material is granted. On the other hand, it is also recognized that fuller disclosure encourages settlement.[80] Balancing these competing interests, the courts have held that the public is best served by rigidly confining within narrow limits the withholding of material or evidence relevant to litigation on the basis of privilege.[81]

The rationale for litigation privilege provides an essential guide for determining the scope of its application. Its purpose is to protect from disclosure the statements and documents that are obtained or created particularly to prepare one's case for litigation or anticipated litigation. It is intended to permit a party to freely investigate the facts at issue and

---

76 *Mosley v. Spray Lakes Sawmill Ltd.*, [1996] A.J. No. 380 (Alta. C.A.); *Grant v. Downs (1976)*, 135 C.L.R. 674 (Austl.) and later adopted by the House of Lords in *Waugh v. British Railway Board*, [1979] 2 All E.R. 1169 at 1183.
77 *Blair v. Wawanesa Mutual Insurance Co.* (2000), 98 A.C.W.S. (3d) 298, (Alta. Q.B.).
78 *Mosley v. Spray Lakes Sawmill Ltd.*, above note 76.
79 *Waugh v. British Railway Board*, above note 76.
80 *Mosley v. Spray Lakes Sawmill Ltd.*, above note 76.
81 *Blackstone v. Mutual Life Assurance Co.*, [1994] 3 D.L.R. 147 (Ont. C.A.).

determine the optimum manner in which to prepare and present a case. The litigation may already be pending or simply contemplated. Canadian courts have made it clear that it is not enough that preparation for litigation be a substantial purpose for preparing a document. Rather, it must be the dominant purpose. Although the principle can be stated succinctly, its application is often more difficult.[82]

10.3.1.1 The Dominant Purpose Test

The task of applying the test to documents for which privilege is claimed is not an easy one. The task of balancing disclosure and candor in the discovery process against privilege for . . . investigating facts and developing information for the purpose of properly instructing counsel in a case which is virtually certain to be headed for litigation appears . . . to satisfy the dominant purpose test rule . . . Material will be privileged only if the only reason for its existence is for the purpose of supplying it to legal counsel.[83]

The dominant purpose test has two parts. First, it must be determined when the document was created. If a document was created before litigation was contemplated, it is not privileged. To satisfy this part of the test, it has been held that there must be a "definite prospect of litigation."[84] Second, if a document is created after litigation is contemplated, it must be shown that the "dominant purpose" for which the document was produced was its submission to a legal adviser for use in contemplated litigation.[85]

It has been held that a lawsuit need not have been initiated nor a lawyer retained to establish that at the time of creation the dominant purpose of a document was its use in litigation. However, the purpose cannot be determined from subsequent events that indicate that the statement is now useful for litigation.[86] It has further been held that at some point in the information-gathering process, the focus will shift such that its dominant purpose will become that of preparing the party for whom it was conducted for anticipated litigation. In other words, there is a continuum during which the focus on the inquiry changes from a dominant purpose of investigation to a dominant purpose of preparation for litigation.[87]

Determining the timing of a change from a dominant purpose of investigation to a dominant purpose of preparation for litigation is a difficult one. Each case must be analyzed on its own facts. It has been recognized that investigations can occur for reasons other than preparation for litigation. Investigations can be initiated to avoid litigation, to determine whether litigation will be a likelihood, or to fulfil an obligation under a contract that requires it. For these reasons, litigation privilege has been carefully confined to narrow

---

82 *Mosley v. Spray Lakes Sawmill Ltd.,* above note 76.
83 *Tsprailis v. Western Union Insurance Co.* (1989), 32 C.P.C. (2d) 325 (Alta. Q.B.).
84 *Walters v. Toronto Transit Commission* (1985), 50 O.R. (2d) 636 (H.C.).
85 *Ontario (Ministry of Finance) v. Ontario (Assistant Information and Privacy Commissioner),* [1977] O.J. No. 1465 (Div. Ct.); *McDonnell v. Lopuch (*1993), 11 C.P.C. (3d) 376 (Alta. Q.B.).
86 *Mosley v. Spray Lakes Sawmill Ltd.,* above note 76.
87 *Hamalainen v. Sippola* (1991), 3 C.P.C. (3d) 297 (B.C.C.A.).

limits to preserve the public interest in full disclosure. The onus of proving that the privilege applies should rest squarely on the person claiming the privilege.[88]

Examples of cases where documents prepared by investigators in the private sector have undergone this analysis are plentiful. For example, in an Alberta personal injury case, the motor vehicle accident was investigated by the defendant insurance company's adjuster. Because the accident was serious, the defendant's insurer instructed its adjuster to conduct a preliminary investigation notwithstanding no claim had been made. The report of the adjuster was never sent to a lawyer and the file was closed. Months afterward, the plaintiff filed a claim. During the subsequent litigation, the plaintiff made a request for disclosure of the adjuster's investigation report. The court held that while litigation may always be a reasonable possibility where there is a serious accident, it could not be said that actions taken by the adjuster were done to prepare for litigation. Therefore, the dominant purpose of the investigation report was not for litigation, and the report was ordered produced.[89]

In another Alberta case, a plaintiff brought action against the insurance company for payment of the proceeds of a life insurance policy on the life of one of its employees. During the course of litigation, the plaintiff requested the reports of the defendant's private investigator be disclosed, arguing that the initial purpose of retaining the private investigator was to determine if it should accept or reject the claim. The defendant argued that it was not obliged to disclose the reports because the private investigator was retained by outside counsel in the contemplation of litigation. The court found that while the defendant retained outside counsel because it was cognizant that if it denied the plaintiff's claim litigation would likely follow, it was equally clear that one of the main purposes in retaining outside counsel was to investigate all aspects of the claim. Accordingly, although one of the "substantial purposes" of retaining outside counsel was in contemplation of litigation, another "substantial purpose" was to examine the claim itself. Accordingly, the documents were not acquired and generated solely for the purpose of litigation. Consequently, the documents were not covered by litigation privilege.[90]

10.3.1.2   The Substantial Purpose Test

There has been some controversy on the proper test to use for the past forty years. Some courts have held that the substantial purpose test, not the dominant purpose test, should be applied concerning litigation privilege.[91] Other courts held the proper test of litigation privilege is the dominant purpose test notwithstanding earlier decisions that adopted the

---

88   *Mosley v. Spray Lakes Sawmill Ltd.*, above note 76.

89   *Ibid.*

90   *Adams Motors Ltd. v. Transamerica Life Insurance Co. of Canada* (1992), 5 C.P.C. (3d) 170 (Alta. Q.B.).

91   *Keuhl v. McConnell* (1991), 3 C.P.C. (3d) 22 (Ont. Gen. Div.); and *Werner v. Warner Auto-Marine Inc.* (1990), 44 C.P.C. (2d) 175 (Ont. H.C.J.).

substantial purpose test.[92] Most recently, the courts, following an English House of Lords decision on this topic,[93] have recognized the "dominant purpose" test.[94]

The following sections discuss litigation privilege as it applies to a private investigator's reports, to surveillance films and videotapes, and to witness statements.

10.3.2 Investigator Reports

In addition to discussing how the dominant purpose test has been applied to a private investigator's reports, this section also discusses the waiver of privilege by disclosure of such reports.

10.3.2.1 The Dominant Purpose Test

Investigative reports may be protected by litigation privilege. Where a report was prepared at the request of a solicitor, it has been held that for it to be privileged, the question is not only if it was prepared after retaining counsel, but rather if the "dominant purpose" for preparing it was for legal advice or for use in litigation.[95]

Cases where privilege was found not to attach to a private investigator's report include where a court found that a substantial purpose for retaining outside counsel was to consider the possibility and ramifications of litigation and equally to examine the claim itself.[96] Likewise, where a court found that litigation did not become a reasonable prospect until after the discontinuance of benefit payments, and where a private investigator's report was prepared prior to that date, privilege did not attach and the report was required to be disclosed.[97]

Occasionally, conditions are put on the disclosure where the dominant purpose has not been met. Where an arbitrator ordered an employer to produce to a union all existing notes, memoranda, reports, and summaries prepared by the employer and the private investigators retained by the employer relating directly to the grievor, the arbitrator required the union to enter an undertaking not to disclose any information to anyone other than their counsel.[98]

Cases where privilege was found to attach to a private investigator's report include a situation where a private investigator prepared a theft investigation report for an insurer prior to counsel being retained. The court held that its dominant purpose was for litigation

---

92 *Heritage Clothing (Canada) Ltd. v. Sun Alliance Insurance Co.* (1985), 4 C.P.C. (2d) 154 (Ont. H.C.J.); and *Falconbridge Ltd. v. Hawker Siddeley Diesels & Electrics Ltd.* (1985), 3 C.P.C. (2d) 133 (Ont. H.C.J.), referring to *Blackstone v. Mutual Life Assurance Co.,* [1944] 3 D.L.R. 147 (Ont. C.A.).

93 *Waugh v. British Railway Board,* above note 76.

94 *Canadian Pacific Ltd. v. Canada (Competition Act, Director of Investigation and Research),* [1995] O.J. No. 1867 (Gen. Div.); *Nova v. Guelph Engineering Company* (1985), 30 Alta L.R. (2d) 183 (C.A.).

95 *MacDermott v. Atlantic Mutual Life Assurance Co.* (1989), 91 N.S.R. (2d) 408 (S.C.T.D.).

96 *Adams Motors Ltd. v. Transamerica Life Insurance Co. of Canada,* above note 90.

97 *Saprai v. Carter,* [1993] B.C.J. No. 1797 (S.C.).

98 *Re AFG Industries Ltd. and Aluminum, Brick and Glass Workers International Union, Local 295G* (1998), 71 L.A.C. (4th) 67 (Ontario) (P. Knopf).

because, given the amounts involved, the defendant knew that the claim was definitely headed for the courts because no insured could abandon or walk away from a claim of those proportions.[99]

Where a private investigator prepared an arson investigation report for an insurer, a court has held that its dominant purpose was for litigation. The court further held that since the nature of the private investigator's involvement was to gather facts to assist counsel, he could not be called to testify at a discovery requested by the plaintiff.[100]

Where a spouse referred to a private investigator's report in an affidavit and gave copies of the report to an expert witness, a court held that the dominant purpose requirement of contemplation of litigation was proven because it was actually prepared during ongoing family law child custody litigation.[101]

If privilege for a document is claimed at discovery, it cannot be later used at trial without leave of the court.[102]

10.3.2.2 Waiver of Privilege

Waiver of privilege becomes an issue when a private investigator's report is disclosed to a third party. Pertaining to medical experts, where a lawyer discloses the contents of a private investigator's report he had commissioned to a medical doctor, the disclosure does not destroy the report's privileged character if the disclosure to, and the discussion with, the medical doctor is also done in contemplation of litigation.[103] However, where a lawyer voluntarily waives privilege and discloses a medical report that makes reference to a private investigator's report, the privilege attached to the private investigator's report is also waived and it too loses its privileged character.[104]

Privilege is not necessarily waived if a witness unwittingly discloses information to a private investigator. It has been held that where a defendant admits on a discovery that a private investigator's report was commissioned in preparation for litigation to impeach the credibility of the plaintiff, the defendant has not waived his privilege with respect to the private investigator's report.[105]

In a British Columbia case, the owner of a hockey team took twenty-five witness statements and forwarded them to an insurance adjuster assigned by the defendant to the file. The plaintiff, meanwhile, hired his own private investigator who convinced the insurance adjuster to show him the statements he had obtained. Upon the private investigator's request for copies of the statements, the defendant's counsel instructed the adjuster and the witnesses to have no further contact with the private investigator. The plaintiff brought a

---

99 *Laxton Holdings Ltd. v. Madill* (1988), 34 C.C.L.I. 172, rev'g (1987) 26 C.C.L.I. 110 (Sask. C.A.). See also *Tsprailis v. Western Union Insurance Co.* (1989), 32 C.P.C. (2d) 325 (Alta. Q.B.), pursuant to Rule 194(2) of Alberta Rules of Court.
100 *Webber v. Canadian Surety Co.*, [1992] N.S.J. No. 80 (S.C.).
101 *Robertson v. Robertson*, [1996] M.J. No. 417 (Q.B.).
102 Rule 30.09 of the Ontario Rules of Civil Procedure.
103 *Pelletier v. McAuley*, [1980] B.C.D. Civ. 3612-02 (S.C.).
104 *Stafford v. Webb*, [1997] 71 A.C.W.S. (3d) 239 (Man. Q.B.).
105 *McDonnell v. Lopuch* (1993), 11 C.P.C. (3d) 376 (Alta. Q.B.).

motion for disclosure arguing the defendant had waived privilege by allowing the private investigator to read the witness statements. The court, however, held that the party seeking disclosure must prove that the possessor of waiver knew of the existence of the privilege and that it was voluntarily waived. The court found that the adjuster had no intention of waiving the insurer's client's privilege, nor did he have authority to do so. Accordingly, the defendants were not required to produce the statements.[106]

10.3.3 Surveillance Films and Videotapes

Issues of privilege and surveillance videotapes include the document and communication debate, the dominant purpose test, the extent of disclosure required, the timing of the required disclosure, and the waiver of privilege.

10.3.3.1 The Document and Communication Debate

There has been debate whether videotapes are communications and therefore subject to the rules of privilege,[107] or actions with no intent to convey information and therefore not communications subject to the rules of privilege.[108] Similarly, there has been debate whether surveillance videotapes are a form of *viva voce* evidence of a private investigator or a document requiring production.[109] It is now widely accepted that surveillance photographs and videotapes are "documents" similar to witness statements and therefore are subject to the rules of privilege.[110]

10.3.3.2 The Dominant Purpose Test

Normally, if surveillance is undertaken on instruction from counsel, it attracts litigation privilege.[111] Where the surveillance is not at a lawyer's instruction, the same rule may not apply.

---

106 *Zapf v. Muckalt*, [1995] B.C.D. Civ. 3612-22 (S.C.).

107 *Paquet v. Jackman* (1980), 24 B.C.L.R. 287 (S.C.).

108 *Chmara v. Nguyen* (1992), 77 Man. R. (2d) 261 (C.A.): "There is no evidence that the plaintiff intended to convey any information to the defendant or his agent; or that she was aware that her activities were imparting information to anyone. In my view, her activities as recorded in the video tapes were simply not communications."

109 *Fobel v. Dean* (1989), 76 Sask. R. 87 (Q.B.), pursuant to Rule 212 of Saskatchewan Rules of Civil Procedure; *Murray v. Woodstock General Hospital Trust* (1988), 64 O.R. (2d) 458 (H.C.J.), aff'd (1988), 66 O.R. (2d) 129 (Div. Ct.), pursuant to Rules 30.09 and 31.06 of Ontario Rules of Civil Procedure; where a court held that surveillance videotape is a kind of *viva voce* evidence, and though surveillance evidence is through the medium of a video, it does not alter its character; *Fobel v. Dean, ibid.*, pursuant to Rule 212 of Saskatchewan Rules of Court, where the court held that the video is not a "document" in the context of the Rule requiring disclosure.

110 *Iannucci v. Heighton*, [1994] B.C.J. No. 1721 (S.C.). See also Rule 30.01 of Ontario Rules of Civil Procedure.

111 *Breau v. Naddy*, [1995] P.E.I.J. No. 108 (S.C.).

For example, in a situation where video surveillance was undertaken within two months from the date of an accident, where no lawyers were involved, no action had been commenced, and the adjuster through the private investigator was merely gathering facts on film upon which he could evaluate the plaintiff's claim, a court held the dominant purpose of the surveillance was not in contemplation of litigation.[112] Where a court found that litigation did not become a reasonable prospect until after the discontinuance of benefit payments, and where a private investigator's surveillance tapes were prepared prior to that date, privilege did not attach, and the surveillance videotapes were required to be disclosed.[113] Where video surveillance was undertaken the day a claim was made, a court held that the dominant purpose was not litigation, but rather investigation or evaluation.[114]

10.3.3.3 The Extent of Disclosure Required

Partial disclosure of privileged surveillance videotapes is another contentious legal issue. There is controversy over how much should be disclosed and when it should be disclosed. Older cases held that while the videotapes themselves may be protected by litigation privilege, the facts disclosed on the films are the proper subject of discovery,[115] and their content should be disclosed by affidavit.[116]

Not all courts, however, have agreed with this position. In Nova Scotia, for example, it has been held that to require disclosure of the factual content of a surveillance video or an investigator's report would effectively require the whole of the privileged document to be divulged.[117] In Alberta it has been held that where a document is privileged, the privilege should not be whittled away by compelling questions about it on an examination for discovery.[118]

Under the new rules in Ontario, a series of cases have resulted in a list of what information contained on surveillance videotapes must be disclosed. This list includes

1.   the name of the investigator and the investigation company;

2.   the dates of any surveillance, including the time and length of observation;

3.   the place of the surveillance;

4.   the place where the photographs and/or videos were taken;

5.   the type of camera or other information as to how the recording or photography was completed;

---

112 *Richter v. Yee*, [1992] B.C.J. No. 2944 (S.C.).

113 *Saprai v. Carter*, [1993] B.C.J. No. 1797 (S.C.).

114 *Iannucci v. Heighton*, above note 110.

115 *Paquet v. Jackman* (1980), 24 B.C.L.R. 287 (S.C.); *Ohl v. Cannito*, [1972] 2 O.R. 763 (H.C.J.), pursuant to Rule 326 (Ontario's old Rules of Practice).

116 *Spatafora v. Wiebe* (1973), 1 O.R. 93 (H.C.J.), pursuant to Rules 326 and 347 (Ontario's old Rules of Practice).

117 *MacDermott v. Atlantic Mutual Life Assurance Co.* (1989), 91 N.S.R. (2d) 408 (S.C.T.D.), pursuant to Rule 31.15(1). The court further noted the Rules of Civil Procedure are different in Nova Scotia than in Ontario.

118 *McDonnell v. Lopuch* (1993), 11 C.P.C. (3d) 376 (Alta. Q.B.).

6. a synopsis of the relevant activities and observations; and

7. a list of persons who also witnessed what was documented on the videotape.[119]

The detail of the synopsis of the relevant activities and observations is also contentious in Ontario. Although some courts have stated a defendant does not need to provide a running account of everything on the film,[120] other courts have held that a detailed synopsis of both the video surveillance evidence to be led at trial and that not to be relied upon must be disclosed.[121]

One Ontario practitioner has stated that normally at discovery, when questions are asked about surveillance evidence, counsel is obliged to tell the other party something about it if they have such evidence. Dates, times, and particulars of activities and observations must be shared, but not the film or video evidence itself. He also commented that with mediation becoming increasingly important as a way to resolve disputes, the strategic value of showing the mediator and the other party the surveillance could be worthwhile.[122]

10.3.3.4 The Timing of Disclosure

Issues that arise with regard to the timing of the release of privileged information on surveillance videotapes include the before or after discovery debate, the release of information during an actual discovery itself, and the use of undisclosed information at trial.

10.3.3.4.1 The Disclosure before or after Discovery Debate

It has been argued that if information is privileged, a plaintiff should not be allowed to obtain indirectly what it cannot obtain directly. If full disclosure were made before trial, the plaintiff could tailor his evidence to dilute the impact of the observations.[123] One Ontario court stated:

> It must be remembered that the purpose of such surveillance is either verification or contradiction. A trial is a search for truth and surveillance is a tool used in pursuit thereof. A truthful witness will not suffer by having been under surveillance; prevarication and exaggeration may be exposed. Full disclosure in advance may well enable the untruthful witness to avoid

---

119 *Sacrey v. Berdan* (1986), 10 C.P.C. (2d) 15 (Ont. Dist. Ct.), pursuant to Rules 30.01(1)(a) and 31.06(1)-(3); *Nolan v. Grant* (1986), 8 C.P.C. (2d) 253 (Ont. H.C.J.), pursuant to Rules 30.09 and 31.06.; *Murray v. Woodstock General Hospital Trust* (1988), 64 O.R. (2d) 458 (H.C.J.), aff'd (1988) 66 O.R. (2d) 129 (Div. Ct.), pursuant to Rules 30.09 and 31.06; *Maggio v. Lopes* (1988), 29 C.P.C. (2d) 284 (Ont. Master), pursuant to Rules 30.09 and 31.06; *Patterson v. Wilkinson* (1988), 89 D.L.R. (4th) 444 28 C.P.C. (2d) 250 (Ont. H.C.J.), pursuant to Rules 30.09 and 31.06; *Weiss v. Machando* (1988), 65 O.R. (2d) 201 (H.C.J.), pursuant to Rules 30.09 and 31.06; and *Ceci v. Bond* (1992), 89 D.L.R. (4th) 444 (Ont. C.A.), pursuant to Rules 30.09 and 31.04(3). [All rules cited are from Ontario Rules of Civil Procedure.]

120 *Nolan v. Grant, ibid.*, pursuant to Rules 30.09 and 31.06; and *Maggio v. Lopes, ibid.*, pursuant to Rules 30.09 and 31.06, Ontario Rules of Civil Procedure.

121 *Niederle v. Frederick Transport Ltd.* (1985), 50 C.P.C. 135 (Ont. H.C.J.), pursuant to Rule 30.02(1) of Ontario Rules of Civil Procedure.

122 C. Kentridge, "Surveillance Must Be Used with Caution" *Law Times* (1–7 June 1998).

123 *Maggio v. Lopes*, above note 119.

the effect of surveillance by tailoring his or her evidence to dilute the impact; indeed, it is the very type of claimant in respect of whom surveillance is indicated that such attempted deception is likely to occur.[124]

Following this line of logic, other courts have ordered plaintiffs to complete their examinations for discovery before the defendant's disclosure of surveillance information.[125] It has been held that where the credibility of the opposing party is an issue, it may be withheld until after discoveries so that the witness may give honest answers to questions asked relating to his capabilities and activities.[126] Another court summed up the issue this way:

> In my view, the surveillance information, including the films, is not necessary to enable the plaintiff to answer truthfully questions put at his discovery. In this perspective, it seems to me the purpose of disclosure is more so than any other factor to enable him to adapt or tailor his evidence. The position of the defendants give rise to the real likelihood that the disclosure sought would be used, at least in part, to allow the plaintiff to adapt his evidence to the information disclosed. In my view, what is necessary to disclose here is the fact of the surveillance, including its form, not the facts disclosed by a descriptive process of what was filmed and observed.[127]

Although seemingly the majority of cases permit the withholding of videotape surveillance evidence until after discoveries, there are cases where courts voiced an opposite opinion. One court held that a defendant's motion to postpone disclosing to the plaintiff particulars of its surveillance and investigation should only be allowed if there is a real likelihood that the plaintiff will tailor his evidence if disclosure is made.[128] Another court ordered the defendants to provide surveillance information prior to the plaintiffs' examination for discovery, ruling that possible prejudice resulting from the disclosure, unlike real prejudice based on a demonstrated foundation, was insufficient to permit its withholding.[129]

10.3.3.4.2 Disclosure during Discovery

Where a concern was raised that surveillance information disclosed on discovery of the defendant might be provided to the plaintiff, a court ordered that the examinations be held

124 *Murray v. Woodstock General Hospital Trust*, above note 119.
125 *Weisz v. Gist* (1986), 12 C.P.C. (2d) 190 (Ont. Dist. Ct.), pursuant to Rule 30.09 and 31.06; *Cowan v. Wilk* (1988), 17 W.D.C.P. 196 (Ont. Dist. Ct.); and *Calogero v. Tersigni* (1985), 49 O.R. (2d) 508 (Ont. H.C.J.), pursuant to Rule 34.04(3) [all rules from Ontario Rules of Civil Procedure].
126 *Iannucci v. Heighton*, above note 110.
127 *Daruwalla v. Shigeoka*, [1992] B.C.D. Civ. 3613-01 (S.C.). See "B.C. Surveillance Videos Need Not Be Disclosed before Discovery: Judge" *Lawyers Weekly* (3 July 1992) at 11.
128 *Gumieniak v. Tobin* (1987), 16 C.P.C. (2d) 126 (Ont. Dist. Ct.), pursuant to Rule 31.06(1); *Ceci v. Bond*, above note 119, pursuant to Rules 30.09 and 31.04(3); *Taylor v. Fry* (1996), 29 O.R. (3d) 714 (Gen. Div.), pursuant to Rule 31.04 [all rules from Ontario Rules of Civil Procedure].
129 *Paulin v. Prince* (1987), 21 C.P.C. (2d) 152 (Ont. Dist. Ct.), aff'd (1987), 23 C.P.C. (2d) 319 (Ont. H.C.J.), aff'd (1988), 31 C.P.C. (2d) 281 (Ont. Div. Ct.), pursuant to Rule 31.06 of Ontario Rules of Civil Procedure.

on the same day and that there be no disclosure to the plaintiff of information obtained from the defendant.[130]

10.3.3.4.3 The Use of Undisclosed Privileged Evidence at Trial

Where the rules of disclosure were not complied with, some courts permitted surveillance evidence to be used to impeach the credibility but not as substantive evidence,[131] and other courts ordered a defendant at the outset of the trial to disclose information regarding surveillance films taken of the plaintiff.[132] Where the existence of the videotapes was not disclosed until after discovery, it was held that a plaintiff would be allowed to call reply evidence to explain it.[133] Where defendants deliberately withheld video surveillance evidence from the plaintiff until trial in order to achieve surprise, a court held the evidence to be inadmissible.[134]

Where a private investigator was ordered to disclose a file's notes and reports, and only disclosed a report that was drafted on the basis of notes of other investigators, it was held that there was a breach of disclosure rules. However, as the plaintiff must have known that such notes existed and did not request them, he was not entitled to have the investigation file declared inadmissible, but rather only permitted an adjournment to review the undisclosed notes.[135]

10.3.3.5   Waiver of Privilege

Where a surveillance videotape was shown to a defence expert and referred to in his report, the court ordered production of the videotape. The court held that privilege had been waived by the delivery of the tapes to the defence expert. In this case, the videotape was shown to the defendant's medical expert but not the plaintiff's medical expert before trial. The defendant argued greater weight should be given to the defendant's expert's report and testimony. The court held that by invoking privilege, they were accomplishing indirectly what they were prohibited from doing directly. The court found the mischief attempted by the defendant was getting before the trier of fact in the form of medical reports conclusions that one might draw about the plaintiff's credibility from a review of the videotape without producing the videotape itself. The court held it is for the trier of fact to draw his or her own conclusions after reviewing the tape. The court also held that to give

---

130 *Costa v. Melo* (1992), 13 C.P.C. (3d) 159 (Ont. Gen. Div.).

131 *Jones v. Heidel* (1985), 6 C.P.C. (2d) 318 (Ont. H.C.J.), pursuant to Rules 30.07 and 30.09; *Giroux v. Lafrance* (1993), 19 C.P.C. (3d) 12 (Ont. Gen. Div.), pursuant to Rules 30.01, 30.03, 30.09, & 31; *MacDermott v. Atlantic Mutual Life Assurance Co.* (1989), 91 N.S.R. (2d) 408 (S.C.), pursuant to Rule 31.15(1); *Patterson v. Wilkinson* (1988), 28 C.P.C. (2d) 250 (Ont. H.C.J.), pursuant to Rules 30.09 and 31.06 [all rules from Ontario Rules of Civil Procedure].

132 *Niederle v. Frederick Transport Ltd.* (1985), 50 C.P.C. 135 (Ont. H.C.J.).

133 *Machado v. Berlet* (1986), 57 O.R. (2d) 207 (H.C.J.), following the rule known as *Browne v. Dunn* (1894), 6 R. 67 (H.L.), pursuant to Rule 30.09 of Ontario Rules of Civil Procedure.

134 *Clark v. O'Brien* (1995), 52 A.C.W.S. (3d) 1048 (N.S.S.C.). The evidence should have been disclosed under Nova Scotia's Civil Procedure Rule No. 20.08.

135 *Turner v. Economical Mutual Insurance Company* (14 May 1999), F.S.C.O. Judgment No. A-012411 (Ont. F.S.C.), pursuant to Rule 37.1 of the Dispute Resolution Code, 3d ed.

full weight to the defendant's medical expert's report, the plaintiff's medical expert must be able to comment upon the video surveillance as well.[136]

Where a defendant, against whom a case has been dismissed, gave surveillance documentation to a remaining defendant, the court held the documentation was not privileged. There is no joint privilege if a document is created solely for the first defendant.[137]

10.3.4 Witness Statements and Witness Names

In insurance litigation, where a defendant hired a private investigator to interview certain people with regard to the plaintiff's potential loss of income resulting from a personal injury accident, the court held that the plaintiff was entitled to the names and addresses of all potential non-expert witnesses.[138] However, in one case, a court refused to require the defendant to provide the names and addresses of everyone interviewed during an investigation by the defendant where the defendant did not intend to rely upon the interviews at trial.[139]

In criminal litigation, where a defence lawyer mentioned that he hired a private investigator to interview witnesses, the defence lawyer did not release privileged information and the private investigator's interviews remained protected by litigation privilege.[140]

In regulatory litigation, where a defendant retained a private investigator to interview a plaintiff's former employees, a court ordered disclosure, holding that no privilege attached to statements made by one party to an opposing party or their agent. The fact that these were former employees of the plaintiff did not take the present case outside of this exception.[141]

10.3.5 Freedom of Information Requests

In an Ontario case, an individual sought copies of all invoices received from private investigators engaged by the Ministry of Industry, Trade and Technology, the Ontario Development Corporation, and the IDEA Corporation with respect to investigations, as well as copies of all reports prepared by investigators for the aforementioned organizations. The Ontario Information and Privacy Commissioner refused access to these records. On appeal, the Commissioner held that as the dominant purpose of the private investigators' reports was for use in litigation, the records were subject to the litigation privilege and exempt from disclosure. As for the invoices, they were closely associated with the reports and therefore also exempt from disclosure.[142]

---

136 *Binkle v. Lockhart* (1994), 24 C.P.C. (3d) 11 (Ont. Gen. Div.), pursuant to Rules 30.02 and 33 of Ontario Rules of Civil Procedure.

137 *Tremblay v. Daum* (1994), 29 C.P.C. (3d) 219 (Ont. Gen. Div.).

138 *Woong v. Jung* (1989), 16 A.C.W.S. (3d) 53 (B.C.S.C.), pursuant to Rule 27(22) of the Supreme Court of British Columbia Rules.

139 *Nolan v. Grant* (1986), 54 O.R. (2d) 702 (H.C.J.), pursuant to Rules 30.09 and 31.06 of Ontario Rules of Civil Procedure.

140 *R. v. Samra* (1998), 41 O.R. (3d) 434 (Ont. C.A.).

141 *Alberta v. Stearns Catalytic Ltd.* (1991), 81 D.L.R. (4th) 347 (Alta. C.A.).

142 *Re Ministry of Industry, Trade and Technology*, [1989] O.I.P.C. No. 89.

10.3.6 Anton Piller Orders

It has been held that the seizure of privileged documents during the execution of an *ex parte* Anton Piller order does not amount to an involuntary waiver of privilege.[143]

10.3.7 Privilege and Defamatory Statements Made during Investigations or Trial

Absolute Privilege: Absolute privilege attaches to statements made during the course of a trial or in preparation for trial. In an Ontario defamation case, a defendant brought a motion for summary judgment, arguing that the alleged defamatory statements were made when a private investigator interviewed him as a potential witness in the course of judicial proceedings, the judicial proceedings being a separate action the plaintiff had with the defendant. The plaintiff did not become aware of those statements until later when they were republished by third parties in the course of the original proceedings. The court held:

> The immunity in the doctrine of absolute privilege must extend to all steps in contemplation of litigation including statements made by a potential witness even if he or she is never called upon to testify . . . It matters not whether a potential witness is interviewed by a lawyer or by an investigator hired to gather evidence in the course of judicial proceedings . . . The purpose of the doctrine of absolute privilege is to encourage witnesses to give their evidence without fear of being subject to a defamation action at a later date.

The court held that the doctrine of absolute privilege does not protect statements made by a witness in court that are unrelated to the matters in issue. Absolute privilege also does not apply to investigations that are nothing more than "fishing expeditions." The court further held that absolute privilege cannot be extended to statements based on hearsay evidence.[144]

Qualified Privilege: Qualified privilege is another form of privilege to be considered. Occasions of qualified privilege arise when a person has an interest or a duty — legal, social, or moral — to make a communication to another person, and that person has a corresponding interest or duty to receive it.[145] On such occasions, a person is entitled to make untrue defamatory statements about another without liability provided he or she does so honestly believing the statements are true and provided they are made without malice or any indirect or improper motive.[146]

Where a business person was asked questions by a private investigator retained by a competitor business person, the court held:

---

143 *Sunwell Engineering Co. v. Mogilevsky* (1986), 8 C.P.C. (2d) 14 (Ont. H.C.J.), leave to appeal to Ont. Div. Ct. refused.
144 *Larche v. Middleton* (1989), 69 O.R. (2d) 400 (Gen. Div.).
145 *Adam v. Ward*, [1971] A.C. 309 (H.L.).
146 C. Gatley, *Gatley on Libel and Slander*, 8th ed. (London: Sweet & Maxwell, 1981) at 185.

The mere fact that an inquiry is made about the character or position of another does not necessarily render the answer privileged . . . But where a person who is asked a question touching on the character, financial position, or responsibility of another, *bona fide* believes that his inquirer is asking the question not to gratify idle curiosity, but for some other purpose in which he has a legitimate interest of his own, it is not merely his right but his duty to answer, and if he does so in the honest belief that his answer is true and without malice towards the person whose character or position is the subject-matter of the inquiry, his answer is a privileged communication . . . It is in the general interest of society that correct information should be obtained as to the character of persons in whom others have a legitimate interest, and that person should be able to give it without exposing himself to an action of libel or slander.

The court found the words of the business person were protected by the defence of qualified privilege because the private investigator had a legitimate interest and because there was no malice in the information he provided.[147]

10.3.8 Privilege and Search Warrants for a Private Investigator's Files

As mentioned above, privilege belongs to the client and only he or she can waive it. In a Saskatchewan case, a private investigator was retained by a lawyer to conduct an interview of the lawyer's client. The police later obtained a search warrant for the private investigator's notes and tapes. The private investigator brought a motion to quash the search warrant on the basis that his conversations with the client were subject to solicitor-client privilege. The court, however, held that the privilege was that of the client. Since the client had not asserted his privilege, it did not extend to the private investigator.[148]

10.3.9 Privilege and Illegally Obtained Evidence

In an English case, a defendant sought discharge from a Mareva (asset freezing) injunction imposed together with an Anton Piller (search and seizure) order. The defendant requested disclosure of privileged documents on the ground that the plaintiff had employed private investigators who breached the *Data Protection Act (UK)* and various Swiss banking laws in investigating his finances and assets.

The court held the clash of public interests was between legal privilege and combatting crime and fraud and protecting the victims thereof. In dealing with these opposing principles, the court reasoned that if investigative agents employed by solicitors for the purpose of litigation were permitted to breach legislation or to indulge in fraud or impersonation without any consequence, it would be improper for a court to sanction such conduct. The court noted that the primary option for a person who has suffered from a private investigator's breach of criminal or civil law is a separate prosecution. The court also noted the primacy of the principle of vindicating the truth with the aid of relevant evidence rather than excluding it on the basis that it was improperly obtained. The court held, however,

---

147 *Larche v. Middleton*, above note 144.
148 *Re Michael F. Robinson* (1983), 10 W.C.B. 132 (Sask. Q.B.).

that as to the extent of disclosure required, in cases where evidence is obtained through criminal or fraudulent conduct by private investigators employed by solicitors for use in, and relevant to, issues in litigation, it is discoverable and not protected by legal privilege. The court further noted that when solicitors condone criminal or fraudulent conduct for the purposes of litigation, such conduct should be treated the same as advising on, or setting up, criminal or fraudulent transactions yet to be undertaken.[149]

10.3.10 Breach of Privilege by Private Investigators

In an Ontario case, a private investigator was found by a court to have breached a solicitor's privilege with his client. During an adjournment, a private investigator who had been retained by the plaintiff's lawyers approached the defendant's lawyers and disclosed his findings. The plaintiff's counsel informed the court of the private investigator's conduct. The court ordered the defendant's lawyers removed from the record stating that "the court must protect privileged information from improper use by an opposing party."[150]

10.3.11 Private Investigators as Disclosure Agents for Lawyers

Where a criminal defence lawyer sought to have a private investigator he retained review disclosure documents in his stead, the court held there are very strict limitations on access as it pertains to the laws of privilege. The court held that persons who are in attendance for the purpose of the disclosure should be limited to either counsel or other counsel acting as agent for counsel for the accused.[151]

Another court, however, did not comment negatively when a Crown provided access to a private investigator retained by defence counsel. In this case, the private investigator was given unrestricted access to the entire police investigation file consisting of two banker's boxes and four filing cabinet drawers at the police detachment, as well as police logs from a telephone tap investigation. The files also contained information of other suspects, crime-stopper tips, statements from various witnesses, and Centre of Forensic Science reports.[152]

10.3.12 Reciprocal Disclosure in Criminal Litigation

It is well settled law that the Crown must make complete and open disclosure to the defence in criminal litigation. The reciprocal is not true of the defence.[153] Notwithstanding this principle, there was an occurrence where a Crown sought to obtain defence disclosure of witness statements obtained by a private investigator retained by the defence. The trial judge

---

149 *Dubai Aluminium Co. Ltd. v. Sayed Reyadh Abdulla S. Nasser Al Alawi*, [1998] T.N.L.R. No. 920 (England & Wales Q.B.).
150 *Appleton v. Hawes* (1990), 47 C.P.C. (2d) 151 (Ont. H.C.J.). See "Plaintiff's Doctors Can Be Called to Testify for the Defence, Court Rules" *Lawyers Weekly* (21 June 1991) at 27.
151 *R. v. M.C.*, [1993] O.J. No. 1130 (C.J.).
152 *R. v. Malott*, [1993] O.J. No. 2825 (C.J.).
153 *R. v. Stinchcombe* (1991), 8 C.R. (4th) 277 (S.C.C.).

allowed it. The Quebec Court of Appeal, however, held that while the Crown has the right to cross-examine a witness called by an adverse party on a previous statement, it does not give the Crown the right to obtain a statement that is in the possession of the defence. The court further held that statements made to defence lawyers or their agents are privileged.[154]

10.4   LITIGATION COST AWARDS

Under English and Canadian law, there is a principle that at least part of the costs of litigation should be shifted to the losing side by an award known as party-and-party costs. In each province, there are published scales of costs for the preparation of court documents by a lawyer and for standard payment for each hour of preparation for presentation of a case and for each appearance or day in court. Accordingly, when a plaintiff wins a case for damages, a court will award "x dollars damages plus costs" against the defendant. Conversely, if the defendant successfully defends the action, a court will dismiss the claim "with costs"; that is, party-and-party costs against the plaintiff. If the result of the action is a mixed one — for example, a plaintiff's claim succeeds in part and is rejected in part — the costs may be apportioned, or each party may be left to pay its own costs.

The fee a client pays a solicitor is almost always greater than an award of party-and-party costs. Therefore, even when a client wins a case with an award of costs in his or her favour, these costs will ordinarily cover only a portion of the fee charged by his or her lawyer. But the winner is considerably better off than the losing side with respect to the costs of the litigation; the loser must pay party-and-party costs to the other side, the fee of his or her own lawyer, and, of course, the amount of the judgment. Included in the determination of costs are disbursements. The quantum of disbursements may include the costs for an investigation.

This is a very simplified review of the law of costs. The law of costs is actually quite complex and considers factors such as the timing, quantum, acceptance, and rejection of offers. It also considers the conduct of the parties to the case. Costs are generally a matter of judicial discretion that are usually determined following the event; that is, awarded to the successful party, with a secondary determination as to whether there is any appropriate reason to deprive a successful litigant of his costs.

For a thorough review of the law of costs, reference should be made to the leading Canadian text, *The Law of Costs*.[155] However, even this book does not include a discussion of costs as it applies specifically to services rendered by private investigators. For this reason, a review of this topic is included here.

---

154 *R. v. Peruta and Brouillette* (1992), 78 C.C.C. (3d) 350 (Que. C.A.), referring to s. 10 of the *Canada Evidence Act*, R.S.C. 1985, c. C-5. See also D.M Tanovich & L. Crocker, "Dancing with Stinchcombe's Ghost: A Modest Proposal for Reciprocal Defence Disclosure" (1993) 26 C.R. (4th) 333. See also C.B. Davison, "Putting Ghosts to Rest: A Reply to the 'Modest Proposal' for Defence Disclosure of Tanovich and Crocker" (1995) 43 C.R. (4th) 105.

155 M.M. Orkin, *The Law of Costs* (Aurora: Canada Law Book, 1987–) [looseleaf].

10.4.1 Lawyers and the Use of Private Investigator Services

It is common for law firms to retain private investigators as opposed to having their clients retain them. The reasons given normally are to ensure the private investigator is reputable, to properly instruct the private investigator as to what information is needed and how to properly obtain it, and to preserve solicitor-client privilege and avoid disclosure during examinations for discovery.[156]

However, while lawyers frequently wish to retain the private investigator, they sometimes ask the private investigators to bill the client directly for their services. This often rubs both the client and the private investigator the wrong way. If the private investigator is to bill the client directly, the private investigator normally wishes to meet with the client directly, something the lawyer will often try to prevent.[157] If the client is going to be billed by the private investigator directly, he does not like to pay the lawyer's "administration" fee for the lawyer acting as a "go-between."[158]

10.4.2 Provincial Cost Rules and Private Investigators Generally

The rules pertaining to the cost awards for private investigators are governed by each province's rules of civil procedure. In some provinces, a general rule has been interpreted pertaining to the use of private investigators. For example, in Alberta it has been held that all reasonable and proper expenses including the use of a private investigator should be allowed.[159] In British Columbia, it has been held that a private investigator's fee is not an allowable cost award if the work could be done by a solicitor or his or her staff.[160] In Saskatchewan, it has been held that a court may allow reasonable expenses resulting from the obtaining of evidence.[161] And in Ontario, it has been held that a court may allow for expenses that are properly and necessarily incurred for the continuation of an action, but not for services that were eventually thrown away.[162] It has also been held that the inter-

---

156 *Kucher v. Chowne*, [1997] A.J. No. 367 (Q.B.).
157 Private investigators have also been frequently heard to complain that lawyers either are late at paying their bills or simply do not pay at all. This has led to many private investigators keeping an informal list of lawyers from whom they will not accept contracts. This is another reason why many private investigators require that they meet with the client or refuse to take the case. See *Pankhurst v. Matz* (1991), 71 Man. R. (2d) 271 (C.A.); and *Mattson & Associates Ltd. v. McCloy, MacKay* (1980), B.C.D. Civ. 3651-01 (S.C.).
158 *Kucher v. Chowne*, above note 156.
159 *Kassam v. Dragish* (1991), 49 C.P.C. (2d) 174 (Alta. Q.B.), pursuant to Rule 600(1)(a) of Alberta Rules of Civil Procedure.
160 *Noble v. Wong* (1983), 148 D.L.R. (3d) 740 (B.C.C.A.), pursuant to Rule 57(4) of British Columbia Rules of Civil Procedure.
161 *Ellenchuk v. Ellenchuk* (1972), 24 D.L.R. (3d) 235 (Sask. Q.B.), pursuant to Rule 563 of Saskatchewan Rules of Civil Procedure.
162 *Appleton v. Hawes*, above note 150, pursuant to Rule 58 of Ontario Rules of Civil Procedure. Here the investigators billed $416,000.

pretations of the various provincial provisions depend on the facts of each particular case.[163] The following is a review of cost awards categorized by various services that private investigators offer to the legal community.

10.4.3 Witness Statements

Before 1981, the cost of the investigator's report indicating the contents of witness statements was allowed as a reasonable disbursement in preparation for litigation.[164] Shortly thereafter, two cases held that the costs of the investigator's report for interviews of witnesses friendly to the plaintiff were not allowable because no special skills were required.[165] Thus, the "special skills" test was born. In both of these decisions, it was indicated that circumstances may exist where the retaining of a private investigator to interview witnesses is justified under a costs analysis.

Noble v. Wong[166] is a case often cited on the issue of taking witness statements and costs awards for the services of private investigators. This was a personal injury case wherein a private investigator submitted a $547 invoice. The court held that the investigator's fee for attending at the scene to time the traffic lights and his fee for obtaining photographs were properly taxable. However, the taking of statements was not. The court held that the rule in British Columbia is that only interviews that require the "special skills" of a private investigator are recoverable in a civil litigation matter.

At the initial taxation hearing in *Noble v. Wong*, the court held that the private investigator went well beyond interviewing witnesses and rendered services normally provided by a lawyer. The court held the investigator's interview of the plaintiff did not contemplate an interview by the lawyer because the report included a full description of the plaintiff and witness profiles. The report also set out summaries of the evidence and concluded with an opinion on the liability of the parties to the action. The court held that to permit costs awards for such conduct could lead to investigators doing work that, by law, is reserved to lawyers.[167] The court stated:

> This is not to say it is improper for solicitors to use para-legals, law students or investigators for work that such people are capable of performing, and passing the saving on to the client. That question is not before us. The question here is whether, having someone else do the work, that other person's bill can be taxed as a disbursement on a party-and-party taxation. I think that it cannot if the work is of the kind normally done by the solicitor or his staff.

The Court of Appeal upheld the trial judge's decision.

---

163 *Powar v. British Columbia Ministry of Transport*, [1995] B.C.D. Civ. 3598-06, [1995] B.C.J. No. 706 (S.C.).

164 *Bowers v. White* (1977), 2 B.C.L.R. 355 (S.C.).

165 *Bell v. Fantini* (1981), 32 B.C.L.R. 322 (S.C); *Hall v. Strocel* (1983), 34 C.P.C. 170 (B.C.S.C).

166 1983), 148 D.L.R. (3d) 740 (B.C.C.A.), aff'g (1982), 38 B.C.L.R. 246 (S.C.).

167 See also *Hall v. Strocel*, above note 165; *Fawall v. Atkins* (1981), 28 B.C.L.R. 32; *Bell v. Fantini*, above note 165.

There have been a number of reported cases that have followed *Noble v. Wong*.[168] A few peculiar applications of the rule have also been reported. In one case, a solicitor carried on business in Vancouver and the witnesses were located in Courtenay on Vancouver Island. The court followed the decision of *Noble v. Wong*, notwithstanding it was a poor use of the solicitor's time to attend the witness's location to take statements.[169] In another case, a court held that the plaintiff could have obtained a copy of the RCMP file to obtain statements rather than interview the RCMP officers and incur the expense of private investigators.[170]

In summary, the ultimate test for whether a disbursement, including the costs of retaining an investigator, is recoverable is whether in all the circumstances it was reasonable. Expenditures for investigator's reports are not considered reasonable unless it is established that the matters investigated call for the "special skills" of an investigator. To put the matter another way, if the work in question can be done by a lawyer, the cost of hiring an investigator to do it is not recoverable.

Although most courts have followed this principle, its reasoning is contentious. At the Court of Appeal in *Noble v. Wong*, the dissenting judge arguably gave a more balanced assessment of the issue. Anderson J.A. held:

> In my view the learned trial judge erred in holding that interviewing and taking statements from witnesses are services normally provided by a lawyer to his client. To so hold is to fail to distinguish between "preparation for trial" and the investigatory or fact-gathering process.
>
> The tariff provides partial indemnity in respect of services performed by a lawyer in conducting the litigation process. Thus, if witnesses are interviewed for the purposes of discovery or trial or are interviewed for the purposes of considering settlement, such work can not be "farmed out" and charged as a disbursement. Such work is the work of a lawyer and it would be improper and unethical to delegate this work to a lay person, however skilled.
>
> On the other hand, the fact-gathering process is not normally a process conducted by lawyers. It certainly is not a process exclusively reserved to lawyers. In so far as personal injury claims are concerned, the investigatory process is not conducted on behalf of defendants by lawyers but by skilled adjusters who are employed at all stages of the proceeding to make a complete and thorough investigation of the facts relating to the claim of the plaintiff or potential plaintiff.
>
> Such an investigation invariably includes interviewing and taking statements from witnesses. I do not criticize the use of investigators and adjusters in the fact-gathering process. Lawyers are not trained as investigators and, in any event, are not equipped to carry out investigatory tasks. Special skills are required in interviewing and obtaining statements from witnesses at the investigatory stage. That is why the work of interviewing and obtaining

---

168 *Streifel v. First Heritage Savings Credit Union*, [1992] B.C.J. No. 1459 (S.C.); *Tatar v. Kusch*, [1994] B.C.J. No. 1983 (S.C.).

169 *Hall v. Strocel*, above note 165.

170 *Asham v. Forsythe* (1998), 76 A.C.W.S. (3d) 707 (B.C.S.C.). See also *Powar v. British Columbia Ministry of Transport*, above note 163.

statements from witnesses is conducted by skilled and experienced police officers in the criminal law field. The prosecutor takes no part in the fact-gathering process.

It does not make sense, in my opinion, to discourage plaintiff's counsel from using investigators and adjusters in the investigatory process when it is obvious that the use of investigators and adjusters by defendants' counsel have provided counsel with invaluable assistance in defending claims brought against their clients. In a case of any magnitude, it would seem to be folly for the plaintiff's counsel not to employ a skilled adjuster or investigator to seek out and interview all witnesses.

In my view the proper test to be applied is as follows: "Was the work carried out by the investigator reasonably required to enable the party to properly advance or defend his claim?"

In each case the registrar will have to determine, in light of all the circumstances, whether the work done was of an investigatory nature or not. I am of the opinion that the registrar cannot hold that the disbursement was not reasonable merely because on the facts before him, special investigatory skills were not required. It is not possible for counsel or the investigator to know whether the investigation will be difficult or whether the witnesses sought to be interviewed will be unfriendly or evasive.

In summary I hold as follows: (1) The interviewing of witnesses and taking of statements as part of the investigatory process are not exclusively or normally services which can only be performed by a lawyer and such services are not carried out as "preparation for trial" . . . (2) If a report is obtained from an investigator as part of the fact-gathering process and was reasonably necessary to enable a party to advance or defend a claim, the cost of such a report is a reasonable and proper disbursement pursuant to Rule 57(4) of the rules.

Concurring with Justice Anderson's comments, an Alberta judge held this pointless distinction is motivated by some desire to hold costs down and an assumption that disbursements are recoverable on a cost-plus basis while legal fees are not.[171]

10.4.3.1   Special Skills: Unidentified Defendant

Immediately following the decision of *Noble v. Wong*, another court in British Columbia provided reasons for not following the trend. The court held that costs for the private investigator were reasonable because the identity of one of the defendants to the action was not certain. The court acknowledged that while lawyers sometimes conduct investigations, particularly of a routine nature, they cannot be considered to be professional investigators, and it is not in their client's best interest to delve into investigations that are not routine.[172]

10.4.3.2   Special Skills: Lawyer as Witness

A second reason for a lawyer to retain a private investigator to take witness statements is to prevent the awkward situation where the lawyer could find himself or herself at trial as a witness. Such a situation could arise if the defendant qualified or denied his or her earlier statement. The lawyer would then be in the impossible position of being both counsel

---

171 *Kassam v. Dragish*, above note 159.
172 *McCann v. Moss* (1984), 47 C.P.C. 207 (B.C.S.C.).

and witness on the same case. The court noted that this difficulty does not arise with "friendly" witnesses.[173]

10.4.3.3   Special Skills: The Hostile Witness

In a British Columbia case, a plaintiff retained a private investigator to interview ten witnesses. Four of the witnesses were considered to be hostile. The plaintiff claimed all the private investigator's expenses should be included in the determination of costs. The court held only 40 percent were allowable, the 40 percent representing the interviews conducted with the hostile witnesses.[174]

10.4.3.4   Special Skills: Numerous Witnesses and Witness Locates

Awarding costs for witness locates performed by a private investigator has been considered reasonable in Alberta.[175] Awarding costs for finding witnesses to determine a defendant's floor-sweeping practices in a personal injury case has been considered reasonable in British Columbia.[176] Interviewing potential witnesses and members of the military regarding the plaintiff's claim for future loss of income has been considered reasonable in Alberta on the basis that the information was not readily available elsewhere.[177]

Although awarding costs for the taking of statements from "friendly" witnesses has not been considered reasonable, the locating, organizing, and taking statements in cases where there are numerous witnesses has. In an Alberta action, the plaintiffs sued the defendant broadcasting company and a number of its employees for defamation arising from a series of news broadcasts that related to the business conduct of the plaintiffs. The claim was for $15,700,000 and the trial lasted thirty-seven days with seventy defence witnesses. The action was dismissed and the defendants sought indemnification for costs in the amount of $1,400,000 of which $252,751 was for private investigation fees. The defendants presented accounts rendered over the course of six years from private investigators retained to locate, interview, and maintain contact with more than 100 prospective witnesses. The Court noted that the accounts themselves were brief but the supporting documentation was voluminous.

In awarding solicitor-and-client costs against the plaintiffs, the court held that the nature and size of the case dictated that the defendant's plea of justification would require a great number of witnesses. The size of the claim dictated that the defendants be proactive in locating witnesses and that they not merely wait for volunteers to come forward to prove the truth of their allegations. It was proper in this case to assign the task of locating, interviewing, and maintaining contact with witnesses to private investigators. The court held:

---

173 *McCann v. Moss, ibid.*
174 *Allen v. Homan*, [1998] B.C.J. No. 46 (S.C.).
175 *Kassam v. Dragish*, above note 159.
176 *Parsons v. Canada Safeway Ltd.* (1995), Victoria No. 93/2114, (B.C.S.C.) [unreported].
177 *Noel v. Dawson*, [1999] A.J. No. 176 (Q.B).

This was a mammoth undertaking which required specialized expertise and capabilities of a professional investigative service. It is not the type of work which could be performed effectively, conveniently or economically by barristers.

Notwithstanding this characterization of the task of the private investigators, the court held there must be some limit upon the recovery of investigative costs. The court deemed a fair recovery of investigative costs is the amount actually incurred in relation to persons called as witnesses at trial. Recovery of costs for those witnesses not called was deemed to be unwarranted.[178]

Instead of seeking to recover a private investigator's fees for taking witness statements in the costs remedy, such costs have been successfully obtained under the heading of special damages in an Ontario defamation action.[179]

10.4.3.5 Special Skills: Subcontracting

In a British Columbia case, a court held that the "handling" fee to locate a Nova Scotia investigator to take a statement from a "friendly" witness was not a reasonable expense. Pursuant to the ruling in *Noble v. Wong*, the court held that counsel for the defendant could have made arrangements for local counsel to take the witness statement. The court held that no "special skill" was required to conduct this interview and therefore no award for costs should be made.[180]

10.4.3.6 Employees Who Take Witness Statements

Where a litigant used its own employees to take witness statements instead of hiring a private investigator, a British Columbia court held that the portion of an employee's salary spent on this task does not qualify as a disbursement that may be recouped in a cost award.[181]

10.4.4 Surveillance

It has been held that when deciding whether the costs of a private investigator are proper disbursements, the standard to be applied is whether the disbursement is proper in the sense of not being extravagant, negligent, mistaken, or a result of excessive caution or zeal.[182] The test is whether the expense is necessary to fully and properly prepare for trial.[183]

A number of factors have been identified in making this determination. It has been held that the surveillance must focus on a central issue of the litigation.[184] If the surveillance is

---

178 *Sidorsky v. CFCM Communication Ltd.* (1995), 27 Alta. L.R. (3d) 296 (Q.B.), additional reasons to (1994), 23 Alta. L.R. (3d) 116.

179 *L.K. v. E.J.S.* (1997), 43 O.T.C. 206 (Gen. Div.).

180 *Powar v. British Columbia Ministry of Transport*, above note 163.

181 *Canada (Attorney General) v. B.C. Ferry Corp.* (1981), 134 D.L.R. (3d) 29 (B.C.C.A.).

182 *Van Daele v. Van Daele* (1983), 56 B.C.L.R. 178 (S.C.).

183 *Morrissette v. Smith* (1990), 39 C.P.C. (2d) 30 (B.C.S.C.).

184 *Dineley v. Mollison*, [1999] B.C.D. Civ. 770.15.55.00-01 (S.C.); *Tatar v. Kusch*, [1994] B.C.J. No. 1983 (S.C.); *Niznick v. Johnson* (1961), 28 D.L.R. (2d) 541 (Man. Q.B.); *461 King Street West Ltd. v. 418 Wellington Parking Ltd.*, [1994] O.J. No. 1620 (Gen. Div.).

used for a purpose that is not critical to determining liability or quantum of damages, it should not be the subject of a cost award.[185] Further, to be awarded costs, it is not necessary that the surveillance videotape or reports be used during the trial. Rather, the test is whether the videotape evidence or reports were necessary to prepare for trial.[186] It has also been held that the use of local investigators is reasonable, while using investigators from outside a provincial jurisdiction is not.[187]

The time spent on surveillance factors into determining if a cost award is reasonable. In a personal injury case, surveillance conducted over a seven-day period followed by a four-day period has been considered reasonable so as not to give a false impression as may occur from a snapshot in time.[188] However, in a domestic case, a court held that only the first three days of a fourteen-day surveillance were necessary for the court to make the finding it did and that only one investigator, instead of the three used, was necessary to undertake the surveillance.[189]

Mistakes made by private investigators may also be reflected in the cost awards granted by a court. In an Ontario case, a plaintiff was able to prove that the private investigator had videotaped the wrong person. This situation was aggravated by the private investigator when he attempted to minimize the impact of his carelessness during cross-examination. The court held the defendant's cost award was to be reduced because the mistake of the private investigator had resulted in unnecessary litigation.[190]

Improper conduct by private investigators has resulted in costs awards against their clients. In a case from Alberta, a court found that the private investigator had improperly edited the surveillance tape with intent to mislead. In increasing the costs award by 60 percent against the defendants for their private investigator's "reprehensible" conduct, the court held:

> If I had had evidence of a deliberate attempt . . . to deliver misleading surveillance evidence by either party, I would not have hesitated in ordering special costs against the party tendering such evidence. Such conduct would clearly be reprehensible . . . and deserving of rebuke . . .
>
> In my judgment it is important to consider conduct which may preclude early resolution or unduly protract litigation in determining what recovery of costs is just in all of the circumstances.

In an Ontario personal injury case, a court refused to grant the defendant security for costs when it was revealed the alleged malingering plaintiff was photographed in his bed-

---

185 *Stephens v. Aviation Products Co. Ltd.* (1981), 34 N.B.R. (2d) 694 (Q.B.); *Ross v. Kobelka* (1996), B.C.J. No. 1751 (S.C.).

186 *Dineley v. Mollison*, above note 184; *Powar v. British Columbia Ministry of Transport*, above note 163; *1307347 Ontario Inc. v. 123058 Ontario Inc. (c.o.b. Golden Seafood Restaurant)*, [2000] O.J. No. 5032 (S.C.J.).

187 *Dineley v. Mollison*, above note 184.

188 *Powar v. British Columbia Ministry of Transport*, above note 163.

189 *Ellenchuk v. Ellenchuk* (1972), 24 D.L.R. (3d) 235 (Sask. Q.B.).

190 *Parkes v. Kaneff Properties Ltd.*, [1997] O.J. No. 2037 (Gen. Div.).

room. The court stated "solicitors of this court do not hold back bedroom curtains so that the occupants may be surreptitiously photographed."[191]

There may be cost ramifications for not disclosing surveillance videotapes until the point of trial. In an Alberta case, a court held that had the videotapes been disclosed before trial, the plaintiff would have had the information required to determine whether to accept the settlement offer. Accordingly, the plaintiff was entitled to her party-and-party costs up to the date of the offer, and the defendant was entitled to its costs thereafter.[192]

10.4.5 Criminal Record Checks and Criminal Defence Investigations

In a British Columbia case, a court held that a review of *Criminal Code* charges against one of the parties to a claim conducted by a private investigator was a task that could have been performed by a solicitor. Accordingly, a costs award for the private investigator's services was not justified as reasonable.[193]

Where a defendant to a criminal and civil action retained a private investigator to successfully defend allegations of sexual assault where police had conducted their own investigation, it was held that the hiring of a private investigator was a tactical decision and not "muck-raking." The court therefore allowed the expense in its costs award.[194]

10.4.6 Weather and Road Condition Checks

In British Columbia, it has been held that a weather check and road conditions investigation conducted by a private investigator are activities that could have been performed by a solicitor. Accordingly, an award of costs was not justified as reasonable.[195] By contrast, in Alberta such tasks have been held to be a reasonable and proper expense of a private investigator.[196]

10.4.7 Child Custody and Abduction Investigations

In a British Columbia family custody case, a husband submitted evidence obtained from a private investigator that his spouse was not a suitable parent. The court held that the evidence was not of sufficient quantity or quality to bring about a change in custody. The spouse requested solicitor-client costs against her husband for bringing the application. The court, however, held that while the husband may have been hasty in taking action in

191 *Davidson v. Keewatin Town* (1990), 45 C.P.C. (2d) 64 (Ont. H.C.J.). See also C. Kentridge, "Surveillance Must Be Used with Caution" *Law Times* (1–7 June 1998).
192 *Laube v. Juchli*, [1997] A.J. No. 1029 (Q.B.).
193 *Powar v. British Columbia Ministry of Transport*, above note 163.
194 *D.P. v. L.E.*, [1998] B.C.J. No. 2950 (S.C.).
195 *Powar v. British Columbia Ministry of Transport*, above note 163.
196 *Kassam v. Dragish*, above note 159.

reliance upon the private investigator information, it cannot be said that he was motivated by anything other than the best interests of the children.[197]

The courts have not awarded costs for child locates in the reported cases reviewed. In one British Columbia case, a father paid $4,000 to a private investigator to locate his child. Instead of awarding costs, the court reduced the maintenance payments the father owed until the costs of his private investigator were recouped.[198] In another British Columbia case, a mother paid $40,000 over eight years to private investigators to locate her abducted children. On the issue of costs, the court held that the expense was not incurred for the purpose of defending the child-custody application. The court suggested that the expense could properly be recouped through a claim for damages for economic and consequential loss. The court further noted that such an entitlement is recognized in Article 26 of the *Hague Convention on the Civil Aspects of Child Abduction*, which had been adopted into law in British Columbia.[199]

10.4.8 Domestic Investigations

In an Ontario divorce case, a court awarded costs to a spouse not only on the basis that she was successful at trial, but also because of the tactics employed by her husband and his investigator. The court found that retaining of a private investigator to obtain evidence of his wife's infidelity was undertaken in an obvious attempt to prolong the litigation. The court further found that the private investigator's zealousness to destroy evidence possibly in the possession of his client's wife was so ludicrous as to be deserving of cost sanctions.[200]

10.4.9 Injunction Motions against Private Investigators

In an Alberta case, the defendants failed in an application for an interlocutory injunction against the use of a private investigator by the plaintiff. The plaintiff moved for costs for the motion. The defendant argued that costs should be in the cause.[201] However, the court awarded costs for the motion to the plaintiff. The court held that the defendant's concern about the use of private investigators was entirely severable from the issues in the litigation. The court further held that the motion did not advance the litigation and only increased its costs. Notwithstanding these criticisms, the court held that if the defendants became ultimately successful in the litigation, they would be entitled to costs, including costs of the motion for an injunction relating to the private investigator.[202]

---

197 *Smith v. Smith*, [1983] 23 A.C.W.S. (2d) 187 (B.C.S.C.).

198 *Thorne v. Thorne*, [1985] B.C.D. Civ. 1635-02 (S.C.).

199 *Kowey v. Kowey*, [1986] B.C.D. Civ. 1545-03 (S.C.).

200 *Firestone v. Firestone* (1979), 25 O.R. (2d) 314 (H.C.J.). In this case, the investigator burned down the agency of a fellow investigator who he believed had incriminating photos of his client.

201 "In the cause" means that costs should not be determined until the end of the action, and then on the normal basis of determining costs (i.e., to the successful party).

202 *Berube v. Wingrowich*, [1997] A.J. No. 1043 (Q.B.).

10.4.10   Human Rights Cases

Where plaintiffs brought action against the defendants under human rights legislation for failing to rent an apartment to them because they were of East Indian ancestry, they also argued for the cost of a private investigator they had retained to determine if the apartments in question were still for rent after they had been refused accommodation. The Human Rights Council denied this charge. The Council held that a private investigator was not required to find out the availability of the suites; any Caucasian friend could have done that for them.[203]

10.4.11   Unlicensed Investigators

In a Saskatchewan case, a plaintiff appealed the decision of a taxation officer who had rejected his claim for the costs of a private investigator who had secured evidence of the defendant's adultery. The private investigator was not licensed. The taxation officer rejected the costs request because section 13 of Saskatchewan's PISGA provides that no person may bring or maintain an action for the recovery of fees for private investigators unless at the time the action arose the person was licensed as a private investigator. The taxation officer held that to allow the claim for costs would be to allow the private investigator to do indirectly what he could not do directly. The court agreed and held the taxation officer was correct to refuse the fees of the investigator in this case.[204]

---

203 *Taber v. Stanford Construction Ltd.* (1996), 25 C.H.R.R. (B.C.C.H.R.).
204 *Waschuk v. Waschuk* (1969), 4 D.L.R. (3d) 78 (Sask. Q.B.).

PROVINCIAL CONTACT INFORMATION FOR LICENSING

Alberta

Alberta Justice
Ministry of the Solicitor General
Public Security Division
10365 - 97th Street, 10th Floor
Edmonton, Alberta T5J 3W7
Tel: (780) 427-3457
Fax: (780) 427-5916

Mr. Cal Wrathall, Administrator
E-mail: cal.wrathall@just.gov.ab.ca

Ms. Jeannie Kotyk, Deputy Administrator
E-mail: Kotykj@just.gov.ab.ca

British Columbia

Ministry of the Attorney General
Security Programs Division

P.O. Box 9217, W400
4000 Seymour Place
Victoria, British Columbia V8W 9J1
Fax: (250) 387-4454

Mr. Tony Heemskerk, Registrar
E-mail: Tony.Heemskerk@ag.gov.bc.ca

Mr. Dean Benson, Deputy Registrar
E-mail: Dean.Benson@ag.gov.bc.ca

Ms. Cathy Drever, Information Clerk
Tel: (250) 387-6987
E-mail: Cathy.Drever@ag.gov.bc.ca

Manitoba

Criminal Justice Division
Law Enforcement Services
530 - 405 Broadway, Woodsworth Building
Winnipeg, Manitoba R3C 3L6

Tel: (204) 945-2825
Fax: (204) 945-2217

Ms. Charlene Muloin, Registrar
Tel: (204) 945-2934
E-mail: Cmuloin@jus.gov.mb.ca

New Brunswick

New Brunshwick Department of Public Safety
Private Investigators and Security Services Licensing Commission
Licensing and Registration
P.O. Box 6000
Fredericton, New Brunswick E3B 5H1

Tel: (506) 453-2429
Fax: (506) 453-3044

Ms. Rita Richard-Clark, Licensing Officer
Email: Rita.Richard-Clark@gnb.ca

Newfoundland

Department of Government Services and
Lands Trade Practices Division - PISGA
P.O. Box 8700
St. John's, Newfoundland A1B 4J6

Tel: (709) 729-2732
Fax: (709) 729-3205

Mr. Craig Whalen, Administrator
Tel: (709) 729-2725
E-mail: Cwhalen@mail.gov.nf.ca

Ms. Carole Laing, Deputy Administrator
Tel: (709) 729-5879
E-mail: clainge@mail.gov.nf.ca

Nova Scotia

Department of Justice
Police and Public Safety Services
5151 Terminal Road, Ground Floor
P.O. Box 7
Halifax, Nova Scotia B3J 2L6

Tel: (902) 424-2124
Fax: (902) 424-4308

Ms. Karen Forsyth, Coordinator, Private Security Industry Programs
E-mail: forsytke@gov.ns.ca

Ontario

Ministry of the Solicitor General and Correctional Services
Private Investigators and Security Guards Section
25 Grosvenor Street, 9th Floor
Toronto, Ontario M7A 2H3

Tel: (416) 326-0050
Fax: (416) 326-0034

D/S Gerry Gibson, Deputy Registrar
Tel: (416) 362-0032
E-mail: gerry.gibson@jus.gov.on.ca

Prince Edward Island

Department of Community Affairs and Attorney General
Consumer Services
161 Maypoint Road, Box 2000
Charlottetown, Prince Edward Island C1A 7N8

Tel: (902) 368-5536
Fax: (902) 368-5198

Mr. Eric Goodwin, Manager
E-mail: Ewgoodwin@gov.pe.ca

Quebec

For Private Investigation Agency Licences:

Direction des Affaires Policières
2525 Blvd. Laurier
Sainte-Foy, Quebec G1V 2L2

Tel: (418) 646-6617

General e-mail: dappc@secpub.gouv.qc.ca

Ms. Pierrette Legere, Registrar
E-mail: pierrette.legere@msp.gouv.qc.ca

Ms. Denise Bilodeau
E-mail: denise.bilodeau@msp.gouv.qc.ca

For Private Investigation Agent Licences:

Grand Quartier General
C.P. 1400, Succersale "C"
Montreal, Quebec H2L 4K7

Tel: (514) 598-4584
Fax: (514) 598-4230

Captain Guy Asselin

Saskatchewan

Department of Justice
Private Investigators and Security Guards Program
1874 Scarth Street, 7th Floor
Regina, Saskatchewan S4P 3V7

Tel: (306) 787-5496
Fax: (306) 787-8084

Mr. Brian Miller, Registrar
Tel: (306) 787-8084

Yukon Territory

Yukon Justice
Box 2703
Whitehorse, Yukon Y1A 2C6
Tel: (867) 667-5111
Fax: (867) 667-3609

Ms. Carol Cameron, Licensing Officer
E-mail: Carol.cameron@gov.yk.ca

PRIVATE INVESTIGATOR ASSOCIATIONS CONTACT INFORMATION

Alberta

Alberta Association of Private Investigators
Box 56006
115 - 1935 32nd Avenue N.E.
Calgary, Alberta T2E 7C8

Tel: (403) 818-8440
Web site: http://www.alberta-investigators.org

Mr. Don Wilkinson, President
E-mail: donwilkinson@home.com

British Columbia

The Private Investigators Association of British Columbia
P.O. Box 34503, Station "D"
Vancouver, British Columbia V6J 4W4

Tel: (604) 878-4388
Web site: http://www.piabc.com
E-mail: Info@piabc.com

Mr. Don Defehr, President

Newfoundland

Newfoundland Security Guards and Private Investigators Agencies Association Ltd.
P.O. Box 23105
St. John's, Newfoundland A1B 4J9

Tel: (709) 722-6408

Ms. Debbie Reddy, Secretary/Treasurer

Ontario

Council of Private Investigators - Ontario
814 Berkshire Drive
London, Ontario N6J 3W2

Tel: (519) 641-1521
Web site: http://www.cpi-ontario.com
E-mail: director@cpi-ontario.com

Mr. Charlie Robb, Administrative Manager

Quebec

Association of Security and Investigation Agencies of Quebec
2100 rue de l'Eglise
Montreal, Quebec H4E 1H4

Tel: (514) 761-7121

Mr. Daniel Simon (Eastern Quebec)
Tel: (418) 681-0609

Ms. Jeanette Bardeau (Western Quebec)
Tel: (514) 990-1722

Mr. Robert Champagne (Western Quebec)
Tel: (514) 937-7487

CODES OF ETHICS AND MISSION STATEMENTS OF PRIVATE INVESTIGATOR ASSOCIATIONS IN ALBERTA, BRITISH COLUMBIA, AND ONTARIO

ALBERTA

Mission Statement

The Alberta Association of Private Investigators will encourage and foster the highest ethical standards to promote and inspire public confidence in the profession.

Code of Ethics

The Alberta Association of Private Investigators adopts the following Code of Ethics and mandates its acceptance and observance by its members:

- All work will be performed with due diligence in a responsible and professional manner.
- Each member will maintain confidentiality of information.
- Each member will work in accordance with the law.
- Each member will ensure that all persons paid to assist in investigations are advised of this Code of Ethics and that they are expected to adhere to it.
- Each member will strive to determine that a client has a legitimate purpose to instruct an investigation.

Standards of Practice

No part of this document is intended, nor shall it be inferred, to supersede any rules, regulations, laws or by-laws of the *Private Investigators and Security Guards Act* of Alberta.

STANDARD I – WORK WITHIN THE LAW

Members of the Alberta Association of Private Investigators will:

(1.1) Maintain appropriate licence requirements.

(1.2) Conduct investigations in accordance with the law.

(1.3) Comply with all lawful orders of the courts and to testify to matters truthfully, accurately, and without bias or prejudice.

(1.4) Refrain from insinuating or representing oneself as a member of Law Enforcement.

(1.5) Consider all legal issues raised during the course of an investigation and review these with the client.

STANDARD II – MAINTAIN CONFIDENTIALITY

Members of the Alberta Association of Private Investigators will:

(2.1) Pledge to maintain client confidentiality of the information gathered during the course of an investigation subject to the agreement with the client and/or as required by law.

(2.2) Treat with discretion and respect those whom we are called upon to investigate. Ensure that contact with anyone regarding the investigated individual is discreet, respectful, non-threatening and non-judgemental.

STANDARD III – MAINTAIN PROFESSIONAL STANDARDS

Members of the Alberta Association of Private Investigators will:

(3.1) Submit objective, unbiased and complete reports, including all relevant information.

(3.2) Refrain from creating evidence by having a person engage in any activity or action they would normally not do, thus incriminating themselves falsely.

(3.3) Ensure the accuracy of all photographs, video or audio evidence obtained during the course of the investigation.

(3.4) Ensure that anyone under the age of majority is interviewed in the presence of and/or with the permission of their legal guardian.

(3.5) Make reports of progress to the client by the method and with the regularity previously agreed upon.

(3.6) Refrain from accepting referrals where a potential conflict of interest exists.

(3.7) No member will at any time make false or misleading claims to professional qualifications not possessed.

(3.8) [Will not] engage in marketing that is factually inaccurate and [will] avoid exaggerated claims as to costs or results.

(3.9) Members will ensure that, prior to accepting an engagement, all objectives of the client are understood and that the client is fully aware of anticipated costs and completion of assignment.

(3.10) Will employ only licensed investigators in all aspects of investigative work except in an administrative capacity.

(3.13) Co-operate with law enforcement and governmental agencies without breaching client confidentiality.

STANDARD IV – PROFESSIONAL RESPECT

Members of the Alberta Association of Private Investigators will:

(4.1) Not deny equal professional services or employment to any person for reasons of multicultural diversity and physical challenges. Members shall not be party to any plan or agreement to discriminate against a person or persons on basis of the above.

(4.2) Be obligated to report breaches of legal, ethical or questionable conduct on the part of any member where it is believed such conduct will bring discredit to the profession and/or be detrimental to its members.

(4.3) Comply with the instructions from the referring firm:
(a) refrain from contacting the referring firm's client without permission;
(b) pay promptly for all work conducted by other investigative firms;
(c) any inference regarding competitors must be rendered with strict professional integrity and courtesy.

(4.4) Will not use any information obtained during the course of an investigation for personal gain or personal advantage.

STANDARD V – PROFESSIONAL DEVELOPMENT

Members of the Alberta Association of Private Investigators will:

(5.1) Maintain competency in all individual fields of expertise.

(5.2) Promote any educational programs intended to raise the standards, efficiency and effectiveness of the private investigation industry.

STANDARD VI – RESPONSIBILITIES TO THE PROFESSION

Members of the Alberta Association of Private Investigators will:

(6.1) Comply with the Code of Ethics and Standards of Practice of the Association as amended from time to time and with any order or resolution of the Board of Directors or its committees under the Bylaws of the Alberta Association of Private Investigators.

(6.2) Not make false or malicious statements about another Association member.

(6.3) Be subject to disciplinary action for any offence which constitutes a breach of professional conduct.

(6.4) Ensure all dues will be paid in full. Failure to renew membership may result in the removal of the member from the Association.

(6.5) Have membership in the Association denied or revoked if obtained by means of fraud and/or other irregularity. A member shall notify the Association immediately regarding a person who has obtained membership by means of fraud or other irregularity.

(6.6) Comply with all requests of the Board of Directors of the Alberta Association of Private Investigators to produce within a reasonable time frame, any requested information in the member's possession, custody or control, in matters related to potential breaches of the Association By-laws, Code of Ethics, and Standards of Practice notwithstanding the rules governing confidentiality or the Freedom of Information and Protection of Privacy Act.

(6.7) Not make public statements or comments, which may be interpreted as representing the Alberta Association of Private Investigators or its views, except when authorized by the Board of Directors to act as an official spokesperson for the Association.

(6.8) Maintain adequate liability insurance.

BRITISH COLUMBIA

Code of Ethics

Preamble

The Private Investigators' Association of British Columbia has adopted a Code of Ethics and Professional Conduct developed by the Association. The PIABC Code of Ethics provides rules and principles of professional conduct and ethics by which members will conduct themselves in discharging their professional duties and responsibilities. Any member who contravenes any of these rules and/or principles shall be accountable to the Ethics Committee and the Board of Directors of the Association. PIABC members shall be mindful of their responsibilities to the Private Investigation Profession and shall carry on their work with fidelity to clients or employers, with fairness to employees and with loyalty to the Association, in a manner worthy of a Professional Investigator.

Private Investigators have an important role to play in society. In performance of that role the investigator's actions have an effect on the welfare of other people. Because of their social responsibilities, members of a profession are obligated to act in the interest of these other parties who have a stake in the nature and quality of professional activities. These stakeholders include employers, clients, various identifiable third parties, and the public at large. Therefore, the professional organization and its members have a stake in the performance of individual members. The Code of Ethics applies to the behaviour of members of the Association when they either perform the role of a private investigator or represent themselves as members of the Association.

RULES OF PROFESSIONAL CONDUCT

A. Responsibility to Society

1. Discredit

Members shall not knowingly misrepresent themselves, their duties, or credentials. Members shall conduct their businesses with honesty, integrity, and uphold the highest moral principles and avoid conduct detrimental to the profession. Members shall guard their professional reputations and that of their professional associates. Members shall at all times uphold the Constitution, By-laws, and the Code of Ethics of the Private Investigators' Association of British Columbia.

2. Unlawful Activity

Members shall not engage in any unlawful or unethical practice. The member shall refuse to participate in practices which are inconsistent with the standards established by regulatory bodies regarding the delivery of services to clients. Members in all cases shall counsel against any illegal or unethical course of action.

3. Criticism of a Member

Members directing any discussion and comments or criticism toward a fellow member/investigator/security professional or organization shall do so in a positive and constructive manner. When asked to comment on current or past matters that are or have been managed by another investigative member or firm, the member, if he/she believes that the situation was handled wrongly or badly, shall not make any comments of a questionable or derogatory nature toward the handling member before speaking with that member and giving that member an opportunity to respond.

4. Reporting Acts Detrimental to the Profession

A member shall report to the Association any situation of which the member has sufficient personal knowledge and which the member thinks may be detrimental to the profession.

5. Compatible Activities

A member may engage in any profession, trade, industry, office or duty except where these undertakings are detrimental to the public good or to the standards of the profession.

B. Trust and Duties

1. Confidentiality

Members shall not disclose or use any confidential information concerning the affairs of any client, former client, employer, or former employer. Members shall treat as confidential and safeguard privileged communication and information that is obtained in the course of practice. Professional files, reports and records shall be maintained under conditions of security, and provision shall be made for their return to the client or their destruction when appropriate. A member is not forbidden to disclose the employers'/clients' affairs where properly acting in the course of the duties incumbent on a member, or where disclosure is compelled by a process of law.

2. Conflict of Interest

A member shall, when providing services on behalf of a client or employer, be free of any influence, interest or relationship in respect of the client's affairs which impairs the members' professional judgement or objectivity, or which, in the view of a reasonable observer, may have that effect.

3. Resolution of Conflict of Interest

Upon becoming aware that a conflict of interest exists a member shall either eliminate the circumstances that cause the member to be in contravention or resign from the engagement.

4. Information Used for Personal Advantage

A member shall not, without an employer's or client's consent, use confidential information relating to the business of the member's employer or client to directly or indirectly obtain a personal advantage.

C. Due Care and Professional Judgment

1. Competence

The member shall render only those services that the member is competent and qualified to perform. A member shall not promise or offer services or results he/she cannot deliver or has reason to believe he/she cannot provide.

2. Professional Development

The member should maintain technical competency at such a level that the recipient receives the highest quality of service. It is further the member's duty to avail themselves of opportunities to learn more about their profession.

3. Terms of Engagement

Members, where required, shall carry professional liability insurance for their own protection and the protection of affected third parties. Members shall not undertake to counsel on legal issues.

D. Deceptive Information

1. Known Omission

Members shall make all his/her reporting based upon truth, fact and observation to the best of his/her abilities and belief.

2. Altered Information or Evidence

Members shall not purposely alter video or any other evidence to exaggerate or misrepresent the information obtained during the course of their investigation.

E. Professional Practice

1. Advertising

A member shall not seek to obtain clients by advertising, or other form of solicitation that is false or deceptive, includes the use of harassing conduct, creates an unjustified expectation of favourable results or contains self-laudatory statements that are not verifiable.

2. Contracting to Other Members

All services shall be provided in a timely fashion and shall respond to the purpose of the referral. All business members accepting assignments from other members are forbidden to contact the client directly, unless specifically instructed to do so. Members are responsible for all proper fees and expenses incurred by another agency for work undertaken under his/her instructions. Members will undertake to pay promptly for services rendered by another member

F. Responsibilities to the Profession

1. Compliance

A member shall comply with the by-laws and the Code of Ethics and Professional Conduct of the Association as amended from time to time, and with any order or resolution of the Board or its committees under the by-laws.

2. Disciplinary Action

A member shall be subject to disciplinary action for any offence which constitutes a breach of professional conduct.

3. Membership Obtained Fraudulently

A member shall not obtain admission to membership by means of fraud or other irregularity. A member shall notify the Association immediately regarding a person who has obtained membership by means of fraud or other irregularity.

4. Legal Action against a Member

When possible a member shall, before entering into a legal action against another member which might discredit the profession, give the Association as much notice as is possible of such an intention, outlining the basis of the proposed action.

5. Assistance of the Board

Members shall, when required, comply with the request of the Board, or its committees in the exercise of their duties in matters of the by-laws or the Code of Ethics and Rules of Professional Conduct, and when required produce any documents in the member's possession, custody, or control, subject to rules governing confidential information described in Section B (1).

6. Public Statements

Members shall not make public statements or comments which may be interpreted as representing the Association or its views except when authorized to act as an "official spokesperson" for the Association.

ONTARIO

Code of Ethics

1.0 Interpretation and Definition

1.1   No part of this document is intended, nor shall it be inferred, to supersede any rules, regulations, laws or by-laws of the *Private Investigators and Security Guards Act* of Ontario.

1.2   For the purposes of this document, a member is either an individual investigator or an investigative agency providing services in the Province of Ontario.

1.3   The Council is the Council of Private Investigators — Ontario (CPIO).

2.0 Objectives of the Code of Ethics

2.1   The Code of Ethics is directed at three primary intentions of the Council:

2.1.1   Ensuring and safeguarding the quality of investigative services provided by members of the CPIO to its clients;

2.1.2   Achieving an orderly and courteous conduct among members of the CPIO;

2.1.3   Developing and maintaining a positive attitude toward the investigative profession by:

2.1.3.1   Non-members of the Council;

2.1.3.2   Law Enforcement and other regulatory officials;

2.1.3.3   Clients and other members of the public.

3.0 General Standards of Conduct

3.1   Reputation of the profession:

3.1.1   Each member will regard him/herself as a member of an important and respectable profession;

3.1.2   Each member will ensure that his/her reputation, that of each council member, and that of the investigative profession as a whole is maintained at all times;

3.1.3   No member shall engage in any investigative activity for which he/she is not reasonably competent or qualified.

3.2   Compliance with the Code:

3.2.1   Each member shall adhere to, and respect, this Code of Ethics.

3.3   Integrity and Due Care:

3.3.1   Each member will conduct due diligence to ensure that the credentials of a client(s) are verified and that they have a lawful and moral purpose to instruct an investigation;

3.3.2   Each member will ensure that all employees and other persons paid to assist in investigations adhere to, and respect, this Code of Ethics and accept responsibility therefor.

3.4   Confidentiality of Information:

3.4.1   Each member will respect the privacy of clients and their lawful confidence;

3.4.2   Each member will ensure adequate security and safeguarding against inadvertent or negligent disclosure of private information.

3.5   Fees or Remuneration:

3.5.1   No member shall take personal or financial advantage of information gained by virtue of either a professional client relationship or a relationship with a member.

3.6   Membership Dues:

3.6.1   All dues will be paid in full when due. Failure to renew membership may result in the removal of the member from the Association.

3.7   Advertising:

3.7.1   No member will at any time make false or misleading claims to professional qualifications not possessed.

4.0 Relations with Fellow Members

4.1   Courtesy and Consideration:

4.1.1   Each member will work together with all members of our Association towards the achievement of the highest professional objectives of the Council and to observe the teachings of truth, accuracy and prudence;

4.1.2   Where convenient, practical, and in the interest of the client, members are encouraged to solicit the services of another member;

4.1.3   A member who accepts an engagement, whether by referral of an associate member or otherwise, from the client of a member who has a continuing relationship with that client, shall ensure that such relationship is not jeopardized;

4.1.4   No member shall make false or malicious statements about another council member.

5.0 Organization and Conduct of a Professional Practice

5.1   Disclosure of Conflicts:

5.1.1   Members shall, at the earliest convenience, disclose to a client any influence, interest or relationship, pertaining to an investigative engagement, which would be seen by an average observer to impair the member's professional judgement or objectivity.

5.2 Terms of Engagement:

    5.2.1 Members shall ensure that, prior to accepting an engagement, all objectives of the client are fully understood and that the client is fully aware of anticipated costs and completion of assignment.

5.3 Unconsidered Opinions:

    5.3.1 No member shall provide an opinion for which he/she is not fully qualified.

5.4 Reports:

    5.4.1 All reports to clients shall be objective and unbiased and should not provide unsolicited opinions which are not supported by fact;

    5.4.2 Each member shall be forthcoming, truthful, and professional in disclosing investigative findings.

6.0 Disciplinary Procedure

6.1 Violation of By-Laws, Code of Ethics or Practice Standards:

    6.1.1 Upon review by the Ethics Committee and/or the Disciplinary Committee, sanctions may be issued as follows:

        6.1.1.1 Written warning;

        6.1.1.2 Probation of membership to the Association;

        6.1.1.3 Expulsion of membership to the Association.

    6.1.2 The Ethics Committee reserves the right to notify civil authorities and/or provincial regulators.

7.0 Jurisdiction and Membership

7.1 Jurisdiction of Ethics Committee:

    7.1.1 The role of the Ethics Committee will be to:

        (a) act as a mediator in minor disputes between members, either corporate or indvidual, when mutually acceptable,

        (b) investigate ethical violations and accusations, and

        (c) resolve matters or recommend action by the Disciplinary Committee.

    7.1.2 Membership to the Ethics Committee will be rotated at regular intervals with every member being given an equal opportunity to serve.

ONTARIO

Code of Privacy

I. Declaration

A.   Council of Private Investigators - Ontario hereby declares that every Member of the Council respects individual privacy and recognizes an obligation to use best efforts to protect individual privacy to the greatest extent possible in the course of carrying out licensed activities under the *Private Investigators and Security Guards Act* (the Act). Every Member conducting an investigation shall use the means least intrusive to individual privacy under the circumstances of a particular case.

II. Collection of Information

A.   No Member shall collect information on behalf of a client unless the collection is:

1.   expressly authorized by law, including the Act,

2.   used for the purpose of law enforcement,

3.   necessary to the performance of a lawfully authorized activity, including an authorized activity under the Act, or

4.   to preserve, protect, or defend the legal rights of a client under common law, federal or provincial statutes.

B.   Members shall obtain personal information only to the extent relevant to the purposes for which that information is to be used, and only to the extent necessary for those purposes.

III. Use of Information

A.   No member shall use personal information in his/her custody or control except:

1.   for the purpose for which it was obtained or a consistent purpose;

2.   for the purpose of law enforcement; or

3.   to perform a lawfully authorized activity.

IV. Disclosure of Information

A.   No member shall disclose personal information in his or her custody or control except:

1.   to the client, or pursuant to the direction of the client that retained the investigator or the Council of Private Investigators - Ontario company that collected the information;

2.   to an officer or employee of the Council of Private Investigators - Ontario company who needs the personal information in the performance of his/her duties; or

3.   as required by law.

V. Client Agreement

A.   When accepting an assignment from a client, Members shall advise the client of the terms of the Privacy Code and of the Members responsibility to conduct all inquiries in accordance with the Code.

VI. Security of Personal Information

A.   Personal Information shall be protected by reasonable security safeguards against such risk as loss, unauthorized access, destruction, use, modification or disclosure of data.

REPORT ON TRAINING AND STANDARDS FOR PRIVATE INVESTIGATORS

REPORT OF THE BEST PRACTICES AND TRAINING SUB-COMMITTEE TO THE PRIVATE SECURITY INDUSTRY ADVISORY COMMITTEE

by William Urquhart

(22 April 1999)

OBJECTIVE

The objective of this committee is to evaluate existing professional practices and training of Private Investigators in Ontario, and to provide recommendations to assist in establishing an authoritative standard for investigative training, leading to an overall enhancement of standards of practice.

FOCUS

Private investigators in Ontario who fall under the licensing provisions of the province's *Private Investigators and Security Guards Act* (the Act), of which there are believed to be currently approximately 3,400, plus those new applicants to the industry. (How those provisions are to be interpreted has been the subject of study previously by this committee.)

REFERENCE SOURCES

A.   The Legislation governing Private Investigators in all provinces and territories of Canada, and the licensing practices in those jurisdictions

B.   An overview of similar legislation in the U.S.A.

C.   Ontario Commission of Inquiry into the Confidentiality of Health Information, *Report of the Commission of Inquiry into the Confidentiality of Health Information* Commissioner Horace Krever (Toronto: The Commission, 1980)

D.   Council of Private Investigators — Ontario, Survey, November 1996, of licensed agencies in the Province of Ontario

E.   Consultations with Greg Sones of Policing Services in the course of his 1996 study of the Private Investigation Industry as a preliminary to formation of PSIAC

F.   Consultations, with Rob Gerden, Private Investigation Industry Study directed by former Registrar Len Griffiths

G.   Moylen, J. and R. Pitre, (1996), *The Canadian Security Sector: Training and Education*

H.   Gerden, R.J., Private Security, (1998), *Private Security: A Canadian Perspective*

I.   Groot, N., *Legal Liability of the Canadian Private Investigator*

J.   Canada Life Assurance Company, survey re: Vendor Selection Process

K.   Consultations with Private Investigation Agency operators in all provinces of Canada except New Brunswick and P.E.I.

L.   Anecdotal evidence of sub-committee members

M.   Information as supplied by the Registrar's office, and statistical information in the possession of the Registrar's office respecting complaints received.

N.   Ontario Ministry of Education and Training

OBSERVATIONS

1. The legislation governing private investigators and procedures for licensing individual investigators across the country are essentially identical, with the regulators in most jurisdictions having no authority to stipulate training. With respect to qualification to be a licensed private investigator, the response was fairly uniform, "there are no training or experience requirements to become a private investigator . . ." There are three notable exceptions.

British Columbia

As a co-operative effort of the licensing body in that province (Ministry of the Attorney General), the Private Investigators Association of British Columbia, the Justice Institute (the equivalent of the Ontario Police College) and that province's Ministry of Skills and Labour, there is being developed a basic training program. It is expected to become a prerequisite for licensing of private investigators. Investigators in and out of PIABC expect membership in PIABC will become a condition of licensing. PIABC is also participating in the development of the program for administration through Douglas College in that province.

Notable are:

- A branch of the licensing body conducted the surveys of the industry, the results of which provided part of the guidance for the course undertaken; and

- The Ministry of Skills and Labour provided funding under a partnership arrangement with PIABC, on the understanding this was an industry driven initiative.

Another factor unique to this province's situation is the dominance of the Insurance Corporation of British Columbia as a user of private investigative services. That entity has subjected its service providers to a level of scrutiny beyond the average of what is likely to be encountered in any other jurisdiction. The fact of it being a government organization may also have prompted the level of interest brought by the other relevant branches of government.

Newfoundland

In addition to the requirements common to most other jurisdictions, one must in this province:

- [To gain an agency licence] become a member of the Newfoundland Security Guards and Private Investigators Agencies Association Limited; and

- If acting as [a private investigator], have successfully completed or be willing to enroll in a compulsory course offered in correspondence format through College of the North Atlantic. There is a provision for assessment of other security training programs offered through accredited training institutions other than College of the North Atlantic and exemptions for persons with certain background.

The represented training in the course referred covers powers of arrest, ethics, communication skills, relevant legislation, the court system, etc. with possibly more emphasis on security guard training than for a private investigator.

Ontario

Section 7 of the Act states:

(1) The Registrar, or anyone authorized by him, may make such inquiry and investigation as he considers sufficient regarding the character, financial position and competence of an applicant or licensee and may require an applicant to try such examinations to determine competence as the Registrar considers necessary.

(2) The Registrar may require further information or material to be submitted by an applicant or a licensee and may require verification by affidavit or otherwise of any information or material then or previously submitted.

2. Investigators range in experience and training from none on both counts to many years as investigators in the public and private sectors with the most in-depth of training for investigators, including what is relevant for private investigators. The type of work they do varies as widely too. The only thing all have in common is that they all went through the same procedure to be licensed. At one end of the scale, it was obvious the applicant knew how to investigate. At the other, hopefully there was an undertaking by the agency to teach the applicant, a presupposition that because an agency licence has been granted, someone in the agency is competent as a private investigator and able to teach those skills.

3. In the survey by the Council of Private Investigators of agency operators, one question was: "What should be the major concern of private investigators in this province?" While the answers varied, more than 63% of those responding had major concern for ethical standards and training in the industry.

4. In the Canada Life Survey, of the 20 agencies graded as superior in Ontario through an initial screening process, only two were found in follow-up, on-site inspections and interviews to have any formal orientation and training for their new staff members and only one had a formal method of ongoing training.

5. There are in Ontario, approximately 13 registered private vocational schools that appear by their names to be offering training in private investigation. There are additionally several training organizations offering programs of potential relevance to private investigation. Most if not all of the province's 25 Community Colleges offer a Law and Security Administration Program or similar which include courses represented as being relevant to a career in private investigation. Some offer training directed specifically to investigation.

6. Sheridan College offers a two-year diploma program, Investigations, Public and Private which has this term a first-year enrollment of over 40. There are additionally a variety of other organizations offering training relevant to private investigation, including seminars of a few days or less, the offerings of correspondence schools and longer term programs such as offered by the Association of Certified Fraud Examiners leading to professional designations.

7. Some of the above is taken by those already engaged in careers in investigation, whether for police, another public sector or in a private capacity where licensing is not required. Individuals engaged in those careers also receive a variety of training designed specifically for their occupation. Portions, but not all of that training is relevant to a career in private investigation as well.

8. Anecdotal information from Agency employers suggests both public and private educational institutions lack effective screening for individuals suitable to the occupation as private investigators. In the case of the public institution, they may not feel able to restrict admission to a program if the individual has met the academic criteria. Like private institutions, although less direct, they are also under an economic pressure to accept applicants.

9. In their 1996 survey for the Industrial Adjustment Committee on the Security Sector, Moylan and Pitre found that the many courses of study available to students in the security field do not provide the student "with a fair assessment of their worth in the market place nor does it give the employers a standard assessment by which to judge quality of programs." They further observed, among other things, that:

   ◆ Professional relationships between the security industry and the providers of security training and education are weak at best; and

   ◆ Training and education programs are operating in a void, with no relationship between institution and industry.

10. There is a great diversity in the industry for the types of services offered and a lack of any professional body to which members of the industry uniformly subscribe. Among those organizations dealing with varied aspects of investigation are:

   • The International Association of Special Investigation Units
   • The Canadian Association of Special Investigation Units
   • The Canadian Association of Fire Investigators
   • The Association of Certified Fraud Examiners
   • The Council of Private Investigators — Ontario
   • The International Association of Arson Investigators
   • The International Association of Auto Theft Investigators
   • The American Society for Industrial Security
   • The Association of Forensic Investigators
   • The Canadian Society for Industrial Security
   • The Council of International Investigators

Not all of these permit full membership to private investigators; some are for profit and some have qualification requirements beyond what can be met by the majority of Ontario private investigators. The only organization seeking to represent the interests of private investigators in Ontario specifically is the Council of Private Investigators — Ontario, an Ontario non-profit corporation. Membership is available to anyone holding a valid Ontario PI licence.

11. Rates for a few in private investigation can be as high as $300.00 per hour but in 1997, the WPSIB tendered for surveillance work and found 80 firms meeting their criteria, willing to provide services for between $45.00 and $55.00 per hour, with no allowance for travel time, or appearance at hearings. More recently, one of the largest consumers of investigative services in the automobile insurance industry advised it would pay the equivalent of $55.00 per hour for investigative services, and found itself able to be selective in the agencies it chose, while in Vancouver, the Insurance Corporation of British Columbia will pay $75.00 per investigator hour for surveillance services. If in-store security, or strike work, the hourly rate charged by an agency may be less than $25.00 per hour.

12. Beyond what may come to the surface through a complaint, or in the screening at licence renewal time, there is no outside audit of the competency of the individual licensee. Provided his or her employment remains profitable to the agency, it is conceivable they could have a career of many years without an alteration in their level of competency.

13. Final judgement before employment as to one's suitability for licensing, and to work as a private investigator rests with individuals whose background is primarily policing. While this has application in a wide variety of circumstances, it is also unresponsive to a wide variety of work done in private investigation and the environment in which such work is carried out. Examples include civil liability for an unfortunate result, conflict of

interest situations, intellectual property, business intelligence, access to information sources, etc.

14. There is a perception by some that police and policing services are mistrustful of private investigators and this may work against a co-operative effort for the benefit of the industry, and in turn the public.

COMMENT

While the statistical information in the possession of the registrar's office concerning complaints is not yet available, it is understood to be in large about unlicensed investigators and so has little bearing on the practices and training of licensed private investigators. Further, anecdotal evidence would indicate a significant portion of the public, including regular users of private investigation services are not aware of licensing requirements for private investigators nor of to whom they may complain in the event of a complaint about an investigator.

It may be said by some that the marketplace has a way of culling those of substandard abilities; it apparently does, if the impression of a significant turnover in licensees is true. But it is also suspected that only the most sophisticated of consumers, such as the legal profession, large companies and institutions, all of whom are frequent users of private investigation services, are reasonably equipped to judge the quality of the product they receive. Anecdotal information suggests those least able to afford the services of a private investigator are also least able to judge the quality of the work received. They may gravitate toward a less qualified, poorly equipped, perhaps unlicensed agency, sometimes under a mistaken impression of what a private investigator can do in their particular circumstance.

Private Investigators and Agencies providing Private Investigators in this province are regulated to some degree under the Act, its Regulations and by General Guidelines developed by the Registrar's office. Those documents provide some limited guidance as to what one will and will not do in the performance of their work but they provide almost no prescriptions as to how a private investigator will do his or her job. This is quite unlike any other profession that places one in a position of trust.

♦ Lawyers undergo extensive uniform training and testing before being allowed to practise and continue to be governed by such publications as the Rules of Civil Procedure, dictating how one aspect of their work will be done, including the forms that will be used to do it;

♦ Chartered Accountants also are subject to an apprenticeship and uniform testing and have the C.I.C.A. Handbook for guidance.

♦ Real Estate Agents must complete a uniform course of study before being allowed to take an exam for licensing.

♦ Insurance Brokers follow a program of similar intent to Real Estate agents

♦ Independent Insurance Adjusters, although not necessarily subject to a uniform prerequisite study program, undergo testing for knowledge and competency to be licensed.

In all of the above examples, there are varying degrees of government regulation and involvement in the testing for competency. There is also in every case mandatory requirement for membership in a professional body, which includes in its mandate continuing professional development and defines codes of practice, if one is to engage in that profession.

The ease of licensing is believed to perpetuate an economic climate that works against professional development.

It is a generally accepted rule of thumb that a professional office, such as for accountants and lawyers, must be able to charge three times what it pays its professional staff. That allows coverage for wages, benefits and other elements of overhead and a structured training program and a reasonable return on investment, including for entrepreneurial risk. In a properly equipped investigation agency, the investment required and the fixed costs are at least as much as in an accounting or law firm. However, as evidence already referenced indicates, many agencies are anxious to receive work for which they would be paid less than $60.00 per hour.

Another rule of thumb in a professional office is that one must devote significantly more than 40 hours to their work week in order to produce more than 30 hours of billable time, while allowing for vacations, etc. The efficiency rate in some lines of investigative work (e.g., surveillance, store security and strikes) can be easily greater, but work availability and hourly rates can also be less.

Natural consequences of these economic conditions include:

a) Many part-time investigators;

b) Many looking upon investigative work as a supplement only, such as for a pension, or that will be taken from time to time in an agency that is primarily for guards;

c) When work is available, many will take it without regard to overtime and other mandatory benefit considerations;

d) Schemes are entered into that endeavour to avoid the requirements that exist in an employee/employer relationship;

e) There is no budget within many agencies for professional development;

f) The individual investigator is not making enough to be able to afford professional development, or even take the time from work to attend for such, and sees no future worth in such an investment anyway; or

g) Having acquired investigative experience in another sector, some may view themselves above any need for further learning.

h) With competition in the industry driving down hourly rates, junior staff is relied upon to conduct the bulk of the work and "trial and error" becomes the primary form of training. Those who are trained by co-workers often receive their co-workers' "bad habits" in addition to whatever other unsubstantiated and anecdotal information is currently in practice.

At the other end of the scale are prominent firms able to attract the most skilled of investigators, often engaged in very complicated investigations. With charge-out rates from $80.00 per hour for a researcher, to more than $300.00 per hour for a senior person, they and their staff can afford and probably recognize the need for continuing professional development.

These same firms will routinely represent that they are able to provide services across the country, and they do accomplish that by subcontracting to other agencies glad to receive work at the lower rate.

CONCLUSIONS

It is submitted that as private investigation places one in a position of public trust, it just makes sense there be established best practices and training standards. It is believed past studies by the Ministry have supported that view.

It is the opinion of this committee that there should be competency requirements met by anyone seeking to work as a private investigator. However, the committee also realizes that development of testing that would have widespread application across the entire spectrum of private investigation is not a realistically achievable goal, except as respect to ethics.

It is self-evident that those on a very basic level, most lacking in any significant training, are the ones most in need of it. They have the most day-to-day contact with the public and they have the least practical access to meaningful professional development.

This does not rule out the appropriateness of some uniform testing, for all licensees, namely with respect to ethics.

It is finally submitted that the Ministry already has at its disposal the means to initiate desirable change.

RECOMMENDATIONS

1) That a standing committee be formed with equal representation from the private investigation industry and from policing services division to:

   a) Identify a non-profit corporation whose goals and representation identify most closely with the objective of continuing professional development for private investigators;

   b) Develop a basic curriculum, probably through a tender process, in which all applicants for licensing as a private investigator must show proficiency as a condition for licensing;

   c) Identify an institution or institutions qualified to teach the curriculum, who will be identified as such to prospective licensees, and who will be subject to audit;

   d) Identify or develop a program for testing on ethical issues suitable for administration to all licensees, current and applying; and

   e) Develop a system of probationary and graduated licensing to be granted in keeping with one's qualifications, and to limit their work accordingly.

2. That continuing membership in the aforementioned non-profit corporation be made a condition of licensing for all private investigators in the province (a term to be implemented as soon as practicable after the company is identified);

    a) The membership dues would go in part toward the expenses and to otherwise fairly compensate, including for their time, the representatives from the private sector to the standing committee; and

    b) The corporation would assume other responsibilities as from time to time identified and its budget allowed, in keeping with its represented goal of professional development.

3) That existing provisions of the PI&SGA, Sections 7(1) and (2) be applied to:

    a) Implement the proposed mandatory testing of new applicants;

    b) Require production of proof of membership in the corporation; and

    c) Require proof of successful completion of ethics testing of all licensees.

SELECTED BIBLIOGRAPHY

BILEK, A.J., J.C. KLOTTER, & R.K. FEDERAL, *Legal Aspects of Private Security* (USA: Anderson Publishing Company, 1982)

Black's Law Dictionary, 6th ed. (St. Paul: West Publishing Co., 1990)

BLAKE, S., *Administrative Law in Canada* (Toronto: Butterworths, 1997)

BROWN, C., *Insurance Law in Canada* (Toronto: Carswell, 1999)

BURNS, P., "The Law and Privacy: The Canadian Experience" (1976) 54 Can. Bar Rev. 1

CAMPBELL, C.M., ed., *Data Processing and the Law* (London: Sweet & Maxwell, 1984)

CASTEL, J.-G., *Canadian Conflict of Laws* (Toronto: Butterworths, 1997)

CORNISH, J.L., *The Criminal Lawyers' Guide to the Law of Criminal Harassment and Stalking* (Aurora: Canada Law Book, 1999)

Crankshaw's Criminal Code of Canada, 8th ed. (Toronto: Carswell, 1992)

DIAS, R.W.M., & B.S. MARKESINIS, *Tort Law*, 2d ed. (Oxford: Clarendon Press, 1989)

EKOS RESEARCH ASSOCIATES INC., *Privacy Revealed: The Canadian Privacy Survey* (Toronto: 1993)

EVANS, J.M., et al., *Administrative Law: Cases, Text, and Materials* (Toronto: Emond Montgomery, 1989)

FLEMING, J.G., *The Law of Torts*, 7th ed. (Sydney: The Law Book Company, 1987)

FRIDMAN, G.H.L., *The Law of Torts in Canada*, 2 vols. (Toronto: Carswell, 1989)

GEDDES, E.F., "The Private Investigator and the Right to Privacy" (1989) 17 Alta. L. Rev. 256

GERDEN, R.J., *Private Security: A Canadian Perspective* (Toronto: Prentice-Hall Canada, 1998)

GOLDSTEIN, E., *Visual Evidence: A Practitioner's Manual* (Toronto: Carswell) [looseleaf]

GROOT, N.J., *Legal Liability of the Canadian Private Investigator* (Toronto: Andijk Inc., 1998)

GURRY, F., *Breach of Confidence* (Oxford: Clarendon Press, 1984)

HARTMAN, J.D., *Legal Guidelines for Covert Surveillance Operations in the Private Sector* (Toronto: Butterworths, 1993)

HAWKINS, D.J., & E. KONSTAN, *The Canadian Private Investigator's Manual* (Toronto: Emond Montgomery, 1996)

493

HEUSTON, R.F.V., & R.A. BUCKLEY, *Salmond and Heuston on the Law of Torts*, 21st ed. (London: Sweet & Maxwell, 1996)

HOGG, P.H., *Constitutional Law of Canada*, 3d ed. (Toronto: Carswell, 1992)

JEFFERIES, F., ed., *Private Policing and Security in Canada* (Toronto: Centre of Criminology, University of Toronto, 1973)

JOHANSEN, D., *Federal and Provincial Access to Information Legislation: An Overview* (Ottawa: Law and Government Division of the Parliamentary Research Branch, July 1997)

JONES, D.P., & A.S. DE VILLARS, *Principles of Administrative Law*, 3d ed. (Toronto: Carswell, 1999)

JUSTICE (BRITISH SECTION OF THE INTERNATIONAL COMMISSION OF JURISTS), *Privacy and the Law* (London: Stevens & Sons Limited, 1970)

KLAR, L.N., ed., *Studies in Canadian Tort Law* (Toronto: Butterworths, 1977)

KLAR, L.N., *Tort Law*, 2d ed. (Toronto: Carswell, 1996)

KREVER, H.J., *Report on the Commission of Inquiry into the Confidentiality of Health Information* (Toronto: Queen's Printer, 1980)

LAMARCA, G., "Overintrusive Surveillance of Plaintiffs in Personal Injury Cases" (1986) 35 Defence L.J. 603

LAW REFORM COMMISSION OF CANADA, PRIVATE PROSECUTIONS (Ottawa: Law Reform Commission of Canada, Catalogue No. J32-1/52-1986)

LAWSON, I., updated and edited by Bill Jeffery, *Privacy and Free Enterprise: The Legal Protection of Personal Information in the Private Sector*, 2d ed. (Ottawa: The Public Interest Advocacy Centre, 1997)

LINDEN, A.M., *Canadian Tort Law*, 6th ed. (Toronto: Butterworths, 1997)

LINDEN, A.M., *Studies in Canadian Tort Law* (Toronto: Butterworths, 1968)

MACIURA, J., & R. STEINECKE, *The Annotated Statutory Powers Procedures Act* (Aurora: Canada Law Book, 1998)

Martin's Annual Criminal Code 2001, annotated by E.L. Greenspan & M. Rosenberg (Aurora: Canada Law Book, 2000)

MINISTRY OF THE ATTORNEY GENERAL OF ONTARIO, *Property Protection and Outdoor Opportunities: A Guide to the Occupiers' Liability Act, 1980 and the Trespass to Property Act, 1980* (Toronto: Queen's Printer, 1980)

MULLAN, D., *Administrative Law* (Toronto: Irwin Law, 2001)

OPPAL, W.T., POLICING IN BRITISH COLUMBIA COMMISSION OF INQUIRY, *Closing the Gap: Policing and the Community* (Victoria: Queen's Printer, 1994)

OSBORNE, P.H., *The Law of Torts* (Toronto: Irwin Law, 2000)

PACIOCCO, D., & L. STUESSER, *The Law of Evidence*, 2d ed. (Toronto: Irwin law, 1999)

PARKIN, S.L., *Surveillance in the Workplace* (Toronto: Council of Private Investigators, Ontario Professional Development Conference, 12 May 2000)

PELADEAU, P., "The Information Privacy Challenge: The Technological Rule of Law" in R.J. Cholewinski, ed., *Human Rights in Canada: Into the 1990s and Beyond* (Ottawa: Human Rights Research and Education Centre, University of Ottawa, 1990)

PERRIN, S., et al., *The Personal Information Protection and Electronic Documents Act: An Annotated Guide* (Toronto: Irwin Law, 2001)

PROSSER, W.L., *Handbook on the Law of Torts*, 4th ed. (St. Paul: West Publishing Co., 1971)

PROSSER, W.L., "Privacy" (1960) 48 Cal. L. Rev. 383

ROACH, K., *Criminal Law*, 2d ed. (Toronto: Irwin Law, 2000)

ROCK, A.M., "The Anton Piller Order: An Examination of its Nature, Development and Present Position in Canada" (1984-85) 5 Advocates' Q. 191

SHARP, J.M., *Credit Reporting and Privacy: The Law in Canada and the U.S.A.* (Toronto: Butterworths, 1970)

SHARPE, R.J., *Injunctions and Specific Performance* (Aurora: Canada Law Book, 1995)

SHARPE, R.J., & K.E. SWINTON, *The Charter of Rights and Freedoms* (Toronto: Irwin Law, 1998)

SHEARING, C.D., & P.C. STENNING, *Private Security and Private Justice — The Challenge of the 80s: A Review of Policy Issues* (Montreal: The Institute for Research on Public Policy, 1983)

SHEARING, C.D., & P.C. STENNING, *Search and Seizure Powers of Private Security Personnel: A Study Paper* (Ottawa: Law Reform Commission of Canada, 1979)

SMYTH, J.E., D.A. SOBERMAN, & A.J. EASSON, *The Law and Business Administration in Canada*, 6th ed. (Scarborough, Prentice Hall Canada, 1991)

SOLOMON, R.M., & B.P. FELDTHUSEN, *Cases and Materials on the Law of Torts*, 3d ed. (Toronto: Carswell, 1991)

SOPINKA, J., S.N. LEDERMAN, & A.W. BRYANT, *The Law of Evidence in Canada*, 2d ed. (Toronto: Butterworths, 1999)

STENNING, P.C., & M.F. CORNISH, *The Legal Regulation and Control of Private Policing and Security in Canada: A Working Paper* (Toronto: Centre of Criminology, University of Toronto, 1975)

TAKACH, G., "Exploring the Outer Limits: The Anton Piller Order in Canada" (1985) 23 Alta. L. Rev. 310

TAKACH, G.S., *Computer Law* (Toronto: Irwin Law, 1998)

THOMAS, R., *Entrapment Issues: Some Surprising Answers and Dangers* (Austin, TX: National Association of Investigative Specialists, 1997)

WATT, J.D., & M.K. FUERST, *The 2001 Annotated Tremeear's Criminal Code* (Toronto: Carswell, 2000)

WELLS, J.T., et al., *The Fraud Examiners Manual*, Canadian ed. (Austin, TX: Association of Certified Fraud Examiners, 1998)

Wigmore on Evidence, original by J.H. Wigmore, *Evidence in Trials at Common Law*, vol. 5, 3d ed., rev. by J.T. McNaughton (Boston: Little, Brown, 1961)

Winfield and Jolowicz on Tort, edited by W.V.H. Rogers, 13th ed. (London: Sweet & Maxwell, 1989)

TABLE OF CASES

INDEX

s.494: citizens arrests, 114

Deceit, 266–67
Defamation
    criminal offence, 203–6
    distinguished from injurious
        falsehood, 277
    tort, 271–77
Detention by private citizens
    distinguished from arrest, 116
    duty to give reason for, 143
    duty to give right to counsel, 144–47
    duty to give right to silence, 147
    effect of the *Charter*, 122
    searches, 142
Digital number recorders,
    evidence by, 400
    use of, 163–64
Drugs
    investigations of, 185–89
    possession of, 185–89
Duty to report crime
    compounding an indictable offence, 199
    obstructing justice, 193–95
    under the PISGA, 62–63

Electronic surveillance, 157–68
    cellular interceptions, 165
    cordless phone intercepts, 400
    general prohibition, 158
    interception devices, 157, 166
    number recorders, 163–64
    tort award by a criminal court, 158
    tracking devices, 161
E-mail surveillance, 384–85
Employee Discharge
    case reviews, 386–87
    labour surveillance, 368–87
Entrapment
    accepted, 347
    condemned, 347
    criminal covert investigation, 407
    labour surveillance, 383–84
    trespass to chattels, 259–60
Evidence
    admissibility of, 343

illegally obtained, 343–44
affidavits, *see* Affidavits
asset tracing, 413
Charter considerations, 344–45
cordless phone intercepts, 400
derivative, 395–96
duty to turn in to authorities, 195
employee discharge, 386–87
entrapment, 347–83
fabrication of, 195
goals of laws of, 343
illegally obtained, 343, 373–78,
    399–400, 412–13, 452–53
prejudice against PI's, 345
    conduct while testifying, 348–49
    deceased witness, 349–50
    entrapment, 347
    irrelevant information, 347–48
    paid witnesses, 345–346
    success-based retainers, 346
    unlicensed PIs, 346
privilege; *see* Privilege
property seizures, 410–13
    continuity, 410
    garbage
        agents of the state, 411–12
        from curb, 411
        from hotel room, 412
        private investigators, 412–13
        right to seize, 185
statements; *see* Witness statements
surveillance,
    admissibility rules, 354–62
    relevance, 354
    reliability, 355–60
    authentication, 360, 381–82
    prejudicial effect, 361, 382–84
    audio narratives, 362
    Charter concerns, 362–64, 368, 369–71
    collateral use, 386
    current judicial views, 351
    digital, 360
    digital number recorders, 400–401
    domestic, 387
    duration, 359
    editing videotapes, 357, 362